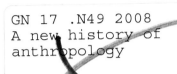

A New History of Anthropology

A New History of Anthropology

Edited by Henrika Kuklick

Blackwell
Publishing

Editorial material © 2008 by Blackwell Publishing Ltd

BLACKWELL PUBLISHING
350 Main Street, Malden, MA 02148-5020, USA
9600 Garsington Road, Oxford OX4 2DQ, UK
550 Swanston Street, Carlton, Victoria 3053, Australia

First published 2008 by Blackwell Publishing Ltd

1   2008

Library of Congress Cataloging-in-Publication Data

A new history of anthropology / Henrika Kuklick, ed.
    p. cm.
  Includes bibliographical references and index.
  ISBN-13: 978-0-631-22599-7 (hardback : alk. paper)
  ISBN-10: 0-631-22599-4 (hardback : alk. paper)
  ISBN-13: 978-0-631-22600-0 (pbk. : alk. paper)
  ISBN-10: 0-631-22600-1 (pbk. : alk. paper)   1. Anthropology–History.
2. Anthropology–Philosophy. I. Kuklick, Henrika.

  GN17.N49 2008
  301.09–dc22

                                            2006034807

A catalogue record for this title is available from the British Library.

Set in 10.5/13pt Minion
by Graphicraft Limited, Hong Kong
Printed in Singapore
by COS Printers Pte Ltd

The publisher's policy is to use permanent paper from mills that operate a sustainable forestry
policy, and which has been manufactured from pulp processed using acid-free and elementary
chlorine-free practices. Furthermore, the publisher ensures that the text paper and cover
board used have met acceptable environmental accreditation standards.

For further information on
Blackwell Publishing, visit our website:
www.blackwellpublishing.com

Contents

Illustrations

Notes on Contributors

Robert Ackerman ("Anthropology and the Classics") is the author of *J. G. Frazer: His Life and Work* (1987), *Selected Letters of J. G. Frazer* (2005), and *The Myth and Ritual School: J. G. Frazer and the Cambridge Ritualists* (2002), as well as numerous essays on the history of anthropology and the history of classical scholarship. Until 2000, he was Director of Liberal Arts at the University of the Arts in Philadelphia. Now retired and living in Britain, he is a Life Member of Clare Hall, University of Cambridge.

Regna Darnell ("North American Traditions in Anthropology: The Historiographic Baseline") is Professor of Anthropology and Director of First Nations [Native American] Studies at the University of Western Ontario (Canada). She has published extensively on the history of Americanist (including Canadian) anthropology and linguistics, Native North American languages and cultures, and cross-cultural miscommunication. She co-edits a series of Critical Studies in History of Anthropology and the *Histories of Anthropology* annual for the University of Nebraska Press. She chaired the 2002 American Anthropological Association Centennial Commission, is a fellow of the Royal Society of Canada, a member of the American Philosophical Society, and received the American Anthropological Association's Boas Award in 2005.

Thomas F. Glick ("The Anthropology of Race Across the Darwinian Revolution") is Professor of History at Boston University. He has written extensively on the comparative reception of scientific ideas, particularly in the Spanish-speaking world and Brazil. He is editor or co-editor of *The Comparative Reception of Darwinism*, 2nd edn (1988); *The Reception of Darwinism in the Iberian World* (2001) and *A recepção do Darwinismo no Brasil* (2003) – all volumes to which he also contributed chapters.

Anna Grimshaw ("Visual Anthropology") is Associate Professor in the Institute of the Liberal Arts, Emory University. She is the author of *Servants of the Buddha* (1992) and of *The Ethnographer's Eye: Ways of Seeing in Modern Anthropology*

(2001).With Amanda Ravetz, she is co-editor of *Visualizing Anthropology: experiments in image-based ethnography* (2004). She is currently working on a book, *Rethinking Observational Cinema.*

Henrika Kuklick ("Introduction" and "The British Tradition") is Professor in the Department of History and Sociology of Science at the University of Pennsylvania. She has published extensively on the history of the human sciences, with emphasis on the history of anthropology. Her publications include: *The Savage Within: The Social History of British Anthropology, 1885–1945* (1991); "Islands in the Pacific: Darwinian Biogeography and British Anthropology." *American Ethnologist* 23 (1996): 611–38; "After Ishmael: The Fieldwork Tradition and Its Future," pp. 47–65 in A. Gupta and J. Ferguson, eds., *Anthropological Locations* (1997); "Fieldworkers and Physiologists," pp. 158–80 in A. Herle and S. Rouse, eds., *Cambridge and the Torres Strait* (1998); "'Humanity in the Chrysalis Stage': Indigenous Australians in the Anthropological Imagination, 1899–1926." *British Journal for the History of Science* 39 (2006): 535–68.

Rena Lederman ("Anthropological Regionalism") has been on the faculty of Princeton University's Anthropology Department since 1981. Author of *What Gifts Engender* (1986) and many articles and book chapters on gift exchange, gendered relationships and language, sociopolitical forms, and historical representations in Papua New Guinea, she has also published on research practices, the bureaucratization of "human subjects" ethics regulation, the politics of disciplinarity, and the dynamics of specialist/lay communication (e.g., "Unchosen Ground: Cultivating Cross-subfield Accents for a Public Voice," in Segal and Yanagisako, eds., *Unwrapping the Sacred Bundle* (2005), and her forthcoming book, *Anthropology Among the Disciplines*).

Harry Liebersohn ("Anthropology Before Anthropology") is Professor of History at the University of Illinois, Urbana-Champaign. He is the author of several books, including *Fate and Utopia in German Sociology, 1870–1923* (1988), *Aristocratic Encounters: European Travelers and North American Indians* (1998), and *The Travelers' World: Europe to the Pacific* (2006).

Christer Lindberg ("Anthropology on the Periphery: The Early Schools of Nordic Anthropology") is Associate Professor of Anthropology at Lund University in Sweden as well as Associate Professor in Comparative Religion at Turku University in Finland. He has been a fellow at the Swedish Collegium for Advanced Study in the Social Sciences in 2003. He is currently scientific editor of *Acta Americana*, and is on the editorial boards of *European Review of Native American Studies* and of *Anthropologicas*. Lindberg is the author of several books pertaining to the history of anthropology, including a biography of Erland Nordenskiöld as well as three collections of biographical essays. He is currently working on a textbook on the history of anthropology and a comparative study of Native American religions.

Jonathan Marks ("Race Across the Physical–Cultural Divide in American Anthropology") is Professor of Biological Anthropology at the University of North Carolina at Charlotte. His primary area of research is molecular anthropology – the application of genetic data to illuminate our place in the natural order – or more broadly, the area of overlap between (scientific) genetic data and (humanistic) self-comprehension. Nevertheless, his interests are wide-ranging, including evolutionary theory, history, human genetics, and the sociology and philosophy of science. His research has been published in scientific and scholarly journals ranging from *Nature* to the *Journal of Human Evolution* to *History and Philosophy of the Life Sciences*. His books include: *Human Biodiversity: Genes, Race, and History* (1995); *What It Means to Be 98% Chimpanzee* (2002), for which he was awarded the W. W. Howells Prize in Biological Anthropology from the American Anthropological Association; and *Evolutionary Anthropology* (1992), which he wrote with Edward Staski. He also received the 1999 American Anthropological Association/Mayfield Award for Excellence in Undergraduate Teaching, and served as President of the General Anthropology Division of the AAA from 2000 to 2002.

Donna C. Mehos ("Colonial Commerce and Anthropological Knowledge: Dutch Ethnographic Museums in the European Context") is a Senior Researcher at the Eindhoven Technical University and Program Coordinator of the Foundation for the History of Technology in the Netherlands. Her book *Science and Culture for Members Only: The Amsterdam Zoo Artis in the Nineteenth Century* (2006) explores relations between science, nationalism, and colonialism in Dutch middle-class culture. She is currently working on the project "Technology and the Civilizing Mission: Dutch Colonial Development in the European Context, 1870–1970," funded by the Dutch Organisation for Scientific Research. She is exploring the circulation of technologies, technical experts, and expertise between and among Western nations and their (ex-)colonies to illuminate new social relations.

H. Glenn Penny ("Traditions in the German Language") is Assistant Professor of History at the University of Iowa. He is the author of *Objects of Culture: Ethnology and Ethnographic Museums in Imperial Germany* (2002), and editor, together with Matti Bunzl, of *Worldly Provincialism: German Anthropology in the Age of Empire* (2003). He is currently working on a book project about the German love affair with the American Indian, which spans the last two centuries.

Robert N. Proctor ("Temporality as Artifact in Paleoanthropology: How New Ideas of Race, Brutality, Molecular Drift, and the Powers of Time Have Affected Conceptions of Human Origins") is Professor of the History of Science at Stanford University and the author of, most recently, *The Nazi War on Cancer* (1999), which won the Viseltear Prize from the American Public Health Association. His research interests coalesce around the history of scientific and medical controversies; he has also written on cancer and environmental policy, tobacco culture, human origins, molecular anthropology, racial hygiene, expert witnessing, and the "social construction of ignorance" (agnotology). He has held positions as Senior Scholar in Residence at the US Holocaust Memorial Museum in Washington, DC (1994), and as Visiting Fellow at the Max-Planck-Institute for the History of Science in Berlin (1999–2000). He is now working on a project on human origins (especially changing interpretations of the oldest tools), a book on "Darwin in the History of Life," a book on figured stones ("Agate Eyes"), and articles on how tobacco hazards came to be recognized.

Barbara Saunders ("The Empire in Empiricism") is Research Professor in the Anthropology Department at the University of Leuven in Belgium, and has published extensively on the nature of color science, the Kwakwa'ka'wakw, museum studies and gender. During 2001–2, she was a Fellow of Clare Hall, Cambridge. Her recent publications include: with J. van Brakel, "Are There Non-Trivial Constraints on Colour Categorisation?" *Behavioural and Brain Sciences* 20 (1997): 167–232; "Revisiting Basic Colour Terms." *Journal of the Royal Anthropological Institute* n.s. 6 (2000): 81–99; *Theories, Technologies, Instrumentalities of Colour: Anthropological and Historiographic Perspectives*, edited with J. van Brakel (2002); *Changing Genders in Intercultural Perspectives*, edited with M.-C. Foblets (2002).

Lyn Schumaker ("Women in the Field in the Twentieth Century: Revolution, Involution, Devolution?") is a lecturer at the Wellcome Unit for the History of Medicine, Centre for the History of Science, Technology and Medicine at the University of Manchester. She is the author of *Africanizing Anthropology: Fieldwork, Networks, and the Making of Cultural Knowledge in Central Africa* (2001), and is currently writing a book on the history of medicine in Africa, *Snake Spirits and Garden Cities: Nature, the Supernatural and the Copperbelt Malaria Programme in Colonial Zambia, 1920–1940*. Her other work on history of anthropology has included "The Director as Significant Other: Max Gluckman and Team Research at the Rhodes-Livingstone Institute, Northern Rhodesia, 1941–1947," *History of Anthropology* 10 (2004); and "A Tent with a View: Colonial Officers, Anthropologists, and the Making of the Field in Northern Rhodesia," *Osiris: A Research Journal Devoted to the History of Science and its Cultural Influences*, vol. 11 "Science in the Field", eds. Henrika Kuklick and Robert Kohler (1996). She is currently joint editor and member of the editorial board of the *Journal for Southern African Studies* and has organized numerous conferences on heritage in Africa and the history of indigenous healing in Africa.

Emmanuelle Sibeud ("The Metamorphosis of Ethnology in France, 1839–1930") is maître de conferences (equivalent to assistant professor) in the History Department of The University of Paris VIII. Her main interests are the cultural history of French colonialism and the history of ethnography in the twentieth century. She is the author of *Une science impériale pour l'Afrique? La construction des savoirs* *africanistes en France, 1878–1930* (2002). With Jean-Loup Amselle, she edited *Maurice Delafosse, Entre orientalisme et ethnographie: l'itinéraire d'un africaniste, 1870–1926* (1998). With Anne Piriou, she edited *L'africanisme en questions* (1997). She is on the editorial committee of the *Revue d'histoire des sciences humaines*. She is currently researching colonial intellectual networks.

Merrill Singer ("Applied Anthropology") is the Director of Research at the Center for Community Health Research at the Hispanic Health Council in Hartford, CT, and a Research Affiliate at the Center for Interdisciplinary Research on AIDS at Yale University. Dr. Singer was the 2004 recipient of the Practicing Medical Anthropology Award of the Society for Medical Anthropology, and was recently appointed to the City of Hartford Mayor's Commission on AIDS. His current applied research projects include a CDC-funded study of sexual risk and communication among inner-city young adults, a CDC-funded study of emergent illicit drug-use behaviors, a NIDA-funded study of unintended messages in oral HIV testing among injection drug users in Rio De Janeiro, and a NIDA-funded study of ethical issues in research among drug using populations. He has conducted anthropological research in the USA, the Virgin Islands, China, Brazil, Haiti, and Israel. He has published extensively on health disparities, public health issues in lower income populations, HIV risk and prevention, factors in illicit drug use and abusive drinking, and health policy issues among Latino populations.

Hilary A. Smith ("Using the Past to Serve the Peasant: Chinese Archaeology and the Making of a Historical Science") received her PhD from the Department of History and Sociology of Science at the University of Pennsylvania, where she is currently a lecturer. Her research is on the history of Chinese science, medicine, and society, and her dissertation focused on changing medical understanding of nutritional disorders in Chinese history, with special attention paid to the late imperial and modern periods.

Nikolai Ssorin-Chaikov ("Political Fieldwork, Ethnographic Exile and State Theory: Peasant Socialism and Anthropology in Late Nineteenth-Century Russia") is a member of the Department of Social Anthropology at the University of Cambridge. He has carried out field research in northern Siberia on the relation between indigenous peoples and the state. His research interests include comparative colonialism; socialist and post-socialist economic systems; systems of taxation; and anthropological theory. His publications include: "Bear skins and macaroni: The social life of things at the margins of a Siberian state collective," in Paul Seabright, ed., *Barter Networks and Non-Monetary Transactions in Post-Soviet Societies*, Cambridge: Cambridge University Press, 2000; and *The Social Life of the State in Subarctic Siberia*, Stanford: Stanford University Press, 2003.

Ivan Strenski ("The Spiritual Dimension") is Holstein Family and Community Professor in Religious Studies at the University of California, Riverside. His most recent work is a historical approach to theories of religion, *Thinking about Religion* (Blackwell, 2006). Three previous books developed the history of Durkheimian theories of sacrifice in terms of their connection with the political, ideological, and religious contexts of France since the sixteenth century. These are *Theology and the First Theory of Sacrifice* (2003), *Contesting Sacrifice: Religion, Nationalism and Social Thought* (2002) and *Durkheim and the Jews of France* (1997).

Introduction

Henrika Kuklick

This collection will appeal to a range of readers, anthropologists and historians prominent among them.[1] For historians, the value of its essays will be their contextualization of anthropological ideas and practices in specific times and places. Anthropologists will find not only discussions of the discipline's major branches but also analyses of portions of its history that rarely feature in its oral tradition – a tradition highly susceptible to "mythicization," as George Stocking has noted (1995: xviii).

The classic typology of historians of the human sciences is Stocking's, a dichotomous scheme of ideal types: "presentists" and "historicists." Presentists, usually practitioners of the discipline they describe, frame their accounts in contemporary terms, often seeking lessons from the past for the present: their tone may be celebratory, as they trace the antecedents of ideas and methods now considered commendable, or mournful, regretting the loss of exemplary practices. Historicists, frequently drawn from other disciplines, are not explicitly concerned with contemporary standards and debates; they show that when we read old texts as if they had just been written, we frequently misunderstand their authors' intended meanings (Stocking 1968: 1–12).

But presentist and historicist approaches are complementary, not mutually exclusive. No matter what their professional training and special interests, historians inevitably ask questions that are important in our age. They know that past concerns were different from our own, but they must also know how contemporary practitioners view their enterprise; the past may appear different in the future, but knowledge of a discipline's present has some bearing on understanding its history. Thus, today's anthropologists should be both served by attention to historical matters of contemporary concern and inspired by historicist accounts, which aim to meet anthropology's time-honored goal of sympathetically reporting distinctive ways of life. And to describe episodes in the development of the human sciences also serves to reveal aspects of the general social orders within which they occurred, addressing questions of interest to all manner of historians.

Remembrance of Things Past

To understand anthropologists' concerns when they contemplate their discipline's identity, we must recognize the characteristics of disciplines as such, including disciplines'
struggles to endure in institutionalized forms. Roughly a third of a century ago, many
anthropologists feared that their enterprise could survive as such only if it subjected
itself to unforgiving introspection (e.g., Hymes 1969). They cherished anthropology's
enduring intellectual and moral commitments – at the very least, to a cross-cultural
purview and identification of the many ways that it is possible to be human – but
feared that the discipline's customary boundaries were no longer defensible.

In a recent essay, James Clifford summarized the mood of yesteryear. Practitioners
could no longer agree "on (1) an empirical object, (2) a distinctive method, (3) an
interpretive paradigm, and (4) a telos, or transcendent object. The object was
'primitive' societies; the method was 'fieldwork'; the paradigm was 'culture'; the
telos was 'Man'" (Clifford 2005: 37). The object, famously termed the "savage slot"
by Michel-Rolfe Trouillot, had a working definition that represented justification
for unequal power relationships, such as those engendered by colonialism. Anthropology's method of (primarily) qualitative analysis based on long-sustained participant
observation was no longer distinctive to it. The culture concept had been appropriated by other disciplines. The objective of studying man – i.e., the human species,
in modern parlance – in all of our aspects now seemed an unrealizable project, a
problem particularly acute for anthropologists in North America, where the traditional
four-field organization no longer seemed viable in many departments; separate institutional niches were being found for sociocultural anthropology, linguistic anthropology,
biological anthropology (including paleoanthropology, the study of the development
of the human species based on fossil records), and archaeology.

How can we make sense of Clifford's disciplinary obituary? It represents heartfelt
sentiments that were widespread but historically inaccurate: disciplines have not been
defined by fixed charters. That a cross-cultural purview is at the core of anthropology is undeniable: it has always been a defining characteristic of the field, whereas other
disciplines may only occasionally adopt it. In general, however, anthropology is no
different from other knowledge-based enterprises. Their pasts and presents are linked
through intellectual and professional lines of descent, but all scholarly fields have had
fluctuating boundaries. Nevertheless, apparent borderlines – as well as cleavages – can
appear extremely important at any given moment.

Anthropologists in Situ: Policing Boundaries;
Restructuring Universities

Just as many contemporary sociocultural anthropologists may feel that they have
little in common with biological anthropologists, many biological/experimental
psychologists have intellectually uneasy relationships with their social psychologist

colleagues and wonder whether psychology's diverse components should go separate ways. It is not unusual for chemists to worry that their field is dissolving; biologists are seizing possession of one portion of it, while physicists are appropriating the remainder. Sociologists, particularly American ones, have been known to quarrel about whether their discipline is defined by its use of quantitative measures. How should they evaluate sociologists who employ qualitative techniques? Perhaps they are really anthropologists!

Arguments about disciplinary purity tend to proliferate in times of scarce economic resources; relative tolerance prevails when all disciplinary factions have access to funds. Consider American sociology in the decades following World War II. Sociologists' professional ideology was that they belonged to a united field: their empirical research was informed by their theory. But this was not the case. Postwar sociologists' so-called "grand theorists," such as Talcott Parsons, conceptualized societies in organicist terms; sociology's fundamental unit of analysis was a social group, and individuals' activities were meaningful because they contributed to the operation of the whole. Meanwhile, many empiricists were nominalists, embracing large-scale survey research, taking the individual as their basic unit of analysis and representing social orders as sums of their individual parts. Sociology's two sides could be *symbiotic*: for example, surveys of such subjects as communication networks, mass media, and public opinion done on contract at Columbia University's Bureau for Applied Social Research represented a financial bulwark for faculty and students. Thus, the discipline was replete with contradictions. But American sociologists could afford to ignore them. They had marketable skills, enjoyed relatively generous funding, and exercised unprecedented international influence.

In no small part, disciplines' current anxieties are functions of changes in institutions of higher education. Arrangements have varied from one country to another, but universities everywhere have become highly dependent on outside grants to finance their faculties' research, whether these grants came from private philanthropies, industries, or government agencies. The ability to attract outside funding has become a condition of permanent employment in many disciplines (which means that individuals must learn to make plausible claims that their research fits their patrons' programmatic goals). Related to funding needs of institutions of higher education were dramatic changes in institutions' personnel rosters during the last third of the twentieth century: administrators became an enlarged percentage of employees, and their role has been to make higher education economically viable. They help to attract and manage funds, and attempt to make academics more efficient (no matter how they define efficiency). In practice, this means that academic administrators have followed a managerial trend evident in all manner of occupational spheres, reducing the percentage of employees who occupy secure positions and increasingly relying on temporary laborers, who work for relatively low salaries and need not be given benefits; unlike many other types of workers, academics are distinguished by having the possibility of gaining full job security – tenure – but the academic profession is becoming less secure in the aggregate, and academics' current occupational difficulties are not unique.

Universities are also dependent on income-generating students, and in recent decades have competed for them among fluctuating populations of persons of traditionally appropriate age. The post-World War II baby boom produced its last large cohort of future student bodies in 1964. Boomers' children constituted the so-called "echo boom," but the echo boom came to an end, forcing administrators to contemplate a future in which new strategies would have to be formulated in order to appeal to a smaller recruitment base. In essence, university managers' task is to minimize uncertainty, and the students they seek to attract and retain may be unpredictable in their demands.

In sum, in the managed university, competing for scarce resources, scholars of any persuasion can feel threatened by those whom they see as encroaching on their intellectual domains, as well as by administrators who may cut their departments' personnel allocations (or even eliminate their departments entirely).[2]

It is not surprising that all manner of disciplines were beset by crises of identity during the 1970s. At this time, the academy's economies suffered and new PhD's employment prospects fell. Moreover, there was also considerable political conflict in the world at large, such as over the Vietnam War – and those academic experts who offered advice in the prosecution thereof were much criticized. Thus, though anthropologists have had distinctive concerns, we must recognize that they have been hardly alone in worrying about the institutional viability and political import of their subject.

Original Sins

For many who problematized anthropology's identity a few decades ago, the discipline's fundamental defect was its gestation in the colonial situation. That is, anthropologists' encounters with exotic peoples became possible through the extension of colonial rule by European and American powers. Certainly, the most vulnerable of aboriginal peoples were those who became minority populations in their own territories, such as those of North America and Australia. But indigenes need not have been official subjects of the states from which Europeans came to witness their behavior, measure their physical traits, and collect specimens of their material culture, which were represented in texts, pictures, and museum displays. The development of the global economic and technological infrastructure that made colonial rule possible had opened new areas for research (see Kuklick 1997). I must stress that visiting Europeans' attitudes to non-Western peoples were not uniform. In particular, visual representations and museum displays exhibited the full gamut of possible attitudes toward exotic peoples (see especially Grimshaw, Mehos, and Penny in this volume).

Moreover, no power relationship can be thoroughly coercive; even prisoners and slaves have developed modes of resistance. The establishment of colonial authority did not protect anthropologists from being regarded as adversarial intruders. Consider, for example, E. E. Evans-Pritchard's frustration when the barely pacified Nuer repeatedly avoided answering his questions, driving him "crazy," producing feelings that he could not resist labeling "Nuerosis" (1940: 13). But anthropologists could turn their imputed association with government powers to their own purposes. When Margaret Mead was working in New Guinea with her then-husband, Reo Fortune, she observed that they were unable to find servants until Fortune "went about from one village to another, unearthed their darkest secrets which they wished kept from the government, and then ordered them to come and carry" (letter of January 15, 1932, in Mead 1970: 308) And therein hangs the tale: anthropologists might elicit subject peoples' "darkest secrets," which could prove useful to colonial regimes. Thus, the charge was made that anthropology had been the "handmaiden" of colonialism (e.g., Asad 1973).

Significantly, virtually from the beginning of the Age of Exploration to now, an apparently consistent political attitude has joined predictions about the fates of non-Western peoples: though their societies might have some qualities Europeans could envy, these peoples were destined to become extinct in cultural, if not necessarily physical terms. Thus, their distinctive characteristics must be recorded for posterity. The cause of what is usually termed "salvage ethnography" can be seen in the scientific pursuits of Captain James Cook, who noted that during the interval between his first (1766–1771) and second (1772–1775) sea voyages, New Zealand's Maoris had suffered from the introduction of European vices, which "disturb the happy tranquility they and their fore Fathers injoy'd [sic]" (quoted in Smith 1992: 99).

Anthropological salvage persists – although I must stress that it does not necessarily have consistent implications. The image of a people untouched by Euroamerican culture excites the imaginations of popular audiences (see, e.g., Marc Lacey, "Remote and Poked, Anthropology's Dream Tribe," *The New York Times*, December 18, 2005). Moreover, non-Western peoples may themselves endorse salvage efforts, such as recording their vanishing languages and preserving their heritage sites.

Among professional anthropologists, however, elegiac tones have long prevailed. Indeed, proto-professional anthropologists of roughly a century ago, such as participants in the 1898 Cambridge anthropological expedition to the islands of Torres Strait (then called Straits), went so far as to instigate re-enactments of ceremonies barely remembered by the oldest islanders. By 1965, Margaret Mead pitied the young anthropologist who might not be able to contribute anything significant to the discipline, unlike the anthropologist of bygone days, who had "the wonderful knowledge that everything he records will be valuable," since "[a]ll of it is unique, all will vanish, all was and is grist to some fellow anthropologist's mill" (Mead letter of December 19, 1965, in 1970: 305). Today, of course, the putative cause of cultural extinctions is not the extension of colonial power but the steamroller of globalization – which might be seen as an extension of the status quo ante.

To recognize the political attitude underlying predicted extinctions is to call into question the epistemological status of anthropologists' observations. That is, it was once a fundamental tenet that anthropologists were able to understand foreign societies because they brought outsiders' perspectives to their observations; by confronting differences between their ways of life and those of the peoples they studied, anthropologists were able to understand distinctive beliefs and practices of other societies as products of situational contingencies, rather than as *natural* phenomena, as the persons who sustained them likely believed. Thus, anthropologists were also primed to recognize their own societies' received wisdom. No later than 1914, W. H. R. Rivers observed

> There is nothing which has a greater tendency to interfere with conventional morality than travel, and especially travel among peoples with manners and customs widely different from one's own. It is the change of attitude towards the conventions of one's own society which produces the broadening of ideas and the tolerance which travel brings in its train. (II, 566; and see Gellner 1988)

Thus, anthropology self-consciously adopted the identity of the "uncomfortable discipline, questioning established positions and proclaimed values" (Raymond Firth in 1981, quoted in Wright 1995: 65). There is an echo of this attitude in the standpoint epistemology associated with contemporary feminist theorists, whom Schumaker discusses in this volume (and anthropologists have always known that men and women researchers have had differential access to male and female social spheres, which is one of the reasons that the discipline has been relatively open to women). But standpoint epistemology differs from celebration of outsiders' perspectives insofar as the possibility of perceptual acuity derives from individuals' social positions rather than their choices and achievements. Contrast this view with that of Rivers: loss of faith in the merits of one's own society resulted from experience that might be deliberately undertaken by anyone.

Were anthropologists arguing in thoroughly disinterested fashion when they claimed that their stranger status in exotic places made them acute observers there, and subsequently capable of dispelling conventional wisdom at home? Obviously not: they were legitimating their discipline's erstwhile definition. But this does not mean that we must dismiss their claims – or aims. In the final analysis, if we are incapable of sympathetic understanding of persons unlike ourselves – whether by virtue of their social status, geographical place, or temporal location – the cause of much scholarship, not just of anthropology, is lost. Unfortunately, the celebration of otherness became a political casualty in anthropology: "the other" became a code phrase for the victim of colonized objectification – a vehicle for projective fantasy.

Consider historians by illustrative contrast. Many, if not all, historians distrust accounts of the relatively recent past made by persons who, by definition, share many of the assumptions of their historical subjects; but historians assume that their distance in time from historical actors will allow them to see the conventional wisdom and power structures of past ages with relatively clear eyes. Anthropologists lost faith in a defensible epistemological stance because it was tainted by its association with colonialism; those based in Western institutions felt uncomfortable defining the non-Western world as their main sphere of inquiry. Thus, in 1979, Maurice Freedman mournfully (and presciently) observed a "wholly depressing" trend: "the study of the 'other', and with it the truly international character of anthropology, could die in a welter of national particularism and self-absorption" (15). This unhappy condition was not permanent, however, not least because anthropology is now practiced in former colonies. And when an Indian anthropologist does research in the Netherlands, she can claim that her perceptual skills are heightened because she does not take for granted many of the assumptions of her subjects (Palriwala 2005).

There are other indications that anthropology has expunged the colonial taint. Those persons who might once have been classified as "primitive" may have spokespeople who are their own, professionally trained "native anthropologists." And authors of anthropological studies of exotic peoples often feel a moral obligation – or are legally compelled – to submit their accounts for consideration to the persons described therein, as well as to professionals' scrutiny (see Lederman in this volume). With relative ease, persons remote from centers of power can acquire the means to produce visual images portraying themselves as they wish to be understood (see Grimshaw in this volume). Indigenes now have moral authority and – in varying degrees – legal rights to affect museum exhibits of their ways of life.

Moreover, anthropologists have expanded their substantive purview considerably. No longer confining themselves to what would once have been euphemistically termed "simple societies," they now consider incontrovertibly complex societies, as well as such ties that bind as transnational associations and relationships within and among complex work organizations – all of which research loci present opportunities to expand our inventory of known behavioral variations (see Lederman in this volume). And they have moved into diverse applied research settings at home as well as abroad, including (but hardly limited to) the school, the corporation, the hospital, the government bureaucracy, and the city street (see Singer in this volume). Moving from the academy into the real world can be dangerous: advice given may not be effective, or it may have unhappy and unanticipated consequences. The spheres of practical anthropological labor may be frivolous as well as important; advising retailers about consumer behavior, say, is quite different from working with the homeless. But the "field" to which the anthropologist takes herself need not be a remote and exotic place (see, e.g., Gupta and Ferguson 1997). Notwithstanding the conservative attitudes preserved in certain anthropology departments, many contemporary anthropologists have taken the entire world as their purview.

"The Past is a Foreign Country"

So begins a novel by L. P. Hartley, *The Go-Between*, and it is not surprising that this sentence (or a slight variant thereof) has served as the title for a number of historical studies. Confronting anthropology's history means recognizing significant differences between past and present practitioners. The discipline has roots in virtually every intellectual quarter. But as an enterprise requiring fieldwork, it descends from the natural history sciences. As such, its literary conventions in the late-nineteenth and early-twentieth centuries were very different from what they became. It was once imperative that fieldworkers open their accounts by setting themselves in the scenes of their inquiries, describing the flora and fauna as well as the diverse persons among whom they found themselves, in order to convey to the reader that they were authentic witnesses, whose testimony was reliable – no matter what specific phenomena they had come to observe (e.g., Haddon 1901; and see Kuklick 1997).

For a number of contributors to this collection, disciplinary discussions about field-work as such have entailed reconsideration of what used to be a standard trope in anthropology's oral tradition: that fieldwork methodology was contrived (or at least independently invented) by Bronislaw Malinowski as a nearly unintended by-product of a historical accident. A graduate student at the London School of Economics, he was visiting Australia to participate in the meetings of the peripatetic British Association for the Advancement of Science when World War I began; he had intended to do field research, but might never have spent as much time as he did in the nearby Trobriand Islands had he not been a citizen of the Austro-Hungarian Empire, classified as an enemy alien and thus unable to return to Britain until the war's end. Malinowski may have publicized his experience effectively, but his was not the first exercise in sustained field research (see esp. Lindberg, Penny, Sibeud, Ssorin-Chaikov in this volume).

Malinowski's most innovative contribution to fieldwork method may have been the conventions of ethnographic reporting he developed, which made fieldworkers the lonely heroes of their stories, abstracting them from their social networks – from their effectively anonymous valued local confidants and support staff, as well as from other Europeans who were residents in their field sites, ranging from missionaries to commercial traders, who taught fieldworkers a good deal about local lifeways. Debunking the legend of the heroic lone fieldworker is more than an exercise in demythol-ogizing the discipline's history – though it is that. It expresses as well as facilitates pedagogic recognition that fieldwork technique is socially embedded practice that can be taught.

Finding pioneering fieldworkers in many locations also involves questioning what has been understood to be the international hierarchy of disciplinary practi-tioners. Until recently, British and American sociocultural anthropology effectively reigned supreme, and at least "for some purposes" they could together be "regarded as variants of a single hegemonic anglophone anthropology" (Stocking 1995: xvii). But this hegemony is itself a historical product. In the early twentieth century, it was arguably variants of the German-language tradition that were internationally hegemonic – and these variants included Boasian cultural anthropology, the dom-inant school in the United States (see Darnell, Lindberg, and Penny in this volume; see also Gingrich 2005: esp. 111–36).

Discrediting the myth of sustained Anglophone anthropological hegemony serves the contemporary cause of those who are making anthropology an increasingly international discipline – as it certainly was in the nineteenth century, as well as, to a lesser extent, in the twentieth century before World War II (see Kuklick 2006). It is worth noting that parochialism has been a function of disciplinary specialty as well as time and place. In the decades immediately following World War II, British social anthropology was aggressively *British*, militantly patroling its boundaries against foreign invaders (see Kuklick in this volume). By contrast, paleoanthropology has been a virtually international enterprise (see Proctor in this volume).

Selecting Problems; Confronting Results

In general, examination of anthropology's past reveals much about peculiarities of intellectual venues – of time, place, and ideology. For example, anthropologists and their forebears were obsessed with the centuries-old problem of defining genuine spirituality, an issue that does not animate contemporary anthropology. Scholars expected to gain understanding of religious belief from comparative cultural analysis. But their conclusions were hardly unanimous. Indeed, many scholars judged that material progress led to spiritual degeneration, rather than that supposedly "civilized" peoples were superior in every way (see Strenski in this volume). The varied ways that Darwinian speculations about race were received in different national contexts tells us much about the political climates of different places (see Glick in this volume). Archaeological inquiries have frequently served political purposes, but these have run the full gamut of available possibilities (see Smith in this volume; see also Kuklick 1991a). And research undertaken for clear ideological reasons has had unintended consequences. The nineteenth-century Russian political radicals who undertook inquiries among Siberian peasants wished to prove that historical trends were inevitably leading to the realization of their ideals. Many of them were enduring forced exile as punishment for their political acts. Alas for the radicals, many of their findings disconfirmed expectations (Ssorin-Chaikov in this volume).

And one must stress that persons apparently joined in a common pursuit have had different motives and effected unrelated ends. The link between anthropology and the classics forged in the late-nineteenth and early-twentieth centuries, described by Ackerman in this volume, was compounded of many elements. There was the straightforward factor of academic politics: relative to the upstart discipline of anthropology, classics had high prestige, some of which might be transferred to the new field. But by the very token of its long establishment, classics was in need of invigoration, and analogizing extant non-Western peoples to those of Ancient Greece and Rome could yield new insights – and also call into question long-cherished beliefs that the Classical Ancients were the intellectual and political progenitors of Western civilization at its best. The histories of ancient empires could also be studied as cautionary tales: rulers of contemporary empires might learn how to avoid the fates of the empires of Greece and Rome.

It is unquestionable that in all of its aspects anthropology had historical connections to colonialism, and many of the contributors to this collection explore these (see esp. Kuklick, Liebersohn, Mehos, Penny, Saunders, Sibeud, and Singer). But the relationships they find are complex and diverse. At one extreme is the relationship between the study of non-Western peoples and political values in the polities that would join to become the German state, where the development of anthropology predated the acquisition of colonial territories and was linked to liberal politics. At the other extreme is the situation in the Netherlands, in which future colonial officials were given formal instruction in practical knowledge about subject peoples and museums were created in which colonies' commercial value was made evident; but anthropology did not develop in the Netherlands as an esoteric discipline until the end of the colonial era. Indeed, in no matter what national context, anthropologists' political views have varied considerably at any given moment and over time. Thus, officials of colonial governments often took exception to anthropologists; officials frequently suspected that anthropologists were subversives, undercutting government authority because they identified with those they studied.

It is important to remember that colonies were not worlds apart from the metropoles; they were joined in a range of social ties. The successes or failures of colonial ventures had political implications for metropolitan regimes, and colonies were sites for innovations that might be brought home. The colonies presented Europeans with a variety of opportunities. Consider the persons A. C. Haddon encountered in the islands of the Torres Strait, which he first visited as a biologist in 1888 and to which he returned as the organizer of the Cambridge anthropological expedition in 1898. Among his contacts were the Bruce brothers, Robert, a barely educated carpenter and wheelwright, who befriended him during his first visit, and John, schoolmaster and magistrate of the island of Mer, whose assistance proved invaluable for his anthropological work; the brothers had come to the islands to escape straitened circumstances in Glasgow. The islands were also full of fortune hunters of many nationalities, including Japanese, hoping to become rich from pearl trading. Among the careers that could be advanced in the colonies were scientific ones, of which geology was perhaps the most notable (and profitable); anthropologists were only one among many types of researchers for whom work in the colonies became vital – both because the colonies represented distinctive natural worlds, enlarging scientists' subject matter, and because the inclusion of positions in the colonies within occupational job structures literally enlarged individuals' opportunities to succeed (see Kuklick and Kohler 1996). But scientific pursuits in colonial places could be quite humble ones, such as those of Alfred Russel Wallace, who collected natural specimens that might be sold for display in gentlemen's houses (for more on Wallace, including his anthropological activities, see Kuklick in this volume). In short, Europeans' connection to colonial power could have been nearly incidental, and Europeans' behavior could range from reprehensible to admirable.

Knowledge for Whom?

Colonial settings were not the only ones in which early anthropology was seen to have value; it led to self-understanding and figured in consideration of domestic political issues (see, e.g., Penny and Kuklick in this volume). But colonial settings were the most notable locales of applied research. Thus, it is significant, as Schumaker observes in this volume, that academic institutions in new states have not abandoned anthropology because of its colonial taint (though they may choose to call it sociology), and continue to train students to do fieldwork; but new policy concerns animate anthropological inquiries in former colonies. Moreover, the reward system of anthropology is differently structured in new states; work framed as purely academic (such as that leading to publication in peer-reviewed journals) enhances status in university settings, just as it does in Euroamerican universities, but research with practical value, such as contract labor for non-governmental organizations (NGOs) is far better remunerated than academic employment – and universities may be dependent for daily operating costs on the funds their faculties contribute when they do contract labor (see Holland 2006). Euroamerican anthropologists might note national/regional differences in disciplinary prestige structures and reconsider their colleagues' relative disdain for applied anthropology, which grew in the post-World War II period and was at an especially high point during the Vietnam War era (see Singer in this volume).

That a substantial proportion of credentialed anthropologists now work in non-academic settings has been taken as a sign of the discipline's decline. Certainly, graduate students in anthropology, like graduate students in other human sciences – economics, political science, psychology, and sociology – must recognize their mentors' view that academic careers are best. But the possibility of diverse types of anthropological careers is really a sign of the discipline's strength. Other human sciences also present students with evidence that should (in various ways and to various ends) provoke introspection and self-understanding, just as anthropology does in its humanistic incarnation. But their viability as disciplines rests in no small part on demonstration that their insights can be useful. And as a substantial literature on the history of knowledge-based occupations has shown, professional workers of every type have greater freedom of thought and action if they have many clients, and need not be the creatures of a single sort of patron (the classic text is Johnson 1972). Psychology has not been exiled from the university because the majority of its PhDs work in applied settings. The human science with the greatest prestige, economics, is that with the greatest perceived practical value – and palpable influence, supplying industries, governments and international agencies with advisors at the highest level. Indeed, it is notable that economists are now competing with anthropologists for a sector of applied research turf: developing strategies to reform self-destructive and antisocial human behavior. When anthropologists' methods prove successful in solving social problems, their discipline's prestige is enhanced. Moreover, anthropology's considerable value as, in Firth's previously quoted words, the "uncomfortable discipline, questioning established positions and proclaimed values," is not incommensurable with its practical application. Anthropologists formally employed to solve social problems may be more effective advocates for their clients than those who have themselves embraced advocacy (see Singer in this volume).

Indeed, the prestige differential between abstract scholarly inquiry and popular recognition is a false one in the real world, though it may seem genuine within the academy. Respect gained in the world at large legitimates disciplines. Consider the career of Franz Boas: he both appealed to popular audiences and became a (indeed, for long

Tom Tierney

Margaret Mead

In office wear

In an evening ensemble

Figure 1   A literal illustration of Margaret Mead's popular recognition, a paper doll included in Tom Tierney, *Notable American Women. Paper Dolls in Full Color* (1989). The other heroines of the collection are Emily Dickinson, Isabella Stewart Gardner, Mary Cassatt, Emma Lazarus, Jane Addams, Juliette Gordon Low, Helena Rubenstein, Willa Cather, Helen Keller, Margaret Sanger, Clare Boothe Luce, Georgia O'Keefe, Margaret Bourke White, Babe Didrikson Zaharias, and Lorraine Hansberry. Reproduced with the artist's permission.

the) dominant figure in the discipline, populating anthropology departments with his students. When he retired, *Time* magazine made his career its cover story, which emphasized the success of his lifelong project to discredit scientific racism (May 11, 1936). Indeed, sociocultural anthropology's popular prestige in the United States surely hit a high point during and after World War II in consequence of the involvement of a substantial proportion of its practitioners in the war effort, participating in activities ranging from setting foreign policy to (there is no ignoring it) the management of Japanese internment camps (see Singer in this volume). Perhaps no anthropological analysis has had a greater policy impact than Ruth Benedict's *The Chrysanthemum and the Sword* (1946), which guided the post-World War II reconstruction of Japan by victorious occupation forces. And certainly no sociocultural anthropologist has been a more prominent public intellectual than Margaret Mead, whose status as such developed before the war but was enhanced by her activities during it. She became an expert witness before Congressional committees, a television personality, and a columnist for the mass-circulation magazine *Redbook*, in which she broadcast her opinions on all manner of subjects; as she herself was aware, her academic colleagues were somewhat disdainful of her because she wrote popular works (she tried to raise their opinion of her by also writing works for strictly professional audiences), but by gaining widespread recognition she served to enhance the value of her discipline in the public eye.

Academic Structures; Public Responsibilities

Rena Lederman suggests that anthropology cannot define its boundaries and mission without attention to the public's understanding of its role: "anthropology's comparative, first-hand point of view is expected to offer answers to questions other scholars and laypeople have about fundamental 'human nature'" (2005: 56). The specific issue she is addressing is whether there is justification for perpetuation of American anthropology's traditional four-field disciplinary structure, and her argument is that intellectually productive exchanges among subfield practitioners are results of such a structure – not just that a four-field department matches popular understandings of anthropology.

The arguments made for subfield fission or fusion fit genres hardly original to our time, invoking essentialist definitions dating to the nineteenth century. At Stanford University, for example, one department split into two in 1998: the Department of Anthropological Sciences, structured along canonical four-field lines but defining the discipline by its *method* rather than its *content*; and the Department of Cultural and Social Anthropology (including archaeology), grounded in the assumption that anthropology's substantive content defies formulation of law-like generalizations, requiring interpretative, humanistic analyses. Stanford's administration ordered the two departments to reunite in 2007. Sociocultural anthropologists who feel that their work belongs among the humanities and biological anthropologists who feel close affinities with population geneticists are reasoning along the lines that divided the Stanford anthropologists. But though arguments about the nature of different types of knowledge systems are fruitful material for the flourishing new specialty of the anthropology of science, I will say no more about them as such.

Nevertheless, the question of what contemporary biological anthropologists and sociocultural anthropologists can say to one another has to be taken seriously. That is because we must consider anthropology's historical contribution to the pseudo-science of scientific racism, which justified such unfortunate policies as slavery and eugenic measures ranging from forced sterilization to attempts to exterminate whole populations. But anthropologists' arguments about race more frequently took liberal forms – including opposition to all of the aforementioned policies. Indeed, anthropologists' most constructive contribution to public discourse was long considered to have been discrediting for all time the "dangerous myth" of significant differences among types of humankind, or "races" (see, e.g., Darnell, Glick, Marks, Penny, and Proctor in this volume; see also Barkan 1992).

Unfortunately, however, the argument that biological and behavioral variation are linked has again become respectable on many fronts. It is an argument that appeals to popular audiences as well as to various types of academics – illustrating the general phenomenon that the line between specialized knowledge and popular belief is always somewhat blurred. Indeed, there are social developments that could not have occurred absent scientific advances – but did not follow from science per se. How else, for example, is one to understand why DNA testing that revealed their Jewish ancestry has led a number of members of a Catholic population of Spanish descent living in the American southwest to either convert to Judaism or to incorporate Jewish elements in their Catholic religious practices (reported in *The New York Times*, October 29, 2005)? Consider the phenomenon of the link between commercialized DNA testing and tourism: travel plans to specific parts of Africa may be based on testing of tissue samples that supposedly reveal persons' geographic origins. And racism of the sort once considered thoroughly discredited is gaining scientific sanction with such recent developments as the recent approval of a drug, BiDil, judged to be especially effective in treatment of heart disease among African-Americans; one assumes that physicians' assignment of African-American identity to persons who will then receive BiDil is likely to be based on such superficial characteristics as skin color, whereas, in fact, DNA testing often reveals to persons that in genetic terms they are not what they appear to be. Of course, persons outside the academy as well as inside it understand races as social constructions rather than natural population units, but that does not mean that racist judgments have not lately gained in respectability (see, e.g., unsigned editorial in *The New York Times*, "Debunking the Concept of 'Race'," July 30, 2005).

Contemporary developments are likely to remind practitioners of science studies of the oft-told story of the acceptance of Gregor Mendel's articles demonstrating laws of heredity unaffected by environmental factors (acquired characteristics were not inherited), which were published in the mid-1860s. But Mendel's laws were ignored until 1900, when they were simultaneously – and independently – rediscovered by three scientists, one in Germany, one in the Netherlands and one in Austria, after which knowledge of them spread throughout the scientific community. Late-nineteenth century scientific work had favored their acceptance. Equally important, there were many outside the world of science whose attitudes were consistent with hereditarianism, representing extravagant expectations that the quality of the human species could be elevated with the application of scientific knowledge.[3] This is to say that hereditarian views became mainstream, although they were not universally accepted. (The famous British polymath, Herbert Spencer, for example, refused to abandon belief in the heritability of acquired characteristics, arguing that human progress was impossible in the absence of this mechanism.)

The moral of this story is not simply that scientific findings will not be accepted until widespread social attitudes favor their recognition. Scientific findings can also inspire social movements – including public opposition to scientific judgments. Consider contemporary campaigns to portray Darwinian evolution in school textbooks as merely a theory, to which "intelligent design" ("creationism" in disguise) should be considered a viable alternative. Using such techniques as those of molecular genetics, scientists have powerful tools for establishing relationships of descent and divergence among species – defining these in ways that challenge many persons' religious beliefs.

In short, popular attitudes and professional developments are together serving to oblige contemporary anthropologists to explicate the relationship between biological and cultural phenomena, rehearsing arguments that once seemed firmly settled. Old controversies, such as whether varieties of humans are members of one species (the doctrine of "monogenism") or are truly different species (the doctrine of "polygenism"), which seemed resolved in favor of the former position more than a century ago, are surfacing in euphemized form in such disciplinary specialties as paleoanthropology – which may best exemplify the relationship between popular and esoteric spheres, since its findings both require mastery of highly specialized knowledge and techniques and are of interest to an enormous popular audience (see Proctor in this volume).

It is the very mixture of enterprises that anthropology may join that allows its practitioners to provide distinctly sophisticated answers to revitalized questions. In this volume, Jonathan Marks argues that sociocultural and biological anthropologists are as intellectually close as (if not closer than) they have ever been, and it is notable that relationships between the subfields are now being forged outside the United States (see Kuklick in this volume). That is, a nuanced understanding of recent work in the biological sciences complements sociocultural anthropologists' recognition of the extraordinary range of possible ways that humans may live – the plasticity of "fundamental 'human nature'." Research indicates that individuals' development both in utero and after birth is shaped by interactions between their biological potentials and environmental factors. That is, humans have survived over time under highly diverse conditions because our brains evolved to facilitate adaptation – sufficiently flexible to be accommodating and innovative. The cross-cultural perspective that has consistently been at the core of anthropology does not permit reductive notions. It is ignorance of societal variation that allows evolutionary psychologists, say, to argue that contemporary humans have an internal programming dating to the evolution of the species, naturally preferring to mate with persons of specific body types in order to maximize the number of their offspring. Likewise, ignorance allows some biologists to argue that persons are genetically programmed to specific types of behavior. In short, subfield practitioners need one another now as much as they ever have in order to make the sorts of arguments that are dear to each.

Conclusion

Some of the contributors to this collection are anthropologists, while others are historians, and some essays in the collection may have special appeal for contributors' disciplinary colleagues. But many essays should have broader appeal – although different intellectual types will read them for different reasons. All readers should appreciate the value of placing ideas and practices in historical contexts. But historians will be pleased to read studies that reveal previously unexposed dimensions of significant phenomena – the political philosophy of John Locke, say, or arguments about slavery, the perennial question of Home Rule for Ireland, the crisis of German liberalism, and that odd creature the intellectual French colonial official. Anthropologists will learn of neglected ancestors and bring a historical perspective to contemporary debates.

Notes

1   For various forms of assistance to me as I produced this collection, I would like to thank Orit Abuhav, Robert Ackerman, Ana Alonso, Rita Barnard, Glenn Bowman, Joshua Berson, Paul Burnett, Brian Daniels, Joseph Farrell, Sarah Fee, Edgardo Krebs, Maneesha Lal, Rena Lederman, Jonathan Marks, David Mills, Howard Morphy, Joy Rohde, Anne Rothenberger, Brent Shaw, Mark Turin, Nathan Sivin, Susanna Trnka, Peter Wade, and Maxim Waldstein.

2   For just two specimens of histories of the university as an institution, see Rüegg 2004 and Graham and Diamond 1997. One should note that the consequences of administrators' efforts to maintain or enlarge the size of their institutions' student populations have not been all negative. Campaigns to enroll persons beyond normal student age and with backgrounds different from institutions' usual recruitment bases create more stimulating learning environments. And consider the coeducation movements of the late nineteenth century and the end of the twentieth century. At both times, all-male institutions opened their doors to women because the size of the cohorts of males available for recruitment as students were relatively small; decisions made for economic reasons contributed to the growth of women graduates' demands for greater recognition of their talents and accomplishments.

3   The movement to improve the human species – eugenics – was not invariably linked to immoral policies, since it included advocacy of public health measures, which would facilitate expression of individuals' inherent potential. The classic work on the subject is Kevles 1985.

1

Anthropology Before Anthropology

Harry Liebersohn

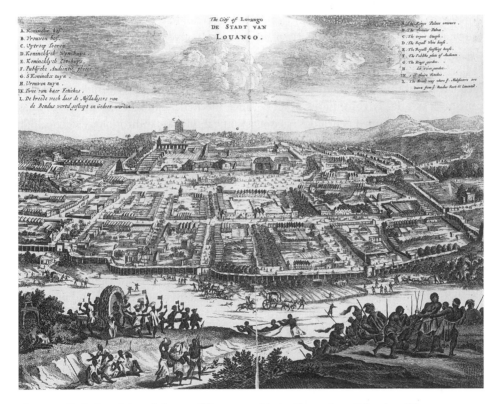

Figure 2   Early imagining of the non-Western world. An illustration of the city of Louango, in present-day Congo, from a book compiled from diverse sources and published in London by John Ogilby in 1670, *Africa*, which was dedicated to King Charles II. In addition to his career as a publisher and bookseller, Ogilby was Master of his Majesties [sic] Revels in the Kingdom of Ireland, and was closely associated with prominent members of the Royal Society. From the editor's collection.

Introduction

How long has the discipline of anthropology existed? How can we differentiate it from predecessors and forerunners? To ask such questions is to attempt to define a distinctive kind of activity, which different practitioners may define differently. Nevertheless, at the base of most practitioners' definitions will be the search for systematic patterns of human variation, no matter where these may be found. For most historians of anthropology, the discipline's foundation was laid in mid-nineteenth-century Euro-America, when evolutionary theorists compared their supposedly superior civilization to other, more "primitive" societies and cultures, which they found both among their own peasants and workers and among the non-European peoples of the world. While the evolutionary paradigm was a loose one, it ordered classes and races on an ascending scale from a "savagery" barely distinguishable from animal behavior to the "civilization" of Northern Europe, with many gradations in between (Stocking 1987). The ethical and cultural value-judgments accompanying this paradigm, which corresponded to the West's political and economic ascendancy over most of the rest of the world until 1914, provoked criticisms and alternative paradigms that shaped the discipline in the twentieth century.

Looking further back in time, we do not discover a neatly defined proto-discipline. History, for example, has a lineage going back to an Ancient Greek muse, Clio; one can speak of a fairly continuous practice since the Renaissance. Philosophy, too, has a long and well-defined genealogy, as does political theory. Anthropology's genealogy is less clear. Who by general agreement is a great seventeenth-century anthropologist to compare with the philosophers Leibniz or Descartes, or an eighteenth-century anthropologist to compare with the historian Gibbon? At first sight, we have few clues. It may be comforting to believe that anthropology is a thoroughly modern discipline, to suppose that before modern times educated Europeans merely relied on learned and folk legend for their opinions about peoples unlike themselves. Close examination, however, reveals that Europeans had valuable discussions of foreign peoples centuries before they had the modern disciplinary label to describe their interests. Herodotus served as a classical source for the ethnographic imagination; travel accounts were a significant genre of medieval writing and were still popular and profitable reading material in the eighteenth century (Kelley 1998; Campbell 1988; Withey 1989: 35–8). Sea captains, scientists, sailors, merchants, settlers, and missionaries offered competing, sometimes hugely successful tales of the wonders they had seen. While some of their accounts were based on brief or casual impressions, others distilled experiences of immersion in and dependence on foreign societies. Critical debate informed their writings; travelers reviewed the claims of predecessors and took their stands on conflicting, hotly contested views of native peoples. Their pre-modern discourse left deep impressions on philosophy, literature, and state policy.

When we try to reconstruct the overall shape of this "anthropology before anthropology," two major eras emerge. One is the period from 1492 to the late seventeenth century, which Anthony Grafton (with Shefford and Siraisi 1992) has characterized as an era of respect for the authority of Europe's "old texts" or learned tradition, which had to be reconciled with the experiences of "new worlds" explored by Columbus and his successors. During this period, conceptions of non-Europeans inherited from classical antiquity and clerical dogma continued to inform Europeans' perceptions and eyewitness accounts of American and other "new worlds." At the same time, something new was emerging: a canon of modern travel writing, which had its own favored peoples for observation, topics of conversation, and categories of analysis, some of them ways of approaching non-Europeans that are still with us. From the late seventeenth to the late eighteenth century, a new kind of concern set the agenda of anthropological conversation. Enlightenment thinkers sought out human nature in its original and (they hoped) universal form among non-literate peoples. Just as the discovery of the Americas stimulated the Renaissance revaluation of inherited conceptions of extra-European peoples, so the systematic exploration of Oceania in the eighteenth century stimulated a self-conscious search for a scientific method of analyzing non-European politics and societies. We will consider these two historical moments in turn: first, the Renaissance era, characterized by a tension between inherited texts and new-world experiences; and second, the Enlightenment era, characterized by a tension between newly acquired knowledge of the Pacific and conventional notions of reason.

It is tempting to imagine that early historical actors' perceptions of the non-European world were distorted by traditional expectations or Eurocentric notions of "reason," whereas we study the world as it is. According to Margaret Hodgen's survey of early anthropology (1964), Columbus observed people of the New World with calm realism, marking a sudden break with medieval fantasy and legend; but for centuries after Columbus, writers only slowly discarded the "baggage" of medieval error. J.H. Elliott casts the relationship between European observers and New World in a more complicated way. Acquiring knowledge was not just a matter of casting off excess baggage. With the best will and the greatest insistence on precise observation, early European observers could not accurately record what they saw; human perceptions and the ability to communicate depend on the existing stock of cultural and intellectual knowledge, and a long process of rapprochement and growing familiarity had to take place before the peculiar contours of the New World could become visible and take their place in a work such as *Cosmos*, the traveler-scientist Alexander von Humboldt's 1845 synthesis of the learning of his time (1972: 3, 18).

Can we plot "progress" in the history of anthropological knowledge, moving from unfamiliarity and error to secure knowledge? As Elliott notes, Humboldt was exceptional in his time for considering the impact of America on Europe rather than vice versa. More broadly, when it came to observing indigenous cultures during the nineteenth century, learned authority was compatible with gross prejudice and systematic distortions. Missionaries and sailors were capable of making valuable observations superior to those of trained scientists on voyages; all of these early observers can continue to inform and instruct us today. The anthropologist James A. Boon offers cautions against any view of steady progress in anthropology. He observes that cultural eras such as the Middle Ages, the Renaissance, or the Enlightenment were as totalities so complex that it is difficult to say which was the more "Eurocentric" or open toward other cultures. For Boon, anthropology does not "progress" so much as it enlarges our conception of humanity (1982: 36–7, 48).

Just as if we were doing fieldwork in a strange part of the world, we need to approach the "pre-history" of anthropology in a subtle and open spirit. To deny ourselves access to its insights is to provincialize ourselves in time; to ask what we can learn from it is to expand our conception of anthropology.

Renaissance Anthropology: Testing Textual Authority

The first important ethnographic document of modern times is the letter that Columbus (1451–1506) sent to his royal masters and their counselors announcing the results of his first overseas voyage. It was printed in Barcelona in the spring of 1493, and subsequent editions soon appeared in Spanish, Latin, French, and German (Vigneras in Columbus 1968: xxi). Columbus's letter is a good example of the juxtaposition of the old and the new. Included in it are a factual summary of the voyage, exclamations of wonder at marvels seen, legends proffered as truths, and an insistence on the truthfulness of his eyewitness report, all of this placed within a framework of triumphant religious faith. The imperial motive was certainly there, inseparable from the announcement of discovery. In a sentence announcing that he had found "very many islands," he went on to state that he had taken possession of all of them for their majesties by proclamation and by unfurling of the royal standard (Columbus 1968: 191). He went forward, he dispatched men, and he failed to find cities and towns, but he found much that inspired wonder. All the islands "are very fertile to a limitless degree." They have harbors "beyond comparison with others that I know in Christendom." Their rivers, "good and large," are "marvelous." The mountains are "beautiful"; "they seem to touch the sky." In particular, the island he named Española was an earthly paradise. The people "all go naked, men and women, as their mothers bore them," a description that makes them neither wild nor sexually charged, but the embodiment of a prelapsarian innocence, comparable to the original human couple frolicking in paradise before the Fall. They are meek and mild; they have no creed but are acutely intelligent; they speak among themselves a common tongue. In other words they are ripe for Christianization – indeed, already inclined toward conversion (Columbus 1968: 192–7). Columbus's world bears the firm stamp of textual authority. The people who inhabit it are shaped by their relationship to it (Grafton with Shefford and Siraisi 1992); within a biblical and theological scheme of things, they have been assigned a place as unformed, intelligent beings who will readily play their part in the divine drama of universal spread of the true faith (Flint 1992).

We now possess another, detailed record of Columbus's first voyage, which went unpublished in his own time, an abstract of his voyage journal. The original copies of the journal were lost, but the abstract, which was discovered in 1791 and published in 1825, seems highly reliable (Vigneras in Columbus 1968: xxi–xxii). It brings us closer to Columbus's initial impressions of the peoples he encountered on Caribbean islands, which were formed on an island "called Guanahani in the language of the Indians." The Europeans saw naked people, and Columbus went ashore in an armed launch. He announced to the gathering crowd that he was taking possession of the place in the name of his royal masters. Then came the first of many exchanges in the fateful meeting of Europeans and Americans:

> ...in order that they would be friendly to us – because I recognized that they were people who would be better freed [from error] and converted to our Holy Faith by love than by force – to some of them I gave red caps, and glass beads which they put on their chests, and many other things of small value, in which they took so much pleasure and became so much our friends that it was a marvel. (1989: 65)

In the first hour of encounter he registered the presence of the marvelous. Again and again he recorded his amazement at all he observed. He bore witness to the intrusion of the unexpected and the new; there is a mixture of prejudice and fresh impressions in his written legacy. Columbus may have been unable to recognize or, later, to admit that he had not found China or India, but he recognized that he was in the presence of something unprecedented. His writing alternates between trying to describe it – which often leads him to fall back on traditional descriptions – and the language of astonishment. As Stephen Greenblatt has observed, wonder was one of the most fundamental European reactions to the encounter with the Americas (1991: 14). Overall, Columbus's writing constitutes a tentative breakthrough to a new mental as well as physical world. He struggles to make old and new fit together, sometimes arguing that the things he has seen confirm the original vision that had led him overseas, at other times giving way to an astonishment that is at least an implicit recognition of something novel and requiring elucidation.

In the generation after Columbus many Spanish theologians turned to Aristotle in order to define the peoples of the New World as natural slaves, peoples who had deficient reason. They were members of a horde, a chaotic mass that failed to maintain proper distance among persons of different social status; wore no clothes; the men were polygynous; and they were idolaters. Trying to understand Indian religious practices, unsympathetic observers concluded that Indians were in the grip of the devil (Pagden 1982: 24–6, 42, 47, 52–3; Cervantes 1994: 5–39). Yet, for the most famous Spanish writer on the peoples of the Americas, Bartolomé de Las Casas (1474–1566), Amerindians were not objects of abstract speculation, but living human beings whom he himself had seen and known. Las Casas traveled to the New World several times, first visiting what is today Haiti in 1502, and subsequently going to Cuba, Venezuela and Mexico (Pagden in Las Casas 1992: xviii–xxiii, xxxvii). He witnessed atrocities, the enslavement of indigenous peoples, and their masters' ruthless contempt toward them. A member of the Dominican order who left Spain for the first time without an inkling of what awaited him, Las Casas worked tirelessly and risked his own life and reputation to call attention to the evils he discovered, never losing his sense of moral outrage. His most famous work, *A Short Account of the Destruction of the Indies* (1552), is an early example of an important genre of anthropological writing, the exposé of colonial abuses. Las Casas's book was put into the service of Spain's European rivals. The English translation published in 1699 promised in its subtitle to relate the Spaniards' "unparall'd Cruelties on the *Indians*" (Las Casas 1699). Yet Las Casas himself wrote as a reformer who was appealing to the monarchy and Spain's ruling class to alleviate evils that contravened their own standards of justice, and would lead to the ruin of their empire if uncorrected (Pagden in Las Casas 1992: xxxvii–xxxix). In a certain sense, Las Casas used the rhetorical manner of Columbus's first letter as well as personal observation and learned debate. He portrays native peoples as childlike, poor, devoid of ambition or greed, and near-naked. "They are innocent and pure in mind and have a lively intelligence, all of which makes them particularly receptive to learning and understanding the truths of our Catholic faith and to being instructed in virtue; indeed, God has invested them with fewer impediments in this regard than any other people on earth" (Las Casas 1992: 10). The depredations of the settlers undermined the Amerindians' opportunity to realize fully their natural goodness through conversion to Christianity. Las Casas was more than an apologist for Christianity, however. His writings also included a stage theory of civilization – one that arranges all peoples in a hierarchy that ascends to full civility, in which human beings live in a peaceful, orderly polity. All had the same beginnings in barbarism, characterized by violence and irreligion. Las Casas's stage theory of social development was an alternative to theories of Amerindians' depravity, an attempt to plead for a recognition of their full humanity (Pagden 1982: 142).

Another remarkable Spanish analyst of indigenous Americans was the Jesuit missionary José de Acosta (1540–1600). Like Las Casas, he knew the New World firsthand, spending time in Peru and Mexico before returning to Spain in 1587. Like Las Casas, he tried to mediate between his experience of indigenous societies and the received categories of Aristotelian social and political theory. Also like Las Casas, he thought Amerindian society deficient, but believed in the possibility of its improvement (Pagden 1982: 147–59). Acosta's *Natural and Moral History of the East and West Indies* is dispassionate and comprehensive, a model for the kind of survey of non-European peoples and places that Enlightenment travelers would produce over a century later. It begins with a long debate with religious and ancient authorities in order to establish the newness of the Americas, concluding that the ancients, including Augustine, Aristotle and Pliny, believed there were no men beyond the Tropic of Cancer, or certainly none between the two tropics (Acosta 1604: 35–6). Acosta also uses his and others' experience of the Americas to refute his contemporaries' prejudices. One of his means is comparison with classical antiquity. He reminds his readers that if there are abominations among the Indians, the same or worse are recorded for the Greeks and Romans (ibid.: 328). Many of their institutions were worthy of great admiration, "whereby we may understand, that they were by nature, capable to receive any good instructions" (ibid.: 432). In some ways, they surpass the societies of classical antiquity and modern Europe; had the Greeks and Romans known the laws and governments of the Mexicans or the Incas, they would have esteemed them (ibid.: 432). Comparing indigenous peoples to the ancients was a rhetorical strategy that others would use for centuries when they wished an educated audience to have a favorable opinion of these peoples; for example, as late as the early nineteenth century, painters alluded to noble classical types in their portraits of North American Indians and Polynesians (Truettner 1979; Smith 1985). The Greeks and Romans (along with the Bible) provided Europe's in-house stock of anthropological knowledge. They served as norms of admirable humanity for moderns, but at the same time their literature and histories recorded practices as strange as any to be discovered around the world.

The chief objective of missionaries such as Las Casas and Acosta may have been to convert the people they met, but missionaries could also be disposed to pay close attention to indigenes' psychological, cultural, and religious life. Such was the case with a French Huguenot minister who traveled to Brazil, Jean de Léry (1534–1613). When Claude Lévi-Strauss first arrived in Rio de Janeiro 378 years later, it was with a copy of Léry in his pocket, "the anthropologist's breviary" (Lévi-Strauss 1973: 81).

The mission that took Léry to the New World was fraught with dangers. It was the first Protestant mission and was led by an experienced soldier, Nicolas Durand de Villegagnon. Arriving in 1557, the missionaries had a falling out with Villegagnon and fled from their island base to the mainland. There they spent two months depending for their survival on the Tupinamba Indians, bluff warriors whom Europeans feared as cannibals. During this stay, however, Léry learned to admire them as generous, witty, intelligent hosts. Returning to France in 1558, he was plunged into an atmosphere of rising hostility between Catholics and Protestants. He was almost killed in the St Bartholomew's Day Massacre during August 1572 and survived a siege inside the town of Sancerre from January to August of 1573, during which the desperate town-dwellers boiled and ate the soles of their shoes to stay alive (Whatley in Léry 1990: xvi–xviii). Civil war was the background for Léry's appreciative memoir of his stay among the Tupinamba, published in 1578, twenty years after he returned to Brazil; his book is not a register of immediate impressions, but a reflective memoir with a strong comparative background.

Jean de Léry speaks to us as a passionate, intelligent man, one who is stung by the criticisms of his mission, alive to the wonders of this world and, of course, ever thinking about the next. He does not fit the comfortable image of an urbane humanist who anticipates ourselves. Rather, his curiosity, his openness to the Tupinamba, and his weariness with his fellow countrymen make him an "anthropologist" open to the New. Wonder is one of the recurring themes of Léry's account (ibid.: xv, xxii, xxvii). When Léry's voyage across the Atlantic begins, he is miserable as he eats worm-infested biscuits and drinks fetid water, but he discovers flying fish, which he had previously thought fictions of travelers' tall tales, and also savors the albacore and learns to distinguish two kinds of porpoise, including one that blows and snorts like a pig (Léry 1990: 15–21). When he reaches the rain forest, he is dazzled by its brilliance and lushness. He writes of America that "everything to be seen – the way of life of its inhabitants, the form of the animals, what the earth produces – is so unlike what we have in Europe, Asia, and Africa that it may very well be called a 'New World' with respect to us . . ." To describe the Tupinamba he turns to the vocabulary of the Golden Age (the pre-Christian notion of a contented first age of humankind) and of the Beatitudes (Jesus' invocation of a condition of spiritual blessing in the Sermon on the Mount). Some Tupinamba live to be a hundred and twenty, and the air and climate of their country are good. Their long lives – "they all truly drink at the Fountain of Youth" – shows "the little care or worry that they have for the things of this world" (ibid.: lx–lxi, 56–7). He and his fellow voyagers are astonished by the Tupinambas' nakedness, and while he is still with Villegagnon they whip the women for refusing to clothe themselves, to no avail. However much he disapproves of their nakedness, and tries to reform them with a violence most of us would find repulsive, he also informs his reader that these naked women do not arouse "wanton desire and lust," in contrast to the French women who revel in artifice (ibid.: 67). The Calvinist minister has his own motives for making a point like this: he is ever the preacher urging his audience to engage in self-reflection. One of Europeans' often-repeated charges was that the peoples of the Americas were cannibals. Léry assures his readers that they are right to feel superior on this point, describing how the Tupinambas killed and ate captured enemies, sometimes after treating them hospitably and providing them with wives for long periods. After enumerating the Tupinambas' cruelties, he asks readers to "think more carefully about the things that go on every day over here, among us" starting with the usurers who (metaphorically) eat everyone alive just as the Tupinamba eat their enemies. He frankly reveals the Tupinambas' atrocities – after all, he went to Brazil to convert them and thus to improve their behavior – but he thinks that the cruelty of moneylenders who oppress widows, orphans, and the poor is worse than the Tupinambas' (ibid.: 131–2). Although he does not sentimentalize the Tupinambas, his theology, and his experience of civil war in France make him skeptical toward European assumptions of moral superiority.

Michel de Montaigne (1533–92) was born just a year before Jean de Léry. An honored public man and for a time mayor of his native Bordeaux, he shared with his Calvinist contemporary a revulsion toward the cruelties of the Wars of Religion between Catholics and Protestants that were tearing France apart, an experience that also heightened his appreciation of strange societies. We do not know whether he read Léry's travel account, but his essay "On Cannibals" (1580) turns to reports on new peoples of Brazil in order to teach his readers to rethink their categories of barbarism and civilization. Brave and faithful, the Brazilians are closer to nature, while Europeans are corrupted by civilization. Their cannibalism, while opposed to natural law, has to be understood as part of a code of martial valor that is itself noble and generous. "We are justified therefore," he writes, "in calling these people barbarians by reference to the laws of reason, but not in comparison with ourselves, who surpass them in every kind of barbarity" (Montaigne 1958: 114). Montaigne's skepticism toward received textual authority, whether classical or religious, denotes an end point of early modern thought, a radical new openness to the fresh knowledge available to Europeans (Grafton with Shefford and Siraisi 1992: 153–7). It represents a new beginning, for in place of textual authority it upholds reason as the measure of all things human. To be sure, Montaigne had a remarkably flexible conception of reason, with wide allowance being given for the varieties of human custom and the eccentricities of his fellow Europeans. Nonetheless he associated reason with an uncorrupted nature and a male warrior virtue that permitted him to admire the Brazilians.

Enlightenment Anthropology: Testing the Limits of Reason

Beginning in the late seventeenth century a distinctive Enlightenment anthropological discourse took shape. It did not represent a neat beginning of modern anthropology; Acosta has a better claim to founder status than Enlightenment theorists, and as we have seen, *Tristes Tropiques* (1955), Claude Lévi-Strauss's famous travel memoir, has one distant inspiration in Jean de Léry's ethnography. It is more useful to think of the eighteenth century as a moment when tensions emerged between a new set of preconceptions and empirical experience. In the Renaissance, those tensions involved the conflict between textual authority and new information streaming back into Europe from the voyages of Columbus and his successors. In the Enlightenment, European conceptions of rationality were tested against the experiences of new generations of travelers.

The outlines of an Enlightenment ethnology emerge in the writings of Louis-Armand de Lom d'Arce de Lahontan (1666–1716). Baron Lahontan was a soldier in French Canada from 1683 to 1693 (interrupted by visits to France in 1690 and 1691). A quarrelsome man who got in trouble with the religious and secular authorities in Quebec, he wrote a history of his years in North America that ridiculed European authorities and praised native peoples for their courage and their love of freedom. His account of his travels is a mixture of vivid reporting on Indian life and tall tales about his adventures. He strikes a new note in an imaginary dialog staged between himself and a Huron named Adario. A local Socrates, Adario identifies the absurdities of Christianity, the immorality of the French and the cruelty and injustice of their laws. Indians lived simply, freely, and happily without any aid from Europeans. Lahontan's "savage" is more rational than his "civilized" interlocutor. At the early date of 1702, Lahontan's *New Voyages to North America* offered a fully formed portrait of the unlettered indigene as the embodiment of reason and critic of European corruption. Lahontan's account, and especially its dialogue with Adario, provided impressive and useful testimony for Enlightenment thinkers (Lahontan 1709; Hayne 1969; Ouellet in Lahontan 1990).

Lahontan's contemporary, Joseph-François Lafitau (1681–1746), came to the study of American Indians from the contrasting perspective of a devout missionary. At age 15 he joined the Jesuit order and went as a volunteer missionary to Canada, where he stayed from 1712 to 1717, spending much of his time deep in the interior in Sault St Louis, and returning to Canada in 1727–29 (Fenton and Moore in Lafitau 1974: xxxi–xxxviii). From the viewpoint of a highly educated Jesuit, Lafitau arrived at comparable conclusions that Huron and Iroquois peoples were rational individuals who inhabited societies infused with admirable ethical principles. Interested in finding vestiges of the earliest, natural religion of man (see Strenski in this volume), Lafitau did not merely apply abstract categories borrowed from his studies; he was an analytical social observer, and respectful of his hosts. Like Lahontan, he noted that they were capable of excellent self-government without being policed by a modern state. He went beyond Lahontan in his analysis of their kinship system, anticipating modern anthropology's concern with kinship (Motsch 2001: 156; Fenton and Moore in Lafitau 1974: xlvi–xlviii, li, lviii, cxviii–cxix). Seen in the context of the eighteenth century, Lafitau's work reminds us that missionary texts could point the way to an Enlightenment perspective. The Jesuit missionary could be as emphatic as the anti-clerical Lahontan in emphasizing the highly developed debating skills of Indians; both men assumed that Indians were in full possession of natural reason, the birthright of every human being.

Jean-Jacques Rousseau built on this widespread belief in natural reason and challenged European self-confidence with the model of primitive society in his *Discourse on the Origins of Inequality* (1755). It is a work that has provoked disagreement as well as admiration ever since it was published (Liebersohn 1998: 24–6). Rousseau identified the central flaw of European society, its fundamental and unanswerable question in an age of self-proclaimed Enlightenment: why did it organize human beings into ranks of legal unequals? The example of indigenous peoples around the world suggested to Rousseau that social hierarchy was unnatural. He argued that social evolution had actually found its equilibrium, the condition in which human beings were happiest, at the midpoint between original anarchy and modern social divisions – in those societies that had language and the family but not yet the arts of metallurgy, the knowledge that came with literacy, and the power of the state. Ever since he wrote the *Second Discourse*, Rousseau has been accused, not without justification, of naïveté and sentimentalization of native societies. There was, however, a methodological originality to the *Discourse on Equality*, which established it in the social scientific canon. The modern French tradition of sociocultural analysis built on Rousseau's vision of societies as unified, intelligible systems. A work such as Durkheim's *The Elementary Forms of Religious Life* (1912), for example, follows Rousseau's method of trying to imagine the essentials of human collective existence by looking at societies that were supposed to represent social life in its simplest form. Also visible in Rousseau's work is the problematic relationship between theoretical model and empirical reality: Rousseau oscillates between model-building and turning to indigenous societies for evidence, sometimes insisting the two processes are distinct, sometimes taking for granted that societies called "primitive" reveal an original, clearer form of the logic of "later" societies such as those to be found in modern Europe. The significance of Rousseau's achievement has been obscured by the ideological controversies that have surrounded his work, held responsible at times for the outbreak of the French Revolution and accused of providing the model for its Jacobin reign of terror. From the standpoint of the history of the social sciences, Rousseau demonstrates the fruitfulness of studying *society* as an entity distinct from nature or the state, and in the *Second Discourse* he turns his readers' attention to the study of non-European societies.

By contrast, British travel writers approached native cultures free of the theoretical ambitions of a Lahontan or a Lafitau, not to speak of a Rousseau. The age of buccaneering produced an outpouring of travel narratives that entertained readers with tales of British derring-do against Spanish and French rivals and also contained serious information about the world of the open seas. One of the best to write in this vein was William Dampier (1652–1715). After a first trip to Jamaica and the surrounding Caribbean from 1675 to 1678, he departed again for Jamaica in 1679 and experienced a series of adventures that took him to Central America, Virginia, Cape Horn, Manila, Formosa, and the north coast of Australia; he returned home in 1691 (Gray in Dampier 1927: xx–xxvii). Neither a visionary like Columbus, nor a man of God like Léry, nor a homespun *philosophe* like Lahontan, nor a well-bred cleric like Lafitau, Dampier went abroad in search of fortune. Though he came home penniless, he had kept a journal that was the basis of his bestselling *Voyage Round the World* (1697). This neither praises nor condemns indigenous peoples so much as estimating their usefulness for European marauders, as in its description of the Moskito people who lived between Cape Honduras and Nicaragua: skilled with lance and harpoon, and fearsome as gunners on European ships, they became valuable allies and guides for the British. Dampier wrote that he and his countrymen let them come and go as they pleased, for if they frustrated them, the Moskitos would "miss" the fish and turtles they were supposed to lance (Dampier 1927: 15–17). His descriptions were entertaining for armchair travelers and instructive for future adventurers. He enjoyed protection in high places and entered into polite society. Dedicating his book to Charles Montague, president of the Royal Society, he declared "a hearty Zeal for the promoting of useful knowledge, and of any thing that may never [sic] so remotely tend to my Countries advantage" (Dampier 1927: 1). Useful knowledge and national interest: these were Enlightenment principles with wide appeal.

Men of letters were not slow to respond with works of fiction that built on the experiences of Dampier and other adventurers. Daniel Defoe, a canny popularizer for the London literary market, based his bestselling adventure novel on the story of a marooned and rescued sailor from Dampier's account. Entitled *The Life and Strange Surprizing adventures of Robinson Crusoe of York, mariner . . . Written by himself,* Defoe's 1719 book was effectively presented as non-fiction; indeed, Defoe's name was not on the title page. Moreover, Defoe promised the reader instruction as well as entertainment. Crusoe's story was supposed to reveal "the Wisdom of Providence in all the Variety of our Circumstances." A deep sense of religious design pervades this fictional narrative of discovery, just as it earlier motivated Columbus and his patrons. Crusoe's relationship to the "native" he met on his island, whom he named Friday, embodied widespread attitudes toward native peoples: a mixture of fear of the demonic (symbolized above all by the fear of cannibalism) and confidence in one's calling to missionize, Christianize, and civilize. This volatile combination of fear and missionary impulse remained characteristic of later, more secularized travel writing. *Robinson Crusoe* also fascinated readers with its detailed, concrete description of life abroad, showing how English industry and common sense could master difficulties and lead to the founding of colonies in far-flung parts of the globe.

Travel writing was not just the province of buccaneers and novelists. European rulers and their scientific advisors mounted an enormous effort over the course of the eighteenth century to make a systematic inventory of the resources of the world, including its non-European peoples. Marginal European powers were among the pioneers in this movement. The Russian Tsars sent German scientists across Siberia to report on the contents of their vast continental empire (Mühlmann 1968: 53). Linnaeus, who wrote a notable ethnography of the Sami people, served as scientific advisor to the Swedish state and sent numerous travelers on extra-European voyages (Koerner 1999). The culmination of this movement toward scientific expeditions came with the three circumnavigations commanded by James Cook (1728–79) in 1768–71, 1772–75, and 1776–80 (the third expedition returned to England the year after Cook's death in Hawaii). Cook came from a modest background, but made his reputation as a land surveyor. The Admiralty had originally singled him out for his surveying and presumed navigating skills. Cook's enterprises were distinguished by the elements they combined. State support; careful formulation of instructions; long preparation and assembling of scientific equipment; the use of trained scientists as participants or advisors; the involvement of armed forces and scientific training for navy and army personnel: these set precedents for later eighteenth-century and nineteenth-century scientific voyages, which generally made intelligence-gathering about indigenous societies an important part of their work. Habits of persistent, method-ical observation made Cook an exact reporter on the societies of such places as Tahiti, New Zealand, Australia, Easter Island, the Marquesas, and Vanuatu. His efforts served imperial ends. Writing without classical flourishes, with little conjecture, he pro-vided reliable information for scientists, commercial actors, and colonizers. Cook's impact on ethnographic writing throughout Europe is immeasurable; he set the standard for subsequent seafaring naturalists (Smith 1985; Mackay 1985; Liebersohn 2006).

Cook's analytic approach was not devoid of presuppositions. He believed firmly in the sanctity of property, and raged about the frequent pilfering that took place on Polynesian islands. Notwithstanding evidence to the contrary, he assumed that punishment would prevent further deviant behavior. He presumed Britain's right to establish strategic outposts for a world empire at convenient points. He expected Hawaiian islanders to conform to middle-class British behavioral norms, and grew increasingly tyrannical when they did not. His murder in Kealakekua Bay, Hawaii in 1779 was surely a consequence of his inability to understand Hawaiian society. Perhaps he was killed because he violated the ritual expectations Hawaiians had for the god they believed him to be; or perhaps his death followed his interference in a local war, in which he was a partisan of the losing side (Sahlins 1985; Obeysekere 1992). Regardless, sub-sequent travelers had good reason to examine non-Europeans' alien ways of thinking if they did not wish to suffer fates equivalent to his.

A young German on board the second Cook voyage, Georg Forster, signaled the turn to a different way of understanding non-European peoples. He began with con-ventional Enlightenment assumptions that Tahitians and other Pacific islanders would conform to the model of rational "natural man," egalitarian in local politics and eager for friendship with gun-toting strangers. Instead, he encountered polities that varied con-siderably from island to island, even though languages were remarkably similar across the vast reach of Oceania from New Zealand to Easter Island. His *Voyage Round the World* (1777) gushed with brotherly love toward the islanders who lived up to his expec-tations of kindness and friendship, and plunged into melancholy at unwonted violence, native or European, that challenged his hopes for a brotherhood of humankind.

While deeply immersed in Enlightenment ideals, Forster's narrative shades into a mood that is recognizably Romantic – a term that he himself occasionally used to describe wild landscapes. It hints at a newly emerging interest in non-Europeans not for their rationality (and therefore their receptiveness to Christianity or colonization) but for their strangeness (Forster 2000).

The close contact between Europeans and non-Europeans in Cook's voyages, then, tested European assumptions about human nature. What is distinctive is that a writer like Forster did not simply demonize native behavior that eluded European categories of rationality, but considered the possibility that it embodied a different kind of logic. A systematic questioning of inherited models of rationality and their application to non-European peoples was proposed by Johann Gottfried Herder, who announced a novel approach to the study of culture in his *Ideas for a Philosophy of History of Mankind* (1784–91). Herder was by training a Lutheran minister, but his earliest intellectual efforts reflected the enlightened literary and philosophical thought of his time. His preface challenged French claims to cultural hegemony and Enlightenment universalism: "Which people on earth does not have some culture? And how deficient would be the plan of providence if every individual in the human race were created for that which *we* call culture and is often just refined weakness?" (Herder 1989: 11–12, trans. H. L.). Thus, Herder suggested repudiation of the notion of one superior culture and opened the way to modern sociocultural anthropology's attempt at unprejudiced understanding of all ways of life. He demanded the creation of a new discipline for the study of mankind in general – which sounds in retrospect like a call for the creation of anthropology (1989: 14). And he boldly asserted that peoples across the globe belonged to one species and could not be divided into "races." Later writers could turn to him for a program for studying folk, marginal, and extra-European cultures. Literatures and national practices that had once been neglected or held in contempt could now be regarded as valuable contributions to the formation of a greater, single humanity.

Herder's writings, and the Romantic currents in anthropology that followed, contained difficulties that would haunt the study of culture throughout the nineteenth and twentieth centuries. One of his starting assumptions was a basic distinction between vital and lifeless cultures. Herder emphasized the environmental conditioning of culture: he attributed both physical and cultural differences among peoples to their climate, topography, and other natural conditions. There was no room in his thinking for fruitful interaction between cultures or for the consequences of migration; each culture was nurtured and strengthened by its deep connection to the soil. The counterpart to praise of what we would today call cultural authenticity – being in touch with one's inner nature and pulsating with creativity – was condemnation of everything else as inauthentic and devaluation of "nomadic," "hunter-gatherer," and "mercantile" peoples and classes as artificial, lifeless, and sterile. Herder's work sometimes seems to take a hermeneutic approach, which tries to enter into the spirit of every time and place, and at other times reads as a xenophobic partitioning of culture into irreconcilable spheres of the organic and authentic versus the inorganic and inauthentic (Herder 1989: 490–2).

Conclusion: Anthropology between Enlightenment and Romanticism

The history of anthropology from 1492 to the early nineteenth century crossed two watershed moments. The first was the transition from the Renaissance to the Enlightenment. It amounted to a decisive rejection of the authority of ancient texts and recognition of the novelty of peoples and places unknown to classical antiquity. This transition was irreversible; no subsequent era has abandoned the authority of experience in favor of text and myth.

The second watershed was far less stable. Enlightenment travelers and thinkers approached the non-European world in search of universal norms and forms of human behavior. Their encounters with the societies of Oceania exemplified their intellectual difficulties. Pacific peoples had no typical form of social organization and little in the way of recognizable religious belief; rather, they confronted visitors with a diversity of social arrangements that made it difficult to arrive at any clear definition of fundamental human nature. By the late eighteenth century, critics such as Herder had repudiated Enlightenment universalism and argued instead for the particularity of cultures. No single metropolis, no single people represented normal humanity; in Herder's vision, each of the many diverse cultures made its contribution to an unfolding of human nature over time. Already in Herder, however, Romantic admiration of the local and the particular had the potential to fashion boundaries among groups that celebrated one culture at the expense of others. The appeal of Romanticism was far from general among European thinkers. The Enlightenment's search for universal norms and for exact measurement and classification did not end in the eighteenth century but continued, transmuted but not abandoned, into the nineteenth century. There was no resolution of the quarrel between universalists and particularists comparable to the earlier victory of empiricists over traditionalists. European industrialization and creation of an integrated world economy seemed to set Europeans apart from all other peoples, accentuating their sense of superiority. Against this background, social theorists proposed universal schemes of human development to explain the differences between European and non-European peoples. At the same time, folklore and language research, which derived from Romantic conceptions of national identity, continued unabated, recording in ever-greater detail the artifacts and structures of individual cultures. The quarrel between Enlightenment and Romantic approaches, transformed over the course of the nineteenth century and yet persistent, was an uneasy legacy to the founders of modern anthropology.

Further Reading

Elliott, J. H. 1972. *The Old World and the New, 1492–1650*. Cambridge: Cambridge University Press.

Lamb, J., V. Smith, and N. Thomas. 2000. *Exploration and Exchange: A South Seas Anthology, 1680–1900*. Chicago: University of Chicago Press.

Liebersohn, H. 2006. *The Travelers' World: Europe to the Pacific.* Cambridge, MA: Harvard University Press.

Smith, B. 1985. *European Vision and the South Pacific*, 2nd edn. New Haven: Yale University Press.

Withey, L. 1989. *Voyages of Discovery: Captain Cook and the Exploration of the Pacific.* Berkeley: University of California Press.

Part I

Major Traditions

2

North American Traditions in Anthropology: The Historiographic Baseline

Regna Darnell

The diversity of traditions within North American anthropology has been underestimated by most historians of anthropology, both North American and foreign. Americanist anthropology cannot be equated simply with the tradition that developed around Franz Boas (1858–1942) and his students, and encapsulated within the geographical boundaries of the United States. Hallowell (1960) identified two core features of this national tradition: its four-field, subdisciplinary scope (sociocultural anthropology, biological/physical anthropology, archaeology, and linguistics) and its focus on the study of the American Indian. In 1960, just before the history of anthropology emerged as a focus of specialization within the North American discipline, Hallowell's overview provided a relatively seamless narrative around which the distinctiveness of American anthropology might be understood by its practitioners. Hallowell envisioned the history of anthropology as an "anthropological problem" (1965), in which anthropologists should take the primary responsibility for telling their own story, as part of their professional socialization and contemporary practice. Hallowell's narrative received an authoritative imprimatur at a conference sponsored by the Social Science Research Council in 1962, which was attended by George W. Stocking, Jr., the dean of American historians of anthropology. Stocking's work has described how the professionalization of Americanist anthropology in universities was effected by the Boasians (Stocking 1968).

Debates about whether anthropology and other social sciences had a paradigm, and therefore could be considered mature sciences, abounded in the decade following the publication of Thomas S. Kuhn's *The Structure of Scientific Revolutions* (1962). Increased reflexivity among anthropologists about their own history – and efforts to find paradigmatic coherence in it – meant that its core narrative slighted diversity, which was paradoxical, given that the discipline had become increasingly diverse and more closely connected to colleagues working in other national traditions after World War II.

Debates conducted within American anthropology concerned who should write disciplinary history – historians or anthropologists – and the relative merits of historicism and presentism as paradigmatic models for the historian. Many lauded Stocking's efforts to set a methodological standard for anthropologists, who were not accustomed to use the techniques of trained historians (such as archival research), whereas others thought that anthropologists could learn historical methods more easily than historians could learn to think like anthropologists (Darnell 1977). If the history of anthropology were to be integral to the contemporary discipline, anthropologists would have to commit themselves to producing ethnographies of anthropological practice that met historians' standards.

The question of historicism vs presentism (Stocking 1968) was less easily resolved. Historicism, understanding ideas in the contexts of their times rather than judging them by contemporary standpoints, was equated by many with the purported objectivity of idealized history. In this view, presentism distorted and foreshortened the past. But some unabashedly adopted a presentist view. For example, Marvin Harris (1968) questioned the hegemony of Boasian anthropology, reconstructing North American anthropology's history as a saga of progress toward his "techno-environmental determinis[t]" synthesis. The Marxist political economy he envisioned as the revitalizable core of evolutionary anthropology had been set back by Boasian "historical particularism." For Harris, revisionist disciplinary history was inseparable from the desirable future of anthropology.

Since the 1960s, however, methodological sophistication has come to be taken for granted, regardless of the disciplinary roots of the anthropological historian. In a post-structuralist milieu of reflexivity and standpoint epistemology (see Schumaker in this volume), historicism and presentism are no longer opposing binaries. Rather, disciplinary historians are careful to situate themselves relative to their subject matters and favored modes of interpretation (Darnell 2001). Stocking himself has adopted rhetoric of speaking from the "centers" of contemporary anthropological discourse – in his own case, from his position at the University of Chicago (Stocking 2001). At his location, however, it is especially likely that one will see the intersection of British social anthropology with the Americanist tradition that developed around Boas, and minimize the analytic utility of the very concept of national tradition.

Early Studies of the American Indian

The identity of America as independent of Europe was constituted in good part by the presence of the American Indian (Deloria 1998). The statesmen founders of the United States were deeply engaged with an imagined "noble savage," at the same time as settlers were displacing the Indians. Thomas Jefferson (1743–1826) exemplifies this ambiguity. He collected Indian vocabularies and excavated a burial mound in Virginia, but Jefferson also held slaves and endorsed Indian removal (Wallace 1999). Jefferson also drew up instructions for the Lewis and Clark Expedition, which would set the stage for American continental expansion. Anthropology, government expediency and Indian Affairs administration were joined long before the professionalization of the discipline.

The study of Indian languages rapidly became the key to classifying the diversity of cultures in Native North America (Bieder 1986). John Pickering (1777–1846) collected existing materials and attempted a standardized alphabet. Peter Stephen Duponceau (1760–1844) described the characteristic grammar of Amerindian languages as "polysynthetic." As an Indian agent, Henry Rowe Schoolcraft (1793–1864) recorded Ojibwe texts and vocabulary. Albert Gallatin (1761–1849), Jefferson's Secretary of the Treasury, prepared the first comprehensive classification of Indian languages in 1836. As governor of the Michigan Territory, Lewis Cass (1782–1866) designed questionnaires to map cultural and linguistic diversity. Thus, talented but untrained amateurs produced a form of linguistics that functioned to classify peoples in ethnological categories, quite unlike the tenor of Indo-European philology.

The study of American archaeology got off to a slow start because there seemed to be no American equivalent of the European paleo-, meso- and neolithic ages. Most eighteenth-century observers took for granted the basic homogeneity of Amerindian tribes, and assumed that they were peoples without history, incapable of change, or certainly of high achievements; for example, there was sustained refusal to acknowledge contemporary peoples as ancestors of the so-called Mound Builders of the Mississippi and Ohio valleys (Trigger 1989). Such assumptions hampered the development of archaeological inquiry (and also strengthened European settlers' belief that they had a "Manifest Destiny" to populate North America, since its aboriginal inhabitants were incapable of developing the land). It was 1927 before the Pecos Classification for the American Southwest used tree ring dates to provide the first reliable chronology for Indian cultures. Goodenough (2002) stresses that archaeology made rapid progress in the 1950s as it contrived new dating methods, with major breakthroughs following the development of radiocarbon dating.

Early studies of the American Indian assumed that physical type would correlate directly with linguistic and cultural diversity. Early anthropometry – (ostensibly) systematic measurement of variations in human physical characteristics – was in certain respects indistinguishable from relatively popular movements. Phrenology, at the height of its popularity in the early nineteenth century, was predicated on the assumption that individuals' character could be discerned from bumps on their heads. The mid-nineteenth-century debates between polygenists (who believed the diverse human "races" to be separate creations) and monogenists (who emphasized environmental modification of human characteristics) were as much theological as scientific. The eugenics movement, which began in the late nineteenth century, appealed to many notable scientists, but its efforts to improve the quality of the human species required popular involvement. Nevertheless, methods of study and analysis were developed and collections of skeletons became available for later analysis. And population genetics would eventually show that the outward characteristics usually thought to define racial differences were merely superficial surface differences among groups.

The Emergence of Americanist Anthropology

Prior to the existence of anything recognizable as a professional discipline of anthropology, the basic parameters of the four subdisciplines were delineated, and beginnings were made in exploring diverse aspects of the American Indian within the geographical boundaries of North America. It was in the late nineteenth century that the professionalization of anthropology occurred in North America: paid positions for scholars with specialized credentials became available; and peers were considered the appropriate judges of the merits of scholars' work. An adequate history must attend to the intellectual ideas and the institutional frameworks and social networks within which anthropological work occurs.

Four major figures define the progress of North American anthropology toward professionalization during this crucial transitional period: Lewis Henry Morgan, Daniel Garrison Brinton, Frederick Ward Putnam and John Wesley Powell. Each, in his way, was grounded in the context of late nineteenth-century America and looked toward the future of anthropology within the inclusive democratic experiment of the post-Civil War nation. The institutional framework for their anthropology centered in learned societies in major cities.

Morgan (1818–81) was a lawyer and businessman based in Rochester, New York, whose contact with the local Iroquois led him to ethnography and, ultimately, to evolutionary theory. His anthropology was avocational, although the Smithsonian Institution published his classical kinship studies. Early contact with the New York Seneca led to his classic ethnography *League of the Ho-de-no-sau-nee* (1851), then to more generalized study of kinship contrasting the classificatory systems of so-called "primitive" societies with the descriptive terminologies of his own civilization (1871), and, finally, to a model of human evolution from savagery to barbarism to civilization based on "primary germs of ideas," with each stage marked by a seminal cultural innovation (1877). Beyond its North American formulation, Morgan's evolutionary celebration of American progressivism and ingenuity was turned to rather different purposes by Friedrich Engels (1884), who used Morgan's ideas to justify socialist revolution.

Brinton (1837–99) was a physician whose primary professional affiliation was with the gentleman scholars of the American Philosophical Society, founded by Benjamin Franklin in Philadelphia "for the promotion of useful knowledge." Technically, his professorship in ethnology, established at the University of Pennsylvania in 1886, was the first such anthropological position in North America, although he received no salary and had no identifiable students (Darnell 1988). Brinton assembled and published a Library of Aboriginal American Literature (featuring his own Mayan textual studies), provided an early classification of North and South American languages, and interpreted myth themes in terms of the "psychic unity of mankind," a mentalist perspective oddly in contrast with his unabashed evolutionary racism. Brinton foresaw the need for professionalization, calling for an academic rather than museum institutional base for anthropology, and supported early national projects; for example, he served on the inaugural board of the *American Anthropologist*.

Putnam, who took up a professorship at Harvard in 1887, was affiliated primarily with the Peabody Museum of American Archaeology and Ethnology, where training for his students centered (Mark 1980). Putnam's strength was in archaeology, although his interests were not confined to it. (He was also a strong supporter of Franz Boas, under whose auspices Columbia became a center of cultural and linguistic anthropology, after Boas's appointment there – initially, in 1896, as a lecturer in physical anthropology.) Putnam (1839–1915) was primarily an institutional leader, organizing departmental and museum collaborations at Chicago around the 1893 World's Columbian Exposition and at Berkeley around the turn of the century.

Powell (1834–1902) was a geologist who turned to ethnology under the auspices of the Smithsonian Institution, becoming director of the newly established Bureau of (American) Ethnology in 1879. Powell's geological surveys in the "arid lands" of the American Southwest earned him the opprobrium of land speculators and politicians when he defined environment, technology and culture as an inseparable package (Powell 1878). Retreat to ethnology and the less politicized scientific environment of the Smithsonian Institution became politic. Powell's geological outlook was consistent with his interest in the cultural practices of the Ute and Shoshone, whose simple technology produced a living from the desert. Although the BAE ethnologists were trained in fields ranging from geology to journalism to theology, they quickly set new standards for scientific research. Powell was able to amass a database for understanding the American Indian by eliciting information from (usually unpaid) amateurs who were in contact with Indians, supplementing their labors with fieldwork by his permanent staff. The Bureau was the first American institution to assemble a team of paid anthropological researchers.

The work of the Bureau centered on the continental United States, consistent with the Smithsonian's mission to acquire and disseminate knowledge useful to the American people. Government sponsorship was pragmatic, geared to settling the Indians on Reservations for effective administration as well as to assimilating them as rapidly as possible. Congress was prepared to support research on Indians in the years of Reservation settlement, but not to encourage a theoretical science of global scope. This meant that Congress's expectations were often at odds with Powell's. Powell's own anthropology, which relied theoretically on Morgan's evolutionary model, was concerned to establish the relationships among Native American peoples and to classify languages. Early BAE research was, in effect, mapping – filling in the blanks in what was known about the Aboriginal peoples of the United States (Darnell 1998a). Powell's method derived from the geological surveys of his early career. As an ethnologist, he encouraged team research on linguistic classification as the paramount means of organizing Indians for national administrative purposes. His 58-unit linguistic classification (1891) provided a baseline for ethnology, as did F. W. Hodge's *Handbook of American Indians North of Mexico* (1906, 1912), as well as the *Handbook of American Indian Languages*, edited by Boas (1911a, 1922), and provided grammars of selected Native American languages geared to typological or "psychological" description, with each language described in its own terms.

Figure 3   Franz Boas in Eskimo costume. Used with permission from the American Philosophical Society.

Many of the institutions necessary for further professionalization emerged out of a pragmatic context (Hinsley 1981). The Anthropological Society of Washington drew together intellectuals from various sciences who were employed by the federal government. The Women's Anthropological Society of Washington set an early role model for women in science: Matilda Coxe Stevenson, Alice C. Fletcher, and Zelia Nuttall were among the early members also affiliated with the Bureau. There were administrative (but often practically irrelevant) distinctions to be made among the Smithsonian and the BAE as its subsidiary, as well as the United States National Museum (the collections of which were part of the Smithsonian's by 1880), but in practice bureaucratic lines were blurred, and diverse projects were supported, ranging, for example, from Frank C. Cushing's work among the Zuni to Otis T. Mason's development of tool typologies.

Franz Boas, trained as a physicist and subsequently as a geographer in Germany, turned to ethnology or cultural anthropology as a result of his 1883–84 expedition in Baffinland. There, Boas found that environment mediated culture rather than determining it – even though the Eskimo lived under extreme conditions (Stocking 1968). He then did fieldwork in a very different culture area. On the Northwest Coast he found diverse peoples who spoke many languages, the richness of their culture having been facilitated by long-term borrowing and interaction. Boas argued that the diffusion of cultural traits and complexes would reveal the history of past migration, settlement, and group interaction. Historical accounts were to be supplemented with "psychology," defined as "the Native point of view." This Native standpoint was accessible through linguistic texts obtained from the contemporary keepers of oral tradition.

The institutional development of American anthropology at the Bureau of American Ethnology was distinctive (although government science was becoming professionalized in Powell's day). Most of the early clusters of professional anthropological work involved collaboration between museums and universities: Harvard and the Peabody Museum, Columbia and the American Museum of Natural History, Berkeley and the Hearst-sponsored Berkeley Museum, Chicago and the Field Columbian Museum, Pennsylvania and the University Museum. Unable to confer academic credentials under Bureau auspices, Powell could not create a professional lineage. Nonetheless, Boas was able to draw upon the Bureau's work in systematizing what had been learned about the American Indian, and utilized its resources in the early years of his own career. Although after about 1904, Boas elided these continuities of subject matter and approach to emphasize the innovation inherent in his own programmatic vision for Americanist anthropology, the continuities are salient in retrospect (Darnell 1998a). Boas was able to build on the fieldwork, the mapping exercises, the increasingly rigorous standards for research and reporting, the development of publication outlets and scientific societies, and the idea of anthropology as a professional science. But the history of the emergence of Boasian anthropology has been colored by Boas's own pronouncements, as well as the memories of his students, for whom anthropology's early institutional history became virtually invisible. Later commentators have emphasized the roots of Boas's theory and practice in his German academic training, as well as his repudiation of the evolutionary approach of Powell and his Bureau.

From his earliest work, Boas embodied the Americanist tradition (Darnell in Valentine and Darnell eds. 1999). First, culture, for Boas, was symbolic thought rather than the observable behavior, which might arise from it. Second, the inseparability of language, thought, and reality placed linguistics at the center of cultural studies. Third, the database for ethnology, linguistics and psychology lay in the collection and translation of native language texts. Fourth, the production of such texts fell within Matthew Arnold's dictum of preserving the best that had been thought in human history (cf. Stocking 1968 on the contrast between E. B. Tylor and Arnold). Fifth, although Boas's later detractors often accused him of studying the moribund memory culture of remnant speakers unaffected by Western contact, the "traditions" entextualized by Boasians' "informants" (today, more appropriately referred to as "consultants" or even "collaborators") demonstrate tradition to be malleable and ever-adapting. "Tradition" is what establishes continuity with the past; it is a process of decision-making in light of what is already known and tested by collective experience. Sixth, textual work led the Boasians to establish intimate personal relationships with their consultants, which over time dramatically altered the ethical parameters of the discipline. Increasingly, Native Americans were acknowledged by outside anthropologists as experts in their own cultures rather than objects of study. Seventh, although Boas and his early students were unable to do protracted fieldwork, constrained by their museum and academic employment schedules, their research focus on "the native point of view" required them to return repeatedly to the same groups and communities over substantial periods of time. Because Native American communities were close at hand, and their members often had access to anthropological writings, the ethic of collaboration was reinforced.

After a peripatetic early career of science writing, museum collection and exhibit management, and Northwest Coast fieldwork sponsored by the British Association for the Advancement of Science and the BAE, Boas gained a position in 1889 at the new Clark University, whose president, the distinguished psychologist G. Stanley Hall, opened it as an institution devoted entirely to graduate training. (Boas received his appointment before he returned from the field.) Although Boas lectured on ethnology, his research and teaching were largely devoted to physical anthropology. Along with most of the Clark faculty, he resigned in 1892; however, he did not join the mass migration of erstwhile Clark employees to the new University of Chicago (where evolutionary anthropologist Frederick Starr was already ensconced). After various, transient work episodes, including participation in preparation of the Native American exhibits at the 1893 Chicago world's fair, a failed attempt to obtain a secure position at the Field Columbian Museum, and a period of unemployment, Boas finally settled in New York in 1895, when he gained a position at the American Museum of Natural History. He retained his affiliation with the museum when Columbia University hired him as a lecturer in physical anthropology in 1896. Boas and his students continued Amerindian work under museum auspices, and he organized the Jesup North Pacific Expedition to compare Siberian and Native American cultures. Few grand conclusions emerged, and Boas's relations with the museum gradually soured, resulting in his resignation in 1905 (Cole 1999).

Thereafter, Columbia's academic program was key to Boas's increasing control over the institutional development of American anthropology. The first cohort of his students spread across the country. Alfred Kroeber went to Berkeley, as did Robert Lowie (after reluctantly departing from the American Museum of Natural History). Edward Sapir moved from Ottawa to Chicago and then to Yale. Moreover, the first generation of Boas's students divided up the scope of cultural and linguistic anthropology as Boas understood it (Darnell 2001), each developing a piece of the theoretical core of the Boasian paradigm. Early in his career, Boas had developed a limited number of central theoretical positions (Boas 1896, 1911a, 1911b); they became standard anthropological wisdom, taken for granted to such a degree that they were no longer recognized as theoretical. First, Boas argued that anthropology had succumbed to the temptation of premature generalization based on evolutionary theories that distorted the realities of cultural diversity revealed by ethnographic research. Second, he asserted that history and psychology were the key approaches to culture, with the former taking precedence initially in order to establish an adequate database for further generalization. Third, he emphasized that race, language, and culture were analytically separate, and that a single typology of cultures could not be established. Boas's students took these axioms as given, and applied them to the study of particular Native American groups. Perhaps because Boas was often reluctant to make his theoretical arguments abstractly or explicitly, his students elaborated his paradigm variously, producing a series of programmatic textbooks during the first quarter of the twentieth century.

Alfred Kroeber (1876–1960) argued that the discipline of anthropology was distinguished from the natural sciences, humanities, and other social sciences by its core concept of culture. Culture, as Kroeber (1917) envisioned it, was "superorganic," having a force beyond the perspective or agency of the individuals composing it. Although this construct of culture has been criticized, and it is not now necessary to justify the existence of anthropology as an autonomous discipline, Kroeber's formulation served to establish that Boasian anthropology had a coherent program and mandate.

Edward Sapir (1884–1939), the paramount linguist among Boas's early students, critiqued the superorganic definition of culture, arguing instead for a standpoint theory of language, society and culture, which emphasized individuals' engagement with cultural norms (Sapir 1999; Darnell 1990). Sapir turned to collaborations with psychologists and psychoanalysts to explore the "impact of culture on personality" and argued that individuals creatively constructed their cultural worlds, each having a (somewhat) distinctive version of his/her culture. Sapir himself did not explore the implications of intra-cultural variability inherent in his position, however.

Paul Radin (1883–1959), another critic of the idea of the superorganic, considered his Winnebago consultants to be "primitive philosophers" (1927). Despite the absence of "systematic" philosophy among North American tribes, he considered the great philosophical questions to be universal, and his own civilization to have no monopoly on their resolution. Radin's conversations with Winnebago philosophers such as Crashing Thunder produced life histories of significant individuals in relation to their cultures, and also produced history from knowledge preserved through oral tradition.

History as imposed by the accidental preservation of documents written by outsiders could never capture the realities of "the native point of view."

Ruth Benedict's *Patterns of Culture* (1934) was a bestseller in its day. Benedict (1887–1948) borrowed a vocabulary from abnormal psychology to characterize the diverse choices made by different cultures from within the biologically given parameters of human potentiality. The cultures of the megalomaniac Kwakiutl, the Apollonian Zuni, and the schizophrenic Dobuans (based, respectively, on the ethnography of her teacher and mentor Boas, her own investigations, and Reo Fortune's work) had equal value in their own terms. Her cultural relativism came to define Boasian anthropology in the eyes of the American public. Despite her psychological terminology, Benedict was primarily interested in broad contrasts among societies, particularly between the Apollonian Zuni and the Dionysian Plains Indians, rather than in the scope that cultural patterns allowed for individual agency. She brought her moral position to bear in consideration of the quality of life in North American interwar society (Geertz 1988).

Sapir's protégé in linguistics, Benjamin Lee Whorf (1897–1941), elaborated his teacher's ideas about how language, particularly grammatical categories, structured the world for speakers (Lee 1996). Whorf's assertions about linguistic relativity, the mutual entailment of "language, culture and reality" (Whorf 1956), often sound deterministic to contemporary ears, as though languages might embody incommensurable views of reality. But Whorf himself saw possibilities for multicultural awareness and cross-linguistic conceptual fertilization. Linguistics, like ethnology, could reveal alternative philosophies.

Margaret Mead (1901–78) brought issues of gender and sexuality into then-contemporary debates about the universality of the American structure of the family and sexual practices. *Coming of Age in Samoa* (1928) sketched an alternative vision of adolescence as a time when young women could enjoy idyllic sexual freedom. Culture, not biology, was responsible for American teenage angst. Mead's work was strongly criticized by the late Derek Freeman (1983) in a peculiar exercise of revisionist history. Freeman worked with adult males who played political roles in a different part of Samoa and more than a generation after Mead had been there; his results do not invalidate the products of Mead's collaboration with young women. Freeman's critique, however, seems motivated more by his sociobiological theory than by Mead's work per se. Whatever the flaws of her pioneering fieldwork, Mead increased the American public's awareness that their own cultural practices were far from universal, and inspired a line of empirical, cross-cultural research in Americanist anthropology on sexual mores (Lyons and Lyons 2004).

Elsie Clews Parsons (1874–1941), a sociologist who converted to Boasian anthropology, was an early critic of the American family and proponent of sexual freedom. Parsons explored the possibilities of individual differences across cultures through life histories; her *American Indian Life* (1922) was a collection of commentaries on a range of Native American cultures by fellow Boasians.

A. Irving Hallowell's fieldwork among the Canadian Ojibwe explored the semantic space of the Ojibwe worldview, emphasizing "the behavioral environment of the self" as a cultural construction (Hallowell 1955). Hallowell (1892–1974) situated his work in the "culture and personality" genre, but his exploration of cognitive categories provided by cultures transcended the interpretive method of those who administered to diverse peoples the Rorschach (inkblot) test (which was intended to reveal individuals' personality characteristics) and the Thematic Apperception Test (which was supposed to measure individuals' perception of interpersonal relationships).

Although there were certainly other important Boasians of the interwar years, these key figures set the research agenda followed by most American anthropologists before 1945.

Non-Americanist Sociocultural Anthropology

The Boasian paradigm dominated American anthropology until the academic expansion that followed the Second World War. Returning veterans were taught by Americanists but found their fieldwork sites around the globe, as America itself became increasingly internationalist (and funds to support research abroad grew). Influence from British and French anthropology increased. Amerindian research was no longer central, although Darnell (2001) has argued that an "invisible genealogy" of Americanist assumptions has persisted and continues to underpin the apparent diversity of anthropology since World War II.

Initially, postwar anthropology seemed to play a valued role in the American move away from ethnocentric isolationism. Many American anthropologists participated in the war effort and advised government agencies on foreign policy. Benedict's *The Chrysanthemum and the Sword* (1946), with its culturally sophisticated program for postwar reconstruction of Japan, exemplifies this productive collaboration.

Work such as Boas's and Benedict's had challenged racism both under Hitler and at home. But cultural relativism was inimical to the anti-Communist, Cold War perspective developed after World War II. Implicit in Boasian cultural relativism were critiques of scientific racism, social inequality, and class hierarchy (Baker 1998; Barkan 1992). During the Cold War, anthropologists' collective reputation as radical activists meant that many found themselves defending their freedom of speech and harassed in employment, while others accused colleagues of communist inclinations (Price 2004). And many anthropologists challenged the ethics of the government, the military, and multinational corporations.

During the 1960s, left-leaning or radical anthropologists effectively followed the precedent of Boas's 1919 protest against espionage by anthropologists (Stocking 1968; Darnell 1998a). They protested against social scientists' involvement in American counterinsurgency movements, especially in Latin America and Southeast Asia. The ethics committee of the American Anthropological Association was forced to respond, largely under pressure from the association's student members, although the profession was still deeply divided over the propriety of scientific distance versus social activism.

A strand of North American sociocultural anthropology focusing on politics as subject matter and as activism developed alongside the Americanist tradition, although it was less visible. Joan Vincent (1990) divides this alternative tradition into six periods. From 1879, with the founding of the Bureau of American Ethnology to 1897, the politics of anthropology revolved around the expansion of the American frontier and the displacement of Native Americans. From 1898 to the end of World War I, an "uneasy" growth of university anthropology and ongoing fieldwork in North America coexisted with the blossoming of American imperialism. Vincent stresses the apolitical character of Boasian ethnography per se, in sharp contrast to the Boasians' activism in social issues, especially anti-racism. The years from 1919 to 1939 were dominated by the Depression and the New Deal, represented in anthropology by John Collier's restructuring of the Bureau of Indian Affairs around Native American cultural maintenance and revitalization. Studies of acculturation, understood as positive adaptation to change rather than assimilation, emerged in this period. Fieldwork in peasant communities, such as that done in Mexico and Guatemala by Robert Redfield (1897–1958) and in Puerto Rico by Julian Steward (1902–72), broke down the assumption that "primitive" societies were isolated from a larger world. From 1940 to 1953, British social anthropology set the standard for the study of political organization; class hierarchy became an important variable for the first time. Moreover, the development of area studies in the post-World War II period facilitated the strategic deployment of anthropological results. Vincent characterizes the period from 1954 to 1973 as romantic, exemplified by Stanley Diamond's (1974) reconsideration of anthropological reliance on the concept of the primitive. Most American participants, however, emphasized activism in opposition to the Vietnam War and to the alliance of military, corporate, and government power underlying it (Hymes ed. 1969). Vincent argues that anthropology since 1974 has moved away from seeing politics as a distinct sphere of inquiry in anthropology, a position perhaps most clearly articulated in the subtitle juxtaposing the "politics and poetics of ethnography" in James Clifford and George Marcus's *Writing Culture* (1986). Most anthropologists, however, have unequivocally rejected an extreme form of postmodernism, arguing that, in the neoliberal era, reflexivity must be mobilized to engage with the real world, both ethnographically and through political activism.

Other streams of anthropological theory also reflected the internationalization of the Americanist tradition. The 1960s were characterized by a polarization of materialist and idealist approaches. Cultural ecology began from nature and moved toward culture, with Leslie White and Julian Steward as the major proponents of a reconstructed evolutionary paradigm. Symbolic or interpretive anthropology coalesced around the work of Clifford Geertz. French structuralism, exemplified by the work of Claude Lévi-Strauss, fit well with American interpretive approaches but went beyond them to speculate on the universal structure of the human mind. Most Anglo-American structuralists employed the method without these speculations (Ortner 1984).

In the 1970s, variants of Marxism became fashionable. Ortner distinguishes structural Marxism, which emphasized culture and ideology over historical inevitability, from the political economy that derived from the world systems model, in which there are no "people without history" (Wolf 1982). Political economy has been encompassed by globalization theory, to which anthropology has contributed critiques based on ethnographies of local resistance. Ortner suggests that a theoretical emphasis on "practice" was the innovation of the 1980s, linking interpretive anthropology to renewed questions about agency and the variety of local structures of social order (Ortner 1984).

Present Trajectories

Cultural anthropology has remained the core of the discipline in North America, despite the range of subdisciplinary specializations. The concept of culture has predominated across the subdisciplines until quite recently. Nevertheless, biological anthropology has looked to evolutionary biology for justification for some considerable time. If there is an overall trend, it has perhaps been toward the study of meaning, not in the narrowly linguistic sense, but as a distinctive feature of social order and social interaction. Goodenough (2002) emphasizes that the anthropological turn to meaning began in linguistics as a structuralist method of analysis of semantic domains in various languages, but was extended, by Lévi-Strauss and others, to the study of culture. Goodenough also notes efforts to systematize cross-cultural research, beginning with the Human Relations Area Files pioneered by George Peter Murdock (1897–1985).

Polarization between "emic" approaches to meaning for members-of-culture and "etic" or comparative approaches, often statistical, has led to a perceived dichotomy between the scientists and the humanists in American anthropology. Those who want anthropology to be a science (e.g., Kuznar 1997) ridicule meaning-oriented approaches as merely descriptive and therefore of little interest for a comparative discipline. The scientific approach is also understood to mean that anthropologists' objectivity is threatened if they do not distance themselves from political activism. By contrast, humanists tend to see fieldwork and a comparative perspective as consistent with public engagement by anthropologists. They talk about context and standpoint, and are less disturbed that so-called postmodernist fuzziness will obscure the real world. For them, ethnographic truths are partial, grounded in the relationship of observer and observed. Their anthropology is more likely to produce questions than answers, but claims disciplinary relevance to widespread problems of contemporary society.

Contemporary linguistics within anthropology has struggled against post-Chomskyan linguistics, with its emphasis on universals wired into the human brain. For Chomsky and his followers, variation among languages is superficial and of limited theoretical interest. Ethnographically – that is, for their speakers – languages' variation is critical. Language is not only a tool for communication but also a way of structuring the cultural world, an Americanist position strongly maintained by contemporary students of Amerindian languages. But linguistics is the most challenged of the subdisciplines, and many anthropology departments no longer offer it as a specialization. Many anthropological linguists have chosen to situate their work in relation to the adequate study of culture and meaning rather than as an independent technical study of particular languages (Briggs 2002; Duranti 2003). Their theoretical synthesis has been productive but its consequence for linguistic anthropology per se may not be.

A culture historic perspective in archaeology paralleled Boasian approaches to culture, and, indeed, explicitly borrowed its culture concept (Willey and Sabloff 1993; Trigger 1989). Evolutionary models have persisted in archaeology more widely than in sociocultural anthropology. V. Gordon Childe's materialist models fit well with American work in cultural ecology, particularly the evolutionary models of Leslie White (1900–75) and Julian Steward (1902–72). White's model was effectively unilinear, with sequences based on levels of sociocultural complexity. Steward's multilinear evolution relied more heavily on local environment and particular developments; his model of band-level societies in the Great Basin provided archaeologists with materialist explanations and analogies. Ethnoarchaeology was an important model linking archaeology and ethnology, although contemporary cultural parallels had to be applied with caution to prehistoric cultures.

Processual or "new archaeology" was developed by Louis Binford in the 1960s. The method was deductive, quantitative, functionalist, and evolutionary, emphasizing ecology and subsistence, supplemented by ethnoarchaeological analogy. Contemporary American archaeology remains polarized between processual and post-processual approaches, the latter most closely associated with the work of Ian Hodder, a Briton now at Stanford. For Hodder and his followers, artifacts are symbolic as well as material, and archaeologists can infer meanings from material evidence, especially with the help of ethnoarchaeology. Efforts at synthesis have begun, but the debates are far from resolved.

Physical anthropologists, who now usually call themselves biological anthropologists, have drawn on scientific advances to reach beyond surface morphology by employing population genetics and mitochondrial DNA analysis, among other techniques. Their questions have shifted from the typology of racial types, now seen to be epiphenomena overlapping across populations, to the particulars of biological and cultural interaction among populations and individuals. Biological anthropologists have been outspoken in challenging the inadequate science of scientific racism. Isotopic analysis has clarified paleo-diets, forensic analysis has drawn on genetic research, and excavation of fossil hominids has complicated the evolutionary record. Biological anthropologists often work in interdisciplinary research teams, and are especially likely to collaborate with archaeologists.

Canadian Anthropology

The hegemonic status of the United States in the unmarked reference to "American" anthropology has been a source of considerable anxiety to Canadian anthropologists, of whom this author is one. There have been a variety of approaches to the history of Canadian anthropology in relation to contemporary identity and practice (Harrison and Darnell, eds., 2006). The differences in the two continental national traditions are not absolute, and under some conditions are elided in favor of a generalized New World contrast to European or Third World approaches. Nonetheless, some dimensions of variation can be suggested.

Scale is the most obvious variable. Canadians as well as Canadian anthropologists are constantly aware of the leviathan to the south. Canadian anthropology is closer to its origins than its American counterpart; the first academic program was not established until 1925 at the University of Toronto. Many of the founders of departments and museums are still active. The profession is small enough that face-to-face interaction is a viable model of peer networks for the Canadian Anthropology Society/Société Canadienne Anthropologie.

Many Canadian anthropologists are ideological refugees, who fled the United States during the Vietnam War years and elected to stay in Canada and to develop a local anthropological tradition, often focusing on the study of Canadian society. Canadian practitioners are flexible on the question of who is a Canadian anthropologist. One may acquire that identity by various routes. These include: place of birth (regardless of later residence or employment); place of training; citizenship (native or naturalized); fieldwork within Canada; professional employment in a Canadian institution. No single definition will incorporate all who claim or are recognized to hold the status of Canadian anthropologist. Respect for diversity is also a key variable in the self-image of a multicultural Canadian state (Darnell 2000).

Canadian anthropology has intensive ties to all three of the major contemporary national traditions – the American because of proximity and partially shared history of dealing with Native peoples; the French (especially in Quebec) because of the two founding nations, whose claims to Canada are constitutionally enshrined; and the British as a result of colonial (and perhaps post-colonial) history. Structural-functionalism in Canada is closer to its British origins than in the United States, where it has been largely Americanized and grafted onto preexisting paradigms. The Humboldtian German tradition imported to the US by Boas has taken root less firmly in Canada, where local anthropologists, especially those in British Columbia, protested the imposition of Boasian hegemony in Ottawa when Sapir became Canada's first professional anthropologist in 1910.

Anti-Americanism has surged and waned but reached its peak in the 1970s, both within the discipline and in Canadian society as a whole. The rapid expansion of academic anthropology in that decade rapidly outpaced the number of available faculty, resulting in extensive foreign hiring, largely from the United States. By the time Canadian PhDs sought positions, the expansion was over. Current cohort retirements have led to another cycle of outside hirings, which many fear will relegate Canadian anthropology to branch plant status.

The subdisciplinary scope of Canadian departments is more variable than its American equivalent (Darnell 1998b). In small departments, anthropology is likely to be associated with sociology, and this association is replicated in several large departments, most notably those at the University of British Columbia and Carleton. Calgary and Simon Fraser have separate Departments of Archaeology and Anthropology. York, like Carleton, restricts its program to sociocultural anthropology. Quebec anthropology maintains strong European and Francophone ties, although this tradition largely fails to affect the Anglophone anthropological mainstream.

Virtually every Canadian department includes at least one specialist in First Nations (Native American) peoples (Darnell 1997). Aboriginal affairs are more salient in Canadian public culture than in the United States, with every province and territory having visible and vocal Native populations. Native Canadians are widely recognized as Canada's Third Founding Nation. Collaboration between anthropologists and Native communities is widespread, and many anthropologists are politically active on behalf of the peoples they work with. The five-volume *Royal Commission on Aboriginal Peoples* in 1996 offered a theoretical model for social change with substantial input from anthropologists.

Nonetheless, Canadian anthropologists have also worked around the globe, as well as in their own society. Overseas fieldwork has been a counteractant to parochialism within Canada, where the study of Canadian society is sometimes seen as independent of work elsewhere. Anthropologists have been champions of cross-cultural perspectives in both policy/theory and practice.

Conclusion

The received metanarrative of American anthropology is a simple one, relying on the dominance of the twentieth-century discipline by the Boasian culture concept and, until after World War II, the study of the American Indian. The actual development of anthropology in North America, however, has been considerably less seamless and more diverse. The subdisciplines have had somewhat separate trajectories and preoccupations. Fieldwork sites have expanded far beyond Native American communities. American anthropologists study complex communities, urban populations, and globalization alongside colleagues trained in other human sciences. But the Americanist tradition that has been the baseline for contemporary diversity within American anthropology has proven itself a hardy hybrid.

The development of cultural studies within the humanities has challenged anthropology's exclusive right to many of its core concepts: participant-observation fieldwork and cross-cultural study of the "Other" in particular. Postmodernism has seemed to challenge ethnographic authority (cf. Clifford and Marcus, eds., 1986), with some claiming that the much-touted new experimental ethnographies are indistinguishable from literary fiction, while others call upon the discipline to return to its natural science roots and reassert its prior representational authority. Advocacy, long a disciplinary tradition, sometimes seems overwhelmed by postmodernist angst over an extreme relativism that paralyzes judgment or action. Recent powerful infusions of feminist theory have brought both standpoint epistemology and identity politics to the forefront of American anthropology. Despite the polarized nature of many of these debates, most practicing anthropologists continue to adhere to a middle ground that welcomes new energy without entirely jettisoning inherited anthropological traditions. The history of anthropology remains, for the most part, an important source of both professional socialization and continuity with established anthropological traditions throughout the careers of contemporary practitioners.

Further Reading

Darnell, Regna. 2001. *Invisible Genealogies: A History of Americanist Anthropology.* Lincoln: University of Nebraska Press.

Hallowell, Irving A. 1960. The Beginnings of Anthropology in America. Pp. 1–90 in F. de Laguna, ed., *Selected Writings from the American Anthropologist, 1888–1920.* New York: Harper and Row.

3

The British Tradition[1]
Henrika Kuklick

Prelude

The first British society devoted to anthropological inquiry was the Ethnological Society of London (ESL), founded in 1843, named after the Société ethnologique de Paris, which had been founded in 1839. (Then, and well into the twentieth century, "ethnology" meant comparative consideration of human groups.) The ESL descended from the Aborigines Protection Society (APS), founded in 1837 with the motto *ab uno sanguine* ("of one blood"), denoting the outlook of reformers who provoked Britain to ban the slave trade in 1807 and emancipate slaves in its West Indian colonies in 1833 and 1838 – Evangelical Christians, who included both Established state church members and Dissenters. APS members thought conversion to Christianity would uplift all "uncivilized tribes" and encouraged collection of ethnographic information to inform enlightened policies. The ESL emerged as a society for scholarship alone. Its major thinker was a physician, James Cowles Prichard (1786–1848), an Evangelical Anglican – though born and raised a Quaker (Stocking 1971).

Persons of Dissenting origins would be prominent in British anthropology through the nineteenth century – as they were in other learned societies. These were then the centers of British intellectual life, not Oxford and Cambridge, the "Ancient Universities," where persons who did not endorse Established church tenets were barred from candidacy for degrees until 1854 and 1856, respectively, and were excluded from faculties until 1871. The first anthropologist in Britain to receive a university appointment, the Quaker E. B. (eventually, Sir Edward) Tylor (1832–1917), who at Oxford became, in turn, keeper of the Pitt Rivers Museum (in 1883), a reader (in 1884), and a professor (in 1896), could not study there during his youth.

Prichard would be recognized as having "place[d] Ethnology on a scientific basis," as was observed in 1848 by W. B. Carpenter (1813–1885), a scientific polymath and his day's leading physiologist (quoted in Stocking 1973: ix). In Prichard's many works, based on such sources as travelers' reports and classical texts of Greece and Rome, his essential narrative was biblical: all humankind descended from Noah's family,

Figure 4 Early participant observation: Captain James Cook and Joseph Banks, the naturalist on Cook's first voyage – and future long-serving president of the Royal Society – watching dancing inside a house on one of the islands Cook called the Society Islands, now French Polynesia. Engraved after a drawing by Sydney Parkinson, 1773. From the author's collection.

who, along with other survivors of God's flood, dispersed to populate the globe. Some degenerated – a process originating with the Fall of Adam and Eve – while others advanced. Variations were selective expressions of innate potentials common to humankind – products of circumstances. Prichard's position was "monogenism," as opposed to "polygenism," which became increasingly influential toward the middle of the nineteenth century; this identified human types as distinct species, created separately, with qualitatively different aptitudes and appearances. Prichard initially thought original humans were persons of color, and linked skin lightening to elevated behavioral standards; ultimately, he speculated that racial variations might be associated with different environments. Regardless, he consistently sought to trace humans' dispersion and establish relationships among populations, relying primarily on linguistic affinities (Stocking 1973).

Prichard called for what is usually termed "salvage ethnography" – as would subsequent anthropologists: exotic peoples' encounters with Europeans inevitably led to the disappearance of indigenes' distinctive characteristics (causes ranged from extermination to Christian conversion); what would soon be lost must be recorded for posterity. Prichard's "On the Extinction of Human Races," delivered to the British Association for the Advancement of Science (BAAS) in 1839, moved the society to publish a questionnaire to guide travelers in collecting information in 1841. More elaborate questionnaires followed, the most notable being the six editions of *Notes and Queries on Anthropology*, issued in 1874, 1892, 1899, 1912, 1929, and 1951, all but the last produced at least partially under BAAS auspices. These questionnaires represented long-established practice of natural historians.[2]

Between 1841 and 1874, virulent disagreement had developed among students of human variation, who were increasingly concerned with race per se – as was Prichard in his late work. Moreover, scientists found it harder to devise a chronology of human history (and the earth itself) consistent with biblical narrative; human fossils discovered in the mid-nineteenth century suggested that the human species might have existed for longer than had been believed. Furthermore, it seemed that then-contemporary "savages" might resemble humans who had lived in Europe in prehistoric times. Disputes about race led a member of the ESL, James Hunt, to form a rival organization, the Anthropological Society of London (ASL) in 1863, named after Paul Broca's Société d'anthropologie de Paris. (Then, "anthropology" denoted emphasis on humans' physical characteristics.) The ASL embraced polygenism, and, though it was anti-Darwinian, hypothesized connections between human and lower animal forms.

The battle between the societies was a scientific scandal – and the proceedings of the ASL could be prurient, since, in contrast to its competitors, they excluded women. Furthermore, when ASL members extended their scientific views to political issues, they took positions that were anathema to ESL leaders. These included: supporting the South in the American Civil War, arguing that slaves were congenitally unsuited to freedom (significantly, the society had a Confederate agent on its Council, who provided it funds), and endorsing the ruthless suppression of an 1866 uprising by black farmers in Jamaica by the colony's governor, Edward Eyre (Stocking 1971).

The dispute engaged some of the most prominent figures in British science – figures whose allegiance lay with the ESL and who were committed Darwinians. And it represented a decisive moment in the development of British anthropology. Notable among the scientists involved were Thomas Henry Huxley (1825–1895) and Sir John Lubbock (eventually Lord Avebury [1834–1913]). Huxley, known as "Darwin's Bulldog," stoutly defended Darwin's model of evolution through the process of natural selection from the time of the publication of *On the Origin of Species* (1859). Lubbock, "Darwin's Mercury" (Clark 1997), Darwin's neighbor and protégé, introduced his reclusive mentor to a host of Victorian celebrities. Both were members of the "X Club," a dining group of nine men convened by Huxley in 1864, which exercised immense influence in the world of Victorian science. The differences between their respective backgrounds testify to the emergence in their time of what Noel Annan memorably termed the "intellectual aristocracy," persons whose status depended more on their accomplishments than on their social origins. Huxley, from a family of modest means and trained as a physician, ascended to the scientific elite, teaching at a number of London institutions and shaping training in biology at every educational level. Lubbock, the third baronet in his family line, enjoyed the wealth of his family's banking firm. But he distinguished himself by his scientific activities, which included archaeology, ethnology, popular science writing, and especially entomology, as well as service as a Liberal member of Parliament from 1870 to 1900; elevated to the peerage, he chose the name of a group of prehistoric monoliths. Lubbock was the ESL's president in 1863, Huxley in 1868.

The Prichardian and Darwinian eras in ESL activities were linked, not least through Huxley, W. B. Carpenter's scientific ally and close friend (indeed, Huxley's anthropological writing referred to Prichardian problems). Moreover, though objections to Darwinism were made on religious grounds – and Huxley famously coined the word "agnostic" to denote religious skepticism – Darwinian explanation of human variation presumed a single human species. Thus, a core idea of late-nineteenth-century anthropology – the "psychic unity" of all varieties of humankind – was compatible with the biblical account of creation. While Huxley was president of the ESL, he oversaw its fusion with the ASL. With Lubbock serving as its first president, the Anthropological Institute of Great Britain and Ireland (AI) was founded in 1871; it would become the Royal Anthropological Institute (RAI) in 1907.

Despite arrangements intended to guarantee ASL representation among Institute officers, the reunion was an ESL triumph. Only one ASL figure, John Beddoe (1826–1911), the society's president in 1869–1870, was prominent under the new dispensation. Yet late-nineteenth-century monogenism was qualified: the single human species was moderately differentiated. Darwinian reasoning indicated that groups of people developed distinctive features as they became isolated from one another in various ways, such as by geographical barriers to contact; some were nearly frozen in prehistoric time. In both physical and cultural terms, groups could be arrayed on a hierarchy of evolution, but all human varieties were related, since all could interbreed. Human groups were not *qualitatively* distinct. The psychic unity of humankind meant that all peoples followed the same course of development. Presented with a given set of circumstances, any population would respond similarly; this was their "independent invention" of an element of evolutionary progress. The *pace* of human groups' evolution varied, not its direction. And ontogeny recapitulated phylogeny: the stages of maturation of the *individual* – the ideal type was the normal European male – followed the course that resulted in the highest of the human *species'* accomplishments, the development of European civilization. The evolutionist scheme was sufficiently flexible to admit a range of attitudes toward European women, however. In 1883, a BAAS committee warned that the human species could grow extinct if women emerged from their condition of arrested development: educated women's pelvic capacity was shrinking, while babies gestated under civilized conditions had increasingly larger heads. By contrast, A. C. Haddon (1855–1940) argued that European men and women possessed primitive physical traits in equal proportions, though not the *same* primitive traits (Jones 1998). For Prichard, the proof of the unity of humankind had been affinities among groups spread over space, whose resemblances revealed processes of diffusion. Tylor, the most important anthropological figure in his day, who acknowledged Prichard as "the founder of modern anthropology" (1910: 108), instead emphasized similarities resulting from independent invention. To answer one of his day's burning questions – whether any given innovation resulted from independent invention or diffusion – Tylor provided an axiom: the more sophisticated an innovation, the greater the likelihood it originated in diffusion.

Anthropology Emergent

Anthropology was now respectable, led by members of the intellectual aristocracy, as is evident from the high percentage of late-nineteenth- and early-twentieth-century anthropologists who were knighted for their accomplishments.[3] They saw their enterprise as natural science. In 1884, they gained a section – Section H – of the BAAS (ethnology and anthropology, separately and together, had previously figured as subsections in various BAAS quarters). Tylor was its first president. Prominent figures included such men as the polymath Francis (eventually Sir Francis) Galton (1822–1911), Darwin's cousin, now best known for his contributions to statistics and for coining the word "eugenics" to describe (and inspire) deliberate efforts to improve the human species, and W. H. (Sir William) Flower (1831–1899), director of the British Museum's natural history departments from 1884 to 1898. A division of labor had been practically effected among physical anthropologists, social anthropologists, linguists, and archaeologists, but their work was theoretically compatible. Some, including Alexander Macalister (1844–1919), professor of anatomy at Cambridge, an archaeologist as well as physical anthropologist, spanned the subfields. Prominent as an ethnologist, Tylor was nevertheless well informed about physical anthropology (e.g., Tylor 1910). It is notable that he planned a book collaboration with E. Ray (ultimately Sir Edwin Ray) Lankester (1847–1929) while the latter was Linacre Professor of Comparative Anatomy at Oxford, from 1891 to 1898 (he then succeeded Flower at the British Museum); their project failed because their friendship ended, not because they considered their areas of expertise irreconcilable.[4]

Concomitant physical and behavioral variations were associated with evolution in material culture. Consider the exhibitions in the Oxford museum established with the financial support and artifacts of General A. H. Lane-Fox Pitt-Rivers (1827–1900). Expressing Pitt-Rivers's principles, which were consistent with Darwinism, they were set up by Tylor, along with H. N. Moseley (1820–1900), the university's Professor of Zoology and Comparative Anatomy, and the recent graduates W. Baldwin (ultimately Sir Baldwin) Spencer (1860–1929) and Henry Balfour (1863–1939) – who would become the museum's Curator. Displays showed evolution progressing very slowly. Modifications made at any given time to any given type of object were so slight as to be nearly imperceptible.

The meaningful division of labor was between fieldworkers and theorists. It was incidental that Huxley, Galton, and Tylor had visited exotic places as young men. Scholarship belonged to "ethnologists of the study" – the term the intellectual gadfly Andrew Lang (1844–1912) applied to his kind, now usually called "armchair anthropologists" – who generated grand theories using all manner of evidence. They attempted to systematize data collection by distributing questionnaires. When E. H. Man, who had spent 12 years as assistant supervisor of the Andaman and Nicobar Islands, presented findings organized by *Notes and Queries'* categories at 1882 AI meetings, he demonstrated the questionnaire's utility (Stocking 1987: 259).

Figures such as Alfred Russel Wallace (1823–1913), co-formulator with Darwin of the concept of natural selection, resembled modern anthropologists; Wallace spent long periods in remote places and analyzed his findings himself. Active in mid-nineteenth-century anthropological circles, Wallace supported himself by selling the natural specimens he collected in the field until physical ailments ended his foreign career. In Britain, however, he hovered on the margins of respectable science (despite warm support from some scientific notables), since paid collectors were viewed as tradesmen (e.g., Raby 2001). Indeed, Wallace's marginality may be inferred from his participation in both ASL and ESL activities, leading Huxley to prevail upon him in 1866 to lead the BAAS anthropology subsection (then in Section D – Biology) on the grounds that Wallace alone could mediate between the feuding factions (see Huxley to Lubbock, August 1, 1866, AP, Add.MS 49641). And other types of marginal figures, stationed in Empire outposts, both served as informants to metropolitan scholars and published ethnographies. Notable were Lorimer Fison, a long-serving missionary in Fiji who collaborated with A. W. Howitt, an expert in geology who occupied prominent government positions in Australia; their most significant epistolary relationship was with the American Lewis Henry Morgan, but they also sent information to Tylor and J. G. (eventually Sir James) Frazer (1854–1941), the last major armchair anthropologist – and expressed some contempt for those who generalized about non-Western peoples without having had contact with them (Stocking 1987: 236).

Armchair scholars did not expect all informants to be equally reliable. But they believed that inconsistencies in the quality of data would matter less if data were available in vast quantities. To these, they would apply statistical techniques such as Galton's, and identify general patterns. Their scholarly approach was exemplified by E. B. Tylor's 1888 "On a Method of Investigating the Development of Institutions, Applied to Laws of Marriage and Descent," which identified correlations among social traits. Scholars' collective project was to map the sequence of stages by which humankind evolved from primordial to modern conditions, each stage constituting a culture complex. When they found traits inconsistent with the supposed pattern of any given stage, they saw these as either "survivals" of past practices or portents of future advances. The expectation that human potential was expressed in an invariant course was counter to Darwinism; modification through natural selection was non-directional – but Darwin himself had Lamarckian lapses, especially when considering humankind. In gross outline, late-nineteenth-century anthropologists' characterizations of primitive peoples were centuries old. What was novel was the degree of detail to which scholars hoped to explicate stages of evolutionary progress.

As peoples advanced, their experiences supposedly included: a shift from unions involving multiple partners to monogamy; a shift in tracing descent from the mother to the father and the specification of exogamous norms; abandonment of nomadic habits for permanent settlement, organized land cultivation, and defined property rights; the emergence of class hierarchy and differentiated social roles; displacement of magical thinking by scientific rationality; and the emergence of monotheistic religion. Tylor's 1888 article exemplified the evolutionist paradigm. It identified the experience of "couvade" – when a child's father sympathetically feels the pains of its mother during childbirth – as behavior denoting change from a matrilineal to a patrilineal kinship system.

The "Reformer's Science"

Tylor often said that anthropology was the "reformer's science"; its findings would enable the "great modern nations to understand themselves, to weigh in a just balance their own merits and defects, and even in some measure to forecast . . . the possibilities of the future" (quoted in Kuklick 1991: 7). Modern habits would inevitably displace the folk customs preserved in remote parts of Britain, which must be recorded; this was "folklore" – a formally organized enterprise with the foundation of the Folk-Lore Society in 1878 – but folklore was the "anthropology of the civilized races," in the words of G. L. (later Sir Lawrence) Gomme (1853–1916). And primitive survivals among modern peoples might be deliberately eradicated – a sometimes daring enterprise. For example, J. G. Frazer challenged Christians' belief in Jesus's virgin birth; Frazer implicitly analogized Christian belief to that of the Australian Arrernte, whom he represented as the most primitive of extant peoples and who were ignorant of the mechanism of reproduction, imagining that women were impregnated by spirits – so that every Arrernte birth was a virgin birth.

Anthropologists' findings also had implications for domestic politics. Notably, they addressed two questions about the British population: Was it composed of distinct races? Was it degenerating in biological terms? To answer the first (as well as to collect information about beliefs and behavior), the BAAS organized and supported two committees: operating between 1875 and 1883 was a "Systematic Examination of the Heights, Weights, and Other Physical Characteristics of the Inhabitants of the British Isles"; the "Ethnographical Survey of the United Kingdom" functioned between 1892 and 1910 (see Haddon 1898: 348–94). Members of these committees were drawn from the anthropological elite, including Galton, Haddon, Beddoe, General Pitt-Rivers, and the archaeologist A. J. (Sir Arthur) Evans (1851–1941). The committees found geographically isolated populations with distinctive physical and social characteristics, but variously blended mixtures of three basic stocks were found throughout England, Ireland, Scotland, and Wales. Thus, Irish Home Rule could not be justified on the grounds that the Irish were so racially distinct that they could not be integrated into British society. The most important physical variations were associated with class, not race: the poor, especially the urban poor, were markedly shorter and thinner.

This last finding had evident bearing on the deliberations of the Inter-Departmental Committee on Physical Deterioration, convened by the government after the South African War of 1899–1901, when 40 percent of those volunteering for military service were rejected on health grounds. Calling on anthropological expert witnesses, the committee issued a report in 1904 that called for social welfare policies, having learned that apparent signs of decline of the population's collective hereditary potential were transient, circumstantial phenomena – functions of deficient diets, housing,

and exercise – not indications that, say, the best British specimens were not repro-
ducing in substantial numbers while the population of the lower orders exploded. Indeed,
one witness, D. J. Cunningham (1850–1909), then professor of Anatomy at Edinburgh,
emphasized that enlarged opportunities for women did not lead to decline in repro-
ductive capacity; liberated women, freed from restrictive corsets and encouraged to
exercise, were healthier.

But at the turn of the century, anthropologists generally shunned research relevant
to British domestic policy. There were individual exceptions, such as Karl Pearson
(1857–1936), the first occupant of the Chair in Eugenics funded by Galton's bequest
at University College, London (UCL). As the Anthropological Institute's Huxley
Memorial Lecturer in 1903, Pearson presented his basic thesis: most variation among
individuals' physical characteristics, temperaments, and aptitudes was hereditary. Because
environmental factors effected remaining variation, their modification could improve
British lives. Pearson and his associates undertook a congeries of studies, including
his *On the Relationship of Health to the Psychical and Physical Characters in School Children*
(1923). Any variation could be important; Pearson's collaborative work with Mary Noel
Kan, *Study of the Data Provided by a Baby-Clinic in a Large Manufacturing Town* (1922),
controlled for class differences that might underlie correlations, concluding that the
healthiest garments for babies were pure wool, followed by pure cotton, followed by
cotton-wool blends.

It would take Nazi uses of scientific racism to reanimate anthropologists' interest
in domestic political concerns. In 1934, the RAI joined the Institute of Sociology
to form a Race and Culture Committee; its 1936 report was inconclusive. But the
BAAS zoology and anthropology sections held a joint meeting in 1936 to consider the
question of "race," concluding that the word had to be eliminated from scientific and
public discourse because it had been thoroughly politicized – echoing the argument
of *We Europeans* (1935), co-authored for a popular audience by Haddon and the
biologist (Sir) Julian Huxley – Thomas's grandson (Barkan 1992: 286–96). Mass Observation, a movement founded in 1936 by an amateur anthropologist, a poet who became
a sociologist, and a filmmaker, came closest to an anthropology engaged with right-
ing the wrongs of British society. Particularly concerned with race prejudice, it
enrolled untrained volunteers to do research and received qualified endorsement
from the anthropologist Bronislaw Malinowski (1884–1942) – and the disapproval of
his students and colleagues (Kushner 2004: 5–10). After World War II, a few anthropologists concerned to affect policy studied race relations in Britain, but their work
had low professional prestige.

Meanwhile, anthropology was gaining university niches. In 1895, Tylor received a
personal professorship – but failed to incorporate anthropology in the undergraduate curriculum; Tylor's efforts made it a "special subject" for examination in Oxford's
Natural Science course, but it had to be added to the roster of subjects already
required – so no students did it. While Oxford's 1899 "Research Degree" statute allowed
the submission of an anthropological thesis for the postgraduate BLitt and BSc
degrees, it was undergraduate education that mattered. Nevertheless, when John
(eventually Sir John) Linton Myres (1869–1954) conducted a survey for the BAAS in

1900 to determine how many universities were teaching anthropology, he found it in some form at eight institutions; with the exception of some courses at Cambridge, Oxford, and UCL, all of the courses belonged in the natural sciences (JLMP, MssMyres 66). By 1906, Oxford had a school of anthropological studies (though it had no permanent chair until 1936; Tylor's successor, R. R. Marett [1866–1943], retired as a reader). By 1907, Liverpool had an – unsalaried – chair in social anthropology (its foundation professor, J. G. Frazer, stayed in place for only five months). By 1908, Cambridge had a board of anthropological studies (though it did not have a professorship of anthropology until 1932), and in 1913 it made anthropology a component of an undergraduate degree. By 1913, the University of London had a (part-time, but permanent) chair of ethnology at the London School of Economics (LSE), occupied by C. G. Seligman (1873–1940), a professional ally of Haddon's; in 1927, Malinowski would occupy the School's first full-time professorship in anthropology.

When Myres surveyed anthropology teaching in 1923, he found eleven universities providing some form of anthropological instruction (JLMP, MssMyres, 67). Most important were the departments at UCL, where all subfields of the discipline were represented and the first PhD was granted in 1925, and the LSE, where the first PhD was conferred in 1927. At the LSE, students could study with Malinowski's teachers, Seligman and the Finn Edward Westermark (1862–1939), as well as with Malinowski himself, who first taught there in 1913 (his LSE degree was a DSc). Not until after World War II would there be university undergraduate degree courses in anthropology alone (not as part of a subject mixture). But anthropology was gaining ground in the interwar period.

The Colonial Connection

Anthropology's academic gains seem correlated with practitioners' turn toward promoting the discipline's utility for colonial rulers – as well as for missionaries and persons doing business in the colonies. Under BAAS and AI auspices, a number of petitions were presented to the government for creation of an imperial bureau of ethnology, beginning in 1896. Instigated by Haddon, the campaign involved such luminaries as Tylor, Lubbock, and C. H. (later Sir Hercules) Read (1857–1929), keeper of British and medieval antiquities at the British Museum. Pointing to the value of anthropological information in governing India, and to official recognition of the utility of anthropology in the United States and the Netherlands, petitioners made familiar arguments: the bureau would serve science by encouraging reports on peoples who were nearing extinction in culture if not in body; anthropological intelligence made administrators more sympathetic to their subjects' views, capable of gaining the consent of the governed so they could turn indigenous institutions to the purposes of their administrative system, "Indirect Rule" (of which more shortly). But the only result of their campaign was a nominal bureau created in Read's British Museum department; it did not receive necessary funds, and become a repository for a few ethnographic reports forwarded through official channels.

Universities had some success marketing their services to colonial officials. The postgraduate Diploma in Anthropology, which could be earned at Oxford (by examination) from 1905 and at Cambridge (by thesis) from 1908, was especially attractive to colonial civil servants, who could complete its requirements during their long leaves at home. In 1908, the Anglo-Egyptian Sudan invited Oxford and Cambridge to develop anthropological courses for its government staff. But the Sudan regime was unique in the British Empire,[5] not least in its patronage of professional anthropologists; it commissioned research by C. G. Seligman and his wife, B. Z. Seligman in 1909, and later employed Seligman's students E. E. (ultimately Sir Edward) Evans-Pritchard (1902–73) and S. F. Nadel (1903–56). And British universities hired a number of ex-colonial administrators to teach anthropology. For example, the first two occupants of Cambridge's chair were retired members of the Indian Civil Service, T. C. Hodson (1871–1953) and J. H. Hutton (1885–1968).

Moreover, some notable colonial officials endorsed anthropology enthusiastically. At the 1914 meeting of the BAAS, for example, the president of Section H, Sir Richard Temple (a baronet), erstwhile Chief Commissioner of the Andaman and Nicobar Islands, mobilized a discussion that engaged (among others) Sudan's Governor-General, Fiji's Governor, the Resident General of the Federated Malay States, and Alexander Fiddian, a long-serving civil servant in the Colonial Office who consistently promoted applied anthropology. Discussants rehearsed the usual refrains. But audience cheers greeted J. G. Frazer's remarks about a war in "Somaliland, with a loss of British life and heavy loss to the unfortunate natives . . . which a competent knowledge of the customs of the natives would have entirely averted" (Anonymous 1914: 72).

The desire to prevent unrest was the most important reason that colonial officials sought anthropologists' help until after World War II. It explained the employment of the first government anthropologist in Africa, Northcote W. Thomas, who between 1908 and 1912 served in Nigeria and Sierra Leone. His unsatisfactory performance would for years serve as a cautionary tale among colonial officials. Most notably, Thomas refused to violate his informants' confidence and divulge information about a secret society in Sierra Leone that would have to be suppressed if it were to be unmasked as a cannibalistic order. In 1921, the Gold Coast (now Ghana) appointed the first full-time government anthropologist in Africa, R. S. Rattray (1881–1938), transferring him from the regular civil service; his charge was to collect information about indigenous tradition to prevent rebellions such as that following government seizure of the Asante chief's Golden Stool – an act betraying ignorance of its significance. Subsequently, a few full-time positions for government anthropologists were established, virtually all occupied by former colonial officers,[6] and civil servants with special interest in anthropology were sometimes "seconded" to undertake inquiries. Men recruited to the Colonial Administrative Service were expected to acquire a smattering of anthropological knowledge; it was included in the year-long course they were obliged to take at either Oxford or Cambridge after 1924 (their predecessors were offered an optional, three-month course in London).

Overall, however, colonial officials were reluctant to seek professional anthropological advice until the World War II era. Then, Britain was engaged in decolonization, and sought anthropologists' assistance in turning colonies into viable independent states. Consider that in 1927 the governors of Britain's East African territories rejected an offer made by the Rockefeller Foundation (RF) to finance an institute to investigate African welfare, possibly headed by an anthropologist. Only Kenya's governor responded positively; he hoped the institute's findings would help him calm Kenya's restive white settlers, who were threatening civil war, reacting to recent government declarations that African interests were paramount in Kenya and that economic development efforts in East Africa must be centered on Africans. (In mooting this African project, as well as later, realized ones, the RF acted on two beliefs: that research on race relations in Africa would improve understanding of the American South; and that action that made the world more peaceful was both a good in itself and beneficial for commerce.) Typically, colonial officials saw anthropologists as useless at best and destructive at worst: anthropologists who upheld scientific standards either investigated problems of no interest to colonial regimes or failed to produce reports in time to address pressing problems; and anthropologists could be subversives, identifying with the peoples they studied.

Governments of virtually independent territories in Britain's empire seemed more receptive to suggestions that anthropologists could be useful. Haddon's lobbying, in particular, persuaded South African and Australian officials to endorse the creation of professorships in 1921 and 1925, respectively, at the universities of Cape Town and Sydney (the latter subsidized by the RF). The first occupant of both of these positions was A. R. Radcliffe-Brown (1881–1955); in both, he instructed government employees – though he taught them theory, from which practical tactics for work with indigenes could be derived. Radcliffe-Brown and his successors at Sydney trained persons bound for service in Papua, an Australian colonial territory after 1906, as well as New Guinea (once Germany's colony), Australia's League of Nations Mandate Territory after 1919. And three of Haddon's students – E. P. Chinnery, F. E. Williams, and (briefly) W. E. Armstrong – served as government anthropologists in Australia's colonies.

Britain's tropical African colonies were significantly different from South Africa and Australia: the latter were white settler societies. Settlers displaced indigenous peoples, sometimes violently, deployed legal stratagems to deprive indigenes of rights to land and developed reserves for them – and also expected indigenes to work for them. In societies in which indigenes and settlers were locked in endless conflict over the legitimate bases of land ownership, anthropologists' knowledge could seem useful. That in both South Africa and Australia there emerged anthropologists who sympathetically defended indigenes' rights and ways of life is another matter.

But Papua and New Guinea were analogous to Britain's West African colonies: these territories were sources of wealth in resources and laborers, but their climates were thought unhealthy for Europeans. And in such settings, administrators could easily find academic anthropologists infuriating. Consider, for example, the exchange between Gregory Bateson, also a Haddon student, and Chinnery, who sought an effective strategy for elimination of headhunting, an official goal. Outlawing the practice would only drive it underground, said Bateson, and such people as his "wicked Iatmul" required "spectacular activities" to give meaning to their usually boring lives. Headhunting might be controlled, however, confined to a yearly season, with a limit set on individuals' kills! (Bateson to Chinnery, May 8, 1935, EWPCP, MS 766/1/1).

Certainly, it is not irrelevant that anthropology's growth as a discipline coincided with the territorial expansion of Britain's Empire, beginning with the international "Scramble for Africa" in the 1880s and ending with the post-World War I acquisition of territories formerly ruled by the Central Powers. And the erstwhile division of labor between fact collectors in the field and armchair theorists at home ended as travel to colonized territories became relatively safe for missionaries, commercial agents, colonial officers, and scientists of various types – not just anthropologists. Now, anthropologists who themselves observed subject peoples claimed a heightened level of expert authority. Evolutionist anthropology seemed ideally suited to colonial rule, since it postulated developmental laws; colonial civil servants, by definition neutral administrators rather than policymakers, often justified their interventions with evolutionist precepts, claiming that they were merely accelerating inevitable progress. But the relationship between anthropology and colonialism was complex.

Into the Field

By the end of the nineteenth century, anthropologists' leading lights doubted the value of information elicited through questionnaires. In the 1892 edition of *Notes and Queries*, C. H. Read pronounced the passing European traveler incompetent to obtain "even superficial answers" to anthropologists' questions. Only persons with "long-continued residence among a native race' " were reliable (97). But scientifically trained fieldworkers would soon claim superiority to long-time residents. For example, the anthropological field trips of W. H. R. Rivers (1864–1922) were brief, and he relied on interpreters. Yet, he argued that his systematic approach elicited information thoroughly as well as rapidly; his "genealogical method" identified details of a people's understanding of kinship, and from these their social structure – relationships often so complex that "Europeans who have spent their whole lives among the people have never been able to grasp them" (1968 [1910]: 107).

In particular, two field studies had revolutionary consequences. One was the 1898 Cambridge Anthropological Expedition to Torres Straits,[7] a seven-man team organized by Haddon and including Rivers, which spent late-April to mid-November on a cluster of islands located between Australia and New Guinea. Participants' special expertise determined their investigative tasks, and research focused on Mer, the island at the greatest distance from mainland Australia; it was assumed that the farther removed an island society was from contact with European culture, the more primitive it would be. (Expedition members also went to Borneo in pursuit of comparative material, but it seemed relatively inconsequential, and was not included in the expedition *Reports*.) Of the participants, one, Anthony Wilkin (1878–1901), in charge of the expedition's photography, died young. Another, Sidney Ray (1858–1939), an expert linguist, was a primary-school teacher. Two, C. S. Myers (1873–1946) and William McDougall (1871–1938), were psychologists. But the most important British anthropologists of the next generation traced their professional lineage to three expedition members: Haddon, who had been unhappily occupying the professorship of zoology at the Royal College of Science in Dublin since 1880 (Huxley had provided a reference); Rivers, medically trained but then Cambridge's lecturer in experimental psychology and the physiology of the senses (who had taught Myers and McDougall); and Myers's friend Seligman, also medically trained. Leading the expedition decisively altered Haddon's career. In 1900, he became lecturer in ethnology at Cambridge; after becoming a Fellow of Christ's College in 1901, he could afford to resign his Dublin post.

The second revolutionary field study was that conducted in Central Australia by an unlikely pair, Baldwin Spencer and F. J. Gillen (1855–1912). Spencer had prevailed over Haddon in competition to become the University of Melbourne's foundation professor of biology. Gillen, an Australian government servant, ended his formal schooling at 12; his official positions included Sub-Protector of Aborigines for South Australia. The pair met as participants in the 1894 Horn Expedition to Central Australia,[8] and did fieldwork together in 1896–97, when Spencer was on summer vacation and Gillen was given leave by the government. *Native Tribes of Central Australia* (1899) was the first of their collaborative productions. Although they left no professional descendants, their work had immense international impact. Like Haddon, they justified their choice of field site on geographical grounds: by virtue of its isolation, Central Australia was a place where old habits had been preserved. This argument was defensible in Darwinian terms, but personal factors mattered; Haddon and Spencer returned to places they had studied as biologists, and Gillen had lived in Central Australia for over two decades.

Spencer and Gillen urged anthropologists to put themselves "into the mental attitude of the native": Aborigines' lifeways might violate European standards of propriety but were adaptive responses to Australian conditions (1899: 48). *Native Tribes* was a first approximation of the comprehensive ethnography produced through participant observation that would become the post-World War I ideal. Spencer and Gillen assumed Arrernte identities and claimed that they had learned secrets previously hidden from whites (though they were barred from some ceremonies). Nevertheless, they described features of Aboriginal life ranging from everyday practices to sacred rituals. Their work appealed to various audiences. In the Australian context, *Native Tribes* implied a liberal political judgment: the considerable variation obtaining among Aboriginal groups denoted innate ability to adapt to various circumstances, indicating Aborigines' capacity for assimilation. In Britain, however, discussion of the book was framed by J. G. Frazer, who had brokered its publication. As I noted earlier, Frazer saw the Arrernte as the most primitive people on earth, and he believed that the origins of religious belief were revealed in the ceremonies that enacted Arrernte totem identities – their identifications with specific animals and plants.

An international debate ensued. Initially, most combatants agreed that totemism must feature in humankind's developmental trajectory, but quarreled over particulars of evolutionary stages. Finally, combatants rejected unilinear evolutionist theory. Frazer's most important assumption – that superior religion was associated with material progress and the development of scientific rationality – was incorrect; as Lang observed, true primitives could be truly spiritual. There were primitive societies without totemism, and it was not routinely linked to specific phenomena. Even the reconstructed evolutionist Marett saw social change as "a differential evolution of culture, according to which some elements may advance, whilst others stand still, or even decay" (1912: 121).

Haddon, like Spencer and Gillen, urged researchers to understand exotic peoples from the "native point of view." And the "genealogical method" Rivers developed for the Torres Straits expedition proved remarkably durable. But though the six volumes of *Reports* Haddon edited – five published before World War I, and the last (volume I) in 1935 – received largely favorable reviews, they were hybrid growths, partly relying on evidence that Haddon solicited from afar. Moreover, teamwork did not become the discipline's ideal method, though it later had some notable practitioners.[9] In the influential 1912 edition of *Notes and Queries* – which guided Malinowski – Rivers decreed that a visiting research team disturbed a primitive people; the very activities anthropologists wished to observe were disrupted. Moreover, because each element in a primitive society was linked to every other, it was impossible to divide research labor efficiently. Ideally, fieldwork should be undertaken by a lone anthropologist, spending at least a year among a group of no more than 500 people, whose society was somehow bounded by geographical factors. Becoming personally acquainted with an entire population, learning their language and living the local life, the anthropologist would develop a comprehensive understanding of a community. As Myres observed in his obituary of Rivers, it was generally agreed that Rivers set the discipline's methodological standards.

Rivers did not meet these standards, but he justified them, explaining how the lone anthropologist became an embodied scientific instrument. In 1865, W. B. Carpenter had observed that the principle of the conservation of force was "among the best established generalisations of physical science," suggesting that "every thoughtful Physiologist must desire to see the same course of inquiry thoroughly pursued in regard to the phenomena of living bodies" (quoted in Kuklick 1998: 168). Rivers accepted this charge, conceptualizing humans as closed energy systems: the ways individuals expended their energies determined the quality of their lives. Administering physiological and psychological tests to the islanders, Rivers dispelled long-held conventional wisdom that primitives were closer to lower animals than evolved Europeans, having acute eyesight and hearing as well as high tolerance for pain: islanders did *not* have *innately* superior sensibilities. Body economies of energy expenditure explained their habits. In order to survive in unimproved nature, islanders honed their observational skills, so as to be able to recognize signs of impeding danger, say, or edible animals looming in the distance. As was indicated by anecdotal evidence of Europeans who had followed the lifeways of primitive peoples, Europeans could develop acute sensory skills – and would simultaneously lose their capacity for sophisticated reasoning. There was the specific issue of the islanders' relative indifference to the color blue:

perhaps it showed some incomplete evolutionary development, since, like European children, islanders preferred red. Indeed, the dark pigmentation of the macula in their eyes fostered a slight insensitivity to blue. But islanders perceived the color. They just did not appreciate it as advanced Europeans did: admiration of blue was an element of aesthetic contemplation of nature, for which they lacked time and energy. It followed that the lone participant observer among an exotic people could experience life as the people did and become a reliable informant.

Conceptualizing the body as a closed energy system was widespread at this time. Indeed, as his diaries reveal, the young Malinowski understood himself in this way both before and during his fieldwork years (Young 2004: passim). What is notable is that Rivers translated a general scientific scheme into justification for a new anthropological method – with theoretical implications. Rivers's model of the person was another means to discredit unilinear evolutionism. Rivers had no doubt that there were higher and lower forms of behavior, but judged that each individual could present the full range of forms. Reasoning as a psychologist, Rivers challenged the unilinear scheme by translating a historical account of social processes (however much they depended on the cognitive skills of individuals) into a model of personality dynamics that allowed any person to advance and regress; his explanatory model was equally applicable to the "shell-shock" patients Rivers treated during World War I and variation among societies.

Practical Anthropology

Did anthropological developments alter colonial rule? The definitive statement of post-World War I colonial ideology was F. D. (Lord Frederick) Lugard's *The Dual Mandate in British Tropical Africa* (1922). Its title invoked the League of Nations' goal for its Mandate Territories: subject peoples as well as colonial rulers should profit from their relationship. But Lugard, whose official positions had included the governorship of Nigeria, the jewel in Britain's tropical African crown, articulated long-established practices. These were termed "Indirect Rule" and were designed both to enable a small staff of British civil servants to govern many colonial subjects and to avoid provoking indigenous protests. Indirect Rule had two basic features: in any given jurisdiction, the traditional leader was an intermediary, implementing government directives following consultation with the British official in charge; and indigenous customs were respected unless they were, in the stock phrase, "repugnant to natural justice and morality."

An important justification for colonial domination was indigenes' supposed characteristic of cruelty to women; women's rights were major issues at the height of British colonial power. Not surprisingly, "repugnant" customs frequently involved women. Thus, *sati*, the (never universal) Hindu practice of immolating a widow on her husband's funeral pyre, was outlawed by agents of British authority in 1829, before British rule was formally imposed after the 1857–58 rebellion. Female circumcision was another objectionable practice. Colonial officials also worried about the damage that might be done by secret societies, say, or by witchcraft. But since officials' primary concern was to maintain order, they often tolerated "repugnant" practices as bulwarks of peoples' moral values. Among others, the Gold Coast government anthropologist Rattray justified female circumcision in these terms, and a congeries of observers, ranging from academics such as Evans-Pritchard to government employees, testified that witchcraft accusations deterred deviant behavior.

Colonial officials needed procedural rules for the daily business of governing. A highly stylized version of evolutionist anthropology served their purposes. Clear lines of local authority enabled a few officials to govern the masses. Officials were instructed to "find the chief," with whom they would negotiate. If a population had no chief, one could be created, since evolution supposedly inevitably led to centralized authority. For example, a traditional religious office could be invested with secular authority, as happened in the Sudan, following Evans-Pritchard's recommendation (though Evans-Pritchard was no evolutionist). Making administration efficient also meant joining polities in larger units based on (often imaginative) judgments of affinities among peoples. The history of more advanced societies indicated that amalgamations were natural: the United Kingdom joined England, Wales, Scotland, and Ireland. As had happened in Britain, progress led to hereditary lines of succession to traditional offices; calm would reign if there were no competition for office when a ruler died. To avert possible conflict, clear rules of property inheritance were defined; progressive evolution led to the emergence of private property. Finally, the assumption that natural progress was gradual underlay many administrative strategies. Traditional social rules compelling colonial subjects to behave in an orderly manner had to be perpetuated. Indeed, the axiom that contact with Europeans invariably had some destructive impact on colonized societies was another reason that colonial anthropology was historicist in orientation. Identification of societies' pre-colonial characteristics might be necessary if natural progress were to be facilitated. Thus were created many historical fictions.

But persons at the highest levels of colonial officialdom observed the unsettling effects of modification of colonized societies. A notable flashpoint was the Eastern Nigerian women's 1929–30 "Aba Riots," provoked by taxation and the imposition of so-called "warrant chiefs," persons whose authority had no traditional basis (who were subsequently removed). Lugard proclaimed that the only sort of anthropology suited to practical application was functionalism, of which Malinowski was then Britain's high priest. (Malinowski had fawned shamelessly over Lugard.) The Colonial Office's permanent civil servants agreed. As one said in 1931, functionalist anthropology addressed "problems which are of immediate and practical importance to the Administrative Officer" (quoted in Kuklick 1991b: 214). Malinowski was consulted about officials' training. But little change occurred on the colonial ground until after World War II. Certainly, both functionalists and evolutionists argued that sudden changes disturbed social order. But recent critics of functionalist anthropology who have understood this feature of its analysis as proof that it was tailored to suit colonial purposes have been ignorant of both the history of anthropological ideas and the realities of colonial rule.

New Theories and Their Audiences

Haddon, Rivers, Spencer, Gillen, and others had in effect contributed to the new under-standing of human biology that gained currency after 1900, when Gregor Mendel's understanding of the mechanism of inheritance was rediscovered. Although the two schools of anthropology that completed for disciplinary paramountcy in Britain in the first decades of the twentieth century – the diffusionists and the functionalists – assumed that social behavior had some relation to biological endowments, they did not see concomitant variations in human nature and culture.

The anthropological school that emerged in time between the schools of the evolutionists and the functionalists was that of the diffusionists, led by the notoriously combative – and eminent – paleoanthropologist G. (later Sir Grafton) Elliot Smith (born Smith, 1871–1937), and his disciple W. J. Perry (1887–1950). At the height of their influence from roughly 1910 to 1925, concerned to explain phenomena of migration and culture contact, the diffusionists were obsessed with the spread of culture from Ancient Egypt. Their fervent adherents were very few. Nevertheless, their fundamental concern was shared by many early-twentieth-century anthropologists. Indeed, it seems obvious that diffusionist phenomena had to be of interest at a time of considerable population movement worldwide. Moreover, the phenomena of change through contact of peoples made sense in Mendelian terms: changes of individuals and societies did not express an inbuilt developmental program; rather, unpredictable changes might occur just as genetic mutations did, and contact among peoples was bound to result in changes.

For example, Haddon understood cultural variation within a geographical area as evidence of a series of migrations by different peoples, identifying migration routes by tracing trait distributions along geographical lines (e.g., 1920). Seligman's 1915 presidential address to Section H outlined his "Hamitic Hypothesis," suggesting that there were cultural links between Ancient Egypt and Black Africa; Hamitic people had been agents of much progressive change in sub-Saharan Africa. Before his death at 24, Anthony Wilkin went "to Algeria to study the problem of the supposed relation-ship, actual or cultural, of the Berbers with the Ancient Egyptians" (Haddon 1901: ix). Moreover, while Malinowski never published his diffusionist speculations, his early analyses of Trobriand Island culture considered that it might be the amalgam of characteristics of successive bands of seafaring immigrants (Young 2004: 468). And Malinowski also gave Haddon information that served the latter's diffusionist argu-ments (Haddon 1920: 11–12). But Haddon, Seligman, and Wilkin did not identify themselves as diffusionists.

The most eminent scientist who did was Rivers, who announced his conversion in his 1911 presidential address to Section H. In fact, Rivers's argument resembled Haddon's: a diffusionist model explained variation obtaining within an area. If, as Rivers argued in his 1914 BAAS address, Australian peoples living in close proximity and in similar environments were at different stages of development, they must represent different immigrant populations (recall that, by contrast, Baldwin Spencer saw Aborigines as a single people who had adapted to the very varied microclimates of

Australia). Rivers stressed the psychological effects of culture contact: an encounter between a people of relatively high culture and an inferior one could so demoralize the latter that they lost their will to live – and might find new meaning in life by embracing a new religion (such as the invaders'). Rivers's diffusionism was nuanced: even if a single band of migrants was responsible for cultural variation within a small geographical area, there were many micro-level differences. Each group within the area would adapt diffused traits to suit its distinctive way of life; indeed, each specific diffused trait would be expressed differently among various groups (1914: II, 573–83). But the diffusionist school also appealed to Rivers because it attempted integrated analysis of human behavior, attending to the interaction of social and biological factors. He was bemoaning anthropology's fragmentation into discrete subfields at the time of his death in 1922.

Although Elliot Smith and Malinowski were to engage in public debate over the relative merits of diffusionism and functionalism, they arguably appealed to somewhat different constituencies (though both claimed their schemes were applicable to colonial administration). Much diffusionist writing was intended for a popular audience, especially books in the series of which Elliot Smith was the general editor, "In the Beginning of Things," of which only one, *Ancient Mariners* (1928), had an anthropologist author, C. Daryll Forde (1904–80) – who was not a career diffusionist. It is probably not irrelevant that Elliot Smith was then supporting his three sons' expensive education (see letter to Wilson, January 25, 1919, DP, Add.MS 56303). Only some of Malinowski's works had general appeal, such as his *Sex and Repression in Savage Society* (1927).

First based at Manchester University and then at UCL, where Elliot Smith became professor of anatomy in 1919 and Perry became reader in cultural anthropology in 1924, the extreme diffusionists told a tale that Rivers accepted selectively: the basis of Western Civilization was the "Archaic Civilization," a complex culture invented only once, in Ancient Egypt, which had been variously elaborated by its recipients as it spread from there. Its global appeal was psychological: it was founded on the fear of death. But historical accidents yielded its constituent elements: elaborate mummification techniques; settled agriculture; metal smelting to produce tools that had peaceful and military uses – the building of stone monoliths as well as the consolidation and defense of the Egyptian kingdom. In combination, these elements resulted in social stratification. The "Children of the Sun" spread the Archaic Civilization; named after their belief system, they migrated in search of supposedly life-giving substances, such as gold, pearls, turquoise, copper, tin, and flint. They built monoliths wherever they went. But there was no intrinsic relationship among monolith building, sun worship, and mummification; therefore, wherever two of these three traits were found together, they could not have been invented independently but must have been introduced by migrants. Haddon found such generalizations particularly offensive when Elliot Smith judged Torres Strait Islanders' mummification practices to be evidence of contact with bearers of the Archaic Civilization (1935: 321–42). Very few UCL students who wrote diffusionist PhD theses went on to academic careers, though Elliot Smith trained respected paleoanthropologists.[10]

Nevertheless, it is not implausible that central concerns of post-World War I British academic anthropology might have been historical change and processes of diffusion. Early diffusionist works were respectfully reviewed, and diffusionists were taken seriously through the mid-1920s. Indeed, Rivers's diffusionism much resembled the Boasian variant – and was compatible with an American-style organization of the discipline that incorporated social analysis, biological anthropology, linguistics, and archaeology, as well as principles for museum displays. Moreover, other British anthropologists were, as Rivers was, strongly committed to maintaining integration of the discipline's subfields. These included the self-styled "Trinity" who dominated anthropology at Oxford through the late 1930s, Balfour, Marett, and the physical anthropologist Arthur Thompson (Mills 2006: chapter 1), as well as leaders of the RAI. British anthropology was far more aggressively scientific than Boasian anthropology, however, and surely would have remained so regardless of its theoretical orientation.

A counterfactual history turns on a quirk of fate: Rivers suffered the disorder that killed him at age 56 – a strangulated hernia – in his rooms in St John's College, Cambridge, on a Saturday, June 3, 1922. Having given his college servant a holiday, he was not found until he was beyond medical intervention. It is highly probable that Rivers would have brokered the funds that enabled British anthropology to professionalize had he lived longer; he and his students would have received the research grants that were channeled through the International African Institute (IAI) – originally the International African Institute for Languages and Cultures – which was established in 1926, largely financed by the Rockefeller Foundation and the main source of anthropologists' support in the interwar period.

And curricula changed slowly. Consider the 1924 examination for the Oxford Diploma in Anthropology. It gave students opportunities to expound all then-available theories – evolutionist, diffusionist, and functionalist – and tested the full range of anthropological subjects. The examination was divided into the following parts: (1) Physical Anthropology; (2) Archaeology and Technology; (3) Social Anthropology; (4) Ethnology (divided into "Physical" and "Technology"); and (5), a "Practical Examination." Under (1), questions included "In what essentials does the character of man's foot contrast with that of the anthropoids?" Under (2), questions included: "Indicate on a map (supplied) the distribution of the principal groups of megalithic monuments. How far can the theory that these groups are intimately connected be substantiated?" and "How far can pottery-making, on historical and technological grounds, be regarded as a formative art free from external influences?" (i.e., Could diffusion be distinguished from independent invention?) Under (3), questions included: "What light do the ritual practices of modern savages throw on the cave-dwellings of Paleolithic Europe?" (i.e., Was evolutionists' unilinear model useful?) and "Describe the matrimonial classes of Australia." (This could be done in any theoretical mode – and the task denoted the centrality of Australian subject matter at the time.) Under (4), one question linked archaeological hypotheses to social evolutionist ones: "How far is the succession of stone, bronze, and iron, in the manufacture of implements and weapons, borne out by a study of prehistoric and primitive cultures?" Among the requirements of Part 5 was demonstration of specific skills, such as measuring and recognizing "various crania and other osteological specimens."

Moreover, it was not just students who were expected to be knowledgeable about all anthropological subfields. Professionals also could be, no matter how specialized was their own research. Consider the pedagogic career of Radcliffe-Brown, recognized as the joint founder with Malinowski of the functionalist school of social anthropology. Writing to Malinowski from Sydney (still a British intellectual colony), he complained that he was required to spend many hours a week lecturing on "the whole field of physical anthropology, archaeology, linguistics, ethnology, and sociology" (August 29, 1927, MP, YUL). (At the time, "sociologists" was the name crusading functionalists used to distinguish their anthropological faction – and Radcliffe-Brown would leave Sydney for Chicago, where he gained American followers.)

But the functionalists' theoretical triumph, which made social anthropology a thoroughly differentiated pursuit, was effected with the aid of funds from the International African Institute. The prime mover behind the IAI's creation was J. H. Oldham (1874–1960), secretary of the Church Missionary Society from 1921 to 1938. The IAI's institutional parent was a committee appointed by the Colonial Secretary in 1923, the Advisory Committee on Education in the Colonies, whose members included Oldham and Lugard. The committee wished to develop educational programs suited to the "mentality, aptitudes, occupations and traditions" of subject peoples to encourage "natural growth and evolution," making the "individual more efficient in his or her condition of life . . . and to promote the advancement of the community as a whole." It consulted American philanthropists who had supported the education of African Americans, including the Rockefeller Foundation, to which it subsequently appealed for funds to create the IAI. When Sir Walter Fletcher, head of Britain's Medical Research Council, persuaded Oldham that the IAI must include anthropologists, Fletcher lamented that Rivers, "our most fertile anthropologist," had suffered an untimely death. Oldham turned for advice to RF employees, who suggested that he contact anthropologists at the LSE (already a recipient of considerable RF support as the embodiment of the foundation ideal, in which the "academic and the actual come together"). Thus, Oldham encountered Malinowski, whom he would describe as the "most creative and original mind in the field" (quotations from Kuklick 1991b: 206, 212, 208).

Rockefeller Foundation support for the LSE and the IAI made Africa the focus of social anthropologists' attention. The most conspicuous non-Africanist among the next professional generation was Malinowski's first PhD student, the New Zealander Raymond (eventually Sir Raymond) Firth (1901–2002), whose education effectively predated the turn to Africa; his fieldwork was in Oceania, like Malinowski's, and he earned his degree in 1927. The RF also figured in the decline of the diffusionist school; until 1925, it had given grants to Elliot Smith. Moreover, the foundation's enthusiasm for social anthropology made the field's allied enterprises less prominent – and less innovative – components of the whole. As Sir William Ridgeway (1853–1926), Disney Professor of Archaeology at Cambridge, observed, archaeologists could not appeal to philanthropists on the grounds that their work would lead to "the alleviation of the sufferings of humanity" (quoted in Kuklick 1991b: 186). Archaeologists preserved styles of reasoning that became unfashionable among British social anthropologists, and they also worked as members of an almost international discipline (Trigger 1968). Meanwhile, physical anthropology continued to tolerate scientific racism – which explained the inability of the Race and Culture Committee to reach consensus.

Malinowski learned to cast his pleas for funds to fit Rockefeller Foundation policy formulae. Applying for an extension of the initial five-year grant to the IAI, for example, Malinowski insisted that funds would not be spent in "the production of useless and merely ornamental research workers, however valuable their research might be academically." In a 1930 letter to a foundation officer, he argued that as anthropology became scientific it could "play the same part in constructive policy as physics and geology have played in engineering." The foundation changed its regulations for fellowships so that Malinowski's students could win them, often using them to do fieldwork after earning PhDs based on library research. Malinowski's famously intellectually challenging seminars were attended not only by the LSE's international coterie of anthropology students (not all of them his students), but also by anthropologists from other institutions, visiting missionaries, colonial officials, European traders, and Africans. And IAI fellowship recipients became leaders of the next generation of anthropologists. They included the South African Meyer Fortes (1906–83), whose PhD was earned in psychology at UCL, Hilda Beemer Kuper (1911–94), Audrey Richards (1899–1984), Lucy Mair (1901–86), and the South African Isaac Schapera (1905–2003), who had studied with Radcliffe-Brown at Cape Town before earning his PhD at the LSE (quotations in Kuklick 1991b: 187, 213).

Certainly, the young Africanists chose research problems likely to be of interest to colonial rulers, such as labor migration and variations in political organization. But Malinowski urged anthropologists to use their expertise in defense of subject peoples. He said in 1930, for example, that all figures on the colonial scene – government administrators; European investors; settlers, and missionaries; and every class of the subject population, from the most Westernized to people in the bush – had "deeply rooted personal interests at stake" that created "irreconcilable differences." (quoted in Kuklick 1991b: 188). Moreover, when professional anthropologists undertook to specify the structure of a traditional political authority so that it could be used as the vehicle for Indirect Rule, their results might not suit administrators. The South African Max Gluckman (1911–75), a student of Evans-Pritchard and Radcliffe-Brown at Oxford, saw his 1943 report on the Barotse ignored by the government of Northern Rhodesia (now Zambia) on the grounds that the structure he identified was too complex. Indeed, functionalists criticized administrators for invoking evolutionist formulae to justify eliminating political traditions that gave indigenes latitude in choosing their leaders.

Malinowski asserted that "in every type of civilisation, every custom, material object, idea and belief fulfills some vital function . . . represent[ing] an indispensable part within a working whole" (1923: 659). "As sociologists," he wrote in 1922, "we are not interested in what A or B may feel *qua* individuals . . . only in what they feel *qua* members of a given community." Moreover, as he insisted in the 1926 *Encyclopaedia Britannica*, "the essence of evolution consists not in a sequence of different forms changing one into another, but in a better adaptation of an institution to its function." Functionalists analyzed societies as "going concerns": societies changed over time, but the origins of given practices were irrelevant; practices might once have had uses quite different from those they served in the present. And when functionalists made historical judgments, these were of little value to colonial officials seeking interpretations of social change: societies were either resilient, adapting to changed circumstances, or they had been "overwhelmed by the white man's destructive force" (Radcliffe-Brown in 1935, quoted in Kuklick 1991b: 222).

Malinowskian functionalism and Radcliffe-Brownian structural-functionalism were somewhat different. As Seligman and Westermarck's student, Malinowki grounded his theory in biological constants: the biological/psychological needs served by all societies' social institutions must be identical, since the pace of biological evolution was incredibly slow. He also attended to individuals' motives. Social forces shaped individuals' desires to deviate from normative expectations, but individuals were not passive slaves to their societies' rules – contrary to the persons portrayed in the sociology of Émile Durkheim, whose theories Radcliffe-Brown made his own. Radcliffe-Brown insisted that social phenomena could not be reduced to such underlying phenomena as individual psychology. (One must note that Rivers, Radcliffe-Brown's anthropological mentor, had observed that at least *some* sociological generalizations could not be translated into psychological ones, but Radcliffe-Brown's Durkheimianism was in some measure an anti-Riversian move.) And Radcliffe-Brown's influence grew considerably after he returned to Britain in 1937 to take up the new Oxford chair, not least because in 1938 Malinowski moved to Yale to escape the hostilities then looming in Europe, and died shortly thereafter, in 1942.

The functionalists' formative experiences surely shaped their views. Recall the backgrounds of Malinowski's teachers at the LSE: Seligman's status was mixed in the terms of British society, since he was both wealthy and Jewish. Westermarck was Finnish. Malinowski had a strong identity as a Pole, though born a citizen of the Austro-Hungarian Empire; from 1795 to 1918, Poland was an imaginary nation, having been partitioned among Prussia, Austria, and Russia, to be reunited after World War I. Radcliffe-Brown was a person of undistinguished British antecedents, whose intellectual accomplishments won him a Cambridge scholarship. Born Brown, he reinvented himself as Radcliffe-Brown during his sojourn in South Africa, and his appointments at foreign universities gave him many opportunities to witness diverse ways of life. Many of the leaders of the next generation of anthropologists came from South Africa, where they experienced the politics of racial and ethnic difference: Africans, Asians, persons of mixed ancestry, as well as whites divided between speakers of English and Afrikaans lived in distinct communities, with differential life chances. Because many of the South Africans were Jewish, their identities were especially complicated. Moreover, a relatively high proportion of anthropologists who took advanced degrees and earned recognition were women, although their gender limited their mobility; consider that Audrey Richards, the first woman to be elected president of the RAI – in 1959 – retired as a reader. In sum, functionalist anthropologists resembled their predecessors insofar as they were not drawn from the traditional British elite, but they were even more marginal figures. Anthropologists' diverse backgrounds and unusual experiences primed them to recognize societies' and subcultures' distinctive habits and norms.

Functional/structuralist analysis could be performed as formulaic puzzle solving. Evolutionist notions were refuted: magical thinking made sense in social contexts; tracing descent through the mother was not antecedent to patrilineal descent, but types of kinship structures were associated with preferences for marital arrangements, with varieties of prescriptive rights and duties, and with patterns of political conflict deriving from links of family ties and resource distribution; decentralized styles of maintaining political order were not inferior (and antecedent) to formal, hierarchical structures, but different ways of effecting cooperation. A people's classificatory system could be analyzed, and relationships thought to be parallel could be described (for example, man is to woman as day is to night, as right is to left, as village is to forest, and so on). Rituals that reinforced social norms were described. In differently organized societies, there were different social sites that repeatedly fostered discord. Patterns of behavior such as labor migration by a specific sector of a population or witchcraft accusations leveled at the more fortunate were associated with systematically differentially distributed privileges. Indeed, the decline in the study of witchcraft, noted in 1972 by an anthropologist whose specialty it was, Max Marwick, was as definitive a marker of the end of an intellectual era as one might find (although not seen as such by Marwick himself). There was not "a simple and narrow orthodoxy," as Jonathan Spencer observes, but agreement about "what was deemed worthy of argument" (2000: 19).

That is, for roughly three decades following World War II, social anthropology looked like a normal science, as famously described by Thomas Kuhn in his *Structure of Scientific Revolutions* (1962): its practitioners focused on solving a set of problems they collectively recognized as significant. Indeed, there was broad agreement that social anthropology was a science, directed toward formulating laws of human behavior, notwithstanding the occasional dissent, such as Evans-Pritchard's. Applied anthropology was now considered antithetical to true science among the anthropological elite, and the dead Malinowski, in particular, was criticized for having argued that anthropology had practical value precisely because it was a science. Anthropologists' services were sought for development projects, and funds for them were available through the Colonial Social Science Research Council (CSSRC), a subsidiary of the Colonial Research Council, which was created in 1944. The prominent anthropologists selected to allocate CSSRC funds considered it their duty to serve disciplinary priorities rather than colonial government officials, relegating applied work to lackluster talents; it is of interest that the elite entertained the proposition that mediocre anthropologists doing applied research might work best in teams (Mills 2005b: 147). Exasperated, the first head of the Colonial Research Council, Lord Hailey, proclaimed in 1946 that the sort of expertise anthropologists possessed was so vital to development projects that if colonial regimes could not find anthropologists to assist them "we must find someone calling himself by a different name who will do so" (quoted in Kuklick 1991b: 14).

Post-World War II social anthropologists were a small group with a strong sense of collective identity. Led by Evans-Pritchard, 11 people organized the Association of Social Anthropologists in 1946; unlike the inclusive RAI, the ASA was selective, adding members by invitation only.[11] Certainly, harmony did not reign. The relative merits of functionalism and structuralism were debated. There were rivalries among major departments – the LSE, Oxford, Manchester, and Cambridge (within which there was notable personal acrimony). There were significant individual disputes. But relative prosperity conduced to a level of mutual tolerance. When the Empire and the CSSRC shut down in tandem, anthropologists feared destitution; instead, they were generously supported by British and American foundations, and after 1965 by Britain's new Social Science Research Council, which was at the "peak of its munificence" in 1973 (Spencer 2000: 19).

Nevertheless, many postwar anthropologists were uninterested in expanding their undergraduate audiences, making their field relatively slow growing. Thus, paradoxically, a degree of disciplinary uncertainty set in just as Britain's higher education system expanded in the 1960s. A few data – not fully comparable – suggest the limited employment prospects available in anthropology departments. In 1951, the ASA had roughly 50 members, and there were around 30 academic positions in social anthropology in Britain. By 1961, the ASA membership had grown to about 140, and there were roughly 50 academic positions. Members numbered roughly 240 by 1968; however, one-quarter of them were based in the commonwealth (Firth 1951, 474; E. and S. Ardener 1965, 300; Spencer 2000: 3, 4; Mills 2005a). By the 1970s, there were about 150 academic social anthropologists in Britain. More than three decades later, there were less than 250 permanent positions in United Kingdom universities, though the ASA had roughly 600 members, 90 percent of them UK-based (Spencer, Jepson, Mills 2005; Mills 2005a).

The era of paradigmatic consensus came to an end in the 1970s, when many anthropological elders, largely professional descendants of Malinowski, retired – and few new appointments were made. By 1986, Tim Ingold judged anthropology "starved of new ideas" and "virtually moribund" (1996: ix). The discipline remained confined to elite institutions, in part because practitioners were uninterested in expansion and in part because there were not enough trained anthropologists to staff new departments. Funding for graduate students was (and has remained) low. Anthropology's stagnation was particularly notable by contrast to the then-contemporary expansion of sociology. Symptomatic of the soul-searching of the time was the organization by Ingold of the Group for Debates in Anthropological Theory (GDAT), leadership of which passed to Peter Wade in 1995. GDAT debates ended in 2000, but until they did they (ideally) occurred annually at the University of Manchester, debating a general proposition. GDAT's first meeting, held in 1988, discussed "Social anthropology is a generalizing science or it is nothing." Subsequent propositions included "Human worlds are culturally constructed" (1990) and "Cultural Studies will be the death of anthropology" (1997). Anthropologists' revitalizing strategies also included attempting to attract more students. There was demand for anthropologists in non-academic settings, particularly in development. Throughout the 1980s, "the only significant growth area in academic anthropology was in more-or-less vocational taught masters degrees." Disciplinary innovations began at the academic periphery, in such new departments as those at Kent and Sussex, to be imitated by the older departments. By the late 1980s, anthropology had become much more publicly visible, and student demand for anthropology courses grew dramatically (Spencer 2000: 14; see also 4–6, 11).

In the 15 years prior to 2005, the number of PhDs conferred in social anthropology each year grew from roughly 50 to roughly 90, though the number of job openings was only 10 to 20 in any given year. Nevertheless, available evidence suggests that roughly 65 percent of UK-trained PhDs find academic employment; a number work abroad (often having returned to their countries of origin), while many work in non-anthropological UK departments. British social anthropology is now an "exporter" discipline. Its doctoral recipients figure in an international labor market, are distributed across the social sciences, and work in non-academic settings, most notably in development agencies and in diverse UK government departments (Spencer et al. 2005).

Is British social anthropology still distinctive? Some British social anthropologists, for whom engagement with American anthropology is anathema, have made common cause with Europeans (e.g., Kuper 2005). In many academic quarters, however, the line between British and American anthropology is blurring, not least because Americans have become a substantial presence in British departments, constituting more than half the faculty in at least one of them (Kent). Moreover, career patterns have changed. PhD students are no longer required to do prolonged fieldwork in a remote site. The "modal doctoral student" preparing for an academic career is a citizen of a European Union state who does South Asian fieldwork, but social anthropologists who work in Britain are as likely to find academic employment as those who study foreign parts (Spencer et al. 2005: 9).

Moreover, departmental structures are changing. Once, the emblem of American anthropology was its four-field character, while social anthropology was autonomous in Britain. Today, a similar range of variation in departmental organizations obtains on both sides of the Atlantic; many American departments have abandoned the four-field structure, while a number of British departments have joined subfields. A few examples of reorganized departments are those at: UCL, which offers specialization in social anthropology, biological anthropology, and material culture; Kent, which has offered training in biological anthropology and social anthropology, as well as in specialties that are somehow related to natural science – conservation ecology (for a time), environmental anthropology, and ethnobotany; Bristol, which includes archaeology, social anthropology, and biological anthropology; and Durham, which covers biological and social anthropology. Moreover, the *Journal of the Royal Anthropological Institute* (entitled *Man* for a time) has consistently defined its purview in holistic terms; throughout its history, its pool of contributors has been international, and it has published articles in all of the fields that figure in the American four-field scheme, though articles in sociocultural anthropology have predominated, not least because sociocultural anthropologists are by far the largest group among practitioners.

Now, persons employed in UK anthropology departments do research everywhere across the globe, theorize in a congeries of modes, and study many subjects their forebears would not have recognized as anthropological. These subjects include (but are hardly limited to): aesthetics; behavioral genetics; civil society; cognitive anthropology and linguistics; diasporas; ecology; formal and voluntary associations; gender; historical demography; human–animal relations; human evolution; identity; local knowledge systems of various sorts; material culture of prehistoric Europe; missionaries; new media of every description; new technologies of every sort; policymaking of every sort; place and landscape; phylogenetic systematics; popular culture of every sort; primate evolution and behavior; diverse health issues; ritual and symbolism in complex societies; tourism; trauma and conflict; and work and unemployment.[12]

Of course, British anthropology has distinctive features, if only because it is practiced within distinctive institutional structures. At every level, from the departmental to the national, there are idiosyncratic characteristics. But it is fair to say that British anthropology today is at least as international as it was in the late nineteenth century. And the range of subjects that interest its practitioners is at least as broad as it was then.

Notes

1 While writing this essay, I have consulted a number of sources, which I cite. But I have presented much of the material in it in previous works, which I do not cite in the text unless I am using quotations drawn from them (Kuklick 1991b, 1996, 1997, 1998, 2006).

2 See, for example, the set of "Queries" circulated in the early 1670s by a Royal Society group who undertook a "Survey of England and Wales," asking respondents to describe such geographical features as natural vegetation cover, land use, mountains, settlements, mines and quarries, and built landmarks (Taylor 1937: 532).

3 Of course, receipt of a knighthood was not a straightforward matter. Some persons rejected titles offered by the Crown, such as Karl Pearson, of whom more shortly.

4 Lankester did not fully date his letters, but contextual clues indicate that correspondence about the unwritten book with its projected publisher took place around 1896–7. See Lankester to Macmillan, June 6, MA, Add.MS 55219.

5 Its sovereignty formally shared by the Egyptian Khedive and the British Crown, its affairs indifferently supervised by the Foreign Office, its control over the area under its jurisdiction precarious (at best) in many places, such as its southern provinces, the Sudan was a unique colonial territory.

6 There was one exception to this generalization: Margaret Field, who came to the Gold Coast to teach secondary school chemistry, but served as a government anthropologist there between 1938 and 1944.

7 Cambridge made the largest single financial contribution to the expedition. Funds also came from the Royal Society (prompted by Frazer and Galton), the BAAS, the Royal Geographical Society, and the territorial government of Queensland.

8 Spencer investigated biological matters and edited the expedition's *Report*, while Gillen served as chief informant for the expedition's anthropologist, E. C. Stirling. Legend has it that Gillen stimulated Spencer's interest in anthropology, but Spencer provided Stirling ethnographic information before meeting Gillen.

9 In the World War II era, Max Gluckman developed a teamwork method involving white social scientists and African assistants that was particularly appropriate (even necessary)

to analysis of the multi-ethnic and multi-racial relationships of the Copperbelt in Northern Rhodesia (now Zambia), but one must stress that the substance of his teams' research was unusual (Schumaker 2001).

10   Of the 12 recipients of PhDs in anthropology from UCL before World War II, the first, the Rev. E. O. James, whose degree was conferred in 1925, was the most successful British academic, retiring as UCL's professor of history and philosophy of religion. Only the Australian A. P. Elkin (1891–1979), became a successful anthropologist: earning his degree in 1927, he returned home, abandoned diffusionism, and worked his way up to the Sydney chair.

11   The ASA required overwhelming agreement that new members were worthy. At first, one dissent sufficed to exclude someone. In 1950, secret voting was introduced, and regulations changed over time. Today, persons may propose themselves for membership or be nominated, but must present evidence of professional accomplishment. Candidates for membership are admitted if they receive at least two-thirds of the votes of those present at the ASA's Annual General Meeting.

12   I culled anthropologists' self-identified research interests from the "Guide to University Departments" in the *Annals of the Association of Social Anthropologists of the UK and the Commonwealth*, 2005.

Further Reading

Kuklick, H. 1991. *The Savage Within: The Social History of British Anthropology, 1885–1945.* New York: Cambridge University Press.

Stocking, G. W., Jr. 1987. *Victorian Anthropology*. New York: Free Press.

Stocking, G. W., Jr. 1995. *After Tylor*. Madison: University of Wisconsin Press.

4

Traditions in the German Language

H. Glenn Penny

During the last two decades, interest in German anthropology has grown among historians of anthropology in the English-speaking world, largely because of its influence in Great Britain and particularly the United States (e. g., Cole 1999; Liss 1990; Stocking 1987). Until recently, however, there were few efforts to reconstruct the history of anthropology in Germany itself. Because of some anthropologists' complicity in Nazi race crimes, the history of the discipline received little attention. Indeed, it was only in the 1980s that German scholars began to probe that past earnestly. The link to colonialism, with its implicit connection to National Socialism, was an early target (Gothsch 1983; Harms 1984; Winkelmann 1966); and scholars tended to hold up Anglophone anthropology as the standard of comparison, revealing, and in many ways enhancing, its hegemonic position in the history of the discipline. Yet this juxtaposition has proven fruitful, calling into question often-stated generalizations about periodization, professionalization, fieldwork, and the relationship between politics and anthropology.

Recent work has revealed a rich world of intellectual inquiry and popular enthusiasm for the sciences of humanity in central Europe during the nineteenth century (Buschmann 1999; Bruckner 1999; Evans 2002; Maner 2001; W. D. Smith 1991; Zimmerman 2001). It has also indicated that German anthropology had a distinctive development pattern. Most histories of anthropology portray colonial interests and a concern to classify the peoples of the world on an evolutionary scale as the factors that shaped the discipline during the nineteenth century, indicating that only during the first decades of the twentieth century did it begin moving towards more pluralistic frameworks (Bunzl and Penny 2003). Nineteenth-century German anthropology and ethnology were self-consciously liberal endeavors, however, guided by a broadly humanistic agenda and centered on efforts to document the plurality and historical specificity of cultures; their practitioners did not focus on Germany's colonial territories and disdained imperial ideology (Penny 2002b). Then, in the early twentieth century, central European ethnologists and anthropologists abandoned their cosmopolitan heritage. A narrowly nationalistic and increasingly racist orientation became dominant during the interwar years, culminating in the eager participation of many anthropologists in National Socialism.

There are, however, some difficulties in attempting to characterize "the" traditions of anthropology in the German language. German anthropology was never centralized. Rather, it was characterized by avid intra-German competition. Despite many British anthropologists' lamentations around the turn of the century about the support that "the Germans" received from their imperial government (e.g., Dalton 1898), the secret to German success was actually Imperial Germany's aggregate nature. Because its constitution left cultural affairs in the hands of the different states, German anthropology, archaeology, and ethnology remained local affairs well into the twentieth century. These disciplines grew out of loose, competitive associations, with multiple centers. They were internationally as much as nationally oriented, and they were dependent on the largesse of municipal and regional associations, which were driven by competitive verve, each attempting to enhance its status and prestige by showing that its area's cultural and scientific institutions were outpacing those in other major German and European cities. Thus, German ethnologists and anthropologists were given resources to compete with their counterparts in Germany and elsewhere to develop the largest institutions, the most extensive collections, and the leading publications (Penny 2002b).

The institutional landscape in the German-speaking lands was also fractured. Museums, rather than universities, became the dominant institutional setting for the ethnographic sciences, which thus focused on material culture, extensive collecting, and salvage anthropology. Museum holdings encompassed the entire world, and artifact displays were organized according to geographical rather than evolutionary principles, with little or no place for physical anthropology. That exclusion contributed to the institutional and professional crisis of physical anthropology by the early twentieth century, and helped maintain the separation in Germany between anthropology and ethnology.

Indeed, a good deal of confusion about the history of German anthropology stems from terminology. While "German anthropology" seems an acceptable shorthand for the fields that comprise the discipline in the United States, these fields are recognized as distinct, if interconnected, disciplines in the German tradition. During the nineteenth century, *Ethnologie* (ethnology) and *Ethnographie* (ethnography) were used almost interchangeably, and neither was eclipsed by the term *Völkerkunde* (also ethnology), which became dominant by the turn of the century. All of them were roughly – but only roughly – equivalent to what we call cultural anthropology in the United States today. Moreover, different people used these terms in different ways: in some cases, *Völkerkunde* and *Ethnologie* were used interchangeably well into the twentieth century; in other cases, *Völkerkunde* was defined as a science focused on people who were illiterate before their exposure to European expansion, and *Ethnologie* was a science that also included literate peoples (Zwernemann 1983: 22–3). The term *Anthropologie* (anthropology) invariably meant physical anthropology, which was the natural history of humans in the nineteenth century, and became the comparative biology of humans by the third decade of the twentieth century (Proctor 1988: 141). For nineteenth-century Germans, "anthropology," as Rudolf Virchow said in 1894, had "nothing to do with culture" (quoted in Massin 1996: 82). Culture was the realm of ethnologists. In this chapter, I will use "anthropology" as a general term, encompassing the discipline in its broadest sense, but I will distinguish between ethnologists (cultural anthropologists) and anthropologists (physical anthropologists), as the historical actors themselves did.

The distinction between ethnology and physical anthropology was consistently maintained in the German tradition. When the *Deutsche Gesellschaft für Anthropologie, Ethnologie, und Urgeschichte* (German Society for Anthropology, Ethnology, and Prehistory) was founded in 1869, it was the leading association of its kind in central Europe. Initially, physical anthropology was at its center. Its older anthropological section had its own publication, the *Archiv für Anthropologie*, founded in 1863, and had a large contingent of supporters, dominated by physicians interested in morphological studies of skeletons and skulls. When the Berlin section of the Society for Anthropology, Ethnology, and Prehistory published the first issue of its journal, the *Zeitschrift für Ethnologie*, Adolf Bastian, the leading figure in German ethnology until his death in 1905, felt the need to distinguish ethnology from physical anthropology, and that distinction remained clear through World War I (Bastian 1869). Because physical anthropology was slighted in the large ethnographic museums that Bastian and his counterparts created across Germany, and had little success establishing itself in the universities, ethnology was the more prominent discipline by the turn of the century (Buschmann 2000).

Despite the divisions and fractures, the history of German anthropology is marked by a fairly clear periodization, shaped largely by the process of professionalization and a series of generational shifts. That periodization frames this essay, which seeks to characterize the dominant trends in each period while also noting some of the striking alternatives.

Travel, Natural Science, and Cosmopolitan Visions Before 1868

German interests in non-Europeans during the nineteenth century were consistent with a range of intellectual and cultural traditions. Humanism, liberalism, pluralism, and monogenism shaped Germans' inquiries, but the *Völksgeist* tradition of Johann Gottfried Herder was perhaps most important (Iggers 1968: 3–29), encouraging many of the individuals who shaped German ethnology to view culture as something that people everywhere possessed, and human diversity as the result of particular histories rather than stages on an evolutionary scale. Educated Germans were guided by the ideal of *Bildung* (intellectual and moral self-cultivation), which encouraged connection with the wider world, leading them to gather knowledge about their world from a wide array of sources, including the flood of travel literature that poured into Europe during the nineteenth century.

Alexander von Humboldt, renowned for his exploration of equatorial America from 1799 to 1804, was the most influential scientific traveler. He produced thirty volumes based on his journeys, reporting his observations of botany, plant geography, zoology, physical geography, and political economy. He also contributed to the sciences of anatomy, mineralogy, and chemistry, and was keenly interested in the relationship between humans and their environment. His masterpiece was the five-volume *Cosmos* (published between 1845 and 1862), in which he attempted a comprehensive description of the universe and a complete account of the physical history of the world – and it made him one of the most successful authors of his day (the original edition of the first volume alone sold over 22,000 copies [Rupke 1997: vii]). His writings helped to establish geography as a scientific discipline, and his example influenced both the lifestyle embraced by aspiring ethnologists like Adolf Bastian and the character and scope of their ethnographic projects (Bunzl 1996: 43–52; Penny 2002b).

Equally important were accounts from many archaeological digs produced by the middle of the nineteenth century (Maner). Many Germans were entranced by the human bones and extinct animals discovered at places like Brixham cave and the Neander Valley, which seemed to explode the biblical time frame of human history (according to which human existence dated to 4004 BCE). Archaeological finds indicated that material artifacts were of critical importance for reconstructing the past. The physicians who became anthropologists hoped to learn about the transformation of human bodies over time; historians and archaeologists hoped to use material finds to push their local and regional histories beyond written records, challenging earlier histories. Much like the promoters of municipally supported ethnographic museums, local archaeologists were engaged in competitive efforts of civic and regional self-promotion, not just in advancing a new science. Their interests led to such widespread digging across the new German state that by the 1880s the federal government created a permit system to regulate excavations (Weindling 1989: 54).

Anthropology, archaeology, and ethnology were supported by a range of scientific associations. All benefited from the wave of association founding that followed the 1848 revolutions, in which mostly liberal-minded citizens across Germany organized locally in the name of progress, public welfare, and the common good. Professionals and businessmen pursued science as one means of obtaining *Bildung* and fostering culture, civic improvement, and public education in their communities. Some eighty new associations devoted to the natural sciences alone were established in the German lands between 1840 and 1870; and in the quarter century following the creation of the Berlin Society for Anthropology, Ethnology, and Prehistory in 1869, 25 anthropological associations were founded across Germany.

In most cases, these associations were governed by Germany's growing middle classes, which were moving into areas traditionally dominated by royalty, and were eager to display their self-cultivation. Within the cities, scientific associations were also strongly tied to civic pride, municipal development, and a desire by leading citizens to exhibit their worldliness (Penny 2002a). This effort to exhibit worldliness by supporting new, international sciences and building connections across the globe supplied one aspect of German anthropology and ethnology's cosmopolitan character; Alexander von Humboldt's penchant for positing total empirical and harmonic pictures of the world and Herder's credo of cultural pluralism contributed the others.

Museums and the Institutional Landscape, 1868–1907

The institutional landscape that shaped German anthropology emerged together with Imperial Germany (1871–1918). The imperial period witnessed an unprecedented growth in the number and size of German universities; but the growth of museums and other scientific institutions outside the universities was equally important (e.g., Johnson 1990). Museums appealed to individuals who wished to participate in scientific associations, but who lacked the training of nineteenth-century educated elites. Prior to the 1870s, an exclusive group of academics, closely linked to classical education and the universities, dominated the cultural sciences in the German-speaking areas of central Europe (Ringer 1969). Scholars' recognition in the 1860s that material culture supplied them with another kind of historical "text" gave a range of young, enthusiastic scientists the opportunity to develop an expertise that could challenge the philologically based knowledge of the universities. And ethnographic museums furnished them with a new culturally respectable space for the production of knowledge.

The career opportunities presented by the arrival of ethnographic museums on central Europe's institutional landscape may be seen by examining the life of Moritz Wagner, who became curator of Munich's ethnographic collection in 1862 and the first director of its ethnographic museum in 1868. Born into a schoolteacher's family in Augsburg in 1813, Wagner traveled extensively, produced a veritable mountain of journalistic and scientific publications, but consistently faced problems finding a place among German-educated elites. Shortly after completing his training as a businessman in Bavaria, he went to work in Marseilles, where he developed an avid interest in North Africa. Returning to Bavaria in 1835, he studied natural history in Nürnberg and Erlangen, and in 1836 joined a scientific commission attached to French troops near Algiers. From there he wrote extensively for diverse German journals and newspapers. Returning to Europe in 1838, he produced a three-volume account of his travels and observations that was well received among natural scientists (Smolka 1994: 54).

Wagner became an editor for the widely read newspaper *Allgemeine Zeitung*, spent time studying in Göttingen, and made contacts with Alexander von Humboldt and Carl Ritter, who helped him gain the support of the Berlin Academy of Sciences for his travels in Africa, Persia, Russia, and southeastern Europe in the 1840s. Disenchanted by the 1848 revolutions, he followed thousands of refugees to the "new world" in 1852, traveling for two years in the United States and Central America, studying the flora, fauna, and persons he encountered. Returning to Europe, he produced more volumes describing his experiences. From 1857 to 1859, he was supported by the king of Bavaria to travel to South America in order to investigate the potential for Bavarian immigration abroad, as well as to conduct his own research. This final venture, which he regarded as bringing him especially close to Alexander von Humboldt, took him through a war between Peru and Ecuador, violent encounters with local populations, and bouts of disease, after which he returned home "tired, sick, half-blinded and financially at his end" (Smolka 1994: 77–8).

Despite his extensive travels and numerous publications, Wagner's repeated efforts to secure a regular university position were unsuccessful, since he lacked the necessary credentials. Although his migration theories ultimately influenced Friedrich Ratzel's *Anthropogeographie* and the field of natural history in Germany (Beck 1951), German-educated elites regarded him as a mere journalist and a dilettante, and he complained until his death in 1887 that the "armchair scholars" in the universities never took him seriously (Gareis 1990: 46–7). With his appointment as curator of Munich's ethnological collections, however, he gained an intellectual credibility and an institutional base from which he could participate in academic discussions about the relationship between geography and human development.

Large museums were also established in Berlin, Hamburg, Leipzig, Stuttgart, and Vienna, and smaller museums were established in Bremen, Cologne, Darmstadt, Dresden, Frankfurt, Freiburg im Breisgau, Kassel, Karlsruhe, and Lübeck. Before 1905, virtually all of the directors of German ethnographic museums shared many of Wagner's characteristics. They were dilettantes, often travelers who had built personal collections, natural scientists who could not gain university employment, or officials elected by municipal governments or local ethnological associations. They seldom taught university courses, and when they did so it was only as lecturers or untenured honorary professors.

The exception was Adolf Bastian, who established and directed the Museum für Völkerkunde in Berlin, the largest and most important of Germany's new museums, and who was the best-known ethnologist in central Europe. Bastian became a lecturer and later an honorary professor at Berlin University, and a number of his assistants were also able to work there. But there was no department of ethnology or anthropology. Not until 1908 was there a university chair, in both ethnology and anthropology, established in the Philosophical Faculty of Berlin University for Felix von Luschan, Bastian's successor at the museum. Only in 1920 was a chair created at a German university dedicated to ethnology alone; established at Leipzig, it was occupied by Karl Weule after he had spent thirteen years as director of Leipzig's ethnographic museum.

Physical anthropologists had similar difficulties establishing themselves in German universities. During the last decades of the nineteenth century, physical anthropology was generally taught at universities by members of the medical faculties or professors in anatomy or pathology. Although a chair in physical anthropology was established in Munich in 1886, occupied by Johannes Ranke, no comparable position was created until Luschan gained his mixed chair of ethnology and anthropology in 1908. In 1903, only six of Germany's 21 universities offered courses in anthropology – and obviously only Ranke's courses were taught by a chaired professor. Moreover, while ethnologists could work in their field if they could secure one of the few permanent positions available in Germany's new museums, most anthropologists could not gain positions in museums, unless they were willing to focus on ethnology; there were few institutions devoted to physical anthropology. Ranke's chair was paired with a directorship of the anthropological institute at the University of Munich, but there were no comparable institutes until 1907, when an anthropological section was added to the anatomical institute in Breslau. Rudolf Virchow, who led the founding of the German Anthropological Society, the Berlin Society for Anthropology, Ethnology, and Prehistory, and who dominated most of the leading anthropological journals in Germany, did not hold a position as an anthropologist; he was Rector at the Berlin University and Professor of Pathological Anatomy. Even Eugen Fischer, who helped reshape German anthropology during the interwar years, languished in an anatomical institution in Freiburg until he occupied the chair that had been Luschan's in 1927. In sum, most physical anthropologists worked in other fields while pursuing their anthropological interests.

Much like Wagner, Bastian attempted to follow in Alexander von Humboldt's footsteps, spending 25 years of his life abroad on a series of expeditions. Unlike Wagner, however, Bastian was independently wealthy, solidly supported by associations and institutions in Berlin, well connected to collectors and scientists abroad, and consequently much more influential. Bastian's activities went beyond the museum. He founded, contributed to, and edited a number of leading ethnological and geographical journals, and he was repeatedly featured in popular magazines. He was prominent in a number of scientific associations, including Germany's foremost geographical society and the Berlin Society for Anthropology, Ethnology, and Prehistory. By 1895, he had over 230 publications to his credit, and by 1905 his books took up three to four feet of shelf space (Tylor 1905). A number of other German scholars also played important roles in the history of this science, including such figures as Friedrich Ratzel, whose views differed from Bastian's; but it was unquestionably Bastian who set the central trends in German ethnology from the 1860s through the 1890s, as he sketched out his vast empirical project, established extensive international networks of collection and exchange, created an ethnographic institution that set the standard for all others, and helped to train a number of Germany's first professional ethnologists. Just as Rudolf Virchow dominated physical anthropology in Germany, Bastian dominated ethnology.

Bastian's ethnology was governed less by an overarching theory than by a set of methodological, and ultimately political, convictions. Like Virchow, Bastian drew on inductive and empirical methods to avoid the classification of data according to predetermined categories, regarding classificatory schemes as works in progress rather than definitive, and he was reluctant to speak in terms of hierarchies or scales of "progress." He and Virchow excluded teleology from their historicism, and they understood differences among people as merely variations on a central theme of a unitary humanity. Thus, they were staunchly opposed to confounding the categories of race, nation, and *Volk*, and to positing a biological link between mental faculty and race (Massin 1996; Evans 2002).

Their methodological commitment to careful, empirical research over "speculative theorizing" prompted both Bastian and Virchow to shun Darwinian schemes and avoid debates about race. Darwin's ideas were widely discussed in Germany, but Germany's leading ethnologists and anthropologists were staunchly anti-Darwinian. Virchow argued in public that Darwinism was dangerous because of its possible association with Social Democracy; but his chief criticism was that it had no solid empirical foundation. As Franz Boas later noted, Virchow's position rested on "the general scientific principle that it was dangerous to classify data that are imperfectly known under the point of view of general theories," and that "the sound progress of science" requires scientists "to be clear at every moment, what elements in the system of science are hypothetical and what are the limits of that knowledge which is obtained by exact observation" (1974). Thus, from 1872 to 1875, when Virchow debated with the zoologist Ernst Haeckel, the best-known of Darwin's popularizers, he was contributing to a discussion about the possibilities of scientific knowledge that had been conducted in Germany since at least the 1850s, arguing that science was defined by method (Kolkenbrock-Netz 1991). For his part, Bastian compared Darwin's postulates about the "genealogy of mankind" to "fantasies" from the "dreams of mid-day naps" (1871: 138). He, too, reserved his strongest criticism for his public debates with Haeckel, condemning Haeckel's popularizations of Darwinism as irresponsible because they presented unsubstantiated theories as established truths; indeed, Bastian thought the findings of his own science too tentative for presentation to the public.

In lieu of a definitive ethnological theory, Bastian had a set of convictions and a three-part plan of action. He argued that "the physical unity of the species man [had already] been anthropologically established"; his project was to locate "the psychic unity of social thought [that] underlies the basic elements of the body social." His method was to analyze the material cultures of peoples everywhere as expressions of the "monotonous sub-stratum of identical elementary ideas" that could reveal the more general history of the human mind (in Koepping, 1983: 176). Because human nature was "uniform all over the globe," whatever regularities could be found should be "in the thought processes of man" (1869: 23–5). His first task was comprehensive, comparative analysis of these thought processes. This procedure would yield empirical laws. Then, these laws could be applied to Bastian's ultimate end – the effort of Europeans to better understand themselves.

Bastian stressed that every group of people shared "elementary ideas" or *Elementargedanken* – which were not directly observable. Having an "innate propensity to change" (Koepping 1983: 86), they always materialized in the form of unique patterns of thought, or *Völkergedanken*, reflecting the interaction of peoples with their environments, as well as their contacts with other groups. *Elementargedanken* were hidden behind humanity's cultural diversity. The *Völkergedanken* that characterized different groups of people emerged within identifiable zones where geographical and historical influences shaped specific cultures. Unique *Völkergedanken*, like "actual organisms," fit within particular geographical provinces, shifting and changing as they came into contact with others. This interaction was the basis of all historical development, and it could be observed most readily in certain geographical areas: on rivers, coast lines, and mountain passes, which Bastian termed "*Völkertore*" (1873: 324). Understanding the unique contexts in which each culture took shape, Bastian (1872) stressed, was critical for gaining insight into the universal character of "the" human being.

Within Bastian's ethnology, the question of human difference was critical. On a basic level, humanity could be divided into two major categories: *Naturvölker* (natural peoples); and *Kulturvölker* (cultural peoples), who were literate, with a recorded past that historians and philologists could examine. But *Naturvölker* were not bereft of history or culture: there were virtually no peoples on earth who were without historical influences. The historical and cultural trajectories among the world's *Naturvölker* were at the heart of Bastian's ethnological project. Indeed, Bastian's focus was on specific differences among natural peoples, not similarities. Understanding their differences was the key to accounting for the general development of *Völkergedanken*. Like his Anglophone contemporaries, Bastian recommended investigations of the most isolated and simple societies, but, unlike them, he did not imagine that analysis of *Naturvölker* would allow ethnologists to describe a progressive course of cultural development; rather, it would reveal a "set of seminal ideas from which every civilization had grown." The seminal ideas would become the "methodological tool for unraveling more complex civilizations." Allowing the formulation of empirical laws regarding the effects of physiological, psychological, and social conditions on the human mind, Bastian's (1869) ethnographic insights could then be applied to Europeans.

Bastian intended ethnographic museums to embody his goals and methods. They should contain material culture from all areas of the world and all periods of history. But displays should not convey pointed narratives (unlike the arrangements of artifacts in evolutionary sequences found in many British and American museums). Geographically organized objects were displayed in cabinets made of glass and steel, which were flooded by natural light from large windows and glass ceilings and positioned so that scientists could move easily among them, gaining overviews of objects from entire regions, and making mental connections among the material cultures of people living in different times and places. Because of Bastian and Virchow's strong institutional positions, their methodological standards prevailed in central Europe. Geographical arrangements, a focus on collecting, the de-emphasis on narratives and pedagogy: all became standard in Germany's larger museums. Bastian's views about collecting and his penchant for massive empirical projects influenced ethnologists well into the twentieth century.

Attitudes toward fieldwork are one important example. The experience of fieldwork did not become an essential credential in Britain until the early twentieth century, but Bastian and Virchow stressed that the best-trained collectors must be sent into the field in their first proposals for the Berlin museum in the early 1870s, and they lamented the dearth of professional collectors in their first guidebooks (e.g., Bastian 1877: 13). They criticized the quality of collections produced by even well-known amateurs, such as Hermann von Wissmann, the first European to cross equatorial Africa (Essner 1985: 42). Bastian himself spent over 25 years of his life abroad, collecting for his museum and contacting people who would continue his collecting. To some degree, he was inspired by Alexander von Humboldt's example and by the value placed on experience within the German tradition of *Bildung*. But he was also committed to an empiricism requiring the best possible materials, which meant that they must be obtained by the best people – persons trained in German universities and museums. In the 1880s, when the first generation of trained ethnologists came of age, Bastian was able to send men like Karl von den Steinen, who became the director of the American section of the

Figure 5   Glass and steel cabinets in Berlin's Museum für Völkerkunde. Photograph used with permission of the museum.

Berlin museum, on repeated field trips. In the following decades, other German institutions quickly followed suit.

There were, however, tensions. Professionalization, for example, quickly divided ethnologists and collectors. There were never enough positions at the museums for all of the applicants, and a museum like Bastian's was often inundated with unpaid volunteers, hoping to gain permanent positions. Aspirant professionals' position worsened in the 1890s, as museums required increasingly detailed information about individual objects; eventually, museum directors proclaimed that only well-trained professionals could procure quality collections (e.g., Thilenius 1907). Even Adrian Jacobson, who led three major collecting expeditions for the Berlin museum in the 1880s, procuring some 16,000 items for it (perhaps one-sixth of its holdings in 1890), and whose collections were celebrated across Europe, was unable to gain a permanent position. He could not compete with younger men with university degrees who had trained in museums before venturing abroad and who were supposedly superior collectors because of their training (Penny 2002b).

German museums competed for both collections and collectors. Museum directors devoted most of their time to acquisitions, building complex networks of accumulation worldwide, and trying to monopolize collecting in as many areas as possible (e.g., Buschmann 2000). Bastian was particularly aggressive. Four years after Germany became a colonial power, he encouraged passage of a federal law requiring that his museum become a clearing house for all items collected by expeditions financed by government funds and by officials in colonial territories. Ethnographic items delivered to Berlin's *Völkerkunde* museum were supposed to be sorted and doubles sent to other German museums. Instead, the Berlin museum hoarded ethnographica from the colonial territories. The directors of other museums, distressed by their lack of colonial materials, eventually joined forces in an attempt to "break Berlin's monopoly." Their efforts led to the creation of a coalition of non-Prussian museums and repeated public confrontations with Berlin's ethnologists and the federal government that continued unresolved until 1914 (Buschmann 1999).

There were also theoretical tensions. Although a number of Bastian's assistants, such as Albert Grünwedel, had questioned Bastian's grand ethnographic project in the 1880s (Buschmann 1999), many younger assistants were looking for theoretical innovations by the turn of the century. A new generation of directors moved into Germany's leading ethnographic museums during the first decade of the twentieth century, and found theoretical inspiration outside of Berlin. Friedrich Ratzel, in Leipzig, had long opposed Bastian's ethnographic project. Drawing on Moritz Wagner's ideas that new species were formed by separation stemming from migration, Ratzel argued that a similar kind of historical descent could explain the similarities of forms and objects found among different peoples, some even thousands of miles apart. He also argued that tracking the diffusion of these forms could lead to a general history of culture (Zwernemann 1983: 5–30). Ratzel alone had been unable to break Bastian's hold on the science in Germany. But the generation that had gained control of museums by 1907 pushed German ethnology in new directions.

Generational Shifts and Theoretical Transformations, 1907–1918

Virchow died in 1902, and Bastian in 1905. And a range of lesser-known individuals who had safeguarded Bastian and Virchow's institutional hegemony also departed. Germany's leading ethnographic museums gained new directors in very short order. Georg Thilenius became director in Hamburg in 1904, Luschan in Berlin in 1905, Karl Weule in Leipzig in 1907, and Lucien Sherman in Munich in 1907. These new directors shared several key characteristics: they were professionally trained, possessed multiple university degrees, and because they had grown up in an age of aggressive nationalism and colonialism, they were also generally less averse to Germany's imperialist goals than Bastian and Virchow had been. Like Willy Foy, the young director of the new ethnographic museum that opened in Cologne in 1906, most did not value the accumulation of empirical data above all else (Foy 1911: 15–16). The new generation was driven by the often-contradictory demands of professionalism, the pressures to democratize science, and general transformations in the public sphere.

At the 1904 meeting of the Berlin Society for Anthropology, Ethnology and Prehistory, Fritz Graebner and Bernhard Ankermann issued the original declarations of the so-called "diffusionist revolt" (W. D. Smith 1991: 140–61). Presenting papers on the *Kulturkreise* (cultural areas) and *Kulturschichten* (cultural layers) of Oceania and Africa, these young assistants from Berlin's *Völkerkunde* museum challenged the old ethnographic project. Drawing on Ratzel's ideas but emphasizing recent work by Leo Frobenius, Graebner and Ankermann encouraged their colleagues to focus their attentions on identifying cultural traits, the manner in which they were clustered in particular geographical areas, and how they might have been distributed. Frobenius had argued that culture was a living object, that human beings were carriers of culture, and that while people die off, cultures continue to live and develop through contact with other cultures; in essence, cultures migrate and evolve, and the goal was to determine the history of cultural areas and identify the order they brought to human life (Zwernemann 1983: 36). Graebner and Ankermann embraced this research program, and the goal of mapping out – often literally – cultural histories, attacking both evolutionary theories and Bastian's concept of elementary ideas (Graebner 1905: 53).

During the following decade, German ethnology was reshaped by the emergence of several different groups of diffusionists, each with its own characteristics (Zwernemann 1983; Marchand 2003). Ankermann remained in Berlin, while Graebner joined Willy Foy in Cologne to set up a museum along diffusionist lines. Father Wilhelm Schmidt and Father Wilhelm Koppers headed another group centered in Vienna. Leo Frobenius persisted in his pursuit of *Kulturkreise*, settling into his own institute in Frankfurt following World War I. There was not a single *Kulturhistorische* school. But the trend among German ethnologists to move toward diffusionist models and away from Bastian's ideals was widespread, and it became pronounced in the decades following World War I.

The diffusionist revolt did not merely usher in a dominant ethnological theory. It signaled a dramatic change in attitudes among German ethnologists and anthropologists about what constituted good science. Bastian and Virchow stressed careful empiricism, avoiding political debates about cultural hierarchy and race. As expressed in museums as well as scientific journals, diffusionist schemes allowed for classification of cultural areas of individual groups along hierarchical lines. While Bastian's museum eschewed hierarchical arrangements for geographical distributions, the diffusionist ideal led to presentation of explicit narratives – exemplified in Graebner and Foy's new museum in Cologne. Bastian's focus on particularities in order to understand human universals was replaced by a focus on characterizing and defining particularized Others. And the new ethnology was more compatible with interests in nation and empire. While few ethnologists became politically engaged, and many insisted that Europeans should respect primitive cultures (Foy 1906: 32), their hierarchies and rhetoric were easily seized upon and deployed by others to support radical nationalism, imperialism, and even racial-biological schemes (W. D. Smith 1991: 160–1).

Similar shifts took place in archaeology and physical anthropology in the early twentieth century. After Virchow's death, a new generation of scholars emerged in archaeology. Virchow had dominated archaeological discussions, drawing in anthropologists and ethnologists, and maintaining methodological discipline. Perhaps because of his interest in his family's Slavic past, Virchow had sought to explore the complicated patterns of settlement by Slavs and Germans across central and eastern Europe before medieval times. He wanted to understand human migration and development, not to identify a German Ur-settlement. Indeed, he stressed as early as 1872 that "modern Germany is no longer the land of the old Teutonic tribes" (Massin 1996: 101), and that the results of his archaeological digs had no bearing on national unity.

Many of the younger archaeologists were uninterested in contextualizing their finds internationally. They focused on a distinctly German archaeology, and many, such as Gustav Kossina, a member of the hyper-nationalist Pan-German league, fashioned a new German past that boosted national pride. Following Virchow's death, Kossina gained considerable influence when he received a chair in archaeology at Berlin that was meant to replace Virchow's chair. His "scientific" narratives became prominent in museums, literature, and schools. Describing age-old migration patterns of "Germanic tribes," identifying traces of German influence across a broad geographic area in Europe, and finding evidence of the tribes' existence in the early Bronze Age (around 1400 BCE), his science legitimated celebrations of the triumph of the German spirit across two millennia and over much of central Europe (Maner 2001: 217–23).

Among physical anthropologists, Virchow's death was followed by a turn toward Darwinism and a radical shift toward "a biological and selectionist materialism more concerned with the inequalities of evolution than the universal brotherhood or spiritual unity of humankind" (Massin 1996: 100). Whereas Virchow was a liberal pacifist, his successor, Felix von Luschan, was a liberal imperialist. Luschan castigated colonial abuses, but he also argued that anthropology had its place in the colonial regime, and admired British imperial management for its success in modernizing colonies and improving the lives of subject peoples without excessive repression (J. D. Smith 2002). He embraced some elements of eugenics, believing that anthropologists should use their science to combat the growth of mental illness and declining birth rates, and was concerned about racial mixing; but retained a liberal position on race. He rejected anti-Semitism and the idea of Aryan or Nordic races, arguing until his death that there was no such thing as race, and no link between biology and culture. Luschan was a transitional figure. In the years following World War I, men from the next generation, such as Eugen Fischer and Otto Reche, pushed German anthropology toward an explicit focus on race (Proctor 1988: 142–5).

All three fields turned away from Virchow's notions of liberalism and empiricism in response to epistemological and professional crises. In particular, younger practitioners in all three fields faced intense competition for a handful of permanent positions; their occupational insecurity was conducive to new outlooks and to efforts to appeal to new patrons. The new directors of Germany's leading museums felt pressure from municipal and regional governments to transform their institutions into places more suitable for general education, to represent narratives such as those Foy articulated in his diffusionist museum. Younger ethnologists, such as Graebner and Foy, holding university degrees and trained in museums, assailed Bastian and Virchow's methods and goals. Young physical anthropologists repudiated craniometry, recognizing that three decades' measurements of skulls had not yielded a single scientific breakthrough, and sought to demonstrate that their field could be useful for the state. Three developments contributed to anthropologists' reorientation: the rise of eugenics; a new interest in biological evolution, encouraged by paleoanthropological finds of early human ancestors and compatible with Darwinism; and, perhaps most important, the rediscovery in 1900 of Gregor Mendel's principles of biological inheritance, which he had posited in the 1860s, and which reshaped discussions of human heredity in the twentieth century.

Interwar and Nazi Anthropology

World War I altered the physical space in which German ethnologists and anthropologists operated. It transformed the institutional landscape in central Europe, and it enhanced tendencies toward a more nationalist archaeology, a physical anthropology that mixed the categories of nation, culture, and race, and an ethnology devoted to tracing the movement of cultural circles, until one culture eventually dominated another.

The war made expeditions to study non-Europeans (their bodies as well as their cultures) practically impossible, encouraging a new focus on Europeans. And German and Austrian anthropologists gained a new field site – prisoner of war camps – which were initially attractive because they offered safe and easy access to non-Europeans from British and French colonies. Once in the camps, however, anthropologists began working (often exclusively) with Europeans (Evans 2002). Their research ultimately destabilized the "European" as a meaningful category. Physiological studies of Russians, Britons, Belgians, Serbs, Indians, and Algerians reduced the distinctions between European and non-European prisoners. Moreover, in the camps, German and Austrian scientists exercised power over their European subjects greater than that European anthropologists had enjoyed in many colonial situations. Their wartime experiences were decisive for anthropologists such as Otto Reche and Egon von Eickstedt. Their work elaborated racialized analyses of Europeans initiated in the camps, and gained considerable support in interwar and Nazi Germany. Both became full professors during the Nazi era. Reche even worked closely with the SS Race and Settlement Office, helping to formulate a Nazi settlement policy for eastern Europe.

Germany's loss of the war led to dissolution of German ethnologists' global networks of collection and exchange. And the museums suffered greatly after the war (not least because a number of their supporters and scientists had been killed). Museum funding was radically cut, and that which was given was often tied to demands from local governments (now dominated by socialists) that the museums focus less on "elite science." In general, employment opportunities declined, so that many young ethnologists and anthropologists – especially those without secure institutional positions – became eager to show that their science had practical value for the state.

The biggest success story was Eugen Fischer. From his place in an anatomical institute in Freiburg, Fischer moved in 1924 to the University of Berlin, where he replaced Felix von Luschan. In 1926, he also became the director of the Kaiser Wilhelm Institute for Anthropology, Human Genetics, and Eugenics – the only section in the Kaiser Wilhelm Institute not devoted to the physical sciences. From this position he became the most powerful figure in German anthropology, establishing the kind of anthropological institute that Luschan had always wanted, but with fundamentally different goals. It placed anthropology at the service of the state, and its inquiries were intended to show that human genetics explained both physical and cultural qualities (Proctor 1988: 155).

In 1925, the German Society for Physical Anthropology was founded, signaling the death of nineteenth-century morphological anthropology, as it had been practiced in the Society for Anthropology since its creation in 1863. Anthropologists' principles now served the cause of "racial hygiene" – a set of medicalized strategies to solve Germany's social and physical problems that included controlling and limiting racial mixing. And within six months of the Nazi seizure of power, Fischer was elected rector of Berlin University; his "appointment as professor at Berlin and director of Germany's most prestigious anthropological institute guaranteed that, for the next two decades, genetics, eugenics, and the study of racial differences would constitute the primary focus of anthropological research" (Proctor 1988: 155). In 1937, the German Society for Physical Anthropology changed its name to the German Society for Racial Research, making its mission explicit. Unsurprisingly, anthropology was one of the few academic fields in Germany that grew during the Nazi period.

Ethnologists had less to offer the Nazis than either physical anthropologists or archaeologists, because of their concentration on "primitive" non-Europeans. Nevertheless, some, such as Wilhelm Mühlmann, made successful careers by linking their science with state interests, adapting to the shifting social and political climate in Germany after 1920. Born in 1904, Mühlmann initially studied physical anthropology and race science, but he moved into ethnology, receiving his doctorate under Fischer and Richard Thurnwald in Berlin in 1931. Although he became known for a sociologically-informed ethnology similar to Thurnwald's and contrary to diffusionism, he wrote a dissertation that incorporated biological standpoints. In the decade after he earned his doctorate, Mühlmann was obliged to take one short-term job after another, and he wrote a series of proposals suggesting how ethnology might be made more useful to the state, recommending courses of action that would centralize the German museums, remove older ethnologists, and provide him steady employment. There were many ethnologists who showed more interest in working with the Nazis, but he did participate in the denunciation of moderate ethnologists in 1937. Attempting to capitalize on the Nazi interest in eastern Europe, he placed much of his research there, working on migration and assimilation, emphasizing the structure of competition among peoples and the importance of inter-ethnic contacts for historical development. In many ways, politics drove his intellectual shifts, and he benefited from his efforts to tie ethnology to the state more than he suffered from them. In 1950 he became professor of anthropology and sociology in Mainz and, later, Heidelberg. He also wrote what was long the standard text on the history of German anthropology (Michel 1995: 141, 150–1; Fischer 1990: 39–43, 220–5; Mühlmann 1946).

While the trajectories of many individual careers after 1918 are clear, the general process of transforming German anthropology was a complicated one. It was marked by the successes of such individuals as Mühlmann, Reche, Eigenstedt, and Fischer, but the older, liberal anthropology was not simply swept away. It took several decades for the new political, social, and institutional contexts to reshape these fields. Felix von Luschan maintained a strong position against race science until his death in 1924; his last book, *Völker, Rassen, und Sprachen* (1922), ended with a list of ten declarative statements that argued, among other things, that there are no savages and no inferior races, and there is only one human species (Rusch 1986: 274). Rudolf Martin in Munich, who occupied Germany's oldest chair of anthropology, maintained a strong anti-racist stance until his death in 1925 (Proctor 1988: 145). A number of older ethnologists also maintained their earlier, pre-war stances. Georg Thilenius, Karl Weule, and Lucien Sherman retained control of their museums until Weule died in 1926, Thilenius retired in 1935, and Sherman was forced to leave his post by the Nazis in 1933. Carl Schuchhardt sustained a strong stance against Gustav Kossina's nationalist archaeology until he resigned his post at the Berlin museum in 1934. Wilhelm Schmidt in Vienna, a nationalist sympathetic to some aspects of Austrian Fascism, remained ardently anti-colonialist and anti-racist throughout the war (Marchand 2003). Frobenius was not a staunch resister of the Nazis, but he did not become their creature; he continued to critique the West until his death in 1938, never lost control of his institute, launched a new periodical that did not conform to Nazi ideals, and became director of Frankfurt's ethnographic museum in 1934. And their principles led a number of German and Austrian ethnologists to emigrate following the Nazi takeover (Riese 1995). The institutional and intellectual transformation of German anthropology was neither immediate nor absolute.

Conclusions

The memory of National Socialism has made the history of German anthropology difficult to reconstruct, and as we think about the history of the discipline we should ask ourselves why this is so. What have Americans and other Europeans gained by forgetting the contributions of German ethnologists and anthropologists to the production of knowledge? Why have historians constructed teleologies from Herder to Hitler and presented the crimes of National Socialism as a natural extension of a peculiarly German anthropology (e.g., Zimmerman 2001)? And why was it not until the end of the twentieth century that scholars in western Europe and the United States began to move beyond the standard question about science and the Nazis: How could such a great intellectual civilization become so corrupt? It is easy to say that we inevitably view the past through the lens of the present. But this does not mean that we cannot attempt to transcend our limitations, to examine the structures that have guided German anthropology's disciplinary history and to elucidate its social impact.

Further Reading

Penny, H. G. and M. Bunzl, eds. 2003. *Worldly Provincialism: German Anthropology in the Age of Empire*. Ann Arbor: University of Michigan Press.

5

The Metamorphosis of Ethnology in France, 1839–1930

Emmanuelle Sibeud

Introduction

In 1937, when Paul Rivet undertook to draft a definition of ethnology for the new *Encyclopédie française*, he lamented the fact that the term "ethnology" had supplanted the word "anthropology" in France. "It is regrettable that the meaning of the word 'anthropology' – which savants formerly applied to a complex of sciences – has become gradually restricted," he said,

> and these days is most often only understood as the study of the physical dimension of the human races. It is even more regrettable that this semantic variation has led certain individuals to the extreme position of wanting to limit the scope of anthropology to that study, which, we have shown, is only one part of its field. The original meaning of the word anthropology having so manifestly changed, it has become increasingly common to substitute the word ethnology for it. This trend started abroad, in Germany, with the creation of the *Zeitschrift für Ethnologie* in 1869 and, in the United States, with the Bureau of Ethnology in 1879. One can regret that usage has brought about these changes in terminology, or debate the etymological meaning of words, but nothing will change the fact that this meaning has become entrenched. (Rivet 1937)

During the nineteenth and twentieth centuries, such terminological fluctuations were recurrent in the development of the social sciences in France. The definitions of ethnology and anthropology were various, by turns being constituted as a set of hypotheses, as distinctive specialties of practices and practitioners searching for internal coherence, and by practitioners' institutional affiliations.

This chapter aims to retrace this history, with its successive episodes of alliances and disputes, over the course of a century, from the 1830s through the 1930s. The modern meaning of the terms anthropology and ethnology, as well as the word ethnography, became fixed between the end of the eighteenth century and the 1930s. In 1839, the Société ethnologique imbued ethnology with a race-based definition. Later, at the beginning of the 1860s, the Société d'anthropologie in Paris gave a broad meaning to the word anthropology, subsuming under it both ethnology and ethnography, and turning each into subspecialties. In the 1910s, however, this intellectual division of labor was problematized by ethnographers; wishing to make field research the basis of knowledge, they began agitating for institutional and epistemological change. During the following decade, the word ethnology was invested with new meaning and reintroduced, used to mark the distinctive change in the social sciences that was effected when they were at last granted official academic status with the creation of the Institut d'ethnologie of the Sorbonne in 1925.

These terminological shifts have fueled partisan readings of the history of social sciences in France. Some scholars have intentionally limited themselves to partial reconstructions, centered around a "founding-father" whom they fortuitously rediscovered. Others have declared that the history of ethnology was different from the history of other disciplines (Jamin 1988), or they have grafted it onto the history of Durkheimian sociology (Karady 1982, 1988). Since the 1990s, historians have begun to question these limited perspectives, choosing to reintegrate the *longue durée* in the study of the history of the social sciences by analyzing their progressive transformation into academic disciplines and by focusing on such broad topics as field research or the complex interaction between social sciences and political power (Blanckaert 1988a, 1995a, 1996a, 2001).

Indeed, it is only through an examination of theories, practices, institutions and learned networks over the long run that one can understand the metamorphosis of ethnology: it failed as a science of race in the mid-nineteenth century, but reorganized itself at the beginning of the 1920s as a science of civilizations. Its metamorphosis was the result of nearly a century of shifts in contents, research methods, and measuring instruments, but its decisive transformation began in the 1910s. Since the long-awaited unification of the field of social sciences coincided with the peak of the French state's colonial project, one must also closely examine the links that formed between the new ethnology and the practices and discourses of domination.

This chapter focuses on two periods in the long institutional history of the discipline. The first is the time of learned societies, which began in 1839 with the foundation of the Société ethnologique, and lasted until 1905. This was a time of fierce schisms and divisions. During the second period, from 1905 to the end of the 1920s, meanwhile, circumstances reversed themselves: institutional structures were revived and ethnology acquired a home in the universities. How are we to account for these changes? To what was the revival due, and what was its nature? I argue that the role of the ethnographic research conducted by colonial administrators in French Africa was consequential. Given this, we must then ask: How significant was the role played by colonial factors in determining the metamorphosis and major changes in French ethnology?

The Time of Learned Societies, 1839–1905

The term "anthropology" has existed in French for centuries, but its original meaning was theological in nature. It was in the 1780s that it acquired its modern definition as the natural history of humankind. The new word ethnology also appeared in the 1780s in French as well as in most European languages, and was introduced in French dictionaries in the 1830s. By 1839, it had acquired the explicit definition of the "science of races," conferred by the Société ethnologique created in that year. This definition persisted until the end of the nineteenth century, when the term disappeared, only to re-emerge in the 1920s with the cultural revolution that transformed ethnology into the science of civilizations. The term ethnography, meanwhile, had appeared in the 1820s, when it rapidly became part of everyday language, denoting the description of peoples and their customs.

William Frederic Edwards's creation of the Société ethnologique in 1839 marked an important step in the evolution of the social sciences. It was not the first learned society for social scientists. At least two had already been created: the short-lived Société anthropologique founded in 1832 by the phrenologist Spurzheim, and the Société des observateurs de l'homme, which was active between 1799 and 1804 (Chappey 2002). However, the Société ethnologique was the first in a continuous line of learned societies that would provide the structures indispensable to the expansion of research in anthropology, in ethnology and in ethnography.

The Société ethnologique chose to study human races, which it assumed were distinct and stable, relying on hypotheses formulated by Edwards as early as 1829. It attempted methodical examination of the intellectual, moral, linguistic and historical characteristics of the world's races. Thus, the Société created a systematic and coherent research program, focusing both on human societies and on persons as biological individuals. After the death of its creator in 1842, it grew weaker, its activities diminishing further after the revolution of 1848, until it finally dissolved in 1862 (Blanckaert 1988b). Nevertheless, its research program of "the scientific study of human races" was taken up and continued after 1859 by the Société d'anthropologie of Paris, created by Paul Broca. The change that had been made in terminology from ethnology to anthropology can be traced to a theoretical shift and to a tactical choice, both of which would insure the success and durability of the new society to the present day. (The change also stabilized the meaning of the terms "anthropologists" and "ethnologists" as they were used in France until the 1930s.) The discovery at this time of pre-historic races seemed to show that racial differences were long-standing, supporting the polygenists' theory that races had distinct origins and destinies. The ethnologists had made it their political and moral project to understand the specificity of each race in order to offer an enlightened management of racial relations, especially within one nation. Now, however, the anthropologists of the Société anthropologique adopted a new program, one which they claimed to be exclusively scientific: the physical description of races and the elucidation of racial hierarchy, based on anthropometric measures. But this retreat into laboratory work reinforced the anthropologists' self-image as qualified savants ready to serve the post-1870 republic in its search for a secular vision of man and society.

Beginning in 1859, the Société d'anthropologie did not restrict itself to anthropometry. Nevertheless, by making biology the basis of his endeavor, Broca introduced a hierarchy among the different specialized fields that made up "anthropology defined broadly"

(Blanckaert 1989). In contrast to the systematic measurements conducted in laboratories by anthropologists, most of whom were trained physicians, ethnographic field studies appeared to be frivolous pursuits, conducted by travelers with no qualifications. Therefore, the transition from ethnology to anthropology in France reflected an increasing gap between the anthropometric study of humans and descriptive works on human societies, near or exotic. Also in 1859, the Société d'ethnographie de Paris was formed; its rationale was vehement denunciation of anthropology's biological reductionism (Stocking 1984).

Of all the practitioners of social sciences during the second half of the nineteenth century, the members of the Société d'ethnographie are probably the most difficult to define because their conception of ethnography was steeped in spiritualist philosophy and literary erudition, and was, as such, quite different from what we now call ethnography. Opposed to the anthropologists' positivism, which had come to include a strong degree of materialism, ethnographers defined their subject as the "philosophy of human history" (Blanckaert 1996b). Aligned with linguists, Americanists and orientalists, they undertook research in linguistics or on great ancient civilizations, but ceded research on those peoples considered to be "savage" to the anthropologists.

The bitter rivalry between anthropology and ethnography colored the entire development of social sciences in France in the last third of the nineteenth century. In 1864 and 1880, respectively, the anthropological and ethnographic societies gained state recognition, and each boasted several hundred members. But during this time, the societies' positions changed relative to one another. While in the 1860s the Société d'ethnographie had a broader social and academic base than the Société d'anthropologie, the latter society was gaining in strength, not least because many of its members belonged to the medical profession, which was then enjoying a distinct elevation in prestige. By the 1870s, the balance of power between the societies had shifted. In 1868, the Société d'anthropologie could boast a laboratory located near the École pratique des hautes études; and in 1876, it was able to create the École d'anthropologie thanks to the patronage of the city of Paris. Although the École d'anthropologie did not issue diplomas, it was a powerful agent for the diffusion of anthropological knowledge and practices (Harvey 1984; Williams 1985). Moreover, its science was compatible with the development of a secular morality, and it was thus given the task of organizing a large exhibition for the 1889 Paris Exposition to show the natural history of humankind, and the different races. By contrast, the Société d'ethnographie shrunk and disappeared around 1903 (although it would be nominally resurrected in 1913 and claim to continue the mission of its precursor/predecessor [Chailleu 1990]).

The creation of the Musée d'ethnographie du Trocadéro in 1878 signaled the first breakdown in the dual division of the branches of the social sciences. The Musée was created at the beginning of France's colonial expansion with the stated goal of gathering material on the "poor inferior humanity" doomed to annihilation through conquest. As Ernest-Théodore Hamy lamented, "White races, during their expansion throughout the world, have watched native races disappear before their eyes almost everywhere in the newly occupied countries, with only a few savants bothering to set down on paper the traits of these poor inferior men before they were wiped out" (1882: 11). The Musée was thus undertaking a pragmatic and descriptive ethnography, which was not officially practiced/sanctioned in France. The Ministry of Education bypassed this problem by tying the directorship of the new museum to the anthropology chair of its mother institution, the Museum of Natural History, This meant that the directorship fell to an anthropologist, Hamy, who was also an Americanist and an experienced museographer (Dias 1991). In addition, the new museum was forbidden by the Ministry of Education from engaging in any teaching, which might exacerbate the quarrel between anthropologists and ethnographers. Hamy was thus made the unhappy captain of a ship with no crew. This shortsighted choice led to a second impasse. The Musée d'ethnographie du Trocadéro did not have the means to train its own researchers or to supervise amateurs doing ethnographic research. In consequence, there was no formal structure for developing the descriptive techniques whose practice was rapidly expanding at that moment: within France, public school teachers were being encouraged to gather the "popular traditions" of their regions (Chanet 1988), and in French Africa, colonial agents were collecting information about subject peoples (Zerilli 1998). Therefore, by the first years of the twentieth century, there were few connections among three obviously related enterprises: a philosophical ethnography that had come to a dead end; an anthropology in a state of crisis due to the problematization of the notion of race; and developing folklorist and ethnographic practices that lacked institutional or academic homes in which they might be made more systematic.

Around 1905, the signs of a crisis in the relations among these overlapping enterprises multiplied. To stem its declining membership, the Société d'anthropologie sought to reform its research program (Wartelle 2004). In particular, it co-opted Marcel Mauss and Arnold van Gennep, specialists in the new field of the history of the religion of non-civilized peoples. However, these figures advocated a complete overhaul of the institutional structures of the social sciences, hoping to put a more academic face on them, and they undertook to act as intellectual gatekeepers. Since 1895, Mauss had been reviewing the international anthropological literature in *L'Année sociologique*, and in 1913 he wrote a long article for the *Revue de Paris* (edited by Lavisse) to inveigh against the inertia of the authorities, whom he held responsible for the sad shape of ethnography in France (Mauss 1913). Van Gennep also had a forum for publication, the "ethnography-folklore" section of the prestigious literary review *Mercure de France*; beginning in 1905, he had used this journal as a vehicle for stimulating a debate that would lead to the institutional and therefore epistemological reorganization of social sciences in the 1910s. His opening piece in 1905 provided a harsh assessment: "Ethnography is discredited today in the very country where it was born in the eighteenth century. It is true that we have a few official ethnographers, but they oppose the adoption of any new methods. We also have a Société d'ethnographie. It is not even worth mentioning. Its journal invites the craziest theories. And since in France few people read other languages, it is easy to hide from the general public the fact that while ethnography has not made much progress in this country, it certainly has elsewhere" (van Gennep 1905: 609).

The Ethnographic Revolution, 1905–1925

The years between 1908 and 1914 proved to be particularly favorable for the social sciences in France. After having been stuck in the same mold for several decades, the social sciences saw, in turn, the creation of a new journal, the *Revue des études ethnographiques et sociologiques* in 1908, and the foundation of four associations or specialized institutes – the Institut ethnographique international de Paris in 1910, the Institut français d'anthropologie in 1911, the resurrection of the Société d'ethnographie in 1913, and the Société des amis du musée d'ethnographie du Trocadéro in 1914.

The *Revue des études ethnographiques et sociologiques* was created by van Gennep, and appealed to self-taught researchers. Van Gennep was in league with Maurice Delafosse, a colonial administrator-cum-scholar, whom he probably met around 1900 when both attended the conferences in the history of the religions of non-civilized peoples taught by Leon Marillier at the Ecole pratique des hautes études (EPHE). Van Gennep had recently begun a thesis on the taboos of Madagascar under Marillier's direction at the EPHE. Delafosse had taken advantage of being on leave from Africa in metropolitan France during the Paris Exposition to supplement the ethnological training he had acquired with Hamy, having been one of Hamy's few unofficial students at the Musée d'ethnographie du Trocadéro (Sibeud 1998). With Delafosse, van Gennep created the Institut ethnographique international de Paris in 1910. In 1914, the new institute boasted almost as many members (225) as the Société d'anthropologie (229). The new institute provided field researchers with a scientific community, and validated their individual works through its internal debates. This first community of ethnographers challenged the old idea that the less a researcher was aware of theoretical debates, the more credible a reporter he was. Furthermore, it made field research the basis of knowledge for the first time, and placed fieldwork at the center of discussions. In the Institut ethnographique, ethnographers gained a forum in which they were epistemologically emancipated, and prominent among them were the administrators/ethnographers from French Africa, persons who gathered around Delafosse. Van Gennep wanted to push for even more radical change, to renounce the approach and findings of physical anthropology in order to establish an ethnography defined as a science of civilizations that rested exclusively on field research. To further his project, he organized a conference on reform in June 1914 at the University of Neuchâtel, where he had obtained a chair in ethnography in 1912 (he only held it for three years, however). At this meeting – the "first international conference on ethnology and ethnography" – the term ethnology was reintroduced, used to describe an enterprise allied with ethnography (van Gennep 1914a).

The re-emergence of the term ethnology provides the key to understanding this episode of dissent among social scientists, brief though it was. The thirty or so ethnographers/administrators from the Institut ethnographique created a small army of researchers, and a force that led to epistemological change in the social sciences. The masses of material they collected in the colonies made their ethnographic practices highly visible. In addition, the ethnographers/administrators were a cohesive group,

Figure 6   Membership card from the Institut ethnographique.

formed by their common professional identity and viewpoint, their solidarity un-affected by ambitions to make careers in academe. (Delafosse was the only exception to the general rule, going from a colonial to an academic career; prior to his death in 1926, he taught at the Ecole des langues orientales vivantes, where his father-in-law, Octave Houdas, taught Arabic; at the Ecole coloniale; and, briefly, at the Institut d'ethnologie.) The colonial ethnographers made common cause with van Gennep in order to make their voices heard. But they also joined more conventional academic networks. In particular, they attended the meetings of the Institut français d'anthro-pologie, which in 1911 gathered the fifty most distinguished experts in the social sciences, including Émile Durkheim, Marcel Mauss, Paul Rivet, Delafosse, and Lucien Lévy-Bruhl. In 1914, they aligned themselves with the general movement that defined a new "ethnological" professional identity, and which led to the creation of the Société des amis du musée d'ethnographie du Trocadéro, whose aim was to rescue the museum from its scientific and financial malaise. They remained distant, however, from the new Société d'ethnographie, which had been resurrected in 1913 by the ministry of colonies in order to monitor all the institutional changes taking place in the social sciences (Sibeud 2002a: 178–83).

Therefore, the revival of the term ethnology marked a period of transition in the social sciences, instigated by an alliance between van Gennep and a network that was peripheral to the life of French learned societies, comprised of the ethnographers/

administrators who were serving in French colonial Africa. Paradoxically, van Gennep was himself an academic outsider, notwithstanding his sound academic pedigree. Mauss, having succeeded Marillier in 1901, became the supervisor of his thesis *Tabou et totémisme à Madagascar* (which was immediately published by the EPHE), defended in 1904. But though van Gennep was the first graduate in religious ethnography in France, he was unable to find a job – since the only available academic position on the history of non-civilized people's religions was already occupied by Mauss. Nevertheless, he and the colonial ethnographers had, through their "ethnographic dissent," contributed to the transformation of the social sciences and created a unified movement for disciplinary restructuring. Of course, there were social scientists who opposed their cause. Until 1914, the Durkheimian network continued to regard colonial administrators with disdain, seeing them as makeshift ethnographers.

Over time, however, Durkheim had come to pay increasing attention to ethnographic data, and Mauss, his nephew as well as frequent collaborator, considered himself to be the leading expert on ethnography (that is to say, on the ethnographic literature) and, indeed, held what was the only available academic position in the subject in 1901, as a lecturer at the EPHE. During the Dreyfus affair, the anthropologists of the Société d'anthropologie had aligned themselves with the Durkheimians, who rejected scientific racism (Mucchielli 1997). Thus, Mauss and Durkheim, who had until that point steadfastly avoided the learned societies comprised of "amateurs," could in the 1910s claim the important legacy of the Société d'anthropologie; at the same time, they held great influence at the Institut français d'anthropologie. Meanwhile, at the EPHE, Mauss was working to create a new group of specialists, persons with impeccable training who could, when the time was right, found the field of "sociological ethnology."

The Durkheimians' plans were foiled, however, by the dissent coming from "outsider" ethnographers. The situation called for institutional reorganization. But Durkheimian sociology did not yet have the sufficient strength to steer, let alone control, events: it had yet to capture institutional positions or field a cadre of trained disciples. In 1913, Mauss reacted by publishing a long article on "ethnography in France and abroad," in which he portrayed himself as the only established academic capable of leading the necessary reorganization of ethnography. At the same time, he sent a proposal to the Ministry of Education calling for the creation of a bureau of ethnology; in it, he made short shrift of ethnography, ceding the domain to the ethnographers/administrators – having, in effect, little choice – and emphasized ethnology, arguing that it could only be entrusted to "graduates of universities and grandes ecoles" (Sibeud 2004a). If Mauss was reluctant to involve himself in training amateur ethnographers, it was because he feared that by so doing he would consign ethnology to the fringe of academe, and thereby jeopardize his students' professional futures.

In 1914, such fears were justified. The Musée d'ethnographie was barely functioning. Its funds had not been increased for years, and Hamy had voluntarily resigned in 1906. The ongoing quarrel between anthropologists and ethnographers had enabled the Ministry of Education to avoid creating any new teaching positions in anthropology or ethnography for over half a century. One must wonder why Mauss had waited so long to act to remedy the disorganized state of French ethnography.

For example, Durkheim and Mauss applauded when the Belgian Sociological Society edited instructions to be given to every colonial officer in the Congo in 1909. But they were not the only sociologists in France looking for a commitment in colonial management. Organicist sociology and sociologists prevailed in the sociological and ethnographic section of the French Colonial congress (held every two years). Durkheim had long ago chosen an exclusively academic strategy, which implied disregard for any association with "amateurs" and learned societies (Karady 1982). He was eager to discuss available ethnographic data in the *Année sociologique*, and so was Mauss. But as important as the theoretical contributions of the Durkheimian paradigm were, the most crucial problem faced by the social sciences at the beginning of the twentieth century was not how to interpret data, but how to produce and characterize data.

Mauss recognized that fieldwork presented an epistemological enigma. He considered the best researchers to be those who shared in the life of the people they studied and themselves analyzed the material they collected. Yet he never repudiated a positivist vision of survey research, sustaining the hope that he could design a perfect questionnaire, so cleverly devised that it would enable all users to be competent sociologists, regardless of their abilities or training. He never attempted to construct such a questionnaire, however. Mauss was not the only social scientist unable to resolve the quandary of fieldwork. Van Gennep, who (justifiably) claimed to be a practitioner as much as a theoretician, undertook an analysis of the epistemological operation of field research based on the researcher's experience of participant observation, which he tested in a colonial situation during a trip through Algeria in 1911–1912 (Sibeud 2004b). He maintained that ethnographers had to "go to the people" and share their daily activities in order to understand observations, and he made a sharp distinction between this "internal study" and the deficient analysis based on inherently distant practices, such as physical anthropology or the study of photographs (van Gennep 1914b, 8). Nevertheless, he also retained a romantic conception of the possibilities of ethnographic intuition, being as attached to certain outdated notions as Mauss was to his positivist ideas. That is, there was an internal inconsistency in his analysis insofar as it was premised on the assumption that the researcher could think outside his own cultural parameters.

Ultimately, no "revelation" from the field came to transform the practices of the ethnographers/administrators in the 1910s or to convince university graduates to give up library research. The sudden emergence of ethnographers/administrators in institutional and theoretical debates only established that something important happened during ethnographic field research. Yet it was the recognition of this enigma and its importance that finally brought together the fieldworkers and the armchair analysts. Furthermore, the movement of colonial ethnographers between their ethnographic institute and the Institute d'anthropologie resulted in the reorganization of the former in 1920, turning it into a forum for frank debate: the Société française d'ethnographie, managed by Delafosse, with the support of Mauss, Rivet and Lévy-Bruhl. This society was especially active between 1920 and 1926 (the year of Delafosse's death). It published the *Revue d'ethnographie et des traditions populaires* and attracted international interest, welcoming J. G. Frazer and Bronislaw Malinowski while they were in Paris in 1922, for example (Sibeud 2002a: 258–64). The reconciliation of fieldworkers and theorists gave ethnology the solid outlines it had been lacking, and in 1925 it was instituted as a discipline at the Sorbonne. In the meantime, however, other intellectual concerns were looming for the ethnologists, namely the contradictions inherent in an ethnology practiced in an imperial context.

Ethnology in a "Colonial Situation"

In1925, Lévy-Bruhl gave the impression that the ethnologists' situation was unproblematic. He wrote that the Institut d'ethnologie was a "flexible, practical, economical" institution that allowed ethnology to advance at the same time that it served colonial regimes (Lévy-Bruhl 1925: 233–4), thereby satisfying the public's vague feeling that science should serve the state. The institute could both train professional ethnologists and provide colonial agents with the curiosity and the tools necessary to gather information for the professionals. It was also given the responsibility of publishing *Travaux et mémoires* and organizing ethnographic field research projects according to the expressed need of colonial authorities. Indeed, though the Institut was located in the Sorbonne, it was in large part financed by grants coming from, in order of importance, the colonial regimes of Indochina, Madagascar, and French West Africa. Thus, in 1925, the status of ethnography was elevated by virtue of two developments: it was made an official academic discipline; and it was officially declared to be a science useful for the practical and symbolic management of the French colonial empire. It is no wonder that some have called ethnology "the daughter of colonialism," and the degree to which its intellectual content was a function of the colonial situation is nowadays of considerable scholarly interest (Conklin 2002b).

Considering the history of the discipline over the *longue durée* – as I have advocated here – reveals several new dimensions to the ties between the discipline's crystallization and its colonial uses. The idea that one needed knowledge about societies in order to control them was definitely not new, and the project of putting "science" at the service of political management was a consistent feature of republican ideology. However, we can see that there was in fact a gap between word and deed: while politicians made speeches to the scientific community extolling the virtues of enlightened patronage, and the savants answered with similar rhetoric, vaunting the social and political utility of their specialized knowledge, implementing such rhetorical claims was never easy. The 1925 declaration of the colonial usefulness of ethnology was not the first instance. As early as 1878, the founding of the Musée d'ethnographie du Trocadéro had been motivated in part by the conviction that the science of ethnology could serve colonization. But this conviction never generated the funding necessary to organize the teaching of ethnography or, failing that, training in ethnographic practices. Similarly, anthropologists' enthusiasm for mounting colonial "ethnographic" exhibitions or organizing the colonial sections in world's fairs did not inspire them to turn toward field research; instead, these activities allowed them to believe that they could conduct their research without going to the field. The utility of ethnography to colonialism was therefore a necessary, but insufficient condition for its institutionalization. Finally, one must dismiss the legend that ethnography's institutionalization was the product of a historical accident, the result of Lévy-Bruhl's friendship with some members of the left-wing administration elected in 1924 (a story that Lévy-Bruhl helped to spread).

To understand why ethnology became a discipline when it did and its relation to colonialism, one must ask what had changed by 1925 and determine the nature of the alliance that led to the creation of the Institut d'ethnologie. The partnership of Mauss, Rivet, and Lévy-Bruhl with the ethnographers/administrators precipitated two structural changes. First, the alliance fostered the creation of a formal methodology for field research, restructuring ethnology as a discipline that could be taught. Delafosse was put in charge of the ethnography class at the Institute, an extension of his teaching duties at the Ecole des langues orientales vivantes and at the Ecole coloniale (he was also highly influential in the Société française d'ethnographie); the first methodological essay on field research appeared in 1925, written by Alfred Metraux, who paid homage to Delafosse as much as to Mauss. Second, when the ethnographers/administrators started to seek validation of their works in the learned Parisian societies, they created a new kind of link between metropolitan France and the colonies as well as a new venue for the application of their work. As early as 1901, French authorities had established research institutes in their colonial territories, notably the Ecole française d'Extrême-Orient in Indochina and L'Académie malgache in Madagascar (affiliated with the Académie française). Determining scientific policy partly through recourse to local research institutions had become common practice in French West Africa in the 1910s. Similarly, the implementation of French colonial rule in Morocco in 1912 was accompanied by a systematic survey.

As governors-general sought experts to sanction their policies, ethnographers/administrators as well as armchair social scientists at home could aspire to the new role of advisors. For example, the ambitious governor-general of French West Africa, William Ponty, commissioned the Ecole d'anthropologie to do a survey of persons of mixed race and had the Société antiesclavagiste de France do a survey of African families in order to reinforce his "race policy" (Sibeud 2002a: 232–8). Moreover, the activities of ethnographers/administrators intersected with those of academics at this time; notably, Durkheim and Mauss involved themselves in policy issues in metropolitan France, and were eager to assume parallel roles in the colonial sphere – and to associate their discipline with research institutions in the colonies. In 1904, Durkheim went so far as to provide his services to the short-lived "Comité for the scientific inventory of French West Africa's riches." In general, the 1910s were good years for persons who belonged to the intellectual networks that had supported Dreyfus, thus bringing considerable political influence to Durkheim and Mauss (Prochasson and Rasmussen 1996).

Before 1914, however, both metropolitan ethnologists and colonial administrations remained uncertain about the acceptable level of cooperation. Mauss, for instance, had some reservations about the consequences of ethnographers' involvement in colonial activities, "As any other science, ethnography can only be practiced in a spirit of absolute impartiality," he said in 1913; "field research can have practical consequences that are often very important, administratively and economically speaking. Yet it should not be undertaken with only these results in mind" (Sibeud 2004a: 121). As a social scientist and as a socialist, he openly criticized current colonial policy as repressive and authoritarian. He wished ethnology to serve a reformist program supported by persons such as the reformist socialist Jean Jaurès and the powerful Ligue des droits de l'homme (Sibeud 2002a: 238–44). But he was also wary of ethnologists' potential subservience to colonial regimes. Like Durkheim, he tried to enter the quite closed colonial networks, and in 1906 accepted the job of drafting ethnographic instructions on behalf of the very colonialist Comité de l'Afrique française. But he did not complete them, and the Comité de l'Afrique française might have been relieved that he did not.

World War I and its aftermath changed ethnologists' relationship to colonial regimes, however. Defeated powers lost control of their subject territories. The League of Nations divided the German colonies and territories of the Ottoman Empire between Britain and France, designating the lands it brought under British and French rule as Mandate territories. On the one hand, this arrangement meant that the League sanctioned the perpetuation of colonial rule. On the other hand, however, the League declared that the rulers of Mandate territories had specific responsibilities and positive goals: to grant colonized populations a degree of self-rule; to promulgate reforms that improved subject peoples' economies and enhanced their welfare; to work toward making Mandate territories capable of independence (however long this might take). Moreover, the League of Nations had powers of oversight (however deficient it might be judged today in exercising them, both in general and in particular cases). At the same time, the third Communist International denounced the very principle of colonial domination, as did communist parties in metropolitan areas and in some colonies. In both France and Britain, the application of "scientific" rationality to the rule of subject territories now appeared to be a means to mitigate both the politicization and criticism of colonial policies (Dimier 2004a). Political authorities were thus in need of credible scientific research and the support of authoritative savants.

The savants, meanwhile, had come to see their collaboration in a new light. The engagement of intellectuals in the war effort had fostered an expansion of the possible relationships between scientific networks and political authorities. Mauss and Lévy-Bruhl, for instance, lent their support in 1915 to the new Comité des études historiques et scientifiques of French West Africa. In postwar France, however, their pre-war calls for colonial reform went unheeded, since the country was preoccupied with the necessity of postwar reconstruction. Finally, the war had produced many casualties among the younger members of the scientific community; Mauss's students were especially hard hit (Marcel 2001). Thus, the ethnographers/administrators were virtually the only persons available to do research at the very moment that field research had come to be defined as the central epistemological focus. Because the pre-war rivalries between ethnographers/administrators and academics had disappeared, the practical need to rely on colonial figures was less problematic to academics than it would once have been. Now certain that they had in the colonies a network of correspondents who defended the distinctive mission and merits of their discipline, Mauss, Rivet and Lévy-Bruhl were able to offer their services to colonial authorities in 1925 with clear consciences, as well as confidence in their institutional security.

The foregoing discussion reveals the complex and evolving nature of events sparked by a string of mutual compromises. It argues against the simplistic idea that the mere accumulation of information about subject peoples in colonial administrative files would have sufficed to solidify ethnology – or even to make it a colonial "invention." If amassing facts alone is sufficient cause, how is it that officially sanctioned questionnaires carried out by prefects under the First Empire failed to translate into tools of domination, as did the regional field studies by public school teachers? The vital question becomes, how is knowledge translated into power? It would be more accurate to speak of ethnology as an "imperial" creation in which both administrators/ethnographers and social scientists had their share. The former chose to channel their findings into forming a new discipline rather than forming pragmatic formulae for domination; the latter sought compromises between their scientific and political commitments. Similarly, one must wonder about the precise ways that political factors shaped the alliance struck in 1925 between academic ethnology and colonial domination.

The Institut d'ethnologie grew out of the "ethnographic rebellion" coming from the ethnographers/administrators. It improved intellectual training for the colonial administrators, but with the goal of providing them an erudite pastime rather than a professional practice (Dimier 2004b). And while Lévy-Bruhl dreamed aloud of the creation of government anthropologist positions equivalent to the few that existed in the British Empire, it was the Institut that was entrusted with the 1931–1934 Dakar –Djibouti expedition, a mission of collecting artifacts and ethnographic information in French-occupied Africa; although highly prestigious, it had nothing to do with the day-to-day activities of colonial management. The Institut functioned more as a moral guardian than as a breeding ground of potential experts – a position that suited the self-images of the committed intellectuals who were its creators.

The Institut d'ethnologie became the partner of the most prestigious intellectual institutions created in the colonies, such as the Ecole française d'Extrême-Orient or the Académie malgache. In French West Africa, it sanctioned an organization of research isomorphic with the colonial administrative hierarchy; the French West African Committee on historical and scientific studies was headed by the governor-general, and its members were divided into three sections – members resident in Dakar who ran the committee; corresponding members in French West Africa, who did its fundamental work; and corresponding members living outside the colonies, who were its scientific managers. By 1925, it included only a single African, interpreter Moussa Travélé, who was a corresponding member. Its works were implemented through colonial channels in a hierarchical fashion, and the entire colonial staff was obliged to assist in the extensive surveys set up by the committee. The Institut d'ethnologie validated this bureaucratization of research by adding its academic imprimatur to the committee's ethnological projects and by using the committee to circulate the

Institute's own questionnaires. It was not merely a question of transposing colonial rules into a new field. The colonial administration purposely used research networks to control its best-educated indigenous subjects. From 1913 on, it asked teachers to draft monographs while they were on vacation. In 1932, it created a prize specifically for research done by native-born scholars. And it gave a job for the study of local customs to a political opponent who was briefly restored to favor (Sibeud 2002b). By training professional ethnologists and giving them the qualifications to manage research networks in the colonies, the Institut d'ethnologie sanctioned a research policy with objectives that it could not always control.

Still, the Institut d'ethnologie was not a thoroughly compromised institution. It upheld a unitary conception of the study of all human societies, regardless of whether they were considered savage or civilized. In so doing, it resisted colonial authorities' desire for compartmentalizing knowledge. (Consider, for example, that the French West Africa's Committee on historical and scientific studies undertook to produce a "French West African science.") The Institut maintained its position even after 1930, when the creation of the Société des africanistes signaled an important change in the social sciences. There had been two independent paradigms, orientalism and Americanism; now, scholarly laborers were divided into multiple research groups, each focused on one "exotic" area defined by essentialist criteria, while those characteristics imputed to the European area (or Europeanized areas) of the world were raised to the status of an implicit model for all social sciences. Against this return to object-based definitions, the Institut d'ethnologie continued to defend methodological universalism. This stance was decisive. And it proved that ethnology was not intellectually restricted by the negotiations that granted ethnologists access to the areas in which they did their research. While it allowed Africanist ethnologists to remain blind to the colonial situation that defined their work, it also allowed for the criticisms from other figures such as Michel Leiris and George Balandier, which began in the 1950s.

The involvement of ethnologists in the machinery of colonial domination marked a decisive stage in the development of their discipline. When ethnology rose to the challenge of confronting contemporary reality, it gave up its grandiose and utopian project of a thoroughly comprehensive social science to become instead one discipline among others, involved in complex and sometimes ambivalent relations with public policymakers in metropolitan France and in its research fields. However, this change grew out of a judgment that was epistemological before becoming political. Because colonial fieldwork stressed that thorough inquiries required that considerable time be devoted to observation and, moreover, dramatized the gap between field researchers and the persons they observed, colonial ethnographic research drew attention to all of the factors that affect the research process. It sustained collective concerns that gave rise to an original methodology. In other words, ethnology became a discipline because it dared to do field research while accepting that its choices had political consequences. Thus, inherent in its methodological identity was what became a persistent feature of its character as a discipline – the chronic tendency to engage in critical self-evaluation and theoretical dispute.

Further Reading

Conklin, Alice L. 2002. The New "Ethnology" and "La Situation Coloniale" in Interwar France. *French Politics, Culture and Society*, 20(2):29–46.

Sherman, Daniel J. 2004. "Peoples Ethnographic": Objects, Museums, and the Colonial Inheritance of French Ethnology. *French Historical Studies* 27:669–703.

Part II

Early Obsessions

6

The Spiritual Dimension

Ivan Strenski

From Religion to the Problems of Religion

While people have tended to *be* religious or to *give expression* to religion for some time, it is only recently that religion itself has become an object of science or the focus of a set of critical problems about its nature and ultimate value. Believers and theologians, we have thus had always with us, *scientific studies* of religion we have not. In this, religion resembles politics, sociability, or the economy, since they too have only recently become subjects of "scientific" inquiry. Political *science*, sociology, economics and the "*science* of religion" ("*Religionswissenschaft*" or "*science religieuse*") are distinctly modern arrivals on the world stage. In the West, religion became such an object of a critical problematic only about 300 years ago. Then, people started systematically asking questions about the character of the first religion, whether religions change, and, if so, whether they did so according to law-like principles, such as evolution or degeneration, and so on (Strenski 2002). The rise of this kind of questioning marks the beginnings of a *naturalistic* or *anthropological* study of religion – an attitude to religion governed by natural reasons, causes, and laws, and free of moral, spiritual, scriptural, or other supernatural authority. The focus of this chapter will be to account for the emergence of such an *anthropological* approach to religion.

Bodin and Herbert

If a distinctive mark of an anthropological study of religion is its method of naturalistic inquiry, its beginnings extend to sixteenth-century Europe among thinkers broadly designated as *Deists* (Preus 1987; Byrne 1989). "Deists" hoped that rational inquiry about religion would uncover the true or original nature of religion – what can also generally be termed *natural religion*. In France, an early articulation of this attitude came with humanist Sorbonne jurist and diplomat, Jean Bodin (1530–96). Witness to the excesses of the French Wars of Religion (1562–1629), Bodin knew well how religion could incite violence. Determined to undercut religion's ability to do so, Bodin shifted the grounds of discourse about religion from the absolutes and supernatural beliefs to rational argument, such as he well knew from his everyday practice of law. Questions about the truth or value of religion needed to be settled by appealing to public evidence, such as in a court of law. On such naturalistic grounds, Bodin suggested that the oldest religion was most likely to be the true one. Whether Bodin was correct or not, his attitude ruled out appeals to extra-rational or private sources of "knowledge" – those that could not be adjudicated by rational consensus (Preus 1987: ch. 1).

A century later, the same naturalistic style of inquiry drew the interest of Edward, Lord Herbert of Cherbury (1583–1648). Although a Protestant, Herbert remained neutral through the religious strife of the English Civil War (Hill 1987: 16). His ambiguity about religious absolutes led Herbert's critics to dub him an "ambidexter" (Hill 1987: 15). Like Bodin in France, Herbert felt that claims to an exclusive, revealed religious truth fed these intractable religious conflicts (Preus 1987: 25). Herbert can thus be linked with the "skeptical" tradition in rejecting claims to absolute knowledge – especially about religion (Hill 1987: 20). To him, Christianity was just one religion among many, none of which was more credible than any other (Hill 1987: 32). In his *De Veritate* (1633), however, Herbert argued that we could reason to the existence of a "universal" religious common ground independent of any particular religion – in effect, a lowest common denominator of beliefs that could be found in all the world's religions (Preus 1987: 23). Herbert was, in effect, arguing for a so-called Natural Religion.

Locke, Hume, and the Deists

Like Herbert, philosopher John Locke (1632–1704) also promoted religious tolerance, notably in his three *Letters on Toleration* (1689–1692) (Locke 1937 [1689]). He also advocated a similar kind of rational religion, but explicitly identified with Christianity, in his *The Reasonableness of Christianity* (1695). Like Herbert and Bodin, Locke felt that reason – here his sturdy empiricism – was sufficient to address the major questions about the nature of religion. Supernatural revelation was not required to undertake such inquiries about religion.

The philosopher David Hume (1711–76), however, was considerably less hospitable to Herbert's idea of a Natural Religion. Religions were wildly diverse, and did not reflect Herbert's supposed natural religious substratum (Hume 1963: 31; Preus 1987: 38–9). Indeed, Hume argued from available empirical evidence that polytheism was probably the primordial religion. Pre-modern folk were "ignorant . . . idolators," not the devotees to Natural Religion that Herbert imagined (Hume 1963: 33–4). Two works, *A Dialogue concerning Natural Religion* (1779) and *The Natural History of Religion* (1757), exemplify Hume's ideas on the universality and uniformity of natural religion (Preus 1987: 92–5). Despite their differences, then, Bodin, Herbert, Locke, and Hume thus began conceiving the study of religion in anthropological or naturalistic terms. Each believed that people could discover the truth about religion – innate or not – by means of the powers of human deductive or inductive reason.

A generation later, the Deists proper – Charles Blount (1654–93), Matthew Tindal (1657–1733), John Toland (1670–1733), and William Wollaston (1660–1724) – argued for even broader application of naturalistic attitudes to religion. They were generally appalled by the Christian claims that revelation had been restricted to a particular period in history. Such apparently arbitrary limitations conflicted with the ideal of divine justice and goodness (Byrne 1989: 53–5). Instead, God must have instead provided a universal natural religion open to all. And, if open to all, such a religion should be rationally understandable to all (Byrne 1989: 52, 53). Blount, for example, held human reason in such high esteem that he saw it as the only judge of truth – something that appeals to super-rational revelation could not gainsay. Christianity thus belongs within the "larger context of the history of religion," bounded all the while by the limits of ordinary human understanding (Byrne 1989: 80).

Critical Historical Study of the Bible and Other Holy Books

Although in current usage the anthropology of religion involves a direct empirical study of living cultures, at one time it had not yet separated itself from the historical-critical study of *texts*. Yet the rise of the historical and critical study of the Bible – the so-called Higher Criticism of the Bible – evidently facilitated the emergence of anthropology of religion (Byrne 1989: 94). The Higher Criticism of the Bible broke new ground in the study of religion by submitting the Bible to the same kind of rational and naturalistic scrutiny as any piece of literature. Given the centrality of the Bible for Western religious consciousness, one can imagine how important was the impact of the Higher Criticism. Consider only the impact of Higher Criticism of the Bible for critical understanding of fundamental religious notions like "myth." The idea of "myth" itself arose in part because biblical critics queried the status of such biblical events as the flood in Genesis, asking whether it were mere "myth" or real "history." What lay behind or beneath the pious readings of the central document of Christianity? The upshot of this and other sorts of critical inquiry was to reinforce the critical approaches to religion already initiated by Bodin, Herbert, Hume, and the others. If the very word of God could be put under the microscope, then any kind of religious data was in principle a candidate for the same kind of naturalistic questioning. Taking his cues directly from the biblical critics, Friedrich Max Müller (1823–1900), the Oxford philologist, applied the same critical methods to the religious scriptures of India, and by example to religions of all sorts.

Tylor and Müller: From Irenics to Polemics

In at least two ways, the advent of the Higher Criticism practiced by both Müller and the biblical critics had immediate impact on the rise of "anthropology of religion" as the subfield is currently understood. First, the "anthropology" of Edward Burnett Tylor (1832–1917), often cited as the first "anthropologist" proper, was in many ways deliberately worked out to counter Müller's text-critical approach to religion. As Tylor's most rigorously engaged Oxford colleague, Müller forced Tylor to set "anthropology" on a distinctively naturalistic course that dwelt on observed customs and practices, rather than texts. Second, the historical critical methods practiced by both Müller and the Higher Critics of the Bible fed the development of the anthropology of religion associated with William Robertson Smith and Émile Durkheim that Robert Ackerman has discussed in his chapter on "Anthropology and the Classics." To complete this picture of a decisive fork in the road in the naturalistic study of religion, we might usefully review the exchanges between Tylor and Müller.

Born in 1832 into a prosperous middle-class London Quaker merchant family, Tylor followed an eccentric academic career path. He never earned a university degree, but instead systematically studied the work of the great scientists of the day, such as the British geologist Charles Lyell, the German explorer Alexander von Humboldt, and folklorists Wilhelm and Jakob Grimm. Decisive in the formation of Tylor's anthropological career was a journey to Mexico. This issued in Tylor's first book, *Anahuac* (1861), which was followed rapidly by works solidifying his scientific reputation. *Researches into the Early History of Mankind* (1865) dealt with the evolution of culture. *Primitive Culture* (1871) articulated the details of Tylor's "science of culture." Especially as applied to religion and mythology, *Primitive Culture* provided a full discussion of Tylor's theory of "animism," the idea that religion can be explained by the belief that souls inhabit all things and explain their behavior.

The public exchanges between Müller and Tylor seemed always cordial, and frequently laced with compliments. In the mid- to late-nineteenth century, the prestige of Müller's historical philology was quite high, while Tylor's "anthropology" was not particularly so. As anthropologist R. R. Marett (1936: 44) observed: "The concept of a veritable science of language, founded on the use of the Comparative Method became firmly established in men's minds." Early in his career, Tylor therefore curried favor with Müller by praising his scientific work concerning the origins of language and Müller's theory of mythology as "put forth with such skill and marked success" (Tylor 1866: 81; Stocking 1987: 163). For his part, Müller also at first recognized Tylor as an intellectual ally, noting with pleasure that his own comparative philology – "the sciences of language" had given Tylor's anthropology its "first impulse" and trademark interest in the "primitives." Accordingly, Müller specifically applauded Tylor's work in the "early history of the human race" as exemplary of the "good earnest men who care for facts" (Müller 1886: 253).

Yet, despite their common commitment to scientific studies of religion, Müller came gradually to realize that "Mr. Tylor's science" (Müller's words [Stocking 1987: 195]) entailed a total rejection of his "Science of Religion." While Müller never ceased insisting that his "Science of Religion has to deal with facts, not with theories," such assurances failed to blunt Tylor's criticism (Müller 1891: 366). In a veiled attempt to discredit the scientific aspirations of Müller's approach, Tylor contrasts his "animist" to Müller's natural religion hypothesis, by saying that "it has not been necessary for me to assume imaginary or hypothetical states of human culture" (Tylor 1866: 85).

Müller was not without answers to Tylor, even though the future of "anthropology" would belong to Tylor and not to the likes of Müller. Against the rising tide of the prestige of Darwin, Müller ridiculed Tylor's evolutionism, but without much effect. How could Tylor justify regarding children as the logical equivalents of "savages" (Müller 1892: 212)? Was not the assumption of an evolutionary process underlying this equivalence as much a matter of guesswork as Müller's own assumption of primal natural religion as contemplative worship of the infinite? Müller also remained a skeptic about the value of the testimony of native informants. Why are the "savages" assumed to be privileged informants about the dawn of humankind? Would we trust Christians of today to tell us about first-century Palestine (Müller 1892: 217)? Since it was not then obvious that the natives know best, was Tylor's reliance on native information shaky at best? What causal models, hidden determinants or "structures" lay beneath "what the native said" (Müller 1892: 216)? Finally, Müller claimed that his ideal of a single high God, an "Unknown" and "Infinite" being, was also empirical, since it was to be found today in the ethnographic field – even alongside the kind of animistic beliefs cited so often by Tylor (Müller 1892: 218).

At the basis of their differences Müller and Tylor simply disagreed about the course of history. For Tylor, progressive development was obvious; for Müller, degenerative decline seemed everywhere in evidence. This divergence may in turn be linked to the different relation to personal religiosity enjoyed by the two men. Reared outside the established Church of England, Tylor bore non-conformist class resentments against the Anglican establishment, which translated into a complex diffidence about religion. While some of Tylor's fellow scientific naturalists, such as T. H. Huxley, sought a negotiated truce between religion and science, Tylor tended toward a harder line against religion, especially in those "theological" forms that pretended to compete with science as an explanation of the world (Lightman 2001: 345, 348). "Theologians all to expose..." was Tylor's own description of his approach to religion (Stocking 1987: 190–1). For Tylor, religion was now essentially what it had always been – animism – a belief in spirits. As such, no matter how "scientific" modern theologians might think religion to be, it was at bottom still only a form of this "primitive" belief in spirits. The future, in Tylor's view, belonged to science and technology, and a liberation of the human mind from superstitious beliefs in the existence of spirits.

Müller, on the other hand, embodied a sweet Protestant liberalism, and was even given to mystical, yet somewhat gloomy, religious nostalgias characteristic of the German Romanticism of his youthful nurture. Religion had declined from a primal state of Eden-like simplicity and purity into the contentious sectarianism and dry dogmatism of his own day. Behind his scientific pursuits was Müller's desire to recapture this primal religiosity – really a kind of Natural Religion – by tracking it into the oldest religious texts available. In Müller's day, these were assumed to be the Vedas of the Indian religious tradition. By introducing the Vedas to modern readers, Müller felt he could reveal sufficient traces of a primal natural religion that might revive the religious spirits of his age. To Müller, the Vedas did more than celebrate the vast infinite natural expanse of the high heavens or the transcendent life-giving power and energy of the sun; they pointed beyond themselves to their abstract spiritual contents – infinity, eternity, transcendence – the very stuff of his primal natural religion that he felt might attract his religious contemporaries. Behind the mythical representations of old religious texts such as the Vedas, Müller found telling traces of the pure and universal abstractions of primal natural religion to which Müller's scholarship wished to lead his readers.

Against Müller, in effect a latter-day Deist, Tylor took great pleasure in the historical precedent set for his theories by his empiricist forebear, David Hume – distinguished, we will recall, for his slashing criticism of eighteenth-century theories of Natural Religion, such as Herbert of Cherbury's. Proudly, Tylor tells us that Hume's "*Natural History of Religion* is perhaps more than any other work the source of modern opinions as to the development of religion." Tylor reminds us that in *Natural History* Hume argued that polytheism was the most primitive religion and that it recalled something like his animism. Polytheism suggests that there

> is an universal tendency among mankind to conceive all beings like themselves, and to transfer to every object those qualities with which they are familiarly acquainted, and of which they are intimately conscious . . . Nor is it long before we ascribe to them thought and reason, and passion, and sometimes even the limbs and figures of men, in order to bring them nearer to a resemblance with ourselves. (Tylor 1873: 61)

In effect, Tylor was crediting Hume with being the first to propose an animist theory of religion, and also on strictly naturalistic grounds. Tylor thus not only sought to refute Müller's assertions about identity of natural religion, but all such notions resting on other than empirical and naturalistic grounds. In *Religion in Primitive Culture* (1873), Tylor declared:

> Here let me state once for all two principal conditions under which the present research is carried on. First, as to the religious doctrines and practices examined, these are treated as belonging to theological systems devised by human reason, without supernatural aid or revelation; *in other words, as being developments of Natural Religion.* (Tylor 1873: 11; my emphasis)

In a virtual slap at the entire Deist tradition, Tylor asserted, in effect, that animism *was* the real primal natural religion, not Müller's experience of the Infinite. To Tylor's delight, animism did not consist in a straining for unity with some ineffable abstract principle infinite, as Müller imagined. Rather, animism represented the human desire to *explain* the world, and religion for Tylor was conceived as humanity's first feeble, but misguided, attempt at *science* – not at mysticism!

There is no need for improvement of Robert Ackerman's treatment in this volume of Sir James George Frazer (1854–1941) as a founder of anthropology of religion. But on Frazer's relation to Müller one or two points might be made, given that they bear on the role religion has to play in the development of the field. Frazer in effect rejected Müller's spiritual conception of primal natural religion in much the same spirit as had Tylor. Among other things, as Ackerman shows, *The Golden Bough* posed a theory of the evolution of religion that sought to discredit the privileged, revealed status of Christianity by demonstrating that images and motifs regarded as unique to Christianity were not of Christian origin. Frazer's accounts of incarnated divine beings found in many of the non-Christian religious traditions were meant to suggest that Christianity had simply borrowed these pagan motifs and represented them as its own (Frazer 1957: 105–22).

Even more anti-Christian than Tylor, Frazer proposed that a Müller-like Natural Religion was not primal in the evolution of religion. What was primal was the human desire to *control* nature in the interests of fecundity and life, rather than religious worship or mysticism. Magic came before religion in pursuit of this effort of control over nature. (Frazer articulated this view in the second edition of *The Golden Bough*.) When early peoples realized that magic failed to manipulate nature, they turned to supplicating the gods – in effect, to religion. But then humankind came to realize that appealing to the gods failed to insure their control over nature's vicissitudes. Only a man-made, scientifically grounded technology could master nature. No matter how highly evolved it was, religion failed to master nature – just as magic had.

From this point forward, there began to be a divergence between the scholarly lineages of Müller, on the one hand, and Tylor and Frazer, on the other. In large part, today's academic field of religious studies more or less takes its rise from the comparative and philological traditions of Max Müller, while the discipline of anthropology of religion tends to look back to ancestors such as Tylor and Frazer. In our own time, the two streams have been rejoined, at least from the perspective of religious studies, which for at least the last two decades has moved well beyond its philosophical and philological beginnings to embrace methods of ethnographic and ethnological research indistinguishable from "anthropology" of religion so called. In terms of research agendas, while Andrew Lang, R. R. Marett, Émile Durkheim, and early students of religion, typified by Rudolf Otto and Pater Wilhelm Schmidt (even, lately, Mircea Eliade), were still focused on the search for the origins of religion or the primal natural religion (Lang 1908; Schmidt 1912–55; Marett 1914; Otto 1923; Eliade 1957); that pursuit would peter out in the anthropological study of religion of Malinowski's early writings (Malinowski 1948). The discourse of speculation about the origins of religion or the primal natural religion would pass to influential, but protean, theoreticians like Georges Bataille, Walter Burkert, Roger Caillois, Mircea Eliade, or René Girard (Caillois 1950; Eliade 1958; Bataille 1973; Girard 1977; Burkert 1983, 1996).

As a result, the quest for the origins of religion would be radically reoriented. Instead of seeking a *historical* primal natural religion, scholars sought the *experiential* origins of religion. Prominent nineteenth-century leaders in this trend would be Protestant theologian Friedrich Schleiermacher (1768–1834) or William James (1842–1910), both instrumental in shifting discourse about primal natural religion to one about the forms of human *experience* generating and sustaining religion (James 1961 [1902]; Taylor 2002). Likewise, the theories of religion of Durkheim, Eliade, Freud, Jung,

Malinowski, Rudolf Otto and many others really amount to a quest for the origins of religious *experience*, not some hypothetical historical beginning point (Taylor 2002).

Chief among the experiences linked with the origins of the religion is the experience of the sacred. In the hands of a believer such as Otto, the essential religious experiences of the "numinous" or "holy" were experiences of "creature feeling" or "absolute dependence" of devotee upon the divine (Otto 1923: 9–10). For someone like Émile Durkheim, on the other hand, the essential religious experience of these sacred "forces" arose from social life, even though Durkheim described the experience of the sacred much as Otto did. In an address on the feeling of sacredness as the experiential origin of religion, Durkheim said:

> The man who lives according to religion is not only one who visualizes the world in a certain way, who knows what others do not know, he is above all a man who feels within himself a power of which he is not normally conscious, a power which is absent when he is not in the religious state. The religious life implies the existence of very special forces . . . these are the forces which move mountains. By that I mean when a man lives a religious life he believes he is participating in a force which dominates him, but which at the same time upholds him and raises him above himself. (Durkheim 1975: 182)

While anthropologists, properly speaking, might frequently make mention and even owe profound intellectual debts to some of these thinkers, the Girards, Eliades, Batailles and such lie at the margins of the *discipline* of (at least Anglophone) anthropology in the same way Freud did for Melford Spiro or Jung for Victor Turner (Turner 1967; Spiro 1970, 1982).

From the Bible to the Outback

Despite the split that developed between Müller and Tylor, the ideology behind Müller's critical study of sacred texts aided the development of anthropology of religion in the twentieth century. W. Robertson Smith (1846–94) and the later Durkheim provide the main links to this earlier tradition.

Smith learned how to approach ancient and exotic religions and religious texts in Germany from the two leading biblical critics of the day, Paul Lagarde (1827–1891) and Julius Wellhausen (1844–1918). They impressed Smith and through him, Durkheim's *The Elementary Forms*, with the need to study religion in intensely concrete cultural and social contexts – in its *Sitz im Leben*. The study of religion thus required both considerable linguistic or philological skills, and also attention to the world of dense empirical, historical, and social facts. In 1880, Smith even did a stint of field studies in Arabia in order to observe the living religion of real life Semites (W. R. Smith 1880). As a progressive evolutionist, Smith believed that he would find there a religion as close as possible to that of the ancient Israel of biblical times. One could then observe how ancient Semitic religion worked *in situ*, instead of just what one read from biblical texts, and in so doing better understand what the Bible was trying to convey. Smith's classic work – praised by Durkheim – the *Lectures on the Religion of the Semites* (1889) was paired with his 1885 study of Arabian social life, *Kinship and Marriage in Early Arabia*. In this way, the critical methods that Smith learned from Lagarde and Wellhausen made marked contributions to the anthropology of religion.

What Smith thought that he had found in the Arabian back country was a most primitive form of religion akin to that suggested by the biblical narrative, with its talk of sacrifice, sacred precincts, ritual abominations, and the like. Archaic Semitic religious life lacked elegant doctrines or ethical visions, and consisted totally of rituals and social practices (Smith 1923: 213–17). This supported Smith's belief that religion in its earliest stages of evolution merited the description "materialistic" – as something consisting in the main of actions rather than words, beliefs, or even myths. Such early forms of religion were far from anything "spiritual," as Müller and the Deists had assumed about the mystical and philosophical natural religion they considered primary in human history (Smith 1923: 440). For Smith, the glory and reality of religion lay in its future growth beyond ritual, beyond its primitive past. For Smith, the true nature of real religion lay in the spiritual reforming message of the Hebrew prophets, in the ethical monotheism that Smith believed was preached by them and their Christian successors, such as himself (Smith 1923: 439).

In arguing that ritual was the earliest form of religion, Smith parted ways with the Deists. But he also opposed Frazer and Tylor on the nature of mature religion. For Smith, mature religion was basically morality, and not a quasi-technology for *controlling* nature. While for Frazer, religion moved on the same track as had magic – both attempts to control nature, one by human power, the other by appealing to a deity – for Smith, religion and technology moved on different evolutionary tracks. This effectively ruled out the development of religion into technology. Nor, *pace* Tylor's view of animism as primitive science, was religion a particular style of *explaining* human behavior or the world. Religion was substantially and essentially a behavior – ritual in its primitive form and ethical in the form proclaimed by the Jewish prophets and the Protestant Reformers.

At Discourse's End: the Durkheimians and the Professionalization of Anthropology

After the first quarter of the twentieth century, anthropologists generally seem to have lost interest in the discourse on primal natural religion. The spiritual quests for the *primal natural religion* – either to affirm or debunk it – which drove earlier work on religion, no longer seemed interesting. While major twentieth-century anthropologists of religion, such as Clifford Geertz, E. E. Evans-Pritchard, Mary Douglas, Melford Spiro, Victor Turner, Anthony F. C. Wallace or even Claude Lévi-Strauss devoted significant parts of their careers to the study of religion, one would be hard pressed to identify a spiritual dimension directing the works of the entire group. No quest for the primal natural religion or for a religious a priori – again, either to affirm or debunk it – dominated their efforts. Perhaps the last to engage this quest were the immediate predecessors of the major anthropologists of religion of the twentieth century, Émile Durkheim and his school.

An adequate accounting of the contribution of Émile Durkheim and the Durkheimian school to anthropology of religion is well beyond the scope of this article. But the need to reckon this influence is inescapable.

Durkheim was born David Émile at Epinal in Lorraine in 1858. Descended from many generations of rabbis, he followed family tradition and prepared himself for the rabbinate until about age 14. Under the influence of his secular education and the rising patriotism of the period immediately following France's defeat in the 1870–1 war against Prussia, Durkheim became, if anything, more a devoted, even religious, patriot than an adherent to any traditional religion. By the time he left his local secondary school for the Lycée Louis-le-Grand in Paris, he was at least an agnostic, and probably an atheist. There, Durkheim found himself among the cream of French intellectual youth. The future philosophers Henri Bergson and Maurice Blondel were contemporaries as students, as was the future leader of the French socialists, Jean Jaurès, and Pierre Janet, the psychologist.

The appearance in 1912 of Durkheim's classic, *The Elementary Forms of the Religious Life*, signaled a shift in Durkheim's interest from studies of contemporary society to small-scale traditional societies. Before then, Durkheim had published major sociological studies of modern France – *Suicide* (1897) and the *Division of Labor in Society* (1893). This shift had been brewing for some time, since he, along with his closest collaborators, Henri Hubert and Marcel Mauss, had already been writing on some of the standard subjects of the anthropology of religion like myth, ritual, magic, prayer, expiation, sin, sacrifice, the sacred, and such. They had also been in correspondence with and attentive to all the key publications of Frazer, Tylor, Marett, Müller, and other anthropologists of religion.

Durkheim's writing on Australian religion in *Elementary Forms* is couched partly in the older metaphors of a quest for the *origins* of religion and for the *simplest* – most "elementary" – religion, reminiscent of the centuries-old quest for the primal natural religion. In Aboriginal Australia, a society that many felt to be the most "primitive" on earth, Durkheim argued that he had located this *simplest* and most *primitive* form of religious life – "totemism." Like the religion of back-country Arabia studied by Smith, Durkheim saw totemism primarily as an action. It was silent about lofty doctrines or metaphysical meditations that Müller and the Deists felt characterized primal natural religion. Totemism was at first sight the ritual worship of an animate or vegetal species – such as a kangaroo, "witchetty grub," or some plant species. In its ritual *Sitz im Leben*, the totem radiated a manifest religious sense of sacred force, awe, and reverence. It was the focus of an energetic ritual life. At the same time, the totem was regarded as emblematic of the group venerating it, much as a flag symbolized a nation, or a coat of arms, a noble family. Totemism was not then simply what the untutored eye beheld. But just why was it sacred, and why did it radiate such dynamic power throughout the particular Australian group that might venerate it?

Durkheim answered these puzzles by first disposing of the two most readily available explanations of how and why the totem became the center of aboriginal religious life – Müller's "naturism" and Tylor's "animism." The totem did not possess its sacred power because of its natural qualities (Müller) or because a spirit was believed to animate it (Tylor). After all, the natural is nothing more than the mundane, and therefore unable to inspire the reverence characteristic of sacred totems. Neither did Durkheim believe that totems were revered because they were somehow thought to be inhabited by spirits or to be spirits themselves. Totemism had been far too durable and substantial a religion, too integral to sustaining the life of Aboriginal Australians, to be based on the fleeting experiences of spirits – especially as they usually occurred in dreams or hallucinations. Rather, the rationale of totemic worship was the reality that lay behind it, what the totem *symbolized* or stood for. And, that, as one knows, was the totemic *group* who worshiped the totem in the first place! Durkheim audaciously argued that in the simplest religion, people were reasserting the ultimate worth of their own social group and, in doing so, reinforcing its solidarity and strengthening its values. Primal natural religion was society worshiping itself.

In the bargain, Durkheim advanced the theory that religion "functions." Studying cultural or social systems demanded seeking how these cultural and social systems work or hang together to maintain the system as a whole. Religion and religious activities, such as rituals, *function* to maintain the coherence of the group. In this sense, the totemic rites of the Aborigines *function* just as rallying around the national flag does for patriots – to maintain and revive a sense of social solidarity. Like the totem, the national flag is both an object of direct veneration and a symbol of something that goes beyond the physical reality of the flag itself. A totem stands for the core values sacred to the totemic group, the flag stands for the nation and its sacred national values. In activating reverence for it in rituals, patriots, like devotees of totemism, intensify the unity of the group (Durkheim 1995: 228–31).

In comparing patriotism and Aboriginal totemism, Durkheim implied that traditional religious *experience* was not some perception of a realm beyond the human, but an experience of the power internal to social groupings. Durkheim's view about totemism is then best read as a proposal about the fundamental basis of religious *experience*. The *experience* of total dependence felt by traditional believers with regard to God is actually the same feeling had by Aborigines celebrating their totem or that of patriots rallying to their flag. In all cases, it is the power of the social group that engenders these experiences of religious dynamism. Religious experience is therefore real, because these feelings of dependence upon others is real and constitute the main part of the force that inspires faith to "move mountains," as Durkheim (1975: 182) says. We, therefore, generate our own natural religion, and we do it "naturally."

Malinowski (1884–1942) owed much to Durkheim's functionalism and Freud's psychology of the unconscious, even though he had made out that Frazer was his great mentor. Like Durkheim, he first argued not only that societies were systematic wholes, held together by mutually functioning subsystems, such as magic, myth, politics, religion, economy, and such, but that each of these units was absolutely necessary for the continued survival of the whole. This exaggerated crisis mentality may owe much to the hypochondriac nature of Malinowski's personality (Malinowski 1948: 39–41, 46; 1967). But whatever the reasons, this attitude put a particular stamp on Malinowski's way of looking at social wholes: they were organisms in crisis, fragile unities that one disturbed at great risk to those societies. Second, Malinowski felt that the various cultural functions were rooted in biological needs and that cultural functions, such as religion, worked – functioned – by directly addressing biological needs. As such, so-called religious experiences were to be looked on as mere expressions of the biological conditions of human beings in crisis, impelled, as it were, by our biological drive to survive (Malinowski 1948: 51–3).

A choice example of Malinowski's approach is his analysis of a funeral rite in a small-scale traditional society (Malinowski 1948: 47–53). Faced with the death of a member, the survivors realize, perhaps intuitively in such small-scale societies, that each and every death threatens the survival of the entire group. Thus, deaths need to be managed in order to maintain a psychological – and ultimately physiological – equilibrium in the group. Such losses are managed, Malinowski believes, by a strategy of the denial of real death. This unconscious psychological strategy produces various features of religion – the experience of the holy dead, the belief in the immortality of the soul (echoes of Tylor?), the inner feeling of divine providence and care (echoes of Durkheim's experience of our dependence on society?). Malinowski believed such behavior resulted from the inability of humans – simply as biological systems – to adapt easily to the idea of death. The biological aspect of our humanity simply resists permitting us to dwell upon the certainty of our end. We prefer denial of the reality of death to its acceptance. Denial keeps society from disintegration by calming our emotions. It therefore generates – as a biological reflex alone – both the *belief* in immortality and the concomitant religious *experiences* that confirm this belief (Malinowski 1948: 51). Since it generates such religious beliefs and experiences, this strategy of physiologically grounded denial carries us straight to the essence of religion.

Understanding the Way "Natives Think" in the Anthropology of Religion

The view of religion as a kind of noble lie with which Malinowski left us was not, however, to be the final word about religion, even for many of those who followed in the tradition of British social anthropology which Malinowski had done so much to shape. The quest for primal natural religion would not be resumed among anthropologists of religion, but left to a curious breed of historians of religion led by the Romanian expatriot, Mircea Eliade of the University of Chicago Divinity School (Strenski 1987: chs 4, 5). Neither would the quest to see beneath religious *experience* hold much interest for those one might identify as major anthropologists of religion in the second half of the twentieth century. Here I have in mind E. E. Evans-Pritchard, Mary Douglas, and Victor Turner.

These three British anthropologists put aside the undermining of the truth of religious experience or beliefs that haunts the work of the Humes, Frazers, Tylors, Durkheims, Malinowskis, and others. Religion is taken at face value by the likes of Douglas, Evans-Pritchard, and Turner, and explored to reveal what it can tell us about the enlightening ways in which other peoples have constructed or conceived their worlds. Whether this friendliness to religion can be attributed to the fact that Douglas and Evans-Pritchard, at least, were practicing Catholics is a matter for future investigation. A signal article, announcing this change of attitude, comes indeed from Evans-Pritchard – his Aquinas Lecture of 1959, "Religion and the Anthropologists" (Evans-Pritchard 1962: 29–45). In this address, Evans-Pritchard indicted the anti-religious attitudes of his own profession:

> Almost all the leading anthropologists of my own generation would, I believe, hold that religious faith is total illusion, a curious phenomenon soon to become extinct and to be explained in such terms as "compensation" and "projection" or by some sociologistic interpretation on the lines of maintenance of social solidarity . . . I do not know of a single person among the prominent sociologists and anthropologists of America at the present time who adheres to any faith. Religion is superstition to be explained by anthropologists, and not something an anthropologist, or indeed any rational person, could himself believe in. (Evans-Pritchard 1962: 36)

While it is unclear precisely what effect this address had on anthropology, it does not seem accidental that several prominent anthropologists associated with Evans-Pritchard, and indeed Evans-Pritchard himself, show a very different attitude to anthropology of religion than what he indicated in 1959. His *Witchcraft, Oracles and Magic among the Azande* (1937) and *Nuer Religion* (1956) might be seen to illustrate the difference he and his students sought to make against the attacks on religion of Malinowski and his ilk (Eliade 1954; Evans-Pritchard 1956, 1976). If any one feature of the work of the likes of Douglas and Evans-Pritchard can be singled out, it would be an assertion of the priority of understanding over explanation (Douglas 1980: 87–9). If we add the American Clifford Geertz to the newer generation of trans-Atlantic anthropologists of religion, we might even use the term "hermeneutics" to describe this new approach. What Geertz, Douglas, and Evans-Pritchard represent is an anthropology of religion focused on meaning, on mapping the rationality of traditional religious action and thought (Geertz 1973). Evans-Pritchard started us down this road as early as 1937 by defending the rationality of Azande witchcraft beliefs.

> I found it strange at first to live among Azande and listen to naive explanations of misfortunes which, to our minds, have apparent causes, but after a while I learnt the idiom of their thought and applied notions of witchcraft as spontaneously as themselves in situations where the concept was relevant. (Evans-Pritchard 1976: 19)

In the case of Mary Douglas, this understanding of native cosmologies consists in attempts to make coherent and persuasive sense of the apparently irrational beliefs of religious folk in purity or in the power of ritual (Douglas 1970, 1973). In her *Purity and Danger* (1970), Douglas takes on the much-reviled beliefs about defilement and pollution found, for example, in traditional Jewish kosher laws or among Hindus in terms of the impurity and polluting quality of certain castes. What Douglas shows is that these rules are not irrational. They ought to be looked on symbolically, as ways people have for expressing their senses of difference and boundary between themselves and others.

Anthropology of Religion Today

In contemporary anthropology of religion, Douglas, Evans-Pritchard, Geertz, and Turner have dominated the scene from the mid-twentieth century. Many others merit mention, of course, especially if we broaden the interest in religion to encompass work on myth (Claude Lévi-Strauss), sacrifice (René Girard, Georges Bataille, Walter Burkert, Luc de Heusch), ritual (Roy Rappaport, Maurice Bloch), symbol (Roy Wagner, Jack Goody), studies with specific regional foci (McKim Marriott, Milton Singer, Bernard Cohen, Louis Dumont, Melford Spiro, Gananath Obeyesekere, S. J. Tambiah, and many others). The list would swell to an impossibly long one – and certainly an unwieldy one for a single article that seeks some kind of leading thread to sustain its narrative.

What this list shows is how the anthropology of religion has broadened out since the original drive to seek the primal natural religion. Given the extravagant richness of what the generations following Evans-Pritchard have wrought, this broadening has infused great vitality into the field. Still, at the same time, this melding of interests in religion into the mainstream of more compelling agendas in anthropology has made the subject of anthropology of religion harder to discern as a distinct inquiry. Although the data are shallower than one would like, an analytic review of survey articles in the *Annual Review of Anthropology* for the period 1984–2001 reveals a pattern that would not surprise those familiar with the anthropology of religion. There seems at present to be little focused and exclusive anthropological interest in religion. To wit, the term "religion" or "religious" occurs a combined total of 152 times during this span of 18 years in the survey articles of the discipline published in *Annual Review*. The combined total of 152 for the occurrences of "religion" and "religious" in *Annual Review* for the 1984–2001 span is roughly the same rate as the occurrence of a *single* item like "the other" (149 times).

Thus, one may conclude that although the study of religion in its many aspects continues to engage anthropologists, it seems subsumed these days into the more compelling agendas of the day that dictate the kinds of work anthropologists publish and teach. The focus of anthropology of religion has become more diffuse, with no single problem channeling inquiry along a single vector. Whether that is a good or a bad thing, only time will tell.

Further Reading

Collins, Elizabeth Fuller. 1997. *Pierced by Murugan's Lance: Ritual, Power, and Moral Redemption among Malaysian Hindus.* DeKalb, IL: Northern Illinois University Press.

Gellner, David N. 2001. *The Anthropology of Buddhism and Hinduism: Weberian Themes.* New Delhi/New York: Oxford University Press.

Peacock, James L. and Ruel W. Tyson, Jr. 1989. *Pilgrims of Paradox: Calvinism and Experience among the Primitive Baptists of the Blue Ridge.* Washington: Smithsonian Institution Press.

Robbins, Joel. 2004. *Becoming Sinners: Christianity and Moral Torment in a Papua New Guinea Society.* Berkeley: University of California Press.

7

The Empire in Empiricism: The Polemics of Color

Barbara Saunders

Introduction

As a basis for his political philosophy, Locke was driven to create both an epistemology and a philosophy of mind. He was involved in many aspects of the turbulent political life of his time, including, importantly, the founding of new colonies in America. His *Two Treatises* (1690) was, in part, a blueprint for the development of the colonies. What has been realized only recently by Locke scholars is the extent to which his arguments in the two domains – epistemology and political philosophy – had the same structure. In one, the labor of mind was required to transform raw sensations into the abstract thought that was the prerogative of civilized man, and in the other the labor of hands was required to transform raw nature into the "conveniences" of civilized life. In both domains, the raw material – sensation or nature – was the gift of God. The empiricism of his epistemology thus maps nearly exactly onto the developmentalism of his colonial politics. In both cases, man labors, and *should* labor, to improve the divinely given raw material. He "should" implies in the one case a moral philosophy of education and in the other the "civilized" man's right to appropriate undeveloped parts of the globe. One could say that the "work ethic" permeates Locke's thought in both domains. Of course, it seemed to the European that "primitives" were sadly deficient in this respect. It is this which provides an entry for the racism that we now perceive in his thought, even in a domain, a theory of knowledge, where many would be surprised to find it.

In epistemology, Locke and his followers used color as a key example of sensations transformed by labor (abstraction, reflection) into abstract ideas (color categories) and it became the site for the struggle about the definition of reality. His parallel arguments in the political domain argued that Native North Americans, like idiots and "naturals," were not sufficiently developed to discover the truths of experience, were incapable of work, and so were not sufficiently developed to own property:

> There cannot be a clearer demonstration of any thing, than several Nations of the *Americans* are of this, who are rich in Land and poor in all the Comforts of Life; whom Nature

having furnished as liberally as any other people, with the materials of Plenty, i.e. a fruit-ful Soil, apt to produce in abundance, what might serve for food, raiment, and delight; yet for want of improving it by labor, have not one hundredth part of the Conveniences we enjoy: And a King of a large and fruitful Territory there feeds, lodges, and is clad worse than a day Labourer in England. (1690: 41)

When mind and body were united by the moral economy of labor in recognition of God, knowledge and civil society were born. Native Americans, in a state of Nature, had neither.

The long shadow of this account has spawned a paradigm of cognitive science in showing how the various "levels," from cell physiology to "language and culture," can be linked. To create this paradigm, color, which Locke used primarily in his epistemology, has been inserted over the past two centuries into the cognitive domain, and, through politics and "cross-cultural studies," into the colonial domain. The historical development of color science on these foundations has thus, somewhat ironically, made explicit the link that has until recently been overlooked by Locke scholars, namely that corpuscularian essences, narrowly sectarian religious views, and appeals to geopolitical and economic concerns were inherent in the establishment of the field of empiricism.

My purpose in this chapter is to show that far from being a contingent conjunc-ture, groundfloor empiricism (common sense or intuition) and the ethnocentric "denial of coevalness" (Fabian 1983) belong to the same constellation of theories of mind that were proposed in the Anglo-European world between the seventeenth and nineteenth centuries.[1] My general aim is to show that though it undergoes many re-formulations, which strip it of context and historical significance, the influence of this constellation continues today like a gravitational force exercised by a large body at a distance. My particular aim is to show the links between an epistemic thesis (accord-ing to which all knowledge is dependent on and originates in experience), its semantic counterpart (in which abstract ideas stand for experience), and the developmental theory of growth that sets the ground rules for the contemporary ideology of develop-ment. I trace this in philosophy through the works of Locke, Hume, and Mill and in anthropology through Père Lafitau, Rivers, and Berlin and Kay, and show how clarifica-tion of the entanglements may allow some work at the theoretical level directed toward exposing the inner constitution of racism.

Philosophy

Locke's theory of color

Locke's epistemology provides the framework for a theory of mind that is especially significant for anthropology and psychology. These disciplines overlap and intersect in many ways, exemplified with particular force in what may at first seem a minor topic, that of seeing color. This is no accident: to exemplify the workings of "the mind" and its product "ideas," Locke gives a natural history of color in terms of the labor both of "seeing" and "knowing." It is a recurrent example in his and his successors' works, and supplies a paradigmatic structure for his arguments. It provides the kind of understanding that has induced a Euro-American tradition to look for general explanations of color via studies of the languages of the world.

In his *Essay Concerning Human Understanding* (1689), Locke proposes the epistemological thesis that all knowledge rests on "experience." With this he establishes the foundational terms for what I shall refer to as "the field of empiricism." This field can be thought of in terms of two dimensions. One dimension opposes the concept of the newborn human's mind as a blank slate (a *tabula rasa*) to innatism, and is constructed throughout the polemic of the *Essay*. The other dimension opposes relativism to universalism, and emerges in the arguments of his *Two Treatises on Government*.[2] Between them they constitute the necessary elements and preconditions of the field of empiricism: they establish the empirical method, the parameters of a commonsensical "theory of mind" and a theory of development and progress. I suggest that *tabula rasa* versus innatism, and relativism versus universalism form a discursive symbiosis for Locke, which structures a metaphysical picture (the gravitational force) that continues its grip today, albeit in transfigured form.

Locke's epistemology is exemplified by the new empirical sciences resting on the mechanist assumptions of the corpuscularian theory, developed initially by Boyle. Locke's framework, which was appropriated from that of Descartes, allows him to produce an account both of epistemology and civil society that is causally reductionist, yet also emergentist (1690: 80). With this he claims to refute the "innatism" of inborn inequalities of the Aristotelian Catholics and Royalists, and provides an account of differences between individuals and among communities of peoples.

In Locke's epistemology, color finds its equivalent in God-given "natural law" in his *Two Treatises on Government*. Just as color would eventually be explained in terms of primary qualities, so natural law (or ethics), with its basis in experience, would be explained by mathematics. The assurance with which he treats natural law in the *Two Treatises* assumes that its existence, meaning, and content are "plain and intelligible to all rational Creatures" (II, 124). Locke treats natural law like color, as a "positive code" to which all men everywhere conform. Both are governed by God's positive direction, known to all through reason, since reason is "the Voice of God" in man (I, 86). The dictate of reason establishes the first principles of common sense, which are constitutive, given our nature, of achieving any knowledge.

Locke argues that sensations of qualities, supplemented by "reflexion," produce individuated simple ideas. In so far as the qualities that are seen are in agreement or disagreement with the simple idea, it is the differentiations that constitute our knowledge, not the idea per se. Locke is quite clear that in the first instance the differentiations he means concern light, and it is these differentiations that ultimately allow the idea to be produced:

> . . . so after they are born, those ideas are the earliest imprinted, which happen to be the sensible qualities, which first occur to them; amongst which, light is not the least considerable, nor of the weakest efficacy. And how covetous the mind is, to be furnished

with all such ideas ... may be a little guessed, by what is observable in children
new-born, who always turn their eyes to that part from whence the light comes, lay them
how you please. (2.9.7)

The central theme of Locke's *Two Treatises on Government* argues for the foundation
of property and property ownership in terms of labor. Like color, natural law exemplifies the conviction that the universe is to be understood as the rational workings
of the Deity; but on all points natural law must be made to fit with, and be compared
to, the observed facts of the created world and human behavior. The "Law of Nature
... is the Law of Reason" (I, 101). "We are born Free, as we are born Rational"
(I, 61). "The liberty of acting in accord with our own will, not from the compulsion
of others, is grounded on the possession of reason" (II, 63).

Locke counters the arguments for "authority" of the Aristotelians, Tories, and
Royalists: children are born in full equality (II, 55), and attain true freedom when
they reach "the Age of Reason." When he says "in the beginning all the World was
America, and more so than that is now" (1690: 49), Locke is contesting Old Testament
arguments for authority taken to form the basis of "innatism," associated with the authority of traditions and status quo.

According to Locke, a complete account of human development would show that
in the primitive patriarchal Old Testament stage in which we once lived in Europe, we
were like the American Indians. Here he is taking for granted that groups of people
and individuals are completely analogous. The argument is an assertion of the equality
of birth but inequality of true freedom, which requires entering the Age of Reason.
Native North Americans have not yet achieved the Age of Reason, however. It is this
that explains inequality of development. As he says,

> Had you or I been born in the Bay of *Soldania*, possibly our thoughts and notions had
> not exceeded those brutish ones of the *Hottentots* that inhabit there. And had the
> Virginia king *Apochancana*, been educated in *England*, he had perhaps, been as know-
> ing a divine and as good a mathematician as any in it. The difference between him and
> a more improved *English-man* lying barely in this, that the exercise of his faculties was
> bounded within the ways, modes, and notions of his own country. (1.4.12)

This sets up the dilemma of relativism and universalism. It arises because although
neither the innatist nor the universalist would admit degrees of development, the fact
of other cultures or societies nonetheless stood in need of explanation, namely that
God had made them so.

The greater explanatory scope of Locke's relativism within that framework enriches
it by the single developmental trajectory of civil society that married the ethical rights
of the English landed gentry to European thinking, and excluded not only other kinds
of civil society, but its very possibility. The theory required the truth of the one God;
and where unavailable, there was no civil society (Arneil 1996: 210).

Locke's theory of the ethic of labor legitimated and celebrated the superiority of
Anglo-European colonial market agriculture over that of the native people whom it
replaced (Tully 1993: 162). He formulated a thesis in which labor effects changes in

the direction of higher complexity and has an impact on every idea and social structure. For Locke, knowledge and civil society are the historical result of "developmental learning": the one issues in ideas, the other in ownership of land.

Locke's doctrine of the production of empirical knowledge and wealth delineate a moral economy of experiential philosophy and civil society armed with a linear view of life stretching from infant to adult and from savage and tribal to present society. He endows an evolutionary anthropology with temporalized space, stressing that all differences in civil society are "natural."

Hume

Locke established a discursive framework for his successors by drawing consequences for civil society from a theory of mind. This provides a continuity between Locke and Mill via Hume who, despite many differences with Locke, proposed a complex and intricate theory entwined with a hardened, unilinear developmental sequence of human mental capacities. In particular, he shared Locke's view of the relation of empiricism and mathematics, especially in issues of comparison. Mathematics provided the appropriate method in whatever domain. But while Locke displayed a polite attitude to the "Virginia king," Hume left no doubt that Negroes were irremediable – scarcely more than animals. He said:

> I am apt to suspect the negroes and in general all other species of men (for there are four or five kinds) to be naturally inferior to the whites. There never was a civilised nation of any other complexion than white, nor even any individual eminent in either action or speculation . . . Such a uniform and constant difference could not happen, in so many countries and ages, if nature had not made an original distinction betwixt breeds of men.

For Hume, perception is "the mind." To perceive is to feel and to have ideas and, from them, to think and to judge. In his *Treatise of Human Nature* (1739) Hume claims that what we call a *mind* is nothing but a heap or collection of different perceptions, united together by certain relations. It is the notion of "certain relations" which is important because through their unity a "self" or "human being" can be determined. It is also on the basis of the varying degrees of certainty provided by these relations that the arts and sciences can be judged and graded. And it is their epistemological and anthropological complexity and accuracy that underwrites the distinctions "in kind" between the "white races" and the "non-white races." Nature has not endowed the Negroes with such relations of mind that allow culture, science, and the arts to arise.

In general, reasoning is opposed to mere impression as the active to the passive. Active reasoning is the rendering of explicit and clear ideas. What is distinctive for active reasoning is the difference between "perception" and "thought": "All kinds of reasoning consist in nothing but *comparison*, and a discovery of those relations, either constant or inconstant, which two or more objects bear to each other" (1739: 73).

Hume's comparisons are similar to Locke's differentiations. According to Hume, the three kinds of "comparison" that occur are: (1) when both objects are physically present; (2) when only one object is present, and the other is recalled in memory; (3) when neither object is present so that the comparison is purely mental and abstract. In the first case, however, the issue concerns "perception," not "thought," because it is merely passive admission of impressions through sense organs. Hume assumes bizarrely that the Negro has neither memory nor capacity for abstraction, and therefore lacks the realm of higher mental, moral self-constitution and the aptitude for sciences that depend on abstraction. Capable only of passive reception of impressions that are presented to the mind, the Negro's capacity for reason is limited to those things sensually present. Remove the objects, and the Negro mind can neither deduce nor infer their abstract relations through concepts and logical demonstrations (Eze 2000). In order to describe all this Hume often resorts to a very Eurocentric language of commonsense realism. Thus, Hume's racism is more strident than is Locke's (Bernasconi 2003: 147). In the next generation of commentators, especially in Mill, the tensions between the Lockean and Humean views pose conundrums from which there is no easy escape.

Mill

For Mill, who was indebted to Locke for his psychology, the importance of "individuality" as the atom of civil society, derived from, or identical to, self-development, is preeminent and carefully elaborated in *On Liberty* (1869). In common with Locke, Mill could simultaneously sustain an apparent egalitarianism and colonial sentiments, though in Mill's case, the involvement in colonial affairs was direct: in 1823, he followed his father into the service of the East India Company, conducting its correspondence with India in the Department of Native States, and subsequently succeeding the older Mill as Examiner, remaining with the Company until its abolition shortly after the Indian Rebellion of 1857–8. Echoing his father, John Stuart implicitly evoked European standards when he insisted that India's peoples required direction by the civilized peoples represented by colonial rulers (see Goldberg 1993: 35). The moral and human sciences – understood as empirical inductive sciences like the natural sciences – would confirm this. But Mill also initially held that individuals are radically affected by their membership in society, and inevitably formed by the customs, habits, morality, and beliefs of those who raised them. Thus, in his early thinking the possibilities of self-development were relative to the resources of particular societies.

Mill tried to show how experience, acting in accord with known laws of psychology, can explain all our knowledge. The data of experience – sensations and feelings – are intuitively known (as Descartes and Locke had argued). But most important for Mill, "experience" confirms the uniformity of nature, especially in matters concerning causality. Indeed, the law of universal causation is the main pillar of inductive science. Experience yields factual propositions derived from the primitive and natural processes of induction: we note a few limited regularities and predict they will hold in the future.

Like Locke and Hume, Mill held that all we know of objects are the sensations (or impressions) to which they give rise, and their order of occurrence. He was abundantly clear that:

> A sensation is to be carefully distinguished from the object which causes the sensation; our sensation of white from a white object: nor is it less to be distinguished from the attribute whiteness, which we ascribe to the object in consequence of its exciting the sensation. (1834: 33)

It is the capacity for the fine discrimination of "the order of occurrence" that separates humans. Thoughts for Mill are what pass "in the mind itself, and not any object external to the mind, of which the person is commonly said to be thinking" (ibid.: 32). He subscribed to the same reductionist logic and semantic theory as Locke:

> We have a name for objects which produce in us a certain sensation: the word *white*. We have a name for the quality in those objects to which we ascribe the sensation: the name *whiteness*.

But this was only for those who were capable of memory and active reasoning in civil society. In *On Liberty* (1859), Mill considered that it is in the utilitarian interests of subjects-not-yet-civilized to be governed by the civilized until they become sufficiently developed. Goldberg argues that Mill saw equal rights to liberty and justice for all when these rights were abstractly considered, but also judged that the level of "civilized development" of some races rendered their members incapable of the best administration of their resources from the perspective of maximizing the peoples' own utility. Indeed when it came to the colonies, Mill substituted for democratic and public discussion a system by which events experienced and recorded in India were judged elsewhere, transformed into acts of governments and the discourse of authority in other places and times.

How did this fit in with what in Mill's time were thought of as the several races of humanity (Caucasian, Ethiopian, Mongolian, American, Malayan), sometimes just three (the first three, color-coded as white, black, yellow) and the generous, self-sacrificing project of colonialism – of spreading civilization and beneficially Christianizing the globe? Mill referred to the Highlanders and the Basques as "savage relics of past times" who revolve in "their own little mental orbits." In the name of progress, he was happy to see the disappearance of declining languages and obsolete ways of life among Gaelic and other supposedly backward peoples (quoted by Smith 2003: 151). For Mill, a crucial question about the races was: Are they real "Kinds" (by which he meant "logical species")? He equivocated along Lockean lines: "[I]f it shall turn out that the differences are not capable of being accounted for, then man and woman, Caucasian, Mongolian, and Negro, &c. are really different Kinds of human beings, and entitled to be ranked as species by the logician" (1834: 80).

Whether the sexes or races were real Kinds depended upon science – specifically on physiology. There might be innumerable independent differences among the races. But if their differences can all be traced to climate and habits (or, he added in later editions, to some one or a few special differences in structure), they are not, in the logician's view, specifically distinct (ibid.: 80–1). What did Mill think would follow, if the sexes or the races were, in the eye of the logician, real Kinds? He nervously reworked his discussion from edition to edition. If race differences were real, in his sense, then he feared there would be a valid – and not merely a rhetorical – argument against principles of equality. This answer waited upon the findings of the physiologist.

Although Mill opposed the slave trade and contested Carlyle's racist, hierarchized naturalism, Mill's own benevolent developmentalism nonetheless came to err towards neo-scientific racism. His ambivalence over the inherent inferiority of the "native Negroes" transformed gradually from a definition in historical terms to the possible determinism of blood and brain size.

Anthropology

Lafitau

It was particularly in the larger political context of the new sciences, especially the development of colonial infrastructures and the conditions that enabled them, and the social interests therein inscribed, that representations of alien "experience" began to be produced. The influence of Lockean "experience" is obvious in the work of Lafitau, who equated aliens with ancestors in his *Moeurs des Sauvages Amériquains* (1724).

Lafitau developed the detemporalizing, observational distancing devices of empiricism in a systematic way. Although the denial of coevalness had begun to be reinvented in the sixteenth century (from traces in the Ancient writers), by travelers, or compilers of travelers' tales, such as Father José De Acost, in his *Historia natural y moral de las Indes* (1589) and Jean de Léry's inscriptions of his pilgrimage to Brazil in the 1550s (de Certeau 2000), it was Lafitau who developed it into a proto-theory of the unilinear evolution of social and moral institutions dictated by supra-historical principles (Godelier 1988: 73–4).

From Jean de Léry, Lafitau learned that the break between over there and here, between the exteriority of Savagery there, and the civil society here, is a division between Nature and Culture. The alien other is Nature, an object of real exteriority. This other is determined through a translational apparatus of observation, collection, classification, and description. Although Lafitau's discourse does not deal with flora, fauna, and the natural world but with nature as moral, esthetic and religious experience, he nonetheless develops the Natural History episteme, of filling in slots in a table or making points in a coordinate system. It is this that he applies to the Lifeworld. (A notable model of the genre he employs is Linnaeus' classificatory scheme.) He sets up a relation between himself and the Iroquois and between his own present and the ancients. In both cases, he is the subject as well as the other, the object. He creates a synthesis by abolishing his own temporalities, and constitutes scientific explanation through textualization. While his examples come from everywhere, their principles, structures, and functions are universal. Through this style of presentation, Lafitau allows the living Savages to speak on behalf of the dead ancients (de Certeau 1980).

Following Locke's *Two Treatises*, Lafitau used the example of the Iroquois to show that in the beginning all the world was like America, and that the dynamic of history had substituted pragmatic utility for the spectacle of primitive moral expectations and customs. One strategy was to demonstrate a much closer parallelism between savagery and the cultures of Mediterranean antiquity than had been shown before. "I was not content," he said "with knowing the nature of the savages and with learning of their customs and practices. I sought to find in these practices and customs vestiges of the most *remote* antiquity" (Hodgen 1964: 348).

Influenced by Locke's *Essay*, Lafitau developed a method of detached and distancing observation, in order to gather and write down such "facts" as would be transportable, constant and combinable (Latour 1987). Locke's tenacious tenet that the perception of the mind is most aptly explained by words relating to sight was used by Lafitau to make a distinction between reality and fiction – to link the authority of "seen things" with the witnessing and translational activities of the dispassionate observer. To function as a technical discourse, Lafitau plotted a multitude of data over a system of space–time coordinates separate from all meaningful human events. Thus, he replaced the metaphysician's and theologian's discourse with the new scenario of science in which the meaning of what is seen has to be fixed and coded, as "abstract ideas." He used the physical environment of his immediate actuality, that is, empirical observation of outward forms, combined with the Cartesian principles used by Locke, to constitute a "realist" discourse.

De Certeau (1980) compares Lafitau with Lévi-Strauss' ethnographer-as-Lazarus, who returns from the dead to the living, endowed with a knowledge that is unparalleled and incomprehensible to contemporaries. Lafitau's task is to fill in the blanks in knowledge of both halves of the world by the temporal fold of which he is mediator. Lafitau's ambition is to say everything in scientific writing. He naturalizes religion and the principle of "kinship"; and he affirms the dogma of monogenesis in the language of science. Locke's key concept of "labor" is paralleled by Lafitau's development of the thesis of "mother right" (the calculation of descent from the mother, which is both natural generation and natural law) and its classificatory kinship terminology, which were "rediscovered" by Lewis Henry Morgan. Lafitau's achievement was to consolidate Locke's empiricism.

Rivers

By the nineteenth century, the field of empiricism, equated with reason and civilization, encompassed natural philosophy, the natural sciences, and the special sciences of psychology and anthropology. The topic of color continued to be a key example. It was studied by the adjacent disciplines of physiology, experimental psychology, biology, anthropology, philology, and philosophy. Each brought its own methodological resources and ideological resonances to bear. As Mill had insisted, the scientific method – induction/deduction – required empirical laws (generalizations) before it could formulate general laws of nature (or universals). Each discipline took up this challenge in its own way to establish the autonomy of its domain.

Mill's belief that physiology would explain the nature of "race" was widely shared. The thesis of the physiological evolution of the color sense, which had been proposed by Gladstone, Geiger, and the early Magnus was the new form that "innatism" took. However, Leibniz and Kant had already softened the opposition between empiricism and innatism, suggesting that while forms of knowledge were innate their content must be acquired through experience. Whether the innate and empirical hardened so that aliens either had no hope of developing (as Hume's discussion of "the Negro" suggested), or needed the firm hand of colonial government (as Mill suggested), was to be settled by general scientific methodology underpinned by the empiricist thesis of knowledge.

Ramifying into many other discussions, experimental psychology in Germany produced the debates about how to account for color perception between Helmholtz and Hering. German experimental psychology had been dominated by Helmholtz's Lockean view that vision was an experiment constantly performed by the brain with the aid of the eye as a measuring device. This view had been challenged by Hering, who proposed (among other things) a physiological substrate of color sensations working in opposition to one another (red–green, blue–yellow, black–white) in the "visual substance" in order to explain color phenomenology. The empiricist-innatist controversy re-emerged at the heart of the scientific investigation of color (Turner 1993).

The Cambridge experimental psychologist W. H. R. Rivers (in part German-trained) set out to clarify the issues, and undertook anthropological inquiry for this purpose (he would conclude that examination of color names and classifications per se was not a very fruitful approach). That the senses were the source of "experience," and yield, when their products are worked on, knowledge and hence civil society was, thanks to the diffusion of the ideas of Locke, Hume, and Mill, profoundly entrenched. On their authority, such leading figures of nineteenth-century anthropology as Morgan and Tylor never doubted that societies and cultures literally "evolved" following a unilinear path that took them from animal-like primitivity to enlightened civilization. Joining their scheme with the Helmholtz–Hering dispute over empiricism versus innatism, Rivers set out in 1898 to test the "differential discrimination responses" and "color naming behavior" of the islanders in the Torres Strait. (He would later extend this work to experiments on Egyptians [1901], Eskimo (Inuit) of Labrador [1902], the Uralis and Sholagas of India [1903], and the Todas of southern India [1905].) His official conclusion (in line with Virchow 1879, Krause 1877 and Allen 1879) was that differential discrimination and semantic behavior diverged. But underlying this was another conclusion.

Rivers claimed his scientific goal was to study "how far the capacity for appreciating differences goes with the power of expressing those differences in language." Summarizing the results of his color-naming tests of the Torres Strait Islanders, he says, "The languages of these people showed different stages in the evolution of color terminology, which correspond in a striking manner with the course of evolution deduced by Geiger from ancient writings." Referring to the languages of the people of Seven Rivers, Kiwai, Murray Island, and Mabuiag, he continued, "It is interesting to note the order in which these four tribes are thus placed, on the ground of the development of their color language, corresponds with the order in which they would be placed on the ground of their general intellectual and cultural development" (Rivers 1901: 46, 47).

It is noteworthy that the color terms Rivers "found" are the very ones Hering associated with the basic phenomenological color sensations. This correspondence suggests that the color nomenclatures of the different languages are evolving along an innately determined trajectory. Within such a schema, a failure to respond to a Hering color can be interpreted as a kind of evolutionary deficiency. And, in fact, Rivers's results in testing for sensitivity to the color blue indicated that deficiency in color language is associated with deficient sensibility:

> [T]he retina of the Papuan is more strongly pigmented than that of the European. . . .
> The probability that the insensitiveness to blue depended, at any rate partially, on the
> pigmentation of the macula lutea is increased by the fact that the natives were able to
> recognize blue readily on the peripheral retina. (ibid.: 52)

Apparently, "the views of Gladstone and Geiger cannot be contemptuously dismissed" (ibid.: 58).

Empiricism and the Translingual Representation of Modernity

The lack of abstract color names among non-Western peoples became a major cause for the new sciences. Physiological mechanisms were proposed and retracted, as was also a division between physical and cultural evolution; missionaries and colonial administrators were co-opted into large-scale survey work in order to provide empirical data. At stake was Locke's tripartite theory of epistemology, civil society, and development. Was the abstract idea of color innate (i.e., physiological – and thus universal) or was it the product of culture (or civil society and development – and thus relative)? The search for the empirical law of abstract color names had become an empirical test of the Lockean framework itself.[3]

Locke's shadow remains ever present in contemporary color science, which defines color vision as a mode of "seeing light." That is, the experience of color vision is associated with discrimination among different wavelengths of light, regardless of their relative intensities. Nevertheless, color sensation requires processing by the nervous system; the wavelength may be known, and the resulting sensation unknown. Additive color mixing exemplifies the lack of invariant correspondence between wavelength and color: a mixture of two wavelengths can be visually equivalent to a third wavelength. Such visual equivalences of physically different stimuli are termed "metamers" – defined as the set of spectrally different radiations that produce "the same color" under "the same viewing conditions" for a particular creature (Gordon and Abramov 2001: 93). The final goal of contemporary color science is to find the physiological mechanisms for "seeing color." Its definition centers "seeing" in "discriminating" – seeing "differences" and "similarities" of light. "Seeing light discriminations" is the representation of the neurophysiology of the subject that stands between the things themselves and our seeing them (Coulter and Parsons 1989).

Disciplines that study the systems of "seeing light" are radiometry, photometry, and psychophysics; for color, the authority of colorimetry is definitive because the mathematics of metamers works so well (even though their conceptualization, which has been known in principle since Descartes, is now in doubt). It is the "metamer" that functions in this discourse as the techno-theoretical entity that guarantees identity and determines difference, sets the processing isomorphisms of the nervous system in motion, and constrains "categories" and color words. Its (apparent) unity of structure guarantees "correctness," pragmatic success reinforces it, while the discipline itself, within the powerful institution of science, renders inseparable the processes of representing and authorizing. To a large extent, its view of color has become common sense and is held to be intuitively true. This returns us to the problems bequeathed by Locke.

In 1969, Berlin and Kay proposed their theory of *Basic Color Terms*. In a continuing research program, Berlin and Kay and their co-workers set up propositions linking colorimetry, neurophysiology, psychology, and linguistics to unify a cross-cultural developmental scheme of color categorization and semantics. Presenting their work as "new," they formulated their key questions as: If "the color sense" is universal, why is its lexicalization so diverse? Like Magnus (1880), their initial answer was: there is evolution in language. Unlike Magnus, however, Berlin and Kay were preoccupied by a "deeper level" than overt linguistic behavior, a level that revealed "building blocks" or "atoms" or "tokens" in the brain. When linguistically activated, these tokens, structuring the "color space," became a mandatory code to which the original expression "Basic Color Terms" refers. Berlin and Kay proposed Basic Color Terms as a "natural law" or "generative rule" of endogenous growth. BCTs emerge in a continuous, temporalized series, each later stage "transcending" earlier stages in differentiation, marking a metamorphosis along the path towards its end – the full lexicalization of the "color space." Thus, the diversity of color lexica, hitherto thought of as "relative" or "arbitrary" or "random," is overcome: color lexica may superficially differ, but their underlying substructure forms a continuous series.

Nevertheless, even at this deeper level, Berlin and Kay found that languages differ in the number of "tokens" activated. They therefore proposed an even-deeper level of "species-specific bio-morphological structures" that would govern their emergence (1969: 109). Activation occurred in a preordained order, triggered into latency and eventual emergence by its predecessor. This level, the product of evolutionary forces, was related to processes found in society at large, correlated with the "level" of technology.

This reasoning relies on reductive metaphysics, the hypothetical existence of neurological mechanisms and on a form of preformationist embryology in which each stage of development implements the next one until the spectrum is fully named. With this, Berlin and Kay claim to refute relativism and propose instead a "universal" and "evolutionary" perspective on the basis of causal – and thus physiological – mechanisms. Ironically, their "anti-relativism" is identical to Locke's relativism.

In the following diagram, one can find all the elements of Locke's and Mill's theses fixed into what Ingold (1993) in another context calls "an aggressively imperialistic sociobiology."

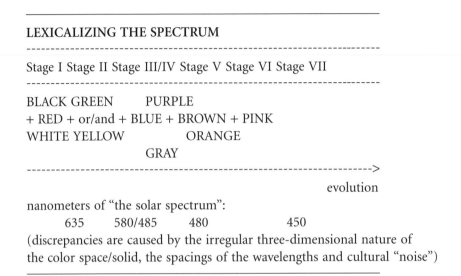

LEXICALIZING THE SPECTRUM

Stage I Stage II Stage III/IV Stage V Stage VI Stage VII

BLACK GREEN   PURPLE
+ RED + or/and + BLUE + BROWN + PINK
WHITE YELLOW   ORANGE
                GRAY

-->
                                    evolution

nanometers of "the solar spectrum":
     635   580/485   480   450
(discrepancies are caused by the irregular three-dimensional nature of
the color space/solid, the spacings of the wavelengths and cultural "noise")

From Locke to Berlin and Kay, "color" provides an operational test, measure, and standard of transhistorical groundfloor empiricism or common sense. It is the tenacity of these arguments that I earlier referred to as a "gravitational force." Locke, Hume, and Mill synthesized epistemology and colonialism and naturalized that synthesis. As historical developmentalism encountered the theories of evolution and the experimental method, the framework hardened so that distinctions between empiricism and innatism and relativism and universalism collapsed. The most striking recognition of this is in a work of Wieviorka (1995: 45), who claims that universalism and relativism provide two logics of racism, and that they are always found in combination (see also Bernstein 1983). We should therefore seek the metaphysical picture that sustains them both. We should also be wary of accounts that employ these terms in opposition. Similarly, we need be wary of employing Euro-American common sense (color) in anything but an explicitly normative way.[4] For otherwise the investigation of cross-cultural color naming can be used to justify the inequality of lifeworlds on empirical, naturalistic grounds.

In this chapter I have attempted to show the religious and Cartesian sources of Locke's justification of color and how these sources not only undergird his discussion of empiricism in general, but are also taken over by his successors working in that tradition. To understand the origins of contemporary color science may help redress or dissolve some of these long-standing problems. C. S. Peirce's criticism of Helmholtz, for example, might also be applied to Locke. He said Helmholtz's theory of color and the materiality of the world was the "pet *petitio principii* of our time" – meaning that Helmholtz thoroughly presupposed what he set out to show (Kevelson 1996: 116). Fodor

(1981) has also noted that a careful reading of Locke on secondary qualities (color in particular) reveals empiricism and innatism to be one and the same. In other words, Locke was also involved in a *petitio principii*. Hacker (1987) suggests that Locke's *Essay* provides all the pieces of the game, which in all essentials is still being played on a board that differs little from that devised in the seventeenth century.

Since "being empirical" is at least part of the credo of most natural and social scientists, I should perhaps be more specific about what is and what is not being critiqued here. "Empiricist" refers to both theory and method. With regard to the theory, my critique has been of the tradition – the principal one – attributed to the "British Empiricists," and has argued that it has by now emancipated itself from the more dubious attendants at its birth in a time of internecine religious and civil conflict and of nascent empire, contrary to the general presumption. These attendants still lurk in the shadows and exercise a surprisingly strong influence. The critique is not – and could not be, the current is too broad – aimed at all "empiricist" theory. It is aimed neither, for example, at William James's "Radical Empiricism," nor at the "platitudinous empiricism" that "restricts itself to the observation that without perceptual experience we can have no knowledge of contingent matters of fact" (Brandom 2000: 23). With regard to methodology, the word "empirical" is often taken to mean little more than "seeing for oneself," as opposed to guessing, or accepting someone else's word. As such, it sounds thoroughly innocuous. But it is not unproblematic. We are always carrying theoretical baggage, which the ideology of "seeing for oneself" helps to hide. I have tried in this chapter to make it more visible. What could be a more unexceptionable empirical enterprise than surveying the color words in a large sample of the world's languages? Yet I hope that my brief history of this enterprise will have persuaded at least some readers that the title of the chapter is more than a pun. The extension of the argument into other domains of anthropology is left as an exercise for the student.

Notes

1   There are other kinds of empiricism, for example the radical empiricism of William James, which escapes much of the argument of this paper because of its anti-dualism. Brandom (2000: 24–5) says: "Classical empiricist philosophy of mind takes immediate perceptual experiences as the paradigm of awareness or consciousness . . . Empiricism attempts to understand the content of concepts in terms of the origin of empirical beliefs in experience that we just find ourselves with."

2   Bernstein (1983: 19) regards the struggle between universalism (or objectivism) and relativism as the great controversy of our time, but also sees it as needs to be superseded because the dichotomy is "misleading and distortive. . . . It is itself parasitic upon an acceptance of the Cartesian persuasion that needs to be questioned, exposed and overcome."

3   For example, Geiger (1871, 1872) and Magnus (1877a) presented the first empirically supported theories of the evolution of color semantics. In contrast, Virchow "tested" their thesis by examining Nubians brought to Germany in 1878 and 1879. Although they displayed "anomalies" of nomenclature, he claimed they were nonetheless able to discriminate

colors in all parts of "the spectrum." Using a method of questionnaire research, he concluded that all peoples differentially respond to the same colors/wavelengths as Europeans
do (1879: 130–1). Krause (1877) too claimed that color nomenclature is completely missing from "underdeveloped languages" while skepticism about discrimination capacities was
unwarranted. Magnus (1877b) agreed with Krause and when asked by the ethnologist Pechuël-
Loesche of the Ethnological Museum in Leipzig to contribute a large "questionnaire-
survey," he presented the evidence from 61 cultures (16 Amerindian, 25 African, 15 Asian,
three Australian, and two European) in which differential responses to color samples were
shown to be "the same" as those of Europeans, although reliable color semantics was absent
(Magnus 1880).

4   Peirce on perception (Bernstein 1964), Sellars on empiricism (1997), and Brandom on the
normativity of concepts (1994, 2000) are important resources here. See also Saunders and
Whittle (2004).

Acknowledgments

I would like to thank Paul Whittle, Charlotte Townsend-Gault, Jaap van Brakel, and Henrika
Kuklick for thoughtful comments on this chapter, although of course all opinions are my own.

Further Reading

Arneil, B. 1996. *John Locke and America*. Oxford: Clarendon Press.
Bernasconi, R. 2003. "Will the Real Kant Please Stand Up? The Challenge of Enlightenment
Racism to the Study of the History of Philosophy." *Radical Philosophy* 117:13–22.
Coulter, J. and E. D. Parsons. 1989. "The Praxiology of Perception: Visual Orientations and
Practical Action." *Inquiry* 33:251–72.
Ingold, T. 1993. "Evolutionary Models in the Social Sciences." *Cultural Dynamics* 4:239–50.
Wieviorka, M. 1995. *The Arena of Racism*. London: Sage.

8

Anthropology and the Classics

Robert Ackerman

Anthropology and classics as academic disciplines have had, and continue to maintain, an intermittent connection, one that is largely the result of their very different
histories and of the disparate movements and tendencies within each. In the West
classics is old (more than five hundred years), whereas anthropology as currently
understood, organized, and practiced is young (little more than a century).[1] Classics
requires a lengthy philological preparation before one can even begin to read with
comprehension and enjoyment, much less attain scholarly standing, whereas the professional apprenticeship in anthropology – fieldwork – is much less protracted and is
now beginning to be no longer compulsory. For centuries a classical education acted
as an explicit class marker, serving to differentiate those who shared a privileged social
background regardless of their actual knowledge of the classical world from those who
did not, whereas anthropology has from its start been both implicitly and explicitly
democratic, and at times even subversive, in its ideology and practice. Finally, because
until about 1940 virtually all educated men (and some women) in the West studied
Latin and Greek in school and often in university as well, if they later became interested in anthropology, they were able, if so inclined, to make informed comparisons
between classical antiquity and the contemporary world. Now that the study of Latin
and Greek no longer constitutes the armature of the school curriculum, and with
classics as a discipline distinctly marginalized within the university, anthropologists
who also know classics and ancient history are rare, which is to say that the influence
of anthropology is much more likely to be felt in classics than vice versa. Since the
1960s, classics has become increasingly permeable to ideas and methods derived from
other fields of study, including those of anthropology; classics is and always will remain
a special interest of only a handful of anthropologists.

Revising the Past

This chapter being a discussion of the relationship between the two disciplines, much
of what follows necessarily constitutes an episode in the history of both. The most

important sustained encounter between classics and anthropology in the English-speaking world took place mainly in Cambridge and Oxford between about 1875 and 1925, a time when a small number of classicists came to believe that anthropology held the key to a new way of realizing the dream of classical philology – "feeling their way into" the mindset of antiquity – and before anthropology had become the academic, professionalized pursuit it is today. To understand how this came to be, we must invoke, over and above the content of the educational curriculum, a number of large-scale cultural, political, and intellectual movements in the eighteenth and nineteenth centuries as context. The most immediate of these, for the scholars in question, was that their own field – classics – in the second half of the nineteenth century in Britain was nearly continuously embattled. The universities' classical faculties were engaged in a running series of skirmishes. Simplifying somewhat, one may say that on the one side were to be found those who saw the ancient texts essentially as linguistic constructions and therefore believed that the main – if not the only – thing necessary for scholarship was a thorough knowledge of the Greek and Latin languages. On the other side were those who accepted that knowledge of the languages was obviously necessary but just as obviously not sufficient, and that the ancient texts could and should be illuminated with light from without, by other disciplines. Over spirited resistance from the pure philologists, first ancient history and philosophy and then epigraphy (the study of inscriptions) and archaeology were successively introduced over the course of the later nineteenth century into the lectures and examinations at Oxford and Cambridge (Stray 1998). Anthropology, at the time thoroughly comparative and evolutionary, was the last of this series of "interloping" presences to enter the classical scene before World War I, and probably the most contentious.

Most classicists took exception to anthropologists' invasions into their intellectual territory; classicists generally believed that comparisons of the peoples and achievements of antiquity with those of the "savage" or "primitive" world were pointless (the two were thought to be essentially dissimilar and thus incomparable) and therefore both misleading and gratuitously demeaning to the ancients. After all, since the Renaissance it had been an article of cultural faith in the West that the Greeks and Romans, our presumed intellectual and spiritual ancestors, constituted miraculous exceptions to the acknowledged barbarism of the ancient world. Now, at the end of the nineteenth century, with ethnographic information pouring into the imperial capitals as an incidental by-product of the rush for empire among the European powers, this information, hitherto largely unavailable, came to be used to undercut the special status of antiquity. Instead of assuming the traditional focus on the "higher sphere" – the art, literature, and philosophy of Greece and Rome – some scholars were going so far as to claim that the beliefs and behavior of the peoples of classical antiquity were not at all unique. Instead, it was asserted, they in fact resembled those of two quite disparate groups who were linked by the fact that neither had yet managed to climb all the way up the ladder of mental evolution: (1) contemporary "savages," whose lives were being documented in detail by the increasing numbers of Western traders, missionaries, soldiers, and explorers resident among them, and (2) Western peasants who, insofar as they continued to live in illiteracy and superstition as they had for centuries, had to that extent not participated in modernity. In other words, the shining Greeks and Romans were, or could be seen as, less than ourselves and in that sense hardly fit to be timeless models of thought and behavior.[2]

Nowhere was this controversy more acute than in relation to the study of ancient religion and mythology. By the middle of the eighteenth century the Scottish philosopher David Hume had already asserted (in his essay "The Natural History of Religion") that religion was a human and not a divine institution, and therefore could and should be analyzed like any other man-made creation. On the Continent, since the 1690s the *philosophes* had mounted a sustained critique of Christianity as the repressive enemy of the unfettered life of the mind. Inasmuch as a frontal assault, at least in Catholic countries, was potentially dangerous for anyone daring to be too outspoken, many writers adopted the transparent device of discussing the beliefs and behavior of primitive peoples as surrogates for Christianity. Either such beliefs were likened to Christianity and then ridiculed, or else they were presented appreciatively as the product of an innate nobility of mind, with the implication that these barbarous nations had somehow managed to arrive at such higher sentiments on their own, without the intervention or guidance of any church. Thus the comparative study of religion had from the start a transparently polemic "edge." (See Strenski in this volume.)

This anti-clerical tendency received an immense impetus in mid-Victorian Britain with the appearance of *On The Origin of Species* in 1859. In a throwaway remark in the antepenultimate paragraph of the *Origin* that must rank among the great understatements in intellectual history, Charles Darwin commented that "much light will be thrown [by understanding evolution] on the origin of man and his history." Although Darwin himself abhorred religious disputation, the publication of the *Origin* caused an intellectual explosion in the 1860s and 1870s; it seemed as if every social and historical practice and institution cried out to be examined anew from the evolutionary point of view (Burrow 1966).

For our purposes the trail-blazer was Edward Burnett Tylor (1832–1917), whose provocatively titled book *Primitive Culture* appeared in 1871 ("provocative" because it had previously been assumed that by definition primitive peoples neither had nor could have any culture worthy of the name). Tylor reviewed the leading human institutions as the products of long evolutionary processes, but it is fair to say that his readers found the chapters on the origins and development of religion and mythology rather more absorbing than those on, say, agriculture and smelting. Educated Christians had been dealt a huge shock by evolution, so that any writer with something stirring or comforting to say on the great subjects of where we had come from, how we had arrived where we are, and where we might be heading was guaranteed a hearing. Indeed, during the last quarter of the nineteenth century readers were confronted by a flood of essays and books that divided into two distinct streams: those by authors who believed that because evolution was obviously the great law of life, religion was just as obviously an outworn stage in human development, to be discarded now that we had moved ahead to science; and those by authors who were unwilling or unable to jettison their faith and therefore attempted to rethink it defensively in the light of evolution.

Within this swirl of controversy the introduction of anthropology into classics came about indirectly, first through the work of William Robertson Smith (1846–94), the Scottish theologian and biblical scholar (Jones 2002). Smith, an intellectual prodigy, was by the age of 23 professor of Hebrew at the seminary run by his evangelical Protestant church, the Free Church of Scotland. Most unusually for someone from his background, he had studied theology in Germany, where he had encountered and embraced biblical criticism, the basic assumption of which was that the Bible we now have, far from being literally the inerrant Word of God, was in fact the result of a lengthy and complex redaction of a number of earlier documents and, thus, was amenable to the same kind of analytical close reading that had been developed over centuries of study of classical texts. Smith, also co-editor of the ninth edition of the *Encyclopaedia Britannica*, took it upon himself in the articles "Angel" and "Bible" to offer a survey of a century of this new way with a biblical text. Because most of his co-religionists in the Free Church had never even heard of biblical criticism, it is not surprising that some of them reacted with shock and horror to the idea that a man preparing their own sons for the ministry was undermining Scripture, and Smith became the defendant in the last significant heresy trials to take place in the British Isles. Although these concluded in a legal stalemate, in the end he had become too notorious for Scotland and accordingly migrated south in 1884 to England, where he became professor of Arabic at Cambridge. There he met and befriended a somewhat younger fellow Scot, also a son of the Free Church, James George Frazer (1854–1941) (Ackerman 1987). Frazer, a brilliant classical fellow of Trinity College, was then searching for a project in which he might immerse himself and by which he might make his name in the scholarly world; for his part, in his capacity as editor Smith was always looking for able contributors. In those days the encyclopedia was published one volume at a time, as completed, so by 1884 Smith had already reached the letter "P". Thus it was that he came to entrust the major articles on "Taboo" and "Totemism" to Frazer. Frazer never looked back. Although he would never abandon pure classical scholarship, in the future he applied himself only to those writers and texts from antiquity that were amenable to anthropological treatment. Indeed, he would become the first person anywhere to occupy a chair of Social Anthropology, in the University of Liverpool in 1908.[3]

Anthropology Emergent

When he met Smith, Frazer had just embarked upon a translation of and commentary on Pausanias, a Greek traveler of the second century CE whose description of "the glory that was Greece" before it was devastated by earthquake and conquest is the most complete that has come down to us. As well as offering descriptions of art and architecture, Pausanias was something of an amateur ethnographer himself, with a special interest in customs and beliefs that persisted in the countryside long after they had died out in Athens. The combination of Pausanias's own folkloristic curiosity and the extensive comparative reading he had done in preparation for the encyclopedia articles convinced Frazer that his new interest in anthropology was not only worthwhile in itself, but would shed light on the classical text, light that was indeed available from no other source. Specifically, as opposed to the worship of the shining Olympian sky-gods we read of in Homer, the Greek rustics encountered by Pausanias seemed mainly to engage in making sacrifices to mysterious subterranean and often malicious beings in order to mollify and thus divert them from carrying out mischief or worse; and as such their superstitious behavior seemed to resemble that of the "savages" described by modern explorers and missionaries and of the benighted peasants who still populated much of the European countryside.

Having come to this conclusion, in 1888 Frazer put Pausanias aside temporarily to write a book whose subject was a curious rite that, we are told, took place in a certain grove at Nemi, outside (ancient) Rome. According to the account by the Roman commentator Servius, if a runaway slave managed to reach the grove, he could remain there until challenged in combat by the next runaway; if the new arrival defeated the former "king of the grove," he would then reign in his place until the next challenge, and so on. Over the next 25 years this book, *The Golden Bough*, would undergo an immense expansion (from two volumes in 1890 to three in 1900 and no fewer than 12 volumes in 1911–15), and would even become (in the one-volume abridgement that Frazer himself prepared) what might be called the first anthropological bestseller; even more remarkably, it remains in print today. Although in its final form the work left the strange goings-on at Nemi far behind and went on to present an encyclopedic survey of the ritual and mythology of the entire "primitive" world, its basic thesis changed little. Frazer accepted Tylor's claim that evolution was to be found as much in our mental and spiritual lives as in the material products of our industries and institutions. Unlike Tylor, Frazer was interested exclusively in the development of the mind, and saw this evolution as passing through three distinct, sequential stages, which he characterized by the worldview that they allegedly embodied: the first was *magic*, in which priests believed they could compel the gods to do their bidding by offering a quid pro quo in the form of animal sacrifice; magic yielded to *religion*, once the priests and the community, having regretfully accepted that they were unable to compel the gods to do anything, prostrated themselves and beseeched the divine powers by means of prayer and sacrifice to aid feeble humanity; and, finally, we arrive at positive *science*, by means of which, having understood and accepted our true position in the (godless) universe, we rational beings can put behind us the fear and trembling arising from foolish notions that had survived from earlier times.

Insofar as mythology was concerned, Tylor (the son of a Quaker family, and perhaps for that reason not disposed to value ritual very highly) then proceeded reductively to equate ancient religion with its beliefs, or mythology, which then was dismissed essentially because it was *mistaken*. That is, Tylor understood mythology as an attempt on the part of superior minds in antiquity to make sense of the world; therefore, like any other product of human reasoning, it was either true or false and could and should be judged accordingly. As Tylor put it in the first manual in English on the subject, *Anthropology* (1881), "Myth is not to be looked on as mere error and folly, but as an interesting product of the human mind. It is sham history, the fictitious narrative of events that never happened" (Tylor 1881: 387).

For better and for worse, however, theoretical consistency never was Frazer's strong point, so at the same time that he accepted Tylor's stern rationalism he also appropriated (without any sense of contradiction) an idea of a quite different kind from his friend and mentor Robertson Smith – that in the religions of antiquity (and unlike Christianity), the creed seems to have been essentially nonexistent. Instead, the important thing was what the worshipers *did* rather than what they *believed*. As Smith put it in his great work, *The Religion of the Semites*,

> This being so, it follows that mythology ought not to take the prominent place that is assigned to it in the scientific study of ancient faiths. So far as myths consist of explanations of ritual, their value is altogether secondary, and it may be affirmed with confidence that in almost every case the myth was derived from the ritual, and not the ritual from the myth; for the ritual was fixed and the myth was variable, the ritual was obligatory and faith in the myth was at the discretion of the worshipper. (1889: 18)

Both these explanations of the genesis and nature of myth and its relation to ritual, along with a third, euhemerism (the idea that the gods originally were real people who once lived heroic lives and that myth is therefore history distorted and enhanced by imagination), jostle uneasily within *The Golden Bough*. Smith's idea (known as "ritualism") would become important to the next wave of anthropologically inclined classical scholars, on whom more below.

Frazer more or less single-handedly created the audience for anthropology among educated readers. It is not hard to see why. He began with the advantage of a subject guaranteed to hold his audience (that is, the origin and meaning of ancient religion and its presumed relation to Christianity), presented it in a highly polished, literary style, and brought to it the industry and erudition traditionally associated with a German savant, as evidenced by the numerous footnotes to be found on every page. Notwithstanding these thickets of notes, which are supposed to stand for and guarantee an objective or "scientific" method, it was not difficult to discern a secularist agenda (Ackerman 1998). At the literal heart of the 12-volume edition of *The Golden Bough* lies a lengthy analysis of the cults of Attis, Adonis, Osiris, and Dionysus, all of them (in Frazer's view at least – modern scholars would disagree about Osiris) dying-and-reviving vegetation gods that characterized the religions of the ancient eastern Mediterranean. Although not a word was said about Jesus of Nazareth, only the slowest reader could fail to notice the missing member of this geographically contiguous set. If Attis, Adonis, and the others were examples of either plain ignorance or of an imperfect understanding of the natural cycle of birth, growth, death, and rebirth, what then was Jesus, and what, therefore, was Christianity? The anti-religious message got through, and the files of Trinity College Cambridge contain many letters to Frazer from readers otherwise unknown to him who thank him for stripping away the mystification surrounding religion and permitting them to see it for the worn-out thing that it was. Despite the near-total eclipse of Frazer's reputation among anthropologists today, he and H. G. Wells must rank as the most important advocates of secularism in the English-speaking world in the twentieth century.

Classicists Resistant

At the turn of the last century Frazer succeeded in demonstrating that anthropology had something useful and important to offer classics, but that message was not greeted with enthusiasm by the great majority of his classical colleagues. To understand this negative reaction, consider for a moment the situation of an Oxbridge classical don around 1900: such a person would have devoted his entire life to acquiring a thorough knowledge of the Greek and Latin languages, and of classical antiquity generally, only to be faced suddenly with an assertion that his preparation was sadly incomplete and that he had now to absorb and make sense of great quantities of new and literally outlandish anthropological data.

One should not dismiss such resistance as mere scholarly irritability or fatigue. So far as classical antiquity was concerned, Frazer's evolutionary epistemological perspective created a serious intellectual problem. An exclusive focus on the long march of humanity up toward the light of rationality will necessarily tend to de-emphasize or blur the special quality of the Greek experience. In this sense, the seemingly objective and therefore "scientific" comparative method was thus inherently biased in that the more advanced was being compared with the less advanced, so that the reader was always being informed about the "primitive" aspect of life in Greece rather than the "enlightened" dimension of life in Africa. Everyone would agree that it is indeed interesting to adduce "parallels" to Greek myth and ritual from, say, Polynesia. But such data become true parallels only when one has already made the crucial assumption that the human mind operates in a similar fashion everywhere regardless of history or geography and therefore has evolved everywhere in the same way, so that Athenians and Apaches are, therefore, comparable in the first place (Ackerman and Calder 1978). This argument seemed to most classicists to assume that which had to be proved, and as a result they were disinclined to give it serious consideration. (Most still are today.)

Even if customs and beliefs did indeed resemble one another among the most geographically and culturally disparate nations and peoples, for the comparisons to be apposite classicists demanded evidence that the evolutionary paths taken by prehistoric Greeks and, say, Polynesians or Africans were indeed identical, and of course none was forthcoming because none existed. If, like Frazer, one believed that like actions bespeak like intentions, one might then read backward from actions to the attitudes purportedly behind them and conclude that one had somehow reconstructed the mental outlook of the ancient world, but this was all excessively speculative. There was nothing in any of this chain of reasoning (or guesswork) that scholars devoted to text would accept as "hard" evidence. Nor was this hostility a manifestation of the particularly embattled situation of British classics; the vast majority of scholars in Germany, the undeniable center of classical studies before World War I, were likewise unmoved by the light that anthropology purported to shine on classical antiquity. Thus Ulrich von Wilamowitz-Moellendorff, at the turn of the twentieth century acknowledged by all as the premier classical scholar in the world, in a letter to Gilbert Murray on September 17, 1912: "The whole modern tendency seems to me to try to explain the adult man from the life of the embryo. It does not interest me much how Hecuba's grandmother felt; nor Plato's for that matter. She was only an old woman and her faith was a hag's" (Beierl et al. 1991: 4).

Starting with the publication of the second edition of *The Golden Bough* in 1900, Frazer's reputation began a long decline. Most of his anthropological contemporaries demurred at what they regarded as his arbitrary definitions of the key terms "magic" and "religion" and the rigidity of his pattern of mental evolution. Classicists continued to esteem his purely classical work, such as the commentary on Pausanias (and later the editions of Apollodorus and Ovid), but also continued to object that the emphasis on the long sweep of evolution devalued the Greek achievement. Even as he came increasingly to be seen as irrelevant by most of his professional peers, however, his popularity with the educated lay audience grew, and *The Golden Bough* in its full 12-volume majesty as well as the one-volume abridgement that he prepared, as well as later books such as *Folk-Lore in the Old Testament*, commanded attention and respect throughout the 1920s and later. (Readers of T. S. Eliot's 1922 *The Waste Land* will recall his assertion, in a note, that his diagnosis of the postwar malaise could be understood only by those thoroughly familiar with *The Golden Bough*.)

Frazer revered facts for their own sake and hoped that his work would survive as a storehouse of data even after his speculations had been discarded (1900: xv–xvi). Although he was appropriately skeptical about his sources, and certainly held some of his informants in much higher esteem than others, in the end he was confident, or at least hopeful, that the "facts" on which he based his suppositions were accurate and, as such, could be thought of as hard, unchanging pebbles of reality. He was undone by his lack of awareness (which he shared with most of his contemporaries) that they instead represented the replies to specific questions that were imbued by the particular interests and prejudices of those asking and reporting them. But it is unfair for us to criticize him for lacking our own critical sophistication. In his own time, it was not his methodological naïveté that undid him. Rather, it was the inadequacy of his psychology and sociology that caused other anthropologically inclined British classicists to look elsewhere for intellectual models.

Blurring Disciplinary Boundaries

The most important of these, known as the Cambridge Ritualist Anthropologists, or Ritualists for short, so called even though one of them (Murray) was at Oxford for most of his career, were Jane Ellen Harrison (1850–1928), Gilbert Murray (1866–1957), Francis Macdonald Cornford (1874–1943), and Arthur Bernard Cook (1868–1952). Although none of them was a literary critic per se, as a group they received their name because in the decade before World War I they asserted, most controversially, that prehistoric Dionysian fertility rituals provided the structural models for Greek drama. To do so they revived and developed Robertson Smith's theory of the primacy of ritual over myth, to which they added a generous admixture from Frazer on Dionysus and his fellow gods of the Mediterranean and from the work of the Continental theorists to be mentioned below.

It should be said, however, that no bright line of demarcation exists between Tylor and Frazer on the one hand and the Ritualists on the other. The Ritualists never ceased to quarry facts from both Tylor and Frazer and agreed with them as well on the importance of evolution and on the value of the comparative method.[4] They were nonetheless dissatisfied with Tylor and Frazer's old-fashioned associationist psychology, which regarded the mind as *tabula rasa*, an entity registering passively and responding mechanically to stimuli that impinged from the outside world, and their individualist sociology, which saw society as an assemblage of discrete rational social atoms acting essentially out of self-interest. For these reasons the Ritualists looked to the Continent for social theory.

The sociology of Émile Durkheim, Henri Hubert, and Marcel Mauss, which emphasized the importance of collective action over individual thought among the "primitives"; the ethnographer and folklorist Arnold van Gennep and his seminal idea of "rites of passage"; and the philosophical "depth" psychology of Friedrich Nietzsche, Henri Bergson, and Sigmund Freud, which asserted that preconscious and unconscious states were as significant as conscious ones, seemed to offer a theory of society and of mind that more adequately described the complexities of human life, both ancient and modern. This conflict should not be confused with the friction that is ever present between successive intellectual generations; from the perspective of a century later, the differences between Tylor and Frazer on the one hand and the Cambridge Ritualists on the other exemplify a shift away from what might be termed the "normal" British positivism of the nineteenth century toward a vitalism and irrationalism that was burgeoning all across Europe at the turn of the twentieth century (Annan 1959; Whyte 1960).

Objections could be raised to calling any of those writers an anthropologist; nonetheless, the Ritualists drew upon them, and all of them had much to say explicitly about "primitive" society and culture. Indeed, Durkheim, Hubert, and Mauss based a number of important books and essays on the descriptions of Australian Aboriginal life that had recently been published by Frazer's great friends W. Baldwin Spencer and F. J. Gillen; Freud used Frazer as his anthropological source in his meta-psychological fantasy *Totem und Tabu* (1913); the all-important concept of *durée*, the "ground of being" too deep for words against which all life is played out, in Bergson's seminal work *L'évolution créatrice* (1907), had a crucial effect on Jane Harrison's later understanding of Greek religion; and Nietzsche's *Die Geburt der Tragödie* (1872) is a direct attempt to "feel his way" in the best romantic fashion into the mind and soul of ancient Greece and thus to intuit directly the origins of tragedy.

At the heart of the Cambridge Ritualists stands the remarkable figure of Jane Ellen Harrison, the first British female classical scholar to attain an international reputation, and as such worthy of some comment in her own right. It was she who brought the others together and collaborated most closely with them, and it was she who acted as their intellectual leader. Educated first at Cheltenham Ladies College, in 1875 she entered the newly opened Newnham College, Cambridge, and thus became a member of the first generation of women to receive a university education in Britain. After an outstanding undergraduate career, she moved to London, supporting herself by writing and lecturing on classical subjects (with some assistance from a family income). She studied Greek vases during visits to museums in Britain and on the Continent and began to publish scholarly articles, gradually making a name for herself in a field with probably the highest intellectual standards of any in the academy (Stewart 1959; Beard 2001; Robinson 2002). Twice rejected for a chair at University College London (Calder 1991), in 1898 she returned to Newnham as its first research fellow. There she produced the body of work that made her the controversial figure that she remains today. She left Cambridge and classical studies in 1922, spending most of the last six years of her life in Paris in the company of one of her former students.

She began her academic career as an art historian, celebrating, in what was then the conventional manner, the idealizing tendency in Greek vase painting. Her "deconversion" from idealism occurred in 1888, when she traveled to Greece for the first time and, peering into the diggers' trenches in the company of Wilhelm Dörpfeld, the leading German archaeologist in Athens, saw for herself how closely and directly Greek vase art reflected and incorporated daily life. It is worth noting that this experience could not have taken place many years earlier, for it was only in the 1880s that the excavation of classical sites in Greece in general, and Athens in particular, got underway in a large-scale organized fashion, with the Germans leading the effort. Two years later, in 1890, in the section on mythology in *Mythology and Monuments of Ancient Athens*, the guidebook that she wrote along with her friend Margaret Verrall, her experience in Greece still plainly resonates. There we find her writing:

> I have tried everywhere to get at, where possible, the cult as the explanation of the legend. My belief is that in many, even in the large majority of cases, *ritual practice misunderstood* explains the elaboration of myth. . . . Some of the loveliest stories the Greeks have left us will be seen to have taken their rise, not in poetic imagination, but in primitive, often savage, and I think, always practical ritual. (iii; italics in original)

It is not known whether she had already read Smith's *Religion of the Semites*, which had appeared in the previous year. Regardless, by 1890 she had turned away from her earlier admiration for the ideal and was already predisposed toward the primitive.

Although the Ritualists as a group wrote many books, by general agreement the two that have lasted, and the two most relevant here as bearing the impress of anthropology, are Jane Harrison's *Prolegomena to the Study of Greek Religion* (1903) and *Themis* (1912). As the title implies, Harrison intended *Prolegomena* as a first installment in her effort to discover how the Greeks arrived at their religious ideas; those who read it, having been prepared by *The Golden Bough* to accept that the shining Greeks were really much more "primitive" than had earlier been believed, would have been immediately struck by differences from, as well as similarities to, Frazer's work. Because

Harrison was always visually oriented – expectable in light of her professional origins as an art historian and archaeologist – her books are filled with illustrations and references to vases and other archaeological finds. By contrast, Frazer, whose many volumes contain not a single illustration (except for the frontispiece, Turner's picture of "The Golden Bough"), is content merely to mention archaeology in his footnotes. Frazer was certainly aware of what the archaeologists were discovering, but the absence of illustrations is of a piece with his overall intellectualist orientation to what the ancients might have been thinking rather than what they made and did. Likewise Harrison's style is much less elaborately literary and much more personal than Frazer's; unlike him, she is unafraid of the pronoun "I," with all the possibilities for subjectivity and vulnerability that implies.

Fortunately, the book's complex argument does not require complete recapitulation for its qualities to be appreciated. Following other scholars, Harrison begins with the distinction between two forms of Greek ritual, the Olympian and the chthonic ("of the earth"). The Olympian layer represents the ritual of an invading people who have superimposed their ideas and observances on the chthonic – the indigenous, subjugated population. The Olympian rites are sunny and optimistic whereas the "rites of the lower stratum are characterized by a deep and constant sense of evil to be removed and of the need of purification for its removal; that the means of purification are primitive and mainly magical nowise affects this religious content" (1903: ix).

Since Harrison's aim is to get behind, or beneath, the Olympian layer, she turns to the festivals because, as Smith had observed, ancient communities prized correct observance over purity of doctrine and as a result festivals changed slowly, if at all. Each of the three chapters at the heart of *Prolegomena* is thus devoted to an analysis of the origin and meaning of a major festival. From the start, Harrison's focus is on the community and its collective religious activity in ancient Greece rather than, as in Frazer, on the importance of the individual thinker within the overall reconstruction of the evolution of the human mind, regardless of time, place, and social circumstance. Her emphasis, as befits a reader of Robertson Smith, is on the sacrifices that constituted the festival's core. These she finds were not tendered to any member of the Homeric pantheon, but instead to what seem to us to be vague ghosts and local demons. The purpose of the book, then, is to trace the all-important step from "demonology to theology, from the sprite and ghost to the human and humane god" (1903: x).

This close reading of the festivals was ground-breaking, and *Prolegomena* was immediately recognized as important. However, at that point in her career Harrison lacked a theoretical way of relating her convincing demonstration of the Olympian overlay on the chthonic substratum to the rest of Greek life. She offered an evolutionary series of stages in what might be termed "the making of a god," but she still needed a social psychology to explain why her account was plausible. She found this when she read Bergson and Durkheim, around 1907 or 1908. Then, the missing pieces fell into place, and she was ready to write *Themis*.

Émile Durkheim, like Robertson Smith, understood primitive religion as essentially collective rather than individual in nature, and as traditional and (in a closed society) obligatory. As already noted, Robertson Smith had offered a sociological analysis of (Semitic) religion, that is, he began with the assumption that it arose from the nature and structure of society itself. From Smith, Durkheim took several other leading ideas: that primitive religion was a clan cult and that the cult was totemic; that the god was the clan itself divinized; and that totemism was the most elementary or primitive, and in that sense original, form of religion known to us. Durkheim analyzed religion as a symbolic system and saw it as an integrated series of "collective representations," his term for ideas shared by the whole of society. These representations are the concrete manifestations of a primitive people's faith in the power that orders the world and maintains it as it ought to be, which is to say the social order itself. Whatever ideas (theology) the primitives have are secondary to the rites that in fact create religious consciousness.

Although Durkheim today is revered as one of the founders of modern sociology and anthropology, Henri Bergson, at least in the English-speaking world, has been largely forgotten, so a word about his concept of *durée* may be in order. Jane Harrison called *L'évolution créatrice*, which she read upon its publication in 1907, one of the three epoch-making books in her lifetime – the others being Aristotle's *Ethics* and Freud's *Totem und Tabu* (1925: 80). Bergson had a direct effect on *Themis* because *L'évolution créatrice* answered a question that had been troubling her for some time. In the introduction to *Themis* she explains that her discontent with the Olympians, which had been growing for a long time, finally began to come clear:

> I saw in a word that Dionysos, with every other mystery-god, was an instinctive attempt to express what Professor Bergson calls *durée*, that life which is one, indivisible and yet ceaselessly changing. I saw on the other hand that the Olympians . . . are not an intuitive expression, but a late and conscious representation, a work of analysis, of reflection and intelligence. Primitive religion was not, as I had drifted into thinking, a tissue of errors leading to mistaken conduct: rather it is a web of practices emphasizing particular parts of life, issuing necessarily in representations and ultimately dying out in abstract conceptions. (1912: xii)

Since the seventeenth century innumerable Western thinkers have speculated about the murky origins of civil society and the consciousness of the earliest humans. Frazer stood in the Enlightenment line of those who were certain that, with the exception of a few choice intellects, the minds of our earliest ancestors were compounds of ignorance and confusion. In contrast, Harrison, Murray, and Cornford, while acknowledging the barbaric aspects of the "primitive" Greece they were describing, intermittently displayed a romantic sympathy for a period when, it seemed, the corrosive, alienating effects of modern self-consciousness were not manifest. Lest it be thought that this sentiment was simply a projection of Jane Harrison's own personality, here are three sentences by Gilbert Murray, in 1897 (before he had met Harrison) on the nature of the gods in Euripides' *Bacchae*:

> Reason is great, but it is not everything. There are in the world things not of reason, but both above and below it; causes of emotion, which we cannot express, which we tend

to worship, which we feel, perhaps to be the precious elements in life. These things are God or forms of God: not fabulous immortal men, but "Things which Are," things utterly non-human and non-moral, which bring man bliss or tear his life to shreds without a break in their own serenity. (272)

There is a great deal more to *Themis* – most notably, the claim that the structure of Greek tragedy arises directly from the form of prehistoric Dionysian ritual, a claim that has been generally dismissed by classicists but had a considerable effect on post-classical literary criticism in the English-speaking world in the first half of the twentieth century (Ackerman 1991a). But space does not permit a fuller exposition here, and enough has been said to offer a sense of the kinds of uses to which anthropology was put by that pioneering generation of scholars.

For the sake of completeness, the narrative is quickly brought to a close. In 1913, Jane Harrison felt as though she and her colleagues were riding a great wave that was cresting all over Europe. As she saw it, the old rationalist worldview was breaking down and large areas of irrational experience that had long been ignored were belatedly being acknowledged (Harrison was one of the earliest partisans of Freud in Britain). In the next year, World War I broke out, and everything she expected and hoped for was at once swept away. Classical studies, anthropology, and the rest of academic life came to a near-halt as scholars in many countries were conscripted into the service of the competing powers.

Disciplinary Differentiation

When the war ended, four years later, the intellectual landscape was no longer recognizable. The collapse of Germany meant, among other things, that classical study suffered dramatically. Anthropology, meanwhile, had undergone a methodological revolution because prolonged fieldwork, which was partly an unplanned result of Bronislaw Malinowski's having been stranded in Australia at the outbreak of war, soon made Frazerian library anthropology seem irrelevant. Moreover, postwar anthropologists became much less interested in contending with classical scholars about the speculative prehistory of Greek religion when numerous existing "primitive" societies cried out for description and analysis.

On the classical side, the Ritualists themselves changed the focus of their work. Harrison forsook Greek entirely, learned Russian, and moved to Paris. Murray, who always felt uncomfortable with the primitive, remained an evangelist for "higher" classical culture by writing and lecturing to those who lacked Greek, and gained an international reputation as an advocate of the League of Nations. Cornford turned to the study of Plato and the pre-Socratic philosophers. A few younger classicists enrolled, more or less, under the Ritualist banner, but for most scholars then, and now, Ritualism was regarded as having had its moment, which had passed. The eminent ancient historian M. I. Finley voiced the consensus in 1966 when, in an issue of the *Times Literary Supplement* devoted to classics, he advised classicists to raise their eyes from the page and *en passant* assessed the value of anthropology for classics as follows: "We all know the standard retort: look at the mess Jane Harrison and even Cornford got into, playing about with Frazer. Let's have no more of that. Indeed not, but Frazer was neither the alpha nor the omega of sociology."

Between the 1920s and the 1950s the connection between classics and anthropology was distinctly on the wane. With a few exceptions (such as George Thomson's *Aeschylus and Athens* [1941]), the energy supplied by the Ritualist episode had dissipated. The turning point for modern classical scholarship was undoubtedly the publication of E. R. Dodds' seminal book, *The Greeks and the Irrational* (1951), followed by the advent of Lévi-Straussian structuralism in Britain in the 1960s, which served to revive the anthropological connection in Anglophone classics, most notably in the work of Geoffrey Kirk (1970). Indeed, for classics, the second half of the twentieth century resembles that of the nineteenth in that in both periods the discipline has demonstrated a continuous permeability to outside ideas and methods. The Cambridge Ritualists were the beneficiaries of ancient history and evolutionary anthropology, but contemporary classicists are able to choose from a longer and more varied menu: structuralism and poststructuralism, Marxism, semiotics, feminism, and "cultural theory." There can be little doubt that for classics, at any rate, anthropology over the past hundred years has been a source of continuing intellectual energy and ferment.

Notes

1 Although anthropology as a distinct field of study within the university is only about a hundred years old, over the last two millennia there have been innumerable travelers and antiquarians with genuine ethnographic interests, and likewise there have been many formal and informal societies and associations devoted to the collection and study of the lore of the "lower" nations. Indeed, the historian Herodotus (fifth century BCE) has often been called the "father" of anthropology. See Liebersohn in this volume.

2 Thus Gilbert Murray (1897: xi): "There is more flesh and blood in the Greek of the anthropologist, the foster-brother of Kaffirs and Hairy Ainos. He is at least human and simple and emotional, and free from irrelevant trappings. His fault, of course, is that he is not the man we want, but only the raw material out of which that man was formed: a Hellene without the beauty, without the spiritual life, without the Hellenism."

3 Almost as soon as Frazer arrived in Liverpool he realized that he had made a mistake in accepting the chair. He was in residence for only five months (April through September 1908) and completed and delivered only his inaugural lecture, *The Scope of Social Anthropology* (London: Macmillan, 1909). He resigned the chair in 1922.

4 In 1909 Cambridge University Press brought out *Darwin and Modern Science*, commemorating the fiftieth anniversary of the publication of *On The Origin of Species*. Jane Harrison, opening her chapter on "The Influence of Darwinism on the Study of Religion," exclaimed, "The title of my paper might well have been 'The Creation by Darwinism of the Scientific Study of Religion' but that I feared to mar my tribute to a great name by any shadow of exaggeration" (Harrison 1909: 494).

Further Reading

Jenkyns, Richard. 1980. *The Victorians and Ancient Greece*. Cambridge, MA: Harvard University Press.

Kuklick, Henrika. 1991. *The Savage Within: The Social History of British Anthropology, 1885–1945*. New York: Cambridge University Press.

Stocking, Jr., George W. 1987. *Victorian Anthropology*. New York: Free Press.

Stocking, Jr., George W. 1995. *After Tylor*. Madison: University of Wisconsin Press.

Stray, Christopher. 1998. *Classics Transformed*. Oxford: Clarendon Press.

Part III

Neglected Pasts

9

Anthropology on the Periphery: The Early Schools of Nordic Anthropology

Christer Lindberg

Introduction: From the Periphery

The contributions of figures in the Nordic states are occasionally included in historical accounts of the formative years of anthropology. The Danish museum curator Christian J. Thomsen is recognized for his influence on museology, and especially for his stone-, bronze- and iron-age typology. The travels in Mexico and Australia of the Norwegian Carl Lumholtz are noted, and the Swedish Hjalmar Stolpe is acclaimed for his archaeological work and his studies of primitive art. Lately, thanks to the research of curators Staffan Brunius at the Ethnographical Museum in Stockholm and David R. Watters and Oscar Fonseca Zamora of the Carnegie Museum of Natural History, credit has also been given to Carl V. Hartman for his archaeological excavations in Costa Rica, as well as for his role as the quintessential museum anthropologist at the Carnegie in the early 1900s (Brunius 1984; Watters and Zamora 2002).

Nevertheless, there has never been proper recognition of two important anthropological schools based in the Nordic periphery: the Finnish Westermarck school and the Swedish Nordenskiöld school. Historians of American, British, or French anthropology may make occasional, casual references to the two schools, but historians rarely suggest that Nordic anthropologists had any major impact on their American, British, or French counterparts. Indeed, over time, knowledge of Nordic anthropologists' contributions to their discipline in its formative years has diminished. In part, historians' neglect of the Westermarck and Nordenskiöld schools is a product of the fact that American and British authors dominate the field of historical writing. In addition, recent Swedish and Finnish anthropologists have tended to identify British social anthropologists as their intellectual ancestors, rather than Nordenskiöld or Westermarck. Historical memory is now being recovered in Finland; following the decline in influence there of Parsonian sociology and Geertzian interpretative anthropology, Westermarck has resurfaced in anthropologists' discussions (Suolinna 1993: 43). In

Sweden, however, where a fundamental split between ethnographic museums and universities occurred in the 1960s, social anthropologists routinely dismiss the Nordenskiöld school as "old museum stuff."

The Westermarck School

In the *International Dictionary of Anthropologists*, Timothy Stroup gives the impression that there never was a Westermarck school, indicating that Edward Westermarck (1862–1939) had no recognized group of followers (1991: 749–50). Yet Westermarck was well placed to gather followers. He was appointed professor of moral philosophy in Helsinki in 1906, and in the following year became professor of sociology at the London School of Economics. In 1926–7, his international reputation encouraged both Helsinki and Turku to create departments of sociology. A number of scholars have recognized the influence of his biologically based conception of social behavior on Malinowski's version of functionalism, but historians have paid little attention to Westermarck's pioneering work as a fieldworker, who did field-based studies in Morocco. Moreover, in Finland Westermarck trained a group of young students whose research was field-based, a contribution that is rarely acknowledged outside Finland and Sweden. In addition to Westermarck himself, three of his students – Gunnar Landtman, Rafael Karsten and Hilma Granqvist – were prominent anthropologists. Together, members of the Westermarck school made some important international contributions to the fields of anthropology, sociology, comparative religion, and philosophy, especially in the 1910s and 1920s.

As is well known, Westermarck and C. G. Seligman were Malinowski's mentors at the London School of Economics. Perhaps Numelin (1947: 89, 138) was being somewhat Finnocentric when he identified Malinowski as more Westermarck's student than Seligman's. In any case, Malinowski repeatedly expressed his gratitude to Westermarck. In one letter to Westermarck, he wrote "how deeply grateful I am for all you have done in the past; for your initial help when I was quite alone and unbefriended in London; for your advice and assistance in bringing out my book and most of all for your personal friendship in which you have honoured me. I am very conservative in my friendship and I value yours very highly for many reasons, not the least because our scientific and general ideas and aims are very much in harmony" (ÅAB: 07/18/1921). Furthermore, Malinowski had reason to thank Westermarck for helping to secure him a position at the London School of Economics (ÅAB: 11/28/1921).

Edward Westermarck was a man of sparkling intellect and critical mind, well read in English, French, and German literature, politically outspoken, with strong anti-Tsarist views – and a man who had the courage to stand up for his ideas. He was a great humanist, whose consistently strong evolutionist perspective must not be confounded with social Darwinism. Throughout his scholarly career, Westermarck stressed the close relationship between nature and culture. This was the central idea in his studies of marriage and family life, in his works on religion, and in his philosophy of morality and emotions. In his *magnum opus*, a revised version of his doctoral thesis, *The History of Human Marriage* (1891), he rejected earlier anthropologists' models of the evolution of family structure, opposing the arguments of such persons as Bachofen, McLennan, and Morgan, who had hypothesized that early humans were promiscuous. To the contrary, Westermarck argued, the family consisting of mother, father, and child must have existed in the very earliest times of humankind. Classifying empirical data to formulate types of marital forms such as monogamy, polygamy, group marriage, marriage by capture, and so on, he showed that similar social forms of marriage existed in very different social and cultural environments, concluding that similarities were to be explained in biological terms (Allardt 2000: 300). Because of human biological character, marriage was a universal social institution: it was required by the growing child's need for prolonged protection by its mother and father. The conclusion of *The History of Human Marriage* was an analysis of early humans' various means for regulating sexuality, which involved an extensive discussion of the incest taboo. Westermarck's explanation of the basis of this taboo, which became known as the "Westermarck effect," suggested that exogamic rules in many societies were not based on kinship per se, but were related to the degree of proximity in which children had grown up together – an argument that he was to repeat in subsequent works.

Another of Westermarck's controversial assertions was his claim that moral judgments are based on emotions, not intellectual rationality, an argument that received its fullest treatment in his provocative *Ethical Relativity* (1932). He found the origin of morality in language, and tried to show that morality moved toward a central position in human culture through biological evolution. He maintained that it was foolish for the social scientist to attempt to determine whether a moral judgment was true or not true. Research in sociology and social anthropology (the latter of which he defined as a branch of the former [e.g., 1936]), was undertaken to reveal the causes and purposes of social phenomena.

In a letter A. C. Haddon wrote to Westermarck (ÅAB 07/20/1908), Haddon insisted on the need for "the intensive study of limited areas" in order to learn ". . . the conditions of existences of a given people – how the environment affects them, how they react on it. But above all we need an accurate and exhaustive study of the psychology, sociology and religion of the people studied." Westermarck was indeed an empiricist, following the Finnish history tradition, and he was certainly a pioneer in the "intensive study of limited areas." In 1898, Westermarck traveled via Spain to Morocco, from which he intended to travel further toward more remote fields. Instead, he decided that Morocco was an ideal fieldwork site; not only was it within easy reach of Europe, but it also was virtually unexplored by anthropologists, and had been untouched by modern civilization (1936). Over the years, Westermarck was to return to Morocco repeatedly. He came to study wedding ceremonies, as well as conceptions of holiness (*baraka*), the evil eye, and evil spirits among the Berber tribes of central and northern Morocco. In 1900, he returned for a period of protracted fieldwork, spending two years and two months in Morocco, and subsequently returned at regular intervals until the outbreak of World War I. In 1923, he was back for a period of intensive work that resulted in the completion of *Ritual and Belief in Morocco* (1926) and *Wit and Wisdom in Morocco* (1930). During his later visits to Morocco, he was stationed in his villa Tusculum on the outskirts of Tangier, working with his key informant, Abdessalam El-Baqqali (Suolinna 1997: 264–5).

Indeed, Westermarck has not been appropriately credited for his articulation and application of the standards of field methodology that have often been assumed to have been pioneered by Malinowski. "Prior to Malinowski doing his fieldwork, Westermarck emphasized the importance of learning the local languages and of getting thoroughly acquainted with the environment, in which one did research" (Suolinna 1997: 276). Judging from Malinowski's *A Diary in the Strict Sense of the Term* (1967), one can surely say that Westermarck enjoyed his fieldwork more than Malinowski did.

Westermarck's student Rafael Karsten was also a pioneering fieldworker. Under severe hardships, Karsten did long periods of field research in South America, making his first field trip to the Gran Chaco area in the Bolivian–Argentine borderland in 1911. He spent over two and a half years in the Amazonian region of eastern Ecuador during the war years of 1916 to 1919, returning to the Shuar Indians (or Jibaro as they were then called) in 1928–29, 1937, 1946, and 1951. Among his best-known publications are *Blood Revenge, War, and Victory Feast among the Jibaro Indians of Eastern Ecuador* (1923), published by the Bureau of American Ethnology, and *The Head-Hunters of Western Amazonas* (1935).

The fact that Karsten's first major fieldwork in Ecuador coincided with Malinowski's fieldwork in New Guinea 1914–15 and the Trobriand Islands in 1915–16 and 1917–18 led me to compare their approaches to fieldwork (Lindberg 1995a). I concluded that the shift in the conception of the ethnographer's role, from that of inquirer to that of participant, did not begin with Malinowski; although other persons in the young Malinowski's professional world described and approximated the participant observer method, Westermarck led directly by example as well as by precept, and Karsten's field research was at least as intensive as Malinowski's. Although covering most aspects of the everyday life of the Shuar, including social and political organization, hunting, trade, agriculture, material culture, and language, Karsten's writings focus on Shuar head-hunting practices. He evidently found this form of ritual warfare so central in their universe that it affected every aspect of their way of life.

Hilma Granqvist studied the lives of women and children in the Palestinian village of Artas for a total of three years in the field between 1925 and 1931. She participated in Westermarck's seminar in London in 1929, and returned to the London School of Economics in 1938 in order to attend a seminar organized by Malinowski. Like Karsten, she was critical of the comparative method of Westermarck and that of her local tutor, Landtman. While Karsten remained descriptive in his ethnography, Hilma Granqvist embraced the ideas of British functionalism, as well as some of British anthropology's methodologies, such as W. H. R. Rivers's genealogical method. Granqvist collected demographic data about the families in Artas. She collected information on all marriages over a hundred-year period from 1830 to 1930. She kept a field diary and carefully noted comments of key figures on the various phenomena in the village (Suolinna 1997: 264–5).

The Nordenskiöld School

Baron Erland Nordenskiöld (1877–1932) was the son of the world-famous Arctic explorer Adolf E. Nordenskiöld, who discovered the Northeast Passage. The younger Nordenskiöld began as a naturalist, making his first expedition to South America in 1899. By the time he made his second South American trip, in 1901–2, his research focus had shifted from zoology to ethnology and archaeology. He began his extensive travels in the Gran Chaco area of Argentina, Bolivia, and Paraguay, which included additional periods of fieldwork in 1904–05, 1908–09 and 1913–14. He lived among and traveled with the Ashluslay, Choroti, Chané and Chiriguano tribes, making archaeological and ethnographic collections for the Swedish ethnographic museums of Stockholm and Gothenburg. He got his professional training from Hjalmar Stolpe, and might have seemed his logical successor. When Stolpe died, however, his position was filled by Carl Hartman. Just before the outbreak of World War I, Nordenskiöld was offered a job at a small county museum in Gothenburg that housed stuffed birds, minerals, and a minor ethnographic collection illustrating the local peasant life. He undertook an ambitious program of collecting, trading, and purchasing, and within ten years had transformed a once-insignificant museum into an internationally important one that specialized in the Indian cultures of South America (Lindberg 1995b, 1997). Moreover, with the aid of a private patron, he secured a position as professor in "general and comparative ethnography" at Gothenburg University. Thus, he was able to tutor a first generation of anthropologists and archaeologists in Sweden, notably Karl Gustaf Izikowitz, Sigvald Linné, Stig Rydén and Henry Wassén. Indeed, the "Nordenskiöld school" counted Alfred Métraux of Paris among its members.

Anthropogeography, the combination of geography and anthropology, the leading progenitor of which was Friedrich Ratzel, was a significant influence on Nordenskiöld's thinking. Ratzel had stressed the interaction between man and nature, emphasizing the topographic and climatic influences upon peoples and cultural forms. In his groundbreaking works *Die Vereingten Staaten von Nordamerika* ("The United States of North America," 1880) and *Anthropo-Geographie oder Grundzüge der Anwendung der Erdkunde auf die Geschichte* 1882, 1891 ("Anthropo-Geography or Basic Traits of the Use of Geology on History"), Ratzel explained similarities in human societies as a result of historical contact and cultural borrowing. He justified his position by stressing that humankind had limited capacities for invention and was inclined to attachment to traditions. Nordenskiöld elaborated Ratzel's ideas, but objected to the uses to which they were put by diffusionist anthropologists. He became particularly hostile to the *Kulturkreise* studies of the "Vienna school," represented by Wilhelm Schmidt and Wilhelm Koppers. Although he was impressed by Schmidt's extensive literary knowledge of all areas of ethnography, Nordenskiöld objected to Schmidt's schematic presentations and dogmatic speculations. Like Westermarck, Nordenskiöld was an empiricist, and by the 1910s he had distanced himself from the philosophical and speculative styles of German ethnography. Instead, he had begun to develop his own version of the empirical cultural history tradition, a middle way between evolutionism and diffusion (Lindberg 1995b). Most of his earlier field reports and investigations were written in German, but from the 1920s and onward he favored French journals, thereby indicating his desire to reach a French audience. However, the bulk of Nordenskiöld's multidisciplinary investigations were published in the ten volumes of his serial publication, *Comparative Ethnographical Studies* (1916–33), including (but not limited to) treatises on the "copper and bronze age in South America" and Amerindian inventions. The decision to write in English was probably a direct result of his increasing interaction with American scholars. The first volume of the series was originally written and published in German, but Nordenskiöld translated it and wrote the rest of the volumes in English. With the assistance of Paul Rivet, arrangements were made to publish *Comparative Ethnographical Studies* in Paris, but for unknown reasons the project was postponed, and the French translations still remain unpublished (Lindberg 1995b).

For Nordenskiöld and his students, the framework of historically oriented anthropology suggested two fundamental questions about the New World's Indian cultures. One, were similar material cultural elements found among various Indian tribes the products of independent invention or diffusion? Two, had cultural elements spread between the Old and New World in pre-Columbian times – a particularly controversial matter? Combining the methods of archaeology, geography, and ethnography, Nordenskiöld was able to develop an analytical approach that utilized collections of material artifacts, cartographic reconstructions, and meticulous research in older literature. In his synthetic method, historical research reconstructed the prehistoric epoch as a sequence of events, and anthropological and archaeological techniques permitted this sequence of events to be traced, based upon its consequences. Nordenskiöld was also convinced that natural factors drove series of changes in culture, which could be plotted by tracing specific historic sequences of adaptation. Regarding the environment primarily as a limiting factor did not preclude the possibility that nature could also function as a cultural stimulant, as was proven by the development of certain human innovations. Thus, it was very important for the Nordenskiöld School to make maps of migrations. Furthermore, Nordenskiöld also paid considerable attention to the causes of migration. War, employment opportunities, water shortages, and religious beliefs were among the factors he analyzed in his mapping of migratory waves, seasonal migrations, and relocations (Lindberg 1995b).

Considering the spatial dispersal of ethnographic artifacts, Nordenskiöld could provide analysis documented by material culture. When he attempted to determine temporal sequences in Indian cultural development, however, he had to use indirect evidence. His primary database consisted of archaeological discoveries, which relied upon relative dating methods in the days before the development of radiocarbon dating. Linguistic data were also of some utility, as were historical reconstructions based upon the later spread of material cultural elements. But his assertion that there had been high cultural forms in the Amazon area that influenced Meso-American high cultures via early migrations was controversial in his day. His reconstruction of chronological sequences in South America was generally ignored until archaeologist Donald W. Lathrap published his work *The Upper Amazon* in 1970. New archaeological discoveries, technological improvements in dating methods, and ethno-botanical research substantiated Nordenskiöld's depiction of pre-Columbian migrations.

In the International Spotlight

To promote *l'étude historique et scientifique des deux Amériques et de leur habitants* and gather scholars working in the fields of anthropology, archaeology, religion, history, ethnology, geography, and linguistics, the first international congress of Americanists was held in Nancy, France in 1875. It was followed by meetings in Paris, Berlin, London, Stockholm, Mexico City, and New York. In the early days of his career, Nordenskiöld had been skeptical about the value of such congresses. But his international contacts expanded when he moved from Stockholm to Gothenburg in 1913, and also when he embarked on his fifth expedition to South America (1913–14). Moreover, when he found that his intellectual exchanges with overseas colleagues were disrupted while World War I raged, he may have realized just how important these exchanges were to him. In 1915, he began contemplating staging an Americanist Congress in Sweden (Nordenskiöld to Rafael Karsten, GUB: 8/20/1915).

Shortly after the end of the war, Nordenskiöld moved to realize this project, seeking the support of his closest friends, the Danish ethnographer Kaj Birket-Smith and Paul Rivet of the Trocadéro Museum in Paris. In July 1920, Birket-Smith wrote to him, "I find the idea of an Americanist Congress in Gothenburg absolutely splendid" (GUB: 7/16/1920). A month later, Nordenskiöld contacted Franz Boas in New York. Both men were distressed by the rejection by many British, French, and American scholars of the possibility that they might have any contact with colleagues in Germany and Austria. Indeed, some French publishers even refused to mail books to German-speaking countries (GEM: 8/19/1920; 10/31/1921).

The suggestion that an international congress of this magnitude should be held in Sweden led to divided opinions both in France and in the United States. Boas sided with Nordenskiöld and Rivet in promoting a Congress in Sweden, while Aleš Hrdlička and William Henry Holmes supported Arnold van Gennep's proposal that there should be yet another meeting in Paris. But Nordenskiöld was determined, knowing that he had the support of German, Austrian, and Dutch scholars. "It must be held in a country that has been neutral during the war," he argued, adding that "members of the congress should be, first and foremost, specialists" (GEM: Nordenskiöld to Boas, 1/23/1922).

Finally, it was decided that proceedings of the Congress would be split between the Netherlands and Sweden. Originally scheduled for 1922, the 21st Congress of Americanists was not convened until August 1924. Papers pertaining to North and Central America were presented in the Hague, and lectures and discussions about the Inuit and South American peoples took place in Gothenburg. This division made sense because Nordenskiöld was an authority on South American Indians, while a number of Danish scholars were specialists in Eskimo studies. A post-seminar was planned for

Copenhagen, and yet another international meeting in Prague was put on the agenda (GEM 12/7/1921; 2/22/1924).

Worldwide problems impeded the staging of the Congress. The world economy was very unstable, and while postwar Europe suffered from economic depression, unemployment, epidemics, and starvation, it was difficult to raise the funds necessary to assemble an international group of scholars. In a local newspaper, a frustrated Nordenskiöld complained: "How will it be possible for an Austrian scholar to go to Sweden under the present economic situation?" To a few scholars, including Waldemar Bogoras of Leningrad, he managed to offer modest travel grants (GEM 5/20/1924). A special invitation was extended to John Cooper of the Catholic University in Washington, who was, according to Nordenskiöld, "one of the few scholars who really have a great knowledge of the old Spanish sources" and the compiler of some excellent biographical works on Tierra del Fuego. Boas suggested that Edward Sapir was equally deserving of treatment that would place him in a prominent role at the Congress (GEM 12/27/1923; 5/24/1924; 7/4/1924; 7/19/1924); in the end, however, only Cooper was able to come to Sweden.

Nevertheless, the Congress became a multidisciplinary event, with representatives from social and cultural anthropology, ethnography, archaeology, linguistics, geography, history, and physical anthropology. Franz Boas was "the Great Man" and Karl von den Steinen the "Grand Old Man" of the Congress. Swedish newspaper coverage was extensive, with articles describing Rafael Karsten as "a profound researcher" and Max Uhle as "the foremost expert on American antiquities." Presenting reports from the Fifth Thule Expedition led by Knud Rasmussen to the Hudson Bay area in 1921, the Danish scholars Kaj Birket-Smith and Therkel Mathiassen gained considerable attention both in the media and at their Congress workshops. Other prominent participants were Stewart Culin of the Brooklyn Museum, Theodore Koch-Grünberg of the Linden Museum of Stuttgart, and Nordenskiöld's close friend Paul Rivet.

During the week of the Congress, more than 80 presentations were given, notable among them Karsten's "The Preanimistic Theory in the Lights of South American Beliefs," Métraux's "Sur un mode Américain du rite du Balancement" ("Concerning an American Rite of Balance"), and Max Uhle's "Der mittelamerikanische Ursprung der Moundbuilder und Pueblocivilisationen" ("The Middle American Origin of the Moundbuilder and Pueblo Civilizations"). Matters covered included patterns of migration, social and political organization, religion and witchcraft, as well as astronomy and mathematics. Intensively debated were historical questions about the relationship between the Old and New World: about migration from Asia to America (the origin of the "Indian race"); about the discovery of America; and about the possibilities for cultural exchanges in pre-Columbian times. Congress participants' theoretical discussions were dominated by concepts of evolution, diffusion, cultural areas, and cultural elements. There was an obvious split between a European view of diffusion (the *Kulturkreis* theory) and an American cultural history based upon historical connections and diffusion within the American continents. The German/Austrian position was held by Schmidt and Koppers, while the American version was represented by Boas, Clark Wissler, and Robert Lowie. Within the framework of a *New History of*

Anthropology, it is quite interesting to note that at this major international conference in 1924 there was yet no trace of what Adam Kuper (1983: 1) has referred to as the "functionalist revolution," which has for him been denoted by Malinowski's appointment as a reader at London School of Economics in that year. Obviously, the Anglo-American variants of diffusionism were consistent with the ideas that were shared by most Continental European anthropologists at the time, despite the differences that obtained among different groups of diffusionists. It is of some interest that Robert Lowie would later say of Nordenskiöld that he was able to steer "a middle course between an outdated evolutionism and an extravagant diffusionism," coming "closer" than most scholars elsewhere "to the attitude commonly assumed in this country" (1933: 160).

At the Conference, Nordenskiöld seemed to be everywhere at once, and "displayed solicitude for the individual comfort of the foreign guests that will be gratefully remembered" (Lowie 1933: 159). Between sessions, he guided groups around the museum, proudly presenting a new archaeological collection made in the Amazon area of Rio Tapajus by Curt Unkel, whom Nordenskiöld characterized as "one of the best in the field," and reporting "that he has been adopted among the Guarani tribe under the name of Nimuendajú" (Göteborgs Handelstidning 11/8/1924).

The 21st International Congress of Americanists was a tremendous personal success for Nordenskiöld. The curator of the American Museum of Natural History wrote him a letter stating: "from everyone who visited Gothenburg I hear the most enthusiastic reports, not only of the success of the congress, but of your museum, which is uniformly admired as the best in Europe if not in the world" (GEM: Mason to Nordenskiöld 12/31/1924). Melville Herskovits of Columbia University praised Nordenskiöld's serial publication, *Comparative Ethnographical Studies*, saying "I only wish that I may be able to write such a work regarding Africa" (GEM 1/7/1925).

The Decline of the Westermarck and Nordenskiöld Schools

Nordenskiöld was at the peak of his career, making full use of his international contacts, his American colleagues in particular. He and Robert Lowie made an agreement to edit and compile a two-volume *Handbook of South American Indians*. The contributors were to be mainly European scholars, including Rivet, Métraux, Karsten, and Nordenskiöld himself. Alfred Kroeber invited him to be a visiting professor at Berkeley, and Nordenskiöld took advantage of the opportunity that this overseas visit provided to make a sixth expedition to South America; on this occasion, he went to Panama and Colombia. Doing research among the Cuna Indians, he was breaking new ground, most notably in his collaboration with his informant, Ruben Pérez Kantule. Unfortunately, however, his health was failing, and he died in 1932 at the age of 55. Although several of his students made distinguished careers as museum curators and archaeologists, his death marked the end of an era. Lowie managed to take over the sponsorship of Nimuendajú research in the Amazon, but publication of the *Handbook* took far longer than had been anticipated. Eventually edited by Julian H. Steward and published by the Bureau of American Ethnology in seven volumes, it became an American enterprise, rather than a European one (although it did include contributions by Métraux and Claude Lévi-Strauss).

As is said in proverbial Swedish folk-wisdom, it is difficult to become a prophet at home. After Nordenskiöld's death, his professorship in "general and comparative ethnography" was eliminated, and it took more than 25 years before anthropology re-entered the curriculum at the University of Gothenburg. With the exception of Izikowitz, his students pursued their careers in the ethnographic museums of Gothenburg and Stockholm. Thus, they were all marginalized in the 1960s when the "modern Swedish anthropology," inspired by the works of Malinowski and Radcliffe-Brown, disassociated itself from the ethnographic museums (Lindberg 1995b). Replacing the old Ethnographical Museum in Gothenburg, a Museum of World Culture was opened in December of 2004. Obviously trying to distance itself from its historical legacy, the new museum pays no homage whatsoever to Nordenskiöld, or to any of his students. From a single small display, almost hidden in a corner of a stairway, the visitor may sense that the museum has a history by looking at a desk with an old typewriter, a few books, and some museum catalog cards scattered about. There is also an installation by an American artist who was commissioned to select a collection of old photographs from the archives. Knowing nothing about the actual collaboration between Nordenskiöld and Kantule, or the strong friendship between the Gothenburg scholars and the Cuna Indians, the artist created a representation of colonial relationships. This installation is an insult to Nordenskiöld as well as to the Cuna people.

Even if Nordenskiöld's enduring legacy to general anthropology was limited, his teaching and fieldwork experience made him a decisive influence in various quarters. His work is still held in high esteem by scholars specializing in South American archaeology and ethnography. His innovative museum exhibits, which combined the use of artifacts, regional descriptions, maps, and photographs, were highly influential. Rivet patterned the collections of Trocadéro (later Musée de l'Homme) after his example, and so did Birket-Smith in the ethnographic collections of the National Museum of Denmark (Lindberg 1997; Vildé 1938–39; Wassén 1932). As a fieldworker, Nordenskiöld influenced both his students and later generations of Swedish Americanists. The highest homage to him was paid by Alfred Métraux, who always spoke of Nordenskiöld as his great teacher, best friend and inspiration (not Marcel Mauss, who might seem a more probable influence).

At the time of Nordenskiöld's death, the Finnish school was also in decline. Regarding Westermarck as one of the leading theorists of the evolutionary school, Émile Durkheim was one of the first to question his writings on marriage and morals. (Westermarck wrote his books in English and Swedish, and it was Arnold van Gennep, alienated from Durkheim's circle, who translated and promoted Westermarck's works in France [see Sibeud in this volume].) But the most decisive rejection of his approach was in Britain, where Malinowski and Radcliffe-Brown's functionalist social anthropology rejected any attempts to reconstruct the unknown past, proscribing all considerations of hypothetical historical origins (see, for example, Radcliffe-Brown 1931). Westermarck replied in his 1936 Huxley Memorial Lecture that he and the functionalists were arguing at cross-purposes: for them, consideration of the origin of an institution meant determining its causes, whereas he was concerned to understand its historical development. His friend R. R. Marett congratulated Westermarck on his lecture, remarking , "Well, we are all getting old, but are not 'done' yet, and have something to say to the younger generation" (ÅAB: Marett to Westermarck, 10/30/1936).

Although not a dogmatic evolutionist, Westermarck was never able to abandon his comparative approach; nor was he able to provide insight into economic and political conditions, and how these influenced the development of customs and ceremonies (Suolinna 1997:268). Westermarck died in 1939, but it was his students who had to confront a changing intellectual climate both in Finland and abroad. Under the banner of "a new sociology," the empirical and comparative approaches of Westermarckian ethnology were abandoned in favor of more philosophical and theoretical positions. None of Westermarck's students managed to pursue a successful international career. Wars and troublesome relations with the Soviet Union contributed to the relative isolation of Finnish academe. Nevertheless, Westermarck's students failed not only by virtue of their limited international contacts but also because of conditions at home. Landtman secured a professorship in sociology, but did no more fieldwork. Karsten ruined his reputation as an able scholar and fieldworker in numerous polemical debates with Nordenskiöld, Rivet, Stirling, and others. Granqvist's thesis, *Marriage Conditions in a Palestinian Village* (1931–35), aroused only marginal interest in her home country, notwithstanding the good reviews it received in international sociological journals. In fact, even with Westermarck's strong support, she was deliberately marginalized in the university by her colleagues, not least by Landtman. Every chance for an academic career was effectively foreclosed when her application for an associate professorship was unsuccessful. Still, she managed to publish three important scholarly works after World War II – *Birth and Childhood among the Arabs* (1947), *Child Problems among the Arabs* (1950) and *Muslim Death and Burial* (1965). Lately, her works have received renewed attention, evaluated in international forums by Zilberman (1991) and Suolinna (1997).

Suolinna (1998) concludes that the stagnation of the Westermarck school was the result of Westermarck's failure to encourage his students to explore new perspectives; he had become an overbearing and therefore constraining force in scholarly discussions. Westermarck's behavior as an elder statesman may have been an important reason for the decline of the Westermarck school, but I would like to stress institutional factors – which figured in the decline of the Nordenskiöld school as well as that of the Westermarck school. Simply by virtue of their geography, Finnish and Swedish scholars are easily marginalized. Scholars in small countries have difficulties getting research grants, assuming prominence in anthropological associations, and placing their articles in international journals. Both Westermarck and Nordenskiöld faced the difficulty of establishing ethnography as a significant scientific field. Westermarck's strategy, as noted above, was to regard it as a branch of sociology, sometimes called ethno-sociology. The anthropology of the Westermarck school moved across the borders of philosophy, sociology, and history of religion, but did not secure an

Figure 7   Trivializing the past: the historical legacy of Erland Nordenskiöld and the former ethnological museum is confined to a small glass box situated in a corner of a staircase. Visiting artist Fred Wilson was given free range to "excavate the museum's subconscious" by the Museum of World Culture. Nordenskiöld's name is not mentioned, and none of the permanent collections from South America are currently on display at the museum. Photograph by the author.

independent status until much later. Nordenskiöld was confronted by the same difficulty. It was impossible to do ethnography within the Swedish university curriculum in the early twentieth century; thus, his institutional base was of necessity in the museum. The Swedish university discipline of social and cultural anthropology was not established until the 1960s, and the new generation of scholars felt compelled to distance their discipline from any "stone-age" museum tradition.

Further Reading

Lowie, R. H. 1937. *The History of Ethnological Theory*. New York: Holt, Rinehart and Winston.
Voget, F. W. 1975. *A History of Ethnology*. New York: Holt, Rinehart and Winston.

10

Colonial Commerce and Anthropological Knowledge: Dutch Ethnographic Museums in the European Context

Donna C. Mehos

Introduction

The links between ethnographic collections in European museums and academic anthropology that may appear obvious today did not necessarily exist in the past. While anthropological interest influenced the emergence of museums, people outside the realm of universities collected and studied the ethnographica of major museums long before anthropology emerged as a discipline. For centuries before the rise of professionalized specialized scientific disciplines, amateur practitioners pursued and produced natural knowledge, amassed significant private collections, and developed skills that equaled or surpassed those of naturalists who taught in the academy (Impey and MacGregor 1985). The history of ethnographic museum collections must be seen in the context of the natural history tradition that included the study not only of plants, animals, rocks, and minerals, but also of exotic peoples.

In the nineteenth century, new museums housing massive collections were founded in cities across Europe. Individuals sold or donated their collections to municipal and national governments, as well as to private associations, forming core collections of these novel institutions. Missionaries spreading Christianity and civil servants administering colonial authority collected natural and ethnographic objects from across the globe, as did adventurous travelers, ships' captains engaged in colonial trade, and naturalists on state-supported scientific expeditions. In the period of European overseas expansion, the natural history of exotic corners of the earth arrived in European institutions in thousands of packing cases reflecting arbitrary, rather than systematic, collecting practices. Early ethnographic museums, zoological gardens, and natural history museums, sometimes combined within one institution, were more closely related to overseas expansion than to academic pursuit.

In this chapter, I explore the nineteenth-century origins and early histories of two contemporary ethnographic museums in the Netherlands: the *Tropenmuseum* in Amsterdam and the *Rijks Ethnologie Museum* in Leiden. Both of these collections were direct results of colonial commercial interests of the state and of private enterprise, a practical characteristic less common in other European museums. While colonialism no doubt played direct and indirect roles in most European ethnographic museums, in the Dutch case, the principal goal that motivated early museum promoters was the improvement of trade rather than intellectual interest in exotic peoples or human evolution. Also typical in the Netherlands was the significant private – rather than state or municipal – capital and initiative necessary to found not only ethnographic museums but also scientific and cultural institutions in general (Mehos 2006). Compared to other European countries, Dutch national museums emerged only after considerable lobbying and fundraising by the motivated elites. Monumental cultural institutions such as orchestral halls, and art and science museums appeared relatively late in the Dutch urban landscape, in contrast to cities where national and municipal authorities invested in and supported the arts and sciences. Despite the state's reluctance to fund museums, the enterprising Dutch, in their efforts to profit from colonial commerce, amassed huge collections in various areas of natural history that were envied by foreign visitors.

In the nineteenth-century period of museum building, European museum staff commonly embarked on study trips to visit collections outside of their own countries. Directors and curators evaluated and compared foreign museums and made recommendations for developments in their own. For example, A. H. Lane-Fox Pitt-Rivers traveled to continental collections when he was contemplating methods of ethnographic display for his own vast collection. Later, he criticized his own government for failing to build an important national ethnographic museum on the scale of those found in other European cities (Chapman 1985: 24), echoing comments made earlier by British naturalist W. H. Fitton after his visit to the impressive *Rijksmuseum van Natuurlijke Histoire* in Leiden (Mehos 2006: 80). L. Serrurier (1846–1901), director of the *Rijks Ethnologie Museum*, traveled to London collections, made explicit comparisons with Parisian exhibit style, and ultimately developed a display system that reflected Adolf Bastian's in the renowned Museum für Völkerkunde in Berlin (Effert 2003: 209–11). In 1913, during the planning stages of Amsterdam's *Koloniaal Instituut* (precursor to the *Tropenmuseum*) building, the director of its Trade Museum traveled to no fewer than 14 museums – all in Germany (Dekker 1913). Although in previous years he had visited institutions in other countries, they merited little attention in his official report, suggesting that he considered German museums exemplary. Museums received much international attention, yet local, regional, and national contexts greatly influenced their development.

Early French anthropological museums, supported to a great degree by the state by the late nineteenth century, included the physical anthropology collections used for research and teaching at both the *École d'anthropologie* and the prominent *Musée d'histoire naturelle*. The first state ethnographic museum with public displays, the *Musée d'ethnographie* in the Trocadéro Palace, opened in 1879, housing ethnographica that had been displayed in the 1878 Universal Exposition in Paris as well as collections of the *Société d'ethnographie*. All of these Parisian museums, as well as their research and teaching, declined in the last decades of the nineteenth century as the level of funding fell. Not until the second decade of the twentieth century, with rapid French colonial expansion, did the study of ethnography revive and the new state institution, the *Musée de l'homme*, take shape. It was to be the new institutional base uniting French physical anthropological and ethnographic studies and collection, in particular, to study the peoples of French African colonies and to collect their material culture. Ultimately, the museum opened in 1938 with the goals of producing scientific knowledge and diffusing it responsibly to the masses. While recognized as a colonial museum intending to contribute to French colonial prowess, and likely to have imparted an ideology of imperialism, its promoters were not – like the Dutch – motivated directly by commercial interests (Conklin 2002a).

The British Museum housed the only national ethnographic collection in nineteenth-century Britain. Much of it originated in the eighteenth century and was in poor condition by the mid-nineteenth century, receiving little priority in the museum. This unfortunate situation was remarked upon by Pitt-Rivers, who himself brought together the most important ethnographic museum in Britain. As a young military officer and advanced amateur interested in natural history, he began purchasing objects in the mid-nineteenth century. Rarely traveling far or collecting in the field, Pitt-Rivers developed a large network of travelers and dealers from whom he bought ethnographica. He also made facsimile reproductions of artifacts in other collections. Typical of elite naturalists in this period, he sought intellectual interaction as a member of, for example, the Royal Geographical Society, the Ethnological Society of London, and the Anthropological Institute. Pitt-Rivers used his increasingly substantial collection to study the historical development of human culture, and he arranged it to reflect his interpretation of cultural evolution. Given the poor ethnographic displays in the British Museum, Pitt-Rivers sought exemplars for his private museum in Continental museums, that in Leiden in particular, with its geographical organization (Chapman 1985). After decades of maintaining his personal museum, Pitt-Rivers loaned his collection to the South Kensington Museum in the 1870s, and in 1882 he offered it as a gift to Oxford University. Oxford accepted the collection, built a museum for it, and in 1883 hired E. B. Tylor as museum keeper. The following year, Oxford appointed Tylor as a reader in anthropology, thereby institutionalizing anthropology in a British university for the first time. While Pitt-Rivers is known for the museum bearing his name, and for his theoretical contributions to evolutionism based on material culture, the connections of this collection to colonialism were indirect. Clearly, his objects were less likely to have been collected had there been no colonial expansion. However, he aimed to illuminate the evolution of general human culture – Western and non-Western societies.

Ethnographic museums became the sites where German ethnology emerged. Conceived both before German unification in 1871 and before the acquisition of German colonies in 1884, museums in German states were not direct expressions of either colonialist or nationalist sentiment (Penny 1999, 2002b, 2003). Cosmopolitan orientations and civic pride motivated the founders and promoters of museums in Berlin, Leipzig, Munich, and Hamburg when cultural policies and initiatives developed on the regional level rather than being dictated by the Reich. Pioneered by Adolf Bastian and his contemporaries, the German ethnographic project fostered scientific studies of objects to unveil the unity of humankind and to understand the European self; the museums were expected to become "libraries of 'mankind'" (Penny 2003: 101), and their exhibits of material culture would instruct public visitors. By the end of the nineteenth century, many contemporaries considered German collections, particularly Berlin's *Museum für Völkerkunde*, the most significant in the world. Ultimately, increasing the size of collections became an end in itself; by 1900, these massive collections could barely be contained within museum buildings (Penny 2003: 103) – a common problem in nineteenth-century museums.

Not all ethnographic museums aimed to produce the same kind of anthropological knowledge in this period before the specialized discipline of anthropology found an institutional home in European universities. In general, anthropological knowledge was produced in various contexts and intended to reach diverse goals. Medical doctors in universities, state research institutions, or scientific societies studied collections of human bones to understand comparative human anatomy, or the physical anthropology of the nineteenth and early twentieth century. Ethnographies, written and studied by amateurs, academics, world travelers, and colonial administrators, described exotic cultures and languages as well as ethnographica. Similarly, comparative ethnology – in some languages and usages synonymous with ethnography – was practiced and read by people with diverse backgrounds, goals, and institutional ties. Taken together, physical anthropology, ethnography, and/or ethnology, and the institutions in which they flourished constitute the rich historical foundation upon which today's academic anthropology arose. This study brings to the foreground the colonial context of early ethnography and collections of ethnographica and demonstrates Pels's and Salemink's position that "[n]ot all ingredients of academic anthropology have been produced at academic locations" (1999: 7).

Museums in the Netherlands

I now turn to a consideration of the particular national context of the Netherlands in comparison to other leading colonial powers. Influenced by national, regional, and local differences, ethnographic museums arose throughout Europe as varied expressions of colonial expansion. Scientific, geographical, and military expeditions, the founding of monumental museums that housed collections from far corners of the world, evolutionary theory, and financial interests in colonial commerce contributed to the increasing interest in exotic, often colonized, peoples, material culture, and human cultural change in general. Institutions founded to exhibit ethnographic collections took on many forms and formulated varied goals in different contexts. In the museums I investigated, the Dutch explicitly expressed their goals and expectations of how artifacts and ethnographic knowledge would contribute to their imperial and commercial ambitions. Even in contexts in which these practical goals remained implicit or did not exist, trade and colonial power made possible the rise of museum collections.

What is today Amsterdam's major anthropological museum, the *Tropenmuseum* (Museum of the Tropics), is one department of the *Koninklijk Instituut voor de Tropen* (Royal Institute of the Tropics) that was founded in the early twentieth century as the *Koloniaal Instituut* (KI, Colonial Institute). Initiated by captains of (colonial) industry and supported by government agencies, the KI fused pre-existing private museum collections to form the basis of a new museum. The Amsterdam *Zoologisch Genootschap* Natura Artis Magistra (Zoological Society *Natura Artis Magistra*) donated its significant museum collection to the new KI, as did the *Koloniaal Museum* (Colonial Museum) of the *Nederlandsche Maatschappij ter Bevordering der Nijverheid* (Dutch Society for the Advancement of Industry) in the nearby city of Haarlem. The explicit goals of the latter were to exhibit colonial natural resources and products derived from them as well as to investigate scientifically tropical products for their commercial potential – an effort to stimulate Dutch colonial trade. Amsterdam's private zoological society devoted its attention to the advancement of natural history. Neither pre-existing institution had formal ties with academic ethnology. While the new KI did develop academic links, it was the promotion of trade, rather than ethnology, that dominated its agenda.

Commonly called *Artis*, Amsterdam's zoological society, founded in 1838, promoted natural history in an innovative institutional form by displaying a significant *living* animal collection (Mehos 2006). Specializing in zoology, *Artis* was a private society financed by Amsterdam's comfortable classes who, as members, enjoyed exclusive access to the zoological garden, natural history and ethnographic museums, library, and aquarium. The zoo's possession of both zoological specimens – dead and alive – and ethnographica reflected nineteenth-century conventions in natural history, as did the joint research of amateurs and professionals. A wealthy society, in its first years and at great expense it purchased a significant private collection for its natural history museum and a considerable collection of living exotic (and fierce) animals from a traveling circus for the zoological garden. While *Artis* continued to purchase specimens for display, donations added considerably to the natural history collections. Soon, not only zoological specimens but also ethnographica arrived at the zoo.

In general in the nineteenth century, donations played a crucial role in the expansion of museum collections. *Artis* was no exception. It received natural objects from across the world: living leopards, Javanese apes, and gazelles for the zoo; birds' nests, mammalian horns, and shells for the natural history museum; shields, swords, and jewelry for the ethnographic collection; and scientific books, reports, and bulletins for the library. Dutch burghers traveling abroad, colonial civil servants, including the Dutch Minister of the Colonies, and foreign dignitaries sent valuable gifts that *Artis* accepted gratefully and displayed to its members. While the precious and unique collections at this Amsterdam institution grew at a phenomenal rate, neither the natural history museum nor the ethnographic museum maintained a systematic acquisition policy. Their collections were therefore the result of arbitrary donations.

Artis's collections displayed empire and colonial nature to the Dutch at home in Amsterdam (Mehos 2006). The prosperity of its members and of *Artis* resulted, to a great extent, from colonial trade, as did the displayed objects and animals. The ethnographic museum exhibited not only artifacts made by indigenous populations but also, for example, models of factories run by the Dutch on Java. This museum instructed Amsterdammers about both colonial nature and European presence in colonies. In 1883, when *Artis* received many objects that had been displayed by the Dutch in *De Internationale Koloniale en Uitvoerhandel Tentoonstelling* (International Colonial and Export Exhibition), the *Artis* museum was bursting at the seams. Its new museum opened in 1888, coinciding with the fiftieth anniversary celebrations of the zoological society. Soon thereafter, *Artis* entered discussions that would lead to the founding of the independent KI to which it would donate its entire ethnographic collection.

The *Nederlandsche Maatschappij ter Bevordering der Nijverheid* (Dutch Society for the Advancement of Industry) was founded in 1836, in Haarlem, just a few miles away from Amsterdam. This society aimed to promote Dutch economic development, in general and, more specifically, to bring attention to the unexplored potential of colonial natural resources for commercial development and trade (Kok 1989: 142). In 1864, it founded the *Koloniaal Museum* (KM) and the secretary of the society, F. W. van Eeden (1829–1901), was given the task of bringing together a collection of colonial specimens. As at *Artis*, the museum's collection developed from donations. In fact, from its planning stages, the KM expected to build its collections exclusively from donations (Politiek 1994: 19). There was no lack of interest as the donations to the KM arrived by the hundreds at Van Eeden's home. Here he arranged, cataloged, and described the numerous wood samples, pigments, food sources, fibers, and oils that quickly filled his own attic, where he worked before the museum quarters were completed. By 1870, 2,700 objects and samples had been collected and the museum departments had been organized. Exhibit halls opened to the paying public in 1871 in the *Paviljoen Welgelegen,* a former palace that also housed museums of industrial design and of contemporary art.

The museum aimed to increase public awareness of and enthusiasm for colonial industrial development. It exhibited natural materials, their industrial applications, and production processes, and gave demonstrations of native products and production techniques to stimulate consumption of colonial wares. For example, it organized courses for lay audiences on tropical agriculture and industry, and hoped thereby to recruit industrialists not yet occupied in colonial trade. While the KM exhibited ethnographica, for example, in demonstrations of indigenous methods for weaving baskets, ethnography was discussed only when it was considered useful for colonial industry. Ironically, ethnography and geography were disproportionately represented in the KM collections relative to the goods and indigenous techniques it chose to emphasize. The donations it received reflected the personal interests of donors rather then the objectives of the society that saw no practical advantage of ethnography for colonial commerce (Politiek 1994).

Despite its appeal to the public, the KM's primary goal remained the promotion of colonial trade and industry. This practical museum aided Dutch businesses by performing research and providing knowledge for Dutch entrepreneurs, for example, by authenticating products and unmasking impure, forged ones. It published hand-books, the journal *Tijdschrift der Maatschappij voor Nijverheid en Handel*, and the KM *Bulletin*. In these publications, descriptions and chemical characterizations of com-mercially promising plants appeared, as did chemical studies or improved processing techniques of successful products such as rubber, sugar, coffee, and chocolate.

Soon the KM suffered from lack of both space and financial resources to expand. Its Governing Council (*Raad van Bestuur*), comprised of captains of industry, hoped to increase financial support. Facing resistance to continue this project in the provin-cial capital of Haarlem, the Council decided, in the early years of the twentieth century, to move the collection to Amsterdam. As plans for the move took form, so, too, did an ambitious scheme devised by the council's chair, J. T. Cremer (1847–1923), president of the *Nederlandsche Handel-Maatschappij* (Dutch Trade Association) and former Minister of the Colonies, and H. F. R. Hubrecht, parliament member and vice chairman of the Amsterdam Chamber of Commerce (*Kamer van Koophandel*). They proposed the founding of a colonial institute that would function as the Dutch center for colonial research, knowledge, and education on a much grander scale than the KM had imagined. In 1910, a definitive decision was reached to found the *Koloniaal Instituut*, and fundraising by Cremer and Hubrecht commenced.

Colonial Commerce, Ethnology, and Academic Knowledge in Amsterdam

To found the *Vereeniging* (Association) *Koloniaal Instituut* in 1910, Cremer sought to secure 1,000,000 guilders as financial backing from companies and individuals before approaching the state for subsidies (Taselaar 1998: 167). Within two months, 960,000 guilders had been raised, and more than 1.3 million guilders had been acquired from individual founders, two state ministries, the city of Amsterdam, the Amsterdam Zoo *Artis*, major companies and financial institutions conducting colonial trade, and 23 individuals by the end of 1911 (Taselaar 1998: 169). In that year, the Ministry of the Colonies and the Ministry of the Interior, the Province of North Holland, and the city of Amsterdam agreed to support the institution with annual subsidies (Hasselman 1926: 10). At the end of 1918, the capital backing of the KI reached 1.7 million guilders (Taselaar 1998: 169). The new *Comité van Voorbereiding* (Planning Committee), with Cremer as chair and Hubrecht as vice-chair, was responsible for articulating the KI goals, planning an institutional organization, and drafting statutes. Building on the relatively modest trade museum of the KM, the committee of the KI developed ambitious objectives to become the "... central colonial institution for science, education, trade and industry ... where science and practice reach out to each other ..." (quoted in De Balbian Verster 1926: 14). What shape did the committee give to the new institution that would be open to the public and how would it serve the public and private investors who shared their vision for a Dutch center for colonial knowledge?

Like the KM, the goals of the KI were "the collection and advancement of know-ledge regarding our overseas territories; in particular: the promotion of commercial, agricultural, industrial and other interests that arise from both the motherland and the colonies under Dutch control" (statutes reproduced in Hasselman 1926: 87). The KI's ideological position mirrored the state's ethical policy, the Dutch civilizing mission in which both the welfare of the colonized peoples and the interdependence of the Netherlands and its colonies took on an increasing importance. The official vision of the KI, articulated in a booklet by the institute's secretary C. J. Hasselman, empha-sized the unity between the Dutch state and its colonies, referred to together as the Entire Netherlands (*Geheel Nederland*) (1926: 79). The Dutch no longer saw their colonies as territories to exploit but rather as "equal parts of a unified whole (*samenhangend geheel*) . . . the motherland and colonies" (1926: 79). The booklet appeared in 1924; it would be reprinted, revised, and translated into English, French, and German to reach international audiences. Similarly, at the opening ceremony of the new building in 1926, J. C. Konigsberger, Minister of the Colonies, described the KI as "the embodiment of the Dutch sense of unity (*eenheidsgedachte*) that promises to become the center of a net that in many areas – Motherland, East, and West – binds us together" (1926). Expecting continued support of the KI by the Dutch people, Hasselman believed that "[t]he flourishing of this institution shall also be the measure (*maatstaf*) of the love of the Netherlands for its colonies" (1926: 85).

The KI was organized into three departments. One, the Department of Tropical Hygiene (*Tropische Hygiëne*), co-founded with the municipality and situated in the new Medical School Laboratory of the Municipal University of Amsterdam, was the first Dutch tropical medicine institute. Two, the Trade Museum (*Handelsmuseum*) incorporated the KM collection and also exhibited tropical products, colonial natural resources, and related industries to promote and maintain Dutch international markets for tropical wares (Hasselman 1926: 43). Like the medical school, it had a laboratory for scientific research and disseminated knowledge. The third department, the Ethnology Museum (*Volkenkunde Museum*), assembled the collections from *Artis*, the ethnographica of the KM, and other smaller collections. It strove to display every-day life and the socioeconomic conditions of all indigenous groups living in Dutch colonies (Politiek 1994: 83–4). While the Trade Museum aimed to produce and share information of economic value like its counterpart in Haarlem, the new Department of Ethnology would increase public awareness about the subjects living under Dutch colonial rule, marking a significant change from the KM (Politiek 1994: 99). In Haarlem, ethnographica illustrated the production processes of native wares, yet the new museum exhibited images of indigenous groups and ranked cultures hierarch-ically according to perceived levels of "civilization." Members of the public learned of the "backwardness" of their colonial subjects and of the superiority of Europeans, a characteristic common in European ethnographic museums. Supporting research on indigenous cultures, the KI expected to improve the living conditions of native popu-lations and to aid in their social progress – completely consistent with the Ethical Policy. More important, the KI envisioned ethnographical studies, like the research in the Trade Museum, as leading to practical knowledge to improve methods of colonial rule.

To manage the Ethnology Museum, the KI sought a knowledgeable director with experience in the Indies, appointing J. C. van Eerde, a high official in the Ministry of the Colonies and former civil servant in Sumatra and Lombok who had published widely based on his colonial experience (Taselaar 1998: 174–5). Van Eerde embodied the ideals of the KI, where he disseminated his practical knowledge in an annual lecture course first given in 1917. This popular three-month introductory course in Indology (*Indologische Leergang*) attracted students entering East Indian commerce and medical students matriculating in the Institute of Tropical Hygiene. He taught ethnography, the Malaysian language, the government organization (*staatsinstelling*), and geography – the latter in relation to agriculture, mining, commerce, and transport (Politiek 1994: 93). In this same year, the KI facilitated his appointment as professor of ethnology (*Volkenkunde*) at the Municipal University of Amsterdam. Van Eerde also held appointments at the *Handelswetenschappen* (Business Faculty) in Amsterdam and taught at the *Nederlandse Handelshogeschool* (Dutch College of Commerce) in Rotterdam. Van Eerde's academic appointments, and his teaching at the KI, demonstrate that his practical colonial knowledge was valued in institutions of higher education.

The role of the KI in initiating and supporting van Eerde's academic appointments also illustrates how this practical KI institution and its staff, though specialized in commerce and colonialism, acquired legitimation and academic credentials. The ethnographic department developed contact with the university by subsidizing the professorships of their staff members. The museum's physical anthropologist, J. P. Kleiweg de Zwaan, was appointed professor of anthropology and prehistory at the Municipal University of Amsterdam. The economist, G. Gonggrijp, held various chairs at the *Nederlandsche Handelshogeschool* (Dutch College of Commerce) in Rotterdam and a chair at the University of Amsterdam financed by the KI (*Gedenkboek* 1932: 589). The KI created links with the academy by appointing a Scientific Committee comprising the Leiden professors A. W. Nieuwenhuis (discussed below) and C. Snouck Hurgronje, and the Amsterdam professor Sebald Rudolf Steinmetz (1862–1940), "the pioneer of ethnology in Amsterdam" (Heinemeijer 2002: 227). Formally linked with the KI, Steinmetz, professor of political geography, ethnology and ethnography of the East Indies, did not use collections for his comparative sociological studies of societies (van Wengen 2002b: 971). This may appear curious, but it was typical.

While academic specialists in colonial subjects, neither the Scientific Committee members nor the museum staff based significant research on museum ethnographic collections. In fact, when the Ethnology Museum chose to support a major multi-year research project that included museum as well as academic experts, it was for the study of customary law, or *adat*, which ultimately led to the publication of many volumes and was marked as a significant contribution to knowledge (Ellen 1976: 317). *Adat* studies, like the study of tropical products, yielded practical information that served colonial interests. It did not shed light on the collections of the museum or the material culture of colonized peoples. Thus, the broad goals of the KI and the advancement of the utilitarian knowledge it fostered reveal that the ethnographic collections played a secondary role in the production of ethnographic knowledge at the KI. While academically responsible, the ethnology museum collections and exhibits educated the Dutch public about empire. Taken together, as Taselaar (1998: 208) clearly states, "[The] activities of the institute . . . give a good image of the ideological orientation of the Netherlands colonial lobby."

Nineteenth-century Origins of the *Rijksmuseum voor Volkenkunde*

Today, the *Rijksmuseum voor Volkenkunde* (National Museum of Ethnology) in Leiden plays an important role for both professional anthropologists and the public. It maintains a formal relationship with the state-supported Leiden University, and academic scholars contribute significantly to the museum's research planning and implementation. In the past, the university and this national museum maintained tenuous links. They shared few intellectual interests, research ideals, or goals, even though the university emerged as the center for academic studies of the Netherlands East Indies. While the state played a critical role in the origin of the museum's collection in the nineteenth century, the university and its scholars remained relatively uninvolved in the museum for many decades. Ethnographic objects did not inform their studies. Rather, scholars in the university specialized in such subjects as (Southeast) Asian languages, geography, and indigenous legal systems, or *adat* law. Museum staff, often not academically trained, maintained, cataloged, and described the collections. Gradually, academic interest turned to the study of ethnographica. Ironically, when the field of anthropology successfully professionalized and the discipline became institutionalized in Leiden, its strength was in theoretical investigations of social structure in which objects played a decreasingly important role – a more general phenomenon seen in the history of the discipline elsewhere.

   The history of the Leiden museum was fraught with tensions between the museum, university, and state. As collections grew, negotiations for a new larger museum generated conflict. Proposals to move the museum to a larger city and to change the nature of the museum were accompanied by arguments to keep it in Leiden because of its importance for university teaching and research. Ultimately, the museum remained in its original location.

Philipp Franz von Siebold's Japanese Collection and Museum

The collection in Leiden, similar to that in Amsterdam, arose from the state's economic interests. The museum's founder, the medical doctor Philipp Franz von Siebold (1796–1866) (Tjon Sie Fat and van Vliet 1990), amassed his private collection while serving the Dutch government. Stationed in Japan between 1823 and 1830, von Siebold was commissioned to provide medical service to the small Dutch population there, to assemble natural historical information, and to develop insight into the Japanese people that would aid the Dutch in maintaining and expanding their exclusive trade relations (Effert 2003: 118–24). He also sent botanical samples to Java

to enrich the colonial state's botanical garden, Buitenzorg (Effert 2003: 119). After returning in 1830 to the Netherlands, where he cataloged and published his descriptions
of the collection, von Siebold offered to sell his ethnographica to King Willem I and
suggested that the state found a national ethnographic museum by combining his
own Japanese collection with the existing Chinese and Japanese collections in the
Koninklijk Kabinet van Zeldzaamheden (Royal Cabinet of Rarities) in The Hague.
The king, though sympathetic in principle, refused. At that time, the state had few
resources. Furthermore, the national government invested little in science and culture.
Rather, it maintained a laissez-faire policy that encouraged private initiatives in
cultural and scientific institutions (Hart 1988). Thus, von Siebold opened his private
museum collection, exhibited in his residence, to the public in 1837. He expected it
to be a place for the study of ethnography, and to be of interest and importance
for "missionaries, civil servants and officers, merchants, and seamen" involved in
colonial endeavors (quoted in Effert 2003: 140). Given van Siebold's commitment to
promote trade with Japan, his collection represented primarily raw and processed
natural resources (Effert 2003: 140–4), thus resembling the museums that later would
be founded in Haarlem and Amsterdam.

   In 1838, the government did purchase the collection and thereby provided some
relief for von Siebold, who faced serious financial difficulties supporting his own research
and publications. However, state ownership neither changed the conditions of the
museum nor influenced von Siebold's role in maintaining it. While the state officially
owned the collection, it did not build a museum, Von Siebold's quarters could barely
contain the large collection. As he pursued the goal of developing a general ethnographic museum that would extend beyond Japan to the rest of the world, so that he
might reconstruct human history (Effert 2003: 140–4), his home became increasingly
(over-)filled. In the 1840s his financial difficulties forced him to move to a more
modest home, and housing conditions for the museum collection worsened. The
problem of housing this increasingly large, formally national collection remained into
the next century.

Collection Growth

The Leiden museum collection grew phenomenally throughout the century. The
museum received donations representing many distant geographical areas, though the
Dutch colonies and regions with a pronounced Dutch presence were most prominently
represented. Private individuals donated objects from their travels, as did colonial civil
servants, military officers, and missionaries. The museum became the repository
for objects collected in scientific expeditions and plundered from villages in military
actions in the Indies (van Wengen 2002c: 24–31, 37–42; 2002a: 83–4). Pre-existing
collections merged with those in Leiden, including the teaching collection of the
colonial section of the *Koninklijke Akademie* (Royal Academy of Civil Engineers) in
Delft when it closed in 1864, and the Royal Cabinet from The Hague that von Siebold
originally hoped to include in his museum in 1883. In addition, material that had been

exhibited at international colonial exhibitions, including the *Internationale Koloniale en Uitvoerhandel Tentoonstelling* (International Colonial and Export Trade Exhibition) in Amsterdam in 1883 (Bloembergen 2001), was donated to the collections of both *Artis* and Leiden. This ethnographica was gladly received and even solicited by the Leiden museum directors, who had few funds for acquisitions. While most of the Amsterdam exhibition was packed away in boxes, its full-scale indigenous buildings were rebuilt in Leiden as an open-air museum – although the Javanese peasants originally accompanying them had returned to the Indies (van Wengen 2002a: 84–5).

In 1859, von Siebold left the Netherlands for Japan, and his *Japansch Museum* came under the directorate of Conrad Leemans (1809–93) of the (national) *Museum van Oudheden* (Museum of Antiquities) in Leiden. Leemans soon had the Japanese collection moved to a more suitable building, where it was exhibited in the newly named *Rijks Japansch Museum von Siebold* (National Japanese Museum von Siebold). However, this new space could not accommodate the growing collection, and it moved again to quarters with more exhibition space. This was still not ideal. Leemans formally requested a new building from the national government in 1862. Not only did the state categorically refuse, but it also suggested that Leemans send extra material to *Artis* for its well-known ethnographic museum. Finding this option unacceptable, Leemans simply created space in the attic (van Dijk 1992: 353). In 1864, the Japanese Museum was renamed the *Rijks Ethnographisch Museum* (National Ethnographic Museum) to reflect its new, less specific geographical focus (Effert 2003: 193–5). While Leemans attempted to make the collections accessible for university education, his attempts failed, and he argued that cramped quarters made it impossible for professors to use a teaching collection in the museum (Effert 2003: 197–8). In 1880, Leemans resigned from his directorship and was succeeded by the museum curator, Lindor Serrurier, a trained lawyer and expert in Japanese who had turned to museum work. During Serrurier's tenure, the problem of space reached new proportions, as did tensions with the state over housing for the museum.

Serrurier both inherited and escalated the storage problem of his predecessors. During the course of his tenure, and as a result of his success in soliciting acquisitions to illustrate phases of development in human societies, the collections increased fivefold (van Wengen 2002a: 86). Eventually, the collection was stored in four different buildings, making it virtually inaccessible. Serrurier made several attempts to secure state funding for a new museum as he struggled for acceptable exhibition and work facilities. In the late 1880s, he collaborated with university administrators to develop a new museum plan in which they argued that the museum – at home only in Leiden – was exclusively pertinent to scholarly research. Despite support from Parliament, this appeal failed. Soon thereafter, Serrurier changed his position and argued that the professors at the university made little use of the collections and therefore the collections would be of more service to the public in a larger city (Serrurier 1895: 5–10). He preferred Amsterdam, and hoped to fuse his museum with that of *Artis*, where he would gladly take over the directorship. He would also consider moving his museum to The Hague. While it is not known what motivated Serrurier's apparent change of opinion, his reconfiguration of the museum's goals – from academic study to public exhibition – may have been a strategy to increase chances of government support for a new building. His proposals for a public museum received little support from Parliament (van Wengen 2002c: 66–7). In fact, during Serrurier's directorship, the Ministry of the Interior (*Binnenlandse Zaken*) made repeated attempts to move the collection to The Hague and to transform it into a museum for art and industrial design, arguing that the decorations on the ethnographica would provide an inspiring resource for Dutch industrial designers. The university and city council, however, argued that the museum depended on university scholars in Leiden – the center of colonial education and knowledge. In 1896, in the heat of these debates, Serrurier quit in frustration.

Serrurier was succeeded by the accomplished museum curator J. D. E. Schmeltz (1839–1909). Prior to his move to Leiden, Schmeltz curated the renowned private museum of J. C. Godeffroy in Hamburg (Penny 2002b: 5). At the time of his promotion to director, Schmeltz served as the editor and supervised the editorial office of the *Internationales Archiv für Ethnographie*, a publication project initiated by Adolf Bastian, the director of the ethnographic museum in Berlin (van Wengen 2002c: 41–2). As museum director, Schmeltz carried on Serrurier's goal to create a general ethnology museum and faced the chronic problems of space and what van Wengen describes as a political "tug of war" (*touwtrekken*) (van Wengen 2002c: 66). When, again, the state commissioned an evaluation of the museum, the appointed committee reached no consensus and individual dissenting members wrote their own opinions as separate appendices in the official report (*Rapport der Commissie* 1903). After Schmeltz's death in 1909, the new director H. H. Juynboll (1867–1932) faced another unsuccessful attempt by the state to move the museum and leave only a teaching collection in Leiden (van Wengen 2002c: 72–4). Juynboll concentrated his efforts and those of his staff on cataloging and describing the massive collections, spending decades to produce a 23-volume catalog of the East Indian collection. Ironically, while the university, the Leiden City Council, and Leiden loyalists in parliament fought to keep the museum in the university town, little professorial research was performed on the museum collections. In 1929, when the funding for a new museum was realized, the state appointed J. C. van Eerde of the KI (described above) – rather than a university professor – to oversee the plans to rebuild the academic hospital into the new museum, to create public exhibit space, and to move the collections. When Juynboll died in 1932, Van Eerde acted as interim director until his own death in 1936. The new building opened in 1937 with W. H. Rassers (1877–1973) as director. Given the *Leidenaars'* vehemence and success in keeping the museum in the university town of Leiden, how realistic were Serrurier's complaints that university students and staff lacked interest in the ethnographic collections?

Ethnographic Knowledge and Research at Leiden University

In the period under discussion, Leiden University emerged as the center of Netherlands East Indian studies, particularly after colonial civil service education was reshaped into an academic program and moved from the Royal Academy in Delft to Leiden in 1864 (Fasseur 2003). Subjects taught to the budding bureaucrats by professors of ethnography included languages, literature, history, religions, and *adat* law. Despite the founding of the first Dutch professorship in ethnography in 1877, few relationships developed between the museum and the university that fought so hard to keep the collection in Leiden. The first to hold the chair, P. J. Veth (1814–95), never traveled to Southeast Asia but wrote and edited descriptive encyclopedic works based on written sources (van der Velde 2000). His successor, the evolutionist G. A. Wilken (1847–91), pursued similar comparative work (Schefold 2002: 75–80), producing descriptive ethnographies of Dutch colonies that betray the practical nature of this early Dutch anthropological scholarship (Ellen 1976: 312–13). Similarly, after Wilken, J. J. M. de Groot (1854–1921), a Sinologist, wrote descriptive ethnography explicitly in the interest of empire (de Groot 1891). De Groot's successor, the evolutionist and physician A. W. Nieuwenhuis (1864–1953), worked with ethnographica more than his predecessors, though not necessarily in the museum context. Holding the chair from 1904 until 1934, Nieuwenhuis had previously coordinated the collection of ethnographic data and natural history specimens in state-supported scientific expeditions through Borneo, some of which were political in character and intended to aid the colonial state (Schefold 2002: 82–5). While, unlike his predecessors, Nieuwenhuis actively collected and studied ethnographic objects in the field and used them for teaching material when he lectured in the Leiden museum, his study of the material was performed in the field rather than in the museum (Nieuwenhuis 1904: 41). That the nearby museum hardly played a role for leading academics brings into question assertions made about the scholarly advantages of keeping the museum in Leiden.

The appointment of two academically trained curators in the second decade of the twentieth century marked a significant turn for both the museum and the university. J. P. B. de Josselin de Jong (1886–1964), having conducted fieldwork (including archaeological) in the Americas and completed a dissertation on ethnolinguistics, began his studies of the museum's Antillean archaeological collection in 1910 (Effert 1992: 18–27). In 1935, he left for a university appointment, succeeding Nieuwenhuis as professor of ethnography. The second curator, W. H. Rassers, expert in the languages and literature of the East Indian Archipelago, began at the museum in 1918, when he based his dissertation research on museum objects to explore Javanese cultural expression. Throughout his career, Rassers worked in the museum studying the collections and ultimately became director of the museum in 1937. Rassers and de Josselin de Jong, who developed a close and productive relationship, founded the influential Leiden school of structural anthropology (Ellen 1976: 319–21; Schefold 2002: 85–9; Effert 1992).

In their studies, Rassers and de Josselin de Jong – and the Leiden structuralist school – combined empirical fieldwork, and a holistic view of culture. Influenced by Durkheim and Mauss, they explained cultural phenomena through analyses of social structure and explicitly criticized the evolutionary views of their predecessors in Leiden (De Josselin de Jong 1960: 6–9). Rassers continued to develop structuralist theory, at times using museum objects to support his theoretical position (van Wengen

2002c: 78). In de Josselin de Jong's long and successful university career, he moved away from the study of objects and developed theoretical models based on ethnographic fieldwork. Despite Rassers's exceptional use of objects (Schefold 2002: 87), social theory based on field ethnography, rather than on material culture, signaled the importance of the structuralist school and the insignificance of the museum collections for the production of knowledge.

De Josselin de Jong's professorial predecessors neither studied museum objects nor did they engage in social theorizing. As Ellen argues, as long as the state needed practical knowledge, theoretical developments were suppressed. Leiden structuralist anthropology did not serve colonial administrative needs in the ways that, for example, investigations of *adat* law did. Only when ethnologists no longer directly aided the state bureaucracy did they entertain purely academic theoretical notions. Thus, anthropology arose as a specialized professionalized discipline in the Netherlands when it became politically unnecessary (Ellen 1976: 320–1). Although criticized by some who deemphasize the utility of pre-professional Dutch ethnology for the colonial state and emphasize professionalized intellectual and institutional (university) history – in particular, the structuralist school (Hüsken 2002; Prager 1999; De Wolf 1999) – Ellen's view of the practical nature of early Dutch anthropological inquiry remains plausible when we consider the colonial context in which it arose.

Rassers and, in particular, de Josselin de Jong have been heralded as the founding fathers of modern Dutch anthropology because they contributed to the development of anthropological theory – the hallmark of scholarly work. However, this perspective privileges theoretical work in the academy over the pre-professional ethnographic knowledge gained, in the Dutch case, for utilitarian purposes. If we acknowledge its historical heritage, today's anthropology is the successor to nineteenth-century physical anthropology, ethnography, and ethnology, and de Josselin de Jong is not the father of Dutch anthropology. Long before de Josselin de Jong wrote ethnographies, scores of people – civil servants, missionaries, naturalists, and museum curators – collected, cataloged, described, and displayed ethnographica. They also studied and taught indigenous languages, customs, and technologies. Various institutions commissioned the production of this knowledge – the state, private enterprise, museums, technical schools, and universities. Dutch anthropology had many fathers – and probably some mothers.

Given the utilitarian nature of early Dutch anthropological knowledge, the vast collections amassed to promote commerce were not critical to the production of specialized academic anthropological knowledge, either in the early period when the university scholars trained colonial bureaucrats or in later decades when structuralists trained field researchers. The founding in 1914 of the first Dutch university anthropology department, the Institute of Ethnology of the University of Utrecht, supports this argument. The city of Utrecht housed no ethnographic collection, a situation some scholars have found "remarkable" (Vermeulen and Kommers 2002: 8–9). They also observe that, though understudied, museums played a significant role in the development of Dutch anthropology (Vermeulen and Kommers 2002: 36). However, in the historiography dominated by a disciplinary perspective that ignores the ethnographic tradition and its many practitioners in the nineteenth century (Vermeulen 2002), this role cannot be explained. In this national context where museums and academic anthropology developed independently of each other, museum collections were simply not prerequisites for university study or research, and, therefore, had little influence on the development of academic anthropology.

Conclusion

A diversity of relationships between ethnographic museums and university anthropology arose in different national contexts, influenced in part by employment possibilities for anthropological experts. Students trained in the Netherlands enjoyed career opportunities in the colonial civil service or entered the world of private enterprise. They rarely moved between the university and the museum. Yet in the American case, museums were the most important employers of university-trained anthropologists until World War I (Stocking 1985: 114). The situation in the Netherlands also contrasts with, for example, those in Scandinavian and German-speaking countries, where anthropology remained largely museum-based for decades after World War II, and in France, where the *Musée de l'Homme* remained a prominent teaching and research center (Frese 1960: 68). De Josselin de Jong was an exception when appointed to the Leiden chair, but he did not return to the museum or to studies of material culture. Rather, he founded a school and promoted a methodology that rendered museums irrelevant to anthropological inquiry. Just as was the case in Anglo-American anthropology, theoretical and field ethnography devalued museum ethnography and collections, and superseded studies of material culture.

Museums of European colonial powers also diverged in their geographical foci and intellectual goals. In the Netherlands, where utility figured prominently, both museums and academic anthropology focused on Dutch colonies or regions significant for overseas trade. Similarly, in Belgium, the Museum of the Congo (founded in 1897, now the Royal Museum of Central Africa) developed expertise on Africa, and devoted 30 percent of its exhibit space to economic aspects of trade and tropical products (Royal Museum of Central Africa 2006). In contrast, the Pitt Rivers Museum, intending to display human evolution in Western and non-Western societies, collected artifacts from all over the world, just as German museums, located in a country with fewer direct colonial connections, collected and displayed objects from near and far to illustrate general human development. Uniquely, the Paris museum ultimately united anthropological studies of exotic cultures with those of French regional culture, or folklore.

The histories of European ethnographic museums in their national contexts shed light on the diversity of collecting practices and uses of objects for study and education, the types of knowledge produced, the levels of cooperation between museums and universities, and the roles of museums on the development of academic anthropology. More important, they illuminate a site for the production of the ethnographic tradition and variety of knowledges critical to our understanding of the history of

Figure 8   Entrance to the Department of Tropical Products of the Royal Institute of the Tropics, as seen today. Originally the Trade Museum, this department was renamed in the heat of the Indonesian revolution in 1947. Photograph by the author.

academic anthropology. Museums are one non-academic ingredient in the history of anthropology (Pels and Salemink 1999).

The two Dutch museums to which I devoted especially detailed attention faced decline in the middle decades of the twentieth century as structuralist anthropology developed. Their collections – the displayed material embodiment of empire, acquired because of overseas expansion, and used to instruct the public and to advance trade – lost meaning as the nation's colonial presence declined. The KI suffered from the loss of generous capital support from industry in the financially troubled 1930s. Its situation worsened with the outbreak of World War II, the Japanese invasion of the Netherlands East Indies, subsequent decolonization, and the rise of the Indonesian nation. Forced to redefine itself (Kreps 1988), the KI has become today's Royal Institute of the Tropics (see Figure 8). The loss of colonial power forced academic change in Leiden. The Leiden museum which, throughout its history, lacked consensus about its utility, also faltered. The museums, like their counterpart practical anthropology, became politically unnecessary.

Acknowledgments

I would like to thank Henrika Kuklick and Judith Schueler for their comments on earlier drafts of this paper. My research was supported by the Dutch Organisation for Scientific Research, grant number 360-53-020.

Further Reading

Bouquet, Mary, ed. 2001. *Academic Anthropology and the Museum: Back to the Future.* New York: Berghahn.
McDonald, Sharon, ed. 1998. *The Politics of Display: Museums, Science, Culture.* London: Routledge.
Schefold, Reimar and Han F. Vermeulen, eds. 2002. *Treasure Hunting? Collectors and Collections of Indonesian Artefacts.* Leiden: CNWS Publications.

11

Political Fieldwork, Ethnographic Exile, and State Theory: Peasant Socialism and Anthropology in Late-Nineteenth-Century Russia

Nikolai Ssorin-Chaikov

In 1928, Soviet ethnographer Vladimir Bogoraz addressed the Committee for Assistance to the Peoples of the Northern Borderlands of the All-Soviet Central Executive Committee of the USSR (which oversaw the state's indigenous policies between 1924 and 1936). It was an occasion for Bogoraz to praise his recently deceased colleague Lev Shternberg, crediting him and his like-minded "comrades" with having developed a new form of ethnography. In the 1890s, Shternberg lived in a Siberian town, Alexandrovsk, where he researched the indigenous Giliak for five years. According to Bogoraz, the new ethnography required both language study and, more importantly, long-term, "stationary" research – conducted in a specific place – as opposed to the wide-ranging and short surveys that were then usual ethnographic practice. In passing, Bogoraz noted that this new method was made possible by the "leisure that the comrades then enjoyed" (Ssorin-Chaikov 2003: 52).

This "leisure that the comrades then enjoyed" was no leisure of scholarly gentlemen of independent means or armchair Victorian anthropologists. Bogoraz's reference was to imprisonment and political exile in Siberia. Shternberg and Bogoraz were among dozens of Russian anthropologists whose academic careers began in such "leisure" that followed their involvement in left-wing political activism. In the late nineteenth century, activists from all parts of the spectrum of Russian radical politics – from nationalists to orthodox Marxists – experienced Siberian exile. Most of the activists who turned to ethnography were participants in *narodnichestvo* – "populism," or "peasant socialism" – a socialist movement with a name derived from the word *narod*, meaning "people," "peasantry," "uneducated classes." *Narodnichestvo* activists believed in the socialist nature of the Russian peasant community (*mir*), opposing the development of industrial capitalism in late-nineteenth-century Russia; and their research in and after exile was continuous with their political fieldwork before it. This was the so-called *knozhdenie v narod*, "going to/living among the people" or "going peasant" – undertaking the socialist agitation that led to arrests.

While the Russian intelligentsia had been interested in the "people" throughout the nineteenth century, in the era of the abolition of serfdom and other social reforms of the 1860s a distinct and "new type of student of popular life" emerged – the "ethnographic populist" (*etnograph-narodnik*). "[I]nspired by the idea of serving the people," this student conceived politically engaged research as a form of service. Siberian exile was students' punishment for their activism, but their contact with actual life conditions made some of them "real experts" on "the people" (Pypin 1891: 346).

This chapter is about the relationship between what these scholars/activists meant by "the people" and by being "real experts." I discuss how "the people" were understood as a source of modernity's social alternatives. For Russian populists, the peasant community or Siberian "primitive socialism" had what modern society lacked – specifically, the free association of producers on land held in common and, more generally, direct sociality of the relationships between producers.

Hence, there was a distinctly socialist notion of field site. Rather than a remote location where "otherness" could be imagined in the colonial, capitalist, and disciplinary gaze (Gupta and Ferguson 1997; Fabian 1983), this was a place of teleological revelation and expectation, from which the radical incompleteness of modernity was visible. Meanings of being a "real expert" on the people followed from the radical incompleteness of modernity. Critique was the only meaningful attitude toward it, and displacement was the only "authentic" form of presence within it. Indeed, exile and undercover revolutionary propaganda were the only specific forms of fieldwork that were true to it. Furthermore, the site from which this vision of the people could be voiced was also often a literal and literary displacement: much populist writing was done in political exile in western Europe, with some of the most influential work being published pseudonymously in Russia.

The ethnography and politics of peasant socialism significantly complicates our understanding of the history of anthropology. They point to the role of critical theory and radical activism for a time period usually characterized by historians of anthropology as an era in which "armchair" anthropologists articulated "establishment" views. They point to a defect in the two key assumptions that engendered the "historiographic turn" in anthropology since the mid-1980s: first, that the un- or pre-critical "colonial situation" was required for the development of anthropology as a "field science" (Asad 1973; Stocking 1991; Gupta and Ferguson 1997), and, second, that this development can be reduced to the critical encounter of classic evolutionary theory, with its ideology of universal progress, with the "cultural relativism" of nineteenth-century Romantic thought (Stocking 1987; Herzfeld 1987).

The history of Russian/Soviet anthropology has been written from the point of view of this interplay of evolutionary and nationalist narratives of difference. Tokarev (1966) and Gellner (1975, 1988) examined the enduring evolutionary legacy in Russian/Soviet anthropology that is visible, for example, in Engels's praise of Lev Shternberg and his account of Giliak (Nivkh) kinship because it was "empirical proof" of the practice of "group marriage" hypothesized by Lewis Henry Morgan (Engels 1995 [1892]). Recently, the eruption of post-socialist ethno-nationalism has called attention to the academic enunciation of nationalist ideologies in Imperial Russia and the Soviet Union (Tishkov 1992; Suny 1993; Slezkine 1994; Knight 1995; Martin 2001; Hirsch 2005; but see also Gellner ed. 1980). This interplay between "otherness as backwardness" and "otherness as uniqueness" is also rehearsed in the discussions of Russian Orientalism (Clay 1995; Brower and Lazzerini 1997; Khalid 2000). In this context, there are some studies that highlight the populist ethnographers' contribution to fieldwork methods (Krupnik 1996; Solovei 1998). Yet the full range of implications of their intellectual and political projects for anthropology remains underexplored (but see Grant 1999).

By looking at populist anthropology, my goal in this chapter is to draw attention to it as a distinctive locus of modern anthropological discourse. In this discourse, "otherness" is not "backwardness" or "uniqueness," and it is not a problem that was to be analytically solved (ordered and classified) from the vantage point of a "a great historical confidence" of the modern "self" (Mitchell 1991: 7). Here, "otherness" is a solution for *modernity* understood as a problem. "Otherness" is here a tool for res-olution of the tension between modernity "as it is" and modernity "as it should be." Two implications of this understanding underscore my argument below.

The first is for the understanding of "otherness" in the context of modernity "as it is" – that is, in the context of all that was "wrong" with it. In this regard, the populist ethnography is an unacknowledged part of the genealogy of the post-1960s "political economy" approach in anthropology and its critique of the state and colonial projects. The populist ethnography that I discuss below revealed the role of the state and colonial systems in the construction of local customs and communities. I focus in detail on an ethnographic case of Russian Northern peasant community organization – first, as it was discussed by two populist writers, and, second, as it figured in the broader landscape of ethnographic debates in late-nineteenth-century Russia, which extended to the Russian "state school" of legal studies. Uncovering a rich and complex discourse on "state" and "community" that informed the ethnography of populists and their interlocutors, I chart the emergence of a historicizing mode in nineteenth-century anthropology.

The second implication is for the understanding of "otherness" as a window on modernity "as it should be." I open the discussion below with the imagination of socialism as a peasant community, and I conclude, via the state theory of community, with the emergence of a peculiar form of positivism – of "truth-as-fairness" – as a more general anthropological method. In this vision, modernity is "the other" world of "truth-as-fairness." It is estranged from itself – from modernity "as it is" – and is im-agined in a pure form only in a displaced yet analytically privileged condition of exile (cf. Malkki 1995). This chapter is a description of how modernity as an imminent social order – the world "as it should be" – underscores multiple displaced conditions which form "overlapping disjunctures" (Appadurai 1996) of repressive state and capitalist systems, cultural worlds of the oppressed, and travel trajectories of socialist theorists.

Background: Late-Nineteenth-Century Russia and the Peasant Community

By 1881, Karl Marx had reached the conclusion that the rural community would provide the "the fulcrum of social rebirth" in Russia. If only it was "freed from all impediments to its spontaneous development," it could serve as an alternative to capitalist modernity (Marx 1955 [1881]: 411–12). Marx's argument cites anthropologist Lewis Henry Morgan, who ended his *Ancient Society* with a prediction that the destruction of capitalism would end with a return to the highest form of the "archaic" type of property – collective production and collective appropriation – a modern version of the "liberty, equality and fraternity of the ancient gens (clans)" (Morgan 1963 [1877]: 561–2). Marx puts this also in terms of a more general critical intervention in the Victorian evolutionary perspective. In his view, Sir Henry Sumner Maine had erred when he saw the demise of the village community as inevitable; rather, it had been damaged by the policies of British rulers of India. In the Russian case, Marx also had very specific "impediments to spontaneous development" of the peasant community in mind.

In 1861, the Russian government had abolished serfdom, a state juridical system in which peasants were the personal property of feudal landlords. Peasants received citizenship rights – the rights of self-government within their social estate, namely, in local councils and peasant district (*volost*') courts. In reality, however, their emancipation was limited. Most land remained feudal property. Peasants received land allotments "for indefinite use," but these ultimately remained the property of their former masters. Peasants had a right to purchase their land from their landlords, yet few did. They clung to the "indefinite use" of land and to "traditional" forms of agriculture, neither transforming themselves into private farmers nor abandoning the land altogether for urban working-class occupations.

Historians of the emancipation of serfs explain peasants' behavior by the multiple and complex communal bonds among individual peasant families, the unwritten "custom" of communal land tenure (Kornilov 1905; Wcislo 1990; Worobec 1991). Significantly for my argument here, these "customs" inspired much debate at the time of emancipation; these debates were central for emerging Russian socialism and Russian anthropology; and Marx's writing on the Russian peasant community figured in this debate. Did "peasant habits" explain the slowness of Russia's capitalist development at the end of the nineteenth century? Or did its characteristics stimulate imagination of social alternatives to capitalism? Marx's dilemma was whether Russia should follow the recommendation of liberal economists, who believed that the transition to capitalism required the destruction of the rural community, or whether Russia could both manage to benefit from the technological yields of capitalism and develop its own historical features. Ironically, his own views in *Capital* (1976 [1867]) and the views of his Marxist followers in Russia overlapped with the liberal economic perspective. Thus, his approach to the peasant community in Russia was a reformulation of his views on peasantry in *Capital*. Furthermore, in this reformulation, he provides a good summary of the literature, including ethnographic and economic sources that he read in Russian.

Marx summarized his day's extensive Russian literature on the peasant community, which grew rapidly from just a few publications in the mid-1850s to 372 titles between 1876 and 1880 and over 2,000 by 1904 (Tokarev 1966: 291). Following this literature, Marx defined the Russian rural community as consisting of private households integrated in a complex way. It was based on the parcel system of holding of arable land, which was constantly re-partitioned among community members, while remaining communal property, as well as the existence of undivided communal right to forest, pastures, and other non-cultivated land. The rural community "owed its vitality to the dualism of its structure" – its communal property and its private households (Marx 1955 [1881]). The tension between its private and collective elements might lead to its decline, but it was equally likely that the communal element might prevail. It was the tension between the individual and collective elements of communal organization that made the rural community, for Marx, "the sprout of socialism," which might divest itself of its "primitive" features and become an element of collective production on a national scale. In his writing, Marx reproduced the prevailing view that the tension between the individual and communal elements in Russian peasant society was structural, and not a function of the operation of evolutionary processes. For Marx, this was critical when he considered "what is to be done" with the community in order to make it the "fulcrum of Russia's social rebirth." One could encourage the individual elements in the communal structure, or the collective ones.

From Exile to Political Fieldwork

Prior to the 1860s, academic understanding of "primitive life" in Russia belonged to the domain of comparative philology. Subsequently, Russian anthropology emerged as a form of knowledge about "contemporary savages" gathered through fieldwork. In part, the educated classes became interested in ethnography in association with their growing interest in natural history: in 1863 the "Society for the Students of Natural Sciences, Anthropology and Ethnography" was founded at Moscow University; and in 1867 it put out an All-Russian Ethnographic Exhibit (Tokarev 1966: 286).

The view of community that prevailed among the Russian ethnographers whose work Marx used had a different point of origin. In the 1860s, members of literary circles also became interested in "the people," understood as "peasants" and "uneducated classes." Ethnographic essays appeared in the *Sovremennik* ("Contemporary") and the *Otechestvennye Zapiski* ("Home Notes") and other literary journals. They were written in the genre of "critical realism" and emphasized social inequality (Tokarev 1966: 278–9). Two key publications shaped intellectual trends (and eventually influenced Marx's views). The first was V. V. Bervi's series of essays, "The Conditions of the Working Classes in Russia," published in the radical journal *Delo* ("Action") in the 1860s. The second was "Letters from the Village" by A. I. Engelgart, published in *Otechestvennye Zapiski* ("Home Notes") in 1872–82. Engelgart's "Letters" were particularly important for the "critical realism" of ethnography, since they pointed to the fragmentation of communities and the emergence of economic inequalities in the village, contradictory land tenure and inheritance practices, and pronounced gender hierarchies.

Bervi's and Engelgart's literary voices were both conditioned by political displacement. Bervi adopted a pseudonym "N. Flerovskii," and Engelgart wrote his "Letters" in exile when he, a professor of chemistry in St Petersburg, was forced to resign his job because of his political views, expelled from the capital, and settled on his small family estate in the Smolensk Province.

Indeed, at this time most Russian critical thought was produced under conditions of exile, political emigration, and literary disguise. The key point of populist social theory – that the rural community could provide a basis for socialism in Russia – was originally made by Alexander Herzen, who was writing from Paris and London. Herzen's idea derived from an influential discourse that had flourished among Russia's educated elite since the 1840s, but which had originally centered on the question of Russia's uniqueness in relationship with the West (the position of the so-called "slavophiles"). Herzen, concerned with the lack of political liberties in the Russian Empire, was initially opposed to slavophile ideology, finding it conservative and apologetic of the established order. Observing rapid and brutal capitalist development in the West, he changed his mind. "The economic principle of the community is the complete opposite of the famous thesis of Malthus: it allocates a place at the dinner-table to everyone" (1956 [1850–51]: 259; see also Herzen 1956 [1851] and 1957 [1854]). In the late 1860s, anarchist Mikhail Bakunin, also in political exile in western Europe, called for peasant revolts in agrarian countries such as Spain, Italy, and Russia. In his polemics with Marx in the First International, Bakunin developed his theory of socialist statelessness, exhorting the "radical youth" of Russia to "help" people to "organize" revolt and "seize all the land" from state and feudal landlords and "form, on this land, free rural communes based on collective property" (Kornilov 1905).

In Russia, these ideas gained intellectual currency in the broader milieu of the educated classes after the appearance of Petr Lavrov's *Historical Letters* (1906 [1869]), published under a pseudonym and written in the Russian North – to which Lavrov was exiled following his arrest for participating in the underground organization "Land and Freedom." In 1870, Lavrov escaped to Paris, where he joined the First International and the Paris Commune uprising. In 1873, Lavrov founded the radical newspaper *Vpered!* ("Forward!"), which became one of the most important voices of political populism, advancing the argument that the lived experience of small landed communities and worker's cooperatives had prepared the Russian people for socialism (e.g. Lavrov 1907).

"Forward!" captured a mood that was, however, broader than socialist: "With all the diversity of manifestations of this mood, from revolutionary radicalism to mystical quietism, . . . the common striving [was] to unite with the people, work for the good of the people . . . everybody referred to 'the people,' talked about 'closing with' or 'going to' the people" (Pypin 1891: 349). The ethnographic writing that I examine in detail below (Sokolovskii 1877; Shcherbina 1879, 1880; Yefimenko 1884) was produced in the context of the "going to the people" campaign of the 1870s. A participant in this campaign, Sergei Kovalik, recalled a sense of "urgency" among the radical youth in the numerous secret societies and networks ("circles," *kruzhki*) that mushroomed in St Petersburg, Moscow, Kiev, Odessa, Saratov and other cities in the early 1870s: "it was time to go" (Kovalik 1928: 130–3). The purposes of "going to the people" were multiple. Some wanted to do "small deeds," such as starting schools and providing charity and medical help in the countryside. Others agreed with Bakunin, who argued that the peasantry was ready for rebellion (Itenberg 1965), and hoped to motivate peasants to seize land from state and feudal landlords. From the pages of "Forward!," Lavrov called for patience and for long preparation for revolutionary agitation.

Radicals who attempted to act were in the minority. Still, there were hundreds of young members of populist "circles" who "in the spring, 1874, . . . departed by railway from the centers to the provinces. Every young man carried a false passport issued in the name of a peasant or a petty bourgeois [*meschanina*], had a coat or [other] peasant clothing packed, if not already worn . . . and a few revolutionary books or brochures." Some of them settled on their home estates, others in "places where they had some connections," but most moved to the Volga basin, where they expected to find the "most favorable soil for their revolutionary activity" (Kovalik 1928: 133).

This activity consisted of urging revolt, and it was carried out in two main forms – the "fleeting" and the "settled." Those agents who moved rapidly from one village to another apparently experienced considerable psychological difficulties, as they attempted to play their role so well that peasants did not suspect that they were gentlemen in disguise. Indeed after spending as many as two years "among the people," some of them became relatively convincing (ibid.: 136). If the purpose of the "fleeting" mode was to find already existing spots of peasant discontent, the "settled" work was aimed at raising local consciousness: "the propagandist made acquaintances among nearby peasants or workers, at first as if without any particular purpose, and, then, little by little, starting conversations on revolutionary topics" (ibid.: 137; see also Deitch 1920; Raskol'nikova 1926).

This campaign continued through the 1870s, but ended in failure. The Tsar's political police easily distinguished gentlemen from peasants, arresting key agitators (Itenberg 1965: 384–99). The populists complained that the "peasants listened but did not understand" (Kovalik 1928: 139), generally failing to respond to populists' critical voices. Peasants mistook revolutionaries for state agents and reported them to the police (Itenberg 1965: 277). One Verevochkina from the Orienburg circle, who visited rural areas "under the pretext of picking berries," was initially welcomed; subsequently, it was rumored that she was a witch. In the only place in which populists succeeded in organizing peasants, the Chigirinskii region, they did so not by raising socialist consciousness but by circulating a letter in November 1876 which purported to be a directive from the Tsar ordering the peasants to form oppositional "secret societies" (ibid.: 151; Deitch 1921: 73–9). Mass arrests followed.

The Rural Community in the Russian North: A Case Study

Apparently, "intuitive socialists" ("the people") did not easily forge political unions with "ideological socialists" (the intelligentsia). But how was the ethnographic imagination of this generation of activists and scholars affected by populists' failure to close the gap between themselves and "the people"? These failures demonstrated "the power of the state over peasant consciousness." Thus, from the late 1870s, the state became the main target of populist revolutionary practices. Increasingly, populists abandoned their efforts to foster peasant revolt and undertook political terrorism aimed at top state officials. Persons on their "black lists" included Tsar Alexander II, who was assassinated on March 1, 1881. The state also became a prominent theme in the ethnographic writing to which many of populists turned after their arrests, imprisonment, and exile to the Russian North and Siberia.

For example, Sergei Kovalik was exiled to Verkhoiansk, where he stayed from 1882 to 1892, and published ethnography about economic conditions among the Verkhoiansk Yakut (1895). Historian of Russian ethnography Pypin observed, "Youthful carelessness" – a euphemism for political agitation – "has drawn Muscovite Rybnikov from his travel in southern Russia to the Olonetskii province [of the North]; and, in a similar way, the southerner Chubinskii found himself in Archangel" (1891: 347). Another political fieldworker of the 1870s, Dmitrii Klementz, was exiled to Minusinsk, in southern Siberia, and spent years working for the local natural history and ethnography museum (Klementz 1886). In 1893, he organized a long-term research project with ten other political exiles, including Vladimir Bogoraz, the "Sibiriakov Expedition," funded by the goldminer and industrialist I. M. Sibiriakov, which explored socioeconomic conditions in the areas adjacent to the goldfields of the Lena river basin (Mainov 1929: xii).

I now turn to two case studies that illustrate the populist polemic about the nature of the Russian rural community: the writing of the populist ethnographers Fedor Alexeievich Shcherbina and Alexandra Yakovlevna Yefimenko. Both worked in the northern parts of European Russia. Shcherbina was exiled to the Viatka and Vologda provinces in 1874–77. Yefimenko, a teacher in rural Kholmogory, near Archangel, married an exiled populist, Petr Yefimenko.

In the 1870s, the North attracted ethnographic interest because "the original" Russian rural community had supposedly survived there. This ancient community was the "district" (*volost'*), a political and agrarian union of several villages. As was argued in the influential book published by historian P. A. Sokolovskii in 1877, *Outline of the History of Community in Northern Russia*, this old Russian union was analogous to the German "mark," a unit of communal land tenure that was formed by conquest of land by a "clan" or "tribe" during the Germanic territorial expansion of the time of Tacitus. Sokolovskii followed the same logic in explaining Slavic colonization of southeast Europe during the early middle ages (1878). In central Russia, this "district community" disappeared with the expansion of feudal land tenure; it was preserved only in the northern periphery of the Russian state and among the Don and Ural Cossacks (Sokolovskii 1877).

Shcherbina and Yefimenko presented a counter-argument: the northern rural community was a recent construct, and should be seen at least partly as a product of particular state policies, rather than as a survival of a stateless social form. For example, Shcherbina observed that the northern peasant community was shaped by a relatively recent state system of land accounting, which made explicit a legal distinction between communal and private land use. He put forward a research question: "Who was the real creator of these forms of property, and what were the consequences of their creation?" (1879: 44–5). In a similar polemic, Yefimenko formulated the goal of her study, which contrasted sharply with the search for primordial survivals pursued by other anthropologists: "The time has come to put the dogma of the primordial and primitive origins [*dogmat ob iskonnosti i pervobytnosti*] of the rural community through a rigorous historical critique [*istoriko-kriticheskomu analizu*]" (1884: 373).

In these ethnographers' work, the Russian North did not represent an idyllic repository of original communal lifestyles, but was a product of colonial expansion; peasant settlers took the land "purchasing or simply seizing land" from much less numerous Finnish-speaking groups (ibid.). In the fourteenth and fifteenth centuries, the main agent of colonization was the Novgorod Principality, and the main form of this colonization was the "half system" (*polovnichestvo*, from Russian *polovina*, "half"). Wealthy Novgorod clans (*boiare*) hired agents, who ran the villages of colonists, sharing with the Novgorod investors approximately half of the profit collected from fur trading settlers or from taxation (Shcherbina 1879: 55; Yefimenko 1884: 195). The lands the colonists occupied were regarded as the property of the Novgorod investors, and the colonists as their "tenants." After Novgorod was conquered by Moscow in 1479, this land was seized from the Novgorod lords and declared the "Tsar's" or "state" property (*gosudareva zemlia*), although some of the state concessions for trade and industrial use followed the "half" model, such as the concession of the wealthy Stroganoff family of Ural entrepreneurs (Shcherbina 1879: 47–50).

The "district [*volost'*] community," according to Shcherbina and Yefimenko, emerged as a unit of state taxation (*gosudatevo tiaglo*) on this state land. Yet, in the process of formation of the "district" as a state unit, these areas underwent various stages of colonization, related to the "slash-and-burn" rural cultivation cycle in which individual family properties were integrated into larger communal structures. Clearing the forest by burning made it the property of a given individual family, but "in about forty years" the cleared land became communal property (Yefimenko 1884: 201). Shcherbina (1879: 73–5) cites five categories of land, which differed in terms of ownership status as well as in terms of stages of colonization. The first category was "God's land," that is, "free, unoccupied, empty," in the colonists' usage, the right to which "was given only by labor" of clearing and cultivation. It is noteworthy that, according to Yefimenko, this "God's land" was also a general definition of the land in peasants' usage: "The land is the Grand Duke's [that is, the Grand Duke of Moscow], but the toil [*posilie*] is my father's and mine"; "the land is God's and Novgorod's," but "theirs" is the labor invested in it (1884: 198–9). "God's," "Novgorod's" or "Grand-Duke's" land was contrasted with "human land" – the land that was already property of a given "commune" (*mir*) or "society" (*obchestvo*), distinguishing it from the land of other communities – which was not subject to redistribution within the community. "New" land (*novina*) was the still uncultivated part of this land, which became communal "allotment" (*nadel*) after cultivation. The final category was "private" land or "subject of property" (*sobstvennaia zemlia*), which did not circulate within the community.

The structure of the community was defined, according to Shcherbina, through the taxation category of the "head" or "adult person," which was the smallest unit of accounting of land allotment within the community, the estimate of work capacity of a given family, and the unit of taxation: "the one who uses the communal property in larger proportion than the 'head' allotment allows, or carries less taxation duties [*povinnostei*] . . ." is "the adversary" (*suprotivnik*) of communal interests and "the enemy of its tranquility." This structure of sharing of communal resources and obligations was sanctioned by the head tax of 1719, and formed "a solid basis of popular life by the end of the 18th century" (Shcherbina 1879: 194, 44).

These studies belied the populists' view of the "organic" rural community, which persisted as the basis of their political ideology in the 1880s and was criticized by Russian Marxists. Yet views such as Shcherbina's and Yefimenko's were much more widespread among socialist students of rural life than Marxist critics acknowledged. They were evident in both ethnographic and historical peasant studies (e.g. Shcherbina 1880; Kaufman 1908; Vasilchiakov 1881; Semevskii 1881), underscored the interdisciplinary analysis of the rural community produced in 1878 by the Imperial Free Economic Society (Tigorov 1879), and influenced ethnographic understanding of cultural differences in the Russian colonial context. For instance, participants in the Sibiriakov Expedition focused on the role of state taxation in construction of indigenous communal structures in Siberia (Vitashevskii 1929a; Levental' 1929; Mainov 1898), as well as illustrating the "embryology" of the law in a more traditional evolutionary sense (Vitashevskii 1929b; see also Yefimenko 1877).

Theories of Community and Anthropology of the State

I have argued that acknowledgment of the role of the state in construction of local communities resulted from populist field experience, both political and ethnographic. This also demonstrates that the populist discourse was not an autonomous one, illustrating the continuity of ideas on the nineteenth-century political and anthropological "left" from Marx to Herzen and Russian peasant socialists. Now I will examine a continuity on the "right" of this discursive field – between populist ethnography and the so-called "state school" of Russian social thought of the 1850–70s, which legitimated Tsarist absolutism and the state approach to the construction of "community" and "people." My purpose is to outline the broader landscape of ideas where political and ethnographic populism figured both as ethnographic discourse and as a theory of political action.

Some of the conclusions of Yefimenko and Shcherbina look similar to those of the key figures of the Russian "state school," historians of law Boris Nikolaevich Chicherin and Konstantin Dmitrievich Kavelin. Just as Marx was, these scholars were influenced by Hegel. However, Marx used Hegelian methodology to envision modern social processes through a theory of commodity, while these theorists were more orthodox Hegelians, explaining social processes through the theory of the state.

Yefimenko and Shcherbina's writing accords with the central thesis of this theory – that the Russian state created communities for "fiscal purposes." Even the "people," with its linguistic and cultural unity, was, from this point of view, the product of state construction, rather than a pre-existing "organic" basis of the state, as Romantic nationalists ("slavophiles") suggested (Chicherin 1858: 285–6, 369). In particular, what appeared to be peasant collectivism was an invented tradition, a mode of control imposed by the state from the thirteenth century onwards. The central element of this mode of control consisted in the so-called "circle binding" (*krugovaia poruka*) – collective ("circle") responsibility for rural individuals' tax returns. This collectivism was formally legislated in the seventeenth century; and it constituted an internal enclave of communalism within the larger system of state and feudal land ownership (Kavelin 1989b [1859]; Chicherin 1899). Specific communal structures "on the ground" were constructed in tandem with state forms. Thus, it was possible to theorize the social organization of peasant communities and of the state administration in the same analytical language, in which individuality and collectivity, community and the state were subject to similar historical processes.

For example, in examining the social dynamics of the peasant community, Yefimenko argues that they cannot be theorized either as a system of "communal holding" or as conglomerates of individual parceled holdings (*obschinnoe vladenie* versus *podvorno-uchastkovoe vladenie*). Individual parcels of land were inherited within an extended family (*pechische*), in which each member had equal rights in all different portions of land and other property. Once the parcels were inherited, they could be sold to buyers both within and outside the village community. The community was a product of economic co-operation and taxation (one of the terms applied to a community member was "share-holder" [*skladnik*]); yet the communal bond was so strong that "the individual holder" was "a moral representative of an ideal whole of the village" (Yefimenko 1884: 220).

This historical balance of communal and individual share-holding was not clearly defined, however. Indeed, the "state school" never conceptualized share-holding as private property, rather it viewed it as parceling a communal plot in the complex classification of land within the cosmology of work and power. According to Yefimenko, the clear juridical definition of communal holding was a result of state intervention and, specifically, of state annexation of land in the North after the fifteenth century (ibid.: 374–6). As Shcherbina explained, the relationship between individual and communal property was itself a social construct. Until the eighteenth century, the boundaries between these different regimes of property were "blurred"; historically, even "the very notions of private property were different"; and the concepts of "property in general were fluid and unclear" – so that land was frequently transferred from individual to communal property, and strong communities coexisted with large-scale (but not feudal) individual holdings (1879: 48–50).

While the codification of communal and individual property forms was a state project, the political framework of the state itself was transformed, according to the "state school." Russian medieval politics were equally characterized by unstable and fluid juridical conditions. For Kavelin, the case of the Novgorod Principality, the chief agent of peasant and merchant expansion to the North, exemplified these conditions. It "was composed of many distinct communities, and each of them repeated the main features of the Novgorod community as a whole":

> Novgorod was governed at the same time by a *kniaz* ["prince"] and a *veche* ["communal council"]. Although opposite by essence, both institutions coexist; and their relations to each other are not specifically determined. There is no constant state structure: a new prince encounters new conditions. . . . The prince is elected by the Novgorod community [selected from one of the aristocratic clans of neighboring principalities]; he depends on the will of the community: he may be expelled from the city any time . . . There are plenty of overt limitations to his power, but it is not regulated in its essence. History made the city suspicious of the power of the prince, but the lack of state order prevented from capturing this [suspicion] in strict juridical terms. At the same time the communal council is no less unsettled a form . . . To make a decision, the council did not demand a majority vote or unanimity; it acted somewhat uncertainly "together" – as today peasant community meetings operate. Those who did not agree with the crowd were [harshly] punished . . . Usually, there was one council; but sometimes two of them hold hostile meetings at the same time. (Kavelin 1989a [1847]: 37)

This political system "reveals the same uncertainty, the same lack of the rigid juridical social order . . . which characterizes the basic lifestyle in the ancient period" (ibid.). Kavelin analogizes this to "primitive . . . kinship relations." They existed as uncodified norms, which could be arbitrarily violated (Kavelin 1859 [1848]: 81–2). Yet neither kinship nor these political arrangements are equivalent to the primordial "state of nature"; they are products of "the first act of consciousness," which generalized "both this randomness" and "the blind outer necessity" of kinship or political arrangements. The acceptance of this "randomness and the blind outer necessity" was in fact "something opposite to these two phenomena." "The acceptance of their determinations as the eternal objective law . . . reveals that this very generalization, this very acceptance was the first expression of the desire to exist under reason, to liberate oneself from the power of blind accident" (1859 [1848]: 59).

Kavelin contrasts the "ancient kin-based community" and the Novgorod political system – which were, in his view, the products of this "first act of consciousness" – with the Muscovite system, the power of which came to a peak in Central Russia in the sixteenth and seventeenth centuries. His explanation of historical change was common among nineteenth-century anthropologists everywhere: there is a shift from "kinship" to "political" organization: the integrity and power of the state [*derzava*] take precedence over the interests of a family. But, he argues, the Moscow "idea of the state" is expressed as a form of family, and state structure takes the shape of the house-hold of the Moscow Grand Prince (1989a [1847]: 47). Important for his argument, however, the state only appeared to resemble "ancient patriarchy." The strong and grow-ing modern state was "subordinated to rules, to juridical formality, and calculated with mathematical precision" (Kavelin 1859 [1848]: 81). It is such a state that creates the regime of serfdom, in which "*servant* is an honorable title that should be earned and conferred" (ibid.), "private life is ruled by the head of the family – the master of serfs; . . . a significant part of the rural population is subservient to private holders and clergy"; and all other people are divided among the inherited ranks [*chiny*], such as merchants, soldiers and the landed aristocracy. "With respect to different obligations to the Tsar," these ranks "are in the same subordination to their rank as the estate and patrimonial peasants to their holders" (Kavelin 1989c [1866]: 220–1). It was under this Muscovite system and its historical heir, the Russian Empire (1700–1917), that the juridical form of peasant corporate community was created.

As this state grew in terms of its military power and territory – in the seventeenth century it included Siberia and stretched to the Pacific Ocean – and as it adopted the universalist Christian symbols of Byzantium (in the sixteenth and seventeenth centuries) and of the Roman Empire (in the eighteenth century), it became, Kavelin argues, an entity in-and-for itself: "[u]nderneath the Grand-Prince patrimony over the state, there appears the abstract moral subject that has . . . its own rationality" (1989a [1847]: 47–8). After Peter the Great, the state as "the abstract moral subject" appro-priated the cultural language of the Enlightenment, and the state form of "Grand-Prince patrimony" eventually gave way to the form of the state that implemented "rational" reforms from the top – what Kavelin calls "the emancipation of pure reason" (1989c [1866]: 202).

It was at this stage that the state universalized its fiscal system in the form of "head tax" and codified peasant communal landholdings and relationships. Second, the emergence of "pure reason" is a teleological process; "pure reason" does not exist in the present, but will emerge in the future. In the 1850s, Chicherin and Kavelin called for drastic top-down reforms to address social conditions, stimulated by intense public debate about the causes of economic backwardness, revealed by Russia's defeat in the Crimean War (1854–56). If the state was the main agent in enslaving the people in the system of ranked serfdom, they argued, emancipation was its "natural duty" and "moral imperative" (Chicherin 1899: xv–xx).

In other words, it was the development of the state form that led to the distinction between the state and society "as they are" and "as they should be" from the stand-point of "pure reason." At this point, the state school came close to populism analyt-ically, and elaborated philosophical foundations of "pure reason" in a peculiar form of positivism. The populists initially called for reforms initiated not at the top but from the bottom. Yet their politics rested on similar grounds. In populist social theory, "society as it should be" was not merely an ideal or a political program. Moral and political judgment also served as a Kantian categorical imperative. Thus, for example, populist Petr Lavrov argued for "positivism" in the social sciences, which "should include subjective moral judgment" and which "necessarily" entails "the

204 Nikolai Ssorin-Chaikov

evaluation of social forms" and plotting "the most desirable [*zhelatel'neishego*] course of history" (1906: 50).

Lavrov, along with populist social theorist Mikhailovskii, argued for deliberate social transformation on the basis of a perceived profound difference between the natural and social sciences: natural sciences deal with regular phenomena, the social sciences with particular ones. The "truth" of natural sciences could be a verifiable knowledge condition, while the social sciences could not transcend "subjective experience," and should be held to the standard of "truth-as-fairness," by the ideals of fairness and morality (see Mikhailovskii 1922 [1869]). If rural communities were products of state construction and "slash and burn" colonization, and were by the late nineteenth century ridden with internal inequalities, it was the moral imperative of "truth-as-fairness" that assumed an idealized communal form as a model for the socialist future.

Conclusion: Situating Socialist Anthropology

By looking at populist anthropology, my goal in this chapter has been to draw attention to a very distinctive anthropological tradition. Uncovering a rich and complex discourse on "state" and "community" that informed the ethnography of populists and their interlocutors, I charted the emergence of a historicizing mode in nineteenth-century anthropology. Historical ethnographies of Yefimenko and Shcherbina exemplify such a mode, as do works of the "state school" theorists. This mode is different from both the evolutionary perspective and the nationalist vision of cultural wholeness. It considers historically specific phenomena without reducing them to reified cultural roots. "Historical critique [*istoricheskaia kritika*]," argued Kavelin, is akin to geology, as it looks for the "remnants of the vanished historical world." But "custom" is not a "petrified fossil" that "keeps its form forever." Because "custom is not unchangeable like fossils, . . . it is hardly possible to separate it into distinct elements." Thus, historical critique is presentist: one should approach "custom . . . as a source of contemporary life," rather than "using it as a means to explain the past" (1859 [1848]: 36–9). For Shcherbina, too, the historical critique of community and communal property is a presentist exploration of the creators of the communal forms of property and about the lives and relationships these forms engendered (1879: 54). Cultural forms are not "petrified fossils," they are processes, and their ethnographic understanding is a presentist and subjective recognition of living communities rather than the reconstruction of the abstract stages of all humanity.

The presentism of anthropology as historical critique entails a particular form of ethnographic holism as well as the teleological notion of "truth-as-fairness." Kavelin formulated this ethnographic holism in terms of opposition between objective ("comparative") and individualizing methods. The comparative method depends, he argued, on the isolation of "elements" of a given phenomenon. But this process of isolation paradoxically both enables and precludes analysis. Taking study of a particular human face as an exemplar of the tension between analytical methods, he observed that "considering the features of this face separately, we would certainly find exactly the same features on some other face; and the more minute is the analysis, the more fruitless are its results," the less we understand the individuality of a face. Instead, we describe "a general, abstract face – the sum of features that belong to some extent to all of humanity." Alternatively, one could "consider all features of this face in its unity, in its organic wholeness . . . The study of how the features relate to the whole brings us to the goal which cannot be reached by analytical and comparative study of these features taken separately" (1859 [1848]: 46).

This tension between the universalizing procedure of "isolation of elements" and considering these "elements" in "their relationship to the organic whole" underscores much of the history of anthropology. What makes this particular history distinct is that the relationship of "elements" to the "organic whole" is a relationship to the future "truth-as-fairness." This historicizing mode should be understood, therefore, in relation to "subjectivist positivism" that has been studied as a basis for populist radical action (Superanskii 1901; Itenberg 1965). "The ideal of fairness and morality" was an important legitimizing concept for both populist political agitation during the 1870s and political terrorism in the 1880s. However, the sociological concept of "truth-as-fairness" is also crucial in understanding the populist theory of community. The egalitarian peasant community remained the social ideal for the populist movement despite – perhaps, because of – the failures of "political fieldwork" and ethnographic primordialism. The disjuncture between the idealized peasant community of populist theory and the realities of rural life reinforced the populist social ideal, rather than challenging it. It was this disjuncture that justified the "truth-as-fairness" of populism and the "pure reason" of the "state school." It admitted of both the populist political vision of "organic community" and ethnographic accounts that belied this idealized vision.

Ironically, the disjuncture between the ideal and the real also sustained the populist belief in the efficacy of individual action by members of the educated elite – "the role of personality in history," which was famously criticized by Plekhanov (1956). Indeed, the near-socialist "people" of the populist imagination of the 1860s and 1870s in the writings of Lavrov, Bakunin, Herzen, and others gave way to the notion of the "crowd," with its pathological susceptibility to mass hypnosis, as in the later writings of Mikhailovskii (1998 [1882]), just as theories of imminent peasant revolt give way to those of change initiated by political agencies remote from peasant communities. This brings me to a paradoxical observation. If one of the goals of populism was to "close the gap" between the radical intelligentsia and "the people," the radical intelligentsia's politics and practices of knowledge were contingent on this gap. This contingency is visible in the radicals' privileging of a viewpoint belied by the actual social relationships and cultural idioms that populists strove to understand and reform. From this standpoint, the "subjectivist positivism" of Russian populists was not very far from the "positivist objectivism" of Comte and Durkheim and of classic twentieth-century anthropology. However, this contingency also looms in the deficiencies of Russian modernity that the populist "truth-as-fairness" was to remedy. The gap between the populist intelligentsia and "the people," then, made possible both populist political fieldwork and the ethnographic gaze.

Further Reading

Gellner, Ernest. 1988. *State and Society in Soviet Social Thought*. Oxford: Basil Blackwell.

Shanin, Teodor, ed. 1984. *Late Marx and the Russian Road: Marx and the Peripheries of Capitalism*. London: Routledge and Kegan Paul.

Slezkine, Yuri. 1991. "The Fall of Soviet Ethnography." *Current Anthropology* 32: 476–84.

Ssorin-Chaikov, Nikolai. 2003. *The Social Life of the State in Subarctic Siberia*. Stanford: Stanford University Press.

Using the Past to Serve the Peasant: Chinese Archaeology and the Making of a Historical Science

Hilary A. Smith

Archaeology is an important part of China's international cachet. These days, no tour to China would be complete without a visit to the Ming tombs in Beijing or to Xi'an[1] to see the terracotta warriors buried with the first Qin emperor. Terracotta soldiers, Tang dynasty ceramics, and the like are featured in exhibitions at museums throughout America and Europe, both in permanent collections and in high-profile touring exhibitions. The objects of Chinese archaeology fit easily into the global culture of collection and exhibition. However, the practice and theory of Chinese archaeology have not been so easily assimilated to a global culture of archaeology. Since the early twentieth century, Western commentators have been remarking that Chinese archaeologists do not do things in quite the same way that Western archaeologists do (Hedin 1943; Loewe 1976; Howells and Tsuchitani 1977; Falkenhausen 1993; Guldin 1994).

This is partly because no truly international discipline of archaeology existed then, or exists now. The institutional alignments of archaeology – with anthropology or with history, for example – vary widely from one country to another. Indeed, many Chinese archaeologists would be surprised to find an essay about their discipline in a history of anthropology. In their institutes, archaeology is a "historical science" and anthropology a "social science," a subtle difference in rubric that reflects large differences in prestige and funding as well as in intellectual orientation. For its part, Chinese *anthropology* has historically been mostly *minzuxue*, "nationality studies," the study of China's 55 officially recognized minorities. While *minzuxue* examined the non-Han other, archaeology focused on Han heritage. (The great majority of the Chinese population – today, over 90 percent – belongs to the Han nationality.) Institutionally, the two have had little to do with one another, although of the two disciplines, archaeology enjoys the greater prestige and funding.[2] To call archaeology a subcategory of anthropology ignores their relative importance in the Chinese academy (Kelly 1979; Olsen 1987). Both, like other research fields, are centered Soviet-style in central research institutes; university departments are primarily teaching organizations.

In the early twentieth century, Western archaeology was looking outward, marshaling the world's people, past and present, into a broader evolutionary narrative. By contrast, Chinese archaeology looked inward, searching for foundations within Chinese culture on which to build a modern nation. The respective places of China and the Western industrial powers in the early-twentieth-century world order likely contributed to their archaeologists' different perspectives. Western nations, after all, were emerging from a century of industrialization and imperial expansion; China was emerging from a century of repeated defeat and imperial collapse.

Decades later, under communist leadership, Chinese archaeologists turned the story of the origin and development of Chinese civilization into an example of a universal pattern of social development. In their reading, the broader narrative illustrated by the development of Chinese culture was a Marxist story of evolution from primitive society through slave society, feudalism, capitalism, and socialism. Unlike the narratives of biological and social evolution in vogue in the West earlier in the century, Marxist evolution put the People's Republic of China – and, by implication, the Chinese people – at the front of the evolutionary parade. This chapter will examine how this "alternative archaeology" arose (Trigger 1984).

The Birth of Archaeology in China: A Hybrid of Chinese Historiography and Imported Field Practice

Chinese archaeology did not begin as a straightforward imitation of any single foreign tradition of archaeology. Instead, Chinese scholars perceived Western field archaeology as a complement to China's own strong historiographical tradition, choosing from among the foreign models of archaeological inquiry they observed, and then using the form of field investigation they had chosen to help elucidate and correct Chinese history.

Chinese foundations

As modern Chinese histories of archaeology tell it, the earliest predecessors of the archaeologists were the paleographers (*jinshixue jia*, "metal-stone-study specialists") of the late Qing dynasty (1644–1911) (Xia 1986; Chen 1997). These scholars, as the name suggests, studied ancient inscriptions on bronzes and stone stelae. They were interested in the development of styles of writing and forms of expression, and tended to focus on the text rather than the object on which it was inscribed. Their work in classifying script forms prefigured the systematic typology that would be so important in later archaeological work.

The paleographers' counterparts in historical studies were those who, like them, practiced evidential scholarship (*kaozheng*). Late Qing evidential scholarship attempted to illuminate the original meanings of the Confucian classics, using rigorous philological methods. By the nineteenth century, classical scholars' interpretive bent had turned away from statecraft and self-cultivation and toward the empirical. Determining the dates, provenance, and historicity of the contents of classical texts became more important than expounding on the moral lessons or philosophical truths they offered (Elman 1984). Since they were already accustomed to looking for such empirical data, Chinese scholars quickly understood how field archaeology might add to their own philological work. Studying the material culture of the past supplemented evidential scholarship and paleography, rather than supplanting it.

One of the clearest examples of this phenomenon was a very influential series of articles published a few years before the first Chinese-led excavations in the 1920s. The articles, later compiled into seven volumes entitled *Gu shi ban* (in translation, Debates on Ancient History), critically reassessed the historical reliability of pre-Han dynasty classics (before 206 BCE). Edited by Gu Jiegang, *Gu shi ban* included contributions from some of the most illustrious post-Qing dynasty scholars, such as Hu Shi and Ding Wenjiang. These authors read the Confucian classics as specimens of literature rather than as sacred texts, earning themselves a popular reputation as iconoclasts – the "Doubters of Antiquity," *yi gudai zhe* – in the process. The Doubters did not deny that the past and that its textual traces were important, but they insisted that what the classics revealed involuntarily about the circumstances surrounding their production was as significant as what the classics declared explicitly to be the truth about the past. Their project, then, was to discover what classical authors were not consciously trying to tell them: when the text was written; what texts were being produced at the same time; what the predominant genres of the time were. In other words, their work was quite similar to the philological projects that Qing evidential scholars had undertaken. The difference was that in addition to textual exegesis, Gu's circle drew on archaeological, geographical, and geological evidence.

The new breed of Chinese intellectuals in archaeology, then, were largely driven by dedication to their own heritage of historical scholarship. There was little sense that archaeology had anything to do with fitting China into a global narrative, as western anthropologists and archaeologists were concurrently trying to do.

Foreign foundations

To the twentieth-century intellectual descendants of China's paleographers and historians, foreigners' field activity in China provided two models of archaeology for observation and possible emulation. One, a product of the international power dynamics of the nineteenth century, was the conquest model of scientific investigation; the other, with precedents almost as old as imperial China itself, I will call the mission model. Practitioners of both types intended to draw Chinese data into the scope of their global narratives about humanity and history, whether by casting Chinese fossils as the "missing link" between pre-human hominids and humans or by describing Chinese social organization as intermediate between primitive and industrialized societies. Not coincidentally, representatives of the same western countries, as well as Japan, also wanted to draw China into their countries' spheres of economic and political influence. The influence of Japan on Chinese archaeology deserves much more attention than it can receive in this short chapter: the Chinese admired the Japanese as an example of Asian resistance and even superiority to the industrialized West; but after the Sino-Japanese War (1894–5), Japan began to resemble the Western imperialist powers in its political relationship with China, taking Taiwan and extracting concessions and indemnities. Thus, I have grouped Japan with the Western nations in the discussion of conquest science below. One of the central concerns in both types of research was to assess comparative degrees of "advancement" among pre-modern societies and, by extension, among modern ones. Thus, while paleontologists investigated fossils in order to define China's place in the evolution of modern humans, Western historians at the turn of the century theorized that Chinese civilization derived from the civilizations of Egypt, Babylon, India, or Central Asia (Chen 1997).

The conquest model of archaeological fieldwork arrived in China in the form of extensive, multi-focal expeditions. Some of the most prominent examples of these were: the investigations of Torii Ryuzo, the Japanese archaeologist in northeastern China, starting in 1895; those of Aurel Stein, working for Britain in Xinjiang at the turn of the century; and the Carnegie Institution Expedition, an American scientific mission through eastern China in 1903–1904. Such expeditions thrived during a period of weak Chinese governments, reaching their heyday in the waning years of the Qing dynasty and in the early years of the Republic (1911–1949). Expeditions after the fall of the Qing dynasty included: the Tokyo Geographical Society's 1911–1916 foray, which collected geological specimens from as far afield as Tibet; the 1927–1935 Sino-Swedish Expedition headed by Sven Hedin; and the American Museum of Natural History's 1922–1930 expeditions to northern China and Mongolia in search of the "missing link" in human evolution. These investigations were funded by foreign governments, institutes, and corporations, and were supervised by foreigners in Chinese territory, generally with little input or participation on the part of the Chinese themselves.

My term "conquest science" draws on the titles of popular accounts published by early-twentieth-century expedition leaders, such as Sven Hedin's *A Conquest of Tibet*, the sensationalistic report of his 1904–1909 expedition, or *A New Conquest of Central Asia* by American adventurer Roy Chapman Andrews. Moreover, "conquest science" reflects the way many of the Chinese elite perceived foreign-led expeditions, as various examples of imperialist powers compromising China's sovereignty.

One reason for their suspicion was that in these expeditions the materials collected were usually not analyzed near the sites of collection, or anywhere in China, and they were generally exported without permission or compensation. The locus of knowledge production in conquest science was abroad. Artifacts and other data were generated in China, but they did not become *knowledge* until they were analyzed abroad and described in scientific papers or monographs published in Stockholm and Washington, London, and Tokyo. This evinced not only a bias in favor of the laboratory and museum as sites of knowledge production, but also exclusion of China from the implicit list of countries that could articulate reliable knowledge.

By the 1920s, conquest science was on the decline. This was partly because Western field science was beginning to turn away from extensive expeditions and toward intensive single-site excavations. In China, it was also partly due to increased resistance from the Chinese. In 1927, prospering under the first period of relative stability since before the Opium Wars (1839–1842), a group of Chinese scholars in Beijing, calling themselves the "Union of Scientific Corporations of Peking," was sufficiently organized to oppose a foreign-led expedition; the group even obliged the expedition leader to sign a contract making concessions to their concerns.

The leader was the Swede Sven Hedin, who had participated in several earlier expeditions to western China, and he anticipated no obstacles when he and his team of foreign scientists arrived in Beijing in 1926 for an expedition funded largely by the Swedish crown prince and Lufthansa Airlines. Lufthansa was interested in establishing a Beijing–Berlin airlink and hoped that the expedition would smooth the way both practically, by locating appropriate places for refueling stops, and diplomatically. Like Hedin, the sponsors had not anticipated any objections, and certainly not organized resistance, on the part of the Chinese.

Organized resistance is precisely what they got, however. The Union of Scientific Corporations of Peking, composed of representatives of prominent Beijing universities, the Central Observatory, the History Museum, the Beijing Library, the Art Museum, and other institutions, insisted on negotiating a contract with Hedin before allowing him to set off for Xinjiang in northwest China. The details of the contract vividly demonstrate Chinese intellectuals' fears about expeditions such as Hedin's.

The Union stipulated that no artifacts could be removed from China; everything found must be sent to Beijing and remain there. Another concern expressed in the contract was that sensitive data collected during the expedition might be useful for war or imperialist ambitions. Thus, the contract specified that no maps over a scale of 1:300,000 could be drawn and that no wireless stations could be established. Ultimately, the Union's worry turned out to be misdirected, though not unfounded: it was not the Swedish and German explorers making maps in Xinjiang whom they needed to fear, but the Japanese explorers who had been making maps in Manchuria and central China – maps that undoubtedly proved useful to the Japanese during their invasion of central China in the late 1930s.

One of the most hotly contested points in the contract was the proposal to incorporate Chinese scholars at every level of the expedition. This was highly unusual; Chinese typically had no intellectual influence in foreign scientific expeditions. There were always Chinese on an expedition's payroll, but they were employed in such roles as cooks, dynamiters (who used a preferred mode of excavating objects), and ricksha runners. Until the late 1920s, the respective roles of Chinese and foreigners in the projects of conquest archaeology were clearly delineated: it was the Chinese who carried, dug, blasted, cooked, and interpreted, and the foreigners who coordinated, directed, planned, and analyzed. Chinese scholars were not included in a decision-making capacity on a conquest science expedition. In fact, on Roy Chapman Andrews' 1921 "Missing Link" expedition, the Chinese, far from being participants in the conversation about human evolution, were jokingly perceived as potential *objects* of the investigation. In China, Andrews writes, "the familiar American joke was continually in our ears: 'Don't endure sandstorms out there in the desert. I saw a Missing Link pulling a ricksha this morning'" (Andrews 1961).

By contrast with such expeditions, the mission investigations represented a more familiar style of foreign participation in Chinese intellectual life, in which the foreigners cooperated with, and sometimes even subordinated themselves to, Chinese academics, investigating questions of interest to the Chinese. A detail in the negotiations between Hedin and the Union of Scientific Corporations of Peking succinctly captures the perceived difference between the two styles of research. As the Union explained it, the English word "expedition" offended because it "was considered to be derogatory and applicable only among uncivilized peoples." They therefore requested that Hedin change the name of the Sino-Swedish Expedition to "The Scientific *Mission* to North-Western China" (Hedin 1943).

It was a telling distinction. Missionaries on the seventeenth-century Jesuit model, unlike expedition leaders, were historically aware that the Chinese among whom they worked were a civilized people, and that to influence them required becoming civilized oneself in their eyes. The Jesuits were convinced that the most effective way to win converts was to persuade the most powerful members of a society and rely on their influence to further propagate Christianity. The missionaries ingratiated themselves with Chinese emperors by demonstrating the usefulness of their sciences, particularly astronomy. Since the prediction of irregular heavenly events such as eclipses and comets were assumed to portend good or ill for the emperor's continued mandate to rule, the missionaries' astronomical knowledge earned them a place in the imperial bureau of astronomy (McKnight 1992: 75). Such positions were available to them in part because they learned the Chinese language, wrote treatises in Chinese, and mastered the forms of ritual etiquette important among the elite. The Jesuits are only the best-known example of this type of advisor; Indian and Islamic astronomers had held similar positions in the bureau of astronomy many centuries before the Jesuits appeared on the scene (see Spence 1969; Jami 1994).

In the 1920s and 1930s, though the imperial court no longer existed, the role of scientific advisor to the Chinese elite persisted. It was no longer played by Jesuit missionaries but by scientists of many different nationalities and persuasions, such as the Swede Johan Gunnar Andersson, employed by the Chinese Geological Survey from 1914; the Canadian Davidson Black, an anatomist who directed the excavations of Peking Man fossils in the 1920s; and Franz Weidenreich, a German anatomist who became the head of the Cenozoic Research Laboratory after Black's premature death in 1934. All three men belonged to the eclectic international group whose most renowned accomplishment was the discovery and analysis of the Peking Man bones at Zhoukoudian beginning in 1926. The foreign scientists who excavated Peking Man worked side by side with Chinese colleagues, some of whom they had trained themselves, and spoke highly of their Chinese colleagues' skill and devotion. Like their Chinese counterparts, and unlike practitioners of conquest science, they were integrated into Beijing life. Some of them, such as Andersson, were even supervised by Chinese scientists: Ding

Wenjiang when Andersson began work for the Geological Survey, and Wang Wen-hao when Ding moved on to other work a few years later.

With the opening of the Rockefeller-funded Peking Union Medical College in 1921 and the Cenozoic Research Laboratory in 1926, Beijing became a locus for the production of significant paleontological knowledge (Ferguson 1970: 62–5). George Barbour, another of Beijing's erstwhile foreign residents, described the intellectual ferment occurring there thus:

> As many nationalities were represented in the polyglot scientific group to be found there in the late twenties and early thirties as at any time in the city's long history. The Academia Sinica, the Peking Union Medical College, the Chinese Geological Survey, and the various educational and missionary institutions acted as magnets to attract a steady stream of outstanding specialists from other lands. (1965)

For Davidson Black, the head of the anatomy department at Peking Union Medical College (PUMC) and one of the principal Peking Man investigators, no place was more congenial than Beijing for working on human paleontology. Black was offered positions at a number of Western universities, including his own alma mater, the University of Toronto, and he refused them all, preferring to stay at PUMC to work. He cited the unparalleled opportunity for cooperative international work when he declined the other job offers; for him, Beijing was no "hornet's nest" of provincial Chinese interested in their own advancement, as some foreign scholars perceived it (Hedin 1943), but a place with an intellectual environment conducive to producing new knowledge.

By contrast, Black found that far from encouraging new paleontological knowledge, established academic centers in the West often resisted it. When he left China in the late 1920s for an American and European tour in which he presented the newly-discovered Peking Man teeth as evidence of a possible humanoid ancestor, he was disappointed in the coolness of the reception he received. After a particularly disheartening presentation to scientists at Columbia University, Black longed to return to Beijing, where the finds had seemed exciting and significant (Hood 1964). In the end, through the many volumes of analysis that Black, his colleagues Franz Weidenreich, Pei Wenzhong, and others published in the *Paleontologia Sinica*, the official publication of the Geological Survey, the wider scientific world did come to recognize the finds as exciting and significant, but initially Black encountered suspicion of knowledge that hadn't emerged from a known Western site of knowledge production.

By making themselves a part of life in Beijing, working side by side with Chinese colleagues, and publishing reports in both English and Chinese, men like Andersson and Black were actually following a long-established pattern of foreign participation in Chinese intellectual life. It is no surprise, then, that the earliest independent Chinese excavations more closely resembled the Peking Man excavations of the 1920s, with their intensive focus on a single site over a period of years, than the extensive expeditions that preceded and coincided with them.

Anyang and beyond: Chinese archaeology takes root

Conventionally, Chinese archaeologists have touted Li Ji's 1926 excavations at Xiyin and Anyang as a landmark in the development of archaeology in China because they are the first known example of fieldwork directed by a Chinese scholar rather than a foreigner (Liu et al. 2000; Chen 1997). Scholarship on Chinese archaeology therefore usually casts Li Ji as the father of Chinese archaeology.

Born in 1896 in Hubei, Li grew up during a tumultuous period of Chinese history. In his childhood he experienced the final economic and political disintegration of the Qing dynasty, which had been teetering for decades, followed by 15 years of warlord rule with which the Nationalist government initially could not compete. Li graduated from the prestigious Qinghua Xuetang (later Qinghua University) and immediately went to the US to study. In 1923 he earned a PhD at Harvard in anthropology, completing a dissertation entitled "The Formation of the Chinese People," published under the same title a few years later (Li 1928). The dissertation exemplifies the commonsensical combination of physical anthropology with historical record that would characterize Li's approach throughout his career. In it, he concludes that the modern Chinese people derive from the commingling of the "we-group" and the "you-groups" of traditional Chinese historiography – that is, the people who considered themselves full members of the Middle Kingdom and those they labeled barbarians. Li ignores the question that Western anthropologists and antiquarians had been asking for centuries, namely: what great civilization did Chinese civilization *derive from*? Egypt? Babylon? What, in other words, did the Chinese owe to Western history? For Li, the "formation of the Chinese people" was a question best answered by physical data (modern Chinese compared with skeletal remains) viewed along with the rich historical record that was useless to non-Chinese-speaking scholars. He pieced together a people's past not only by measuring living Chinese bodies, but also by extracting data from Chinese historical records on the proliferation of surnames, the accumulation of city walls, and the movements of populations.

After finishing his dissertation, Li returned to China and participated in foreign-led excavations in Henan before beginning his own at Xiyin (Li credits Dong Zuobin with being the first to investigate the Xiyin site, but Li's reputation is more widespread outside China than Dong's). At Xiyin and Anyang, Li and his colleagues excavated the oracle bones that had been used to perform divination as early as 1200 BCE.[3] The objects of study themselves, bearing what is still the earliest-known form of Chinese writing, confirmed the uniqueness and antiquity of the Chinese past. As it had done for the paleographers and evidential scholars who preceded him, Chinese history set the parameters of inquiry for Li.

By 1929, one year after the Nationalist government founded the History and Philology Research Institute as a branch of the Academia Sinica, Li had become the director of its archaeological section. Li was thus one of the first representatives of truly *national* archaeology in China – sponsored and overseen by the government and not by a foreign-funded or foreign-directed institute such as the Peking Union

Medical College. His continued work at Anyang proved seminal: it was there that he trained many in the next generation of Chinese archaeologists. Once a national archaeology had been established, it became the obvious way for patriotic young scholars to obtain their training.

In 1937, circumstances changed drastically. After years of controlling Manchuria, the Japanese army invaded the cities of coastal and central China with startling rapidity. Many academic and research institutions, among them the History and Philology Research Institute, were forced to move repeatedly to avoid the chaos of the conflict. In the space of three years, the Institute moved from Nanjing to Changsha to Kunming to Li Village, Sichuan Province. Almost immediately after fighting with the Japanese ceased, civil war broke out between the Nationalist and Communist factions in China. By the time the wars came to an end, archaeology on the mainland had suffered many losses. The world-famous Peking Man bones vanished in 1941, never to be recovered, and the History and Philology Research Institute moved to Taiwan, taking Li Ji and other prominent scholars, as well as a great many artifacts. All the important sites remained on the mainland, however, including many whose names are now known across the globe. The stage was set for a new era.

The Golden Age: A New Archaeology for New China

After the Chinese Communist Party ousted the Nationalists in 1949, Chinese archaeology came, for the first time, to be guided by a global evolutionary narrative. PRC archaeologists interpreted data according to a Marxist-Leninist understanding of how human society progressed from a primitive state to socialism, considered the most advanced form of social organization.

The application of a global narrative, however, did not bring Chinese archaeology closer to concurrent Western traditions than it had been before. In the 1960s and 1970s, when the Cultural Revolution gave Marxist evolutionism its firmest hold on Chinese archaeology, the so-called "New Archaeology," originating in the US, was sweeping through the Western archaeological world. This was a movement away from the tendency to simply inventory and classify "archaeological assemblages" and toward an understanding of patterns in the evolution of human societies or in the responses of human societies to specific environmental circumstances (Caldwell 1959; Binford 1962). New Archaeologists were concerned with the evolution of human societies in response to pre-existing constraints, particularly ecological ones. They did not allow much room for human agency, since culture was thought to develop out of necessity in the face of environmental pressures. Nor did the practitioners of the New Archaeology deem history very important in their analysis; the unpredictable details of particular historical contexts seemed incidental to understanding transcultural patterns of human response. The New Archaeology, with its fatalism about the development of social organization, thus tended to naturalize the status quo.

By contrast, the operative force in Maoist social evolutionism was human behavior, based on human choice. This form of evolutionism was based on the idea that, within the limits set by the form of production, better things are possible with the exercise of human will and effort. Considering the relative power of the US and China at this time, it seems appropriate that American neo-evolutionism naturalized the existing world order, while Chinese Marxist evolutionism suggested the certainty of change, even revolution.

The Harvard scholar K. C. Chang (Zhang Guangzhi), perhaps the most prominent observer of archaeology in China, wrote that the 1960s and 1970s ushered in the "Golden Age of Chinese Archaeology," a label Chinese archaeologists and historians themselves have continued to use. It seems obvious why this period deserves such a complimentary tag: it is justified by a roster of impressive discoveries. Even someone familiar with only the best-known Chinese artifacts would find that most of them were unearthed in the 1960s or 1970s, from the famed army of terracotta warriors in Xi'an, which first came to light in 1974, to jade and gold burial shrouds from the second century BCE, discovered in 1968. Then there is the cache of manuscripts and artifacts that has been such a boon for historians of the Han dynasty (206 BCE–CE 220) and the pre-Han, unearthed in 1972–73 at Mawangdui. If the measure of archaeology's success is the volume and value of items unearthed, there is no doubt that the 1960s and early 1970s were a golden age.

Yet behind the Golden Age lurks the specter of the Great Proletarian Cultural Revolution (1966–1976), reminding us that these years had a profound influence on shaping the very *nature* of Chinese archaeology, not just its visibility. In the 1960s and 1970s the discipline secured its place as a powerful symbolic endorsement of the new order. Archaeology came to be associated with nation-building in the People's Republic, both ideologically and literally.

There was, first of all, an intimate link between archaeological excavation and the growth of infrastructure. Most archaeological projects from the first decades of the People's Republic, as today, were "salvage archaeology" projects. In other words, they were projects begun when the construction of roads, factories, mines, and dams revealed long-buried artifacts and threatened the survival of the sites (Xia 1983). Chinese peasants took on a greater role in the archaeological enterprise as the number of salvage sites increased. It was peasants, after all, who were out in the countryside leveling ground for roads and setting the foundations of buildings. The archaeologists therefore made great efforts to turn the Chinese peasantry into archaeologically and "paleoanthropologically aware citizens" (Chang 1977), who would notify the authorities when they came across artifacts in the course of their work. Spotting and reporting archaeological finds were patriotic responsibilities just as important as building roads and dams. Peasants often participated in the excavation of such "salvage" sites once they were discovered, usually doing the grunt work. As the number of artifacts burgeoned, local and regional museums began to open; by 1957 there were 72 museums in China, both regional and national (Li et al. 1999). Exhibits in local museums displayed human fossils and artifacts as illustrations of the evolution of society along Marxist lines. They provided the peasantry with a form of class education that seemed all the more persuasive because they themselves – or people like them – had helped discover and excavate the objects displayed. Museums thus forged a strong symbolic connection between the physical process of nation building and the reconstruction of the nation's past.

Peasants had been involved in archaeology early on, of course. For thousands of years, farmers had undertaken their own excavations. In the aftermath of a battle or a bad stretch of weather that had ruined the crops, they sometimes banded together to dig up oracle bones or other artifacts to sell or trade to wealthy collectors and connoisseurs (Li 1977). In the nineteenth century, expedition leaders had relied on peasants' local knowledge of both history and topography to find and exploit the richest deposits of artifacts. In the PRC, though, the state's emphasis on their obligation to report finds to officials instilled in farmers a deeper sense of involvement. Suddenly, digging up bronzes or carrying equipment had a deeper significance than simply keeping the family's rice bowls full; it was a way of revealing the truth about China's past and contributing to its future glory (Faison 1998).

It was not just farmers whose relationship to archaeology changed. Archaeologists' background and education changed as well. Many of the archaeologists who had risen to prominence in the 1920s and 1930s were gone, having left for Taiwan in 1948. A new generation ascended in the 1950s, educated differently from their elders and predecessors. Although the most prominent of the older archaeologists remaining in the PRC, such as Xia Nai, had the cosmopolitan educational backgrounds and international connections typical of Li Ji's generation, young archaeologists were likely to have been trained in China and the Soviet Union and to have few foreign contacts. Many of the young archaeologists had trained at Anyang under Li Ji, in fact, and had been educated in the fledgling national institutes that were forced to move repeatedly during the war with Japan.

The tumult of the civil war had also disrupted institutional continuity. Having lost Academia Sinica to Taiwan, the government of the People's Republic promptly set up a new academic center in Beijing, the Chinese Academy of Sciences (the Institute of Archaeology now belongs to the Chinese Academy of Social Sciences, which was established in 1977). Much remained the same, however, despite the transition of authority from the Nationalists to the Communists. Most important, the place that archaeology held in the new Chinese Academy of Sciences (CAS) approximated the place it had held in the Academia Sinica, where it had been one of three (later four) branches of the Institute of History and Philology. In the CAS, too, archaeology fell under the rubric of the "historical sciences," and was not classified with "social sciences" such as sociology and anthropology.

Governmental support for archaeology was demonstrably enthusiastic, given the scale of projects and publications undertaken during the first three decades of the People's Republic. By 1959, three major scholarly journals devoted to Chinese archaeology were in circulation: *Archaeology* (*Kaogu*), *Journal of Archaeology* (*Kaogu xuebao*), and *Cultural Relics* (*Wen wu*), published by the CAS's Institute of Archaeology. Moreover, though archaeologists as a group did not live through the Cultural Revolution unscathed, the Institute of Archaeology was one of the few intellectual centers that did not close down. Still, publication of all archaeological journals ceased between 1966 and 1972. As in universities and other research institutes, mass criticism sessions were held at the Institute, and also in the few university departments of archaeology then in existence. And archaeologists, like other urban intellectuals, were sent to the countryside to learn from the peasants through labor. But the volatile political tides of those years did not affect archaeological work as adversely as they did work in other disciplines. Before 1973, when Chinese sociologists and anthropologists gradually began to be "rehabilitated" into respectability in the eyes of the government, Chinese archaeologists working in state-funded institutes were obtaining the technology for radiocarbon dating, the first results of which had been published in the West as early as 1949, but which was an expensive technology in a poor country (Institute of Archaeology 1992; Taylor 2000). Furthermore, the anthropologist Greg Guldin concludes from his interviews with Chinese archaeologists and anthropologists that the criticism sessions in archaeology departments were mostly pro forma affairs that left few lingering resentments compared with those in other work units (Guldin 1994). That archaeologists weathered the vicissitudes of China's "ten lost years" as well as they did suggests that they made themselves appear essential to the construction of the New China. How did a discipline devoted to reconstructing the past thrive under a regime determined to break with everything old?

In archaeology, as in most occupations, there was a slogan from Mao to guide and exhort the workers in their endeavors. From 1972 until a few years after Mao's death in 1976, "Use the past to serve the present" (*gu wei jin yong*) appeared in bold print in the archaeology journals as well as in the introduction to most catalogs and excavation reports. Interpreting their finds through the lens of Marxism, as "using the past to serve the present" encouraged them to do, enabled archaeologists to legitimate Communist rule and resolve, at least on the surface, a widespread ambivalence toward China's past. Before the nineteenth century, there had been no need for Chinese historians to emphasize China's uniqueness or to suggest that China's heritage was glorious; nothing could have been more self-evident to the elite members of a vast empire. By 1911, however, with China's sovereignty and solvency fatally compromised, it began to seem that China's uniqueness lay as much in its "backwardness" (*luo hou*) as in the glory of its former dynasties. Accordingly, many of the early twentieth-century modernizers tended to emphasize China's uniqueness in the negative, as something that impeded national progress. Many others argued that China's heritage was its best source of independence and strength. In Republican China, policy debates often centered on the question of whether China's past was its glory or its shame.

The leaders of Communist China inherited the Nationalists' ambivalence toward the past. Clearly, there was nothing quite like China's continuous historical record, corroborated by increasingly rich archaeological evidence. But if the material trappings of the Chinese past simply attested to a "feudal" and "superstitious" heritage, why would the government of liberated China devote labor and money to preserving them? What use had a poor people perilously close to war for ancient bronzes, jade jewelry and texts?

The leaders' answer was that artifacts provided object lessons in Communist history for peasants and intellectuals alike. Even a regime determined to break with the past needs to define the past from which it intends to depart. Archaeologists interpreted artifacts, in combination with the historical record, as evidence of China's progression from a primitive society to a slave society to a long-lived feudal society, and their evidence was accompanied by Marxist-Leninist interpretations in the many new provincial museums. Chinese archaeologists even found evidence in prehistoric burial patterns that their society had undergone an early change from matriarchy to patriarchy, a feature of Lewis Henry Morgan's model of social evolution on which Engels depended. All artifacts and ruins were interpreted as confirmation of the laws of historical evolution as described by Marx, Lenin, and Mao.

Conveniently, "Marx-Lenin-Mao Zedong thought" (*ma-lie-maozedong sixiang*) provided archaeologists with a paradigm for resolving ambivalence about the past. Old (imperial) China had not been composed of one homogeneous mass of Chinese, after all, but of two classes of people: decadent landowners; and oppressed laborers and peasants. During the 1960s and 1970s, it was said that the latter were the people who had made the opulent artifacts, and the former were the people for whom the artifacts had been made. A 1971 article in the English-language magazine *Eastern Horizon* grimly sums up the significance of recent discoveries: "These finds show how the feudal ruling class wallowed in luxury and dissipation and how the labouring people were brutally exploited and oppressed." But the anonymous writer also pointed out that the finds "show the great wisdom and skill of the Chinese labouring people of that period" (1971: 25). Another archaeologist, analysing the famous Buddhist frescoes in the caves of Dunhuang, in northwestern China, explains that the "skilful artisans, who exhausted their energies generation after generation on the creation of the Dunhuang frescoes, were rewarded, in return, with the earthly hell of feudalistic society." Still, he concludes, the Dunhuang frescoes are "treasure houses of ancient culture" and "reveal the incessant and organic evolution of Chinese art" (Chang 1984). This was a deft solution of the problem of uniqueness as well as an instant justification for the whole enterprise of archaeology.

Framing their interpretations in terms of Marx-Lenin-Mao Zedong thought allowed Chinese archaeologists to reconcile the notion of Chinese uniqueness and even superiority with the fact of China's poverty and weakness in modern times. Thus, the archaeologists of New China settled upon an interpretation of material culture that supported a Communist reading of history without devaluing ancient artifacts themselves or undermining their own work in finding and preserving them.

On a figurative level, then, the objects of archaeology were "nationalized," attributed to faceless, ancient laborers with whom citizens of the People's Republic could identify. Ironically, though, excavations tended to focus on recovering goods from the tombs of the wealthy rather than investigating the actual living conditions of common people. As Lothar von Falkenhausen (1993) has observed, "even though the scholarly world might learn more from the excavation of a Bronze Age village than from the tomb of yet another royal figure," the latter type of project has been more common among archaeologists in China. Falkenhausen attributes this obsessive focus on the culture of the elite, even today, to a strong historiographical bias in Chinese archaeology.[4]

Archaeologists in the Golden Age continued the nationalistic inclinations of early twentieth-century archaeology but channeled them into a particular kind of national pride, a pride consonant with both the iconoclasm of New China and reverence for a long and glorious heritage. Under a strongly nationalistic government whose relationship with intellectuals was extremely volatile, enhancing the national import-ance of archaeology became a strategy for survival, one that Chinese archaeologists managed to deploy effectively.

Conclusion

In this chapter, I have tried to set the development of the "historical science" itself in a historical context. To understand how Chinese archaeology has developed and why it has taken the institutional forms that it has taken, it is necessary to consider the history of its interaction with other national traditions of archaeology, as well as the broader political climate in which finds were made. Given that it developed during periods of national vulnerability, it is not surprising that the questions Chinese archaeology first asked were introspective: inward-looking rather than expansive, or expansionist, like early Western forms of archaeology. Chinese archaeology strove to explain the origins of the Chinese people, of Chinese civilization, and of the Chinese polity, with the assumption that all of these things were unique in human history. Even when Chinese archaeologists adopted a Marxist narrative under Communist leader-ship, they continued to focus on the exceptionalism of Chinese history, endorsing a party authority that touted Maoism as unique.

In recent years Chinese archaeologists have begun once again to work closely with foreign scholars. Many Chinese archaeologists today spend time training abroad, as Li Ji's generation did. Yet the historiographical proclivities of Chinese archaeology remain consistent with what they have been in the past, and conspicuous fault lines of disagreement between Chinese and the various Western archaeologies persist. One flashpoint, for example, is the question of whether *homo erectus* fossils found in China represent an evolutionary dead end or the ancestors of present-day Mongoloid races (Sautman 2001; Etler 1994). Another is the question of the historicity of the Xia dynasty (before the sixteenth century BCE, according to Chinese historians), putatively the first Chinese dynasty. Despite a large-scale project sponsored by the Chinese govern-ment, most Western archaeologists still believe no persuasive evidence of the Xia exists (Eckholm 2000). Given the differences in their historical foundations, Chinese archaeology and its Western counterparts may not simply be examples of different regional accents of a single language, but something closer to dialects that are only partly mutually intelligible.

Notes

1   The Chinese names and words in this essay have been romanized according to the widely used Hanyu Pinyin system. Where the Chinese name is part of an English name for which a different romanization is still more common, (e.g. Peking Man), I have left it in the older Wade-Giles system.

2   The Institute of Archaeology was one of the original research institutes of the Chinese Academy of Social Sciences when it became independent of the Chinese Academy of Sciences in 1977. Even today, there is no institute of anthropology of similar prestige.

3   For more on oracle bones and pyromancy, see D. N. Keightley. 1978. *Sources of Shang History: The Oracle-Bone Inscriptions of Bronze Age China.* Berkeley: University of California Press.

4   Communist Chinese leaders' disdain for the Chinese "peasant" may also factor into this propensity. Myron Cohen (1993) has written that the category "peasant" (*nongmin*) to describe rural Chinese is a twentieth-century invention freighted with prejudice about ordinary Chinese as ignorant, superstitious, and incapable of governing themselves.

Further Reading

Fikesjö, Magnus, and Xingcan Chen, eds. 2004. *China before China: Johan Gunnar Andersson, Ding Wenjiang, and the Discovery of China's Prehistory.* Stockholm: Museum of Far Eastern Antiquities.

Guldin, Gregory Eliyu. 1994. *The Saga of Anthropology in China: From Malinowski to Moscow to Mao,* 1 vol. *Studies on Modern China.* Armonk, NY: M. E. Sharpe.

Lu, Tracey Lie-dan. 2002. "The Transformation of Academic Culture in Mainland Chinese Archaeology." *Asian Anthropology* 1:117–52.

Part IV

Biology

13

The Anthropology of Race Across the Darwinian Revolution

Thomas F. Glick

Three theoretical issues in biology – polygenism, hybridism, and recapitulation – were particularly salient in nineteenth-century anthropology. Here I will examine these three issues in five national settings – the United States, England, France, Germany, and Brazil – across the Darwinian revolution of nineteenth-century biology. The publication of Darwin's *On the Origin of Species* in 1859 was significant in the anthropology of race, not because it changed anyone's mind but because it provided a theoretical framework for orienting research and presenting results that lent legitimacy to a wide range of arguments already in existence. Although the modern concept of race has clear eighteenth-century European antecedents, American concerns set the tone for the nineteenth-century debate. The Americas had been a living laboratory for racial theory that Europeans visited with great enthusiasm. The interplay between European and American writers and theorists provides an interesting dynamic for the development of the anthropology of race and the ethnology that contributed to it.

Polygenesis in the United States: Before Darwin

Polygenesis was the idea that human races did not share common descent but originated in different sites, each race created in perfect adaptation to its habitat. The universal interpretation of Genesis had been that all human beings were descendants of Adam and Eve. Racial differentiation was usually explained as a result of slow adaptation to environment (thus, some supposed that if blacks were to live in temperate climates for a sufficiently long period, their skin color would whiten). In the New World, the tripartite ranking of the proximate races – white, Indian, and black – made for a richer, though much more nuanced, discussion of race.

The architects of American polygenism were Samuel George Morton, George R. Gliddon, and Josiah C. Nott, referred to collectively as the "American School." Their theory, as it developed in the 1840s, was that historical and archaeological evidence demonstrated the permanence of the races, which therefore should be considered different species of the genus *Homo*. Separate creation was assumed. After Morton's death,

Nott and Gliddon brought out a selection of his writings titled *Types of Mankind, or Ethnological Researches* (Morton 1854), which became the standard account of polygenesis. Also contributing to *Types* was Louis Agassiz, the Swiss geologist and biologist, who had come to America in 1847. It was Agassiz who completed the scientific argument for polygenism, whose American opponents had viewed it simply as an excuse for slavery, as well as contrary to Christian orthodoxy. (Paradoxically, many southern, theologically orthodox conservatives rejected the polygenism of "scientific racism" as immoral before the Civil War, but subsequently succumbed to racist sentiment; see Genovese 1998: 82–3, 93, 95.) Agassiz's view rested on a paradox, "that the unity of species does not involve a unity of origin, and that a diversity of origin does not involve a plurality of species" (1850: 113). What he meant was that the races of mankind were like swarms of bees, created separately in already organized social groups, fitted for the environments for which they were created (1850: 128). The races, then, were specially created each in the environment that they inhabited over historical time.

Morton and Gliddon viewed anthropology as an applied science, the findings of which would have practical application in the management of racial diversity (Gossett 1965: 77). Although they did not articulate their arguments for the sole purpose of justifying slavery, their doctrine suited the purposes of slaveholders and the politicians representing them. Nott, in his introduction to *Types of Mankind*, recounts with considerable pride the consultations that Gliddon and Morton afforded John C. Calhoun, when the latter as Secretary of State was negotiating with France and England over the annexation of Texas, and looking for arguments supporting Texas' entry to the Union as a slave state (Morton 1854: 590–1).

If the races of humanity constituted special species, then the concept of hybridity had to be redefined. According to the predominant theory of hybridity, if mixed-race individuals were truly hybrids, they would be sterile, but mulattos clearly were not. Morton and Nott retooled hybridity by asserting that there was a gradient of inter-specific sterility and fertility that would diminish in hybrid lines over a period of time (Gossett 1965: 76). They assumed that racial hybrids had weakened constitutions. In contrast to them, a younger anthropologist, Lewis Henry Morgan, favored a kind of "whitening," at least with respect to Indians: the children of mixed Indian and white marriages would become more attractive over the generations, and the resultant hybrid race would "improve and toughen" our own (Thomas 2000: 47–9).[1] And, as we shall see, hybridization was viewed more positively in other cultures.

Darwin's Anthropology

Darwin had deliberately avoided the issue of mankind in the *Origin of Species,* saving a fuller discussion for the *Descent of Man* (1871). Darwin's view of human history as expounded there is a compendium of natural-man theory, inspired mainly by Thomas Hobbes and Adam Smith. (Darwin himself admitted his intellectual indebtedness.) So, in the famous chapter on "Moral Faculties," he speaks of the "never-ceasing wars of savages" (2004: 155), who were organized in primal hordes. He then invokes "sympathy" – a natural impulse in human beings, according to both Adam Smith and Jean-Jacques Rousseau – which gives the first impulses to benevolent action and which subsequently "developed through natural selection as one of the most important elements of the social instincts."

In *Descent*, therefore, Darwin sets out what Patrick Tort has called a theory of the "reversive effect of evolution" (1996: I, 1334–5), whereby social instincts are reinforced in the struggles of primitive hordes. Those groups displaying more "sympathy" – that is, in modern sociological language, those who displayed the greatest social cohesion – would be advantaged in the struggle for life over those who had less. The advantage, however, is a social, not a biological one (even though Darwin thought that the instinct for sympathy would become fixed hereditarily over generations). Human ethics and morality have tended to defeat natural selection with each advance of civilization.

Once society emerges, therefore, culture acts to check the action of natural selection (Darwin 2004: 161). And here Darwin shows himself to be a moderate, rather than an extreme "social Darwinist." Societies clearly do things contrary to the best interests of the species, such as dispatching the most physically fit men to die in wars. And, inasmuch as "progress is no invariable rule," he warns that nations can degenerate as well as progress. The ancient Greeks, he observed, "ought, if the power of natural selection were real, to have risen higher in the scale, increased in number, and stocked the whole of Europe" (166). Development depends on many concurrent favorable circumstances: "Natural selection only acts tentatively" (167). It is not an iron rule, but a probabilistic one. This is an important point. As Steven Jay Gould, Ernst Mayr, and others have taken pains to reiterate, evolution was not for Darwin a teleologically mandated journey from lower to higher.

Social Darwinism was not based on Darwin's notions of the evolution of social forms as laid out in the chapter on "Moral Faculties" in the *Descent of Man*. To the extent that it was Darwinian at all (as opposed to ideas derived from the thought of Herbert Spencer), social Darwinism had been tricked out of the *Origin of Species*, where Darwin does not infer from the processes of human evolution how the mechanism of the survival of the fittest might be applied to human social order.

Darwin was famously opposed to slavery, the subject of violent arguments he had while traveling as a young man on the *Beagle* with the ship's Tory captain, James FitzRoy. His letter to his sister Catherine, sent from Maldonado, Uruguay, expresses the views he conveyed to FitzRoy (while simultaneously displaying his inability to suppress a racial-sounding slur against Portuguese slaveholders):

> What a proud thing for England, if she is the first European nation which utterly abolishes [slavery]. – I was told before leaving England, that after living in Slave countries; all my opinions would be altered; the only alteration I am aware of forming is a much higher estimate of the Negros character. – it is impossible to see a negro & not feel kindly towards him; such cheerful, open honest expressions & such fine muscular bodies; I never saw any of the diminutive Portuguese with their murderous

countenances, without almost wishing for Brazil to follow the example of Hayti ... (*Correspondence*, 1: 312–13, May 22, 1833)

He was also opposed to polygenist accounts of the origins of mankind, and kept himself informed on Agassiz's anti-evolutionary defense. As early as 1850, he was privately criticizing Agassiz's views on ideological as well as scientific grounds. He wrote to his cousin W. D. Fox, "I wonder whether the queries addressed to [name omitted] about the specific distinctions of the races of man are a reflexion from Agassiz's Lectures in the US in which he has been maintaining the doctrine of several species – much, I dare say, to the comfort of the slave-holding Southerns" (*Correspondence*, 4: 353, September 1, 1850). A decade later, he wrote to Charles Lyell, commenting on Agassiz's appeal to the multiplicity of dog varieties as a model of human polygenism,

> I do not think multiple origin of dogs goes against single origin of man. . . . On coinci-
> dence of colour alone, so fleeting a character, does not go for much in his comparison
> of man & anthropoid apes. All the races of man are so infinitely closer together than to
> any ape that . . . I sh^d look at all races of man as having certainly descended from single
> parent . . . Agassiz & Co. think the Negro & Caucasian are now distinct species; & it is
> a mere vain discussion, whether when they were rather less distinct they would, on this
> standard of specific value [whether in dogs the differences arose in state of nature or
> under domestication], deserve to be called species. (*Correspondence*, 8: 378, Septem-
> ber 23, 1860; see also Darwin to Lyell, September 28, 1860, *Correspondence*, 8: 397)

In the early days of the American Civil War, Darwin wrote to Asa Gray that he knew no one who was not favorable to the Northern cause, adding that "Some few, & I am one, even wish to God, though at the loss of millions of lives, that the North would proclaim a crusade against Slavery" (*Correspondence*, 9: 163, June 5, 1861). In 1863, a bitter debate erupted between the pro-Confederacy Anthropological Society of London (whose president was the polygenist James Hunt) and the Ethnological Society (whose president was the Darwinian John Lubbock). Darwin followed this debate closely (see Darwin to Joseph Hooker, May 1863, and Thomas Huxley to Darwin, July 2, *Correspondence*, 11: 15 and 12: 67). Hunt sought to justify slavery with a scientific argument. When, in this debate, he declared that "the Negro" was not of the same species as white Europeans, he was attacked by T. H. Huxley. The following year, Hunt brought out his translation of Carl Vogt's defense of an evolutionary hierarchy of races, *Lectures on Man*. Vogt, an evolutionist, argued that the Negro is intermediate between apes and men. The London Anthropological Society was modeled on that of Paris. Like its French counterpart, the leadership was polygenist and opposed to evolution, yet perfectly willing, for ideological motives, to back the work of polygenist evolu-tionists (Harvey 1983: 291; Di Gregorio 1984: 168).

When Darwin's ideas (from *Origin*) were applied to society, there was a widespread Malthusian conclusion to the effect that if fecundity were the main criterion of fitness, then the poor would have an advantage in the future evolution of mankind (Claeys 2000: 236), an argument promiscuously mixing biological, social, and cultural criteria. In the course of the 1860s, Darwin looked for an alternative explanation for human fitness and, through his readings of Alfred Russel Wallace and Francis Galton, found such a criterion in intelligence. Groups with more advanced culture were likely to prevail over those more primitive, civilization over savagery. So Claeys concludes (237) that by the mid-1860s Darwin had himself become a social Darwinist, although he recognizes that Darwin's concept of "race" was colored by his notion of social class. Weikhart (1995) advances as proof a letter from Darwin to Heinrich Fick, a law professor in Zurich, in which Darwin opines that if Trade Unionism treats all its members equally, biological competition will be excluded, although he notes too that "temperate frugal workmen will have an advantage and leave more offspring than the drunken and reckless."

The problem with all such arguments is that the variables are not defined. Human society inevitably introduces social and cultural factors alongside biological ones. Darwin's argument in *Descent* is more sophisticated. Here groups, not individuals, have the edge, and selection among groups is on the basis of capacity for sympathy – an individual trait that has a collective effect of inducing group cohesion and solidarity.

Recapitulation

Recapitulation, the notion that the development of the fetus recapitulates the phylogenetic history of that species, was a cornerstone of post-Darwinian evolutionary theory and became, after 1859, a primary support of scientific racism. To persons who accepted the characterization of "primitive" people as childlike in comparison to civilized Europeans, recapitulation made it possible to view such groups as lower in an evolutionary hierarchy than Europeans, and to equate living primitive races with our hominid ancestors as sharing the same phylogenetic level. For Sigmund Freud, there was a fourfold parallelism between prehistoric hominids as our ancestors, currently living primitive groups, children, and neurotics (Gould 1977: 158) – to which Cesare Lombroso added some kinds of criminals – all representing the same phylogenetic level.

Gould (1977: 126–35) gives many examples of recapitulationist arguments for racial hierarchization, noting that "Biological arguments for racism may have been common before 1859, but they increased by orders of magnitude following the acceptance of evolutionary theory" (127). The primitive-as-child dominated this kind of evolutionary discourse, to the point where recapitulationists used quality of mind as the primary marker of racial ranking, more than any physical criteria. Carl Vogt, in his 1864 *Lectures on Man* (cited by Gould 1977: 128), concluded: "In the brain of the Negro the central gyri are like those in a foetus of seven months, the secondary are still less marked. By its rounded apex and less developed posterior lobe the Negro brain resembles that of our children, and by the protuberance of the parietal lobe, that of our females."[2] Anthropologists, like the American Daniel Garrison Brinton, had no difficulty positing racial hierarchies on the basis of the biogenetic law: "The adult who retains the more numerous fetal, infantile or simian traits, is unquestionably inferior to him whose development has progressed beyond them. . . . Measured by these criteria, the European or white race stands at the head of the list, the African or negro at its foot . . . All parts of the body have been minutely scanned, measured and weighed, in order to erect a science of the comparative anatomy of the races" (Brinton 1890: 48). But, of course, anatomy mattered far less in these hierarchies than did inferences drawn from social recapitulation whereby civilizational attainments of non-European races were compared with those of Europeans and hierarchizing conclusions were drawn.

Polygenesis in the United States: After Darwin

When Darwin's theory reached the United States, the polygenists of the American school were able to fit their preconceptions into Darwin's monogenic model with surprising ease. The way they did this was to recognize the fluidity and impermanence of species that Darwin described and then to say that blacks constituted an "incipient species," thereby saving all of the data and conclusions from comparative anatomy and physiology that had been marshaled to support polygenism. Darwinism further explained why the races had not changed over the course of human history, the time frame having been too short to record such change. So Josiah Nott could declare a compatibility between polygenist arguments for the inferiority of blacks and Darwinism (Gossett 1965: 232–3).

Darwin thought that primitive peoples were fixated at a lower stage of evolution (albeit culturally, not so much biologically), and had thus predicted that the "lower" races would, over time, disappear when brought into competition with the higher ones. Such a view was commonplace throughout the nineteenth century. Thus did scientific racists in the post-Civil War United States anticipate the decline of the free black population. In the last decades of the nineteenth century writers on race were obsessed with racial demographics and keenly sought evidence for the decline of black numbers. In this exercise, the census of 1890 was a key document, setting off speculation that American blacks would soon disappear. Economist Francis A. Walker perceived a slower rate of increase in the black population compared to the white and a tendency for them to concentrate in a diminishing area of the South (Gossett 1965: 245–6). The 1890 census came at a time when social theory had to have an evolutionary component in order to be taken seriously. Another economist, German-born Frederick L. Hoffman, also forecast the coming extinction of the black in America, mixing social Darwinist theory with that of degeneration. He espoused strict Spencerian laissez-faire, arguing that misguided social policy, artificially preserving the unfit, would interfere with the natural workings of the struggle for life (ibid.: 249–51). The same conclusion had long been drawn in the case of Amerindians both before and after the reception of Darwinism. In an 1823 Supreme Court decision, John Marshall had declared that the melding of peoples subsequent to conquest would not take place in the United States, owing to the racial qualities (such as savagery and nomadism) of the Amerindians, which were not subject to change. In his concurrence with

Marshall's decision, Justice Joseph Story promoted similar views, and predicted the extinction of the Indians as a result of competition with Europeans (Malcomson 2000: 64–5). Later, Darwinism would lend an evolutionary patina to established views of racial hierarchy.

Morton was the prime American representative of a European rage for cranial measurement that was popularized by Anders Retzius (1796–1860) and formed the basis for a variety of typologies of human groups. The idea was that each race had a distinctive head shape which could be measured and worked into a typology of human races, using numerical formulae such as that embodied in Retzius's cranial index. Morton had a huge collection of skulls of 1,000 or more specimens (which he called his "cranial library"). He named his approach "craniometry" and argued in his *Crania Americana* (1839) that there was a gradient of races based on brain capacity with whites at the top, Amerindians in the middle, and blacks at the bottom. Brain size, in his view, was an indicator of intelligence and therefore a good predictor of behavior. Owing to their deficient brains, American Indians could never become civilized: primitives with a "peculiar and eccentric moral constitution . . . Their minds seize with avidity on simple truths, while they reject whatever requires investigation and analysis" (Thomas 2000: 41–2).

Polygenesis in France

The role of polygenesis in French anthropology can be appreciated from the debate in the Société d'anthropologie de Paris, founded in 1859 as representing both positivist and polygenist views (Harvey 1983). The Society's founding spirit was the neuro-anatomist Paul Broca (1824–80) who, the previous year, had laid out his views on human evolution in a series of lectures at the Société de Biologie on human and animal hybridity, hybridity providing the theoretical justification for polygenesis.

The issue of hybridity was seen as crucial because if the races of mankind were truly separate species, as some polygenists held, then they should be inter-sterile; since they obviously were not, an argument developed that in many cases of cross-breeding, first generation hybrids were not as fecund as either parent stock, and if cross-breeds continued to interbreed with each other, they would become less and less fecund with each generation (unless, on the model of the "in and in" method of stock-breeding, the cross-breed were bred to a pure member of the parental stock).

Broca addressed the issue in an 1864 monograph that begins by opposing the grim predictions of writers like Nott and Arthur de Gobineau, who had predicted that mixing of races brings inevitable disaster, even threatening the very extinction of the human species. Broca responded that such predictions are obviously wrong when one regarded the "power of prosperity" of the United States, where Anglo-Saxons had been overrun with immigrants with no loss of vitality. Broca inquired under what circumstances do crossed races display diminished vitality, and found only contradictions. The problem was that, like all types, human types are abstractions, conceptualized on the basis of whatever traits one stresses. Polygenists had personified such abstractions, giving real existence to what are just ideal types. Monogenists proposed five main varieties of human beings, distinguished mainly by skin color. But Broca dissented from their view that all human races can produce prolific cross-breeds. Even when Broca was convinced that infecund crosses could be documented (children of Negro women and white men were rarely vigorous, he asserted), he suggested that climate may account for infertility. He concluded that there are too many intermediate degrees of fecundity to state any conclusion with certainty (Broca 1864).

Darwin had observed that hybrids and mongrels revert to one or both parent types after an interval of two or more generations. This happens because crossing encourages the reappearance of traits long retained, but not expressed (Darwin 1868, ch. 13). The notion that interbreeding of half breeds over time results in decreased fertility was also known to breeders and reported by Darwin (ibid.: 118–19).

With regard to methodology, Broca stressed anthropometric methods of craniology and comparative anatomy in the elaboration of racial typology. Broca and his polygenist associates engineered an award to Carl Vogt, a leading Darwinian, in 1867, in spite of the latter's opposition to polygenism. Vogt had written authoritatively on the simian origins of mankind. By 1870, Broca's position had shifted in the direction of accepting evolution, but with a multiple origin model, in order to preserve polygenism (Harvey 1983: 296–7). When members of the Society formed a teaching arm, the École d'Anthropologie in 1876, Broca became the first holder of the chair of general anthropology. When he died in 1880, leadership of both the Society and the School passed to a group of "scientific materialists," evolutionists who opposed polygenism. These materialists were at first Darwinian, then shifted towards a neo-Lamarckian position. They were politically on the left and very influential in French politics of the 1880s. The complex interplay of ideas and ideology made the French reception of Darwinism quite different from that in other Catholic countries, where there tended to be a binary polarization between free-thinking anti-clerical Darwinists on one side, and obscurantist Catholics, led by clergy, on the other. In France, the debate among anthropologists reflected instead a response "to a fluctuating political, social and philosophical situation in which the scientific issues in turn shift both meaning and direction" (Harvey 1983: 304). Thus, the influential and greatly respected Catholic anatomist and anthropologist Armand de Quatrefages, who understood the role of natural selection in the shaping of populations, was placed in the paradoxical position of having to support Darwin against the polygenist evolutionists of the Société d'Anthropologie.

Physical Anthropology in Germany

German physical anthropology only became Darwinian in the 1890s. Before then, German anthropology had been generally liberal on racial matters. The leading voice of physical anthropology throughout the last third of the nineteenth century was the pathologist Rudolf Virchow, who was liberal in politics and anti-Darwinian in biology. He was the leading figure in the foundation of the first German anthropological society, the Berliner Gesellschaft für Anthropologie. This Society, as well as the regional societies that sprouted up in its wake, all relied on the German scientific diaspora, whose members submitted observations and specimens from outposts around the world for analysis and classification.

From its inception, German physical anthropology, led by Virchow, was monogenist, although Virchow argued against descent from apes. Anthropologists uncomfortable with monogenism either had to "animalize" the "lower" races or attempt a modification like H. Klaatsch's "bigenic" model, which proposed a gorilla origin for a Western racial line, and an Eastern line stretching back to the orangutan. On the whole, anthropologists of this period opposed political anti-Semitism. Virchow's political position was to insist on the distinction between a race and religion. On the basis of his celebrated pigmentation study of German schoolchildren, Virchow had found enough fair-skinned, blond Jews (11 percent) to bolster his contention that Jews were not a race in the anthropological sense; he referred to them as a "national race" that could be assimilated. He opposed Teutonic racial nationalism and the "Pan-Aryan dogma" (Massin 1996: 87–91). Virchow's death in 1902 made it harder for anthropologists to resist the rising tide of racist theory (see Proctor 1988).

In spite of the anti-evolutionary monogenism of German anthropology (and it is interesting to note that religion apparently was not an issue here), "most anthropologists continued, without any sense of contradiction, to hold an evolutionary view of races and cultures. Accepting the generalized cultural progressivism of their day, they assumed that there was an evolution from savagery to full humanity" (Massin 1996: 97).

Virchow ranked the races on the basis of his anthropometric study of skulls, which permitted a hierarchical ranking of races by the cephalic index (the ratio of the length of the skull to its breadth, a measure that supposedly indicated brain size and which was also used by the leading German Darwinist, Ernst Haeckel [1834–1919]). Virchow was instrumental in obtaining agreement from all German anthropologists on how the measurements were to be taken. He adopted Hermann von Ihering's standardized scheme (later called the "German horizontal") whereby a horizontal line of measurement was drawn from the bottom of the eye-socket to the top of the ear orifice. The German horizontal was adopted in the "Frankfurt Agreement" of 1883, which made it more difficult for anthropologists to induce subjective apriorisms into their measurements (Zimmerman 2001: 88–90). Virchow's typology of races was completely static, lacking any historical or evolutionary narrative. For him, as for most other German anthropologists, races may not have been species, but the boundaries between them were fixed because their distinguishing characters were the result of the specific climates in which they lived. Thus, climatic determinism became a way to retain monogenism while adopting, for all practical purposes, polygenist criteria.

Virchow had used his influence to keep Darwinians out of influence in academia generally and anthropology specifically (Massin 1996: 115). But enough paleontological evidence of the common ancestry of simians and human beings had accumulated by the time of Virchow's death that German physical anthropologists soon recast their field in Darwinian terms. The Darwinian view of race that Virchow had so long opposed, on both moral and scientific grounds, was that long espoused by Ernst Haeckel.

Haeckel followed a Darwinian trope in arranging human "species" – 12 of them, comprising 36 "races" in all, in his scheme – in phylogenetic trees. Haeckel was a nominal monogenist while, according to his own lights, favoring a polygenist logic. The monogenists were right in a broad sense, though in a narrow sense the polygenists were right, "inasmuch as the different primaeval languages have developed quite independently of one another" (Haeckel, 1876: II, 304, and see 308). Haeckel's appropriation of the evolution of languages, which lent itself to depiction in a tree-like form, was by no means unique; it had been a standard argument of cultural evolutionists, including Wilhelm von Humboldt, the brothers Grimm, and, after 1859, Haeckel and Friedrich Max Müller (see Leeds 1988: 456, 460). Haeckel regarded language as the most distinctive marker of humanity and, on that basis, it could be said that the various races, although derived originally from a common stock, originated "independently of one another, by different branches of primaeval, speech-less men directly springing from apes, and forming their own primaeval language" (304). For Haeckel, the most important physical marker of race, along with skin color and cranial form, was hair. So his classificatory tree of humanity was mainly based on language and hair type. Filiation of language was evidence of a phylogenetic relationship. He thought "Papuans" to be the most primitive of all living races, closest to the "original form" of woolly-haired men.

Haeckel had influenced early European social psychologists such as Gustave Le Bon, according to whom Haeckel had correctly assumed the

> justifiable position that savages were closer to animals than they were to the individuals of advanced civilizations. Primitive peoples, in other words, had more affinities with the animal world from which they had sprung directly, than with men of advanced societies who had psychically and psychologically outpaced primitive men in their rapid ascent up the evolutionary tree and were, consequently, more biologically remote from their animal forbears. (as characterized by Gasman 1998: 156)

> Likewise the unit of analysis in the sociology of Ludwig Gumplowicz, a polygenist social thinker influenced by Haeckel, is the group or race, the social equivalent of a species. Among these, only the Germans are highly evolved. (as characterized by Gasman 1998: 174, 181)

Darwinism, that is, natural selection, "eclipsed" for 30 years as the most important mechanism of evolutionary change, reasserted itself in German anthropology in the mid-1890s "and the fundamental question of the 'hierarchy of races' and 'existence of superior and inferior races' acquired again a central position in anthropology" (Massin 1996: 99) – replacing the old craniometry.

As evidence accumulated, the idea of a static head type was undermined, convincing many of the plastic nature of head shapes and of races. In practice, it was impossible to find anything resembling pure racial types by craniometric measures, even though J. Ranke held in 1891 that the human craniological series distributed throughout humanity in gradual, uninterrupted transitions. A Lamarckian assumption that all shared was that "the level of culture could influence the volume of the brain and thus the size and shape of the skull" (Massin 1996: 111). This turned an older proposal on its head: first, shape of skull influenced mental capacity; later, mental capacity influenced skull shape. Indeed, Virchow had thought that race was a purely mental construction, that as anthropologists had come to apply statistical methodology, races had lost any reasonable biological meaning, and all one could talk about were clusters of variations "within the typical norm" (ibid.: 113).

Brazil

In Brazil the racial polemic was at the core of the heated ideological debate attending both the replacement of the Empire by the Republic and the abolition of slavery. There were quite a few polygenists, but those who were monogenist, whether because of Darwin or the Bible, adapted polygenist language to stress racial differentiation. Out of this ideological mélange came a double law of miscegenation: (1) it is adaptive: Europeans must miscegenate (with blacks) to ensure survival in the tropics. (2) it is degenerative.

According to Silvio Romero (1851–1914), the most important intellectual historian in late-nineteenth-century Brazil, the intellectual movement that characterized *fin-de-siècle* Brazil began in the mid-1870s with the confluence of Republican politics and the replacement of Comtean positivism by Darwinism, Spencer, and German monism. More precisely, the French defeat in the Franco-Prussian War stimulated the abandonment of French intellectual models, Comtean positivism in the first place. At the same time, the perceived need to define Brazilian nationality was strengthened by war with Paraguay.

In any case, Darwinism leads ineluctably into the thicket of Brazilian high culture of the early Republican era because the two main shapers of that culture, Tobias Barreto (1839–1889) and his student Romero, were outspoken Darwinians. What "Darwinian" means in this context is that Barreto and Romero (until the late 1890s), following Haeckel, thought that the struggle for existence covered *all* processes of culture and social life; literary production, for example, had no meaning or value outside of the environment that produced it. Environment here means climate plus culture, culture being a read-out of race. Climate is important because, according to the theory, Europeans *had to miscegenate* in order to survive in the tropics. Indeed, this was a common Darwinian trope in Brazil. The social historian Euclides da Cunha also stressed that miscegenation with "inferior races" had been necessary for Europeans in Brazil in order to appropriate the biological resistance offered by peoples already adapted to tropical climates. For da Cunha, the result was an atavism, a retrograde people, but not a degenerate one (Costa Lima 1988: 174–5).

In Latin America, as elsewhere, there was a tight link between Darwinism and Positivism. There were no Darwinians there who weren't also positivists. (In Brazilian political/intellectual parlance of the late nineteenth century, "positivism" meant Comtean positivism; the Spencerian brand was called "evolutionism.") But there is an important distinction to be made between European positivism (of whatever type) in places like England, France, or Germany, where positivism was a kind of seal on the achievements of the Scientific Revolution and the Enlightenment, an assertion of the primacy of science in the hierarchy of authorities. Positivism was highly rhetorical in character, and while it wasn't a philosophy of science in the strict sense, it provided a language in which the general objectives of science could be expressed.

But in Latin America there was no such established scientific tradition; indeed, in many of the twenty countries of the region there was no science to speak of, especially in the first half of the nineteenth century. So positivism – whether Comtean or Spencerian – was *programmatic* in Latin America. Positivists looked for ways to implant science, through the foundation or alteration of institutions that had the capacity to change those societies. In Brazil, positivist programs centered on the issue of nationality or race and the "scientific" approach to it.

Romero noted that directly after the fall of the Empire and instauration of the republic in 1889, you couldn't find persons calling themselves monarchists; instead, they identified themselves as Comtean positivists. Noting that the Military School had been a Comtean stronghold, Romero observes wryly it was the first time in history that an entire army had been recruited to defend a school of philosophy (Romero 1895). Moreover, there were no universities in Brazil until 1920; to earn a doctorate, one had to go to Coimbra, in Portugal. The institutions that served as the principal centers of Darwinian irradiation in Brazil between 1875 and 1900 were the law school in Recife, the medical school in Bahia, and the National Museum in Rio de Janeiro. All were self-consciously evolutionist, Darwinian in their emphasis on selection in human populations, Haeckelian in their insistence on a hierarchy of races, and Spencerian in their opposition to metaphysics. They shared the obsession for defining the nation that characterized all Brazilian positivists.

The leading lights of Recife were Tobias Barreto and his disciple Silvio Romero. Barreto was a Germanist (he even published a German daily for a while in Recife) and a staunch Haeckelian. In an 1880 article on "Haeckelism in Zoology," Barreto demonstrated his detailed acquaintance with German evolutionary biology (the article is a review of a minor work by a German anatomist critical of Haeckel and Darwin's theorizing). He discussed the role of deduction in science, citing the philosopher of science William Whewell, dismissed the anatomist as a hyper-empiricist who has reduced morphology to a purely nominal science, and so forth (Barreto 1966: 204–14). Barreto and Romero saw Haeckel's approach as one that furnished the weapon with which to attack Comtean positivism (following in the spirit of Spencer's critique of Comte's school as a substitute for religion). Although Haeckel was himself a vitalist of an idiosyncratic sort, he was read in Brazil and in Latin America generally as an arch materialist, and Barreto and Romero picked up the anti-teleological note in Haeckel's monism (there is no continual or inevitable social progress in Haeckel's view; see Gasman 1998: 28). Romero pushed this line in his attack on the Comteans, *Doutrina contra doutrina* (1895). In the School of Recife's analysis of the requirements of the civil and criminal codes (largely their work), the unit of analysis was race. Haeckel furnished the basic view that informed all Brazilian conceptualizations of race in the 1870s and 1880s: for Haeckel, as we have seen, races were distinct species. Through Haeckel, a polygenist conceptualization of race was grafted onto a monogenist evolutionary model (Gasman 1998: 14; Schwarcz 1999: 187).

Romero took literally Haeckel's insistence on the total coincidence of human beings and their environment (see Gasman 1998: 18). Thus, for Romero, climate is basic. In order to survive in the tropics the Europeans *had* to miscegenate, because the hybrid *mestizo* was better adapted to the environment (Candido 1988: 59). But then the resulting mestizo society is in a bind, because it is culturally degenerate. In his *History of Brazilian Literature* (1902–3), he argued that Brazilian writers develop ontogenetically in the context of the phylogeny of their ancestors, as they adapted to their particular environments (Candido 1988: 76). Romero had picked up cultural recapitulationism from evolutionist social theorists like Gabriel Tarde and Henry Sumner Maine, but abandoned this line in the 1890s, just as Barreto was abandoning Haeckel for a more philosophically nuanced neo-Kantianism. Romero's parting shot was a sharp critique of the cultural recapitulationist line, in which colonies were said to revert to an older phylogenetic stage, then recapitulate the successive ones, a sequence for which, he argued, there was no historical evidence (Romero 1901).

The program of the Bahia Medical School, the second center of Brazilian Darwinism, was to develop a program of public health and to write racially conceptualized public health legislation for the Republican congress to enact. Darwinian biology had been introduced there in the 1870s by a German professor, Otto Wucherer, and Haeckelian insights were applied to public health issues by his student R. Nina Rodrigues. If, for Romero, miscegenation was generally positive, for Nina Rodrigues it was reprehensible, the source of physical, mental, and cultural degeneracy. Nina focused on the nation's disease, not on diseases of the individual. Believing races to be fundamentally different, Nina pushed for craniological identification of racial groups pursuant to a reform of the criminal code according to an evolutionary logic: he wrote in 1894 that races at different levels of evolution could not be held to a single standard (Schwarcz 1999: 264). The central axis of medical legislation was the relationship between degeneracy (produced by miscegenation) and criminality (hence, the vogue for the evolutionist criminology of Lombroso and Enrico Ferri) (ibid.: 260, 287). "It is said that we have proven among us the mestizos are incapable of perfectibility," the *Bahia Medical Gazette* editorialized in 1886, "imprisoned as they are in an advanced state of decline" (ibid.: 301). One solution was to let the weaker mestizos (and all Indians, culturally inferior by definition) select out, by a natural process (ibid.: 269). Nina Rodrigues subscribed to the same evolutionary hypothesis accepted by Romero, da Cunha and others of the same generation: the regressive political ideas (that is, monarchist ones) of the rebels of the "backlands" testified to their "inferior evolutionary stage," owing to which they could not replace a concrete ruler (a monarch) with an abstract form of government (a republic).[3]

Behind these disparate appreciations of miscegenation were differing views of hybridism. The negative view was that the more primitive side will be dominant in interracial breeding, Broca (1864: 19) had opined that in the case of two primitive races, the more numerous side will absorb the less numerous. Many Europeans in the colonies believed that they would be overwhelmed by the indigenous masses through miscegenation. For example, one Thomas Hutton, an Englishman in India, wrote an interesting letter to Darwin " . . . Nature abhors what is called civilization as much as she does a vacuum. – That is to say in other words, that Nature remains true to herself, and endeavours to avoid all that is *artificial*. – The European is decidedly a highly cultivated and therefore artificial breed; – the native of India on the other hand, is almost a child of nature. – Hence when these two races intermix, Nature makes violent efforts to retain the simple and true, and to reject the artificial and false blood" (March 8, 1856, *Correspondence*, 6:52). This was a common opinion, an inference derived from the observations of animal breeders, and it was linked to degeneration theory. Hence, Nina Rodrigues concluded that miscegenation inevitably produced a weaker race and that "whitening" was scientifically impossible.

So between the jurisprudential school of Recife and the Bahia Medical School, racial theory was converted into an ideology of national culture, one which in the 1930s, divested of its biological and environmental determinism, Franz Boas's student Gilberto Freyre would make into a positively pitched national ideology in *The Masters and the Slaves* (Schwarcz 1999: 308).

The third center was the National Museum in Rio de Janeiro (the Museu Nacional), which had the feel of a research university. It had natural and social science departments, and, until the 1890s, the nation's first and only experimental biological laboratory. Under the directorships of Ladislao Netto (1874–1893), a Darwinian botanist, and his successor João Batista Lacerda (1895–1915), the National Museum entered its golden age, with a staff of talented foreign naturalists. The head of the geology section was an American, Orville Derby, who also ran the national Geological Survey. The Swiss biologist Emilio Goeldi headed the natural history section. And among a group of "traveling naturalists" were two distinguished German biologists, Fritz Müller and Hermann von Ihering. Von Ihering, an evolutionist but not a believer in natural selection, had been one of the architects of German physical anthropology before immigrating to Brazil, as noted above. Lacerda and von Ihering were both hard-line racists. Lacerda was a polygenist who, following Nina Rodrigues, wanted to "whiten" blacks and mestizos through European immigration. Von Ihering claimed that all hybrids were decadent, and caused a scandal by advocating that an Indian group inhabiting an area targeted for a new road should be exterminated. Note that Darwin was cited as the source *both* for the claim that hybrids are more resistant *and* for the claim that hybrids are unstable. Von Ihering was not only the man who had devised the common standard of craniology, he was also the link between Virchow and Brazilian anthropology.

There were two setpieces of the anthropological literature: *sambaquis* (kitchen middens) and Botocudos (a tribe that Lacerda in particular viewed as extremely "savage" and retrograde). Müller showed some interest in *sambaquis*, but primitive peoples seem not to have interested him professionally (even though he must have had contact with Botocudos, who lived within the western perimeter of his study area). In any event, Virchow had a network of German informants and collectors, residents for the most part in Santa Catarina province, who sent him materials found in the *sambaquis*, the most important being skulls and axes. Virchow appears not to have dated these finds

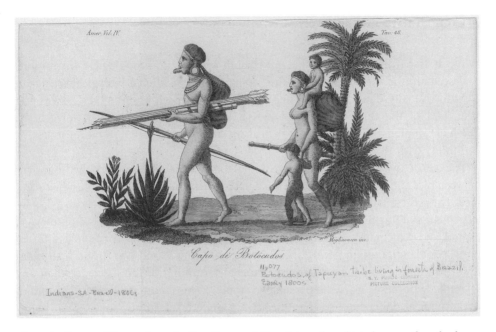

Figure 9 Image of Botocudos, who Brazilian semi-Darwinians thought to be near-throwback hominids and who were adduced as examples of human society at the lowest level of evolution. Published circa 1830. 807451: "Capo de Botocudos". *Il costume antico e moderno, o, storia del governo, della milizia, della religione . . .* ; by Giulio Ferrario, 1823–1838. Firenze: Batelli. print. Picture Collection, The Branch Libraries, The New York Public Library, Astor, Lenox and Tilden Foundations.

but did validate the middens as human creations, the work of primitive agricultural-ists (Castro Faria 2003).

The museum also offered courses open to the public, famously attended by the science-loving emperor, Pedro II. Lacerda gave a course on anthropology, treating the "great general questions of monogenism, polygenism, and transformism." In his zoology lectures, João Joaquim Pizarro liked to scandalize the women in the audience with "exaggeratedly radical transformism," emphasizing points of contact between humans and monkeys (Lopes 1997: 185–7). In the 1880s, the Museum was generally identified as a center of evolutionary biology, where *everyone* was an evolutionist, and where the Linnaean concept of the species was pronounced dead (ibid.: 190).

In Brazil, evolutionism, particularly in its Haeckelian form, was readily turned into an ideology because it was used to confirm the prior conviction of the elites that there were qualitative differences among human groups which allowed them to be classified hierarchically from inferior to superior. The social, the cultural, and the biological inevitably fused to form a seamless theory of social organization: while some argued that the atavistic results of miscegenation could be reversed by the same mechanism of importing Europeans to "whiten" the inferior races (*embrancamento*), the same effect could be achieved through the imposition of European culture, which was enough to "whiten" a mulatto like Barreto or a black (Costa Lima 1988:178).

A Comparative Perspective

While it is hardly surprising that nineteenth-century anthropological institutions coalesced around the issue of race, they appropriated or filtered biological science in a distinctive way. The reigning concepts were hierarchical, both before Darwin and after, and of the three biological issues noted, Darwin had rejected polygenesis, but had adopted the other two – hybridism and recapitulation – more or less in continuity with the pre-evolutionary understanding of them.

The debate over race was, of course, vitiated by an inability to mark the boundary between race and culture, or between biological, social, and cultural factors as they affect race. The great debate over race passed the Darwinian divide with scarcely an acknowledgement that anything had changed. Race was an issue marked by lack of ontological control, and that control would be gained slowly and with continuing conceptual difficulty until "population thinking" introduced some clarity after World War II. Social attitudes toward race have, on the whole, been more determining of racial science than any scientific hypothesis. Darwin's personal example, to his credit, no doubt did more to advance racial understanding than the science undertaken in his name.

Nineteenth-century racial thought drew from common sources which, to some extent, hearkened back to deterministic ancient Greek climate theory, and which new evolutionary perspectives did little to alter. National distinctions in the post-Darwinian discourse of race have to do, first, with the racial breakdown in individual American nations or with the colonial experiences of the European powers. Second, the disciplinary cultures of national schools of anthropology determined both methodological and theoretical approaches.

In all national settings, to the extent that a method was applied, the emphasis was on cranial measurements, which were justified as the best means to achieve a quantifiable delineation of racial groups: Sven Arrhenius had been right about them. However, ideas informing the interpretation of cranial data were not standard, and varied from society to society. Belief in polygenesis was not necessary in order to create a racial hierarchy, Ernst Haeckel furnishing a good example of a committed monogenist who insisted on a hierarchy of racial groups.

This essay has focused mainly on Brazil because it was a museum of racial science: for European physical anthropologists it provided an inexhaustible supply of data. Virchow had an army of German engineers there supplying him with skulls, von Ihering – who devised an influential standard norm for cranial measurements – held an important museum post, while the National Museum in Rio was a center of discourse on evolution in general and on evolutionary anthropology in particular. The influence of Haeckel here, as elsewhere, was enormous, the more so because Tobias Barreto, an extremely influential scholar of jurisprudence, cultural theorist, and a Germanophile devotee of Haeckel, promoted a distinctive line on the application of evolutionary thought to race: while he ranked the races in the usual manner, he introduced a novel twist: *mestiços* were better adapted to life in the tropics than their European progenitors. Through his student, Silvio Romero, his ideas were widely diffused.

In the United States, the political struggle over slavery determined the broad contours of racial "science," with greater focus on the black population (rather than on Amerindians) with intent to substantiate politically generated views on their supposed lack of fitness for freedom. Here, as in Brazil, naturalists could not escape the "national discourse" on race and identity.

Finally, we might ask which figures directed the debate. In Brazil, they were professors of law and medicine and museum scientists. In Germany and France, they were physical anthropologists, some of whom had medical training. In the United States, public opinion was a powerful force in molding and validating the positions of the so-called American School, whose leaders (again including some persons with medical training) were single-minded about the racial significance of craniology. When the transition from the Morton–Glidden–Nott nexus to Agassiz was completed, Agassiz's university status was a perfect conduit for the diffusion of European racial hierarchy schemes with the stamp of university approval, though also with any Darwinian interpretation (after 1859) filtered out.

Notes

1   Based loosely on Morgan's *League of the Ho-de-no-sau-nee, or Iroquois* (1881) and *Ancient Society* (1877).
2   Darwin's observation with regard to birds, that adult females were morphologically similar to adolescent males of the same species, was soon broadened, via recapitulation, to include human females. It informs Freud's view of women, but was a commonplace of German evolutionary biology when Freud studied it in the 1880s.
3   "A locoura epidêmica de Canudos" (1897), cited by Costa Lima, 1988: 238 n. 29.

Further Reading

Gasman, D. 1998. *Haeckel's Monism and the Birth of Fascist Ideology*. New York: Peter Lang.
Gould, S. J. 1977. *Ontogeny and Phylogeny*. Cambridge, MA: Harvard University Press.
Schwarcz, L. M. 1999. *The Spectacle of the Races: Scientists, Institutions and the Race Question in Brazil, 1870–1930*. New York: Hill & Wang.
Thomas, D. H. 2000. *Skull Wars: Kennewick Man, Archaeology, and the Battle for Native American Identity*. New York: Basic Books.

14

Race Across the Physical–Cultural Divide in American Anthropology

Jonathan Marks

The first generation of American physical anthropologists, known worldwide as the "American School," functioned as apologists for the Confederacy. Southern politicians greatly appreciated the works of Samuel George Morton, Josiah Nott, and George Gliddon (Hrdlička 1914; see also Glick in this volume). After the Civil War, the field all but disappeared. It was resurrected at the end of the nineteenth century by Franz Boas at Columbia, and slightly later by Aleš Hrdlička at the Smithsonian Institution and Earnest Hooton at Harvard. Boas came to Columbia as a physical anthropologist, an expert on measuring schoolchildren and collecting Eskimo skeletons. On his recommendation, the Smithsonian hired Hrdlička in 1902; Hooton came to Harvard in 1913.

At Columbia, Boas promoted liberal scientific humanism, as had his mentor, Rudolf Virchow. In practical terms, this meant that the study of biological differences and processes was sharply differentiated from the study of cultural-historical differences and processes. Virchow had found Ernst Haeckel's politically inflected Darwinism to be unscientific and repugnant (Massin 1996); Boas would likewise find Charles Davenport's politically inflected Mendelism to be scientifically valueless (Boas 1916).

Eugenics and the Anthropological Divide

The intellectual struggle between Boas and Davenport has been little discussed, although they were both founders of their academic disciplines in America – anthropology and human genetics, respectively. Both were New York-based. Both had doctorates in science. And both wrote paradigmatic works in 1911, reaching opposite conclusions about the same issue: the relationship between primitive and civilized folk. Davenport's *Heredity in Relation to Eugenics* argued for a Mendelian basis of cultural supremacy. Boas's *The Mind of Primitive Man* argued that cultural dominance rested on historical contingency.

Davenport made genetics the key science of the modern world: it both explained observed phenomena and promised to provide solutions for social problems. His friend

Madison Grant endorsed practical strategies for curing social ills – eugenics – based on the assumption that populations with inferior germ-plasm were clearly identifiable: the poor should be sterilized, and immigration from southern and eastern Europe should be curtailed. Grant's *The Passing of the Great Race* was well received both by geneticists, such as MIT's Frederick Adams Woods, and by politicians as diverse as Theodore Roosevelt and Adolf Hitler.

In January 1926 the informal "Eugenics Committee of the USA" was succeeded by a formal organization, the American Eugenics Society. Within it, a large "Advisory Council" of scientists, clergy, physicians, philanthropists, reformers, and politicians served under a Board of Directors that included Madison Grant. Its first president was the Yale economist Irving Fisher. Davenport wanted Grant to be its second president, but Fisher objected that "our committee is criticized more for his membership than anyone else, I think and it seems to me that it would be bad policy to make him President especially at the start" (June 10, 1926, CDP).

Evidently, Grant's Nordicism, racism, and xenophobia were controversial, despite his strong reputation among many politicians and academics. One of his most vocal critics was Boas, who wrote a damning review of *The Passing of the Great Race* for *The New Republic*. Hrdlička, the founding editor of the *American Journal of Physical Anthropology*, asked Boas to review the second edition of the book, saying that "what you said was so good that I hoped you would write another similar review." Unfortunately a review was never published, and Blakey (1987) makes a case for Hrdlička opportunistically playing off both sides.

In 1926, the AES Advisory Council included the geneticists Castle and East (Harvard), Conklin (Princeton), Guyer (Wisconsin), Holmes (Stanford), Jennings (Johns Hopkins), Walter (Brown), Woods (MIT), Wright (Chicago), and Little (Michigan; later, Jackson Laboratories). Notably missing was Thomas Hunt Morgan, the pioneering *Drosophila* geneticist, who worked in the same building as Boas at Columbia. In deference to Henry Fairfield Osborn, President of the American Museum of Natural History, Morgan did not confront the eugenicists, but published some oblique criticisms in the mid-1920s (Allen 1978; Kohler 1994). The first geneticist-defector from the eugenics ranks was Herbert Spencer Jennings, who reanalyzed the eugenical data presented to Congress (purporting to show a gradient of criminality among the populations of Europe from northwest to southeast) for the social work periodical *The Survey* in 1923. The most newsworthy defector was biologist Raymond Pearl (also of Johns Hopkins), whose widely publicized 1927 critique in H. L. Mencken's *The American Mercury* ultimately cost him a position at Harvard (Glass 1986).

America's two most prominent physical anthropologists also sat on the AES Advisory Council. As early as 1923, however, Hrdlička had complained to Irving Fisher, "During the last five years by mischievous publications such as Grant's and others, a great deal of mal-information has been spread and intolerance aroused among our own people" (June 7, 1923, HP). By contrast, Hooton remained an outspoken advocate of the eugenics program well into the 1930s. When Madison Grant sent Hooton his *Conquest of a Continent* in 1933, Hooton wrote to him, saying, "I don't expect that I shall agree with you at every point, but you are probably aware that I have a basic sympathy for you in your opposition to the flooding of this country with alien scum" (November 3, 1933, HP). Not until 1936 did Hooton write to the Executive Secretary of the AES to have his name removed from the Advisory Council.

Hooton was nevertheless anxious to differentiate his own physical anthropology from that of the Nazis. He tried "emphatically to dissociate the finding of his science from the acts of human injustice which masquerade as 'racial measures' or 'racial move- ments' or even 'racial hygiene'" (1936: 512). More significantly, Hooton worked with Boas to draft a resolution condemning the Nazi Nuremberg Laws, circulating it to seven prominent human biologists; but only Hrdlička signed it (Barkan 1992: 314). Indeed, until the 1939 meetings of the American Anthropological Association, the members of the AAA had declined to pass a resolution condemning the Nazis, largely on the grounds that it was perceived to be sponsored by Boas, presumably an interested party as a person of German Jewish origin. Ultimately, the AAA passed such a resolution, officially written by Hooton and presented by Fay-Cooper Cole of the University of Chicago.

Hooton's actual views, however, were hard to specify. He stood nearly alone among American physical anthropologists in criticizing Nazi physical anthropology, but also sponsored the British botanical geneticist and racist R. R. Ruggles Gates, as well as William R. Sheldon, who sought to correlate body form with personality traits. Gates was an unapologetic polygenist, insisting that humans should be seen as comprised of several different species because the interbreeding criterion for the demarcation of species was irrelevant; he was held in utter contempt by the gen- eticists J. B. S. Haldane (1962) and Theodosius Dobzhansky.[1] In his Foreword to Gates's 1948 book, Hooton coyly disavowed the conclusions that followed; and privately to Robert Yerkes, while not praising the work, Hooton characterized Gates far too mildly as having "not fallen under the influence of the Boasian school of anthro- pology which insists upon discounting racial differences" (July 12 1949, YP). And many were perplexed by Hooton's sponsorship of Sheldon, whose *The Varieties of Human Physique* (1940) was dedicated to Hooton; Hooton's own students saw little merit in the entire endeavor.

The Postwar Years

Madison Grant died in 1937. The Eugenics Record Office was closed by its chief patron, the Carnegie Foundation, in 1940. Franz Boas died in 1942. Aleš Hrdlička died in 1943. Charles Davenport died in 1944, as sitting president of the American Association of Physical Anthropologists (having been nominated by Hooton). Only Hooton was left to represent the "old guard," and Hooton himself, like many Americans, had migrated politically to the right (which may partially explain the sentiments expressed in the correspondence quoted above). A new generation of American cultural anthropolo- gists emerged to be the antagonists of the scientific racists.

On the political scene, however, the Nazi menace had been replaced by the Com- munist menace. Prior to World War II, the Nazis were not principally the enemies of American democracy, but of Communism – and, indeed, the Nazis had directed their strongest political invective against the Communists. It was thus reasonable for American intellectuals who came to maturity in the 1930s, and who opposed both the racism at the core of Nazi ideology and the racial inequalities in America, to gravitate toward the Communists, the strongest enemies of Nazism. Of course, much Communist sympathy among American intellectuals dissipated with the non-aggression pact signed by Hitler and Stalin in 1939.

During and after World War II, the intellectual burden of anti-racism was picked up by the heirs of Boas in cultural anthropology. Notably, two cultural anthropologists, Ruth Benedict and Gene Weltfish, co-authored a pamphlet called "The Races of Mankind," which had been solicited by the USO for distribution to American soldiers, and which was intended to inform soldiers about the ideological issues dividing the Allied and Axis powers. It was withdrawn, however, after the chair of the House Military Affairs Committee, Andrew J. May of Kentucky, judged its strident egalitarianism un-American; ultimately, he had it declared subversive. As early as 1944, the cultural anthropologist Ralph Linton (who was not in the Boasian intellectual lineage, and famously hated Ruth Benedict) reported to the FBI that Boas had been a Communist, and had been surrounded by Communists, including Weltfish (Price 2004: 111). Weltfish's career was to suffer in the anti-Communist frenzy of the postwar period; in 1953, two weeks before she was forced to testify before Senator Joseph McCarthy's committee, she lost the job she had held at Columbia since 1936.

Certainly the most vocal and influential exponent of anti-racist anthropology was the enigmatic Ashley Montagu (Sperling 2000). Born Israel Ehrenberg in London's East End, he began by studying physical anthropology informally with Sir Arthur Keith, and later studied cultural anthropology formally with Bronislaw Malinowski at the London School of Economics. At this time, he reinvented himself as Montague Francis Ashley Montagu. In 1931, he emigrated to the United States, writing a letter introducing himself to Hooton at Harvard, in which he cavalierly misrepresented his credentials:

> I am twenty-six, educated at Cambridge, Oxford, London, Florence, and Columbia. M.A., Ph.D., etc. fifteen anthropological publications. Recommended very generously by Sir Arthur Keith, who has furnished me a too-glowing testimonial which you may see if you wish. Sir Arthur once told me that I can always say that he will speak for me, so I may as well mention this too, for if you hold him in as great respect as I do, this should be impressive. (December 28, 1931, EHP)

In fact Montagu had not matriculated at either Cambridge or Oxford. He would not earn a PhD for several years, and it would be in cultural anthropology, under the supervision of Ruth Benedict. Nevertheless, he got a job teaching anatomy to dental students through Hrdlička. In 1941, he launched his first attack upon the central concept of physical anthropology – race – combining the Boasian approach with the arguments advanced in Britain by the biologist Julian Huxley and the anthropologist Alfred Cort Haddon in their *We Europeans* (1936). Montagu maintained a cordial correspondence with Hooton, whose sponsorship (or at least benign neglect) would be needed for any advancement in physical anthropology.

Meanwhile, in the wake of revelations of Nazi horrors UNESCO's president, Julian Huxley, sought to have a formal statement issued about race. An international panel of anthropologists was assembled under Arturo Ramos, a Brazilian anthropologist, who died suddenly, leaving Montagu acting as "*rapporteur*" (Barkan 1996). The resulting UNESCO Statement on Race was issued in 1950, and left the "old guard" biologists and physical anthropologists sputtering about the divide between cultural and physical anthropology. To them, it was evident that the Statement had been drafted principally by cultural anthropologists – and authored by its *rapporteur*, Montagu (Stewart 1961). As one of the angered physical anthropologists wrote, the original statement

> was drawn up by eight men, one each from seven countries with Ashley Montagu as rapporteur. Only one, save the rapporteur, is a physical anthropologist – Juan Comas of Mexico. The United States was represented by a Negro sociologist, E. Franklin Frazier; France by Claude Levi-Strauss, a Jewish sociologist, the UK by Morris Ginsberg, profession unstated.[2] Not a single expert on race had anything to do with it. There were no Germans or Austrians.
>
> It was sent to about 90 scientists, including myself. Darlington, Sir R. Fisher, Genna (Italy) and I "are frankly opposed to the statement". (Carleton Coon to Sarah Dees [undated], CP)

Darlington and Fisher were notable names to drop, being well-known for their conservative political views. It was not surprising, however, that there were no Germans or Austrians. Consider that the leading German physical anthropologist was Eugen Fischer, who had joined the Nazi Party in 1940 after years as a collaborator. In *Science*, the expatriate Franz Weidenreich declared that Fischer merited trial as a war criminal (1946; see also Goldschmidt 1942). But the conservative backlash against the 1950 statement was powerful, particularly in England. The British journal *Man* published a long series of critical comments on it; and in response, a second UNESCO Statement on Race was drafted in 1951. Anxious lest the meeting be dominated by "out-and-out racists," which would result in a "pretty sad" statement (Dobzhansky to Montagu, February 24, 1951, AMP), the anti-racist scholars arranged to have the liberal geneticist L.C. Dunn serve as *rapporteur*. The second statement emphasized the biological aspects of debates about race – and principally the indeterminacy of many key issues, such as intelligence. Even so, many senior physical anthropologists and biologists took exception to this statement. Their criticisms were solicited and published as *The Race Concept: Results of an Inquiry*, by UNESCO. Notable among the few physical anthropologists and geneticists who failed to respond to UNESCO's solicitation was Hooton.

Montagu had successfully undermined the concept of race, central to physical anthropology, but at enormous professional cost. Untenured at Rutgers, he was a prime target for the McCarthyites. Succumbing to political pressure, Rutgers summarily fired him, and he found all other academic avenues blocked. He was forced to earn his living as a lecturer and writer.

Mainstream physical anthropologists, Hooton's former students, were less intrigued by any possible deterministic relationships between the head and the mind than Hooton had been. None elaborated his facile (if industrious) contributions to criminology (Hooton 1939a, 1939b). One (Carl Seltzer) kept somatology alive; and another (Carleton Coon) kept racial studies alive. The others explored diverse issues, from local variation in skull form to population genetics, and the malleability of the human body. The student who epitomized the generational change in the field was Sherwood Washburn, who wrote a thesis in 1940 on the anatomy of monkeys, and then moved to New York to take up a position at Columbia University's Medical School.

At Columbia, Washburn befriended the evolutionary geneticist Theodosius Dobzhansky. Together, they organized a major conference at Cold Spring Harbor on "The Evolution of _Homo sapiens_," bringing together leading physical anthropologists – among them a goodly number of Hooton's former students, as well as Hooton himself. Their objective was to effect a major shift in theoretical and empirical focus from abstract races to real populations. Washburn recalled that Hooton took him aside, to say "Sherry, I hope I never hear the word 'population' again!" (personal communication).

In the following year (1951), Washburn published his most famous paper, describing the shifts that had taken place within his cohort – from the race to the population, from categorization to function, from typology to plasticity, from static classification to evolutionary dynamics, from speculations about heredity to genetic studies, and from humanity's discrete divisions to the underlying common history of the species (Haraway 1988). This was a "new physical anthropology." Adopting the biologists' Evolutionary Synthesis, physical anthropologists subtly but crucially reconceptualized race. It was now understood as a mega-cluster of populations, not an essentialized form. This facilitated the study of race genetically, as it was, for example, by Boyd (1963) and Cavalli-Sforza, which meant identifying people as parts of races, rather than races as inhering within people.

Hooton had employed a fundamentally Platonic idea of race, "a vague physical background, usually more or less obscured or overlaid by individual variations in single subjects, and realized best in a composite picture" (1926: 79). But much rethinking was required when a race was considered to be a cluster of people, rather than an underlying abstract essence they shared. Claims such as "some persons who appear to be white show definite negroid or mongoloid skeletal features" (Hooton 1926: 78), or that a prehistoric skull from Colorado might be "pseudo-Australoid" (Hooton 1930) – became nonsensical, once race was redefined in terms of ancestry and geography. The specialist now focused on adaptation and relatedness, no longer on racial diagnosis and identification.

Indeed, to focus on the issue of race now reduced simply to assuming there were natural global divisions of people, then asking how many there were and where to draw the lines among them. Frederick Hulse (1962) argued compellingly that race was no more than a transient pattern of the gene pool. And, of course, in the real world of migration and admixture, to focus on race effectively required reimagining the racial world of 1492 (or perhaps of 1492 BCE), rather than analyzing the racial world of 1960.

The Racial World of 1960

With the accession of the Nazis and their troubling ideology, Hooton and Hrdlička had laid claim to the "real" scientific study of race, although their writings were permeated with the popular prejudices of the day. For example, Hrdlička (1930: 170) summarized the aptitudes of the races in tabular form, noting that "musical ability" was in blacks "well represented, but not of high intellectual order" (he was apparently not much of a jazz fan). By the 1960s, however, the racial issues of interest to the public were civil rights in America and decolonization in the rest of the world. Those anthropologists best able to contribute to consideration of these movements were cultural anthropologists, and consequently discourses of race were replaced by discourses of ethnicity and nationalism (Baker 1998).

And yet, as the civil rights movement advanced, there were still many who saw egalitarianism as Communistic, and, indeed, as un-American. Among them was a wealthy textile magnate called "Colonel" Wickliffe Draper, who had established a philanthropic scientific endowment named "The Pioneer Fund" in 1937, with Charles Davenport's protégé, Harry Laughlin, as its first president. The previous year, Laughlin had been awarded an honorary degree from Nazi-controlled Heidelberg University, for his inspiration in drafting model eugenic sterilization laws. The possibility that he might accept it in person was scandalous even to Davenport (Kevles 1985).

With Draper's financial support, Davenport undertook work in the 1920s to show that miscegenation in Jamaica had produced an inferior hybrid race; even other eugenicists judged this research to be egregiously flawed (Castle 1930; Pearson 1930). By the 1950s, Draper was using the Pioneer Fund to channel financial assistance to opponents of integration and civil rights within the academy, and even to scholarly non-academicians. In 1959, some of these activists incorporated the International Association for the Advancement of Ethnology and Eugenics (IAAEE), and shortly thereafter began publishing *Mankind Quarterly*, with Draper's backing (Tucker 1994, 2002; Winston 1998). Prominent among these activists were Columbia University psychologist Henry E. Garrett, UNC anatomist Wesley Critz George, and a sometime historian and former president of Delta Airlines, Carleton Putnam.

Garrett had testified for the defendant in 1953 in the famous *Brown vs. Board of Education* trial. In the first volume of the *Mankind Quarterly*, he ranted against "the equalitarian dogma," crediting it not to Thomas Jefferson but to the Communists, anthropologists, and Jews, and particularly to Franz Boas. Under the editorship of an obscure Scottish nobleman named Robert Gayre, *Mankind Quarterly* listed Garrett and the geneticist Ruggles Gates (see above) as associate editors.

The journal immediately ignited a controversy in the scientific community. The British physical anthropologist Geoffrey Harrison (1961: 163) reviewed it angrily in *Man*: "Few of the contributions have any merit whatsoever, and many are no more than incompetent attempts to rationalize irrational opinions." Likewise, the Mexican physical anthropologist Juan Comas (1961) wrote an extended critique in *Current Anthropology*. Santiago Genoves (1961) brought *Mankind Quarterly* to the attention of the readers of *Science*.

The Yugoslav anthropologist (and Dachau survivor) Božo Škerlj resigned from *Mankind Quarterly*'s editorial board upon discovering its ideological stance, and criticized the journal in *Man*, only to be sued by Gayre and Garrett for associating them with Nazi ideologies.

Carleton Putnam had become an active spokesman for segregation in the late 1950s. His National Putnam Letters Committee took out large pro-segregation advertisements in major newspapers, often written as open letters to the president – for example, in *The New York Times* on January 5, 1959. In 1961, the Public Affairs Press released Putnam's short book, *Race and Reason: A Yankee View* (originally titled *A Warning to the North*), which not only made the argument against integration, but also followed Henry Garrett in laying the blame for the idea at the feet of anthropologists, Communists, and Jews (even more explicitly than Garrett had), and reviling Franz Boas in particular. But Putnam went further, and discussed the qualifications of different types of anthropologists to issue authoritative pronouncements on race. Anthropologists came in two varieties, cultural and physical. The equalitarian movement had been led by the cultural anthropologists, although it was the physical anthropologists who were the experts on racial biology (1961: 51–2).

Apparently, Putnam had at least one ally within the anthropological community, tutoring him on the state of the field, at least as that ally saw it. And Putnam acknowledged as much:

> Besides intimidation there has, of course, been a false indoctrination of our younger scientists, although some hope on this score may be found in the following statement in a letter to me from a distinguished scientist younger than I am, a scientist not a Southerner, who is a recognized international authority on the subject we are considering: "About 25 years ago it seemed to be proved beyond a doubt that man is a cultural animal, solely a creature of the environment, and that there is no inheritance of instinct, intelligence or any other capacity. Everything had to be learned and the man or race that had the best opportunity for learning made the best record. The tide is turning. Heredity is coming back, not primarily through anthropologists but through the zoologists. It is the zoologists, the animal behavior men, who are doing it, and the anthropologists are beginning to learn from them. It will take time, but the pendulum will swing." (1961: 50)

To Putnam, the proposition that different groups of people had roughly equivalent intellectual endowments, and were entitled to equal opportunities and rights, was radical. It was not radical, however, for most anthropologists, whether cultural or physical. The American Anthropological Association quickly passed a resolution introduced by its outgoing president, archaeologist Gordon Willey, condemning Putnam's book (Margolis 1961). The following spring, the American Association of Physical Anthropologists passed a similar resolution, introduced by Stanley Garn.

The president of the AAPA was Carleton S. Coon of the University of Pennsylvania, who had been Hooton's second doctoral student. He later recalled the events of that business meeting:

I was involved in that I was related to the author through both the Carletons and the Putnams. He had sent me a copy, and I had read it. I had seen nothing actionable in it
. . .

I asked the audience how many had read Carleton Putnam's book? Just one. What did he think of it? Not much. How many had heard of it before? Only a few hands were raised. Yet these people were prepared to vote to censure Carleton Putnam. . . .

There they were, some of them old and trusted friends, apparently as brainwashed as Pavlov's puppies, or as most of the social anthropologists . . .

I told my fellow members that I would no longer preside over such a craven lot, and resigned the presidency. I would leave them to vote whatever resolution they wished, but not in my name. (1981: 334–5)[3]

Coon's story was more than a little disingenuous, however. His resignation was not accepted. While he was still president of the AAPA, he published his *magnum opus* on race. Originally pretentiously titled *On the Origin of Races* to evoke Darwin, Coon's book lost its initial preposition at some point along the way, and was published in October 1962. Its central premise was that the five types of humans (Caucasoids, Mongoloids, Australoids, Congoids, and Capoids [i.e., those from the Cape of Good Hope]) evolved into modern *Homo sapiens* from *Homo erectus* at different times; and, further, that this provided a deterministic, naturalistic explanation for the different "levels of civilization" each had attained.

Coon and Putnam: A Family Affair

Since the time of Madison Grant, the Boasians had successfully repudiated explanations of "civilization" that involved nature rather than history – so Coon's thesis seemed uncomfortably retrogressive. Although Hooton had always been a little uneasy with the Boasian wall separating social history and biological evolution, he had generally kept his doubts to himself.

Carleton Putnam, however, had devoted considerable energy in 1962 to editing and publishing a pamphlet by the anatomist Wesley Critz George on the intellectual inferiority of blacks, commissioned by the Governor of Alabama, distributed by the Putnam Letters Committee, and underwritten by the Pioneer Fund. He now actively promoted the work, in another open letter advertisement in *The New York Times*, this one addressed to President Kennedy and published on October 3, 1962. Cultural anthropologist Morton Fried of Columbia wrote in to quote both the AAA and AAPA resolutions against Putnam, but was blindsided by the response published in the *Times* on October 24 by Garrett and George.

[I]n his new book, "The Origin of Races," published Oct. 15, Carleton Coon, one of the foremost physical anthropologists, presents evidence indicating that the white race passed from the stage of Homo erectus to Homo sapiens 200,000 years before the Negro and is therefore 200,000 years ahead of him on the ladder of evolution.

One need look no further than the introduction to "The Origin of Races" to find these words: "It is a fair inference . . . that the subspecies which crossed the evolutionary threshold into the category of Homo sapiens the earliest have evolved the most, and that the obvious correlation between the length of time a subspecies has been in the sapiens state and the levels of civilization attained by some of its populations may be related phenomena.

Although Garrett and George's letter was published on October 24, it was dated October 14, actually the day before the publication of the book they were quoting. Coon himself was soon besieged by colleagues and journalists wanting to know what he had meant, and how the segregationists had been able to pounce upon what he had said so quickly.

The truth was uncomplicated. Putnam and Coon had been corresponding since 1960, when Coon began assisting Putnam in the preparation of the latter's *Race and Reason*. Putnam's extended quotation from a "recognized international authority" was taken from a letter from Coon dated June 17, 1960 (CP), and deliberately disguised. On May 17, 1962 Putnam had sent the anatomist George "sheets of quotations from Coon's book"[4] (George to Putnam, May 19, 1962, GP). And just a few days later, Putnam told George that he wanted "to go over *The Biology of the Race Problem* [i.e., George's pamphlet] with you paragraph by paragraph. I now have the Colonel's comments as well as Coon's." With the publication of *The Origin of Races*, and Coon's help with both Putnam's *Race and Reason* and George's *The Biology of the Race Problem*, the segregationists had good reason to count Coon an ally.

Moreover, following Ruggles Gates's death, Coon was invited to join the editorial board of the *Mankind Quarterly*. There were affinities between Coon and Gates: Coon's racial taxonomy (which split sub-Saharan Africans, and lumped Americans with Asians) was identical to the one presented by Gates in *Human Ancestry*, but at a lower taxonomic level; and Gates had acknowledged Coon's assistance in reading and commenting on his 1948 book (see Eckhardt 2000). But Coon politely declined *Mankind Quarterly*'s invitation, although not because the journal was an appalling disgrace to scholarly studies of human variation, but because it would look bad: "I will be very glad to get your monographs and also your magazine, to which I would be happy to subscribe," he wrote, "but I fear that for a professional anthropologist to accept membership on your board would be the kiss of death, here in the so-called land of the free and home of the brave" (Coon to Gayre, November 6, 1962, CP).

Coon's book received favorable notices from Hooton's successor at Harvard, William Howells, from the distinguished biologists Ernst Mayr and George Gaylord Simpson, and from many others. Coon even retrofitted his earlier work to accommodate *The Origin of Races*. He revised *The Story of Man*, reducing the number of races identified in it from six to five, and changing the order in which they evolved, upon which his new book's radical conclusions were predicated. Coon had bluntly written in the first edition that "The Mongoloids are probably not as ancient as the Negroids" (1954: 198); this flatly contradicted the thesis articulated in *The Origin of Races*, and he deleted it in the new edition.

The rumors about Coon's connections to the segregationists had been swirling for months in the academic community. Stanley Garn, who had worked with Coon at Harvard, had co-authored *Races* (1950) with him, and had also put forward the AAPA motion to condemn Putnam's work, noted that "Carleton Putnam, racist pamphleteer and a cousin of Carleton Coon, leaked cryptic hints well before the Mississippi insurrection" [in the fall of 1962, when a black student named James Meredith tried to matriculate at the University of Mississippi] (Garn 1963).

As a full-time propagandist, Putnam certainly was not going to keep his newly acquired scientific arguments secret. Putnam had written privately months earlier, "When the President of the American Association of Physical Anthropologists, a magna cum laude graduate of Harvard and a native of New England, states that recent discoveries indicate the Negro is 200,000 years behind the White race on the ladder of evolution, this ends the integration argument" (Putnam to James A. Moss, June 4 1962, CP). Putnam's public addresses and pamphlets led Sherwood Washburn, the president-elect of the American Anthropological Association, to write to Coon, "I certainly hope that there is some way you can answer the weird political distortions which he makes from your evolutionary views. The less Putnam appears to be scientifically respectable, the better for all of us" (August 8 1962, CP). Coon would not repudiate Putnam publicly or privately, however. While the segregationists were already citing his forthcoming work, Coon adopted a self-protective posture of scientific detachment in his reply to Washburn: "We have no business getting involved in domestic social and political issues, particularly as an association" (August 18 1962, CP).

Many of the reviews of Coon's book, while favorable, noted that segregationists were invoking him, and politely (often condescendingly) averred that they were doing so improperly or inappropriately – as indeed Washburn had put it to Coon. *The Saturday Review* asked the distinguished evolutionary geneticist Theodosius Dobzhansky to review the book, and Dobzhansky wrote a polite, albeit critical, review, sending an advance copy to Coon as a professional courtesy. Coon, who had written obsequiously to Dobzhansky a few months earlier that the latter's ideas were very similar to those expressed in his own forthcoming book (May 26 1962, TDP), now read his own insecurities into the review and reacted vituperatively: "You accused me of 'mischievously' altering my style so as to provide easy quotes for political people. That is libel" (Coon to T. Dobzhansky, October 25, 1962, CP). Coon prevailed upon the editor of *The Saturday Review*, Norman Cousins, to pull Dobzhansky's review and to publish an excerpt from his own book (Coon 1981, 353).[5] Dobzhansky's review came out in *Scientific American* and *Current Anthropology*.

Dobzhansky was in fact an ideal person to help relieve the pressure on the anthropological community, being an interested outsider (his research was on the evolutionary genetics of the fruitfly, *Drosophila*), and of great scientific stature. In his homeland, Dobzhansky had been deeply affected by the politicization of biology through the agency of Stalin's geneticist, Trofim D. Lysenko. He had begun his career in America working with Thomas Hunt Morgan, the only geneticist of prominence to have resisted the lure of the eugenics movement, and had become involved with the anthropological community in New York, working on projects with Ashley Montagu, Margaret Mead, and Sherwood Washburn. Being a "real" biologist, non-Jewish, and an émigré from the Soviet Union, he was particularly immune from the segregationists' charge of undue influence of a Jewish/Communist/Cultural-Anthropological conspiracy.[6]

This was a juncture at which the solidarity of biological and cultural anthropology was crucial, and it was fortunate that the incoming president of the American Anthropological Association was a biological anthropologist, Sherwood Washburn. Washburn had been Coon's teaching assistant at Harvard, and had a testy relationship with their common mentor, Hooton. Hooton had been irked by Washburn's first paper on race, and could hardly have missed the fact that the "new physical anthropology" was effectively a repudiation of his own work.

Washburn, as a non-Boasian, was also well suited to chide Putnam for "greatly exaggerat[ing] the role of Boas in American anthropology" (Washburn to Putnam, December 5 1961, GP). Putnam fumed back, "It is not sociologists, nor cultural anthropologists, who are best qualified to speak on this subject, but physical anthropologists and geneticists" (Putnam to Washburn, December 12 1961, GP) – apparently unaware of the academic specialty of his correspondent! And obviously, if one of the central issues was the comparison and relative evaluation of the accomplishments of different groups of people, then the cultural anthropologists were indeed the most appropriate experts (Diamond 1962; Steward 1962).

Dobzhansky had already published a thunderous review of Putnam in the *Journal of Heredity*. Between Washburn and Dobzhansky, then, the two most highly respected "physical anthropologists and geneticists," invoked by Putnam, were in fact actively repudiating his work, even before the publication of *The Origin of Races* tied it to Coon's.

As a respected professional colleague, Coon had to be handled differently from Putnam, and Washburn agreed to address the "race issue" in his 1962 AAA presidential address (Washburn 1983: 19; DeVore 1992: 422). Washburn's address, subsequently published in the *American Anthropologist* (Washburn 1963), provided the community essentially with a "position paper" written by a leading physical anthropologist, thus undermining both the possibility that Coon spoke authoritatively for the subfield, and the argument that the AAA represented only cultural anthropologists, who differed from, and erred against, physical anthropologists in their understandings of race.

A tradition developed among Coon's friends that Washburn's presidential address had been a vehement personal tirade against Coon, and that the published version was much more polite (Shipman 1994). Washburn vigorously denied this rumor, but did not keep a copy of his address. But not only would that have been counterproductively indecorous for an issue of such delicacy, it would also have been unnecessary. Washburn's strategy was simply to define Coon and his work out of modern anthropology, as he had, in effect, been doing for over a decade.

At the annual meeting of the American Association for the Advancement of Science in February 1963, Dobzhansky acted as discussant in Stanley Garn's symposium on race, and

> closed by referring to the adverse use of Coon's theory by racist propagandists. He remarked that this demonstrates that scientists can no longer remain in ivory towers, unconcerned

with the impact of their pronouncements, and that, indeed, it is naïve and irresponsible for them to pretend they can. (Leacock 1963)

In private, Coon and Dobzhansky had been conducting a heated correspondence for months (Jackson 2001). Coon finally responded publicly in *Science* to Dobzhansky's "charge, repeated many times since my book came out, that I wrote it irresponsibly, naively, or mischievously. I wrote it without evasion or provocation and as truthfully as I was able, fully aware of the abuse that would follow, but not expecting an officious rebuke from a man of Dobzhansky's stature as a scientist" (Coon 1963).

It is worthy of note that Coon did not attempt to protect himself under the shield of "academic freedom" – as professors subsequently associated with the *Mankind Quarterly*, Pioneer Fund, and their satellite organizations, would do. Coon's argument was that he could not be held accountable for whatever use people made of his work. But that position had become untenable, not least after J. Robert Oppenheimer's widely-quoted comment in 1947 that "physicists have known sin" for their development of nuclear weapons.

Coon never maintained that Putnam and the segregationists had misquoted or misused his work, which implies that they were drawing what he saw as proper inferences from it. And Coon was happy to send his academic enemies into the hands of the red-baiters. As he wrote to anthropologist Harry Turney-High of the University of South Carolina, "it seems to me that somebody should do [two] things: (1) investigate the communist influence on American anthropology via Bella Dodd [a Catholic lawyer for the Communist Party], Boas, and the Boasians. . . . (2) find out why Ashley Montagu changed his father's name retroactively in Who's Who and whether or not he has ever carried a [Communist Party] card."

After Putnam and Coon

The immediate academic reaction to the disputes over Putnam and Coon was that physical anthropology largely abandoned thinking about race as such, replacing it instead with population genetics. Thus, to the extent that race was a "real world" issue that students came to college engaged with, and opinionated about, physical anthropology effectively withdrew and relegated academic racial discourse to the population geneticists on one side and to the cultural anthropologists on the other. Cultural anthropologists' position had been laid out by the Boasians; but the population geneticists' position was naively ambiguous, sometimes denying the very existence of race (Lewontin 1972), and sometimes using race as an unproblematic analytic category (Nei and Roychoudhury 1974). Academic physical anthropologists turned their backs on the race concept, although it remained viable in forensic anthropology, in its "applied" connection to law enforcement – largely disconnected from theory (Brace 1995).

The Pioneer Fund, however, continued to find and support scientists whose work echoed the themes that had aroused Wickliffe Draper's interest in the likes of Charles

Davenport, Harry Laughlin, Henry Garrett, Carleton Putnam, and Wesley Critz George. As late as 1980, the Pioneer Fund gave money to reprint an excerpt from Carleton Coon's work (Lombardo 2002). They now made a subtle shift, however, by supporting work that seemed to affirm the general inheritance of behavior. This would be convergent with the racist agenda on the assumption that there is an easy translation between the reasons that different people act in different ways *within the same group*, and the reasons that *groups of people* act differently from one another. This elision of the sources of within-group and between-group variation became central to the arguments of Arthur Jensen, the Berkeley psychologist, one of the major beneficiaries of the fund in the 1960s. His student, Thomas Bouchard, began a widely publicized study of twins at the University of Minnesota, with the generous help of the Pioneer Fund. *The Mankind Quarterly* remained in print, edited by Roger Pearson (Lynn 2001; Kenny 2002; Lombardo 2002).

By 1970, Arthur Jensen and William Shockley – the Stanford physicist who was also a Pioneer beneficiary – were putting new spins on familiar stories, Jensen arguing for the innateness of IQ differentials, and Shockley for meaningful variation in the overall genetic value of human groups. Their scholarly opponents were principally population geneticists, such as Stanford's Luca Cavalli-Sforza and Harvard's Richard Lewontin (a Dobzhansky student).

In the late 1980s, a Canadian psychologist named J. Philippe Rushton, supported by the Pioneer Fund, made news with a theory that misapplied ideas from population ecology: Human races, he argued, had undergone divergent selective pressures on life-history variables, which could be inferred by IQ, head size, self-reported measures of sexual activity and sexual anatomy, lawlessness, and, of course, civilization. When his work, along with that of several other Pioneer Fund grantees and *Mankind Quarterly* contributors, was cited in the bestseller *The Bell Curve* (Herrnstein and Murray, 1994), it brought the journal under renewed public scrutiny, as well as the fund itself (DeParle 1994; Lane 1994; Littlewood 1995; Marks 2005).

Jon Entine's *Taboo: Why Black Athletes Dominate Sports and Why We're Afraid to Talk About It* (2000) repeated some familiar charges: scholarly discourse on race is stifled by a liberal-Jewish-anthropological conspiracy.[7] One of Entine's principal sources was Berkeley physical anthropologist Vincent Sarich, whose own book *Race: The Reality of Human Differences* (Sarich and Miele, 2004), presented the same charges. While Sarich and Miele do not mention the Pioneer Fund, they discuss uncritically the work of its modern beneficiaries: Philippe Rushton, Richard Lynn, and Arthur Jensen. Then they speculate on what the "discovery" that indigenous Africans have a mean IQ of 70 might imply about Africans, rather than questioning what it might imply about the quality or character of the science that produced this figure.

There is no little irony in being able to counter their arguments by quoting none other than Earnest Hooton (1940: 107), assessing the implications of controlled adoption studies:

> These data might be interpreted as indicative of the fact that intelligence is not innate but environmentally controlled. Or they may reveal that intelligence tests test principally

the environment of the testees and the intelligence of the testers. As Juvenal might have said, "Who shall test the testers themselves?

... [T]o me the principal result of these fascinating experiments is to confirm a strong suspicion that diagnoses of superior or inferior intelligence cannot be made from intelligence tests (at any rate upon the testees).

Unsurprisingly, these modern neo-racist writers cite one another, acknowledging the complementary nature of their positions. Thus, the "2nd Special Abridged Edition" of Rushton's book – mass-mailed to social scientists – begins with plaudits for Entine. Sarich and Miele also praise Entine, after dismissing a century of anthropological progress – and then proceed to laud Rushton. Political scientist Charles Murray, co-author of *The Bell Curve*, provided blurbs for the works of Rushton and Sarich-Miele. Jon Entine became an adjunct fellow of the American Enterprise Institute – Charles Murray's base – in 2002. The same year, Philippe Rushton assumed the presidency of the Pioneer Fund.

Conclusions

The "four-field approach" had been in place in anthropology for over a century, originally instituted as a means of comprehensively "othering" the now-pacified American Indians. Its call to be "holistic" (i.e., anti-reductive) that emerged in the early 1960s (e.g., Mandelbaum et al. 1963) was to some extent a call to harmonize the polarity of the "physical" versus "cultural" studies that was now being exploited by the segregationists. Paradoxically, Carleton Coon was probably the closest to a generalist anthropologist the discipline had seen since Boas himself.

I think that the history of anthropology bears out the conclusion that consideration of race does not divide anthropology along subdisciplinary lines, and probably never has. Boas's position was nuanced, and evolved considerably during his lifetime, but was part of a liberal German tradition shared, for example, by Felix von Luschan (Smith 2002). Hooton's views were likewise nuanced, and changed during his lifetime.[8] Ralph Linton, outside the Boasian lineage, discussed race and discussed the anthropological subfields in a 1938 paper, but did not suggest that they mapped on to one another.

The anti-racist Benedict–Weltfish pamphlet, which was so threatening to Southern legislators during World War II, assumed the existence of races, but challenged the ranking of their innate intellectual capacities. The modern view, that human variation is clinally structured, and that race is principally a cognitive category rather than a natural one, was still controversial by the late 1960s. And while Carleton Coon had many friends and colleagues who were reluctant to criticize his work, his most devastating critics were nevertheless his fellow biological anthropologists. As the distinguished anatomist Wilfrid E. Le Gros Clark (1963) observed:

It seems that Dr. Coon places too much confidence in the ability of anatomists to distinguish one race from another by reference to single isolated skeletal remains; for

example, he believes that "Any good anatomist can tell the skeleton of human races apart."
If this is the case, the present reviewer is certainly not a good anatomist.

Carleton Putnam, likewise, does not seem to have had much support in any quarter
of anthropology. Although he may have tried to turn physical anthropologists against
cultural anthropologists by claiming that the latter had no expertise on race, he was
pilloried by both types.

We are unlikely to return to the days when Franz Boas, Clark Wissler, and Alfred
Kroeber could sit on the editorial board of the *American Journal of Physical
Anthropology* (in 1918). Biological and cultural anthropology are certainly not
converging methodologically or intellectually, but race is not one of the principal
elements on which they disagree. To the extent that race is still occasionally taken to
be a natural category, it is generally only among narrow classes of applied physical
anthropologists.[9] Physical anthropologists are still more attracted to biologized
theories – for example, to sociobiology in the 1970s and to evolutionary psychology
in the 1990s – but the issue of race itself is now far less divisive in anthropology than
it was to earlier generations. Consequently, at present there may be more agreement
among the practitioners of all subfields of anthropology when the subject is race than
there is on any other subject (Mukhopadhyay and Moses 1997).

Acknowledgments

I thank Amanda Mims for research assistance with the Wesley Critz George material. I thank
George Whitney for access to materials on the American Eugenics Society. I am grateful for
comments on this manuscript from Susan Sperling, Bernice Kaplan, John J. Jackson, Leonard
Lieberman, and Henrika Kuklick.

Notes

1 As a botanical geneticist, he was familiar with the problem of applying Ernst Mayr's "biological species concept" to plant species, which are capable of extensive cross-fertilization.
Decades later, the distinguished plant geneticist G. Ledyard Stebbins would describe the
BSC with considerable justification as "zoocentric" (personal communication). See also Osman
Hill (1940).
2 Coon's characterizations here are worth noting, given the conspiratorial beliefs of the
scientific segregationists (see below). Claude Lévi-Strauss is possibly distantly descended
from the Biblical tribe of Levites, but could hardly be described as a "Jewish sociologist"
by anyone familiar with his life and work; and Morris Ginsberg was a prominent British
sociologist.
3 In his autobiography, Gabriel Lasker presents a different picture of events. He recalls Coon
denying kinship with Putnam to the AAPA executive committee, and the floor vote on the
resolution to have been "something like ninety-one 'aye' and one 'nay'." "[N]obody joined
Coon in the vote against the motion, and Coon stormed out of the room" (1999: 148–9).

4   This referred to Coon's revised edition of *The Story of Man*, which he adjusted to accommodate his new theory. This volume was published several months before the *Origin of Races*, and the significance of the changes escaped Stanley Garn's (1962) review in *Science*. See below.

5   Based on Mead's (1963) attempt to mediate the situation, Jackson (2001) makes a case for the *Saturday Review* pulling Dobzhansky's review for procedural reasons, but this interpretation is supported by neither Dobzhansky's nor Coon's perceptions.

6   That did not stop the segregationists, however, from regarding Dobzhansky, at various times, as a crypto-Jew, crypto-Communist, and crypto-Boasian.

7   According to Entine, "I think the taboo is a reflection of white racism, liberal white racism. Also partly Jewish. All the thinkers who talk about it, men like Richard Lewontin, Steven [sic] Jay Gould, Jonathan Marks, they're all of my generation, '60s Jews who carry the weight of the Holocaust on their shoulders" (*The Philadelphia Daily News*, February 3, 2000). By coincidence, Entine's book is published by a descendent of the publishing house that handled Carleton Putnam's works: Public Affairs Press.

8   The "alien scum" to whom Hooton referred in his correspondence with Madison Grant, presumably subsumed impoverished Russian Jewish immigrants of the early twentieth century, and not the assimilated German Jews. Hooton's first graduate student, Harry L. Shapiro (who ultimately became Curator of Anthropology at the American Museum of Natural History, and remained loyal to his mentor), was in the latter category.

9   Forensic anthropologists have tended to be the noteworthy exception, crudely synonymizing the observation of gross skeletal variation and the existence of formal races. Now there are also "corporate geneticists," who market their determination of individual racial affiliations to the public. This is a marriage of high technology and low theory, and its success hinges on the ability to translate complex genetic patterns into simple folk idioms of kinship, including race; see Koenig et al. (2007).

Further Reading

Barkan, E. A. 1993. *The Retreat of Scientific Racism*. New York: Cambridge University Press.

Jackson, J. J., Jr. 2006. *Science for Segregation: Race, Law, and the Case Against Brown v. Board of Education*. New York: NYU Press.

Marks, J. 1995. *Human Biodiversity: Genes, Race, and History*. New York: Aldine de Gruyter.

Tucker, W. H. 2002. *The Funding of Scientific Racism: Wickliffe Draper and the Pioneer Fund*. Urbana, IL: University of Illinois Press.

15

Temporality as Artifact in Paleoanthropology: How New Ideas of Race, Brutality, Molecular Drift, and the Powers of Time Have Affected Conceptions of Human Origins[1]

Robert N. Proctor

Introduction

When did humans become human? Did this happen five million years ago or 50,000 years ago? How sudden was the transition, and is this even a meaningful question?

Strange as it may seem, there is radical disagreement over the timing of human evolution, understood as the coming-into-being of the language-using symbolic cultural creature of today. No one knows whether speech, consciousness, or the human aesthetic sense are fairly recent phenomena (developed around 50,000 years ago) or 10 or even 50 times that old – though it now seems that recency enjoys the upper hand. For many years, it was fashionable to project "humanness" (whatever that might mean) into any and every hominid scratched out by a paleontologist; Lucy was "our oldest ancestor," an australopithecine "woman" (versus "female"), and even older hominids were sometimes granted humanity. Today, however, it is more common to see the australopithecines as far more chimplike; humanness is often not even granted to *Homo habilis* or *erectus*, the earliest in our genus (itself a semiarbitrary designation), and there are those who do not want to see the Neanderthals or even early *Homo sapiens* as "fully human."

What is going on here? What makes us want to grant or withdraw humanity from a given or presumptive ancestor? What is the evidence one way or another, and what general issues are at stake?

Here I would like to explore some of the separate lines of inquiry leading to the idea that humanness is relatively recent – perhaps 200,000 years old in a *biological* sense and even younger than this in a *cultural* sense, judging from the best-established dates for the first ornamentation, abstract or representational art, compound-tool use, deliberate grinding and polishing, and many other (presumed) signs of human symbolic intelligence.

To avoid getting bogged down in definitions, let me operationalize "humanness" by equating it for the moment with language and culture – recognizing that these categories themselves are not so secure: witness the recent work on "chimpanzee material culture," which casts the traditional sociosymbolic, anthropological concept in an altogether novel light (De Waal 1999; McGrew 1992). Let me blackbox some of these definitional issues for now, to make sure I convey the novelty implicit in recent thinking with regard to human recency.

Only two or three decades ago, for example, it was widely thought that the two- and three-million-year-old hominid fossils being found in Africa had "culture" in the anthropological sense – including folkways and mores, fables and religion, and so forth. Humanness in the wake of the 1950 UNESCO Statement on Race was pushed back further into the middle Miocene – as when Pilbeam, Simons, and many others suggested that *Ramapithecus* circa 14 million years ago was a "hominid" and "tool-user" – and therefore human in some deep and inclusive sense. The equation of hominid and humanity fit with older ideas of humans as an evolutionary "breed apart": only humans use tools, tool use implies language, language implies culture, language and culture are unique to humanity, and so forth. The equation also had certain advantages for career-conscious fossil-finders, since it was surely preferable to have found some kind of human rather than some kind of chimp.

This consensus – equating hominid and humanity – has been broken in the past few decades, the transformation being visible in a number of different fields. In the 1970s and 1980s, for example, one often heard that the Acheulean handaxes found over much of the terrain of the Lower Paleolithic, more than a million years ago, were evidence of complex foresight, planning, and a primitive appreciation of symmetry and proportion. Early *Homo erectus* populations were presumed to be linguistic creatures and to have a basic appreciation of aesthetics (Edwards 1978) or even mathematics (Gowlett 1984). Wynn claimed that the manufacture of handaxes required a stage of intelligence that is typical of "fully modern" adults (1985: 41). The more common view today is that these artifacts were produced through a sequence of operations that did not necessarily have the "handaxe" as an end-in-view – and that their makers need not have been capable of speech (Noble and Davidson 1996: 196–9).

A second example: mastery of fire has long been thought to be commensurate with human evolution, and in the 1970 and 1980s evidence of human-controlled fire was pushed back to 1.4 or even 1.6 million years ago in Britain and in Africa. Today, however, there is a great deal of skepticism about these early dates, derived from the difficulty of distinguishing anthropogenic from accidental fire. Scholars have not been able to find the carbon signatures of human-made fire in the seabeds downwind of the hominid sites of Africa (Bird and Call 1998: 767–9), and there is skepticism even with regard to the once-solid claims for anthropogenic fire at the 500,000-year-old *Homo erectus* site at Zhoukoudian, south of Beijing, where "Peking Man" was long thought to have built great hearths (Weiner et al. 1998: 251–3). Fire was clearly being kindled in the Upper Paleolithic (James 1989), but it may prove impossible to confirm earlier dates. There is also the widely publicized discovery of biological (i.e., phylogenetic) recency – the idea that humans had a common ancestor with chimps as recently as 5 or 6 million years ago. This close temporal kinship was not discovered until the 1960s (Sarich and Wilson 1967) and not widely accepted until the 1980s – by which time it had also been shown (independently, by Richard Lewontin) that racial differentiation cannot be very old (Lewontin 1972; 1974: 152–7). Sarich reemphasized the animal in our humanity, while Lewontin showed the triviality of racial distinctions. Sarich moved up (and diminished) the break with apes, Lewontin moved up (and diminished) the separation of races from one another.

I want to explore some of the origins of the idea of human recency, an idea that captures two rather different, but intertwined phenomena. First of all, there is the trend in the past few decades to push forward the dates for many of the qualities we often regard as central to being human (speech, control of fire, conscious ritual, and so on). Early hominids have become "less human," insofar as some of the earliest dates for traits once seen as "modern" have not withstood scrutiny. Second, though, what we include in the category of human has also undergone some interesting changes. Tool use, for example, is no longer considered the *sine qua non* of humanity, and we recognize that it is possible for an ape to be bipedal and for "humanness" to be a quality that we grant to more than one species. It is the connection between these changing ideas – recency and humanness – that I intend to explore.

My argument will be that the temporal retreat from humanness can be understood as the outcome of a number of different evidentiary, conceptual, and ideological pressures, having to do with changing understandings of race, time, and brutality. The retreat has partly to do with Jane Goodall et al.'s celebration of nonhuman tool use (Goodall 1963) and, to a lesser extent, the rise of "pop ethology," evolutionary psychology, and sociobiology, all of which champion the animal in man. But there are several other key transitions that warrant an accounting. I want to focus on three of these transformations, or "crises" or turning points, each of which has given force to the idea that humanness may be relatively recent:

1. Archaeology – the crisis in interpretation of the oldest tools, specifically the Oldowan and Acheulean assemblages of the Lower Paleolithic, the oldest tools to have epochal names attached to them and the oldest to count as evidence of hominid or human "culture." (Chimpanzee cultural traditions have thus far been treated only ahistorically, since there is little archaeological evidence of chimpanzee tool use – though Frédéric Joulian has found evidence of chimps using hammerstones and anvils to crack nuts for at least 200 years [Joulian 2000]. The historicity of nonhuman primate culture remains remarkably undertheorized and under-researched.) A key question here is whether Oldowan and Acheulean artifacts can be considered evidence of a cultural "tradition" in any interesting sense (Binford 1985: 322). An argument can be made that they cannot, given their apparent stability and uniformity over vast stretches of time and

space (Ingold 1993b). Oldowan tools persist for roughly a million years in Africa (from 2.5 to 1.5 million years ago) and Acheulean tools even longer (from 1.5 million to 200,000 years ago). The argument has been made that one reason these tools are so stable is that their users were not transmitting knowledge of their use by means of abstract symbols (language) and that some other mechanism must account for their endurance. One possible implication is that their inventors were not yet human in some significant sense (e.g., lacking language), but that some kind of nonlinguistic transmission may have been involved. Consider those Japanese macaques who copied the inventive Imo, who sorted grain from sand by tossing both into the water: grain floats (Kawai 1965 and, for a critique, Galef 1990).

2. Paleontology – a crisis deriving from the recognition of fossil hominid phyletic diversity, another innovation of the 1960s and 1970s, following spectacular South and East African hominid fossil finds (*Zinjanthropus*, *habilis*, Lucy, and others), suggesting that more than one species of hominid must have coexisted at many points in the course of hominid evolution. Many paleoanthropologists today place the total number of hominid species at about 20 in four or five distinct genera: *Australopithecus* and *Homo*, of course, but perhaps also *Paranthropus* and *Ardipithecus*, and now *Kenyanthropus*, *Orrorin*, and *Sahelanthropus*. Hominid diversity seems to have peaked about two million years ago when three or four, or possibly even more separate hominid species coexisted on the planet (and all in East Africa). Fossil hominid diversity was not accepted without a struggle, however: ideological resistance was enhanced by the liberal re-evaluation of *race* after World War II, when a consensus began to emerge that the humans living today are more or less equal in terms of cultural worth and standing in the Family of Man. The dogma that only one hominid species could exist at any given time – the "single species hypothesis" – was consistent with the 1950 United Nations Educational, Scientific, and Cultural Organization's "Statement on Race," which branded race an unscientific category and "man's most dangerous myth" (Ashley Montagu's epithet).

3. Molecular anthropology – a crisis stemming from the recognition that all living humans have descended from a small group of Africans who lived roughly 150,000 years ago. "Modern humans" are therefore relatively recent in a *biological* sense, though nothing is necessarily implied about *cultural* recency, a nontrivial distinction, albeit one that not all parties will concede. This "Out-of-Africa" scenario has received immense coverage in the popular press, not only through its vivid emblem of an "African Eve" but also through the clarity of its opposition to the multiregional or regional continuity hypothesis, according to which the *Homo erectus* populations in different parts of the world didn't go extinct (as proposed by the mitochondrialists) but rather survived and gave rise to the separate, but commingling populations of *Homo sapiens* that eventually evolved in those regions. The molecularist, sequence-based recency thesis (with strong supporting fossil evidence) has become the dominant view, partly through the strength of its molecular methods, but also through increasing evidence of temporal coexistence of *Homo sapiens* and *Homo neanderthalensis*. The multiregional model has also been discredited by associating it (unfairly, in many cases) with the old, tainted idea of polygenism – the argument that human races are separate (and

unequal) species – extreme forms of which conceptualized races as separate creations (in the pre- and anti-Darwinian version) or had whites descending from chimps, blacks from gorillas, and yellows from the orangs (e.g., Klaatsch 1910: 567).

All three of these transformations – archaeological, paleontological, and genetic – have contributed to rising belief in human recency. Other scientific trends have been at work: There is the collapse of certain key elements of older conventional wisdom, including the uniformitarian gradualism that precluded dramatic changes in life and the earth. Neocatastrophism has become fashionable, as in Gould and Eldredge's punctuated equilibrium or recent efforts to argue that the explosive growth of human creativity around 50,000 years ago (the "Big Bang of the Mind") may have sprung from some sort of neural mutation (Klein 1999). Recency is not the same as suddenness, however, and the idea of recency has become at least as popular among anti-Gouldians as Gouldians. Indeed, two anti-Gouldian aspects of this thesis have proven especially provocative: that language capacities may have developed relatively late in human evolution (Davidson and Noble 1993); and that the human cultural "Big Bang" may have been close to the point of human racial differentiation and dispersal, raising the specter that some races may actually have become "human" earlier than others – a common idea among segregationalists and polygenists as late as the 1950s and 1960s (Coon 1962). These (potentially racist) hypotheses may be dismissed with a proper chronicling of the events in question.

I now turn to a consideration of changes in archaeology, moving then to a discussion of paleontology, race, and genetics, followed by some concluding remarks on temporal retreats as cultural artifacts, conflicting notions of "evidentiary prudence," and some of the stakes involved in contested notions of prehistoric humanity. One of my claims will be that the racial liberalism of the 1950s and 1960s was partly responsible for delaying the recognition of fossil hominid diversity by 10 or 20 years.

Refiguring the Acheulean

In 1797 John Frere, a former high sheriff of Suffolk, discovered a number of curious artifacts in a brick-clay pit in the parish of Hoxne. In a letter published three years later in *Archaeologia*, Frere described the implements as "weapons of war, fabricated and used by a people who had not the use of metals" (Frere 1800).

Historians have often commented on the failure of Frere's contemporaries to recognize the antiquity of human artifacts. His paper went essentially unnoticed for more than 50 years, until the Prehistoric Revolution of 1859, when from diverse angles (and fairly suddenly) it was recognized that humans were of great antiquity. By Frere's time, most paleontologists had abandoned Archbishop Ussher's estimate that creation had occurred in 4004 BC, but the absence of human remains in geologic deposits had made it unfashionable to argue for the deep antiquity of humanity. It was not until the 1850s that human antiquity was widely recognized, the key event being the acceptance by English and French geologists of the authenticity of the Acheulean "handaxes" (as they were later called) found by Boucher de Perthes in the gravels of St Acheul, northwest of Paris. Boucher's vindication was interestingly coincident with the publication of Darwin's *Origin of Species*, though the latter book seems to have had little immediate impact on the question of human antiquity. The foremost collector of and protagonist for these early tools, Boucher de Perthes, was in fact a biblical catastrophist who argued that humans had probably been created and destroyed several times before Adam was created.

Acheulean tools are remarkable in several respects, quite apart from their beauty and symmetry, qualities that have earned for them recognition as the first traces of a hominid (human?) aesthetic sense. The oldest are about 1,500,000 years old and the youngest about 100,000, and they are remarkably uniform over vast reaches of time and space (Isaac 1977: 219). Handaxes are found over most of the range occupied by *Homo erectus*, from the Pleistocene gravels of England (though not in Ireland, scoured clean by glaciers) to the open-air sites of northern Spain, Algeria, and Morocco, to the famous *erectus* sites of Africa and as far east as southern China.

Acheulean tools are difficult to interpret, however. *Homo erectus* is generally assumed to have made them, but there are several other candidates, including *H. habilis*, *H. rudolfensis*, *H. antecessor*, *H. heidelbergensis*, *H. ergaster*, and perhaps others (though whether these really are all separate species has also been called into question). Moreover, it's not really clear what could be meant when the Acheulean is called a "culture" or a "people" – especially if different species are using these tools. Can different species share a common culture? Paleontologic and ethnic categories are blended here, nature and culture. Some scholars treat the Acheulean as a *chronologic* or *periodizing category* (like "Pleistocene"), others use it simply as a *tool-type designation* ("Acheulean handaxe"), while still others imply a certain kind of people ("the Acheuleans"). Classificatory ambiguity is hard to resolve because the artifacts were produced for so many hundreds of millennia as to have become distributed as quasi-geologic objects.

For many years after the Prehistoric Revolution, it was argued that Acheulean tools were "axes" or "hatchets" (eg., Lyell 1863: 112–17), a plausible interpretation for the time, given their symmetry and size and cutting edge, which often extends around the entirety of a specimen. Perhaps they were weapons, as pictured in Louis Figuier's 1870 *L'homme primitif*, which shows club- and axe-wielding savages from "the period of extinct animals" fending off an attacking cave bear. Images such as these drew from well-established iconographic traditions predating the discovery of prehistory, from the medieval knight or woodsman to older images of primeval man as Adam or Hercules (with club and skin) or the more or less noble savage (Moser 1998: 135).

Such identifications became harder to defend, however, when it became clear that none of the "axes" used in the Lower Paleolithic had ever been *hafted*. None displays any of the wear patterns that result from having been mounted to a handle or shaft (de Mortillet 1897). This raises an interesting and unresolved question: Why was there no hafting, nor any other use of compound tools prior to the Middle Paleolithic (no spear with a stone tip, knife with grip, rock with strings, and so on)? Could this have something to do with the late evolution of language? Might compound tools be the artifactual counterpart of language?

Paleoanthropologists remain divided on how to interpret handaxes. J. Desmond Clark suggested their use as bark-stripping tools, while others have proposed digging or throwing scenarios. Experimental archaeologists have shown their usefulness in processing large animal carcasses; the idea of myriad diverse nonspecific uses has also been proposed (cutting, digging, scraping, hammering, chopping), making handaxes the "Swiss army knives" of the Paleolithic (Schick and Toth 1994: 258–9). The neurobiologist William Calvin imagines handaxes as "killer Frisbees," used in efforts to obtain meat by, say, being thrown at animals gathered around a waterhole (Calvin 2002: 138–41). Evolutionary psychologists have speculated that "handaxes" may even have been sexual lures, bragging points made by men to attract females (Holmes 1998).

A rather different approach has been to argue that Acheulean tools are not in fact as uniform as they seemed initially (Gamble 1999: 134). There are Acheulean sites without handaxes, handaxes made from elephant bone, and Acheulean-like *coups de poing* that persist into the Late Mousterian that were probably used by Neanderthals. Scholars have also argued that the *procedures* by which they were made are more important than the *final shape* they assumed, and that the variability in shape may have something to do with the types of rock available for use. Still others have argued that hominids may have used "handaxes" as blanks for the production of flakes, which would make them not tools at all, but simply discarded cores. Not tools, but trash!

So even though Acheulean tools were identified as Stone Age artifacts more than two centuries ago, they remain somewhat mysterious – more so now even than when first recognized as evidence of "the antiquity of man" in the middle of the nineteenth century. The difficulty is partly that we now know that "humans" (in the species-specific sense) cannot have been making them (*Homo sapiens* appears in the fossil record only at the very end of the Acheulean's duration in archaeological deposits). It may even be that who- or whatever made them was more like a creative chimp than a modern human. Chimpanzees and other primates are known to have invented myriad forms of tool use (nut hammering, fishing for ants with sticks, potato washing, etc.) and may even transfer "knowledge" of how to make and use such tools from one group to another (Whiten and Boesch 2001). Acheulean tool-makers may have been hominids without the use of language – or even, if MacLarnon's analysis of the anatomy of *Homo erectus* is correct, physically incapable of speech (1993; but compare the critique in DeGusta et al. 1999). Modern humans' ability to recombine tools for novel uses may have something to do with our possession of language – our ability to combine and manipulate abstract symbols (Noble and Davidson 1996). The fixity of Acheulean "designs" over vast spans of time would seem to suggest a feeble recombinatorial symbolic capacity (language), regardless of whether tool techniques were spread by diffusion or independent invention.

A diffusionist pre-language model, for example, would suggest that handaxe design passed around the world by (silent) imitation from one group to another, with little variance ("drift") in the particulars of handaxe size or shape. Had handaxes had a "purely symbolic" function, we might expect greater variance over time and space (Wynn 1995). But had these "tools" been independently invented, over and over again, the archaeological record could still exhibit its remarkable uniformity, if the confines of use, method, and material were narrow or the device fell into some kind of adaptive optimum. In either case, handaxe use may have been closer to chimp ant-dipping and leaf sponging than to, say, sonnet writing or H-bomb building.

Is it possible that the first hominid creations that are genuinely beautiful, displaying symmetry and undeniable skill, were made by creatures that were not yet fully human? The idea of "fully human" seems oddly teleological in this context – we don't talk about creatures being "fully cockroach" or "fully chimpanzee." Evolutionist thinking suggests that there is no essence of humanity, no fixed or final form, but narratives of arrival, liberation, and completion are seductive and satisfying. And so the Acheulean remains enigmatic, a misfit in the black–white binary world that requires us to keep a gulf between nature and culture, man and beast.

Racial Liberalism, the UNESCO Statements, and the Single-Species Hypothesis

Understandings of hominid diversity have undergone a profound shift in recent decades from a conception that there could be only one kind of hominid at any given time to the view that the past 30,000 years or so are actually rather unusual in having only one. (Forget the Neanderthals: the newly discovered *Homo floresiensis* lived until circa 13,000 years ago, or even later, making our present solitude still more recent.) Many paleoanthropologists now believe there have been more than 20 different species of hominids since our last common ancestor with chimps (Tattersall 2000), the apparent peak being roughly two million years ago when as many as half a dozen different hominid species coexisted in Africa, just prior to the *Homo erectus* exodus.

This is a dramatic change from the common view of the 1950s and 1960s, defended by C. Loring Brace and others, that the human cultural/ecological niche was so narrow – and entry barriers so great – that only one kind of hominid could exist at any given time (Brace 1964). Humans filled the "cultural niche," and that was that. This older idea was partly an outcome of the fear of excluding extinct hominid species from the ancestral Family of Man, but it was also interestingly consistent with older, gradualist, ladder-like phylogenies deriving from a secularized variant of a divinely ordained species hierarchy. The single-species hypothesis popular in the 1950s, 1960s, and 1970s envisioned a linear nonbranching evolutionary sequence according to which *Australopithecus* begat *erectus*, *erectus* begat Neanderthal, and Neanderthal begat *sapiens*. Most of our newer family trees since the 1970s, thanks partly to Gould, are bushy, with many false starts and dead ends (extinctions) – and with more than one species of hominid living concurrently (eg., Johanson and Blake 1996).

What accounts for the rise of the single-species hypothesis and (now-passé) reluctance to appreciate fossil hominid diversity? Gould and others have stressed the perennial bias of uniformitarianism, with its *scala naturae* progressivism and preference for linear "chains" over diversifying "bushes" (Gould 1997, 2002), but changing local sensitivities also have to be taken into account. I have already mentioned Brace's odd ecological rationalization, but we should also recall that the exposé of the 1912

Piltdown hoax in the early 1950s forced paleoanthropologists to come to grips with a much narrower range of hominid skeletal morphology. (Piltdown Man had a modern human cranium attached to an orangutan jaw.) Yet another impulse was the growing concern over the out-of-control proliferation of hominid taxa. "Lumpers" such as Ernst Mayr contributed to the hypothesis with his effort to reduce the clutter of hominid generic names. Mayr maintained that the proliferation of hominid generic titles made little taxonomic sense, and proposed that the zoo of names circulating at that time (*Australopithecus, Plesianthropus, Paranthropus, Pithecanthropus, Eoanthropus, Sinanthropus, Paleoanthropus*, and others) be reduced to a single genus, *Homo*, defined by upright posture. Mayr also maintained, following Dobzhansky and with race clearly on his mind, that "never more than one species of man existed on the earth at any one time" (Mayr 1950: 112).

Mayr's pronouncement has to be read against the backdrop of changing views of race. Ever since Linnaeus, and interestingly unperturbed by Darwin, racial theorists had squabbled over how many different natural varieties humanity could be divided into. Darwin in his *Descent of Man* had noted the absurdity of such exercises, with Virey distinguishing 2 races of man, Kant 4, Blumenbach 5, Buffon 6, Hunter 7, Agassiz 8, and so forth. Disturbingly far into the twentieth century, human phyletic trees showed a jungly bush of racial diversity, as when Grafton Elliot Smith distinguished separate branches for Negroes, Mongols, Mediterraneans, Nordics, Alpines, Australians, and the now-extinct Neanderthals and Rhodesian Man, all portrayed as having evolved along separate tracks for hundreds of thousands of years (Proctor 1988).

The history of ideas of diversity cannot be seen as progressive triumph of bushiness over linearity, however. Diversity has come and gone and come again, keeping different kinds of political company. Racial diversity became unfashionable after the revelation of the crimes of the Nazis (and, eventually, with campaigns to end racial segregation and discrimination), but fossil hominid diversity was also underplayed as attitudes toward the ancestral (or extinct) hominid "other" were held to have implications for contemporary race relations. The 1950s was not a time to exclude certain types of fossils from the fold of humanity.

One sees this clearly in changing views of the australopithecines. Prior to World War II, these small-brained African creatures (first discovered by Raymond Dart at Taung in South Africa in 1924) were more often seen as apes than as hominids. Part of the problem was the widespread notion – contra Darwin – that early man must have arisen in Asia; there was also the cerebralist, Piltdown-era prejudice that early humans must have had very large brains (like Piltdown Man). It was not until after the war that the australopiths were recognized as hominids. Their elevation to hominid status was clearly helped by the inclusive atmosphere of the postwar era (Cartmill 1993: 201), though a cynic might also wonder whether the global calamities of these decades didn't help spawn the view that humans can have very small brains.

The single-species hypothesis was dealt its first solid blow in 1959, when Mary Leakey discovered the 1.8-million-year-old *Zinjanthropus* at Olduvai Gorge in Tanzania, a fossil (now known as *Australopithecus boisei*) with such hyperrobust features (including large flat grinding molars) that it was hard to imagine as just a bigger, male version of the gracile (and female) australopithecines (the original version of the single-species hypothesis.) *Homo habilis* ("handy man"), found at Olduvai in the early 1960s, further undercut the assumption of a single-stalk, nonbranching evolutionary tree. *Habilis* was clearly more "human-like" than *Australopithecus*, yet much older than had been imagined for our genus – about 1.75 million years by potassium–argon dating. This was the first real evidence that *Homo* must have lived contemporaneous with the australopithecines, threatening the reigning assumption that early, ape-like hominids had been fully, steadily, and universally replaced by more human-like hominids. The story became more complex in 1974, when Donald Johanson found a 3.2-million-year-old hominid he dubbed *Australopithecus afarensis*; Lucy's skeleton was only 40 percent complete, but clearly indicated that "humans" walked upright more than three million years ago. Humanness was being disaggregated, temporally: some parts of humanity were now appearing only very recently (art, symbolism), while others were being pushed back very far (notably upright posture).

New hominid species have continued to be discovered in Africa at a rate of about one per year for the past dozen years or so. A 4.2-million-year-old fossil christened *Australopithecus anamensis* was found in 1995 by Meave Leakey and Alan Walker of Johns Hopkins; the 4.4-million-year-old *Ardipithecus ramidus* was found in 1994 by Tim White in Ethiopia. Newer finds include the 6-million-year-old *Orrorin tugenensis*, the 3.5-million-year-old *Kenyanthropus platyops*, and the 6- to 7-million-year-old *Sahelanthropus tchadensis*. No one knows whether any of these were our direct ancestors: in a rather trivial sense they almost certainly were not, given the bushiness of hominid lineages and the fact that most such lineages eventually perish. The bush became bushier in 2004, when a new hominid species was found on Flores Island in Indonesia; the diminutive *Homo floresiensis* ("Hobbits") lived until only 13,000 years ago or even later, and present us with a fabulous example of what is known as "insular dwarfing." Finds such as these make it harder to say what does or does not constitute humanity. But efforts to taxonomize in this realm are also fraught with difficulties. Breeding experiments cannot be done, which makes it hard to guarantee that two separate fossilized individuals really were separate species. There are also professional pressures favoring "splitters," insofar as it is better for one's career to have found a new species than yet another example of someone else's already discovered sort. Similar pressures encourage the imputation of humanity to one's finds, since it is clearly better to have found an early "man" than a rather late or precocious ape. The automation of phyletic reconstruction via the increasingly popular techniques of cladistics has also encouraged "splitting": Willi Hennig's 1966 *Phylogenetic Systematics* (translated from the German text of 1950) moved a generation of paleontologists toward splitting – as one might expect from a book written by an expert on beetles (the Coleoptera order contains an estimated 300,000 species). Arthropod body parts are more obviously digital, especially by contrast with mammalian features, which are more often analog.

The trend since the 1970s, however, has been to argue that hominids prior to *Homo sapiens* were not as human as once thought. To the reasons already mentioned I would add a retreat from some of the more optimistic assessments of chimpanzee cognitive capacities of the 1960s and 1970s and an increasing appreciation that it is not such a bad thing to be "not fully human." (Recall Gandhi's famous comeback, when asked what he thought of Western civilization: "It would be a good idea.")

There has also been the growing sense that it is not necessarily "racist" to believe that non-sapient hominids were radically different from us. Here it is important to appreciate the ideological obstacles faced by those who wanted to emphasize fossil hominid diversity. Prominent among these was the liberal anti-racialist sentiment of many postwar anthropologists. Shock and horror over events in Nazi Germany led UNESCO to sponsor two collaborative analyses of the race concept (for details, see Marks in this volume). The canonical resolution of the race issue became: race as usually conceived does not exist; peoples everywhere are equal in terms of intellectual and cultural worth; differences are due to nurture rather than nature. Michigan population geneticist Frank Livingstone's summary has been widely-cited: "there are no races, there are only clines" (Livingstone 1962: 279).

Looking back, though, it is hard to avoid the conclusion that recognition of fossil hominid phyletic diversity was delayed – perhaps by a decade or more – by fears that this would somehow justify racism. The fear seems to have been that by defining multiple lineages we would open the door to racism, by excluding one or another lineage from the family of man. Brace, for example, was afraid that Neanderthals would be dehumanized by exclusion from the human ancestral line (1964; 2000: 57). And Matt Cartmill recalls that "at anthropology meetings during the 1960s, scientists who questioned the mental capacities or human status of the Neanderthals were sometimes accused of bigotry, as if they had cast a slur on some ethnic group" (1993: 201).

The liveliness of this issue has to be understood in light of the fact that, even as late as the 1960s, human *racial* diversity was still being routinely characterized as taxonomically significant by a number of influential physical anthropologists. Carleton Coon, for example, as president of the American Association of Physical Anthropologists, in 1962 claimed that African *erectus* populations ("Congoids") had actually crossed the threshold to fully human status 200,000 years later than hominid populations in Europe and Asia.

These remain live and difficult practical questions for museum exhibitors and reconstruction artists, who must grapple with the question: how human should I make my Neanderthal or Australopithecus look? Many reconstruction artists in the 1970s, 1980s, and 1990s used human glass eyes to create a certain empathetic resonance with onlookers; but a trend is growing to recognize this as an over-humanizing bias. One solution: darken the sclera! Darkened sclera draw us back from the attentive "whites of the eyes" we associate with humanity, fixated as we are on where everyone else is looking; and we can expect this to be used to calibrate where a particular hominid should fit in the man–beast continuum.

Molecular Anthropology

Today, the notion of modern humans developing slowly and separately in different parts of the world over a period of about a million years is known as "multiregionalism," understood as an alternative to the "replacement" or "Out-of-Africa" model – the idea that fully modern humans emerged rather suddenly circa 200,000 years ago in Africa, from where they (eventually) spread throughout the world, replacing (without interbreeding with) the *Homo erectus* populations they encountered.

The two sides are loosely (but only loosely) represented by different disciplinary traditions. Multiregionalists, led by Milford Wolpoff at the University of Michigan, tend to rely on evidence from physical anthropology, whereas several of the most prominent out-of-Africanists have been molecular geneticists – notably the diaspora from Allan Wilson's Berkeley lab in the 1980s (though their position was articulated prior to the development of sequencing tools – see Stringer and Gamble 1993). Multiregionalists point to continuities in physical type as evidence of regional continuity; out-of-Africanists point to nucleotide divergence as evidence of bottlenecks and human biorecency, as well as to anatomical evidence. There are also ideological divides, though not always those reported in the popular press, where the tendency has been to gloss the debate (slanting toward the mitochondrialists) as "we're all Africans" versus "racial divisions are really deep." Wolpoff is not Carleton Coon (see Marks in this volume).

One current struggle is over how to grant early hominids (e.g., the Neanderthals) dignity. Multiregionalists lament the Neanderthals' derogation as the implicit opposites of modern humans, protesting also the "Eurocentric bias" implied in paying so much attention to whether these particular creatures – numbering perhaps 10,000 at any given time – suffered "replacement," noting that even if hominid populations were replaced in Europe, this tells us nothing about the rest of the world (Wolpoff and Caspari 1997: 270–8). Their critics counter that the Neanderthals are no less respectable for having gone extinct; their dignity should not hinge on their ability to breed with *Homo sapiens* (Tattersall 1995, 2000) – a question that is impossible to resolve (Marks 2002).

Both camps have leveled the charge of racism against their opposites. Out-of-Africanists have accused multiregionalists of exaggerating racial divisions (conceived as going back as far as a million years in some early "candelabra models"); multiregionalists have accused Out-of-Africanists of implying a total and perhaps violent replacement of *Homo erectus* (or Neanderthals) by *Homo sapiens* – an idea reported in sensationalist articles in the popular press. Each side has also branded the opposing camp as "old-fashioned." Multiregionalists hear in Out-of-Africa echoes of a "replacement model" with imperialist overtones (triumphalist sagas often featured Europeans as merely the most recent of races to have established supremacy in colonized lands). Out-of-Africanists find in Wolpoff's multiregional model vestiges of the hoary specter of polygenism. Multiregionalists see the debate in terms of "harmony" versus "violence"; the replacement theorists see a world of "recent unity" versus "deep racial divisions." Multiregionalists have also objected to what they see as the near-biblical suddenness of the events required by an Out-of-Africa narrative.

Since the 1990s, the evidence has been almost all in favor of the Out-of-Africanists. The multiregionalists' idea of populations evolving in similar directions over vast distances sounds suspiciously teleological, and multiregionalists also have no technical wonder comparable to sequencing in their scientific repertoire. The original mitochondrial evidence has also been joined by evidence from the Y chromosome and elsewhere (Underhill et al. 2000). Since its inception in the early 1960s, the form of comparative biochemistry known as molecular anthropology (Zuckerkandl 1963) has yielded spectacular laboratory triumphs, providing new dates for the origins of birds, the colonization of land by plants, and a date of about 500,000 years ago for the last common ancestor of our lineage and the Neanderthals (Krings et al. 1997). Molecular techniques have revolutionized the study of phylogeny (Goodman 1996), and with new techniques of rapid sequencing, such as pyrosequencing, we can expect to have the complete Neanderthal genome in fairly short order.

Contrary to Ayala's claim that genetic sequences contain "virtually unlimited" information about evolutionary history (Ayala 1995), however, there are clearly limits to what can be learned from such techniques. Molecular anthropologists may fix the dates for the human–chimp split, the origins of *Homo sapiens*, and migration events of various sorts (including out of Africa), but we are not likely to find out much from nucleotide sequences alone what it was like to live as a Neanderthal or *Homo erectus* (though some information on diets may eventually emerge from the burgeoning field of molecular coproscopy, analyzing ancient feces). We are unlikely to learn from genetic sequencing who could talk with whom, or what they might have discussed. And we may not want to restrict "humanness" to membership in the taxon *Homo sapiens*. If by "humanness" we mean something other than our biological specificity – such as capacity for language or culture – "humanity" may have existed among a number of different species, and might even pre- or post-date the origins of *Homo sapiens* by a substantial period. Much here remains uncertain.

Temporality, Origins, and Evidentiary Prudence

Origin stories are famously narratives of conquest, triumph, or tragedy. Paleoanthropology presents us with "allegories of quest, allegories of comparison" (Conkey and Williams 1991: 104). It also often serves as a kind of exercise in defining our identity, exploring how we came to be what we are – rather than, say, what we might have been or once were and no longer are. We tend to define origins in terms of endings, seeing origins as moments of liberation (of the hand from the ground, for example), or completion (Landau 1991; Leroi-Gourhan 1993).

Temporal orderings feature prominently in most human origins stories: scholars have struggled over whether big brains came before bipedalism, whether species coexisted or followed one another, whether home-site provisioning or carnivory or watercraft are relatively new or profoundly old. And we learn a great deal about the chronology of specific bones, sites, or artifacts from analysis of faunal remains, stratigraphic superposition, and techniques exploiting the regularity of radioactive decay or flipflops in the earth's magnetic field (Klein 1999). Many parts of culture do not fossilize, however, which means that it may be impossible to learn how far back into the past they may have existed. In the absence of empirical indicators, events are often pushed forward or backward in time to fit with a "story" that may include fossil, archaeological, or genetic evidence, including evidence in dispute. Such pushes are cultural artifacts in their own right, revealing our own interpretive biases.

For many years in the historical sciences, there have been professional pressures to "push back" dates for the origins of fire, art, and other cultural perishables, not only because scholars gain glory in finding the "oldest evidence" for a particular phenomenon but also because scientists collectively have had to defend themselves against popular threats to their antiquity project (most notably from creationists). The new emphasis on recency can be seen as a retreat from some of the long-standing time-deepening urges of several historical disciplines. Paleolithic archaeology developed with the recognition of the "high antiquity" of human artifacts, for example, just as paleontology developed with the recognition of "deep time."

This new move to (relative) recency reverses the "antiquity urge" of a number of historical sciences, but it also challenges the old archaeological maxim that "absence of evidence is not necessarily evidence of absence." There's a certain positivist minimalism in the diminished hope that stronger evidence of cultural sophistication will eventually turn up in, say, the Middle or Lower Paleolithic. One thing keeping such hopes alive is the room for honest disagreement (alongside inherent uncertainties). Absence of evidence is not evidence of absence, but preservation biases can make it difficult to come to reliable generalizations. For example: no one yet knows how *Homo erectus* arrived at Flores Island in Indonesia 800,000 years ago, and unless the archaeological record gets very much better, it will be difficult to say whether the migrants simply drifted over on accidental rafts (peat mats or log jams) or navigated on some kind of watercraft. The two scenarios presuppose radically different cognitive and industrial capacities of early hominids.

Yet another reason interpretations remain in flux is that there are different senses of what it means to *err on the side of caution* in the characterization of early hominid capacities. Tattersall, for example, has argued in favor of human recency by pointing out that we have "no strong reason for inferring that much of a cognitive gap existed between the early hominids and the living apes." Evidence may someday emerge of more sophisticated cognitive abilities in the australopithecines, but until then "it is probably most prudent to view these early hominids much more as 'bipedal apes' in cognitive as well as anatomical qualities" (Tattersall 1998: 121). Why, though, is this the more "prudent" view? Whether a certain inference is considered the more prudent or responsible one depends on what one imagines to be in danger. On the question of when humans became human, there are interestingly opposite senses of the nature of empirical excess, overstatement, and caution.

Defenders of recency say that complex behaviors should not be inferred where they are not visible: what cannot be proven must be doubted (Binford 1985). We also have to resist projecting our sense of the present onto the life of the past, "creating our origins in our own image" (Isaac 1983). Tattersall adds that it is "safer to assume primitiveness than derivedness unless there's proof to the contrary" (personal communication). "Humanness" is the derived character, so safety dictates a judgment of nonhuman until proven otherwise. Those wanting to find humanness going back very far, by contrast, perceive a danger in underestimating the complexity of the past, perhaps to glorify the present. Gowlett (1984: 168), for example, cautions against the tendency to "assume the primitiveness of the earlier archaeological record, rather than to test it for complexity." Gamble and Roebroeks postulate for the Middle Paleolithic a recognition of the same "internal dynamism" that is "currently accorded to the Upper Palaeolithic" (1999: 11). Gowlett cautions that the australopiths and early *Homo* could suffer the same denigration once suffered by the Neanderthals, and that: "We must now make quite sure that a similar reduction does not happen to the hominids of the Lower Pleistocene, unless indeed it is the correct interpretation" (1984: 171).

We can think of these as two different ways to appreciate complexity or even two different kinds of openmindedness – to the possibility that humans in the present may be more *unusual* than we have thought, and therefore rarer in a temporal sense (i.e., more recent), or to the possibility that humans in the past may have been more *complex* than we have thought, and therefore more like us. The two conceptions involve different stories of the old ways and the new. Those who regard early hominids as human argue that human ancestors were once regarded as primitive or savage brutes, or even members of some inferior race, but that we have only recently begun to appreciate the complexities of paleolithic cultures. We have *minimum* estimates of early hominid cultural experience, and modesty (or humility) would suggest that our discoveries of hominid complexity will grow with time and research. By contrast, for those who hold that humanity is fairly recent, the complaint is that people have been rash to conclude that early hominids were like hominids today. Now, however, we are more careful not to read our present into the past. Both views recommend caution, but their different conceptions of what is at stake (or in danger) lead to very different assumptions about the past.

I believe that the question as originally posed, "When did humans become humans?," is not really an empirical one. Humans are not just biological but cultural creatures, and, as such, we have contrived definitions of "humanness" to elevate ourselves over other creatures. Humans are animals with a seemingly inexhaustible capacity for self-aggrandizement, involving ourselves in exercises in self-definition and self-deception. Anthropologists may eventually fix dates for the onset of upright posture, fire-making, food sharing, grandmothering, accurate throwing, and so forth, but the emergence of humanity cannot be defined by any one nor all of these. So long as we do not restrict our definition to biological specificity (as in the capacity to interbreed and produce fertile offspring), we have considerable latitude. We might choose to include all symboling creatures, or all upright hominids, or all hominids in our line since our last common ancestor with chimpanzees. We may choose to include *erectus*, or not. But our choice of whom to include among humanity is ultimately a moral one.

Note

1   This is a revised and abbreviated version of a paper first published in *Current Anthropology* 44 (2003): 213–39.

Further Reading

Corbey, Raymond and Wil Roebroeks, eds. 2001. *Studying Human Origins: Disciplinary History and Epistemology*. Amsterdam: Amsterdam University Press.

Moser, Stephanie. 1998. *Ancestral Images: The Iconography of Human Origins*. Foreword by Clive Gamble. Ithaca: Cornell University Press.

Walker, Alan and Pat Shipman. 1996. *Wisdom of the Bones: In Search of Human Origins*. New York: Knopf.

Part V

New Directions and Perspectives

16

Women in the Field in the Twentieth Century: Revolution, Involution, Devolution?

Lyn Schumaker

Stranded in the Zambian countryside in late 1992, I caught a lift in a transport truck on its way to Lusaka. In the cab were the driver, a young boy, and a woman who looked to be in her early forties. A self-styled "businesswoman," she had taken up informal trading to support her family. During the journey, she and the driver argued about her involvement in trade. Dismissing the driver's beliefs about its impropriety, she demanded, "*Who* is a woman?," challenging his definition of woman. This question returns each time I return to the field or sit down to write about African women – and women anthropologists.

One must not conflate the history of women in anthropology with the history of sex and gender as areas of study. Even when men dominated anthropology, biological sex, sexuality, male and female behavior, and the sexual division of labor constituted important research topics. Anthropologists have always been concerned with human differences of all kinds, sex and sex roles included. Equally important, the concept of gender itself is a historical artifact, emerging as a strategy of women in the mid-twentieth century to argue against the claims of physical anthropologists and some of the neo-evolutionists of the time, a strategy used to cut the purported link between biological sex and culturally prescribed sex roles and restrictions. This project reached its peak in the 1970s with the general acceptance of the term "gender" as part of anthropology's terminology (borrowed from feminist literary theorists who used the concept in early critiques of the gendering of language). Similarly, the recent late twentieth-century move to de-essentialize biological sex is in part a strategic response to evolutionary psychology's current project to *relink* biology with behavior and the growing influence of this project on popular and scientific attitudes toward women, work, and sexual identity.

Reviews of feminist ethnography and histories of women in anthropology exhibit an imbalance of attention given to women's ethnography over women's fieldwork, privileging female anthropologists' writing over their field experiences. For example, Kamala Visweswaran's "Histories of Feminist Ethnography" (1997) assesses the changing agendas of feminists as ethnographers. Her historical periodization of the concept of gender has much to recommend it, but despite her discussion of feminist anthropologists' sense of identification or disidentification with the women they study, she herself says little about the field contexts or academic contexts that shaped these ethnographies and the concepts of gender that guided them. Nor is there much in the literature she considers.

By "field context" I mean not simply the studied society, but also the larger national and international, colonial and postcolonial contexts of fieldwork that are mentioned but rarely explored in sufficient depth to understand the position of the fieldworker and the responses she receives from her subjects. Women, like other fieldworkers, must be placed in the context of the people and projects who share the field with them, including missionaries, development workers, administrators, and entrepreneurs (Schumaker 2001). Observations about these field contexts can be found in memoirs of fieldwork, where they rarely get adequate theoretical weight or depth of analysis, but usually function as "apt illustrations" or amusing anecdotes of the anthropologist's life in the field.

The task of historically contextualizing gender and biological sex must be addressed in relation to the field as anthropology's key site of knowledge production. This is a history that has yet to be written – about the ways women have influenced the trajectory of the discipline and its valuation of fieldwork during the twentieth century. I will outline this history, from the fieldwork revolution of the interwar period through the institutional entrenchment of anthropology in Western universities in the 1960s. I will also suggest the outlines of anthropology's subsequent experience of academic involution from the 1980s to the present – the inward-turning critiques that were, in part, a response to new managerial regimes in the universities and the increasing insecurity of academic careers. Related to this is the discipline's so-called retreat from fieldwork as its defining method. Finally, I will consider the choices anthropology now faces with respect to women, fieldwork, and the study of sex, gender, and sexuality.

Revolution

In many ways, the history of anthropology in the twentieth century has been the story of women's entry into the discipline and the interaction of this phenomenon with anthropology's defining methodological moment, the emergence of participant-observation fieldwork. The fieldwork revolution received a great deal of attention, thanks to Malinowski's talent for self-promotion. The revolution in anthropology's self-perception effected through the inclusion of women proceeded much more quietly. Nevertheless, the subsequent histories of both women and fieldwork have been intertwined throughout the twentieth century, and women have profoundly changed the discipline's identity.

Prior to World War I, women participated in anthropology in small numbers, similar to their participation in the wider range of sciences called "natural history," which included anthropology. A few, such as Brenda Seligman and Elsie Clews

Parsons, achieved recognition for their work. But none achieved the rare and privileged status of the so-called armchair anthropologists – the great male theoreticians of the age, such as Frazer and Tylor. And women were not accepted into the most influential area of nineteenth-century anthropology – physical anthropology – which in its guise as craniology was used to justify European racial and class hierarchies and, especially, the exclusion of women from education, medicine, and the sciences.

Elsie Clews Parsons is an example of one of the few women who engaged in anthropological fieldwork before World War I, continuing her career well into the interwar period. Parsons studied sociology, not anthropology, but she moved gradually away from her Columbia sociology circles and into the orbit of Franz Boas and his students. Her fieldwork in the American Southwest began when she and her Congressman husband traveled there in 1910 for leisure and his government business. He had resisted her earlier desire to spend their honeymoon in this promising fieldwork destination. An egalitarian feminist determined that one should have the right to be masculine or feminine, passionate or sexless, Parsons saw fieldwork as a strenuous masculine adventure. Despite her informant-based veranda style of collecting folklore, and her archaeological style of collecting artifacts, she also observed ceremonies and dances – all three of these activities consonant with the Boasian diffusionist approach rather than the (later) Malinowskian participatory and (contemporary) Riversian experimental styles. Nevertheless, she unselfconsciously engaged in participant observation when she allowed Native American healers to apply their medicines and exorcism practices to her own person (Hare 1985).

By the 1920s and 1930s the fieldwork revolution championed by Malinowski, but developed as well by Rivers and Haddon in Britain and Spencer and Gillen in Australia, could have led to the field becoming a last bastion of masculine adventure. Indeed, arguments about the dangers of participant observation for women anthropologists were made, but these could not be defended within anthropology's larger colonial context. The interwar period witnessed the domestication of colonial frontiers, as well as the American Western and Southwestern frontiers, with women arriving as nurses, clerks, and teachers to join the missionary and settler wives who had long occupied these frontiers. Exclusion of women from anthropological fieldwork would have been inconsistent with the general domesticating trend.

Women's entry into the field in the interwar period also derived from changes in the discipline's self-perception and career structure. When Boas and Rivers directed anthropology away from the search for the biological factors previously thought to explain human diversity, they raised the possibility that anthropologists should not only consider their subjects in a new light but also reconsider who qualified for membership in the profession. This was partly due to the pressures of more egalitarian educational systems in Europe and North America, which admitted more women and other members of previously excluded groups onto the lower rungs of professional ladders. Moreover, many professions, such as medicine and teaching, provided better career opportunities for women (and educated members of the indigenous populations) in the colonies and dominions than in the metropoles (Lal 1996). The colonies and dominions also provided routes to better academic positions for women anthropologists, who found it easier to rise to the top of non-metropolitan research institutes and university departments, as exemplified in the career of Winifred Hoernlé at the University of Witwatersrand in South Africa.

Although anthropology, like other professions, may have become more welcoming to women, its method of participant observation is not in itself necessarily egalitarian or open to diversity amongst its practitioners. The characteristics attributed to middle-class Western women in the late nineteenth and early twentieth centuries, however, overlapped with the set of characteristics deemed necessary for successful participant observation. Participant observation demanded skills of sympathy, tact, and adaptability. These traits were included in the Victorian ideal of womanhood and the late nineteenth-century feminist conception of the genius of woman – traits of child-like adaptability familiar from craniology's image of woman as juvenile or primitive (Fee 1979). Not all women used this argument, however: Elsie Parsons, for example, stressed the flexibility of both men's and women's personalities.

Women fieldworkers also benefited from the generally held assumption that they could gain greater access to women's lives than male anthropologists – a point made as early as 1884 by Edward Tylor, who encouraged men to include their wives in fieldwork for this reason (Visweswaran 1997: 597). Boas echoed this sentiment in his early acceptance of women students before World War I, for he "assumed women had access to areas of social life men did not have; he considered women more 'intuitive' and skilled in interpersonal relationships and urged them to collect data on the 'emotional' expressive sides of life" (Modell 1984: 181). Indeed, some male anthropologists stressed the necessity of having women fieldworkers study women in highly sex-role-differentiated societies, such as those found in Australia.

Meanwhile, in the metropolitan academic centers, the 1920s and 1930s saw the first significant numbers of women studying with the leading anthropologists of the day. These women did fieldwork in a wide range of settings. Boas's students (and those he mentored jointly with Elsie Parsons and, later, Ruth Benedict) did fieldwork within a range of Native American societies in the Western and Southwestern US, as well as in Brazil, Melanesia, Mexico, and the Caribbean, while Malinowski's male and female students claimed the British colonial African field and other territories within the imperial orbit.

Because of this timing, women figured among the pioneers of fieldwork in settings such as central Africa and Papua New Guinea, places where anthropologists studied human societies systematically for the first time during the interwar period. Because they engaged in fieldwork when participant observation was new to anthropology, they joined the earliest interpreters of the significance of that method for the discipline. They also developed new subject matter through its use – for example, Margaret Mead on sexuality and child development in the Pacific and Audrey Richards on nutrition and work in Africa.

Women researchers may have had a particular interest in these topics and may also have been seen as having a particular facility for the type of fieldwork involved – asking questions about intimate relations in adolescence and marriage or discussing women's cultivation of millet and recipes for typical meals. Nevertheless, nutrition and work, as well as sexuality and child development, figured among the most important topics across the human sciences in the interwar period, essential for colonial development plans, as well as for Western governments' growing social welfare programs at home (Worboys 1988). These were not the "ghettoized" domestic-related topics familiar to later feminists. Rather, their prominence signaled the interest of colonial administrations keen to reverse demographic decline and resolve labor problems in Africa and Melanesia. Male anthropologists also found these topics of interest: Max Gluckman used Richards's agricultural and labor migration work as a model for aspects of the Rhodes-Livingstone Institute's research in British Central Africa; and Boas himself collected "blueberry pie recipes from the Northwest Coast Indians" (Schumaker 2001: 80–6; Modell 1984: 181).

Women's changing status in the discipline also shaped their experiences of fieldwork and views of the societies they studied. The position of women in anthropology in the interwar period, though improving in terms of their access to higher education, was hardly secure. Few academic posts existed even for men, and the career structure of the discipline had not yet settled into the pattern we now take for granted. Social and cultural anthropology in Britain and North America were still in the process of establishing themselves as academic disciplines, and their leading proponents justified their approaches and sought funding for research on the basis of a wide range of arguments for the theoretical importance of the discipline or the usefulness of its knowledge for metropolitan social concerns or colonial government needs. Like male anthropologists, women anthropologists acquired funding for fieldwork in those places seen as the most appropriate for certain kinds of theoretical and/or practical work, and their perceptions of the field were shaped by the scholarly networks they relied on and by the communities of administrators, settlers, and missionaries who guided them or clashed with them in the field.

Unlike male anthropologists, however, women entered the field with interests and goals shaped by their lower status in the Western societies from which they came and the difficulties they encountered while making places for themselves in the discipline and in the universities, funding councils, and government institutions where social scientists sought jobs. Hoernlé and Richards remained fixed largely on colonial and African interests and did not reach high positions in Britain (though Richards's Colonial Office post was a significant achievement for a man or a woman in a discipline which, at the time, had few high academic posts (Schumaker 2001, 128). Ruth Benedict waited a considerable time before receiving a permanent academic job despite her important work at Columbia and Barnard. This was at least partly because Boas gave more support to women without other sources of income, and only after Benedict was no longer supported by her husband did she receive the compensation and formal recognition she deserved (Modell 1984: 167–8). Indeed, a woman anthropologist's status as a married woman and/or mother figured significantly in her evaluation both by male colleagues and by women students entering the discipline. Benedict's anxieties about balancing marriage and career, and her position as a role model for women students, emerge poignantly in her biography and in memoirs of fieldwork by her former students (Modell 1984; Golde 1970, 1986).

"Bored by Babies at Home and Abroad . . ."

World War II made a lasting difference to the integration of women into anthropology, both in the academy and in the field. Male anthropologists of the war generation often had their education interrupted by military service. Hence, academic space was opened for women who had acquired qualifications before or during the war, who were able to enter the profession at a senior level and take up fieldwork opportunities in greater numbers. In the early postwar years, when well-funded development programs in the colonies translated into more work for social scientists, Elizabeth Colson, for example, began work at the Rhodes-Livingstone Institute in 1946 as the most highly qualified member of its team after the director, Max Gluckman (who had received his doctorate before the war). Gluckman did not hesitate to recommend her as the next director when he later left for an academic post in Britain. Nevertheless, though a few women benefited from wartime opportunity, men continued to dominate the field, predominating in overall numbers in both research institutes and universities.

Another major postwar area of disciplinary expansion, nascent forms of development anthropology, also favored male anthropologists. This emergent field blossomed in the 1960s in response to decolonization and new theories of "economic take-off" applied to former colonies. The applied development sciences emerged mainly from decolonizing colonial agricultural and labor departments, spheres dominated by men, and applied development work became one of the major alternative sources of employment for redundant technical officers. When professional anthropologists joined this emerging field as employees and consultants, men dominated in numbers well into the 1970s. At that point, however, the "women in development" movement argued that the perspective of female anthropologists was essential to bringing women into the development process, an argument made urgent by emerging concerns about the failures of development in some parts of the world.

Postwar government policies that subsidized war veterans' access to university education also meant that men with interrupted careers rapidly caught up after demobilization, and, as a result, the ratios of women to men in the academy declined after the 1940s across most disciplines. This was part of a broader postwar push to reward men for war service and show gratitude by quickly reintegrating them into society, displacing women from the industrial and managerial work they had taken on during the war. Also associated with this were broader cultural and intellectual changes in Western societies; the 1950s saw the emergence of exaggerated gender differentiation in clothing and popular culture, and a variety of forms of neo-evolutionism emerged in the academy. Although in anthropology most of these theories focused on cultural rather than biological evolution, they nevertheless gave prominence to various forms of sex-role differentiation similar to earlier biologically justified forms. Hunter-gatherer studies, for example, were generated by postwar concerns about human aggression and focused on "man the hunter," ignoring, until much later, women's and men's gathering activities and women's role in the evolution of agriculture.

Women anthropologists responded to these cultural and intellectual trends in a number of ways. The feminism of the interwar period and early postwar years used socialist, Marxist, or eugenic arguments that increasingly stressed equality of treatment for women: equal political rights – the suffrage movement; equal access to education and jobs; and equal sexual freedom – the birth control movement (for Parsons's eugenicism see Visweswaran 1997: 600). There was a general (if uneven) shift from the earlier strategy of many nineteenth-century feminists, who had accepted the notion of separate male and female social spheres but emphasized the special talents that made women better than men for particular roles or activities.

Women anthropologists in the early postwar years, though they may have sometimes justified their presence in the field by pointing to their ability to discuss intimate matters with both male and female subjects, often insisted that their sex was irrelevant for the writing of ethnography. They took a "difference-blind" approach to women's rights, part of a more general shift exemplified by the United Nations Declaration of Human Rights of 1948. The women anthropologists who contributed to Peggy Golde's collection, *Women in the Field* (1970), show the influence of both of these interwar and early postwar feminist approaches, in different degrees, depending on the ages at which they began their education and fieldwork.

Margaret Mead's contribution to Golde's collection provides a good example. With a career spanning the interwar and postwar periods, she discusses episodes from fieldwork between 1925 and 1967 and her training by Boas and Benedict at Columbia in the 1920s. Her essay argues that women are often better fieldworkers than men because they find it easier to gain access to both men's and women's activities. Nevertheless, she always qualifies her generalizations, saying that local responses to female versus male fieldworkers may be different in cultures she does not know (Mead 1970: 322). Hers is not an argument based on the notion that women gain insight based on a universal femininity; instead, individual women can be more masculine or feminine in their interests as fieldworkers – those who take an interest in children versus those who are "bored by babies at home and abroad" (323). Choice of topic and individual personality are to Mead more important than any talent inherent in a particular sex, and access to information is limited on the basis of sex primarily because most societies make certain areas of life the exclusive territory of one or another sex. Women's greater loneliness during fieldwork – which Mead repeatedly mentions in her account – stems from constraints on women's activities imposed on them by both the societies they study *and* the colonial societies to which they might retreat for relief from fieldwork.

In other essays, women approaching their first fieldwork emphasize the importance of equality of treatment within the academy and their breaking of stereotypes of femininity found in their home society as well as the society they are studying. For example, Ruth Landes ascribes to Boas and Benedict a difference-blind view in their selection of students and their deployment of men and women to the field: "These two scholars appeared to distinguish, not the sexes, but only ability. It was their overriding concern. Never before had I met it in a working situation . . ." (Landes 1970: 120). She then discusses her fear as she approached her first fieldwork, in Brazil in

1939, a fear based on previous female *and male* experiences – the earlier deaths of a "girl anthropologist" and a "man anthropologist" during fieldwork (120). (Her use of the term "girl" is not due to internalized sexism, since her account reflects the determination of young women after World War I to challenge the restrictions of "Victorian womanhood"; their use of the word "girl" signals a boyish adventurousness young women could claim in that period, not the diminutive connotations the word acquired during the 1950s.)

Similarly, Laura Nader (who studied at Harvard with Clyde Kluckhohn) and Gloria Marshall (an African-American anthropologist who studied at Columbia in the early 1960s) do not invoke any universal female abilities when they describe differences between men and women as fieldworkers. Both avoid generalizations, and though Nader is "tempted" to say that women have greater access to both sexes, she believes this may be due to women *in Western culture* being "better able to relate to people than men are" (Nader 1970: 114). Both point to examples of their ability to move outside the sex roles given to women in their field sites, and Marshall sees her "relative insulation" from men in one field site as due to the way she presented her research interests – as focused on women, not men (Marshall 1970: 183).

The first edition of Golde's *Women in the Field* was published in 1970, shortly after the beginning of women's studies in late 1969 and on the cusp of major changes in anthropology departments in the US that would lead to more academic jobs for women. The period before 1970 had witnessed an actual decline in women's jobs in top anthropology departments, with half having no women at all (Golde 1986: vii). The gains that women would make in anthropology departments after 1970 are reflected in the publication of a second edition of Golde's collection, demanded by the growing interest in gender as a topic in anthropology courses.

The discussions of fieldwork in Golde's second volume (which adds only two new essays) appear dated to late twentieth- and early twenty-first-century feminists because of their different mix of "difference-blind" versus "special talents" arguments for women's legitimacy as fieldworkers. Both arguments would also be used in the 1970s and 1980s, though with a greater emphasis on special talents following the rise of feminist standpoint theory. The variety of experiences recounted in Golde's volume show that women and men have different sets of opportunities and difficulties in fieldwork, depending on the demands of both the anthropologist's home society and the studied society. Most of the women represented in Golde, however, seem optimistic that these are largely subject to the fieldworker's self-presentation and negotiating ability. Feminist standpoint theory, however, would revive arguments that women's special talents or unique experiences suited them better than men for work with women subjects.

Involution

During the 1970s, debates among feminist philosophers often centered on the issue of which model was most appropriate for understanding women's lower position in

Western society and/or all societies. Some thinkers preferred class-based models, which assumed that the most important distinctions between humans arose from differing histories of privilege or poverty. The application of a class model to male/female social relations led to analyses that stressed the overall equality of men's and women's physical and mental capacities, playing down any differences as minor – the minimum differences required for biological reproduction. Women might have less physical strength, different psychology and intellectual interests, as well as lower position within contemporary social and political hierarchies, but these attributes stemmed from a combination of socialization and discrimination. Thus, sexism had led to an exaggerated emphasis on minor biological differences in what was essentially a monomorphic species.

The application of a cultural model produced a very different picture. Although they assumed the same biological differences, cultural feminists posited a distinctive "women's culture" focused around mothering and assumed to be universal to women in different societies and different historical periods. Women's psychological and intellectual capacities derived from their cultural difference from men. Women could be seen as having a radically different relationship with nature and were often equated *with* nature by men – as in Carolyn Merchant's (1980) environmental history – as well as by some women in eco-feminism and deep ecology. Similar to the nineteenth-century feminists who made the "genius of woman" arguments, cultural feminists stressed women's intuitive capacities; some even linked feminine intuition to female biology, using research from cognitive science that claimed to prove that behavior is determined by sex-linked differences in the brain.

This stress on intuition influenced the arguments of women fieldworkers in anthropology in the 1980s: Some argued that a woman was able to penetrate the male realm of the society she studied because of her superior social skills, while at the same time a man was incapable of gaining a deep understanding of women in the society he studied, because he lacked the necessary intuitions about female experience (examples include Rosaldo and Lamphere 1974; Cesara 1982; Behar and Gordon 1995; but see Visweswaran 1997: 610–11 on Rosaldo). The 1980s saw the development of a parallel strand of work on women in science that explored women scientists' approaches in terms of the socialization of girls, women's different psychology, or their different perspective resulting from their lower position in patriarchal societies. A classic example of this genre is Evelyn Fox Keller's (1983) treatment of the female geneticist Barbara McClintock, whom Keller saw as having a distinctively feminine view of the organisms she studied, as well as a feminine scientific style.

Feminist standpoint theory usually combined elements of both cultural feminism and class analysis, seeing women as having a shared standpoint or perspective based on (if not always innately determined by) their biological sex. All women were seen as members of the same sex because of their biological characteristics, whereas gender was seen as culturally constructed, with its multiple categories potentially open to both sexes. Women, as a biologically defined group, shared a standpoint in much the same way that a particular class shares a position in a hierarchy, with its particular understandings and interests, even worldview, deriving from that position.

In anthropology, the career of Edith Turner exemplified this cultural turn in the study of sex and gender and in the justifications some women used for their special abilities as fieldworkers. In the late 1940s and early 1950s, Turner participated equally in fieldwork and analysis with her husband, Victor Turner. Her burden of childcare, however, restricted her ability to write or pursue an academic career until much later. Within anthropology the greater valuation of published theoretical work over other types of anthropological activity meant that her fieldwork was devalued even when acknowledged by her husband and colleagues. While Victor Turner became famous for his work in symbolic anthropology, Edith Turner remained invisible except within their closest professional circles. Her research achieved recognition only after she began publishing autobiographical accounts of fieldwork and her own independent research on women (Engelke 2004: 35–6, 44–5).

Both the autobiographical direction of Turner's work and her reflections on the field fit well with anthropology's growing recognition of women within the discipline in the 1970s and 1980s, with new ways of looking at women as subjects of research, and with newly emerging reflexive approaches. Turner's autobiographical focus on her experiences "at home in the field," as well as her emphasis on her intuitive understanding of her women subjects, also fit well with standpoint theory's focus on women's unique experiences and universal differences from men (Schumaker 2001: 124, n. 17). Thus, despite the fact that her earlier fieldwork took place in the immediate postwar period, Turner saw her work as a woman in the field and in the discipline very differently from the women anthropologists represented in Golde's volume. The cultural feminism of the 1980s could accommodate Turner's claims for an intuition-based understanding of her subjects' experiences more comfortably than the earlier more difference-blind feminist views.

In the 1990s, however, standpoint theory began to be challenged, both in anthropology and in historical work on the origins of biological and medical/psychiatric concepts of sex and sexuality. According to this emerging work, sex and gender are relational. That is, any particular gender can only be understood within the totality of possible genders within a society (Schumaker 2001: 124; Roper and Tosh 1991: 2, 15). Therefore, women anthropologists cannot claim special insight into the lives of women of other cultures. Insight can only be justified by examining the many dimensions within which particular women anthropologists may share their subjects' experiences, conceptual categories, or perceptions. Most important of all is the mix of sexes and genders recognized within the studied society. The mere fact that women may share a physical process, such as menstruation, childbirth, or menopause, cannot be assumed to indicate a shared experience or even a shared recognition of the process (for menopause see Locke 1993).

Summarizing recent critiques of standpoint theory, Visweswaran states:

> Standpoint perspectives rely upon a notion of the sex/gender system, which assumes women are all members of the same "sex" notwithstanding different gender identifications produced by culture, for to produce a "women's standpoint," which is shared by women regardless of culture, is to rely upon the only thing women share in common: biology . . . (609, citing Jagger 1988)

Biological sex, however, is also a Western concept, which must be examined as such rather than simply applied to other cultures and societies (Moore 1994; Butler 1990). Furthermore, biological sex interacts with other important categories, both in the West and in the developing world, mediated by colonial and postcolonial hierarchies. Ann Laura Stoler (1992) has analyzed this dynamic interaction for gender, class, and race in colonial settings.

Standpoint theory and the emerging critiques of its assumptions were successive phases of a more general inward-looking period in anthropology from the late 1970s to the present. They belong to a larger disciplinary concern with the nature of the anthropological "self" that acts as the research instrument in participant observation and, especially, the "authorial self" that produces ethnography. Anthropology's period of growing reflexivity began, however, as a response to changes in the economic and social context of the discipline in the West and a decline in practitioners' emphasis on fieldwork. And, as in the fieldwork revolution of the 1930s, women in the 1980s acted as full participants in these trends.

The Retreat from the Field

Women's gains in Western universities in the 1970s had been due as much to economic prosperity as to the political and legal challenges mounted by the women's movement. The massive expansion of tertiary education in the industrialized nations that had begun in the 1960s led to significant proliferation of academic jobs. In the late 1970s, however, a variety of economic factors slowed university expansion and the related expansion of opportunities for women. Universities became subject to market forces introduced by Western governments interested in reducing expenditure for tertiary education. This resulted in a more business managerial model applied to academic jobs and productivity (Martin 1998). A growing popular critique of professional expertise also affected the academy, particularly when this critique was embraced by conservative governments in the US and Europe, which were intent on reining in universities' potential as breeding grounds for dissent. Moreover, during this time, most professional groups, including anthropologists, subjected themselves to internal intellectual and political critiques (Kuklick 2002).

In anthropology this internal critique, or reflexive turn, has been paralleled by a so-called "retreat from the field." The latter was supposedly initiated by the decolonization of many African and Asian countries in the middle of the twentieth century, accompanied by indigenous critiques of colonial and neo-imperial science that made former colonial field sites less welcoming to anthropologists (see Werbner 1984). Nevertheless, it is likely the retreat was more a change of topics, sites, or types of fieldwork rather than a reduction in the total amount of fieldwork, given the rise of development anthropology and medical anthropology in this period and their deployment throughout the developing world. But anthropologists did exhibit a growing interest in "anthropology at home," in the discipline's internal critique, and in textual analysis of anthropological writing. These trends toward activities that could be more easily carried out in the academy rather than in distant field sites were encouraged by the increasing insecurity of careers in the 1980s and 1990s; an increasing percentage of teaching was carried out by temporary employees, and postdoctoral academics took increasingly longer periods of time to find secure positions.

This trend has had a disproportionate effect on women academics in Western universities because of their career breaks for child-rearing and other continuing disadvantages with respect to men. And accompanying these economic changes of the 1970s and the 1980s was an increased valuation of so-called "women's topics" across the disciplines – housework, child-rearing, and sexual politics – topics that could be explored in one's home society, as well as abroad. Indeed, work on these topics in Western societies, using anthropological perspectives and participant-observation methods, promised new insights – and at less expense to a woman anthropologist's career than that caused by absence from the academy to do fieldwork abroad.

Thus, as was the case with the earlier participant-observation fieldwork revolution and the changes effected when women first joined the discipline in significant numbers, questions about the nature of anthropology itself and about who should participate in its work – in the academy and in the field – have emerged in this period of involution. Debates about sex and gender increasingly included men and non-Western women anthropologists. Some also began to ask anthropology to encompass the views of the subjects of research and of others outside the profession, questioning in the most basic way the boundaries of the discipline. This has led to calls for decentering anthropology and devolving its fieldwork and theorizing.

Devolution

In the area of sex and gender, moves to expand the boundaries of anthropology and reconsider the identity of the anthropologist have taken three new directions in recent years. The first direction continues the focus on the sex or gender of the fieldworker. Unlike the essays in the Golde volume and most 1980s scholarship, however, the debate now focuses on the roles of, and reactions to, male, as well as female, fieldworkers, in response to the emergence of masculinity studies in the late 1980s. That sex or gender have a determining effect on access to research subjects has now also been questioned by men who report experiences that do not fit the stereotypes of the male fieldworker; scholars have also begun to recognize that they must include a wider range of factors, in addition to sex and gender, that can affect the fieldworker's sensitivity to aspects of the studied culture (Whitehead and Price 1986). More attention, too, is now being paid to the sexuality of the fieldworker and, sometimes, to the research subjects' responses to the fieldworker's sexual identity (Whitehead and Conaway 1986; Kulick and Willson 1995).

The second new direction in this area is a response to non-Western scholars' demands that sex and gender must be re-evaluated from perspectives outside Western categories and assumptions, including those of Western feminists. This concern has been stimulated, in part, by the example of African-American feminists who have questioned the white middle-class bias of earlier feminist ethnography (Visweswaran

1997: 612–13), but it is also a response against the intensifying globalization of Western categories in recent decades, felt most strongly in countries of the developing world. I would argue that this critique – at the moment mainly confined to sex and gender categories – must be extended to biology, and we must use it, urgently, to understand the history of interactions between Western and indigenous categories in the developing world. Spurred by concerns about HIV/AIDS, human rights, identity politics, and poverty eradication, new medical, political, and economic movements have brought about a rapid dissemination of Western assumptions about biology and anatomy to the developing world. Local understandings are increasingly swept aside by international health and development organizations, evangelical Christian missions, and Western feminist and gay rights organizations which, despite obvious contradictions among themselves, share a Western model of biological sex and human anatomy.

What is lost in the resulting clashes between these often humanitarian and well-intentioned organizations is that people in different societies may perceive biology and anatomy in ways that differ radically from the assumptions that shape Western medical, religious, and human rights interventions. Understanding different perceptions is vital because much else that is important in a society's approach to medicine, religion, human relationships, and relationships to the environment can devolve from its understanding of human biology. Research on non-Western ideas of biology and their role within different cosmologies has begun (for examples, see Moore, Sanders, and Kaare 1999). This is a new direction in research that needs more attention from Western and non-Western researchers sensitive to the continuities and hybridities of indigenous biology (for example, Davis 1999).

The third new direction involves the devolution of research on sex and gender to a wider range of researchers – part of a more general call to fully integrate developing world scholars and "indigenous anthropologists" into the discipline and to make anthropology more accessible. As one non-Western scholar puts it,

> . . . anthropology should not only be demystified, it should be people-oriented and popular, representative and reciprocal. Its intellectual historicity should be integrative and relational and its sentiment humanitarian and messianic. Its method should be equitable and its objective commitment, equity. (Karim 1996: 135)

Science studies have contributed to this new direction by pointing to the ways that science is produced as much by nonscientific agents as by scientists. Scientific theory and fieldwork in all disciplines are now seen as the product of the interactions among a range of workers, rather than resulting from a process that takes place in the mind of a single scientist or group of scientists fully trained within a discipline. Scientific theories emerge from the diverse range of people and activities centered on particular sites or institutions, such as museums, research institutes, or field sites (Griesemer 1990; Schumaker 2001). Science, exploration, development, and medical work are all prosecuted through the agency and interpretations of a range of scientific auxiliaries and culture brokers (Pang 2002; Hunt 1999).

As Moore has argued, recognition should also be given to the research subjects them-selves, whom anthropology has so far failed to take seriously as producers of theory:

> Deconstructionism argues, of course, that all theories are partial, and there is thus no distinction between the local theories of anthropologists masquerading as comparative social science and those of the people being studied. However, this position occludes the point about the production of knowledge and of how that production is valorized. Anthropologists, for all their concern with local understandings and specificities, do not habitually view the people they work with as producers of social science theory as opposed to producers of local knowledge. (1996: 3)

I also suggest that a historical form of devolution can be employed to rethink past ethnographies, using alternative perspectives captured in the memoirs and biographies of people outside the discipline who shared the ethnographer's field site (see Handler 2004). Within this area, a vital but nearly untapped source for revising our theories about biological sex and gender are anthropologists' spouses and significant others.

Anthropologists' wives, whether joining in their husbands' fieldwork, working as professional anthropologists themselves, or concentrating solely on creating a home in the field, found themselves on the front line of negotiating a place for their hus-bands and families within a different culture (see Pang 2002). Implicitly, but also often explicitly, anthropologists' wives developed theories of the multiple societies in which they were embedded – the studied society, the colonial society, and the small, com-petitive society of anthropologists in and out of the academy. Their memoirs and oral historical accounts abound with observations and analysis of the relationships, statuses, and etiquette of these worlds. They often contain challenges to Western valuations of sex and gender and also relate sex and gender issues to the racial and class antagonisms they experienced during fieldwork. The array of women associated with the Rhodes-Livingstone Institute, for example, provides a range of perspectives on colonial European and African societies, from Elizabeth Colson's analysis of African responses to the fieldworker's clothing to Frances Barnes's medical view of Ngoni birth-ing practices to Edith Turner's and Ruth van Velsen's acute observations of colonial settlers' assumptions about anthropologists' living arrangements (Schumaker 2001).

Furthermore, wives in the field create the field site through their domesticating labor, an activity often remarkably similar to what research assistants and research subjects must do when an anthropologist is among them. Research assistants and subjects also manage the situation and create a cross-cultural world around the anthropolo-gist, the point of which is not exclusively the theory that the anthropologist seeks to produce (though the resulting ethnography may be locally meaningful). Rather the most important point is often the interaction involved in fieldwork itself, the local consequences of the fieldwork situation, and the long-term commitment of the anthropologist. From this wider range of perspectives, fieldwork is not simply instru-mental – not just a method for producing anthropological theory. Rather, fieldwork is what constitutes anthropology for the majority of the people involved in it: Anthropology *is* what happens in the field.

Figure 10   Photograph of Ruth van Velsen, wife of the social anthropologist Jaap van Velsen, in their vanette on Great East Road, Northern Rhodesia, setting off for their field site in Nyasaland, early 1950s. From the author's collection, given to her by Ruth van Velsen.

Issues such as these have been raised by those who today argue for a more engaged anthropology, a "messianic anthropology" or an "anthropology on the front lines" (Harries-Jones 1996; MacClancy 2002). One of the most important front lines today is that of sex and gender. Sex, sexuality, and gender identities have become an area of contestation in the West and in the academy, and this identity war has spread to the developing world. The re-gendering of the world's societies in terms of currently popular Western categories is limiting men's and women's choices, especially where Western educational, activist, and religious campaigns linked to the HIV/AIDS epidemic have had a major impact. This is a front line that demands engaged fieldwork and a diverse range of fieldworkers to rethink Western and indigenous biological categories. It also requires us to do more anthropology "at home" – an anthropology of Western categories of sex and gender. Finally, we must begin to do an anthropology in and of the discipline of anthropology itself and of the academic contexts that shape its research on sex and gender.

Conclusion

The rethinking of sex, gender, and biological categories in the twenty-first century must include anthropology as an academic discipline which, in the West, participates in generating these categories. Fieldwork on anthropology, as a hierarchically structured small society embedded in Western universities and dependent on their funding and production agendas, is the real "at home" anthropology that women (and men) must now pioneer.

Ideally, this project will go beyond the reflexivity of the past two decades, which has produced challenging ethnography and some improvements in (mainly) Western women's careers. This internal shift has taken place, however, without changing the basic structures of the academy or the larger society. Can we renew that overarching 1970s feminist goal of transforming society's structures and hierarchies through feminist critiques, rather than merely finding ways for women to participate more fully within disciplinary structures as they are? And can we find the courage, not simply to include the subjects of research in this project, but to follow their lead?

Further Reading

MacClancy, J., ed. 2002. *Exotic No More: Anthropology on the Front Lines*. Chicago: University of Chicago Press.
Moore, H. L., ed. 1996. *The Future of Anthropological Knowledge*. London: Routledge.
Schumaker, L. 2001. *Africanizing Anthropology: Fieldwork, Networks, and the Making of Cultural Knowledge in Central Africa*. Durham: Duke University Press.
Visweswaran, K. 1997. "Histories of Feminist Ethnography." *Annual Review of Anthropology* 26: 591–621.

17

Visual Anthropology

Anna Grimshaw

Introduction

Writing in his essay "The Camera People," Eliot Weinberger offers an amusing image of the visual anthropologist at work:

> [t]here is a tribe, known as the ethnographic filmmakers, who believe they are invisible. They enter a room where a feast is being celebrated, or the sick cured, or the dead mourned, and, though weighted down with odd machines, entangled with wires, imagine they are unnoticed – or, at most, merely glanced at, quickly ignored, later forgotten. Outsiders know little of them, for their homes are hidden in the partially uncharted rainforests of the Documentary. Like other Documentarians, they survive by hunting and gathering information. Unlike others of their filmic group, most prefer to consume it raw. (1994: 3)

This humorous characterization expresses a view that is prevalent both inside and outside the discipline of anthropology – namely that ethnographic filmmakers are weighed down by technical encumbrances; they produce large quantities of boring footage that show strange people doing strange things (usually at a distance); and that they are theoretically and methodologically naïve.

Weinberger's image of the visual anthropologist at work has remained a popular stereotype, even though the field has greatly diversified from its original focus in ethnographic film. The origins of visual anthropology as a subdiscipline lie in the 1970s. The demarcation of a distinctive collection of interests and activities was part of anthropology's expansion and fragmentation as a discipline as it became consolidated in the postwar academy. Particularly significant was the publication of Paul Hockings's edited volume, *Principles of Visual Anthropology* (1975). Writing in its Preface, Hocking expressed his hope that the book would legitimize a range of activities that were taking place on the edges of the textual discipline. Ethnographic film and, to a lesser extent, photography became central to definitions of the subdiscipline.

However, despite the attempts by Hockings and others (Heider 1986; Rollwagen 1988) to render visual anthropology academically respectable, it has continued, as one commentator puts it, to be a somewhat "unruly" and "disorderly" enterprise (Ginsburg 1998). Straddling the academy and a broader world of media production, this liminality has been a source of visual anthropology's strength *and* weakness. Linked to practice outside the academy, visual anthropologists have been able to engage with a range of experiments and collaborations unconstrained by the limitations, hierarchies, and specializations of academia. This has often been at the cost of intellectual consolidation, serving to undermine broader disciplinary acknowledgment of its theoretical potential.

For those of us who consider ourselves to be visual anthropologists, it is surprising how suspicious some of our colleagues are about our field of practice. From Maurice Bloch's often-quoted remarks (1988)[1] to those by Fabian (1983), Hastrup (1992), Weiner (1997), and Watson (1998), there is a level of resistance that is distinguished by its emotional undertow. Robert Gardner has probably provoked the discipline more than other figures in the field. In particular, his film *Forest of Bliss* generated a flurry of controversy that was notable by the intensity of debate, polarizing "textual" and "visual" scholars (Loizos 1993). Certainly many anthropologists regard visual materials as merely a passive counterpart to more conventionally articulated arguments. For example, more often than not ethnographic film is used as an introductory form of anthropology, illustrative of theoretical work developed by means of textual forms. Visual anthropologists, however, have long argued for the interrogatory, unsettling potential of image-based inquiry. In response to the prevailing skepticism of their colleagues, they robustly challenge charges of theoretical and methodological backwardness by claiming the opposite – their prescience. It can be argued that leading figures in the tradition of ethnographic cinema, for example, the French filmmaker Jean Rouch working in the context of West Africa, began to address the politics of representation some several decades before his textual counterparts. *Writing Culture* (Clifford and Marcus 1986), the book that most represented anthropology's moment of self-consciousness, was published some 30 years after Rouche pioneered an innovative cinematic practice that called into question established disciplinary assumptions.

The origins of what Lucien Taylor (1996) calls anthropology's "iconophobia" are to be found in the particular history of the discipline as it developed into its modern form. But equally they are linked to anthropology's location within a certain kind of European intellectual discourse. For the discipline's ambivalence about vision can be understood as part of the more widespread anxiety about vision that Jay (1993) has highlighted as a consistent thread in twentieth-century thought.

This essay takes ethnographic film as its point of departure. Its centrality to visual anthropology as a subdiscipline has generated a particular range of debates. A brief survey of key figures and developments in the American, British, and French traditions, from the end of the nineteenth century to the present, brings into focus many of these debates. Today, however, the hard-won status of visual anthropology as a subdiscipline faces challenge – as much from those working within it as those outside.

Many visual anthropologists have become impatient with the existing divisions of academic labor. Not only is the visual field of investigation now understood to be much bigger and more complex than hitherto acknowledged; but anthropology itself has become the subject of visual inquiry (Grimshaw 2001; MacDougall 1998). If the former involves studying the proliferating forms of visual culture, the latter is a reflexive practice that addresses questions concerning ethnographic techniques, knowledge and forms of representation.

Nineteenth-Century Visual Practice

Visual techniques and technologies were central to the Victorian project of anthropology. Initially linked to a paradigm that arranged peoples and cultures according to a complex evolutionary schema, the camera was used to provide primary data for the construction of speculative theories about the development of human society. What Pinney calls photography's "quantifying and reality appropriating capacities" harmonized with the "realist and quantitative aspirations of mid-nineteenth century anthropology" (1992: 260). Photography seemed to promise a more reliable and objective way of gathering evidence, facilitating comparison between sets of data collected from different areas of the world. Existing methods were idiosyncratic and largely unsystematized; and they increasingly posed problems for an intellectual endeavor driven by principles of measurement, classification and hierarchy.

The problem of evidence was particularly acute for nineteenth-century anthropology because the roles of theorist and fieldworker were sharply demarcated. Gentlemen scholars like Sir James Frazer, who never left the comfort of their Oxbridge studies to encounter native society first-hand, depended upon a motley collection of travelers, explorers, missionaries, and colonial officials for their research material. Hearsay or reported speech was now supplemented by evidence yielded by the camera. Visual data produced in this way were considered to be more direct and reliable; and, as a consequence, the camera quickly became a critical tool in the shoring up of the scientific credentials of data supplied by amateurs from the field. Anthropologists were part of a growing army of investigators that included geologists, botanists, explorers, government inspectors, and for whom the task of recording and mapping was to be conducted in as scientific a manner as possible.

The importance of the camera to anthropology was manifold (Edwards 1990, 1992, 2001). Not only was it considered to minimize the subjectivity of the observer; but the fieldworker could be trained to produce images according to very specific criteria. The task was not just to collect more reliable evidence; it was also to generate standardized data that could be organized into categories as a preliminary to classification and comparison. To this end, detailed guidelines were drawn up that served to instruct amateur fieldworkers in how to use the new recording technology. Between 1874 and 1920, the publication *Notes and Queries in Anthropology* established itself as the indispensable manual of the fieldworker, containing practical advice on all aspects of data collection – including the role of the camera.

Alison Griffiths, in her book *Wondrous Difference* (2002), identifies three different kinds of photographic production. The first, *anthropometric* photography, is perhaps most identified with nineteenth-century anthropology. Its focus was the type. Animated by the principle of taxonomy, individuals were photographed as physical specimens in highly controlled environments. The native subject was objectified; and his or her individuality suppressed in the interests of representing the whole. Physical appearance was the basis for theories about culture, intelligence, and evolution. The instructions for this kind of data collection were exceptionally precise, requiring the subject to be photographed unclothed against a neutral context so as to enhance appreciation of physical characteristics. In many cases, the body was placed against a grid or other measuring device and images would be made according to a set number of angles.[2]

Over the course of the nineteenth century, however, a different kind of photograph began to emerge from the field. It was marked by a certain informality, reflecting a growing interest in what Pinney calls "the quick and the living" over the "still and the silent" (1992: 78). Everard im Thurn, a botanist turned anthropologist and one-time Governor of Fiji, became a prominent advocate of this second kind of photographic practice. Criticizing anthropometric photography as the documentation of "lifeless bodies," he suggested instead that the anthropologist's camera be used to express something of living culture of people being studied. Central to this new approach was an acknowledgment of the relationship between the photographer and the subjects of his practice. This, in turn, implied the forging of a new relationship between observer and subject, one that could admit the fundamental humanity of native peoples. Im Thurn recognized the importance of gaining the trust of fieldwork subjects and their collaboration. His own photographs, as Griffiths (2002: 101) remarks, are notable for their candor.

The third kind of photograph was the picture postcard. Over the course of the nineteenth century, popular demand grew for images of "primitive" peoples. Commercially produced photographs were distinguished by a "soft-focus pictorialism" that was created in the studio and involved the use of stylized backdrops that served to both idealize and exoticize the native subject. Griffiths (2002: 121) notes that for all their rhetoric of science, many anthropologists drew on a wide range of photographic images, including popular or commercial ones as illustrative counterparts to speculative writing. The constant movement of pictures across different domains reflected a more general fluidity in late nineteenth-century intellectual culture that subverted any neat division between the scientific and the popular. Moreover, it is important to remember that the entire project of photographing native life was conducted not in a climate of disinterested science – quite the contrary. There was an extreme urgency to it.

Leading Victorian anthropologists believed that native peoples were rapidly disappearing. But their determination to record customs and ways of life before it was too late was driven less by a general benevolence and more by the necessity of such evidence in the construction of European society's "primitive" origins. In the service of this salvage enterprise, turn-of-the-century anthropologists like Haddon or Boas advocated the use of the most up-to-date scientific equipment. There was, of course,

Figure 11   A. C. Haddon and Sidney Ray, members of the Cambridge Anthropological Expedition to Torres Straits, with Pasi and his family on the beach at Duaur, 1898. Used with permission of the University of Cambridge Museum of Archaeology and Anthropology.

a certain irony in this situation. Haddon's response to what he perceived to be the plight of the Torres Strait Islanders was to launch his famous fieldwork expedition (Herle and Rouse 1998). His team of Cambridge scientists set out to record native customs and practices before they died out, but the enterprise to save "primitive" man was also part of his destruction. The paradox was symbolized in the prominent role accorded to the camera in salvage anthropology. For the new recording technologies that Haddon and his scientific contemporaries so enthusiastically embraced were deeply implicated in the transformation of that which they sought to preserve.

Haddon's 1898 Torres Strait expedition is often cited as a critical moment in the history of visual anthropology. It yielded four minutes of moving film as well as an important collection of photographs and other sorts of visual evidence. Questions of vision were central to the object, methods and forms of inquiry – marking the expedition as simultaneously modern and archaic. Haddon and his team were representative of the change in ethnographic practice that brought together the previously separate roles of fieldworker and theorist in a single person. This new turn in ethnographic inquiry had important consequences for the role of the camera in the twentieth-century project.

The photographs yielded by the Torres Strait expedition are highly varied. They include the classic anthropometric type, other kinds of highly structured, carefully composed scenes and also more informal portraits. What is interesting, as Edwards (2001) reminds us, is how Haddon's use of the camera enables us to address problems about the changing status of evidence in anthropological endeavor and to explore the complex dynamics of early modern fieldwork practice. The surviving film footage marks the beginning of ethnographic cinema. It is particularly notable for its striking resemblance to the films shot by the Lumière brothers that were exhibited, along with their invention (the cinematograph), in Paris and London in 1895. The theatrical framing, the focus on whole, continuous sequences of action and the direct engagement of film subjects with the camera marks Haddon's Torres Strait film as an example of "the cinema of attractions" (Gunning 1990).[3] There are, in fact, a number of distinctive single-shot "films" within the brief four minutes of footage. One of the important questions raised by this material concerns the status of re-enactment, native subjects staging or performing activities for the purposes of ethnographic recording. Long considered an archaic practice, recent critical work has rendered it a much more interesting and complex phenomenon than previously acknowledged. For, as Edwards (2001) notes, re-enactment serves to animate buried history, re-presenting aspects of the past through performance that makes visible or brings back into consciousness social practices that have long been suppressed by missionary or colonial activity.

Critics of visual anthropology often point to the positivist roots of the modern project. It is important, however, to recognize that the camera was deemed problematic from the very beginning. The Victorian anthropologists, while committed to scientific endeavor, were never complacent, placing naïve faith in the available technology. Instead, as many commentators have pointed out, turn-of-the-century scientists – including the anthropologists – were deeply worried about the status of evidence. The camera did not solve this problem, it merely entered into the equation (Daston and Galison 1992). Jay goes further, arguing that the camera, "the most remarkable technological development of the human capacity to see, at least since the development of the microscope and telescope in the seventeenth century, helped ultimately to undermine confidence in the very sense whose powers it so extended" (1995: 344–5). The crisis of ocularcentrism, which Jay takes to be a distinguishing feature of twentieth-century Western thought, reverberated throughout anthropology as it began to take shape as a modern discipline.

From Surface to Depth

The displacement of vision from its central place as an object and method of anthropological inquiry is associated with the rise of the Malinowskian project. For conceptual attention shifted focus from surface to depth, from visible manifestations of culture to concerns with social structure. Crucially, too, there was a transformation in the role of the fieldworker. The Victorian men of science, with their impressive array of instrumentation, were replaced by a single ethnographer, carrying only a notebook and pen. The camera quickly disappeared from this model of ethnographic practice, becoming "just another ancillary tool in the fieldworker's arsenal" (Edwards 1992: 4). But if image-based techniques and techniques were banished, at best relegated to an illustrative function, vision continued to function as an important metaphor for knowledge. "Going to see for yourself," the mantra of modern anthropology, involved a very different kind of scientific enterprise than that pursued by Haddon and his contemporaries.

The carefully ordered world of the latter, the late-Victorian optimism tied to a belief in the inevitability of progress, was shattered by the Great War. Confidence in sight as the noblest of the senses and a privileged source of knowledge about the world was also destroyed. World War I was the graveyard of the eye:

> The Western front's interminable warfare . . . created a bewildering landscape of indis-
> tinguishable, shadowy shapes, illuminated by lightning flashes of blinding intensity;
> and then obscured by phantasmagoric, often gas-induced haze. The effect was even more
> visually disorienting than those produced by such nineteenth century technical innova-
> tions as the railroad, the camera or the cinema. When all that the soldier could see was
> the sky above and the mud below, the traditional reliance on visual evidence for
> survival could no longer be easily maintained. (Jay 1994: 174)

Malinowskian anthropology emerged in the aftermath of this profound historical moment. No longer harnessed to an Enlightenment vision and its technologies that promised to render the world visible and knowable, the new fieldwork-based project was nevertheless built around a particular conception of vision. It involved the cultivation of a way of seeing. It was about the cleansing of the ethnographer's eye, the recuperation of vision such that he or she could "see again" or "see for the first time" (Grimshaw 2001). In such a project, there was no place for the camera. For here vision is the *visionary*. It involves intuition, insight, moments of revelation that cannot be achieved by means of technology but only by surrendering the body to radical sensory transformation. Indeed the camera becomes redundant, as the fieldworker is now inscribed in a manner akin to the photographic process itself: "[t]he anthropologists' exposure to data . . . occurred during a period of inversion from his normal reality, a stage which is formally analogous to the production of the photographic negative when the all-important rays of light which guarantee the indexical truth of the image are allowed to fall on the negative's emulsion" (Pinney 1992: 82).

The new relationship between vision and experiential knowledge in anthropological inquiry was established with the publication in 1922 of Malinowski's classic text, *Argonauts of the Western Pacific*. In the same year, the filmmaker Robert Flaherty released his classic documentary, *Nanook of the North*. There are many intriguing parallels and tantalizing points of connection between these two works. Nevertheless there is no evidence that suggests they were ever considered to be part of the same project. *Nanook of the North,* Flaherty's portrait of an Inuit family's struggle for survival in the harsh landscape of the Canadian Arctic, exemplifies the strengths and weaknesses of the filmmaker's distinctive approach toward the documentation of native life. The humanism of the work, the acknowledged collaborative relationship between director and subject, and Flaherty's commitment to long-term immersion in Inuit culture as the precondition for its representation, are important features that have endured over the years. At the same time, though, *Nanook* has long been a focus for criticism on the grounds that it is deeply flawed and ethically problematic. In particular, accusations concerning Flaherty's manipulations (his staging of events and re-enactment of long-abandoned practices) and his simplistic vision of native society continue to haunt the project of ethnographic cinema today (Rony 1996; Ruby 2000).

Many of the criticisms leveled at *Nanook* can also be made with respect to Malinowski's work. But the exclusion of Flaherty from anthropology's twentieth-century narrative is linked to questions about ethnographic authority and the establishment of a distinctively *modern* enterprise. The early promise of a synthesis between film and anthropology, so enthusiastically endorsed by Haddon, was not to be achieved. For following the Malinowskian revolution, anthropology became pre-eminently a literary endeavor. Moreover, the evolution of the project as "a disciplined form of inquiry" and its consolidation within the academy depended on a policing of professional boundaries (Clifford 1988; Kuklick 1991b). Malinowski, and his contemporaries, were anxious to distance themselves from their Victorian counterparts whose use of visual techniques and forms were associated with racial classification, salvage anthropology, and with the culture of collecting and museum display. Moreover, anthropology presented through visual forms came to be identified with the popular. The professional and scientific credibility of the discipline depended on a rejection of both art and entertainment. Nothing was more threatening to assertions of ethnographic authority than the image of an anthropologist with a camera. This was an uncomfortable reminder of the shaky foundations upon which such claims were made, blurring as it did the lines between anthropologists and their rivals – journalists, for instance; or worse, much worse, tourists. Figures like Flaherty, despite the developed ethnographic sensibility of his practice, were firmly excluded from this new scientific enterprise. In terms of ethnographic cinema, however, Flaherty's work is as critical – and as controversial – as that of Malinowski within mainstream anthropology.

Filming Science

Although modern anthropology became established as a pre-eminently literary enterprise, image-based work continued to develop and flourish on the edges of the textual discipline. The use of a camera, harnessed to a scientific agenda reminiscent of turn-of-the-century anthropology, was particularly associated with Margaret Mead. Trained by Franz Boas, who shared many of the same concerns as his British counterparts like Haddon, Mead began to actively explore visual techniques and technologies in the context of fieldwork conducted with Gregory Bateson during the 1930s (Jacknis 1988). Together, they sought to develop an innovative methodology appropriate to their investigation into certain cultural practices in Bali and New Guinea. The camera's role was envisaged as an interrogatory rather than an illustrative one, posing rather than resolving ethnographic questions. Important, too, in the conception that Mead and Bateson had of the value of still and moving film in fieldwork activity was their recognition of the limitations of language in conveying or translating aspects of social life. The juxtaposition of different kinds of fieldwork materials (written, visual, aural) was integral to the evocation of what Bateson called "ethos", that is, "the intangible aspects of culture" (1942: xi). Later, in the context of World War II, Bateson and Mead used visual materials in what was known as "the study of culture at a distance." Initially, this involved the development of an anthropological approach toward the interpretation of film (for example, Nazi propaganda). Subsequently it encompassed a study of forms of visual communication, understood not as descriptions but as cultural statements about the world.

The potential of the early Bateson and Mead work was never fully realized, since each moved on to pursue other projects separately. Nevertheless, Mead continued to work with the footage shot by Bateson in Bali and New Guinea, editing it into a series of short films called "Character Formation in Different Cultures." The principle around which Mead organized visual materials was "sequence filming." It involved leaving intact whole blocks of film footage. If one of Mead's main ideas about the camera's role in fieldwork practice was to generate research materials or the research film (a body of data that could be stored in archives to be analyzed by other scholars), another was about the urgent recording of what she believed were rapidly disappearing cultural practices.

Margaret Mead was a central figure in the emergence of visual anthropology as it developed into a field of specialist interest and techniques within American anthropology. Her preoccupations and problematic location within the professional discipline importantly shaped its intellectual agenda. Mead's visually based work with Bateson was certainly interesting, but the important questions about method, epistemology, and form implicit in the Bali and New Guinea project were not seriously pursued. Left in the hands of Mead, they were reduced to a simple scientism harnessed to a salvage paradigm. Mead's high public profile and the skepticism she provoked among most university-based anthropologists played a significant part in the marginalization of visual anthropology. For with Mead at the helm, it was easy to dismiss the enterprise as theoretically naïve, popularizing and animated by old-fashioned salvage and museum-based concerns.

Many of the key figures gathered by Paul Hockings in his book, *Principles of Visual Anthropology*, were people closely associated with Mead and influenced by her passionate commitment to the use of the camera in modern fieldwork. These included John Marshall, Timothy Asch, Asen Balikci, Robert Gardner, and Karl Heider. From the outset they were burdened by problems originating in Mead's project. Hence much energy was expended in seeking to legitimate ethnographic film, in particular, as a respectable kind of scientific endeavor.

The work of Timothy Asch, for example, reveals many of these problems – specifically the belief in the camera as an objective recording instrument capable of yielding research data. Declaring "[it] is the opinion of many in this field that the camera can be to the anthropologist what the telescope is to the astronomer or what the microscope is to the biologist" (quoted in Loizos 1993: 17), during the 1960s Asch, in collaboration with Napoleon Chagnon, began to shoot great quantities of film footage of the Yanomami Indians. Filming was conducted as a form of documentation, with emphasis placed on preserving the integrity of behavioral sequences. From these materials, Asch and Chagnon edited a number of films, including *The Ax Fight*. The latter is one of the most discussed films in the field of visual anthropology. For, as Winston's (1995) astute analysis reveals, Asch and Chagnon make a whole series of claims in *The Ax Fight* about a particular ethnographic situation that are not sustained by the evidence offered in the film footage. Their attempt to show the different stages by which anthropological understanding may be reached, a progressive movement from chaos to order, from the noisy, fighting "savage" Yanomami Indians to the cool rationality of scientific observers, starkly exposed the shaky foundations upon which Mead's project was built.[4]

Models of Ethnographic Filmmaking

A very different kind of visual anthropology from the one being pursued within American anthropology had already developed in France. Based at the Musée de L'Homme in Paris, Jean Rouch had, since the 1950s, been developing a highly distinctive anthropological cinema built around his notion of the *ciné-transe*. At its center was an active, embodied camera. It served as a transformative agent such that the filmmaker embarked with his subjects and audience on a sort of shamanistic journey (Feld 2003; Stoller 1992).

Rouch began his work in French West Africa as an engineer during World War II. His interest in possession ceremonies led him to study anthropology with Marcel Griaule, whose approach profoundly influenced Rouch's subsequent film practice. In particular, Rouch drew on Griaule's notion of fieldwork as a two-stage process, *documentation* followed by *initiation*, a movement that involved a radical shift in levels of understanding. This model was built around an explicit acknowledgment of the theatrical and disruptive nature of fieldwork. When, in the late 1940s, Rouch began to use a camera as an integral part of his fieldwork investigations, he discovered that not only did it capture aspects of Songhay life but it, moreover, *created* ethnographic realities. For Rouch, the importance of the camera lay not in its recording capacities. His interest focused around the camera's ability to function as a catalyst, generating new kinds of experience and knowledge.

Rouch's early documentation films were quickly supplanted by ones that were predicated on the Griaulean notion of initiation, with the camera being used to radically reorient the ethnographer in the field. The camera became a vehicle for disrupting the conventional categories through which anthropologists order and interpret the world. It was also used to transform the conventional relationships – and hierarchies – between anthropologists, subjects, and audience. The development of this new kind of cinema hinged crucially upon Rouch's abandonment of the conventional apparatus of filming, most notably elaborate technology, the use of a tripod and the employment of a film crew. Working with the camera as an extension of his body ("filming in the first person"), Rouch allowed himself to become "possessed," to enter a trance-like state.[5] His approach involved no pretense of detachment or objectivity – quite the opposite. It was often confrontational and sometimes profoundly disturbing. Rouch was impatient with respect and distance. Through his ethnographic cinema ("science fiction," as he idiosyncratically called it) he sought to forge a new space for intercultural exchange and understanding, one that would emerge from the dissolution of boundaries between self and other, European and African, reality and fantasy.

Rouch's cinematic innovations were linked to an unusual historical moment (Grimshaw 2001). His most audacious work, *Les Maîtres Fous* (1954), which established the distinctive contours of his project, was closely tied to the conditions of West Africa as the former colonial territories struggled for independence. Rouch's impatience with the limitations of cinema and anthropology mirrored the creative energy unleashed against the social and political limitations of European rule by the African subjects of his films. He was pioneering what he idiosyncratically called "science fiction," a series of films that represent a sustained interrogation of established categories of reality and fiction. His classic work of this period (including *Jaguar, Moi, Un Noir* and *Chronique d'un été*) anticipated many of the innovations of the French New Wave. It is marked by a tremendous energy that emanates from his challenge to the assumptions of cinema and anthropological inquiry – in particular, the commitment to science, to the "primitive", to the separation and hierarchy of ethnographer and subjects.

A decade after Rouch's most innovative work, David and Judith MacDougall began to define another course for ethnographic cinema. Unlike Rouch's audacious vision, the work of the MacDougalls was anchored in the notion of "respect" for their subjects and their place in the world. From their early East African work like *To Live With Herds* (1972) to their later *Turkana Conversations* (1976–77) and collaboration with Australian Aboriginal communities (1982–88), their films were painstakingly built from the amassing of small details, sifted and organized such that they coalesced into distinctive patterns, textures and rhythms. The MacDougalls shared with Rouch a commitment to embodied technology (the use of minimal, hand-held equipment) and to the development of close relationships with subjects through a long-term immersion in fieldwork situations. The resulting films, however, could not be more different. If Rouch's work is characterized by a rough, improvised, and exuberant quality, that of the MacDougalls is distinguished by its quiet, minutely observed detail and structural elegance. The contrast reflects fundamentally different conceptions of anthropological cinema. One grows out of an interest in the imaginative as a transformative agent in social life, while the other is rooted in a phenomenologically oriented exploration of lived experience.

From the outset, David MacDougall has been committed to the establishment of an intellectually ambitious visual anthropology. He has emerged as one of the leading figures in the field, using his own film practice as the basis for an extended, critical reflection on questions of anthropological technique and knowledge (1998). The body of work he has created with his partner, Judith MacDougall, is remarkable, paradoxically, in its qualities of consistency and innovation. There is a striking intellectual coherence at the core of their work but the changing location of their practice has shaped their inquiry in distinctive ways.

Any understanding of the MacDougalls' contribution to debates in visual anthropology must start with the question of observational cinema. For the breakthrough in ethnographic film that Colin Young proclaimed in his much-cited 1975 essay has reverberated through the MacDougalls' project from the very beginning. Observational cinema was predicated upon the repudiation of an earlier kind of anthropological filmmaking practice that fragmented ethnographic reality as a preliminary to reassembling it in accordance with a conceptual framework that originated elsewhere. The new approach involved a shift from ideas to life, a movement away from filmmaking as the illustration of an argument, toward an open-ended practice that was anchored in an exploration of experiential perspectives. Instead of talking over subjects or lecturing one's audience, observational filmmakers like the MacDougalls attempted to listen. It required a certain humility and patience on their part, and a willingness to abandon claims to expertise and assumptions of authority. At the center of observational cinema was an ethical commitment. Although it is often reduced to a form of visualism (Fabian 1983), the original sense in which Young used the term "observational" referred to a particular stance on the part of the filmmakers.

The MacDougalls' most celebrated film, *To Live With Herds*, is widely acknowledged as a classic example of observational cinema. It is distinguished by its intimate camera work, by its long takes and by the absence of commentary. Despite their innovative techniques, the MacDougalls continued to be troubled by the inequalities embedded in the filming situation; and they began to investigate the possibilities of a more collaborative or participatory cinema. In place of the distancing stance of the observational camera, MacDougall called for the development of an "unprivileged camera style," one that bears witness to the "event" of the film. By this he means that the filmmaker must acknowledge his or her place in any ethnographic situation. The dynamics of the filmmaking process must be rendered as an inherent part of the final representation. In this way the MacDougalls intended to give both subject and audience access to the process of representation. They sought to reveal how anthropological knowledge is generated in and through relationships and encounters rather than existing as a block of disembodied knowledge apart from intersubjective exchange.

Central to the MacDougalls' collaborative practice was the notion of conversation. It was not about the exchange of prior information; rather, it was about creating the conditions in which new knowledge might arise. The MacDougalls' experiments in participatory cinema were most fully developed in the highly politicized context of Australia's Aboriginal communities. But, after more than a decade pursuing collaborative work, the MacDougalls returned to much more self-consciously authored work. Increasingly, they felt that notions of shared authorship, far from clarifying the complexities of ethnographic encounters, only served to obscure crucial issues of power and knowledge (MacDougall 1995).

The different projects of ethnographic cinema pursued by Asch, Rouch, and the MacDougalls were central to visual anthropology's consolidation as a subdiscipline during the 1970s and 1980s. At the same time, another significant kind of anthropological documentary was being created in the context of British broadcasting. Granada Television's "Disappearing World" series began in 1971 (Loizos 1980). Over the course of 20 years, it established a high public profile not just for visual anthropology, but for anthropology more generally. The early films, like Brian Moser's *The Last of the Cuiva*, reflected a commitment to the documentation of native communities believed to be on the edge of extinction. This initial premise, a classic salvage paradigm of vulnerable cultures facing forces of change and destruction, was gradually modified as the series evolved. Increasingly, television audiences were presented with images of vibrant native cultures whose members were highly conscious of their agency in the world (*Masai Manhood*, for example).

"Disappearing World" was an example of "anthropology on television." On the whole, the films were expository (rather than observational) in style. Their focus derived from the specialist interests of the consulting anthropologists. It was the task of the program-makers to make these academic concerns compatible with the conventions of television – a process of translation that was often marked by conflict and difficulty (Turton 1992). Despite the constraints of broadcast culture and the tensions between anthropologists and their television counterparts, "Disappearing World" was an unusually long-running and innovative documentary series. It attracted considerable public interest over the years and it is widely credited with swelling the numbers of students wishing to study anthropology at university. For these reasons alone, many professional anthropologists remain skeptical as to the intellectual seriousness of the enterprise.

Challenging Visions

Visual anthropologists have long claimed prescience over their textual colleagues in matters of disciplinary self-consciousness. The publication of *Writing Culture* (Clifford and Marcus 1986) is widely acknowledged to mark anthropology's reflexive or postmodern turn, inaugurating a period of intense debate that was founded upon the sustained interrogation of established concepts (culture), methods (fieldwork), and representational forms (monograph). It may be argued that ethnographic filmmakers anticipated this moment some decades earlier. Rouch's early experiments in a shared anthropology began in the 1950s. His innovative approach tested the boundaries of ethnographic knowledge and challenged anthropology's tendency to objectify and deny history or agency to the subjects of its inquiry. The MacDougalls, too, used their filmmaking practice as a basis for examining certain conceptual and methodological assumptions built into anthropological work. Ethnographic filmmaking is, by its very nature, both public and collaborative. The cinema of Rouch and the MacDougalls took shape in highly politicized contexts and the filmmakers themselves were unusually open to the dynamics of the situations in which they were working. Issues of knowledge, power, and collaboration were not side-stepped or bracketed out but they were creatively admitted at the very heart of their respective projects.

During the 1980s, questions about indigenous media emerged as a critical focus for discussion within visual anthropology – and beyond. The MacDougalls acknowledged that the experiments in participatory cinema they began in Africa but pursued more fully with Australian Aboriginal peoples were part of a transitional phase. They represented a moment in which anthropological filmmakers served as a vehicle for the articulation of the social and political aspirations of native peoples. But native peoples were rapidly acquiring independent access to a range of media technologies for purposes of self-expression. The fate of anthropological intermediaries in a fast-changing political situation was prefigured in the MacDougalls' film *Takeover*. A number of other anthropologists had also become involved in developing media initiatives within indigenous communities, abandoning their self-appointed role as spokespersons for subjects, seeking instead to facilitate access to technologies that would enable native self-expression. Most notable was the work of Terence Turner with the Kayapo Indians of north-eastern Brazil (Turner 2002). It was Turner's passionate advocacy of anthropological involvement in the struggle by indigenous people to use video as a means for articulating their own voice that particularly galvanized opposition to the field of visual anthropology. His role as a facilitator generated a great deal of heated debate about empowerment, globalization and the role of the media in cultural change. Prominent critics like Faris (1992) and Weiner (1997) attacked the phenomenon of indigenous media as ineffectual, a gesture of resistance, while at the same time accusing anthropological intermediaries (like Turner) of being naïve, agents, despite their best intentions, of a dominating Western visualist project.

There was a certain conceit in this debate. For whatever insults anthropologists traded amongst themselves, the discipline's traditional subjects were getting on with making their own films. Native peoples were energetically negotiating independent access to media technologies in order to produce and control their own representations. These were not intended for anthropological audiences, but for their own communities, for political purposes and as a challenge to existing cultural stereotypes. The consequences of this kind of activity for conventional notions of culture and tradition became the focus of concern for visual anthropologists interested in exploring a new intellectual terrain – the anthropology of media. Leading commentators, like Ginsburg (1995), started from the position that media technologies were an inescapable part of the contemporary world, bringing together in new ways peoples separated by huge social, cultural, economic, and geographical distances. Drawing on her work in Australia, Ginsburg made the concept of mediation central to the development of a distinctively anthropological perspective toward indigenous media. She foregrounded social process, arguing that: "[a]nalysis needs to focus less on the formal qualities of film and video as text and more on the cultural mediations that occur through film and video works" (1995: 259). What all this independent media activity means for the project of ethnographic film – once a significant site for the representation and mediation of cultural difference – is a pertinent question, as Nichols (1994), Ginsburg (1999), and others have noted. But far from rendering the project redundant, figures like David MacDougall (1998) have interpreted the situation as enriching, leading to the emergence of *intertextual* cinema (films that no longer assert representational privilege but acknowledge rival interpretations of social reality). Today ethnographic filmmakers are part of a vast, contested media terrain. No longer able to claim any special status, their work now jostles for recognition amidst competing representations of culture.

New Horizons for Visual Anthropology

Although visual anthropology has traditionally been dominated by ethnographic film, today it is a broad and highly diverse field. Writing in their Introduction to *Rethinking Visual Anthropology*, Banks and Morphy identify two distinctive foci of interest – the study of "visual systems and visible culture" and the use of the visual as a critical tool in the exploration of anthropological techniques and knowledge (1997: 1). The first set of concerns, what might be called "an anthropology of the visual," is about making manifestations of the visual the object of anthropology inquiry. It encompasses, for example, the study of art and ritual objects, tourist artifacts, body decoration, gardens, photography, performance, computers, indigenous visual production, art and esthetics, exhibition and museum culture, the anthropology of media, and so on. Conceptualized in this way, the project cuts across many of the old divisions that separated ethnographic film from the anthropology of art or the study of material culture. It also connects anthropology to the new and rapidly expanding field of visual culture. Despite a convergence of interdisciplinary interests in the visual, anthropologists continue to offer a distinctive analytical perspective. It is rooted in a commitment to ethnography. The objects of study are not approached primarily as "text." There is instead a concern with practice and with the ways in which people forge historical, cultural, and political identities through changing visual forms. But anthropologists do share with their intellectual counterparts in visual studies the central problem of how to work conceptually with the visual. How can the visual be approached on its own terms, rather than be "linguified" (Taylor 1996), that is translated into a different, *textual*, register? Addressing this question is also at the heart of visual anthropology's other focus of concerns.

A second constellation of interests in the contemporary relates to ethnographic inquiry itself. Understood as an investigation of "visual ways of knowing" (MacDougall 1998), this project is both expansive and reflexive. According to MacDougall: "[i]nstead of simply adding to anthropology's fields of study, it poses fundamental challenges to anthropology's ways of 'speaking' and knowing" (1998: 63). It involves working critically with vision as a metaphor for knowledge that is located in body and in senses. Specifically, visual approaches are used to explore what lies at the edge of discursive understanding; and, as such, they also constitute an interrogation of conventional assumptions about anthropological knowledge. This kind of enterprise is no longer inhibited by textual pressures or by the need to justify itself in the estab-lished terms of a literary discipline. Indeed, it depends on a radical shift of per-spective. Understood in this light, visual anthropology escapes from the confines of "pictorial anthropology," the production of films *about* anthropology (Ruby 1975; MacDougall 1998). The new enterprise is animated by a commitment to anthropo-logical visuality – that is, visual techniques and forms are not placed in the service of textual preoccupations, but are developed through the opening of new avenues of ethnographic inquiry.

Notes

1   In an interview with Gustaaf Houtman, Bloch remarked: "What ethnographic film – and especially the ethnographic films that are being made at the moment – are trying to do is give the idea that if you just stare at people, if you hear their words out of context, you've learnt something about them. This idea that ethnographic film speaks for itself is what is wrong. The kind of things one tries to teach in anthropology is, if you just stare at exotic scenes and listen to the things that people are saying without knowing anything about these people, you understand less about them than if you have never seen them or heard them" (Houtman 1988: 20).

2   For details see Edwards's discussion of the plans drawn up by Professor T. H. Huxley in 1869. As president of the Ethnological Society, he was asked to devise instructions that would establish systematic photographic practice. These required "the unclothed subject to be photographed full length, both front and profile. In the front view, the right arm must be outstretched horizontally, the palm of the hand towards the camera. The ankles should be together 'in the attitude of attention'. In the profile view the left side should be turned to the camera and the left arm bent at the elbow and arranged so as not to obscure the dorsal contour; the back of the hand should be turned towards the camera. In addition to the two full length photographs, full face and profile photographs of the head were recommended. All photographs should be accompanied by a clearly marked measuring rod" (Edwards 1990: 246).

3   Gunning argues that these early films were primarily about "showing" or display, rather than about "telling", the narration of stories. They are markedly exhibitionist in character – showing off of the cinematic apparatus and what it can do. See Gunning (1990).

4   The unease provoked by *The Ax Fight* has now become part of a much broader debate about the politics and ethics of the work carried out by Napoleon Chagnon (and Asch) with the Yanomami Indians.

5   "I now believe that for the people who are filmed, the 'self' of the filmmaker changes in front of their eyes during the shooting. He no longer speaks, except to yell out incom-prehensible orders ('Roll!' 'Cut!'). He now looks at them only through the intermediary of a strange appendage and hears them only through the intermediary of a shotgun microphone. But paradoxically, it is due to this equipment and this new behavior (which has nothing to do with the observable behavior of the same person when he is not filming) that the filmmaker can throw himself into a ritual, integrate himself with it, and follow it step-by-step. It is a strange kind of choreography, which, if inspired, makes the camerman and soundman no longer invisible but participants in the ongoing event" (Rouch in Feld 2003: 99).

Further Reading

Grimshaw, Anna. 2001. *The Ethnographer's Eye: Ways of Seeing in Modern Anthropology*. Cambridge: Cambridge University Press.

MacDougall, David. 1998. *Transcultural Cinema*. Princeton: Princeton University Press.

Ruby, Jay. 2000. *Picturing Culture: Explorations of Film and Anthropology*. Chicago: University of Chicago Press.

18

Anthropological Regionalism

Rena Lederman

There is no doubt about the thematic importance, in contemporary social commentary, of wide-ranging movements of people, things, and ideas; of distant connections and hyphenated designations along with the assertions of rootedness and identification that arguments about these things may provoke reflexively. As a freshly sharpened awareness of our historical circumstances, these emphases pose a special challenge for the several disciplines – e.g., history, literary study, and anthropology – that define themselves around contextual understandings of cultural and historical particulars. They call into question the accepted strategies for demarcating the very contexts of understanding.

Among anthropology's contexts of understanding, the regional (or "culture area") organization of training and research has become particularly problematic. Just as it has motivated a redirection in interdisciplinary Area Studies funding, the challenges associated with awareness of globalization have prompted a rethinking of the regional organization of anthropological fieldwork. However, anthropology's regional commitments are distinctive compared with both Area Studies and related disciplines. This chapter aims to specify that distinctiveness. Detailed consideration of the past generation's productive revisionism suggests that anthropology's regional traditions are diverse not just topically but also methodologically – a fact that both conventional and critical analyses have overlooked (e.g., Bernard 1994; Marcus 1995, 1998; cf. Fardon 1990b).

Generally, this chapter treats regional designations (like "Melanesia") and the anthropological term "culture area" to indicate historically elaborated scholarly discourses and associated fieldworking practices, without necessarily implying the existence of locally meaningful – much less objective – geographical, linguistic, or ethnic categories (although here and there it might: e.g., Dirlik 1998). As "culture area" literatures and field practices go, Melanesianist anthropology is especially interesting because of its central role in the history of the discipline: it is, for this reason (and others), the focus of the last part of this chapter. This literature has offered powerful, contradictory visions of the anthropological project: Melanesian communities have been represented *both* as "islands" of localized variation and microevolutionary development *and* as unbounded, ramifying networks of socio-cultural and material relationships. Invoked as both exemplars of the different and the familiar, Melanesian practices have also long inspired important critical and reflexive arguments about cultural analysis, comparison, and translation (e.g., Wagner 1975; Strathern 1988).

Implicated in foundational scenes of so-called "real anthropology," Melanesia is also complexly implicated in contemporary "post-exoticist" (Clifford 1997) discourse concerning the fortunes of the discipline as a whole. While it may now be freshly problematized, throughout the century-long elaboration of metropolitan academic anthropology Melanesianist ethnography has in fact been vanguard, paradigm, and anachronism all at once (although by no means always and everywhere in the same proportions). This review uses Melanesianist work to estimate the value of the discipline's distinctive style of regional study for its critical voice.

Anthropological Regionalism

Regional specialization has been a central component of Euro/American anthropological training and practice for much of this century. As Fardon (1990a: 24) has pointed out, its importance is evident in the social organization of the field – for example, in its professional associations and journals. Knowing (and being known in) your "place" is important in manuscript reviewing, hiring, and tenure evaluations. The importance of area specialization may vary among the national anthropological communities; individual scholars' area commitments may be weaker in the United States than in Britain, for example. But even in the US those expectations are strong early in individual careers (when most field research gets done).

A Conditional Commitment

Since the early 1990s, we have come to a fresh recognition of the *conditionality* of our regional commitments, however. Appadurai (1986: 358) directed our attention to the "tendency for places to become showcases for specific issues" and, conversely, for these issues (or "gatekeeping" ideas) to stand for whole regions – for example, as in the identification of South Asian ethnography with debates about hierarchy (Appadurai 1988) – even when the concepts derived from parts of those regions or from an entirely different place (e.g., Dresch 1988). We have also come to recognize how a hierarchy of located topics (or thematized places) has structured research in the discipline as a whole (Herzfeld 1987). I will consider these arguments in more detail below. For the moment, their importance is in highlighting the qualified character of regional specialization in anthropology: a mutually constitutive relation between ethnographic locations and comparative/theoretical topics is the legacy of the "culture area" discourses that have motivated anthropological regionalism for a good part of the twentieth century.

The term "culture area" originally referred to regions variously demarcated by turn-of-the-century ethnographic schools in the several national traditions. Credited to Clark Wissler (1938) by Alfred Kroeber (1939), the "culture area approach" was originally used, especially in Germany and the United States, as a classificatory framework for museum exhibits. Geographic contiguity implied relationship (if not necessarily homogeneity). From this perspective, ethnographic surveys and observations within an area promised to yield evidence of trait diffusion and to suggest culture history or patterning for some anthropologists (like Franz Boas, Ruth Benedict, and Melville Herskovitz) or functional determinacies, cross-cultural typologies, or developmental progressions for others (like G. P. Murdock, Julian Steward, or Leslie White).

The key point is that culture areas were at least equally about culture theories as about areas. They operated as heuristics, organizing grounded particulars for theoretical and comparative ends. Disciplinary sense-making styles have shifted over the past few generations: functional and neo-evolutionary frames have been marginalized in the wake of interpretive, historicizing, and critical ones. The relationships that many anthropologists seek to understand are not necessarily face-to-face or particularly personal. Nevertheless, our impulse to rethink anthropological locations – to demarcate "the field" (our space of primary research) in fresh ways – so as to take account of shifting topical interests is consistent with long-standing "culture area" practice.

An Already-global Regionalism

Anthropological regionalism is an already-global local knowledge: globalization was *foundational* for anthropology in ways that set the discipline apart. Thus, even as culture area constructs encoded (and often enough directly supported) racial and colonial hierarchies, they were not aligned with national borders and were at odds with (if not actively subversive of) the interests and naturalizing claims of nation-states (unlike the other social sciences: e.g., Ross 1991). At the same time as they privileged the study of certain peoples and topics, they nevertheless motivated and organized systematic consideration of those which were otherwise marginalized by the metropolitan focus of other disciplines. Finally, while classical fieldwork was indisputably local, the discipline has deployed topically focused ethnography to comparative/theoretical ends. On one hand, unlike in economics or politics, anthropological theory is mediated by a display of "cross-cultural" knowledge; on the other hand, unlike historical or literary studies, area specialization for its own sake can become a disability over an anthropological career.

However much we may now be especially conscious of global movements and interconnections, the phenomena associated with globalization are not new. Transnational movements were by some measures greater in the second half of the nineteenth century, when academic anthropology was just beginning, than during much of the twentieth century (Kristof 1999; Stille 2001). What is more, the centuries-long ramification of a modern "world system" – its ebbs and flows, and complex relation with the history of nationalism – has long been an object of interdisciplinary attention and debate (e.g., Braudel 1982; Wallerstein 1974).

Anthropologists have been swimming in these currents all along. The elaboration of a European world-system was an enabling condition of field-based, comparative analysis (features that have historically distinguished anthropology from the other social sciences: Ross 1991; Wallerstein 1996; Prewitt 2002). What is more, world-system effects have been a deliberate focus of critical, empirical attention in anthropology for a long time, and not just as "heterodox" undercurrents (cf. Gupta and Ferguson 1997). For example, Franz Boas's critique of early twentieth century racial ideologies was based on a policy-motivated study of European immigrants to the US (e.g., Baker 1998). Melville Herskovitz's sustained interest in tracing African-American traditions across the Atlantic was an influential precursor of contemporary studies of the Black Atlantic.

Robert Vitalis reinforces this interpretation indirectly in an article the main concern of which was to provide a critical historical reframing of Area Studies. He argued that viewing the origins of Area Studies simply in a post-World War II Cold War logic obscures the influence of "international studies": one academic reflex of the longstanding recognition of "globalization". Calling the *Journal of Race Development* "the country's first IR [international relations] journal" (2002: 12), he situated this cross-regional, interdisciplinary project before World War I and also specifically within the theoretic of race studies. This framework was prescient for including the US in a global perspective (something that conventional Area Studies never did, but that work sponsored by the Ford Foundation's recent "Crossing Borders" initiative develops) and for resisting a simply state-centered perspective. Vitalis's focus on historical precursors to Area Studies specifically placed Boas and Herskovitz actively and politically in this long history of "international race/relations/studies" (2002: 15). The implication is that a "global" framework was foundational in modern twentieth-century anthropology, however much our recent awareness refreshes our vision of it.

Anthropological Regionalism in Relation to Area Studies

The qualified nature of anthropological regionalism becomes more evident when juxtaposed to interdisciplinary Area Studies, with which it has been engaged in practical ways – though more so in some places (like East Asia) than in others (like the Pacific) – especially after World War II (e.g., Gupta and Ferguson 1997: 9). In the last few years, the funding agencies underwriting Area Studies programs have reallocated their support in favor of attention to phenomena that crosscut traditional areas. But while the challenge to Area Studies has been quite pointed, anthropology finds itself favorably situated by these moves.

Social Science Research Council/American Council of Learned Societies's (subsequently, SSRC/ACLS) post-World War II funding of Area Studies programs was meant to end the parochialism of US social science and humanities scholarship, disciplinarily separated from one another (as well as from non-US-based scholarly institutions) and substantively focused almost exclusively on Euro-American realities (Prewitt 1996c: 31–2). The Councils' postwar funding structures aimed to elaborate linkages among the disciplines on the model of multidisciplinary classics programs that had existed prior to World War II (Rafael 1994). It also aimed to demonstrate the compatibility of "disciplinary" and "area" knowledge (Prewitt 1996b: 34) by setting up conditions meant to further it.

But the practical demands of the resulting institutional structures – notably, language training – created new, regionalized separations. Additionally, because of the organizational subordination of Area Studies programs to disciplinary departments in universities, area knowledge (not to mention cross-areal comparison) remained peripheral to work in economics, political science, and sociology.

An index of its elevation to the mainstream, "globalization" was the explicit motive for SSRC/ACLS's mid-1990s reorganization of their funding strategies and is the rationale for the Ford Foundation's "Crossing Borders" project. The Councils have pulled out of the committed regional specialisms associated with Area Studies, now seen as undermining the study of transnational and other global processes. But they have reasserted their commitment to what Prewitt called "area-based" knowledge: that is, knowledge acquired through foreign "field study" in and of particular places but (contra existing Area Studies tendencies) this time applied to "processes, trends, and phenomena that transcend any given area" (1996c: 31–2). This reorientation is meant to discourage a purely analytic "globalism" that "floats free of history and place" (1996a: 18; 1996c: 40).

Anthropologists are favorably positioned for such research because of the historical legacy of culture area-style regionalism: its contingent, uneven involvement in Area Studies programs and its historical commitment to cross-area thinking. Anthropologists' intertwined commitments both to field-based study of specific human experience in situated circumstances and to cross-area topics mean that disciplinary and area knowledge – to use Prewitt's terms – are integral in anthropology in ways they are not in the other social sciences (2002).

From Armchair to Open Air Comparison

Despite the various ways in which anthropological regionalism already presumes a global frame of reference, significant rethinking has been necessary within the discipline, particularly with regard to how individual scholars demarcate their primary research spaces and conceptualize their readership. Throughout most of the twentieth century, versions of cross-cultural comparison – whether implicit in translation strategies or explicit in analysis – were key means for making local knowledge (both the anthropologist's and his/her informants') meaningful to likely readers of ethnography. This was, however, mostly an "armchair" activity. While fortunate practitioners seized opportunities for fieldwork in more than one place over their careers (e.g., Geertz 1995), juxtaposing relations, practices, and identities within or between regions was what anthropologists did with their own and other ethnographers' published accounts when they were not doing primary (field) research.

This sort of "armchair" comparison has been progressively displaced from its central position in anthropological debate over the past generation. The very distinction between ethnography and comparison has itself been eroded not only by recognition that interpretation/analysis is implicated in description, but also by an intensifying interest in what many anthropologists now recognize as ethnographic objects and sources that traverse areas. Many anthropologists now demarcate their space of primary research (whether or not they call it "the field") so as to focus on relations among people, things, and ideas in socially and geographically separated spaces. The taken-for-granted local/global distinction (as, say, orders of magnitude) has been progressively unsettled as anthropologists fix their sight/sites on institutions and relationships that motivate or mediate the movements and confusions of categories (Hirsch and Strathern 2004).

The result has in some ways been surprisingly close to the Boasian ideal articulated a century ago (Boas 1896; see also Hannerz 1989's use of Kroeber). Joan Vincent associates this ideal with W. H. R. Rivers and his diffusionist allies in Britain (1990). Drawing on Vincent's account of the diffusionist legacy, Gupta and Ferguson construe diffusionism as a "heterodox" alternative to canonical Malinowskian ethnography (1997: 19–22); but the two appear on a more equal historical footing from a Melanesianist perspective. From this vantage, one notes that while Gupta and Ferguson (44) take Margaret Mead as an exemplar of the post-Boasian turn away from diffusionism, even they cannot avoid at least footnoting her involvement in acculturation studies. And one wonders where to "place" Malinowski's own kula travels and heterogeneous sources in this picture (Wax 1972).

As if echoing these earlier interests, much contemporary work involves tracing the historical and contemporary connections among peoples, things, and ideas – what used to be conceived in terms of "diffusion," "migration," and "acculturation" within or across regions – on the basis of archival and field-based knowledge of those connections and their diverse authors. We have by now a wealth of significant ethnographic, historical, and textual studies, beginning at least in the 1970s with attention to colonial and postcolonial political-economic relations and representations, and expanding in the 1980s and afterwards to include transnational media, consumption and other cultural forms.

Reinforcing all this, Marcus's vigorous advocacy of "multi-locale" or "multisited" fieldwork in the 1980s and 1990s has offered a much-needed methodological language in which these projects might be rephrased. While Marcus (1995) characterized his argument as prospective – as if genuine instances had not yet been put into practice – in fact, it is much more usefully viewed as an explicit general articulation of how many anthropologists have in practice been demarcating their research spaces for quite a while. This may be one reason why Marcus's argument for multisited fieldwork is so multi-cited: his terms clearly capture – as familiar reference to "participant observation" or "fieldwork" may not – the heterogeneous sources on which many anthropologists actually rely.

Multiple Fields, Diverse Practices

I have so far discussed characteristics shared by anthropology's regional traditions, by contrast to alternatives. They also diverge, not simply in the now obvious topical ways (Herzfeld 1984; Appadurai 1988) but also in largely unremarked organizational and practical ones. Unfortunately, however, the discipline's methods literatures (both conventional and critical) presume *one* disciplinary practice *as if* it were a vast attic into which individual ethnographers climb to scavenge opportunistically. They rarely warn of differentiation in regional disciplinary practice – reason enough to suspect that *no one set* of prescriptions is likely to meet present challenges as they are faced in particular projects.

A Suggestive Overview

Among their organizational differences, regional discourses have divergent cross-disciplinary inflections insofar as they have each been influenced by differently configured Area Studies communities (or the lack thereof). For example, whereas Africanist anthropologists are likely to be in dialogue with historians, Latin Americanist ethnography has strong political economy influences. In contrast, research in the island Pacific along with Native America and several other anthropological "culture areas" were ignored by Area Studies funders like the SSRC (with potentially interesting implications: see Lederman, 1998: 432, n. 2).

Intra-disciplinary influences among anthropology's regional communities are uneven and shifting. Regional anthropologies have been differently positioned within the discipline as a whole (a point to which I will return). They also engage one another differently. For example, a dense interplay between Africanist and Melanesianist work specifically on questions of sociopolitical structure was arguably foundational for Melanesianists. In contrast, cross-talk among South Americanists and Melanesianists has been thin overall despite early interest in, for example, apparent similarities between features of male cults in these two areas (Gregor and Tuzin 2001).

At least some of this diversity is a function of the uneven regional involvements of the various metropolitan anthropologies. That is, waves of British (or French) anthropology in Africa and Dutch (or American) anthropology in Southeast Asia were associated with partially distinctive field practices, institutional styles, and topical/theoretical emphases. The varied shapes of work across areas is also a historical product of the especially powerful local influence of particular "schools", teachers, and writers (e.g., Max Gluckman for central Africa, Ruth Benedict for Japan, Claude Lévi-Strauss for South America) or of a more decentralized array of influences (as in Melanesia).

What is more, given how directly engaged in the world anthropological fieldwork is, it would be surprising if regional *non-academic* institutions, politics, and sociocultural styles were not also key. For example, Kan (2001) and collaborators explore the importance of naming and adoption not only as *topics to study*, but as regionally distinctive *modes of ethnographic access* to Native American realities and means whereby Native Americans actively constrained what ethnographers might know; whereas, for example, adoption has not mediated ethnographic access this way in the Pacific. That is, regional cultural styles have themselves had a palpable (but largely unremarked) influence on anthropological research *methods*. Similarly, Schumaker's (2001) Manchester/Rhodes-Livingston Institute-centered history reveals the importance of African field assistants as mediators and shapers of the ethnographic encounter in central Africa. By contrast, in a complex, rueful autobiographical reminiscence, Clifford Geertz describes troubles between the interdisciplinary Harvard Social Relations team (a leaderless and "motley band" of graduate students of which he was one) and their local collaborators (1995: 104–9). The research, set up for the team and a score of Indonesian students by their Indonesian professors, followed a style inherited from a previous generation of Dutch scholars: formal, group interviews with rural village officials conducted at an old resort hotel. Having "the presumptuousness to find the arrangements . . . not to their liking," the Americans successfully evaded the collaboration by lighting out for more distant provinces.

In these and other ways, the projects of metropolitan anthropologies encountered regional/national research communities of long or more recent standing, variously placed (or displaced as in the case of Argentina). They have become entangled with divergent artistic, practical, and activist interests (e.g., Hereniko and Wilson 1999; Warren 1998). Any proper history of "regional traditions" in anthropology would need to trace threads along these complex webs (see chapters 2–5 in this volume). Such a history might clarify how and why ethnographers are indeed "no longer at ease" (in all of Chinua Achebe's complex senses) with their familiar orienting distinctions (inside/outside, home/native/exotic/foreign), making more evident the mutual impacts of transnational and regional forces.

Finally, implicated in the rest, regional ethnographic communities have different background expectations about scholarly practice – training, conferencing, publishing – including the conduct of fieldwork itself: e.g., expectations about language competence, conditions for obtaining research permissions (affiliations, cooperation, and other obligations), the duration of fieldwork, and (as noted above) kinds of incorporation into field settings. A commitment to intensive language learning before and during graduate school may be conventional in Middle Eastern studies, but not for those who work in the Pacific (where one often cannot do much until one has arrived). While long-term fieldwork may be commonplace in Papua New Guinea, short trips are the norm in Brazil as a function of an active national anthropological community.

All this appears obvious, once noted. Their obvious particularity and their diversity may explain why disciplinary histories resist being told from the perspective of fieldworking practices and are told instead from a national (especially metropolitan) perspective. Unlike explicit contestation over the comparative method (e.g., Barnes 1987) or over American anthropology's four subfield relations (Lederman 2005), the Babel of regional anthropologies has gone largely unremarked, at least in the US. (Given their training emphases, it is not surprising that British anthropologists are more aware: e.g., Fardon 1990a; Dresch and James 2000.)

A Closer Look

The diversity of anthropology's regional traditions did become more evident with reflexive attention to ethnographic writing in the 1980s. These interventions helped us to appreciate the interdependence of anthropological theory (that is, the relatively explicit assumptions driving and framing cultural and comparative analysis) on the situated contingencies of fieldwork and ethnographic writing.

In his brief but influential response to Sherry Ortner's "Theory in Anthropology since the '60s," Arjun Appadurai (1986: 356–7) observed that Ortner had not explicitly identified "the significance of *place* in the construction of anthropological theory in the period since World War II," whereas, in fact, theory in anthropology derives from "going *elsewhere* [his emphasis], preferably somewhere geographically, morally, and socially distant" from that of the anthropologist. His key argument about the dependence of anthropological theory on distinctive placedness concerned the reliance on "gatekeeping concepts": "concepts . . . that seem to limit anthropological theorizing about the place in question."

Appadurai's argument was motivated by the problematic of hierarchy, in two senses. First, he argued that the discipline marginalizes certain places, privileging others. He argued that anthropology has had a habit of treating "the small, the simple, the elementary, the face-to-face" found in African, South American, or Pacific places as more emphatically "*elsewhere*" than the "complex civilizations" of India or China. Consequently, topics associated with these privileged places – kinship, gift exchange – have been "prestige zones" of anthropological theory. Conversely, Appadurai noted, "complexity, literacy, historical depth, and structural messiness" have been excluded since they are not distinctive to these central "zones" of discourse. Second, Appadurai suggested that the anthropology of civilizations is particularly susceptible to the reductionism of "gatekeeping concepts." Thus, questions about "hierarchy" dominate anthropological work in India (just as the "honor/shame" dialectic dominates Mediterraneanist research, and so on). Admitting that metonymic simplifications also distort work in Polynesia, Native America, and other places that we associate with face-to-face societies, he nevertheless emphasized that they are "especially pronounced in the case of complex societies." In a review of contemporary Indian ethnography, Appadurai (1988) made clear how an obsession with caste had distorted representations of South Asia.

Appadurai's point that apparently general or comparative discourse in anthropology has covertly regional sources and limitations was sharp and fruitful. He outlined an ambitious set of questions (1986: 359) to which we still have no panoramic response: e.g., concerning the impact of founding works and authors, the shifting receptivity of host governments to anthropological work and changes in the priorities of funding agencies, and other complex interplays between local research practice and the dynamics of research institutions in regional and metropolitan centers.

Nevertheless, two aspects of the argument are worth critical reconsideration. The first is the relationship between gatekeeping ideas and regional specialization. The second is the "simple" society/"complex" society dichotomy.

Consider for whom gatekeeping concepts work. Appadurai's brief paper was not specific, but seemed to suggest that they foil the work of specialists (regional field-workers). In a remarkably overlooked collection, Richard Fardon (1990b) addressed this question explicitly a few years later, suggesting that, rather than being important in the critical engagement of regional specialists with one another, gatekeeping constructs may in fact be reproduced as a tactic in popularizing and teaching. It may similarly affect new researchers beginning fieldwork in an area: providing selective entrance into a specialization (the question being what happens once one is "in"). This suggests an important qualification to Appadurai's argument. Gatekeeping simplifications ("lineage" or "caste," "nation," or "class") may be shaped as much by anthropologists' comparativist or theory projects as by their actual regional specialist work. If these concepts are packages designed for comparative analyses and for teaching, then *their effects may be less "gatekeeping" than "exporting."* Are they more like *lingua franca* elaborated to facilitate exchanges in distinctive disciplinary and inter-disciplinary trading zones, and less like regulators of the internal dynamics of regional literatures?

We might pursue this possibility, following the uses of one such construct (see also Fardon, 1990a: 26–7): e.g., "lineage", so complexly entwined in the Africanist colonial history of British structural-functionalism (Kuper 1982), where Dresch (1988) has reminded us it was already derivative. We can follow "lineage" out of Africa to Highland New Guinea where it was applied and contested from the outset (Barnes 1962). While the first generation of Highland researchers, working in the 1950s, approached their work with simplified, "good enough" glosses of Africanist segmentary lineage models as conceptual bridgeheads, the derivation of these constructs was clear.

That is, early Highlands ethnographers were conscious of the exogenous and heuristic character of "lineage." They did not overgeneralize it: rather they noted its cultural particularity as grounds for their own critical and creative contributions. Not only did Melanesianist research make clear the apparent "Africanness" of the lineage model, over the next generation it expanded its challenge by calling the solidity of its Durkheimian sociological bedrock into question as well (e.g., Wagner 1974).

Intensively over the first two decades of Highlands research, the "lineage" idea was applied, bent, modified, qualified, and discarded. Researchers leaned on and debated one another's work, elaborating an internally critical cacophony of comparativist proposals; exploring, qualifying, or rejecting the others' syntheses and systematizations (e.g., see Lederman 1986a). On the one hand, another set of terms – partially derived from *Europeanist* anthropology ("loosely structured" societies, "non-groups", "networks": e.g., Watson 1970; see Boissevain 1968) – were explored. Melanesian language categories ("big names," "lines of power": Strathern 1984) were adapted or used outright. On the other hand, an argument was joined directly with Africanist anthropology, both early on and in what Andrew Strathern (1982) called a "second wave" of African models in the New Guinea Highlands.

The point is that "lineage" was not used as a gatekeeper by specialists in their basic research and critical analysis. Exported from Africa to Highland New Guinea, "lineage" did not limit the questions asked by Melanesianist fieldworkers but acted as a productive irritant. Inter-regional differences – at least as much as the apparent similarities that enabled the use of "lineage" as a bridgehead term – were a stimulus for discussion and research. Finally, not only was the conscious, reciprocal, critical engagement across several regional traditions ethnographically productive, but it definitely did not respect the distinction between "simple" and "complex" societies that Appadurai employed in his argument.

The same can also be said about "the gift," a notion just as ambivalently located in the Pacific as "lineage" is in Africa. If gift exchange acquired a privileged association with Pacific ethnography in the wake of Malinowski's *kula* and Mauss's *hau*, then this has also been the scene of that construct's reworking (e.g., Weiner 1980). As in the case of "lineage," the regional specialist literature qualified this received category by means of an intensive consideration of Melanesian categories and practices, and their entanglements with economic markets. As in the cases of other rich comparativist categories that prompt reciprocal engagements across languages and cultures, "the gift" has been taken up productively in other regional literatures within and outside anthropology, similarly traversing the simple/complex distinction (e.g., Davis 2000; Finley 1965; Titmuss 1972).

This leads me to the second aspect of Appadurai's argument that needs review. Appadurai's argument about the hierarchical ordering of regional anthropologies was built around a problematic but pervasive dichotomy of "simple" and "complex" societies. He suggested that gatekeeping concepts foil the work of specialists in India, China, and other complex societies especially. Arguing that anthropological theory is quintessentially derived from work in the most elsewhere of others, he suggested that one cannot make a truly successful career in "metropolitan" anthropology if one does not study kinship/gift exchange and the like. What is more, while conventional comparative analyses might work using data from simple societies, it was completely inapplicable to complex societies. But this argument had two unfortunate implications. It implied that abstracting small-scale social orders was unproblematic: *as if* Pacific or African communities were *actually* simple, and not themselves characterized by "complexity, literacy, historical depth, and structural messiness" (*as if* they were the same in their differences from complex societies). It also implied that the disciplinary positioning of the several "civilization" discourses were similar, despite their historically salient, politically charged differences: e.g., a variously orientalized Middle East (or Japan), a normalized and bracketed Europe.

These two implications return us to the problem with which this chapter began: that anthropologists may underestimate the differences among their regional literatures. Indeed, "gatekeeping" constructs – as modes of packaging increasingly subtle (inaccessible) regional discourses for non-specialist consumption within and outside the discipline – may help reproduce an illusion of homogeneity in the act of facilitating communication. Appadurai's own argument rolls the contradiction tight: in making the case against the marginalization of South Asian complexity, it accepts the "simple societies" package. But this rhetorical convenience helps reproduce the very stereotype burdening public perceptions of anthropology generally.

The argument also risks running afoul in another way, insofar as the disciplinary position of research in other "complex" societies is different from that of South Asia. A brief comparison of India with Greece might be instructive. Herzfeld (1986) has argued that a key challenge in understanding Greek self-representations is the ready access foreign researchers have to the nationalist "Hellenic" cultural model. But Greek culture is structured in terms of a dialectic between that more public, other-directed, idealized and classically European self-representation and a demotic, insider's model that Herzfeld terms "Romeic" (a version of the gendered "appearance"/"reality" distinction that Ernestine Friedl (1967) drew). Associated (partially) with private social identities, the Romeic model also admits to more recent, non-European (e.g., Turkish) entanglements. Herzfeld emphasizes the relativity of the distinction, their ability to trade valences, and their resonance across Greek discursive domains: within households, between nations.

Herzfeld uses this analysis of Greek self-representations in a subtle critique of the distinctive positioning of Greece (and then Europe) in anthropological discourse, emphasizing a dialectic of contradictory representations simultaneously in play. Set beside Appadurai's argument, this analysis makes clear that the stereotypification and marginalization of the anthropology of Greece and of India have quite *different* rhetorical and political economic dynamics, emerge from different fieldworker positionings (in the Greek case, clearly a version of the local social dialectic), and require different correctives.

At least with respect to the simple/complex distinction, Appadurai is certainly not unique for strategically overlooking the diversity of anthropology's regional traditions in the interest of a tight argument. The oversight is worth mentioning, in this instance, because of its irony. It is as if the South Asian inflections of the critique were obscured in the rush to expose the regionalisms more *generally* implicit in theory. As a way of avoiding the same, my argument moves into the regional literature I know best to develop a final point, accepting the limitations that such grounding also entails.

Melanesianist Regionalism

If the viability of anthropology in the twenty-first century hinges on our response to charges of "exoticism," Melanesianist work would appear to be in the hot seat. The (not strictly academic) image of "Melanesia" – in the figures of Bronislaw Malinowski (e.g., 1922) and then Margaret Mead (e.g., 1935), both able popularizers – has come to stand for anachronism: field studies of small-scale societies that bracket historical currents and extra-local influences to focus on the exotic practices of an homogeneous Self-defining Other. But to what degree is this "Melanesia" present in the actualities of Melanesianist anthropology (or, indeed, in those of Melanesians, as is implied in arguments that our analytical means need now to catch up with a worldly reality in which, e.g., cultures are "no longer" spatially bounded, homogeneous or historically unaware, implying that they once were so)?

A corollary question might be how Melanesianist anthropology might most productively enact disciplinary self-criticism and redirection. In what ways has the emphasis on difference – for which this literature is renowned – lost or retained its critical value? Will studies of resource exploitation by multinationals or of adventure tourism in Melanesia necessarily help dislodge disciplinary and regional stereotypes or will only certain approaches to these topics do? Are studies of mythology, witchcraft, or exchange passé or will their value be renewed?

Globalizing Anthropology in Melanesia

Contemporary Melanesianist ethnography has been struggling with these questions (for bibliographic references relevant to this discussion, please consult Lederman 1998). Recent works on contemporary Melanesia have included monographs and collections on Melanesian historical experience and representations of regional and global relationships; counter-colonial movements and discourses; self-making and personhood; the cultural construction and political economy of contemporary gender interests; the making of national cultures; and the localization and exportation of transnational corporations. Regionally focused works consistently offer theoretically and topically organized arguments that connect local ethnography with discipline-wide concerns about identities, borders, property-forms and our representations of these things. Collections with a Pacific-wide focus contain important Melanesianist contributions on, for example, the social upheaval attendant on the destruction of material culture and creation of Christian households and on the contemporary legacy of colonial "racial" hierarchies. Other recent work has concerned language shift and loss, media and advertising, collective violence, emergent class interests, and the spread of STDs.

Throughout contemporary Melanesian studies, it is common to find detailed ethnographic descriptions elaborated in relation to equally well developed theoretical and comparative framings. That the ethnography connects itself explicitly with larger disciplinary and interdisciplinary trends is nothing new, however. Melanesianist anthropology has typically been extroverted. By and large, these works carry on the regional habit of contextualized and layered analysis of extended case materials, now integrating face-to-face fieldwork with the analysis of media and documentary sources. They seek out the cultural/historical specificities of novel relationships and discourses so as to understand cultural innovations or erosions in the Pacific – or to refresh our perspective on familiar problems present elsewhere.

This literature also acts on the criticisms of ethnographic representation at large in anthropology. Indeed, Melanesianist anthropology has its own history of textual innovation (e.g., Bateson 1936). These have included, for example, intercultural collaborations, multiply-voiced histories of first contact, contextualized biographies, and reflections on the use of other anthropologists' field notes. As Keesing and Jolly

(1992) note, recent work has tended to make explicit the position of the observer, and to attend to Melanesian criticism of the anthropological project (e.g. Dirlik 1998; Hereniko and Wilson 1999; Foerstel and Gilliam 1992). Critical of the literature to which it is contributing – including the regional designation and its boundaries – recent work is engaged directly in a struggle over the contradictory implications of "exoticism."

In that struggle, discontinuities may legitimately be emphasized over continuities. It needs to be emphasized, however, that the boundary between newer Melanesianist work inspired by a transdisciplinary focus on globalization, and older work on colonial and postcolonial transformations and the dilemmas of development, is not so clear (e.g., Worsley 1957). Melanesian anthropology also has a venerable history of applied socioeconomic research, accessible mostly locally (e.g., the Waigani seminar volumes, New Guinea Research Bulletins, Research School of Pacific Studies working papers and the like).

One notable intervention at the juncture between scholarly critique and activism, and frontal assault on the "savage slot," is Lenora Foerstel and Angela Gilliam's collection, *Confronting the Margaret Mead Legacy: Scholarship, Empire, and the South Pacific*. A commentary on marginalizing objectifications and their historical repercussions (not to say fallout), the collection is integrated by its assessment of Mead's work and its advocacy of a nuclear-free Pacific – made necessary by the political invisibility such representations help to create.

What is extraordinary about this analytically unpretentious collection is its combination of passion and complexity: it makes a challenging model for the critique of anthropology within and outside Melanesian studies. The editors and their contributors, about half being Melanesian, present an unrestrained diagnosis of Mead's paternalism together with a feminist appreciation of her attention to sociocultural change and her efforts to popularize anthropology as cultural criticism. In equally complex counterpoint, the collection offers John Waiko's invocation of the value of deeply situated, "insider" knowledge. In his essay, Waiko thoroughly relativizes his own insiderhood by means of an account of his efforts to submit his history dissertation not only to his Australian university committee but also to Binandere community elders. In this way, he demonstrates how *mutually* exotic interests and positionings might be negotiated and articulated.

Mead's and Waiko's active efforts to bridge the chasm between scholarly and lay discourse are both steps toward a "post-exoticist" world: they also enable us to consider the riskiness of such dispersed authority. Waiko's demonstrates the ground to be gained through reflexive engagement, whereas Mead's serves to warn about the historically shifting valences of an effective public voice.

Conventional Provocations

Melanesianist anthropology has been implicated in "heterodox" trends since, so to speak, before the beginning. Malinowski's showmanship may have been key to unseating social evolutionism in British anthropology, but the way had already been cleared for him by W. H. R. Rivers (1914) who converted from evolutionism to diffusionism midway through his analysis of his own Melanesian field materials. Indeed, if diffusionism is nowadays being reclaimed as precursory to contemporary trends, it has roots in Melanesianist ethnography.

Trans-local regionalism, we might say, is an inescapable ethnographic reality in this part of the world. It appears in the work of anthropologists of all theoretical persuasions and several subfields (including linguistics and archaeology): from Mead (1938) – for whom the Arapesh were an "importing culture" – through numerous studies of ritual and exchange systems linking regional populations and village/clan/ island communities in unstable relations of power and value (e.g., Biersack 1995), and onwards to studies of mythopolitical geographies (e.g. Wagner 1967; Rumsey and Weiner 2001).

These ethnographies of regional relationships often explore *indigenous* comparative discourses and relational identities (Lederman 1991a). For example, representations of movement and both "internal" and "external" difference are prominent in accounts of cosmology and myth (e.g., Wagner 1967; Weiner 1988). The syncretic openness or improvisational inventiveness of indigenous discourses (Wagner 1975) is also evident in anthropological histories of first contact, colonial entanglements, political economic articulations, and gender constructions.

Melanesian cultural styles have presented disorienting challenges to key ideas in academic social theory. For example, arguments about modernity, for all their pro- ductivity across the disciplines, presume a modern/post-modern polarity predicated on "the premodern" – a hodge-podge of the exotic, the rural, the timeless – as a shadowy, illegitimate, background term, even within anthropology. Melanesianist ethnography presents images cutting across these distinctions (and at the same time forcing readers to face this otherwise-residual category head-on). Indeed, regional ethnography had a hard time imagining Melanesian cultures as premodern even when developmental progressions *were* fashionable. The ethnographic literature has confronted this challenge in two (related) ways. It has pursued an extreme elabor- ation of regional comparativism (in the form of endlessly dueling typologies, a cacophony of competing models); it has also explored critical translations ethno- graphically, but in ways that engage categories of significance way outside the region.

As far as typology-building goes, rhetorically unstable analogies abound, dismantled sometimes even in the act of construction: for example, local exchange practices and ideas have been called "capitalist" and "entrepreneurial," or they have looked like capitalism's opposite and then, inevitably, both and neither (e.g., Gregory 1982) in multiple ways. Nowadays, as I have suggested, long-standing descriptions of Melanesians' apparently iconoclastic, improvisational cultural style of dealing with novelty is providing fresh angles on transnational policy concerning intellectual and cultural property (Hirsch and Strathern 2004).

Local ethnography has surely succumbed to – even luxuriated in – the com- parativist temptations that these sorts of decontextualizing translations present (Lederman 1991b). But the arguments those efforts have engendered also often motivated another sort of move. Never simply ethnographic even as it was always elaborately committed to contextualized cases, this regional literature has also resisted Us/Them objectifications. Instead, a more complex movement between extra-regional sources and vigorous argument within the regional studies community has fostered progressively more nuanced and constrained (less transparent, more difficult) translations. Accessibility has often been lost, surely (as novice readers testify). However, it is a mistake to diagnose this as "exoticist" involution. These challenging translations enact Trouillot's call for serious attention to diverse (lower-case) others; articulating explicitly with trans-regional social theory, they are an important reason why Melanesianist ethnography retains its destabilizing value in twenty-first-century anthropology.

Conclusion

The recent formation of problem-motivated area organizations by North Americanists and Europeanists suggests that regional discourses have not yet outlived their usefulness as disciplinary means *even as* anthropological projects and audiences expand and change. Like other scholarly products, ethnography is honed by professional networks of readers oriented to one another by a "prior citational world" and by experiential conditions favoring "cross-checking" (Appadurai 1997). Although perceptibly less so nowadays than in the past, regional communities remain as key practical loci of this simultaneously normalizing and innovating sociability (especially early in academic careers), whereas I suspect that the critical influences of other specialist reading/conferencing networks are diffuse or shifting by comparison. There is no doubt that the situation is changing. Nevertheless, while this chapter's larger argument cautions against inferences across areas, its consideration of Melanesianist work suggests that the discipline's regional engagements have an as-yet unexhausted power to inspire and authorize individual anthropologists' contributions both within and outside the discipline.

Further Reading

Dirlik, A., ed. 1998. *What is in a Rim? Critical Perspectives on the Pacific Region Idea*. Oxford: Rowman and Littlefield.
Mirsepassi, Ali, Amrita Basu, and Frederick Weaver, eds. 2003. *Localizing Knowledge in a Globalizing World: Recasting the Area Studies Debate*. Syracuse: Syracuse University Press.

19

Applied Anthropology

Merrill Singer

Introduction

Applied anthropology, the use of anthropological concepts, methods, knowledge, and personnel to address socially defined problems in human life, has a long, complex, and often troubled history. It can fairly be said that applied efforts have resulted in both some of the best and some of the worst work carried out in the name of anthropology. Moreover, for decades, conflict over its practical application has divided anthropology. Overall, partisans fall into one of two camps, which may be termed the "Science as Knowledge" school, and the "Science for Practical Utility" school.

Anthropologists of the "Science as Knowledge" school identify their discipline's mission as understanding diverse pathways in human social life. They assert that to use anthropology to formulate planned social change violates two basic disciplinary principles: *cultural relativism*, which proscribes judging any given society by the values of any other, and *data purity*, the scientific standard that data contamination through researcher activity must be minimized. Both of these principles suggest that intervention is, by definition, not anthropology. Anthropologists of the "Science for Practical Utility" school counter that science does not exist in a social vacuum, and that its fundamental purpose is to apply its findings to solving human problems and improving the quality of human life. We live in a world of cultural contact and resulting social change that often leads to pressing problems, and we, as a result, are obliged to apply anthropology to real world challenges. Controversy notwithstanding, applied anthropology has a rich and consequential history that is as much a part of the story of anthropology as ethnographic descriptions in cultural context, archaeological unearthing of past ways of life, tracing the pathways of human biological evolution, and analyzing human language (Rylko-Bauer, Singer, and van Willigen 2006).

The objective of this chapter is to review applied anthropology's history in light of its conflicted relationship with descriptive/analytic anthropology. While no small number of anthropology textbooks have ignored application, and there remain departments of anthropology in which practice has only a minimal presence in the curriculum (Shankman and Ehlers 2000), we end this volume on the history of the discipline by placing practice at the center of anthropology's future.

Our understanding is predicated on several global social changes to which anthropology must respond. First, we now live an informational world, in which anthropologists cannot write traditional ethnographic accounts of so-called "primitives" without facing lawsuits from those affected or censure from the discipline for derogatory portrayals of indigenous peoples (Martins 2002). Moreover, even basic research can have significant impact on those studied (Gupta and Ferguson 1997). Second, the lines once drawn between the West and the rest no longer seem defensible – if they ever were (Wolf 1982); problems experienced there have had many of their causes here (where much of the responsibility for addressing them also lies). Finally, while it is clear that technology provides some solutions, it creates its own dilemmas, and often cannot address the most pressing human problems and needs. In today's world, practice is not an option for anthropology if it is to survive; it is the discipline's destiny. There remains a significant role for basic ethnographic research, but the place of application in the future of anthropology is certain.

In his 1976 Malinowski Award Address, Edward Spicer asserted that the organization of the Society for Applied Anthropology in 1941 was "one of the most important events in the development of anthropology during the twentieth century," and a number of anthropologists have understood applied anthropology to have played a pivotal role in shaping the general development of the discipline. Nevertheless, the history of applied anthropology cannot be described as an orderly progression through a sequence of stages leading up to contemporary modes of practice (but see van Willigen 2002); rather, it is best described as a chain of somewhat distinct eras of anthropological application.

The Era of Colonialism

As a distinct, institutionally rooted and named discipline, anthropology came into its own during the nineteenth-century era of Euro-American colonialism. As Willis (1974: 122) emphasizes, "White rule with its color inequality is the context in which anthropology originated and flourished, and this context has shaped the development of anthropology." The discipline has made much of its keen sensitivity to and valuing of the native's point of view and associated intimate friendship-building with key informants, causing its colonial heritage to long remain a burdensome memory. Some early anthropologists were guilty as charged by van Willigen (2002: 20) of supporting "control over native populations in internal and external colonial settings," doing ethnographic research that provided data for the formulation of colonial policy and the resolution of problems that hampered colonial administration (Willis 1974). Other early anthropologists were concerned with assessing the negative effects of cultural contact and colonial subordination. That the information provided by anthropologists (of whatever political inclination) was often ignored by colonial regimes does not erase anthropology's history of invoking practical goals to justify the development of anthropological theory and descriptive research.

In Britain, for example, the Ethnological Society of London, founded in 1843, and its offshoot and rival, the Anthropological Society of London, established in 1863, emerged with a policy interest in colonized peoples. Although the anthropological and political views of the two societies were antithetical, both would have endorsed the general principle published in 1866 in the ASL's *Popular Magazine of Anthropology*: "Anthropology, independent of its scientific interest and importance, may and should become an applied science, aiding in the solution of the painful problems which human society and modern civilization proffer, and tending to the bettering of the conditions of man in the aggregate all over the world" (cited in Reining 1962: 595; see Stocking 1971).

In the United States, an important benchmark of the institutionalization of anthropology was the foundation of the Bureau of American Ethnology (BAE), created with an applied mission as part of the Smithsonian Institution in 1879. Its first director, Major John Wesley Powell, hoped to collect data on Indian peoples that would help to address some of the problems they faced as a consequence of forced incorporation into US society; he was sympathetic to their plight, but he hoped to be helpful in "eas[ing] their transition to the next stages of civilization" (Ervin 2000: 15). As Chambers (1985: 15) notes, this was "a period of serious misunderstanding and massive exploitation of the Indian people of the United States." It is also notable that the BAE in its early years employed such persons as James Mooney, who wrote and testified before Congress about the 1890s Ghost Dance religious movement. Mooney's study (1896) was a work of advocacy, sympathetically portraying the movement as a response to the severe hardships Indians faced following their conflicts with the US military and their forced confinement on reservations.

The acknowledged father of American academic anthropology, Franz Boas, did not consider himself an applied anthropologist, devoting his career to establishing anthropology as a research science. Nevertheless, there was a clear policy objective in some of his most important early work, such as his 1908–10 physical anthropological study of immigrants to the United States and their children, a critique of racial determinism that he himself proposed to do for the US Immigration Commission. Throughout his career, Boas was strongly "committed to the promotion of human equality" (Eddy and Partridge 1978: 12). Nevertheless, Boasian academic anthropology did not focus on addressing social problems, but rather on documenting cultural history and patterns. As Bronislaw Malinowski observed (1929: 4), "Even in the study of the fully detribalized and yankified Indian, our United States colleagues persistently ignore the Indian as he is and study the Indian-as-he-must-have-been some century or two back." Typically, Boasians disdained applied research (just as their contemporaries working in the other human sciences often did), although there were certainly exceptions to this rule. The usual attitude was articulated by Kroeber: "Applied physics is engineering and applied anthropology is social work" (quoted in Hackenberg 1988: 172).

Boas's critique of racial determinism was favorably received in Britain (Marett 1927: 92). But British academic anthropologists differed from their American counterparts in seeing little conflict between so-called pure and applied research, at least until after World War II. Malinowski, one of the pioneers of modern ethnographic methodology, insisted that colonial officials would be more effective rulers if they were trained by anthropologists to be sensitive to indigenous cultural patterns (1929), and he also argued that anthropologists' understanding of the colonial situation compelled them to use their knowledge on behalf of subject peoples (1930: 422).

In general, however, following World War II – and coinciding with the beginning of the era in which decolonization became deliberate policy – anthropologists have been inclined to criticize use of the discipline for colonial rulers' purposes, producing a large literature condemning anthropology as the "handmaiden of imperialism" (e.g., Asad 1973; Bonfil Batalla 1970; Gjessing 1968; Willis 1974). Nevertheless, we must recognize that a recurrent theme in anthropological advice to colonial regimes was that "the existing culture of a people must be made the constant point of reference if administrative and welfare work is to be intelligently planned and effective" (Keesing 1945: 392). As Ervin (2000) notes, even those anthropologists who worked within the colonial structure did not offer unquestioning support, sometimes offering harsh criticism of oppressive aspects of colonial rule. Moreover, opponents of colonialism were found not only in the colonies but also in the West; from the earliest days of the development of the discipline, anthropologists have figured among these opponents. Nonetheless, anthropology's association with colonial rule is a problematic element in its past, with which current anthropologists must come to terms. In this process, it is critical to keep in mind that the relationship anthropology had with colonialism was discipline-wide, not the peculiar misadventure of applied anthropology, and the discipline's relationship with colonialism was more complex than some have suggested.

The Era of Eminence: From Hawthorne through World War II

In the 1930s, anthropology found a new application, in industrial management. Prominent in this work was W. Lloyd Warner, originally a student of Australian Aboriginal life, who joined an experimental project headed by the Harvard Business School's Elton Mayo, participating in the creation of the Human Relations school of management. Warner and his team addressed the relationships among fatigue, morale, and productivity in work groups employed at the Hawthorne plant of the Western Electric Company (near Chicago), finding that social relationships, including informal social networks as well as associated values and contexts, were important influences on worker morale and productivity (although the most important factor was economic reward). The Hawthorne study pioneered the use of anthropology for systematic micro-observation of industry, laying groundwork for subsequent applied anthropological work in industrial and business settings (Baba 1986). More broadly, Warner's work on communities in complex societies, along with work done by such figures as Conrad Arensberg and Solon Kimball provided "much of the theoretical and methodological groundwork for the development of applied anthropology" (Eddy and Partridge 1978: 19).

During this era, however, applied anthropologists often had difficulty in having their policy recommendations taken seriously. Thus, Kimball (1946: 16) complained that it was "impossible to gain assent" for proposals for humane and workable policies from the Bureau of Indian Affairs, while Kennard and Macgregor (1953: 834) pointed to "a curious opposition on the part of the [Federal] administration to anthropologists themselves." Many applied anthropologists found that their recommendations were largely ignored because they violated official conventional wisdom (Kendall 1989). This pattern became so widespread that there emerged an enduring sense among many anthropologists that their inputs are neither valued nor rewarded in the wider society.

Without question, World War II fostered a dramatic, albeit short-lived, shift in the public fortunes of applied anthropology. Suddenly, anthropologists were in demand in a range of government programs. Cooper (1947) estimated that three-quarters of all professional anthropologists active at the time worked for some war-related government department or program on a full- or part-time basis. The role of social scientists in the war effort led to a firm sense that anthropology could make significant contributions to solving human social problems. As Linton (1945: 3) stated, the time was ripe for a new synthesis of the sciences that deal with human beings and their problems.

The Committee for National Morale, established in 1939 and charged with maintaining public confidence during the war, included a number of anthropologists, and was the first social scientific contribution to the war effort. Another government body, the Committee on Food Habits, dedicated to improving the quality of the American diet, also attracted anthropologists, including Margaret Mead, who had consistently sought to mobilize public interest in anthropology, and remained supportive of applied work throughout her career. Another significant venue of anthropological employment during the war was the Office of Strategic Services (OSS), which would become the Central Intelligence Agency. Created by President Roosevelt in 1942, the OSS employed several dozen anthropologists in a variety of capacities, from economic forecasters to spies. Among them was Gregory Bateson (Price 1998), who was initially reluctant to work for a government intelligence organization, but ultimately became an enthusiastic intelligence operative in Asia. Wartime anthropologists also participated in the administration of Japanese American relocation camps. Although many believed (with some justification) that they were acting to minimize the worst elements of relocation for the 110,000 Japanese American citizens forcibly detained during the war (Moos 1995), those involved in this work "would later be criticized both from within and outside of the discipline" (Gwynne 2003: 62) because of the inescapable racist (as well as exploitative) motivations that led to the incarceration of most Japanese Americans, but only a few of those persons whose ancestors came from European countries at war with the US.

After the war, a number of American anthropologists participated in the administration of the Trust Territory of Micronesia (35 of the 42 scientists hired for this work between 1947 and 1949 were anthropologists); these researchers conducted various applied studies and influenced government affairs to an extraordinary degree (Fischer 1979). During this period, a number of other applied anthropologists were sent to Latin America as part of US technical assistance programs. Anthropologists' varied experiences in these diverse settings contributed to the incorporation of development and cultural change as key issues of general disciplinary concern.

It was in the context of this era's recognition of the practical value of anthropologists' contributions that the Society for Applied Anthropology (SfAA) was founded in 1941. The first national anthropological organization with an explicit commitment to application, it was led by a number of anthropologists working in the war effort, including Margaret Mead, Gregory Bateson, and Ruth Benedict – whose *The Chrysanthemum and the Sword* (1946), which began as a report submitted to the Office of War Information in the spring of 1945, would become an operating manual for the American troops who occupied Japan after the war. Starting with a nucleus of roughly 50 anthropologists who attended planning meetings, the SfAA became an association that would eventually have several thousand members, publish two journals and a newsletter, and help to maintain and honor a tradition of practice during the difficult postwar years.

The Era of Retreat: Bitter Years and Brighter Moments

Although applied anthropology gained legitimation with the formation of the SfAA after the war, some of its founders began to question its mission. Bateson, in particular, regretted his role in military propaganda work, and felt betrayed by the mistreatment of indigenous peoples by the OSS. Bateson's retrospective assessment of his wartime activities was duplicated by many applied anthropologists, whose concern that they might have prostituted themselves in government service contributed to a postwar turn from and repudiation of applied work (Keesing 1945).

Anthropologists could afford to disdain government employment in the postwar period because the number of academic jobs during the period increased dramatically, along with college enrollments. Underlying the expansion in university positions was government investment in scientific enterprises during the Cold War years. By the beginning of the 1960s, anthropology seemed centered in the academy. Following a pattern anthropologists had themselves observed in their studies of disparate societies, the new state of affairs came to seem both commendable and traditional. The status of applied anthropology declined, relative to analysis of "abstract problems" (Eddy and Partridge 1978: 64). As Foster (1969: 131) observed, "applied research [was] viewed by a majority of anthropologists as less profound, less scientifically valid, and hence less worthy of applause than research seen as having no immediate practical value."

One exception to this general rule was Action Anthropology, a new, highly collaborative, community-based approach to application. Conceived by Sol Tax and his students at the University of Chicago, it developed during a field school to train graduate students at the Fox (also called Mesquakie) Indian reservation in Iowa

(Gearing 1960). Initially, students were expected to focus on traditional aspects of Fox culture, pursuing the time-honored project of salvage ethnographic description of disappearing ways of life. The initiative for an alternative approach came from the students, who realized that the Fox were aware that they faced numerous problems, stemming from the readjustment of war veterans to reservation life and the struggle to maintain a distinct Fox identity. Tax and his students decided to abandon academic distance and work with the Fox to develop solutions. For this purpose, researchers had to remove themselves "as much as possible from a position of power, or undue influence," Tax observed (1970: 110), insisting that decision-making authority should stay within the community, with anthropologists assisting community members to achieve their own vision. Another action anthropologist, Allan Holmberg, led the Vicos Project, designed to implement the right of self-determination and to demonstrate that scientific methods and knowledge could be used to improve the lives of oppressed communities. Holmberg assumed the role of *patrón* (in the name of Cornell University) of a Peruvian *hacienda*. Over a five-year period, Holmberg worked to expand education, health care, and economic capacity, and was eventually able to transfer full ownership to the people of Vicos, concluding that an "interventionist or action approach to the dynamics of culture, applied with proper restraint, may in the long run provide considerable payoff in terms both of more rational policy and better science" (1970: 84).

A number of important works were published during this era that focused on the human side of international economic, technological, and social development, rather than on seemingly traditional cultural patterns. Written by university-based anthropologists, these included *Human Problems in Technology* (1952) edited by Edward Spicer, *Cultural Patterns and Technological Change* (1955) and *New Lives for Old* (1956) by Margaret Mead, *Traditional Cultures and the Impact of Cultural Change* (1962) by George Foster, *The Silent Language* (1959) by Edward Hall, *Man Takes Control: Cultural Development and American Aid* (1961) by Charles Erasmus, and *Cooperation in Change* (1963) by Ward Goodenough. Through these publications, applied anthropology staked its claim in the field of international development as the discipline that seeks "to know what the client community's wants actually are and . . . take[s] them fully into account" in any planned process of change (Goodenough 1963: 38).

The Era of Rebirth: Struggling toward Reintegration of Diverse Anthropologies

The 1970s and 1980s saw the emergence of the "New Applied Anthropology," as Angrosino (1976) has called it, which emphasized the discipline's role in policy, intervention development, monitoring and evaluation, and advocacy, with a particular focus on health, the environment, education, and human rights. And not least because the academic job market collapsed during the 1970s, a growing percentage of recent degree recipients began finding permanent employment outside of the academy in a wide variety of institutions. Some began their own consulting firms, while a noticeable and growing number found employment in private industry. At the same time, applied anthropologists began finding an expanded array of roles in the government, international development programs, charities, and community based organizations.

Massive growth in the number of applied anthropologists – many of them without university affiliations – led to the organization of the National Association for Practicing Anthropologists (NAPA) within the American Anthropological Association (AAA) in 1983. The establishment of NAPA represented recognition of practice as the basis of a full-time career, rather than, as had previously been the case, a turn that any anthropologist's career might take at some point or points. Intermittently in conjunction with the older but still vigorous SfAA (with which it shares many members), NAPA took up the matters of applied ethics, the need for a core curriculum to train applied anthropologists, and the thorny question of licensing. And a number of anthropology departments began to add classes or even develop specialized training programs in applied anthropology, usually at the MA level. With growing numbers of applied anthropologists working in diverse settings and roles, specialized journals were founded to address their concerns, such as *Medical Anthropology Quarterly*, *Anthropology and Education Quarterly*, *Culture and Agriculture*, and *Nutritional Anthropology*. In the twenty-first century, the discipline as a whole has been forced to rethink its public role and its influence on public discourse about pressing social issues, and applied anthropology is gaining recognition as a distinct fifth subfield of the discipline (Baba 1994; Fiske and Chambers 1995).

The size and nature of this subfield are reflected in data gathered by the AAA, showing that as many as half of all degree-holding anthropologists now work in applied occupations (Gwynne 2003), distributed across many sectors, including positions in academe but not in anthropology departments and possibly outside of teaching (44 percent), the private sector (25 percent), government (14 percent), non-profit organizations (11 percent), and international agencies (1–3 percent). Applied anthropologists' work focuses on a range of tasks, including research (37 percent), teaching and training (24 percent), administration and management (28 percent), and program implementation (19 percent) (Baba 1995). The existence of a thriving community of applied anthropologists, engaged in public issues ranging from A for "aging" to Z for "zoo reform," belies the widespread stereotype that anthropology is a cloistered discipline that has "turned in on itself," in which most anthropologists "direct conversations primarily toward other anthropologists" and "rarely engage in extended discussions, as public intellectuals, with those beyond the walls of academia" (Borofsky 2000: 9–10).

The value of applied anthropology is well illustrated by its use in the social response to the AIDS epidemic, a crisis of global dimensions. Anthropologists have made concrete contributions to efforts to control AIDS, which have been publicly acknowledged (including by the Surgeon General of the US, the Director of the NIH Office of AIDS Research, and the Director of the National Institute on Drug Abuse, among others). Anthropologists working in the field of AIDS have: clarified the knowledge and attitudes of populations at risk; discovered specific behaviors and contexts of risk; assessed the utility of epidemiological concepts and constructs; developed, tested, and evaluated intervention models; and spoken publicly on critical policy issues. Anthropologists are consulted regularly about various AIDS issues, especially about risk behaviors and the social and structural factors that shape them. Over 200 anthropologists have participated in AIDS research, services, and policy initiatives. For example, about a dozen anthropologists have played roles in Project RARE (Rapid Assessment, Response, and Evaluation), a national initiative launched by the US Department of Health and Human Services' Office of HIV/AIDS Policy to develop a scheme for rapid community assessment and public health response to the AIDS crisis in African-American and other ethnic minority communities (Bowser, Quimby, and Singer 2007; Trotter et al. 2001). Adapted versions of this scheme have been adopted by the Global AIDS Program of the Centers for Disease Control and Prevention (CDC) and the HIV/AIDS Bureau of the Human Resources and Services Administration, and a number of anthropologists are involved in similar and related work in collaboration with the Ministries of Health in a number of developing countries, implementing anthropological work on AIDS in settings around the globe.

In addition, there is increasing recognition that applied anthropology is neither a-theoretical nor dependent on academic anthropology for theoretical conceptualization of its work. Rather, applied anthropologists, with their involvement in social change, are distinctive sorts of witnesses, with their own contributions to make to disciplinary theory-building (Kozaitis 2000). Notes Starn (1994: 21), "the concept of insight through engagement ... fits the new view that knowledge can be developed from all kinds of positions: close, distant, and in between ... Activism clearly can be a valuable angle of observation and interpretation in the flow of fieldwork." Social action can lead to new understandings in society generally. As Partridge (1985: 147) stresses, while existing cultural understandings guide practice in society, it is also true that "Practical activity ... is the generative act of cultural construction." Thus Schensul (1985: 171), an early action anthropologist, argues, "application of results is as much a part of the social scientific process as replication is a part of the laboratory research process." In short, attempts at planned intervention provide contexts for testing existing theory and for constructing new theory, while improved understanding enables more effective change (Schensul and Schensul 1978). Applied anthropologists can "simultaneously influence policy formulation, local 'action,' and theory" (Schensul 1985: 186).

Contemporary Applied Anthropology

A good example of theoretical development in applied anthropology is provided by "syndemic theory" (Singer 1996; Singer et al. 2006), which was formulated among applied anthropologists at the Hispanic Health Council (HHC) in Hartford, Connecticut in the process of implementing HIV prevention/intervention among low-income and health-disparity populations. This work began at the HHC early in the AIDS epidemic when funding became available to examine factors in HIV risk and prevention among injection drug users. Building on anthropological insights about the nature of culture, as well as specific ethnographic information about the African-American and Latino communities, a team of anthropologists and health service providers developed a project designed to test the efficacy of culturally informed HIV prevention models for African-American and Latino drug injectors (IDUs) (Weeks et al. 1996). Follow-up study showed that after six months IDUs in the project reported a 58 percent reduction in AIDS risk behavior, based on a composite risk index, with men reporting a somewhat greater level of reduction than women; African-Americans reported the greatest drop in risk, and individuals who participated in the full intervention program showed greater risk reduction than those who dropped out. In terms of the comparison of cultural vs. standard interventions, while differences did not achieve significance both African-Americans and Latinos assigned to culturally enhanced interventions reported greater risk reduction.

The initial project was followed by a second, also built around a quasi-experimental design. In the second project, the focus was on testing the effectiveness of a brief, culturally neutral-risk prevention model against a culturally enhanced model (Dushay et al. 2001), based on the hypothesis that intervention that is culturally harmonious with the target population will be more engaging and meaningful, and consequently more effective, in decreasing the kind and frequency of risk behaviors. Analysis of project findings showed a significant drop in risk patterns in both arms of the intervention, with somewhat greater drops in HIV risk among participants in the culturally enhanced intervention on some variables.

Together, the two projects described above successfully provided risk assessment, HIV risk reduction education, and referral to approximately 1,800 (distinct) not-in-treatment drug users, approximately 30 percent of the active injection drug users in the city. Building on the lessons learned from these two studies about drug use, drug users, and HIV risk, a community collaborative, called the COPE (Community Outreach and Prevention Effort) Consortium, composed of community research and service organizations and the Hartford Health Department, was formed to design and implement HIV prevention programs for injection and non-injection drug users as well as other particularly vulnerable, low-income populations in Hartford, including youth, men who have sex with men, the homeless, and minority women. Guiding work in the COPE Consortium was a sense that the magnitude of the AIDS crisis had resulted in a rush to implement prevention efforts, often with little attention to the assumptions about the nature of human behavior or the theories of behavior change implicit in any intervention approach. Also guiding this work was a commitment to upholding the dignity of project participants and to working for systemic change and community empowerment to overcome the kinds of structural barriers and social injustices that create special HIV vulnerability in some populations.

The first of the intervention projects developed by the consortium, Project CON-NECT (Community Outreach Neighborhood Network for Education, Counseling, and Treatment), which was targeted toward not-in-treatment drug users, was successful in reducing drug-related risk by: conducting street outreach to hard-to-enroll populations; offering testing for STDs, TB, and HIV infection; providing culturally appropriate risk reduction, skills building, and prevention resources; and assisting at least 50 percent of participants to enroll in drug treatment by the time of their six-month follow-up interview. Other consortium projects addressed AIDS risk among inner-city adolescents, prison inmates, and HIV-negative individuals who engage in specific high-risk behaviors.

The consortium also became involved in research on syringe access as an AIDS prevention strategy, using findings on community and drug-user attitudes to lobby successfully with the State Legislature for approval and funding of syringe exchange as well as legalization of pharmacy sale of syringes without a prescription. The HHC was selected by the Hartford Health Department to lead an evaluation of the resulting Hartford Syringe Exchange program. Evaluation findings showed that access to clean syringes is associated with significant reductions in risk and that this trend continues as new forms of access are added to previous ones (e.g., over-the-counter pharmacy sale of syringes), a pattern that was not seen in another Connecticut city where pharmacy access preceded syringe exchange (Singer, Weeks, and Himmelgreen 1995). In addition, combining syringe exchange with a program of education/counseling was found to be more effective than either of these two prevention modalities alone.

These years of applied research with injection drug users, including interviews about their health status and blood assays for various infections, in conjunction with earlier work at the Hispanic Health Council in building a city-wide drug treatment system for pregnant women in the city, led to realization that a narrow focus on HIV precluded recognition of the multiple and closely intertwined health problems faced by the urban poor. Discussion of the co-existence of multiple diseases in our study participants and of the noxious social conditions in which these coterminous diseases tended to be concentrated led to recognition of the need for a concept that would treat these health and social phenomena as not only connected but as forming a single disease complex. The term coined to label this concept was *syndemic* (Singer 1996; Singer and Clair 2003).

The term syndemic is used on two levels: (1), to denote the clustering of two or more epidemic health problems by person, place or time (Milstein 2001: 2); (2), to refer not only to the co-occurrence of several diseases or other health problems but also to the health consequences of the biological interactions among diseases. Use of the term points to the critical role of social conditions in promoting multiple interacting and rapidly spreading diseases. For example, syndemic theory draws attention to the fact that contemporary epidemics like TB, hepatitis, and AIDS are not merely co-present in various populations; they are interacting diseases that spread together in consequence of persistently unhealthy living, working or environmental conditions, as well as unjust and oppressive social relationships (Freudenberg et al. 2006; Singer 1999, 2001). Because of its utility in explaining and confronting pressing public health issues, syndemic theory has begun to be adopted by epidemiologists in the public health service (Milstein 2001).

Conclusions: Controversy in Context

Applied anthropology, while dating to the very origins of the discipline as a whole, has followed a crooked path. At several points along the way, it has encountered strong expressions of derision as well as diminished recognition within the discipline. Consequently, applied anthropology's practitioners have been far more defensive about their professional identities than anthropologists working in the discipline's other subfields. In recent years, a number of anthropologists have attempted to declare an end to doubts about applied anthropology's legitimate place within the field. Nevertheless, assertions that applied anthropology is in some sense "not real anthropology" (Simonelli 2001) continue.

Prominent among the critics of applied work over the years have been anthropologists who view the discipline from the "Science as Knowledge" perspective. As Chambers (1985: 140) notes, "anthropologists not involved in applied work sometimes characterize applied anthropologists as 'opportunistic,' confused in their methodology, lacking in theoretical perspective, and overly subjective in their commitment to 'saving the world.'" In truth, all of these criticisms are accurate with reference to *some* work done at *some* points in time under the label of applied anthropology. But such depictions are unjustified with reference to the subfield as a whole – and are no less accurate with reference to *some* non-applied, descriptive/analytic work by strictly academic anthropologists. Certainly, some applied work has been opportunistic, in the sense that it has been undertaken by persons not motivated by either intellectual commitment to their specific applied task or concerned about their work's potential impact on people's lives, but seeking other rewards, the most obvious (and understandable) of these being the financial security of regular employment. At worst, opportunistic applied work, in which inadequate consideration is given to its potential impact on vulnerable communities, can be disastrous. The most notorious example of this sort of work is Project Camelot, a multidisciplinary project initiated in 1964 by the US Army, and funded at an unprecedented level; ostensibly an effort to understand how social tensions can lead to "internal wars" within various nations and how such wars might be averted, Project Camelot was really designed to gather information that could be used in counterinsurgency efforts against popular liberation movements (Horowitz 1967). At its best, however, applied anthropology has earned considerable praise and assembled an honorable list of achievements through work in medical anthropology, environmental protection, education, international development, policy initiatives, and social advocacy.

Generally, however, criticism of applied work is based not so much on egregious examples of unethical behavior but on transgression of anthropology's historic commitment to cultural relativism. However, as Holmberg (1970: 84) accurately asserts, "Even the most 'pure' anthropologist imaginable, conducting his research with 'complete' detachment and objectivity, cannot avoid influencing his subjects of study or in turn being influenced by them." Moreover, apparently arcane research can have unintended consequences. For example, prior to World War II, Cora Du Bois worked on an atoll called Alor that is now part of Indonesia, but was occupied by the Japanese during the war. Because the Alorese had an established relationship with Du Bois, an American, some of them innocently revealed that they hoped that the Americans would win the war – and were subsequently executed by the Japanese military. As Du Bois realized, "There is no end to the intricate chain of responsibility and guilt that the pursuit of even the most arcane social research involves" (quoted in Weaver 1973: 32).

A further basis for uneasiness with anthropology's involvement in planned social change emerges from the postmodern understanding of culture that gained prominence during the era of applied anthropology's rebirth. The postmodern challenge is exemplified by the study of the Arhuaco of Colombia by Hastrup and Elsass (1990). Toward the end of their research project, Hastrup and Elsass were approached by some Arhuacos, women prominent among them, and asked for assistance in initiating a development program to both strengthen Arhuacos autonomy and to affirm the role of women as "defenders of the Earth." Hastrup and Elsass recognized the soundness of the project, but rejected involvement in it because the community was divided between "traditionalists" and "modernists," feeling that their participation would have involved "speaking for" individuals who wanted the project. They concluded that advocacy and by extension all forms of anthropological intervention in social systems was "incompatible with anthropology as a distinctive kind of scholarship" (Hastrup and Elsass 1990: 301). By the standards they articulated, "no 'cause' can be legitimated in anthropological terms. Ethnographic knowledge may provide an important background for individual advocacy for a particular people, but the rationale for advocacy is never ethnographic" (Hastrup and Elsass 1990: 301).

From the perspective of applied anthropology, Hastrup and Elsass's dilemma is instructive, but their arguments are not convincing (Singer 1994). Inaction in an arena of social contestation is itself a kind of action. By not collaborating with the Arhuaco women, Hastrup and Elsass were, in fact, taking sides. In a conflicted social situation, especially in settings in which gross inequalities are the norm, neutrality is, in fact, a kind of partisanship on behalf of the often-oppressive status quo. Moreover, contemporary applied anthropologists try not to "speak for" but rather to advocate "with" vulnerable populations in their efforts to gain rights or access to needed resources. Most applied anthropologists believe that communities "have the *right* to be actively involved in the management of their destinies, to avoid becoming the victims of others' good [or bad] intentions" (Chambers 1985: 23). Furthermore, applied practitioners believe that anthropologists have a professional responsibility to use their skills to provide critical assistance to those struggling to manifest this right and that in doing so they "must approach community members as . . . researcher[s] intent on helping them to bring about their own visions, in their own ways, and [at] their own speeds" (Egan-McKenna 1990: 11). Finally, applied anthropologists argue that engagement with communities is a critically important arena for scientific insight, including the development of knowledge that throws the "findings" of unengaged research into question.

In his 1999 Malinowski Award lecture to the Society for Applied Anthropology, Thayer Scudder (1999) offered several suggestions for putting anthropology to good use in the future. These provide starting points for thinking about the directions that applied anthropology should take in the twenty-first century. Additional suggestions have been offered by Baba (1994) and others. All of these indicate key issues in the future development of applied anthropology (and hence anthropology generally). They include:

- developing a broader awareness of anthropological capacity to respond to human problems and a deepened sense of our responsibility to do so
- achieving better integration of application and theory
- revising the internal prestige structure of the discipline, which currently favors theoretical work conducted through academic institutions in exotic settings over other options
- integrating public interest and applied anthropology as variant expressions of anthropological involvement in the public domain
- clarifying ethical challenges of application in the diverse sociocultural settings in which applied anthropologists work

Applied anthropologists have been working to further these goals. A number of developments indicate that applied anthropology has, indeed, become a fifth field of anthropology. There has been a steady advance in the literature of the field. In particular, general textbooks, edited volumes, specialized manuscripts, position papers, and topical bulletins are being published in growing numbers (Brown 1998; Chambers 1985; Ervin 2000; MacDonald 2002; Wulff and Fiske 1987). Applied anthropology now has a significant number of identified professionals, generates its own techniques and theories, has its own literature, is represented by its own common-interest organizations, and is often the subject of specialized courses taught at both the undergraduate and graduate levels.

These gains notwithstanding, it is likely that controversies in and about applied anthropology will continue in the future. However, as anthropologists assess their role in a rapidly changing world that is a place far different from the one that gave birth to the discipline – a world burdened by global human problems of health, nutrition, production, technology, environment, education, conflict, population growth, and inequality, a world that may well benefit from anthropological insight – the importance of speaking with a unified voice and for synthesis across subfields is likely to lower the barriers that have divided anthropology and diminished its impact in the public arena.

Further Reading

Castro, Arachu and Merrill Singer, eds. 2004. *Unhealthy Health Policy: A Critical Anthropological Examination*. Walnut Creek, CA: AltaMira Press.

Ervin, Alexander. 2000. *Applied Anthropology: Tools and Perspectives for Contemporary Practice.* Boston: Allyn and Bacon.

Podelefsky, Aaron and Peter J. Brown, eds. 2001. *Applying Cultural Anthropology. An Introductory Reader.* Fifth Edition. Mountainview, CA: Mayfield Publishing Co.

van Willigen, John. 2002. *Applied Anthropology: An Introduction,* 3rd edn. South Hadley, MA: Bergin & Garvey.

Works Cited

Archival Sources

Lord Avebury (John Lubbock), Avebury, Avebury Papers (AP), British Library, London
Franz Boas Papers (BP), American Philosophical Society, Philadelphia
E. P. Chinnery Papers (EWPCP), National Library of Australia, Canberra
Carleton S. Coon Papers (CP), National Anthropological Archives, Washington, DC
Wesley Critz George Papers (GP), University of North Carolina, Chapel Hill
Charles Davenport Papers (CDP), American Philosophical Society
Warren Dawson Papers (DP), British Library
Theodosius Dobzhansky Papers (TDP), American Philosophical Society
Earnest A. Hooton Papers (EHP), Peabody Museum, Cambridge, MA
Aleš Hrdlička Papers (HP), National Anthropological Archives
Macmillan Publishers, Macmillan Archive (MA), British Library
Bronislaw Malinowski Papers (MP, YUL), Yale University Library, New Haven
Ashley Montagu Papers (AMP), American Philosophical Society
John Linton Myres Papers (JLMP), Bodleian Library, Oxford
Erland Nordenskiöld correspondence (EMS), Etnografiska Museet, Stockholm
Erland Nordenskiöld correspondence, 1933–1941 (GEM), Göteborgs Etnografiska
Museum/Museum of World Culture, Göteborg, Sweden
Erland Nordenskiöld correspondence (GUB), Göteborgs Universitetsbibliotek, Göteborg
Edward Westermarck's letters and manuscripts (ÅAB), Åbo Akademis Bibliotek, Hand-
    skriftssamlingen, Åbo/Turko, Finland
Robert M. Yerkes Papers (YP), Yale University Library

Published and Secondary Sources

Ackerman, R. 1987. *J. G. Frazer: his Life and Work*. Cambridge: Cambridge University Press.
—— 1991a. *The Myth and Ritual School: J. G. Frazer and the Cambridge Ritualists*. New York:
    Routledge.
—— 1991b. "The Cambridge Group: Origins and Composition." Pp. 1–19 in W. M. Calder
    III, ed., *The Cambridge Ritualists Reconsidered*. Atlanta: Scholars Press.

—— 1998. "J. G. Frazer, Jane Harrison, and the 'Scientific' Study of Religion." Pp. 129–58 in A. Molendijk and P. Pels, eds., *Religion in the Making: The Emergence of the Sciences of Religion*. Leiden: Brill.

—— and W. M. Calder III. 1978. "The Correspondence of Ulrich von Wilamowitz-Moellendorff with Sir James George Frazer." *Proceedings of the Cambridge Philological Society* 204: 31–40.

Acosta, J. de. 1970–73 (orig. 1604). *The Natural and Moral History of the Indies*. Reprinted from the English translation by E. Grimston, and edited with notes and an introduction by C. R. Markham. New York: B. Franklin.

Agassiz, L. 1850. "The Diversity of Origin of the Human Races." *Christian Examiner*, 4th ser., 14: 110–45.

Allardt, E. 1997. *The History of the Social Sciences in Finland 1828–1918*. Ekenäs: Societas Scientiarum Fennica.

—— 2000. "Edward Westermarck: A Sociologist Relating Nature and Culture." *Acta Sociologica*, 43: 299–306.

Allen, G. 1879. *The Colour Sense: Its Origin and Development*. London: Trubner.

Allen, G. E. 1978. *Thomas Hunt Morgan: The Man and His Science*. Princeton: Princeton University Press.

Andrews, R. C. 1961. *Meet Your Ancestors: A Biography of Primitive Man*. New York: Viking.

Angrosino, M. 1976. "The Evolution of the New Applied Anthropology." Pp. 1–10 in Angrosino, ed., *Do Applied Anthropologists Apply Anthropology?* Athens, GA: University of Georgia Press.

Ankermann, B. 1905. "Kulturkreise und Kulturschichten in Afrika." *Zeitschrift für Ethnologie* 37: 54–84.

Annan, N. 1959. *The Curious Strength of Positivism in English Political Thought*. London: Athlone Press.

Anonymous. 1914. "Proceedings of Societies: Anthropological Teaching in the Universities." *Man* 14: 57–72.

—— 1971. "Historical Relics Unearthed During the Cultural Revolution." *Eastern Horizon* 10(5): 25–7.

—— 2005. "Guide to University Departments." Pp. 73–130, United Kingdom, in the *Annals of the Association of Social Anthropologists of the UK and the Commonwealth*. London: The Association of Social Anthropologists of the UK and the Commonwealth.

Appadurai, A. 1986. "Theory in Anthropology: Center and Periphery." *Comparative Studies in Society and History* 28: 356–61.

—— 1988. "Putting Hierarchy in its Place." Pp. 36–49 in Appadurai, ed. *Place and Voice in Anthropological Theory. Theme issue. Cultural Anthropology* 3(1).

—— 1996. *Modernity at Large: Cultural Dimensions of Globalization*. Minneapolis: Minnesota University Press.

—— 1997. "The Research Ethic and the Spirit of Internationalism." *Items* 51(4): 55–60.

Ardener, E. and S. 1965. "A Directory Study of Social Anthropologists." *British Journal of Sociology* 16: 295–314.

Arneil, B. 1996. *John Locke and America*. Oxford: Clarendon Press.

Asad, T., ed. 1973. *Anthropology and the Colonial Encounter*. New York: Humanities Press.

Ayala, F. J. 1995. "The Myth of Eve: Molecular Biology and Human Origins." *Science* 70: 1930–6.

Baba, M. 1986. *Business and Industrial Anthropology: An Overview*. NAPA Bulletin No. 2. Washington, DC: National Association of Practicing Anthropology.

—— 1994. "The Fifth Subdiscipline: Anthropological Practice and the Future of Anthropology." *Human Organization* 53: 174–86.

Baker, L. 1998. *From Savage to Negro: Anthropology and the Construction of Race, 1896–1954.* Berkeley: University of California Press.

Balbian Verster, J. F. L. de. 1926 "Hoe het Groeide." ("How it Grew.") Pp. 14–16 in *Het Koloniaal Instituut*. Artikelen en Beschouwingen ter Gelegenheid van de Officieele Opening door H. M. Koningin Geschreven voor de Telegraaf. (*The Colonial Institute*: Articles and Reflections on the Occasion of the Official Opening by Her Majesty the Queen Written for the *Telegraaf Newspaper*.) October 9, 1926 (reprint). Amsterdam: De Telegraaf.

Banks, M. and H. Morphy, eds. 1997. *Rethinking Visual Anthropology.* New Haven and London: Yale University Press.

Barbour, G. B. 1965. *In the Field with Teilhard de Chardin.* New York: Herder and Herder.

Barkan, E. A. 1992. *The Retreat of Scientific Racism: Changing Concepts of Race in Britain and the United States Between the World Wars.* New York: Cambridge University Press.

—— 1996. "The Politics of the Science of Race: Ashley Montagu and UNESCO's Anti-racist Declarations." Pp. 96–105 in L. T. Reynolds and L. Lieberman, eds., *Race and Other Misadventures: Essays in Honor of Ashley Montagu in his Ninetieth Year.* Dix Hills, NY: General Hall.

Barnes, J. A. 1962. "African Models in the New Guinea Highlands." *Man* 52: 5–9.

Barnes, R. H. 1987. "Anthropological Comparison." Pp. 119–34 in L. Holy, ed., *Comparative Anthropology.* New York: Blackwell.

Barreto, T. 1966 [1880]. "O haeckelismo na zoologia." Pp. 204–14 in Barreto, *Estudos de Filosofia.* Rio de Janeiro: Instituto Nacional do Livro.

Bastian, A. 1869. *Alexander von Humboldt, Festrede.* Berlin: Wiegandt & Hempel.

—— 1871. "Bespr Darwin, The Descent of Man." *Zeitschrift für Ethnologie.* 3: 133–43.

—— 1872. *Die Rechtsverhältnisse bei verschiedenen Völkern der Erde. Ein Beitrag zur vergleichenden Ethnologie.* Berlin: G. Reimer.

—— 1873. *Geographische und ethnologische Bilder.* Jena: Costenoble.

—— 1877. *Führer durch die Ethnographische Abtheilung.* Berlin: W. Spemann.

—— 1886. *Zur Lehre von den geographischen Provinzen. Aufgenommen in die Controversen.* Berlin: E. S. Mitler.

Bataille, G. 1973. *Theory of Religion.* New York: Urzone.

Bateson, G. 1936. *Naven.* Stanford: Stanford University Press.

—— and M. Mead. 1942. *Balinese Character: A Photographic Analysis.* New York Academy of Sciences, Special Publication 2. New York: New York Academy of Sciences.

Beard, M. 2001. *The Invention of Jane Harrison.* Cambridge, MA: Harvard University Press.

Beck, H. 1951. "Moritz Wagner in der Geschichte der Geographie." PhD Dissertation, University of Marburg.

Behar, R. and D. Gordon, eds. 1995. *Women Writing Culture.* Berkeley, CA: University of California Press.

Beierl, A. et al. 1991. *The Prussian and the Poet.* Hildesheim: Weidmann.

Benedict, R. 1934. *Patterns of Culture.* Boston: Houghton Mifflin.

—— 1946. *The Chrysanthemum and the Sword.* Boston: Houghton Mifflin.

—— and G. Weltfish. 1943. *The Races of Mankind.* New York: Public Affairs Committee, Inc.

Berlin, B. and P. Kay. 1969. *Basic Color Terms: Their Evolution and Universality.* Berkeley, CA: University of California Press.

Bernard, H. R. 1994. *Research Methods in Anthropology.* Thousand Oaks, CA: Sage.

Bernasconi, R. 2003. "Will the Real Kant Please Stand Up? The Challenge of Enlightenment Racism to the Study of the History of Philosophy." *Radical Philosophy* 117: 13–22.

Bernstein, R. 1964. "Peirce's Theory of Perception." Pp. 165–89 in E. C. Moore and R. S. Robin, eds., *Studies in the Philosophy of Charles Sanders Peirce*. Amherst: University of Massachusetts Press.

—— 1983. *Beyond Objectivism and Relativism*. Oxford: Blackwell.

Bieder, R. 1986. *Science Encounters the Indian, 1820–1880: The Early Years of American Ethnology*. Norman: University of Oklahoma Press.

Biersack A., ed. 1995. *Papuan Borderlands: Huli, Duna, and Ipili Perspectives on the Papua New Guinea Highlands*. Ann Arbor: University of Michigan Press.

Binford, L. 1985. "Human Ancestors: Changing Views of Their Behavior." *Journal of Anthropological Archaeology* 4: 292–327.

Binford, L. R. 1962. "Archaeology as Anthropology." *American Antiquity* 28: 217–25.

Bird, M. I. and J. A. Call. 1998. "A Million-Year Record of Fire in Sub-Saharan Africa." *Nature* 394: 767–9.

Blakey, M. L. 1987. "Skull Doctors: Intrinsic Social and Political Bias in the History of American Physical Anthropology, With Special Reference to the Work of Aleš Hrdlička." *Critique of Anthropology* 7: 7–35.

Blanckaert, C. 1988a. " 'Story' et 'history' de l'ethnologie." *Revue de synthèse* 4(3–4): 451–67.

—— 1988b. "On the Origins of French Ethnology. William Edwards and the Doctrine of Race." Pp. 18–55 in G. Stocking, ed. *Bones, Bodies and Behavior. Essays in Biological Anthropology*. Madison: University of Wisconsin Press.

—— 1989. "L'anthropologie personnifiée" Paul Broca et la biologie du genre humain, Preface to P. Broca, *Mémoires d'anthropologie*. Paris: Gradhiva, i–xliii.

—— 1995a. "Fondements disciplinaires de l'anthropologie française au XIXe siècle. *Perspectives historiographiques*." *Politix* 29: 31–54.

—— 1995b. "Le premessee dell'antropologia 'culturale' in Francia. Il dibattito sul 'Questionnaire de Sociologie et d'Ethnographie' di Charles Letourneau (1882–1883)." *La Ricerca Folklorica* 32: 51–70.

—— ed. 1996a. *Le terrain des sciences humaines (XVIIIe–XIXe)*. Paris: L'Harmattan.

—— 1996b. "Les deux parties du problème. Renan et l'ethnographie (1848–1865)." *Etudes renaniennes* 10: 62–89.

—— 2001. *Les politiques de l'anthropologie. discours et pratiques en France (1860–1940)*. Paris: L'Harmattan.

Bloch, M. 1988. "Interview with Gustaaf Houtman." *Anthropology Today* 4(1): 18–21.

Bloembergen, M. 2001. *De Koloniale Vertoning: Nederland en Indië op de Wereldtentoonstellingen (1880–1931)*. (Colonial Display: The Netherlands and East India at the World Exhibits (1880–1931). Amsterdam: Wereld Bibliotheek.

Boas, F. 1896. "Limitations of the Comparative Method of Anthropology." *Science* 4: 901–8.

—— 1911a. *The Mind of Primitive Man*. New York: Macmillan.

—— 1911b. "Introduction." *Handbook of American Indian Languages*. Washington: Smithsonian Institution.

—— 1916. "Eugenics." *Scientific Monthly* 3: 471–9.

—— 1974. "Rudolf Virchow's Anthropological Work." Pp. 36–41 in G. W. Stocking, Jr, ed. *The Shaping of American Anthropology, 1883–1911*. New York: Basic Books.

Boissevain, J. 1968. "The Place of Non-groups in the Social Sciences." *Man* n.s. 3: 542–56.

Bonfil Batalla, B. G. 1970. "Conservative Thought in Applied Anthropology: A Critique." Pp. 246–53 in James Clifton, ed., *Applied Anthropology: Readings in the Uses of the Science of Man.* New York: Houghton Mifflin.

Boon, J. A. 1982. *Other Tribes, Other Scribes: Symbolic Anthropology in the Comparative Study of Cultures, Histories, Religions, and Texts.* New York: Cambridge University Press.

Borofsky, R. 2000. *Remembrance of Pacific Pasts: An Invitation to Remake History.* Honolulu: University of Hawaii Press.

Bowser, B. P., E. Quimby and M. Singer, eds. 2007. *Communities Assessing Their AIDS Epidemics: Results of the Rapid Assessment of HIV/AIDS in U.S. Cities.* Lanham, MD: Lexington Books.

Boyd, W. C. 1963. "Genetics and the human race." *Science* 140: 1057–65.

Brace, C. L. 1964. "The Fate of the "Classic" Neanderthals: A Consideration of Hominid Catastrophism." *Current Anthropology* 5: 3–43.

—— 1995. "Region Does Not Mean 'Race' – Reality versus Convention in Forensic Anthropology." *Journal of Forensic Sciences* 40: 171–5.

—— 2000. *Evolution in an Anthropological View.* New York: Rowman and Littlefield.

Brandom, R. B. 2000. *Articulating Reasons: An Introduction to Inferentialism.* Cambridge: Harvard University Press.

Braudel, F. 1982–84. *Civilization and Capitalism: 15th–18th Century.* New York: Harper and Row.

Briggs, C. 2002. "Linguistic Magic Bullets in the Making of a Modernist Anthropology." *American Anthropologist* n.s. 104: 481–98.

Brinton, D. G. 1890. *Races and Peoples.* New York: Hodges.

Broca, P. 1864. *The Phenomena of Hybridity in the Genus Homo.* London: Longman, Green & Roberts.

Brower, D. R. and E. J. Lazzerini, eds. 1997. *Russia's Orient: Imperial Borderlands and Peoples, 1700–1917.* Bloomington: Indiana University Press.

Brown, Peter, ed. 1998. *Understanding and Applying Medical Anthropology.* Mountainview, CA: Mayfield Publishing Co.

Bruckner, S. A. 1999. "The Tingle-Tangle of Modernity: Popular Anthropology and the Cultural Politics of Identity in Imperial Germany." PhD Dissertation, University of Iowa.

Brunius, S. 1984. "Carl V. Hartman: Svensk arkeolog – etnograf i Centralamerika" (Carl V. Hartman: Swedish Archaeologist – Ethnographer in Central America"). Stockholm: Institute of Latin American Studies, Occasional Papers.

Bunzl, M. 1996. "Franz Boas and the Humboldtian Tradition: From Volksgeist and Nationalcharakter to an Anthropological Concept of Culture," Pp. 17–78 in George W. Stocking, Jr., ed., *Volksgeist as Method and Ethic: Essays on Boasian Ethnography and the German Anthropological Tradition.* Madison: University of Wisconsin Press.

—— and H. G. Penny. 2003. "Worldly Provincials: Rethinking German Anthropology, Colonialism, and Race," Pp. 1–30 in Bunzl and Penny, eds., *Worldly Provincialism: German Anthropology in the Age of Empire.* Ann Arbor: University of Michigan Press.

Burkert, W. 1983. *Homo Necans: The Anthropology of Ancient Greek Sacrificial Ritual and Myth.* Berkeley: University of California Press.

—— 1996. *Creation of the Sacred: Tracks of Biology in Early Religions.* Cambridge: Harvard University Press.

Burrow, J. 1966. *Evolution and Society*, rev. edn. Cambridge: Cambridge University Press.

Buschmann, R. 1999. "The Ethnographic Frontier in German New Guinea (1870–1919)." PhD Dissertation, University of Hawaii.

—— 2000. "Exploring Tensions in Material Culture." Pp. 55–79 in M. O'Hanlon and R. Welsch, eds., *Hunting the Gatherers: Collectors, Agents and Agency in Melanesia 1870–1930s*. New York: Berghahn.

Butler, J. 1990. *Gender Trouble*. New York: Routledge.

Byrne, P. 1989. *Natural Religion and the Nature of Religion*. London: Routledge.

Caillois, R. 1950. *Man and the Sacred*. New York: Free Press.

Calder, W. M. III. 1991. "Jane Harrison's Failed Candidacies for the Yates Professorship (1888, 1896): What Did Her Colleagues Think of Her?" Pp. 37–59 in W. M. Calder III, ed., *The Cambridge Ritualists Reconsidered*. Atlanta: Scholars Press.

Caldwell, J. R. 1959. "The New American Archeology." *Science* 129: 303–7.

Calvin, W. H. 2002. *A Brain for All Seasons: Human Evolution and Abrupt Climate Change*. Chicago: University of Chicago Press.

Campbell, M. 1988. *The Witness and the Other World: Exotic European Travel Writing, 400–1600*. Ithaca: Cornell University Press.

Candido, Antonio. 1988. *O método crítico de Silvio Romero*. São Paulo: EDUSP.

Carrier, J. 1992. "Introduction." Pp. 1–37 in J. Carrier, ed., *History and Tradition in Melanesian Anthropology*. Berkeley: University of California Press.

Cartmill, M. 1993. *A View to a Death in the Morning: Hunting and Nature Through History*. Cambridge, MA: Harvard University Press.

Castells, M. 1996. *The Information Age: Economy, Society and Culture*. Vol 1: *The Rise of the Network Society*. Oxford: Blackwell.

Castle, W. E. 1930. "Race Mixture and Physical Disharmonies." *Science* 71: 603–6.

Castro Faria, L. de. 2003. "R. Virchow e as comunicações apresentadas à Sociedade Berlinense de Antropologia, Etnologia e Pré-história (Os relatórios de Kreplin e A. von Eye. A coleção Stegemann)." Pp. 125–43 in H. Domingues, M. R. Sá, and T. F. Glick, eds. *A recepção do Darwinismo no Brasil*. Rio de Janeiro: Fiocruz.

Cervantes, F. 1994. *The Devil in the New World: The Impact of Diabolism in New Spain*. New Haven: Yale University Press.

Cesara, M. 1982. *Reflections of a Woman Anthropologist: No Hiding Place*. London: Academic Press.

Chailleu, L. 1990. "Histoire de la société d'ethnographie. La Revue orientale et americaine (1858–1879). Ethnographie, orientalisme et americanisme au XIXe siècle." *L'Ethnographie* 86: 89–107.

Chambers, E. 1985. *Applied Anthropology: A Practical Guide*. Prospect Heights: Waveland Press.

Chanet, J.-F. 1988. "Maîtres d'école et regionalisme en France sous la troisième republique." *Ethnologie Française* 18, 3: 244–56.

Chang, K. C. 1977. "Chinese Paleoanthropology." *Annual Review of Anthropology* 6: 137–59.

Chang, S. 1984. "Art in the Mogao Caves at Dunhuang." In F. Stockwell and B. Tang, eds., *Recent Discoveries in Chinese Archaeology: 28 Articles by Chinese Archaeologists Describing their Excavations*. Beijing: Foreign Languages Press.

Chapman, W. R. 1985. "Arranging Ethnology: A. H. L. F. Pitt Rivers and the Typological Tradition." Pp. 15–48 in George W. Stocking, Jr., ed., *Objects and Others: Essays on Museums and Material Culture*. Madison: University of Wisconsin Press.

Chappey, J.-L. 2002. *La Société des observateurs de l'homme (1799–1804)*. Paris: Sociétédes etudes robespierristes.

Chen, X. 1997. *Zhongguo shiqian kaogu xue shi yanjiu, 1895–1949* (Research on the history of prehistoric archaeology in China). Beijing: Sanlian shudian.

Chicherin, B. N. 1858. *Opyty po istorii russkago prava* (Enquiries concerning the history of the Russian law). Moscow: Izdanie K. Soldatenkova i N. Shchepkina.

—— 1899. *O narodnom predstavitel'stve* (*On popular representation*). Moscow: Tipografia Tovarishchestva I. D. Sytina.

Claeys, G. 2000. "The 'Survival of the Fittest' and the Origins of Social Darwinism." *Journal of the History of Ideas.* 61: 223–40.

Clark, J. F. M. 1997. " 'The Ants Were Duly Visited': Making Sense of John Lubbock, Scientific Naturalism and the Senses of Social Insects." *British Journal for the History of Science* 30: 151–76.

Clay, C. 1995. "Russian Ethnographers in the Service of Empire, 1851–1862." *Slavic Review* 1: 45–61.

Clifford, J. 1988. *The Predicament of Culture.* Cambridge, MA: Harvard University Press.

—— 1997. "Spatial Practices: Fieldwork, Travel, and the Disciplining of Anthropology." Pp. 185–222 in A. Gupta and J. Ferguson, eds., *Anthropological Locations: Boundaries and Grounds of a Field Science.* Berkeley: University of California Press.

—— 2005. "Rearticulating Anthropology." Pp. 24–48 in D. A. Segal and S. J. Yanagisako, eds., *Unwrapping the Sacred Bundle: Reflections on the Disciplining of Anthropology.* Durham: Duke University Press.

—— and G. Marcus, eds. 1986. *Writing Culture: The Politics and Poetics of Ethnography.* Berkeley: University of California Press.

Cohen, M. 1993. "Cultural and Political Inventions in Modern China: The Case of the Chinese 'Peasant'." *Daedalus* 122(2): 151–70.

Cole, D. 1999. *Franz Boas: The Early Years, 1858–1906.* Seattle: University of Washington Press.

Columbus, C. 1968. *The Journal of Christopher Columbus* translated by C. Jane and with a foreword by L. A. Vigneras. London: Anthony Blond.

—— 1989. *The "Diario" of Christopher Columbus's First Voyage to America, 1492–1493. Abstracted by F. B. de las Casas,* ed. and trans. O. Dunn and J. E. Kelley, Jr. Norman: University of Oklahoma Press.

Comas, J. 1961. "Scientific racism again?" *Current Anthropology* 2: 303–40.

Congrès International des Américanistes. 1925. *Compte-rendu de la XXIe Session, Deuxième Partie, Tenue a Göteborg en 1924.* Göteborg: Göteborgs Museum.

Conkey, M. W., with S. H. Williams. 1991. "Original Narratives: The Political Economy of Gender in Archaeology," Pp. 102–39 in M. di Leonardo, ed., *Gender at the Crossroads of Knowledge: Feminist Anthropology in the Postmodern Era.* Berkeley: University of California Press.

Conklin, A. L. 2002a. "Civil Society, Science, and Empire in Late Republican France: The Foundation of Paris's Museum of Man." *Osiris* n.s. 17: 255–90.

—— 2002b. "The New 'Ethnology' and 'La Situation Coloniale' in Interwar France." *French Politics, Culture and Society* 20(2): 29–46.

Coon, C. S. 1954. *The Story of Man.* New York: Alfred A. Knopf.

—— 1962. *The Origin of Races.* New York: Alfred A. Knopf.

—— 1963. "Origin of Races." *Science* 140: 208.

—— 1981. *Adventures and Discoveries.* Englewood Cliffs, NJ: Prentice-Hall.

Coon, C., S. Garn, and J. Birdsell, J. 1950. *Races.* Springfield, IL: Charles C. Thomas.

Cooper, J. 1947. "Anthropology in the United States During 1939–1945." *Société des Americanistes des Paris Journal* 36: 1–14.

Costa Lima, L. 1988. *Control of the Imaginary: Reason and Imagination in Modern Times.* Minneapolis: University of Minnesota Press.

Coulter, J. and E. D. Parsons. 1989. "The Praxiology of Perception: Visual Orientations and Practical Action." *Inquiry* 33: 251–72.

Dalton, O. M. 1898. *Report on Ethnographic Museums in Germany.* London: Her Majesty's Stationery Office.

Dampier, W. 1927. *A New Voyage Round the World.* London: Argonaut Press.

Danto, A. and S. Morgenbesser. 1960. *Philosophy of Science.* Cleveland: Meridian Press. (contains "The Assayer" by Galileo).

Darnell, R. 1977. "The History of Anthropology in Anthropological Perspective." *Annual Review of Anthropology* 6: 399–417.

—— 1988. *Daniel Garrison Brinton: The "Fearless Critic" of Philadelphia.* Philadelphia: University of Pennsylvania Publications in Anthropology.

—— 1990. *Edward Sapir: Linguist, Anthropologist, Humanist.* Berkeley: University of California Press.

—— 1997. "Changing Patterns of Ethnography in Canadian Anthropology." *Canadian Review of Sociology and Anthropology* 34: 269–96.

—— 1998a. *And Along Came Boas: Continuity and Revolution in Americanist Anthropology.* Amsterdam/Philadelphia: John Benjamins.

—— 1998b. "Toward a History of Canadian Departments of Anthropology." *Anthropologica* 40: 153–68.

—— 2000. "Canadian Anthropologists, the First Nations, and Canada's Self-Image at the Millennium." *Anthropologica* 42: 165–74.

—— 2001. *Invisible Genealogies: A History of Americanist Anthropology.* Lincoln: University of Nebraska Press.

Darwin, C. 1868. *The Variation of Animals and Plants under Domestication.* London: John Murray.

—— 1985– . *The Correspondence of Charles Darwin.* 13 vols to date. Cambridge: Cambridge University Press.

—— 2004 [1871]. *The Descent of Man.* New York: Penguin.

Daston, L. 1982. "Theory of Will Versus Science of Mind." Pp. 88–115 in W. R. Woodward and M. G. Ash, eds., *The Problematic Science: Psychology in Nineteenth-Century Thought.* New York: Praeger.

—— and P. Galison, 1992. "The Image of Objectivity." *Representations* 40: 81–128.

Davenport, C. B. 1911. *Heredity in Relation to Eugenics.* New York: Henry Holt.

Davidson, I., and W. Noble. 1993. "Tools and Language in Human Evolution." Pp. 363–88 in K. R. Gibson and T. Ingold, eds., *Tools, Language, and Cognition in Human Evolution.* Cambridge: Cambridge University Press.

Davis, C. 1999. *Death in Abeyance: Illness and Therapies among the Tabwa of Central Africa.* Edinburgh: Edinburgh University Press.

Davis, N. Z. 2000. *The Gift in Early Modern France.* Madison: University of Wisconsin Press.

de Certeau, M. 1980. "Writing vs. Time. History and Anthropology in the works of Lafitau." Pp. 37–64 in M.-R. Logan and J. F. Logan, eds., *Rethinking History: Time, Myth, and Writing.* New Haven: Yale University Press.

—— 2000. "Ethno-Graphy. Speech, or the Space of the Other: Jean de Lèry." Pp. 129–49 in G. Ward, ed., *The Certeau Reader.* Oxford: Blackwell.

de Groot, J. J. M. 1891. *Over het Belang der Kennis van China voor onze Koloniën, uit een Politiek en Wetenschappelijk Oogpunt.* (On the Importance of Knowledge about China for our Colonies, from a Political and Scholarly Perspective.) Inaugural Address: University of Leiden. Leiden: E. J. Brill.

de Waal, F. B. M. 1999. "Cultural Primatology Comes of Age." *Nature* 399: 635–6.

Defoe, D. 1985 [1719]. *The Life and Adventures of Robinson Crusoe*. London: Penguin.

DeGusta, D., et al. 1999. "Hypoglossal Canal Size and Hominid Speech." *Proceedings of the National Academy of Sciences* 96: 1800–04.

Deitch, L. 1920. *Khozhdenie v narod. Iz vospominanii (Going to the people. Memoirs)*. Petrograd: Gosizdatel'stvo.

—— 1921. Pp. 73–9 in "Zagovor sredi krestian Chiriginskogo uiezda (iz arkhiva III otdelenia)" (The conspiracy among the peasants of the Chiriginsk district: the materials from the archive of the Third Department). In *Sbornik materialov i statei*, Vypusk I, Moscow.

Dekker, J. 1913. *Reisindrukken van den Directeur der Afdeeling "Handelsmuseum." (Travel Impressions of the Director of the Department "Trade Museum".)* Amsterdam: Vereeniging "Koloniaal Instituut."

Deloria, P. 1998. *Playing Indian*. New Haven: Yale University Press.

DeParle, J. 1994. "Daring Research or 'Social Science Pornography'?" *The New York Times Magazine*. October 9: 48–50, 62, 70–1, 74, 78–9.

DeVore, I. 1992. "An Interview with Sherwood Washburn." *Current Anthropology* 33: 411–23.

Diamond, S. 1962. "Culture and Race." *Science* 135: 961–4.

—— 1974. *In Search of the Primitive: A Critique of Civilization*. New Brunswick, NJ: Transaction Books.

Dias, N. 1991. *Le musée d'ethnographie du Trocadero (1878–1908). Anthropologie et museologie en France*. Paris: Editions du Cnrs.

Di Gregorio, M. A. 1984. *T. H. Huxley's Place in Natural Science*. New Haven: Yale University Press.

Dimier, V. 2004a. *Le gouvernement des colonies: regards croises franco-britanniques*. Brussels: Editions de l'Université de Bruxelles.

—— 2004b. "Le commandant de cercle: un 'expert' en administration coloniale, un 'specialiste' de l'indigene?" *Revue d'histoire des sciences humaines* 10: 39–58.

Dirlik, A., ed. 1998. *What Is in a Rim? Critical Perspectives on the Pacific Region Idea*. New York: Rowman and Littlefield.

Dodds, E. R. 1951. *The Greeks and the Irrational*. Berkeley: University of California Press.

Douglas, M. 1970. *Purity and Danger*. London: Penguin.

—— 1973. *Natural Symbols*. New York: Vintage.

—— 1980. *Evans-Pritchard*. London: Fontana.

Dresch, P. 1988. "Segmentation: Its Roots in Arabia and its Flowering Elsewhere." Pp. 50–67 in A. Appadurai, ed., *Place and Voice in Anthropological Theory: Theme Issue. Cultural Anthropology* 3(1).

Dresch, P., W. James, D. Parkin, eds. 2000. *Anthropologists in a Wider World: Essays on Field Research*. New York: Berghahn.

Duranti, A. 2003. "Language as Culture in U. S. Anthropology." *Current Anthropology* 44: 323–47.

Durham, W. H. 1991. *Coevolution: Genes, Culture and Human Diversity*. Stanford: Stanford University Press.

Durkheim, É. 1975. "Contribution to Discussion 'Religious Sentiment at the Present Time'." Pp. 181–9 in *Durkheim on Religion*, ed. W. S. F. Pickering. London: Routledge.

—— 1995 [1912]. *The Elementary Forms of Religious Life*, trans. K. E. Fields. New York: Free Press.

Dushay, R., M. Singer, M. Weeks, L. Rohena, and R. Gruber. 2001. "Lowering HIV Risk Among Ethnic Minority Drug Users: Comparing Culturally Targeted Intervention to a Standard Intervention." *American Journal of Drug and Alcohol Abuse* 27: 504–24.

Eckhardt, R. B. 2000. "The Dangers in Editing Past Human History to Fit Present Methodological Constraints." *Kroeber Anthropological Society Papers* 84: 45–58.

Eckholm, E. 2000. "In China, Ancient History Kindles Modern Doubts." *The New York Times*, November 10.

Eddy, E. and W. Partridge. 1978. *Applied Anthropology in America*. New York: Columbia University Press.

Edwards, E. 1990. "Photographic 'Types': The Pursuit of Method." *Visual Anthropology* 3: 235–58.

—— ed. 1992. *Anthropology and Photography, 1860–1920*. New Haven: Yale University Press.

—— 1998. "Performing Science: Still Photography and the Torres Strait Expedition." Pp. 106–35 in A. Herle and S. Rouse, eds., *Cambridge and the Torres Strait: Centenary Essays on the 1898 Anthropological Expedition*. Cambridge: Cambridge University Press.

—— 2001 "Re-enactment, Salvage Ethnography and Photography in the Torres Strait." Pp. 157–80 in *Raw Histories: Photographs, Anthropology and Museums*. Oxford: Berg.

Edwards, S. W. 1978. "Nonutilitarian Activities in the Lower Paleolithic: A Look at the Two Kinds of Evidence." *Current Anthropology* 19: 135–9.

Effert, F. R. 1992. *J. P. B. de Josselin de Jong: Curator and Archaeologist, A Study of his Early Career (1910–1935)*. Leiden: CNWS.

—— 2003. *Volkenkundig Verzamelen: Het Koninklijk Kabinet van Zeldzaamheden en het Rijks Ethnographisch Museum 1816–1883*. (Ethnographic Collecting: The Royal Cabinet of Rarities and the National Museum of Ethnology). PhD Dissertation, University of Leiden.

Egan-McKenna, G. 1990. "'May I Help?' The Applied Anthropologist and Indian Self-Determination." *Practicing Anthropologist* 12: 7–11.

Eliade, M. 1954. *The Myth of the Eternal Return*. New York: Harper.

—— 1957. *The Sacred and the Profane*. New York: Harcourt, Brace.

—— 1958. *Patterns in Comparative Religion*. London: Sheed and Ward.

Ellen, R. F. 1976. "The Development of Anthropology and Colonial Policy in the Netherlands: 1800–1960." *Journal of the History of the Behavioral Sciences* 12: 303–24.

Elliott, J. H. 1972. *The Old World and the New, 1492–1650*. Cambridge: Cambridge University Press.

Elman, B. A. 1984. *From Philosophy to Philology: Intellectual and Social Aspects of Change in Late Imperial China*. Cambridge, MA: Harvard University Press.

Engel'gardt, A. N. 1987 [1872–1887]. *Iz derevni: 12 pisem (From the village: twelve letters)*. Moscow: Mysl.

Engelke, M. 2004. "'The Endless Conversation': Fieldwork, Writing, and the Marriage of Victor and Edith Turner." Pp. 6–50 in R. Handler, ed., *Significant Others: Interpersonal and Professional Commitments in Anthropology*. Madison: University of Wisconsin Press.

Engels, F. 1942 [1884]. *The Origin of the Family, Private Property and the State*. New York: International Publishers.

—— 1995 [1892]. "A Recently Discovered Case of Group Marriage." Pp. 165–8 in B. Grant, ed., *In the Soviet House of Culture*. Princeton: Princeton University Press.

Entine, J. 2000. *Taboo: Why Black Athletes Dominate Sports and Why We're Afraid to Talk About It*. Washington: Public Affairs Press.

Erasmus, C. 1961. *Man Takes Control: Cultural Development and American Aid*. Indianapolis: Bobbs-Merrill.

Errington, F. 2001. "Colonial Linguistics." *Annual Review of Anthropology* 31: 19–39.

Ervin, A. 2000. *Applied Anthropology: Tools and Perspectives for Contemporary Practice*. Boston: Allyn and Bacon.

Essner, C. 1985. *Deutsche Afrikareisende im neunzehnten Jahrhundert: Zur Sozialgeschichte des Reisens.* Stuttgart: Steiner Verlag.

Etler, D. A. 1994. "The Chinese Hominidae: New Finds, New Interpretations." PhD dissertation, University of California, Berkeley.

Evans, A. 2002. "Anthropology at War: World War I and the Science of Race in Germany." PhD Dissertation, University of Indiana.

Evans-Pritchard, E. E. 1940. *The Nuer.* Oxford: Oxford University Press.

—— 1956. *Nuer Religion.* Oxford: Oxford University Press.

—— 1962. "Religion and the Anthropologists." Pp. 29–45 in his *Essays in Social Anthropology.* London: Faber and Faber.

—— 1976 [1937]. *Witchcraft, Oracles and Magic among the Azande.* Oxford: Oxford University Press.

Eze, E. C. 2000. "Hume, Race, and Human Nature." *Journal of the History of Ideas* 61: 691–8.

Fabian, J. 1983. *Time and the Other: How Anthropology Makes its Object.* New York: Columbia University Press.

Faison, S. 1998. "2 Tales of Who Found Terra-Cotta Men." *The New York Times,* June 25.

Falkenhausen, L. von. 1993. "On the Historiographical Orientation of Chinese Archaeology." *Antiquity* 67: 839–49.

Fardon, R. 1990a. "Localizing Strategies: The Regionalization of Ethnographic Accounts." Pp. 1–35 in his *Localizing Strategies: Regional Traditions of Ethnographic Writing.* Washington, DC: Smithsonian Institution Press.

—— ed. 1990b. *Localizing Strategies: Regional Traditions of Ethnographic Writing.* Washington, DC: Smithsonian Institution Press.

Faris, J. 1992. "Anthropological Transparency: Film, Representation and Politics." Pp. 171–82 in P. Crawford and D. Turton, eds., *Film as Ethnography.* Manchester: Manchester University Press.

Fasseur, C. 2003. *De Indologen: Ambtenaren voor de Oost 1825–1950.* (The Indologists: Bureaucrats for the East 1825–1950). Amsterdam: Aula/Bert Bakker.

Fee, E. 1979. "Nineteenth-century Craniology: The Study of the Female Skull." *Bulletin of the History of Medicine* 53: 415–533.

Feld, S., ed. 2003. *Cine-ethnography.* Minneapolis: University of Minnesota Press.

Fenton, W. N. and E. L. Moore. 1974. "Introduction." Pp. xxix–cxix in J. F. Lafitau, *Customs of the American Indians Compared with the Customs of Primitive Times.* Toronto: Champlain Society.

Ferguson, M. E. 1970. *China Medical Board and Peking Union Medical College: A Chronicle of Fruitful Collaboration 1914–1951.* New York: China Medical Board of New York.

Fiedermutz-Laun, A. 1970. *Der Kulturhistorische Gedanke bei Adolf Bastian: Systematisierung und Darstellung der Theorie und Methode mit dem Versuch einer Bewertung des Kulturhistorischen Gehaltes auf dieser Grundlage.* Wiesbaden: Franz Steiner Verlag.

Finley, M. I. 1965. *The World of Odysseus.* New York: Viking.

—— 1966. "Unfreezing the Classics." *Times Literary Supplement,* April 7, 289–90.

Firth, R. 1951. "Contemporary British Social Anthropology." *American Anthropologist* n.s. 53: 474–89.

Fischer, H. 1990. *Völkerkunde im Nationalsozialismus: Aspekte der Anpassung, Affinität und Behauptung einer Wissenschaftlichen Disziplin.* Berlin: Reimer.

Fischer, J. 1979. "Government Anthropologists in the Trust Territory of Micronesia." Pp. 238–53 in Walter Goldschmidt, ed., *The Uses of Anthropology.* Washington: American Anthropological Association.

Fiske, S. and E. Chambers. 1995. "The Inventions of Practice." *Human Organization* 55: 1–12.

Flint. V. I. J. 1992. *The Imaginative Landscape of Christopher Columbus.* Princeton: Princeton University Press.

Fodor, J. 1981. "The Present Status of the Innateness Controversy," in his Representations. Cambridge, MA: MIT Press.

Foerstel, L and A. Gilliam, eds. 1992. *Confronting the Margaret Mead Legacy: Scholarship, Empire, and the South Pacific.* Philadelphia: Temple University Press.

Forster, G. 2000. *A Voyage Round the World,* ed. N. Thomas and O. Berghof, assisted by J. Newell, 2 vols. Honolulu: University of Hawaii Press.

Foster, G. 1962. *Traditional Cultures and the Impact of Cultural Change.* New York: Harper and Row.

——— 1969. *Applied Anthropology.* Boston: Little, Brown.

Foy, W. 1906. *Führer durch das Rautenstrauch-Joest-Museum der Stadt Cöln.* Cöln: M. Dumont Schauberg.

——— 1911. "Ethnologie und Kulturgeschichte." *Petermanns Geographische Mitteilungen.* 57: 230–3.

Frazer, J. G. 1900. *The Golden Bough,* 2nd edn. London: Macmillan.

——— 1957. *The Golden Bough,* abridged edn. New York: Macmillan.

Freedman, M. 1979. *Main Trends in Social and Cultural Anthropology.* New York: Holmes and Meier.

Freeman, D. 1983. *Margaret Mead: The Making and Unmaking of an Anthropological Myth.* Cambridge, MA: Harvard University Press.

Frere, J. 1800. "Account of Flint Weapons Discovered at Hoxne in Suffolk." *Archaeologia* 13: 204–5.

Frese, H. H. 1960. *Anthropology and the Public: The Role of Museums.* Leiden: E. J. Brill.

Freudenberg, N., M. Fahs, S. Galea, and A. Greenberg 2006. "The Impact of New York City's 1975 Fiscal Crisis on the Tuberculosis, HIV, and Homicide Syndemic." *American Journal of Public Health,* 96(3): 424–34.

Friedl, E. 1967. "The Power of Women." Pp. 42–52 in Jill Dubitsch, ed., *Gender and Power in Rural Greece.* Princeton: Princeton University Press.

Galef, B. G. 1990. "Tradition in Animals: Field Observations and Laboratory Analyses." Pp. 74–95 in M. Bekoff and D. Jamieson, eds., *Interpretation and Explanation in the Study of Animal Behavior.* Boulder, CO: Westview Press.

Gamble, C. 1999. *The Palaeolithic Societies of Europe.* Cambridge: Cambridge University Press.

——— and W. Roebroeks. 1999. "The Middle Palaeolithic: A point of inflection." Pp. 5–21 in C. Gamble and W. Roebroeks, eds., *The Middle Palaeolithic Occupation of Europe.* Leiden: Leiden University Press.

Gareis, S. 1990. *Exotik in München: Museumsethnologische Konzeptionen im historischen Wandel.* Munich: Anacon.

Garn, S. M. 1962. "Mankind in History [review of Coon's *The Story of Man*]." *Science* 136: 868.

——— 1963. Review of *The Origin of Races. American Sociological Review* 28: 637–8.

Garrett, H. E. 1961. "The equalitarian dogma." *Mankind Quarterly* 1: 253–7.

——— and W. C. George. 1964. "Science and the Race Problem." *Science* 143: 913–15.

Gasman, D. 1998. *Haeckel's Monism and the Birth of Fascist Ideology.* New York: Peter Lang.

Gearing, F. 1960. "The Strategy of the Fox Project." Pp. 294–300 in F. Gearing, R. McD. Netting and L Peatte, eds., *Documentary History of the Fox Project: 1949–1959.* Chicago: Department of Anthropology, University of Chicago.

Gedenkboek van het Atheneum en de Universiteit van Amsterdam, 1632–1932 (Anniversary Volume of the Atheneum and the University of Amsterdam, 1632–1932). 1932. Amsterdam: Stadsdrukkerij.

Geertz, C. 1973. *The Interpretation of Cultures.* New York: Basic Books.

—— 1988. *Works and Lives: The Anthropologist as Author.* Stanford: Stanford University Press.

—— 1995. *After the Fact: Two Countries, Four Decades, One Anthropologist.* Cambridge, MA: Harvard University Press.

Geiger, L. 1880 [in orig. language, 1871] *Zur Entwicklungsgeschichte der Menschheit,* Translated as *Contributions to the History of the Development of the Human Race.* London: Trübner.

—— 1872. *Ursprung und Entwicklung der menschlichen Sprache und Vernunft,* 2 vols. Stuttgart: Cotta.

Gellner, E. 1975. "The Soviet and the Savage." *Current Anthropology* 4: 595–617.

—— ed. 1980. *Soviet and Western Anthropology.* London: Duckworth.

—— 1988a. *State and Society in Soviet Social Thought.* Oxford: Basil Blackwell.

—— 1988b. "The Stakes in Anthropology." *The American Scholar,* Winter: 17–32.

Genoves, S. (1961) "Racism and 'The Mankind Quarterly'." *Science,* 134: 1928–32.

Genovese, E. D. 1998. *A Consuming Fire: The Fall of the Confederacy in the Mind of the White Christian South.* Athens: University of Georgia Press.

Gewertz, D. 1983. *Sepik River Societies.* New Haven: Yale University Press.

Gingrich, A. 2005. "The German-Speaking Countries." Pp. 61–153 in F. Barth et al., *One Discipline, Four Ways: British, German, French, and American Anthropology.* Chicago: University of Chicago Press.

Ginsburg, F. 1995. "Mediating Culture: Indigenous Media, Ethnographic Film, and the Production of Identity." Pp. 256–91 in L. Devereaux and R. Hillman, eds., *Fields of Vision: Essays in Film Studies, Visual Anthropology, and Photography.* Berkeley: University of California Press.

—— 1998. "Institutionalizing the Unruly: Charting a Future for Visual Anthropology." *Ethnos* 63: 173–201.

—— 1999. "The Parallax Effect: The Impact of Indigenous Media on Ethnographic Film." Pp. 156–75 in J. Gaines and M. Renov, eds., *Collecting Visible Evidence.* Minneapolis: University of Minnesota Press.

——, L. Abu-Lughod, B. Larkin, eds. 2002. *Media Worlds: Anthropology on New Terrain.* Berkeley: University of California Press.

Girard, R. 1977. *Violence and the Sacred.* Baltimore: Johns Hopkins University Press.

Gjessing, G. 1968. "The Social Responsibility of the Social Scientist." *Current Anthropology* 9: 397–403.

Gladstone, W. E. 1858. "Homer's Perceptions and Use of Colour." Pp. 457–99 in his *Studies on Homer and the Homeric Age,* vol 3. Oxford: Oxford University Press.

Glass, B. 1986. "Geneticists Embattled: Their Stand Against Rampant Eugenics and Racism in America During the 1920s and 1930s." *Proceedings of the American Philosophical Society* 130: 130–54.

Godelier, M. 1988. *The Mental and the Material.* London: Verso.

Goldberg, D. T. 1993. *Racist Culture: Philosophy and the Politics of Meaning.* Oxford: Blackwell.

Golde, P., ed., 1970. *Women in the Field: Anthropological Experiences.* Chicago: Aldine.

—— 1986. *Women in the Field: Anthropological Experiences.* Berkeley and Los Angeles: University of California Press.

Goldschmidt, R. 1942. "Anthropological Determinism of 'Aryanism.'" *The Journal of Heredity* 33: 215–16.

Goldschmidt, W. 2000. "A Perspective on Anthropology." *American Anthropologist* n.s. 102: 789–807.

—— 2001. "Notes Toward a Theory of Applied Anthropology." *Human Organization* 60: 423–9.

Goodall, J. 1963. "Feeding Behaviour of Wild Chimpanzees: A Preliminary Report." *Symposium of the Zoological Society of London* 10: 39–48.

Goodenough, W. 1963. *Cooperation in Change*. New York: Russell Sage Foundation.

—— 2002. "Anthropology in the 20th Century and Beyond." *American Anthropologist* n.s. 104: 423–40.

Goodman, M. 1996. "Epilogue: A Personal Account of the Origins of a New Paradigm." *Molecular Phylogenetics and Evolution* 5: 269–85.

Gordon, J. and I. Abramov. 2001. *Color Vision*. Pp. 92–127 in E. B. Goldstein, ed., *Blackwell Handbook of Perception*. Oxford: Blackwell.

Gossett, T. F. 1965. *Race: The History of an Idea in America*. New York: Schocken.

Gothsch, M. 1983. *Die deutsche Völkerkunde und ihr Verhältnis zum Kolonialismus: Ein Beitrag zur kolonialideologischen und kolonialpraktischen Bedeutung der deutschen Völkerkunde in der Zeit von 1870 bis 1945*. Hamburg: Institut für Internationale Angelegenheiten der Universität Hamburg.

Gould, S. J. 1977. *Ontogeny and Phylogeny*. Cambridge, MA: Harvard University Press.

—— 1997. "Unusual Unity." *Natural History* 106 (April): 20–3, 69–71.

—— 2002. *The Structure of Evolutionary Theory*. Cambridge, MA: Harvard University Press.

Gowlett, J. 1984. "The Mental Abilities of Early Man." Pp. 167–92 in R. Foley, ed., *Hominid Evolution and Community Ecology: Prehistoric Human Adaptation in Biological Perspective*. London: Academic Press.

Graebner, F. 1905. "Kulturkreise und Kulturschichten in Ozeanien." *Zeitschrift für Ethnologie* 37: 28–53.

Grafton, A., with A. Shefford and N. Siraisi. 1992. *New Worlds, Ancient Texts: The Power of Tradition and the Shock of Discovery*. Cambridge: Belknap Press.

Graham, H. D. and N. Diamond, 1997. *The Rise of American Research Universities*. Baltimore: Johns Hopkins University Press.

Grant, B. 1999. "Foreword." Pp. xxiii–lvi in Lev Iakovlevich Shternberg, *The Social Organization of the Gilyak*. New York: American Museum of Natural History.

Gray, A. 1927. "Introduction." Pp. xiii–xxxvii in W. Dampier, W. *A New Voyage Round the World*. London: Argonaut Press.

Greenblatt, S. 1991. *Marvelous Possessions: The Wonder of the New World*. Chicago: University of Chicago Press.

Gregor, T. and D. Tuzin, eds. 2001. *Gender in Amazonia and Melanesia*. Berkeley: University of California Press.

Gregory, C. 1982. *Gifts and Commodities*. London: Academic Press.

Griesemer, J. R. 1990. "Modelling in the Museum: On the Role of Remnant Models in the Work of Joseph Grinnell." *Biology and Philosophy* 5: 3–36.

Griffiths, A. 2002. *Wondrous Difference: Cinema, Anthropology and Turn-of-the-Century Visual Culture*. New York: Columbia University Press.

Grimshaw, A. 2001. *The Ethnographer's Eye: Ways of Seeing in Modern Anthropology*. Cambridge: Cambridge University Press.

Guldin, G. E., ed., 1990. *Anthropology in China: Defining the Discipline*. 1 vol., *Chinese Studies on China*. Armonk, NY: M. E. Sharpe.

—— 1994. *The Saga of Anthropology in China: From Malinowski to Moscow to Mao*. Armonk, NY: M. E. Sharpe.

Gunning, T. 1990. "The Cinema of Attractions – Early Film, Its Spectator and the Avant-garde." Pp. 56–62 in T. Elsaesser ed., *Early Cinema: Space, Frame, Narrative*. London: British Film Institute.

Gupta, A. and J. Ferguson, eds. 1997. *Anthropological Locations: Boundaries and Grounds of a Field Science*. Berkeley: University of California Press.

—— 1997. *Culture, Power, Place: Explorations in Critical Anthropology*. Durham: Duke University Press.

Gwynne, M. 2003. *Applied Anthropology: A Career-Oriented Approach*. Boston: Allyn and Bacon.

Hackenberg, R. 1988. "Scientists or Survivors: The Future of Applied Anthropology under Maximum Uncertainty." Pp. 170–85 in R. Trotter, ed., *Anthropology for Tomorrow*. Washington, DC: American Anthropological Association.

Hacker, P. M. S. 1987. *Appearance and Reality: A Philosophical Investigation into Perception and Perceptual Qualities*. Oxford: Blackwell.

—— 1999. *Wittgenstein*. London: Routledge.

Haddon, A. C. 1898. *The Study of Man*. London: Bliss, Sands & Co.

—— 1901. *Head-Hunters: Black, White, and Brown*. London: Methuen.

—— 1920. *Migrations of Cultures in British New Guinea*. London: Royal Anthropological Institute.

—— 1935. *Reports of the Cambridge Anthropological Expedition to Torres Straits*. Volume I: *General Ethnography*. Cambridge: Cambridge University Press.

Haeckel, E. 1876. *The History of Creation*, 2 vols. London: Henry S. King.

Haldane, J. B. S. 1962. "More on 'Scientific' Racism." *Current Anthropology* 3: 300.

Hall, E. 1959. *The Silent Language*. Greenwich, CT: Premier Books.

Hallowell, A. I. 1955. *Culture and Experience*. Philadelphia: University of Pennsylvania Press.

—— 1960. "The Beginnings of Anthropology in America." Pp. 1–90 in F. de Laguna, ed., *Selected Writings from the American Anthropologist, 1888–1920*. New York: Harper and Row.

—— 1965. "The History of Anthropology as an Anthropological Problem." *Journal of the History of the Behavioral Sciences* 1: 24–38.

Hamy, E. T. 1882. "Introduction." *Revue d'ethnographie* 1: i–iv.

Handler, R., ed. 2004. *Significant Others: Interpersonal and Professional Commitments in Anthropology*. Madison: University of Wisconsin Press.

Hanlon, D. and G. White, eds. 2002. *Voyaging in the Contemporary Pacific*. Oxford: Rowman and Littlefield.

Hannerz, U. 1989. "Notes on the global ecumene." *Public Culture* 1(2): 66–75.

Haraway, D. 1988. "Remodelling the Human Way of Life: Sherwood Washburn and the New Physical Anthropology, 1950–1980." Pp. 206–59 in G. W. Stocking, Jr., ed., *Bones, Bodies, Behavior: Essays on Biological Anthropology*. Madison, WI: University of Wisconsin Press.

Hare, P. 1985. *A Woman's Quest for Science: Portrait of Anthropologist Elsie Clews Parsons*. Buffalo, NY: Prometheus Books.

Harms, V. 1984. "Das Historische Verhältnis der deutschen Ethnologie zum Kolonialismus." *Zeitschrift für Kulturaustausch*, no. 4: 401–16.

Harries-Jones, P. 1996. "Afterword: Affirmative Theory: Voice and Counter-voice at the Oxford Decennial." Pp. 156–72 in H. L. Moore, ed., *The Future of Anthropological Knowledge*. London: Routledge.

Harris, M. 1968. *The Rise of Anthropological Theory*. New York: Thomas Crowell.

Harrison, G. A. 1961. "The Mankind Quarterly." *Man* 61: 163–4.

Harrison, J. and R. Darnell, eds, 2006. *Historicizing Canadian Traditions in Anthropology*. Vancouver: University of British Columbia Press.

Harrison, J. E. 1909. "The Influence of Darwinism on the Study of Religion." Pp. 494–511 in A. C. Seward, ed., *Darwin and Modern Science*. Cambridge: Cambridge University Press.

—— 1912. *Themis*. Cambridge: Cambridge University Press.

—— 1925. *Reminiscences of a Student's Life*. London: Hogarth.

—— and M. Verrall. 1890. *Mythology and Monuments of Ancient Athens*. London: Macmillan.

Hart, Jan. 1988. "Kunst, Regeringszaak? 1848–1918." (Art, Government Business? 1848–1918.) Pp. 67–145 in *Kunst en Beleid in Nederland* (Art and Policy in the Netherlands) 3. Amsterdam: Boekmanstichting/Van Gennep.

Harvey, J. 1983. "Evolutionism Transformed: Positivists and Materialists in the *Société d'anthropologie de Paris* from the Second Empire to Third Republic." Pp. 289–310 in D. Olroyd and I. Langham, eds., *The Wider Domain of Evolutionary Thought*. Dordrecht: D. Reidel.

—— 1984. "L'evolution transformé, Positivistes et materialistes dans la société d'anthropologie de Paris du second Empire a la IIIe République." Pp. 387–405 in B. Rupp-Eisenreich, ed., *Histoires de l'anthropologie*. Paris: Klincksieck.

Hasselman, C. J. 1926. *Het Koninklijk Koloniaal Instituut te Amsterdam: Wording, Werking en Toekomst*. (The Royal Colonial Institute of Amsterdam: Emergence, Activities, and Future). 2nd printing. Amsterdam: Het Koninklijk Koloniaal Instituut.

Hastrup, K. 1992. "Anthropological Visions: Some Notes on Visual and Textual Authority." Pp. 8–25 in P. Crawford and D. Turton, eds., *Film as Ethnography*. Manchester: Manchester University Press.

—— and P. Elsass. 1990. "Anthropological Advocacy: A Contradiction?" *Current Anthropology* 31: 301–11.

Hayne, D. M. 1969. "Lom d'Arce de Lahontan, Louis-Armand de." Pp. 439–45 in *Dictionary of Canadian Biography*, vol. 2. Toronto: University of Toronto Press and Les Presses de l'Université Laval.

Hedin, S. 1943. *History of the Expedition in Asia 1927–1935. Part I: 1927–1928*. Translated by D. Burton. Vol. 23, *Reports from the Scientific Expedition to the North-western Provinces of China under the Leadership of Dr. Sven Hedin: The Sino-Swedish Expedition*. Stockholm: Elanders Boktryckeri Aktiebolag.

Heider. K. 1986. *Ethnographic Film*. Austin: University of Texas Press.

Heinemeijer, W. F. 2002. "A History of Anthropology in Amsterdam: Steinmetz and his Students." Pp. 227–43 in H. Vermeulen and J. Kommers, eds., *Tales from Academia: History of Anthropology in the Netherlands*. Saarbrücken: Verlag für Entwicklungspolitiek.

Henshilwood, C. S., et al. 2002. "Emergence of modern human behavior: Middle Stone Age engravings from South Africa." *Science* 295: 1278–80.

Herder, J. G. 1989. *Werke, vol. 6, Ideen zur Philosophie der Geschichte der Menschheit*, ed. Martin Bollacher. Frankfurt: Deutscher Klassiker Verlag.

Hereniko, V. and R. Wilson, eds. 1999. *Inside Out: Literature, Cultural Politics, and Identity in the New Pacific*. Oxford: Rowman and Littlefield Publishers.

Herle, A. and S. Rouse, eds. 1998. *Cambridge and the Torres Strait: Centenary Essays on the 1898 Anthropological Expedition*. Cambridge: Cambridge University Press.

Herrnstein, R. and C. Murray. 1994. *The Bell Curve*. New York: Free Press.

Herzen, A. I. 1956 [1850–51]. O sel'skoi obshine v Rossii (On the rural community in Russia). Pp. 259–63 in *Sobranie sochinenii* (*Complete Writings*), vol. 7. Moscow: Izdatel'stvo Akademii Nauk SSSR.

—— 1956 [1851]. "Russkii narod i sotsialism." (The Russian people and socialism). Pp. 271–329 in *Sobranie sochinenii (Complete Writings)*, vol. 7. Moscow: Izdanie Akademii Nauk SSSR.

—— 1957 [1854]. "Staryi mir i Rossiia." (Old world and Russia) Pp. 134–200 in *Sobranie sochinenii (Complete Writing)* Volume 12. Moscow: Izdatel'stvo Akademii Nauk SSSR.

Herzfeld, M. 1984. "The Horns of the Mediterraneanist Dilemma." *American Ethnologist* 11: 439–54.

—— 1986. "Within and Without." Pp. 215–33 in Jill Dubitsch, ed., *Gender and Power in Rural Greece*. Princeton: Princeton University Press.

—— 1987. *Anthropology Through the Looking Glass: Critical Ethnography in the Margins of Europe*. New York: Cambridge University Press.

Hill, E. D. 1987. *Edward, Lord Herbert of Cherbury*. Boston: Twayne.

Hinsley, Curtis M., Jr. 1981. *Savages and Scientists: The Smithsonian Institution and the Development of American Anthropology*. Washington, DC: Smithsonian Institution Press.

Hirsch, E. and M. Strathern, eds. 2004. *Transactions and Creations: Property Debates and the Stimulus of Melanesia*. Oxford: Berghahn.

Hirsch, F. 2005. *Empire of Nations: Ethnographic Knowledge and the Making of the Soviet Union*. Ithaca: Cornell University Press.

Hockings, P. 1975. *Principles of Visual Anthropology*. The Hague: Mouton.

Hodge, F. W. 1906, 1912. *Handbook of American Indians North of Mexico*. Washington: Smithsonian Institution.

Hodgen, M. T. 1964. *Early Anthropology in the Sixteenth and Seventeenth Centuries*. Philadelphia: University of Pennsylvania Press.

Holland, D. G. 2006. "Socializing Knowledge: The Production and Circulation of Social Science in Malawi, 1964–2004." PhD Thesis, University of Pennsylvania.

Holmberg, A. 1970. "The Research and Development Approach to the Study of Change." Pp. 8–93 in J. Clifton, ed., *Applied Anthropology: Readings in the Uses of the Science of Man*. New York: Houghton Mifflin.

Holmes, B. 1998. "The Ascent of Medallion Man." *New Scientist,* May 9: 16.

Hood, D. 1964. *Davidson Black: A Biography*. Toronto: University of Toronto Press.

Hooton, E. A. 1926. "Methods of Racial Analysis." *Science* 63: 75–81.

—— 1930. *The Indians of Pecos Pueblo*. Phillips Academy Expedition, vol. 4. New Haven: Yale University Press.

—— 1936. "Plain Statements About Race." *Science* 83: 511–13.

—— 1939a. *The American Criminal: An Anthropological Study*. Volume I: *The Native White Criminal of Native Parentage*. Cambridge: Harvard University Press.

—— 1939b. *Crime and the Man*. New York: Doubleday.

—— 1940. *Why Men Behave like Apes and Vice Versa*. Princeton: Princeton University Press.

Horowitz, I. L., ed. 1967. *The Rise and Fall of Project Camelot: Studies in the Relationship between the Social Sciences and Practical Politics*. Cambridge, MA: MIT Press.

Houtman, G. 1988. "Interview with Maurice Bloch." *Anthropology Today* 4(1): 18–21.

Howells, W. W. and P. J. Tsuchitani, eds. 1977. *Paleoanthropology in the People's Republic of China: A Trip Report of the American Paleoanthropology Delegation*. Edited by Committee on Scientific Cooperation with the People's Republic of China (CSCPRC), CSCPRC Report No. 4. Washington, DC: National Academy of Sciences.

Hrdlička, A. 1914. "Physical Anthropology in America: An Historical Sketch." *American Anthropologist*. n.s. 16: 507–54.

—— 1930. "Human Races." Pp. 156–83 in E. W. Cowdry, ed., *Human Biology and Racial Welfare*. New York: Paul B. Hoeber.

Hulse, F. S. 1962. "Race as an Evolutionary Episode." *American Anthropologist* n.s. 64: 929–945.

Hume, D. 1963. "The Natural History of Religion". In R. Wollheim, ed., *Hume on Religion*. London: Collins.

—— 1974 [1739]. *A Treatise on Human Nature*. London: Dent, Everyman's Library.

Hunt, N. R. 1999. *A Colonial Lexicon of Birth Ritual, Medicalization, and Mobility in the Congo*. Durham: Duke University Press.

Hüsken, F. 2002. "Preface." Pp. vii–x in H. Vermeulen and J. Kommers, eds., *Tales from Academia: History of Anthropology in the Netherlands*. Saarbrücken, Germany: Verlag für Entwicklungspolitiek.

Huxley, J. and A. C. Haddon. 1936. *We Europeans*. New York: Harper and Brothers.

Hymes, D., ed. 1969. *Reinventing Anthropology*. New York: Pantheon.

Iamo, W. 1992. "The Stigma of New Guinea: Reflections on Anthropology and Anthropologists." Pp. 75–100 in Foerstel and Gilliam, eds., *Confronting the Margaret Mead Legacy: Scholarship, Empire, and the South Pacific*. Philadelphia: Temple University Press.

Iggers. G. 1968. *The German Conception of History: the National Tradition of Historical Thought from Herder to the Present*. Middletown: Wesleyan University Press.

Impey, O., and A. MacGregor, eds. 1985. *The Origins of Museums: The Cabinet of Curiosities in Sixteenth- and Seventeenth-Century Europe*. Oxford: Clarendon Press.

Ingold, T. 1993a. "Evolutionary Models in the Social Sciences." *Cultural Dynamics* 4: 239–50.

—— 1993b. "Tools, Techniques, and Technology." Pp. 337–45 in K. Gibson and T. Ingold, eds., *Tools, Language, and Cognition in Human Evolution*. Cambridge: Cambridge University Press.

—— ed., 1996. *Key Debates in Anthropology*. London: Routledge.

Institute of Archaeology, Chinese Academy of Social Sciences. 1992. *Zhongguo kaogu xue zhong tan14 niandai shu ju ji, 1965–1991 (Collected C14 Dates in Chinese Archaeology 1965–1991)*. Beijing: Wenwu chubanshe.

Isaac, G. L. 1977. *Olorgesailie: Archaeological Studies of a Middle Pleistocene Lake Basin in Kenya*. Chicago: University of Chicago Press.

—— 1983. "Bones in Contention: Competing Explanations for the Juxtaposition of Early Pleistocene Artefacts and Faunal Remains." Pp. 3–19 in J. Clutton-Brock and C. Grigson, eds., *Animals and Archaeology 1: Hunters and Their Prey*. Oxford: Oxford University Press.

Itenberg, B. S. 1965. *Dvizhenie revolutsionnogo narodnichestva: narodnicheskie kruzhki i "khzhdenie v narod" v 70kh godakh XIX veka* (The revolutionary populist movement: populist groups and "going to the people" in the 1870s). Moscow: Nauka.

Jacknis, Ira. 1988. "Margaret Mead and Gregory Bateson in Bali: Their Use of Photography and Film." *Cultural Anthropology*. 3: 160–77.

Jackson, J. J., Jr. 2001. "'In Ways Unacademical': The Reception of Carleton S. Coon's The Origin of Races." *Journal of the History of Biology* 34: 247–85.

Jagger, A. M. 1988. *Feminist Politics and Human Nature*. Totowa, NJ: Rowman & Littlefield.

James, S. R. 1989. "Hominid Use of Fire in the Lower and Upper Pleistocene." *Current Anthropology* 30: 1–26.

James, W. 1961 [1902]. *The Varieties of Religious Experience*. New York: Collier.

Jami, C. 1994. "L'Empereur Kangxi (1662–1722) et la Diffusion des Sciences Occidentales en Chine." Pp. 193–208 in Ang, I. and P.-E. Will, eds. *Nombres, Astres, Plantes et Viscères: Sept Essais sur L'Histoire des Sciences et des Techniques en Asie Orientale*. Paris: Collège de France, Institut des Hautes Études Chinoises.

Jamin, J. 1988. "Histoire de l'ethnologie est-elle une histoire comme les autres?" *Revue de Synthèse* 4(3–4): 469–83.

Jay, M. 1993. *Downcast Eyes: The Denigration of Vision in Twentieth-Century French Thought*. Berkeley: University of California Press.

—— 1994. "The Disenchantment of the Eye: Surrealism and the Crisis of Ocularcentrism." Pp. 173–201 in Lucian Taylor, ed., *Visualizing Theory*. New York: Routledge.

—— 1995. "Photo-unrealism: The Contribution of the Camera to the Crisis of Ocularcentrism." Pp. 344–60 in S. Melville and B. Readings, eds., *Vision and Textuality*. London: Macmillan.

Jennings, H. S. 1923. "Undesirable Aliens." *The Survey* 51: 309–12, 364.

Johanson, D. C., and E. Blake. 1996. *From Lucy to Language*. New York: Simon and Schuster.

Johnson, J. A. 1990. *The Kaiser's Chemists: Science and Modernization in Imperial Germany*. Chapel Hill: University of North Carolina Press.

Johnson, T. J. 1972. *Professions and Power*. London: Macmillan.

Jones, G. 1998. "Contested Territories: Alfred Cort Haddon, Progressive Evolutionism and Ireland." *History of European Ideas* 24: 195–211.

Jones, R. A. 1977. "On Understanding a Sociological Classic." *American Journal of Sociology* 83: 279–319.

—— 1981. "Robertson Smith, Durkheim and Sacrifice: An Historical Context for *The Elementary Forms*." *Journal of the History of the Behavioral Sciences* 17: 184–205.

—— 2002. "Introduction" to William Robertson Smith, *The Prophets of Israel and Their Place in History*. New Brunswick, NJ: Transaction.

Josselin de Jong, P. E. de. 1960. "Cultural Anthropology in the Netherlands." *Higher Education in the Netherlands* IV, 4: 3–16.

Joulian, F. 2000. "Techniques du corps et traditions chimpanzières." *Terrain*, 34 (March): 37–54.

Kan, S., ed., 2001. *Strangers to Relatives: The Adoption and Naming of Anthropologists in Native North America*. Lincoln: University of Nebraska Press.

Karady, V. 1982. "Le problème de la legitimité dans l'organisation historique de l'ethnologie française." *Revue Française de Sociologie* 23: 17–34.

—— 1988. "Durkheim et les debuts de l'ethnologie universitaire." *Actes de la recherché en sciences sociales* 14: 23–32.

Karim, W. J. 1996. "Anthropology without Tears: How a 'Local' Sees the 'Local' and the 'Global'." Pp. 115–38 in H. L. Moore, ed., *The Future of Anthropological Knowledge*. London: Routledge.

Karsten, R. 1954. "Some Critical Remarks on Ethnological Field-research in South America." *Societas Scientiarum Fennica: Commentationes Humanarum Litterarum*, 19(5).

Kaufman, A. A. 1908. *Russkaia obshina v processe eio zarozhdenia i rosta* (The Russian community in the process of its emergence and growth). Moscow: Tipografia Sytina.

Kavelin, K. D. 1859 [1848]. "Byt russkogo naroda" (Daily life and material culture of the Russian people). In *Sochinenia K. Kavelina*, vol. 5. Moscow: V tipografii V. Gracheva i Ko.

—— 1989a [1847]. "Vzgliad na iuridicheskii byt Drevnei Rusi" (A perspective on the legal order in Ancient Russia). Pp. 11–67 in his *Nash umstvennyi stroi: stat'i po philosophii russkoi istorii i kul'tury*. Moscow: Izdatel'stvo "Pravda."

—— 1989b [1859]. "Vzgliad na russkuiu sel'skuiu obshinu" (A perspective on the Russian rural community). Pp. 95–123 in his *Nash umstvennyi stroi: stat'i po philosophii russkoi istorii i kul'tury*. Moscow: Izdatel'stvo "Pravda."

—— 1989c [1866]. "Mysli i zametki o russkoi istoriia" (Thoughts and observations on Russian history). Pp. 171–256 in his *Nash umstvennyi stroi: stat'i po pholosophii russkoi istorii i kul'tury*. Moscow: Izdatel'stvo "Pravda".

Kawai, M. 1965. "Newly-acquired Pre-cultural Behavior of the Natural Troop of Japanese Monkeys on Koshima Islet." *Primates* 6: 1–30.

Keesing, F. 1945. "Applied Anthropology in Colonial Administration." Pp. 373–98 in Ralph Linton, ed., *The Science of Man in the World Crisis*. New York: Columbia University Press.

Keesing R, and M. Jolly. 1992. Epilogue. Pp. 224–47 in J. Carrier, ed., *History and Tradition in Melanesian Anthropology*. Berkeley: University of California Press.

Keller, E. 1983. *A Feeling for the Organism: The Life and Work of Barbara McClintock.* San Francisco: W. H. Freeman.

Kelley, D. R. 1998. *Faces of History: Historical Inquiry from Herodotus to Herder.* New Haven: Yale University Press.

Kelly, A. 1981. *The Descent of Darwin: The Popularization of Darwinism in Germany, 1860–1914.* Chapel Hill: University of North Carolina Press.

Kelly, D. A. 1979. "At Last, An Arena: Current Policies in Chinese Social Science." *Australian Journal of Chinese Affairs* 1: 123–36.

Kendall, C. 1989. "The Use and Non-Use of Anthropology: The Diarrheal Disease Control Program in Honduras." Pp. 832–40 in J. van Willigen, B. Rylko-Baur and A. McEroy, eds., *Making Our Research Useful: Case Studies in the Utilization of Anthropological Knowledge*. Boulder: Westview Press.

Kennard, E. and G. Macgregor. 1953. "Applied Anthropology in Government: United States." Pp. 832–40 in Alfred Kroeber, ed., *Anthropology Today*. Chicago: University of Chicago Press.

Kenny, M. G. 2002. "Toward a Racial Abyss: Eugenics, Wickliffe Draper, and the Origins of the Pioneer Fund." *Journal of the History of the Behavioral Sciences* 38: 259–83.

Kevelson, R. 1996. *Peirce, Science, Signs.* New York: P. Lang.

Kevles, D. J. 1985. *In the Name of Eugenics.* New York: Knopf.

Khalid, A. 2000. "Russian History and the Debate over Orientalism." *Kritika* 1: 691–9.

Kimball, S. 1946. "The Crisis in Colonial Administration." *Applied Anthropology* 5: 8–16.

Kirchhoff, A. 1879. "Ueber Farbensinn und Farbenbezeichnung der Nubier." *Zeitschrift für Ethnologie* 11: 397–402.

Kirk, G. 1970. *Myth: Its Meaning and Functions in Ancient and Other Cultures.* Berkeley: University of California Press.

Klaatsch, H. 1910. "Die Aurignac-Rasse und ihre Stellung im Stammbaum der Menschheit." *Zeitschrift für Ethnologie* 42: 565–75.

Klein, R. G. 1999. *The Human Career: Human Biological and Cultural Origins,* 2nd edn. Chicago: University of Chicago Press.

Klementz, D. 1886. *Drevnosti Minusinskogo muzeia* (The antiquities of the city museum of Minusinsk). Tomsk: Tipographia "Sibirskoi Gazety".

Knight, N. 1995. "Constructing the Science of Nationality: Ethnography in Mid-Nineteenth Century Russia." PhD Dissertation, Columbia University.

Koenig, B., S. Lee, and S. Richardson, eds. 2007. *Revisiting Race in a Genomic Age.* Piscataway, NJ: Rutgers University Press.

Koepping, K.-P. 1983. *Adolf Bastian and the Psychic Unity of Mankind: The Foundations of Anthropology in Nineteenth Century Germany.* London: Queensland Press.

Koerner, L. 1999. *Linnaeus: Nature and Nation.* Cambridge, MA: Harvard University Press.

Kohler, R. E. 1994. *Lords of the Fly: Drosophila Genetics and the Experimental Life*. Chicago: University of Chicago Press.

Kok, M. W. 1989. "De Musea in Paviljoen Welgelegen." (The Museums in Pavillion Welgelegen) Pp. 139–50 in F. W. A. Beelaerts van Blokland, et al., *Paviljoen Welgelegen 1789–1989*. Haarlem: Schuyt & Co.

Kolkenbrock-Netz, J. 1991. "Wissenschaft als nationaler Mythos: Anmerkungen zur Haeckel–Virchow-Kontroverse auf der 50. Jahresversammlung deutscher Naturforscher und Ärtze in München (1877)." Pp. 212–36 in J. Link and W. Wülfing, eds., *Nationale Mythen und Symbole in der zweiten Hälfte des 19. Jahrhunderts: Strukturen und Funktionen von Konzepten nationaler Identität*. Stuttgart: Klett-Cotta.

Koningsberger, J. J. 1926. "Een Gelukwensch." (Congratulations). In *Het Koloniaal Instituut. Artikelen en Beschouwingen ter Gelegenheid van de Officieele Opening door H. M. de Koningin Geschreven voor de Telegraaf.* (The Colonial Institute: Articles and Reflections on the Occasion of the Official Opening by Her Majesty the Queen Written for the *Telegraaf Newspaper*.) October 9 (Reprint). Amsterdam: De Telegraaf.

Kornilov, A. A. 1905. *Krestianskaia reforma* (The peasant reform). St Petersburg: Izdatel'stvo P. P. Gershunina.

Kovalik, S. F. 1928. *Revolutsionnoe dvizhenie semidesiatykh godov i process 193kh* (The revolutionary movement of the 1870s and the process of 193). Moscow: Izdatel'stvo Politkatorzhan.

Kozaitis, K. 2000. "The Rise of Anthropological Praxis". Pp. 45–66 in C. Hill and M. Baba, eds., *The Unity of Theory and Practice in Anthropology: Rebuilding a Fractured Synthesis*. Washington, DC: American Anthropological Association.

Krause, E. 1877. "Die geschichtliche Entwicklung des Farbensinnes." *Kosmos* 1: 264–72.

Kreps, Christina Fay. 1988. *Decolonizing the Anthropology Museum: The Dutch Example*. MA Thesis, University of Oregon.

Krings, Matthias, et al. 1997. "Neanderthal DNA sequences and the origin of modern humans." *Cell* 90: 19–30.

Kristof, N. D. 1999. "At this rate, we'll be global in another hundred years." *The New York Times*, "Week in Review," May 23, 5.

Kroeber, A. L. 1917. "The Superorganic." *American Anthropologist*, n.s. 19: 163–213.

—— 1963 [1939]. *Cultural and Natural Areas of Native North America*. Berkeley: University of California Press.

Krupnik, I. 1996. "The 'Bogoras Enigma': Bounds of Culture and Formats of Anthropologists." Pp. 35–52 in V. Hubinger, ed., *Grasping the Changing World: Anthropological Concepts in the Post-Modern Era*. London: Routledge.

Kuhn, T. S. 1962. *The Structure of Scientific Revolutions*. Chicago: University of Chicago Press.

Kuklick, H. 1991a. "Contested Monuments: The Politics of Archaeology in Southern Africa." Pp. 135–69 in G. W. Stocking, Jr., ed., *Colonial Situations*. Madison: University of Wisconsin Press.

—— 1991b. *The Savage Within: The Social History of British Anthropology, 1885–1945*. New York: Cambridge University Press.

—— 1996. "Islands in the Pacific: Darwinian Biogeography and British Anthropology." *American Ethnologist* 23: 611–38.

—— 1997. "After Ishmael: The Fieldwork Tradition and Its Future." Pp. 47–65 in A. Gupta and J. Ferguson, eds., *Anthropological Locations: Boundaries and Grounds of a Field Science*. Berkeley: University of California Press.

—— 1998. "Fieldworkers and Physiologists." Pp. 158–80 in A. Herle and S. Rouse, eds., *Cambridge and the Torres Strait*. Cambridge: Cambridge University Press.

—— 2002. "Professionalization and the Moral Order." Pp. 126–52 in A. Anderson and J. Volente, eds., *Disciplinarity at the Fin de Siècle*. Princeton: Princeton University Press.

—— 2006. " 'Humanity in the Chrysalis Stage': Indigenous Australians in the Anthropological Imagination, 1899–1926." *British Journal for the History of Science* 39: 535–68.

—— and R. Kohler, eds. 1996. *Science in the Field*. Osiris, 2nd series, 11.

Kulick, D. and M. Willson, eds., 1995. *Taboo: Sex, Identity, and Erotic Subjectivity in Anthropological Fieldwork*. London: Routledge.

Kuper, A. 1982. "Lineage Theory: A Critical Retrospect." *Annual Review of Anthropology* 11: 71–95.

—— 1983. *Anthropology and Anthropologists: The Modern British School*, rev. edn. London: Routledge.

—— 2005. "Alternative Histories of British Social Anthropology." *Social Anthropology* 13: 47–64.

Kupperman, K. O. 2000. *Indians and English: Facing Off in Early America*. Ithaca: Cornell University Press.

Kushner, T. 2004. *We Europeans? Mass-Observation, "Race" and British Identity in the Twentieth Century*. Aldershot, England: Ashgate.

Kuznar, L. A. 1997. *Reclaiming a Scientific Anthropology*. Walnut Creek/London/New Delhi: AltaMira Press.

Lafitau, J. F. 1974. *Customs of the American Indians Compared with the Customs of Primitive Times*, trans. and ed. W. N. Fenton and E. L. Moore, 2 vols. Toronto: Champlain Society.

Lahontan, L.-A. 1709. *Nouveaux Voyages de Mr. Le Baron de Lahontan*, 2 vols. La Haye: Frères l'Honoré.

—— 1990. *Oeuvres complètes*, ed. R. Ouellet, vol. 1. Quebec: Presses de l'Université de Montréal.

Lal, M. 1996. "Women, Medicine, and Colonialism in British India, 1869–1925." PhD thesis, University of Pennsylvania.

Lambek, M. and A. Strathern, eds. 1998. *Bodies and Persons: Comparative Perspectives from Africa and Melanesia*. New York: Cambridge University Press.

Landau, M. 1991. *Narratives of Human Evolution*. New Haven: Yale University Press.

Landes, R. 1970. "A Woman Anthropologist in Brazil." Pp. 119–42 in P. Golde, ed., *Women in the Field: Anthropological Experiences*. Chicago: Aldine.

Lane, C. 1994. "The Tainted Sources of The Bell Curve." *The New York Review of Books* December 1: 14–19.

Lang, A. 1908. *The Origins of Religion, and Other Essays*. London: Watts.

Las Casas, B. de. 1699. *An Account of the First Voyages and Discoveries Made by the Spaniards in America*. London: D. Brown.

—— 1992. *A Short Account of the Destruction of the Indies*, ed. and trans. N. Griffen, introduced by A. Pagden. London: Penguin Books.

Lasker, G. W. 1999. *Happenings and Hearsay: Reflections of a Biological Anthropologist*. Detroit: Savoyard Books.

Latour, B. 1987. *Science in Action: How to Follow Scientists and Engineers through Society*. Milton Keynes: Open University Press.

Lavrov, P. L. 1906. *Zadachi pozitivizma i ikh reshenie* (The goals of positivism and their achievement). St Petersburg.

—— 1907. *Narodniki-propagandisty 1873–78 godov* (The populists-propagandists of 1873–78). St Petersburg: Tipographia tovarishchestva Andersona i Loitsianksogo.

Lavrov, P. L. [P. Mirtov]. 1905 [1869]. *Istoricheskie pis'ma* (Letters on history). St Petersburg: Tipographia N. N. Klobukova.

Leach, E. 1969. *Genesis as Myth and Other Essays*. London: Cape.

Leacock, E. 1963. "Anthropology (H)." *Science* 139: 638.

Lederman, R. 1986a. *What Gifts Engender*. New York: Cambridge University Press.

—— 1986b. "Changing times in Mendi: notes towards writing Highland New Guinea history." *Ethnohistory* 33: 1–30.

—— 1991a. " 'Dialectics of the Gift.' Book Review Forum." *Pacific Studies* 14: 142–56.

—— 1991b. " 'Interests' in Exchange: Mendi Big Men in Context." Pp. 71–91 in M. Godelier and M. Strathern, eds., *Big Men and Great Men: The Development of a Comparison in Melanesia*. Cambridge, UK: Cambridge University Press.

—— 1998. "Globalization and the Future of 'Culture Areas': Melanesianist Anthropology in Transition." *Annual Review of Anthropology* 27: 427–49.

—— 2005. "Unchosen Grounds: Cultivating Cross-Subfield Accents for a Public Voice." Pp. 49–77 in D. A. Segal and S. J. Yanagisako, eds., *Unwrapping the Sacred Bundle: Reflections on the Disciplining of Anthropology*. Durham: Duke University Press.

Lee, P. 1996. *The Whorf Theory Complex: A Critical Reconstruction*. Amsterdam: John Benjamins.

Leeds, A. 1988. "Darwinian and 'Darwinian' Evolutionism in the Study of Society and Culture." Pp. 437–85 in T. F. Glick, ed., *The Comparative Reception of Darwinism*, 2nd edn. Chicago: University of Chicago Press.

Le Gros Clark, W. E. 1963. "How Many Families of Man?" *The Nation*, January 12: 35–6.

Leroi-Gourhan, A. 1993 [1964]. *Gesture and Speech*. Cambridge, MA: MIT Press.

Léry, J. 1990. *History of a Voyage to the Land of Brazil, Otherwise Called America*, trans. and introd. by Janet Whatley. Berkeley: University of California Press.

Levental', L. G. 1929. "Podati, povinnosti i zemlia u yakutov" (Taxes, financial obligations and land among Yakuts). Pp. 221–453 in D. M. Pavlinov, N. A. Vitashevskii and L. G. Levental', *Materialy po obuchnomu pravu i po obschestvennomu bytu iakutov*. Trudy Komissii po Izucheniu Yakutskoi ASSR Leningrad: Izdatel'stvo AN SSSR.

Lévi-Strauss, C. 1973. *Tristes Tropiques*, trans. J. and D. Weightman. New York: Atheneum.

Lévy-Bruhl. L. 1925. "L'institut d'ethnologie de l'université de Paris." *Revue d'ethnographie et des traditions populaires* 24: 233–6.

Lewontin, R. C. 1972. "The Apportionment of Human Diversity." *Evolutionary Biology* 6: 381–98.

—— 1974. *The Genetic Basis of Evolutionary Change*. New York: Columbia University Press.

Li, C. 1928. *The Formation of the Chinese People*. Cambridge, MA: Harvard University Press.

—— 1977. *Anyang*. Seattle: University of Washington Press.

Li, J. et al. 1999. "Zhongguo wenwu shi ye wushi nian" zhanlan xunli (Tour of the "50th anniversary of the Chinese relics enterprise" exhibition). *Wen wu* 10: 4–26.

Liebersohn, H. 1998. *Aristocratic Encounters: European Travelers and North American Indians*. New York: Cambridge University Press.

Lightman, B. 2001. "Victorian Sciences and Religions: Discordant Harmonies." Pp. 343–66 in John Hedley Brooke, Margaret J. Osler and Jitse van der Meer, eds., *Science in Theistic Contexts: Cognitive Dimensions, Osiris* 16.

Lindberg, C. 1995a. "It Takes More than Fieldwork to Become a Culture Hero of Anthropology." *Anthropos* 90: 525–31.

—— 1995b. *Erland Nordenskiöld: en antropologisk biografi* (Erland Nordenskiöld: An Anthropological Biography). Lund: Lund Studies in Social Anthropology No. 5.

—— 1997. "El museo – como libro y situación de campo: El visionario Erland Nordenskiöld" (The Museum as a Field of Knowledge: The Vision of Erland Nordenskiöld). *Erland Nordenskiöld: investigador y amigo del indígena*, edited by Jan-Åke Alvarsson. Quito: Abya Yala.

Linton, R. 1938. "The Present Status of Anthropology." *Science*, 87: 241–8.

—— 1945. "The Scope and Aims of Anthropology." Pp. 1–18 in Linton, ed., *The Science of Man in the World Crisis*. New York: Columbia University Press.

Liss, J. E. 1990. "The Cosmopolitan Imagination: Franz Boas and the Development of American Anthropology." PhD Dissertation, University of California, Berkeley.

Littlefield, A., L. Lieberman and L. T. Reynolds. 1982. "Redefining Race: The Potential Demise of a Concept in Physical Anthropology." *Current Anthropology* 23: 641–55.

Littlewood, R. 1995. "Mankind Quarterly Again." *Anthropology Today*, 11: 17–18.

Liu, Qingzhu, Wei Wang, Renxiang Wang, Dexin Zhong, Jiayao An, Zhaili Wu, and Xingcan Chen. 2000. *20 Shiji Zhongguo kaogu xue da faxian (Major archaeological discoveries of China in the 20th century)*, vol. 33, *Archaeology of China II*. Chengdu: Sichuan daxue chubanshe.

Livingstone, F. B. 1962. "On the Non-existence of Human Races." *Current Anthropology* 3: 279–81.

Locke, J. 1937 [1689]. *Treatise of Civil Government and a Letter Concerning Toleration*. New York: Appleton-Century-Crofts.

—— 1975 [1689]. *An Essay Concerning Human Understanding*. P. H. Nidditch, ed. New York: Plume.

—— 1997 [1689]. *An Essay Concerning Human Understanding*. R. Woolhouse, ed. London: Penguin.

—— 2000 [1690]. *Two Treatises of Government*. P. Laslett, ed. Cambridge: Cambridge University Press.

Locke, M. 1993. *Encounters with Aging: Mythologies of Menopause in Japan and North America*. Berkeley: University of California Press.

Loewe, M. 1976. Archaeology in the New China. *China Quarterly* 65: 1–14.

Loizos, P. 1980. "Granada Television's Disappearing World Series: An Appraisal." *American Anthropologist* n.s. 82: 873–94.

—— 1993. *Innovation in Ethnographic Film: From Innocence to Self-consciousness*. Manchester: Manchester University Press.

Lombardo, P. A. 2002. "The American Breed: Nazi Eugenics and the Origins of the Pioneer Fund." *Albany Law Review* 65: 207–61.

Lopes, M. M. 1997. *O Brasil descobre a pesquisa científica: Os museus e as ciências naturais no século XIX*. São Paulo: Hucitec.

Lowie, R. H. 1933. "Erland Nordenskiöld." *American Anthropologist*, n.s. 35: 158–64.

Luschan, L. 1922. *Völker, Rassen, Sprachen: anthropologische betrachtungen*. Berlin: Deutsche Buch-Gemeinschaft.

Lyell, C. 1863. *The Geological Evidences of the Antiquity of Man*. Philadelphia: George W. Childs.

Lynn, R. 2001. *Science of Human Diversity: A History of the Pioneer Fund*. Lanham, MD: University Press of America.

Lyons, A. P. and H. D. Lyons. 2004. *Irregular Connections: A History of Anthropology and Sexuality*. Lincoln: University of Nebraska Press.

MacClancy, J., ed. 2002. *Exotic No More: Anthropology on the Front Lines*. Chicago: University of Chicago Press.

MacDonald, J. 2002. *The Applied Anthropology Reader*. Boston: Allyn and Bacon.

MacDougall, D. 1995. *Conversations with Anthropological Filmmakers*. Cambridge, UK: Prickly Pear Press.

—— 1997. "The Visual in Anthropology." Pp. 276–95 in M. Banks and H. Morphy, eds., *Rethinking Visual Anthropology*. New Haven/London: Yale University Press.

—— 1998. *Transcultural Cinema*. Princeton: Princeton University Press.

Mackay, D. 1985. *In the Wake of Cook: Exploration, Science and Empire, 1780–1801*. London: Croom Helm.

MacLarnon, A. 1993. "The Vertebral Canal." Pp. 359–90 in A. Walker and R. Leakey, eds., *The Nariokotome Homo Erectus Skeleton*. Cambridge, MA: Harvard University Press.

Magnus, H. 1877. *Die geschichtliche Entwicklung des Farbensinnes*. Leipzig: Veit.

—— 1877a. *Zur Entwicklung des Farbensinnes. Kosmos*, 1: 423–33.

—— 1880. *Untersuchungen über den Farbensinn der Naturvölker*. Jena: Fischer.

Mainov, I. I. 1898. *Nekotoriye dannye o tungusakh Yakutskogo kraya* (Some data on the Tungus of the Yakutsk region). Trudy Vostochno-Sibirskogo otdela Imperatorskogo Russkogo Georgaficheskogo Obschestva, vol. 2. Irkutsk: Tipo-litografiya P. I. Makushina.

—— 1929. "Predislovie (Preface)." Pp. i–xlix in Pavlinov, D. M., N. A. Vitashevskii and L. G. Levental', *Materialy po obuchnomu pravu i po obschestvennomu bytu iakutov*. Trudy Komissii po Izucheniu Yakutskoi ASSR Leningrad: Izdatel'stvo AN SSSR.

Malcomson, S. L. 2000. *One Drop of Blood: The American Misadventure of Race*. New York: Farrar Straus Giroux.

Malinowski, B. 1922. *Argonauts of the Western Pacific*. London: G. Routledge and Sons.

—— 1923. "Science and Superstition of Primitive Mankind." *Nature* 111 (January–June): 658–62.

—— 1929. "Practical Anthropology." *Africa* 2: 22–38.

—— 1930 "The Rationalisation of Anthropology and Administration." *Africa* 3: 405–30.

—— 1948. "Magic, Science and Religion." In his *Magic, Science and Religion*. New York: Doubleday.

—— 1955 [1926]. *Magic, Science and Religion*. Garden City, NY: Doubleday.

—— 1967. *A Diary in the Strict Sense of the Term*. London: Routledge & Kegan Paul.

—— 1992. "Myth in Primitive Society." In R. Redfield, ed., *Magic, Science and Religion and Other Essays*. Prospect Heights, IL: Waveland Press.

Malkki, L. H. 1995. *Purity and Exile: Violence, Memory and National Cosmology among the Hutu Refugees in Tanzania*. Chicago: University of Chicago Press.

Mandelbaum, D., G. Lasker, and E. Albert, eds. 1963. *The Teaching of Anthropology*. Berkeley: University of California Press.

Maner, B. E. 2001. "The Search for a Buried Nation: Prehistoric Archeology in Central Europe, 1750–1945." PhD Dissertation, University of Illinois.

Marcel, J. C. 2001. *Le durkheimisme dans l'entre-deux guerres*. Paris: Presses Universitaires de France.

Marchand, S. 2003. "Priests among the Pygmies: Wilhelm Schmidt and the Counter-Reformation in Austrian Ethnology." Pp. 283–316 in H. G. Penny and M. Bunzl, eds., *Worldly Provincialism: German Anthropology in the Age of Empire*. Ann Arbor: University of Michigan Press.

Marcus, G. E. 1995. "Ethnography in/of the World System: The Emergence of Multi-sited Ethnography." *Annual Review of Anthropology* 24: 95–117.

—— 1998. *Ethnography Through Thick and Thin*. Princeton: Princeton University Press.

Marett, R. R. 1912. *Anthropology*. London: Williams and Norgate.

—— 1914. *The Threshold of Religion*. New York: Macmillan.

—— 1927. *Man in the Making*. London: Ernest Benn.

—— 1936. *Tylor*. London: Chapman and Hall.

Margolis, H. 1961. "Science and Segregation: The American Anthropological Association Dips into Politics." *Science*, 134: 1868–9.

Mark, J. 1980. *Four Anthropologists: An American Science in its Early Years.* New York: Science History Publications.

Marks, J. 2002. *What it Means to be 98 Percent Chimpanzee: Apes, People, and Their Genes.* Berkeley: University of California Press.

—— 2005. "Anthropology and *The Bell Curve.*" Pp. 206–27 in C. Besteman and H. Gusterson, eds., *Why America's Top Pundits are Wrong: Anthropologists Talk Back.* Berkeley: University of California Press.

Marshall, G. 1970. "In a World of Women: Field Work in a Yoruba Community." Pp. 167–94 in P. Golde, ed., *Women in the Field: Anthropological Experiences.* Chicago: Aldine.

Martin, R., ed., 1998. *Chalk Lines: The Politics of Work in the Managed University.* Durham: Duke University Press.

Martin, T. 2001. *Affirmative Action Empire: Nations and Nationalism in the Soviet Union, 1923–1939.* Ithaca: Cornell University Press.

Martins, L. 2002. "Commentary on the El Dorado Task Force Report." *Anthropology Newsletter* 43(8): 5.

Marwick, M. G. 1972. "Anthropologists' Declining Productivity in the Sociology of Witchcraft." *American Anthropologist* 74: 378–84.

Marx, K. 1955 [1881]. "Marx to V. I. Zasulich." Pp. 411–12 in *Selected Correspondence,* Moscow: Foreign Language Publishing.

—— 1976 [1867]. *Capital: A Critique of Political Economy,* Volume 1. Harmondsworth: Penguin.

Massin, B. 1996. "From Virchow to Fischer: Physical anthropology and 'modern race theories' in Wilhelmine Germany." Pp. 79–154 in G. W. Stocking, Jr., ed., *Volksgeist as Method and Ethic: Essays on Boasian Ethnography and the German Anthropological Tradition.* Madison: University of Wisconsin Press.

Mauss, M. 1913. "L'ethnographie en France et a l'etranger." *Revue de Paris* 20, 5: 537–60, 815–37.

Mayr, E. 1950. "Taxonomic Categories in Fossil Hominids." *Cold Spring Harbor Symposium on Quantitative Biology* 15: 109–18.

McGrew, W. C. 1992. *Chimpanzee Material Culture: Implications for Human Evolution.* New York: Cambridge University Press.

McKnight, B. 1992. *Law and Order in Sung China.* Cambridge: Cambridge University Press.

Mead, M. 1928. *Coming of Age in Samoa: A Psychological Study of Youth for Western Civilization.* New York: New American Library.

—— 1938. "The Mountain Arapesh: An Importing Culture." *American Museum of Natural History Anthropological Papers* 36: 139–349.

—— 1955. *Cultural Patterns and Technological Change.* New York: Mentor.

—— 1956. *New Lives for Old.* New York: Mentor.

—— 1963 [1935]. *Sex and Temperament in Three Primitive Societies.* New York: Morrow.

—— 1963. "Scientist reviewers beware." *Science* 141: 312–13.

—— 1970. "Field Work in Pacific Islands, 1925–1967." Pp. 291–331 in P. Golde, ed., *Women in the Field.* Berkeley: University of California Press.

Mehos, D. C. 2006. *Science and Culture for Members Only: The Amsterdam Zoo Artis in the Nineteenth Century.* Amsterdam: Amsterdam University Press.

Merchant, C. 1980. *The Death of Nature: Women, Ecology, and the Scientific Revolution.* San Francisco: Harper & Row.

Métraux, A. 1925. "De la méthode dans les recherches ethnographiques." *Revue d'ethnographie et des traditions populaires* 24: 266–90.

Michel, U. 1995. "Neue ethnologische Forschungsansätze im Nationalsozialismus? Aus der Biographie von Wilhelm Emil Mühlman (1904–1988)." Pp. 141–67 in T. Hauschild, ed., *Lebenslust und Fremdenfurcht: Ethnologie im Dritten Reich.* Frankfurt: Suhrkamp.

Mikhailovskii, N. K. 1922 [1869]. *Cho takoe progress?* (What is progress?) Petrograd.

—— 1998 [1882]. *Geroi i tolpa: izbrannye trudy po sotsiologii* (The hero and the crowd: selected works in sociology). St Petersburg: Izdatel'stvo "Aleteya."

Mill, J. S. 1895 [1834]. *System of Logic.* London: Longmans, Green.

—— 1991. *On Liberty* [1859], *and other essays.* John Gray, ed. Oxford: Oxford University Press, 1991.

Mills, D. 2005a. "A Short History of the ASA." *Annals of the Association of Social Anthropologists of the UK and the Commonwealth* 23: 4–5.

—— 2005b. "Anthropology At the End of Empire: The Rise and Fall of the Colonial Social Science Research Council, 1944–1962." Pp. 135–66 in B. de L'Estoile, F. Neiburg, and L. Sigaud, eds., *Empires, Nations, and Natives: Anthropology and State-Making.* Durham: Duke University Press.

—— 2006. *Difficult Folk? A Political History of "British" Social Anthropology.* Unpublished manuscript.

Milstein, B. 2001. *Introduction to the Syndemics Prevention Network.* Atlanta: Centers for Disease Control and Prevention.

Mitchell, T. 1991. *Colonizing Egypt.* Berkeley: University of California Press.

Modell, J. 1984. *Ruth Benedict: Patterns of a Life.* London: Chatto & Windus.

Montagu, M. F. A. 1941. "The Concept of Race in the Human Species in the Light of Genetics." *Journal of Heredity* 32: 243–7.

—— 1967. *The Human Revolution.* New York: Bantam.

Montaigne, M. de. 1958. *Essays,* translated and introduced by J. M. Cohen. London: Penguin.

Mooney, J. 1896. *The Ghost Dance Religion and the Sioux Outbreak of 1890.* Fourteenth Annual Report. Washington, DC: Bureau of American Ethnology.

Moore, H. L. 1994. "On Sex and Gender." Pp. 813–30 in T. Ingold, ed., *Companion Encyclopaedia of Anthropology.* London: Routledge.

—— 1996. "The Changing Nature of Anthropological Knowledge: An Introduction." Pp. 1–15 in H. L. Moore, ed., *The Future of Anthropological Knowledge.* London and New York: Routledge.

——, T. Sanders, and B. Kaare, 1999. *Those Who Play with Fire: Gender, Fertility & Transformation in East & Southern Africa.* London: Athlone Press.

Moos, F. 1995. "Anthropological Ethics and the Military." *Anthropology Newsletter* 36(9): 34.

Morgan, L. H. 1851. *League of the Ho-de-no-sau-nee.* Rochester, NY: Sage and Brother.

—— 1871. *Systems of Consanguinity and Affinity of the Human Family.* Washington: Smithsonian Institution.

—— 1877. *Ancient Society.* New York: Henry Holt.

Mortillet, G. de. 1897. *La formation de la nation française.* Paris: F. Alcan.

Morton, S. G. 1854. *Types of Mankind.* Philadelphia: Lippincott, Grambo.

Moser, S. 1998. *Ancestral Images: The Iconography of Human Origins.* Ithaca: Cornell University Press.

Moses, Y. 1997. "Are Four Fields in our Future?" *Anthropology Newsletter* 38(2): 8–11.

Motsch, A. 2001. *Lafitau et l'émergence du discours ethnographique.* Paris: Septentrion/Presses de l'Université de Paris-Sorbonne.

Mucchielli, L. 1997. "Sociologie versus anthropologie raciale. L'engagement decisif des Durkhemiens dans le contexte 'fin de siècle' (1885–1914)." *Gradhiva* 21: 77–95.

Mühlmann, W. E. 1946. *Geschichte der Anthropologie.* Frankfurt: Athenäum Verlag.

—— 1968. *Geschichte der Anthropologie.* 2., verbesserte und erweiterte Auflage. Frankfurt am Main and Bonn: Athenäum.

Mukhopadhyay, C. and Y. Moses. 1997. "Reestablishing 'Race' in Anthropological Discourse." *American Anthropologist* n.s. 99: 517–33.

Müller, F. M. 1886. "On Manners and Customs." Pp. 253–88 in vol. 2 of his *Chips from a German Workshop.* London: Longmans, Green and Company.

—— 1891. *Physical Religion.* New York: Longmans, Green and Company.

—— 1892. *Natural Religion.* London: Longmans, Green and Company.

Munn, N. 1986. *The Fame of Gawa: A Symbolic Study of Value Transformation in a Massim Society.* Cambridge: Cambridge University Press.

Murray, G. 1897. *A History of Ancient Greek Literature.* London: Heinemann.

Murray, S. O. 1994. *Theory Groups and the Study of Language in North America: A Social History.* Amsterdam/Philadelphia: John Benjamins.

Nader, L. 1970. "From Anguish to Exultation." Pp. 97–118 in P. Golde, ed., *Women in the Field: Anthropolical Experiences.* Chicago: Aldine.

Nei, M. and A. K. Roychoudhury. 1974. "Genic variation within and between the three major races of man, Caucasoids, Negroids, and Mongoloids." *American Journal of Human Genetics,* 26: 421–43.

Nichols, B. 1994. *Blurred Boundaries: Questions of Meaning in Contemporary Culture.* Bloomington: Indiana University Press.

Nieuwenhuis, A. W. 1904. *De Levensvoorwarden onder Volken op Hoogen en op Lagen Trap van Beschaving* (The Living Conditions of Peoples on High and Low Levels of Civilization). Inaugural Address: University of Leiden. Leiden: E. J. Brill.

Nikolai-on [N. Daniel'son]. 1893. *Ocherki narodnogo poreformennogo obschestvennogo khoziaistva* (Essays on [Russian] post-reform national economy). St Petersburg.

Noble, W. and I. Davidson. 1996. *Human Evolution, Language, and Mind.* Cambridge: Cambridge University Press.

Numelin, R. 1947. *Fältforskare och kammarlärde: Drag ur socialantropologiens idéhistoria* (Fieldworkers and Bookish Persons: Notes on the History of Social Anthropology). Helsingfors: Söderström & Co. Förlagsaktiebolag.

Obeysekere, G. 1992. *The Apotheosis of Captain Cook: European Mythmaking in the Pacific.* Princeton: Princeton University Press.

Olsen, J. W. 1987. "The Practice of Archaeology in China Today." *Antiquity* 61: 282–90.

Ortner, S. B. 1984. "Theory in Anthropology Since the Sixties." *Comparative Studies in Society and History* 26: 126–66.

Osman Hill, W. C. 1940. "Classification of Hominidae." *Nature* 146: 402–3.

Otto, R. 1923. *The Idea of the Holy.* New York: Oxford University Press.

Ouellet, R. 1990. "Introduction." Pp. 11–16 in L.-A. Lahontan, *Oeuvres complètes,* ed. R. Ouellet, vol. 1. Quebec: Presses de l'Université de Montréal.

Pagden, A. 1982. *The Fall of Natural Man: The American Indian and the Origins of Comparative Ethnology.* Cambridge, UK: Cambridge University Press.

Pang, A. S. 2002. *Empire and the Sun.* Stanford: Stanford University Press.

Palriwala, R. 2005. "Fieldwork in a Post-colonial anthropology: Experience and the Comparative." *Social Anthropology* 13: 151–70.

Parsons, E. C., ed. 1922. *American Indian Life*. New York: B. W. Huebsch.

Partridge, W. 1985. "Toward a Theory of Practice." *American Behavioral Scientist* 29: 139–63.

Pearl, R. 1927. "The biology of superiority." *The American Mercury* 12: 257–66.

Pearson, K. 1930. "Race crossing in Jamaica." *Nature* 126: 427–9.

Pels, P. and O. Salemink. 1999. "Introduction: Locating the Colonial Subjects of Anthropology." Pp. 1–52 in P. Pels and O. Salemink, eds., *Colonial Subjects: Essays on the Practical History of Anthropology*. Ann Arbor: University of Michigan Press.

Penny, H. G. 1999. "Fashioning Local Identities in an Age of Nation-Building: Museums, Cosmopolitan Visions, and Intra-German Competition." *German History* 17: 489–504.

—— 2002a. "The Civic Uses of Science: Ethnology and Civil Society in Imperial Germany." *Osiris* 17: 228–52.

—— 2002b. *Objects of Culture: Ethnology and Ethnographic Museums in Imperial Germany*. Chapel Hill: University of North Carolina Press.

—— 2003. "Bastian's Museum: On the Limits of Empiricism and the Transformation of German Ethnology." Pp. 86–116 in H. G. Penny and M. Bunzl, eds., *Worldly Provincialism: German Anthropology in the Age of Empire*. Ann Arbor: University of Michigan Press.

—— and M. Bunzl, eds., 2003. *Worldly Provincialism: German Anthropology in the Age of Empire*. Ann Arbor: University of Michigan Press.

Pinney, C. 1990. "Classification and Fantasy in the Photographic Construction of Caste and Tribe." *Visual Anthropology* 3: 259–88.

—— 1992. "The Parallel Histories of Anthropology and Photography." Pp. 74–95 in E. Edwards, ed., *Anthropology and Photography*. New Haven: Yale University Press.

Plekhanov, G. V. 1956. *The Development of the Monist View of History*. Moscow: Foreign Languages Publishing House.

Podolefsy, A. and P. Brown. 2002. *Applying Cultural Anthropology: An Introductory Reader*. New York: McGraw-Hill.

Politiek, H. A. 1994. "Koloniaal Museum en Koloniaal Instituut: Een Onderzoek naar Koloniale Beeldvorming van Twee 'Praktische Instellingen'." (Colonial Museum and Colonial Instituut: Research on the Creation of the Colonial Image by Two "Practical Institutions"). MA Thesis: Free University Amsterdam.

Powell, J. W. 1878. *Report on the Arid Lands of the United States*. New York: Belknap Press.

—— 1891. "Indian Linguistic Families North of Mexico." Pp. 7–139 in *Bureau of American Ethnology Report 7 for 1885*. Washington, DC: Government Printing Office.

Prager, M. 1999. "Crossing Borders, Healing Wounds: Leiden Anthropology and the Colonial Encounter (1917–1949)." Pp. 326–61 in J. van Bremen and A. Shimizu, eds., *Anthropology and Colonialism in Asia and Oceania*. Surrey: Curzon.

Preus, J. S. 1987. *Explaining Religion*. New Haven: Yale University Press.

Prewitt, K. 1996a. "Presidential Items." *Items* 50(1): 15–18.

—— 1996b. "Presidential Items." *Items* 50(2/3): 31–40.

—— 1996c. "International Dissertation Field Research: A New Fellowship Program." *Items* 50(4): 91–2.

—— 2002. "The Social Science Project: Then, Now and Next." *Items and Issues* 3(1–2): 1, 5–9.

Price, D. 1998. "Gregory Bateson and the OSS: World War II and Bateson's Assessment of Applied Anthropology." *Human Organization* 57: 379–84.

—— 2004. *Threatening Anthropology: McCarthyism and the FBI's Surveillance of Activist Anthropologists*. Durham: Duke University Press.

Prochasson, C. and A. Rasmussen. 1996. *Au nom de la patrie. Les intellectuels et la première guerre mondiale.* Paris: La Découverte.

Proctor, R. 1988. "From Anthropologie to Rassenkunde in the German Anthropological Tradition." Pp. 138–79 in G. W. Stocking, Jr., ed., *Bones, Bodies, Behavior: Essays on Biological Anthropology.* Madison: University of Wisconsin Press.

Putnam, C. 1961. *Race and Reason.* Washington, DC: Public Affairs Press.

—— 1962. "Culture and Race." *Science* 135: 966–8.

—— 1963. "Science and the Race Problem." *Science* 142: 1419–20.

Pypin, A. N. 1891. *Istoriia Russkoi etnographii* (The history of Russian ethnography). Tom II "Obschii obzor izuchenii narodnosti i etnographia velikorusskaia." St. Peterburg: Tipographia M. M. Stasiulevicha.

Raby, P. 2001. *Alfred Russel Wallace: A Life.* London: Chatto and Windus.

Radcliffe-Brown, A. R. 1958 [1931]. "The Present Position of Anthropological Studies." In M. N. Srinivas, ed., *Method in Social Anthropology.* Chicago: University of Chicago Press.

Radin, P. 1927. *Primitive Man as Philosopher.* New York: D. Appleton.

Rafael, V. 1994. "The Cultures of Area Studies in the United States." *Social Text* 41: 91–111.

Rappaport, R. 1968. *Pigs for the Ancestors.* New Haven: Yale University Press.

Rapport der Commissie van Advies Betreffende's Rijks Ethnographisch Museum. (Report of the Advisory Committee Regarding the National Museum of Ethnology.) 1903.

Raskol'nikova, F., ed., 1926. *Khzhdenie v narod: sbornik* (*Going to the people: an anthology*). Moscow and Leningrad: Moskovskii Rabochii.

Read, C. H. 1892. "Prefatory Note." Pp. 87–8 to Read, ed., Part II, "Ethnography," in J. Garson and C. H. Read, eds., *Notes and Queries on Anthropology*, 2nd edn. London: The Anthropological Institute.

Reining, C. 1962. "A Lost Period of Applied Anthropology." *American Anthropologist* 64: 593–600.

Riese, B. 1995. "Während des Dritten Reiches (1933–1945) in Deutschland und Österreich verfolgte und von dort ausgewanderte Ethnologen." Pp. 141–67 in T. Hauschild, ed., *Lebenslust und Fremdenfurcht: Ethnologie im Dritten Reich.* Frankfurt: Suhrkamp.

Ringer, F. K. 1969. *The Decline of the German Mandarins.* Cambridge, MA: Harvard University Press.

Rivers, W. H. R. 1901. "Primitive Color Vision." *Popular Science Monthly* 59: 44–58.

—— 1902. "The Colour Vision of the Eskimos." *Journal of the Anthropological Institute of Great Britain and Ireland* 32: 143–9.

—— 1903. "Observations on the Vision of the Uralis and the Sholagas." *Bulletin of the Madras Government Museum.* 5: 3–18.

—— 1905. "Observations on the Senses of the Todas." *British Journal of Psychology* 1: 321–96.

—— 1914. *The History of Melanesian Society*, 2 vols. Cambridge: Cambridge University Press.

—— 1968 [1910]. "The Genealogical Method of Anthropological Inquiry." Pp. 97–109 in Rivers, *Kinship and Social Organization*, introduced by R. Firth and with commentaries by Firth and D. M. Schneider. London: Athlone Press.

—— et al. 1901. *Physiology and Psychology.* Vol. II in A. C. Haddon, ed., *Reports of the Cambridge Anthropological Expedition to Torres Straits.* Cambridge: Cambridge University Press.

Rivet, P. 1937. "Ce qu'est l'ethnologie." In *Encyclopédie française VII, L'espèce humaine.*

Robinson, A. 2002. *The Life of Jane Ellen Harrison.* Oxford: Oxford University Press.

Rollwagen, J. R. ed. 1988. *Anthropological Filmmaking.* Chur, Switzerland: Harwood Academic Press.

Romero, S. 1895. *Doutrina contra doutrina: O evolucionismo e o positivismo no Brasil*, 2nd edn. Rio de Janeiro: Alves.

—— 1901 [1899]. "O haeckelismo em sociologia." Pp. 3–46 in his *Ensaios de sociologia e litteratura*. Rio de Janeiro: H. Garnier.

—— 1902–03. *Historia da Litteratura brasileira*, 2nd edn, 2 vols. Rio de Janeiro: H. Garnier.

Rony, F. T. 1996. *The Third Eye: Race, Cinema and Ethnographic Spectacle*. Durham: Duke University Press.

Roper, M. and Tosh, J. 1991. "Introduction: Historians and the Politics of Masculinity." Pp. 1–24 in M. Roper and J. Tosh, eds., *Manful Assertions: Masculinities in Britain Since 1800*. London: Routledge.

Rosaldo, M. and Lamphere, L. eds. 1974. *Woman, Culture, and Society*. Stanford: Stanford University Press.

Ross, D. 1991. *The Origins of American Social Science*. New York: Cambridge University Press.

Royal Commission on Aboriginal Peoples. 1996. *Report of the Royal Commission on Aboriginal Peoples*. Ottawa: Government of Canada.

Royal Museum of Central Africa. 2006. "Import Export." (Exhibit Label). Tervuren, Belgium.

Ruby, J. 1975. "Is an Ethnographic Film a Filmic Ethnography?" *Studies in the Anthropology of Visual Communication* 2(20): 104–11.

—— 2000. *Picturing Culture: Explorations of Film and Anthropology*. Chicago: Chicago University Press.

Rüegg, W., ed. 2004. *A History of the University in Europe*, vol. 3. Cambridge: Cambridge University Press.

Rumsey, A. and J. F. Weiner, eds. 2001. *Emplaced Myth: Space, Narrative, and Knowledge in Aboriginal Australia and Papua New Guinea*. Honolulu: University of Hawai'i Press.

Rupke, N. A. 1997. "Introduction to the 1997 Edition." Pp. vii–xlii in A. von Humboldt, *Cosmos: A Sketch of a Physical Description of the Universe*, vol. I., trans. E. C. Otté. Baltimore: The Johns Hopkins University Press.

Rusch, W. 1986. "Der Beitrag Felix von Luschan's für die Ethnographie." *Ethnographisch-Archäologische Zeitschrift* 27: 430–53.

Rushton, J. P. 1995. *Race, Evolution, and Behavior: A Life-History Approach*. New Brunswick, NJ: Transaction.

Rylko-Bauer, B., M. Singer, and J. van Willigen. 2006. "Reclaiming Applied Anthropology: Its Past, Present, and Future." *American Anthropologist* 108(1): 178–90.

Sahlins, M. 1985. *Islands of History*. Chicago: University of Chicago Press.

Salomaa, I. 2002. *Rafael Karsten (1879–1956) as a Finnish Scholar of Religion: The Life and Career of a Man of Science*. Helsinki: The University Press.

Sanjek, R., ed. 1990. *Fieldnotes: The Making of Anthropology*. Ithaca: Cornell University Press.

Sapir, E. 1999. *Selected Writings of Edward Sapir. Volume 3, Culture*, ed. by R. Darnell, J. Irvine, and R. Handler. Berlin: Mouton de Gruyter.

Sarich, V. and Miele, F. 2004. *Race: The Reality of Human Differences*. New York: Westview Press.

Sarich, V. M., and A. C. Wilson. 1967. "Immunological Time Scale for Hominid Evolution." *Science* 158: 1200–3.

Saunders, B. and P. Whittle. 2004. "The Normativity of Colour." Unpublished paper.

Sautman, B. 2001. "Peking Man and the Politics of Paleoanthropological Nationalism in China." *Journal of Asian Studies* 60: 95–124.

Schefold, R. 2002. "Indonesian Studies and Cultural Anthropology in Leiden: From Encyclopedism to Field of Anthropological Study." Pp. 69–94 in H. Vermeulen and J. Kommers, eds., *Tales from Academia: History of Anthropology in the Netherlands*. Saarbrücken: Verlag für Entwicklungspolitiek.

Schensul, S. 1985. "Science, Theory, and Application." *American Behavioral Scientist* 29: 164–85.

—— and J. J. Schensul. 1978. "Advocacy and Applied Anthropology." Pp. 121–65 in G. Weber and G. McCall, eds., *Social Scientists as Advocates*. Beverly Hills, CA: Sage.

Schick, K. D., and N. Toth. 1994. *Making Silent Stones Speak: Human Evolution and the Dawn of Technology*. New York: Simon and Schuster.

Schieffelin, E. and R. Crittenden, eds. 1990. *Like People You See In a Dream*. Stanford: Stanford University Press.

Schmidt, W. 1912–55. *Der Ursprung der Gottesidee, eine historisch-kritische und positive Studie*. Münster: Aschendorffsche Verlagsbuchhandlung.

Schumaker, L. 2001. *Africanizing Anthropology: Fieldwork, Networks, and the Making of Cultural Knowledge in Central Africa*. Durham: Duke University Press.

Schwarcz, L. M. 1999. *The Spectacle of the Races: Scientists, Institutions and the Race Question in Brazil, 1870–1930*. New York: Hill & Wang.

Scudder, T. 1999. "The Emerging Global Crisis and Development Anthropology: Can We Have an Impact?" *Human Organization* 58: 351–64.

Semevskii, V. I. 1881. "Ne pora li napisat' istoriiu krestian v Rossii?" (Is this not the right time to write a history of peasants in Russia?) *Russkaia Mysl'* 2: 215–65.

Serrurier, L. 1895. *Museum of Mesthoop?* (Museum or Dungheap?) Leiden and The Hague.

Shackel, P. and E. Chambers. 2004 *Places in Mind: Public Archaeology As Applied Anthropology*. London: Routledge.

Shankman, P. and T. B. Ehlers. 2000. "The 'Exotic' and the 'Domestic': Regions and Representation in Cultural Anthropology." *Human Organization* 59: 289–99.

Shcherbina, F. 1879. "Solevychegodskaia zemel'naia obschina" (The Solevychegorsk rural community). *Otechestvennye Zapiski* 7: 41–84 and 8: 167–209.

—— 1880. "Russkaia zemel'naia obschina" (The Russian rural community). *Russkaia Zhisn'* 5: 1–32 and 6: 72–122.

Shipman, P. 1994. *The Evolution of Racism*. New York: Simon and Schuster.

Sibeud, E. 1998. "Les étapes d'un negrologue." Pp. 166–90 in J.-L. Amselle and E. Sibeud, eds., *Maurice Delafosse. Entre orientalisme et etnographie, l'itinéraire d'un africaniste (1870–1926)*. Paris: Maisonneuve et Larose.

—— 2002a. *Une science impériale pour l'Afrique? La construction des saviors africanistes en France (1878–1930)*. Paris: Editions de l'Ehess.

—— 2002b. "Ethnographie africaniste et 'inauthenticité' coloniale." *French Politics, Culture and Society* 20(2): 11–28.

—— 2004a. "Marcel Mauss: Projet de presentation d'un bureau d'ethnologie (1913)." *Revue d'histoire des sciences humaines* 10: 105–24.

—— 2004b. "Un ethnographe face à la colonisation: Arnold van Gennep en Algerie (1911–1912)." *Revue d'histoire des sciences humaines* 10: 79–104.

Simonelli, J. 2001. "Mainstreaming the Applied Anthropology Track: Connections, Guides, and Concerns." *Practicing Anthropology* 23: 48–9.

Singer, M. 1994. "Community Centered Praxis: Toward an Alternative Nondominative Applied Anthropology." *Human Organization* 53: 336–44.

—— 1996. "A Dose of Drugs, a Touch of Violence, a Case of AIDS: Conceptualizing the SAVA Syndemic." *Free Inquiry in Sociology* 24: 99–110.

—— 1999. "Toward a Critical Biocultural Model of Drug Use and Health Risk." Pp. 26–50 in P. Marshall, M. Singer, and M. Clatts, eds., *Cultural, Observational, and Epidemiological Approaches in the Prevention of Drug Abuse and HIV/AIDS*. Bethesda, MD: National Institute on Drug Abuse.

—— 2001. "Toward a Bio-cultural and Political Economic Integration of Alcohol, Tobacco and Drug Studies in the Coming Century." *Social Science and Medicine* 53: 199–213.

—— and S. Clair. 2003. "Syndemics and Public Health: Reconceptualizing Disease in Bio-Social Context." *Medical Anthropology Quarterly* 17: 423–41.

——, P. Erickson, L. Badiane, R. Diaz, D. Ortiz, T. Abraham, and A. M. Nicolaysen. 2006. "Syndemics, Sex and the City: Understanding Sexually Transmitted Disease in Social and Cultural Context." *Social Science and Medicine* 63(8): 2010–21.

——, M. Weeks, and D. Himmelgreen. 1995. "Sale and Exchange of Syringes (letter to the editor)." *Journal of Acquired Immunodeficiency Disease Syndromes and Human Retrovirology* 10: 104.

Slezkine, Y. 1991. "The Fall of Soviet Ethnography." *Current Anthropology* 4: 476–84.

—— 1994. "The USSR as a Communal Apartment, or How a Socialist State Promoted Ethnic Particularism." *Slavic Review* 2: 414–52.

Smith, B. 1985. *European Vision and the South Pacific*, 2nd edn. New Haven: Yale University Press.

—— 1992. *Imagining the Pacific*. Melbourne: Melbourne University Press.

Smith, G. W. 2003. "Review of Mill on Nationality by G. Varouxakis." *Nations and Nationalism* 9: 150–1.

Smith, J. D. 2002. "W. E. B. Du Bois, Felix von Luschan, and Racial Reform at the Fin de Siecle." *Amerikastudien/American Studies* 47: 23–38.

Smith, W. D. 1991. *Politics and the Sciences of Culture in Germany 1840–1920*. New York: Oxford University Press.

Smith, W. R. 1880. "A Journey in the Hejaz." *Scotsman*.

—— 1889, rev. ed. [1894]. *The Religion of the Semites*. London: Macmillan.

—— 1923 [1889]. *Lectures on the Religion of the Semites* London: A & C Black.

Smolka, W. J. 1994. *Völkerkunde in München: Voraussetzungen, Möglichkeiten und Entwicklungslinien ihrer Institutionalisierung, c. 1850–1933*. Berlin: Duncker & Humblot.

Sokolovskii, P. A. 1877. *Ocherki po istorii sel'skoi obshchiny na severe Rossii* (Essays on the history of rural community in the north of Russia). St Petersburg.

—— 1878. *Ekonomicheskii byt zemledel'cheskogo naseleniia Rossii i kolonizatsiia iugo-vostochnykh stepei pered krepostnym pravom* (The economic life of the rural population in Russia and the colonization of the south-eastern steppes before the Serfdom). St Petersburg.

Solovei, T. D. 1998. *Ot "burzhuaznoi" etnologii k "sovetskoi" entografii: istoriia otechestvennoi etnologii pervoi treti XX veka* (From "bourgeois" ethnology to "Soviet" ethnography: the history of Russian ethnology in the first third of the 20th century). Moscow: IEA RAN.

Spence, J. 1969. *To Change China: Western Advisers in China 1620–1960*. Boston: Little, Brown.

Spencer, J. 2000. "British Social Anthropology: A Retrospective." *Annual Review of Anthropology* 29: 1–24.

——, A. Jepson, D. Mills. 2005. "Career Paths and Training Needs of Social Anthropology Research Students. ESRC [Economic and Social Science Research Council] Research Grant RES-000-23-0220. End of Award Report." Unpublished manuscript.

Spencer, W. B. and F. J. Gillen. 1899. *Native Tribes of Central Australia*. London: Macmillan.

Sperling, S. 2000. "Ashley Montagu (1905–1999)." *American Anthropologist* n.s. 102: 543–88.

Spicer, E. 1952. *Human Problems in Technological Change.* Chicago: University of Chicago Press.

—— 1976. "Beyond Analysis and Explanation: The Life and Times of the Society for Applied Anthropology." *Human Organization* 35: 335–44.

Spiro, M. E. 1970. *Buddhism and Society.* New York: Harper and Row.

—— 1982. *Oedipus in the Trobriands.* Chicago: University of Chicago Press.

Ssorin-Chaikov, N. 2003. *The Social Life of the State in Subarctic Siberia.* Stanford: Stanford University Press.

Stafford, B. M. 1997. *Good Looking: Essays on the Virtue of Images.* Cambridge, MA: MIT Press.

Starn, O. 1994. "Rethinking the Politics of Anthropology: The Case of the Andes." *Current Anthropology* 35: 13–38.

Steward, J. 1962. "Culture and Race." *Science* 135: 964–6.

Stewart, J. G. 1959. *Jane Ellen Harrison: A Portrait from Letters.* London: Merlin.

Stewart, T. D. 1961. "UNESCO Statements on Race." *Science* 133: 1634.

Stille, A. 2001. "Globalization Now, A Sequel of Sorts." *The New York Times*, "Arts and Leisure Section." August 11: B7, 9.

Stocking, G. W., Jr. 1968. *Race, Culture, and Evolution: Essays in the Historiography of Anthropology.* New York: Free Press.

—— 1971. "What's in a name? The origins of the Royal Anthropological Institute (1837–71)." *Man* n.s. 6: 369–90.

—— 1973. "From Chronology to Ethnology. James Cowles Prichard and British Anthropology 1800–1850)." Pp. ix–cx in Stocking, ed., *James Cowles Prichard, Researches into the Physical History of Man.* Chicago: University of Chicago Press.

—— 1984. "Qu'est ce qui est en jeu dans un nom? La 'Société d'ethnographie' et l'historiographie de 'l'anthropologie' en France." Pp. 421–31 in B. Rupp-Eisenreich, ed., *Histoires de l'anthropologie.* Paris: Klincksieck.

—— ed. 1984. *Functionalism Historicized: Essays on British Social Anthropology.* Madison: University of Wisconsin Press.

—— 1985. "Philanthropoids and Vanishing Cultures: Rockefeller Funding and the End of the Museum Era in Anglo-American Anthropology." Pp. 112–45 in G. W. Stocking, Jr., ed., *Objects and Others: Essays on Museums and Material Culture.* Madison: University of Wisconsin Press.

—— 1987. *Victorian Anthropology.* New York: Free Press.

—— ed. 1991. *Colonial Situations: Essays on the Contextualization of Ethnographic Knowledge.* Madison: University of Wisconsin Press.

—— 1995. *After Tylor: British Social Anthropology 1888–1951.* Madison: University of Wisconsin Press.

—— 2001. *Delimiting Anthropology: Occasional Papers and Reflections.* Madison: University of Wisconsin Press.

Stoler, A. L. 1992. "Rethinking Colonial Categories: European Communities and the Boundaries of Rule." Pp. 319–52 in N. B. Dirks, ed., *Colonialism and Culture.* Ann Arbor: University of Michigan Press.

Stoller, P. 1992. *The Cinematic Griot.* Chicago: University of Chicago Press.

Strathern, A. 1982. "Two waves of African models in the New Guinea Highlands." Pp. 35–49 in A. Strathern, ed., *Inequality in New Guinea Highlands Societies.* Cambridge: Cambridge University Press.

—— 1984. *A Line of Power.* London: Tavistock.

Strathern, M. 1988. *Gender of the Gift.* Berkeley: University of California Press.

Stray, C. 1998. *Classics Transformed: Schools, Universities, and Society in England, 1830–1960.* Oxford: Clarendon Press.

Strenski, I. 1985. "Comparative Study of Religions: A Theological Necessity." *Christian Century* (February 6–13): 126–9.

—— 1987. *Four Theories of Myth in Twentieth-Century History*. London/Iowa City: Macmillan/Iowa University Press.

—— 1996a. "Misreading Max Müller." *Method and Theory in the Study of Religion* 8: 291–6.

—— 1996b. "The Rise of Ritual and the Hegemony of Myth: Sylvain Lévi, the Durkheimians and Max Müller." Pp. 52–81 in W. Doniger and L. Patton, eds., *Myth and Method*. Charlottesville: University of Virginia Press.

—— 2002. "Why It Is Better to Have Some of the Questions than All of the Answers." *Method and Theory in the Study of Religion* 14 (Winter).

Stringer, C., and C. Gamble. 1993. *In Search of the Neanderthals*. New York: Thames and Hudson.

Stroup, T. 1991. "Westermarck, Edward Alexander." *International Dictionary of Anthropologists*, ed. Christopher Winters. New York and London: Garland Publishing.

Suny, R. 1993. *The Revenge of the Past: Nationalism, Revolution, and the Collapse of the Soviet Union*. Stanford: Stanford University Press.

Suolinna, K. 1993. "Rituals of Passage in Islamic Folkculture – A Comparison Between Studies by Edward Westermarck and Hilma Granqvist." *Westermarck et la société marocaine*. Rabat: Faculté des Lettres et des Sciences Humaines.

—— 1997. "Focusing on Fieldwork: Edward Westermarck and Hilma Granqvist Before and After Bronislaw Malinowski." *Approaching Religion Based on Papers read at the Symposium on Methodology in the Study of Religion held at Turku, Finland, on the 4th–6th August*. Åbo: Donner Institute for Research in Religious and Cultural History.

—— 1998. "Edward Westermarck in the Light of Correspondence Exchanged with His Students and Colleagues." Paper presented at Marriage, Morality and Emotions: An International Symposium in Helsinki, Finland, November 19–22.

Superanskii, M. F. 1901. *Sotsiologiia N. K. Mikhailovskogo* (*Mikhailovskii's sociology*). St Petersburg.

Taselaar, Arjen. 1998. *De Nederlandse Koloniale Lobby: Ondernemers en de Indische Politiek 1914–1940*. (The Dutch Colonial Lobby: Entrepeneurs and East Indian Politics 1914–1940.) Leiden: Research School of Asian, African, and Amerindian Studies (CNWS) Publications.

Tattersall, I. 1995. *The Fossil Trail: How We Know What We Think We Know About Human Evolution*. New York: Oxford University Press.

—— 1998. *Becoming Human: Evolution and Human Uniqueness*. San Diego: Harcourt Brace.

—— 2000. "Once We Were Not Alone." *Scientific American* 282: 56–62.

Tax, S. 1970. "The Fox Project." Pp. 106–12 in James Clifton, ed., *Applied Anthropology: Readings in the Uses of the Science of Man*. Boston: Houghton Mifflin.

Taylor, C. 2002. *Varieties of Religion Today: William James Revisited*. Cambridge: Harvard University Press.

Taylor, E. G. R. 1937. "Robert Hooke and the Cartographical Projects of the Late Seventeenth Century (1666–1696)." *The Geographical Journal* 90: 529–40.

Taylor, L. 1996. "Iconophobia: How Anthropology Lost It At The Movies." *Transition* 69: 64–88.

Taylor, R. E. 2000. "Origins of a Nobel Idea: The Conception of Radiocarbon Dating." *Chemical Heritage* 18(4): 7.

Thilenius, G. 1907. "Denkschrift über ein hamburgische Expedition nach der Südsee, 1907." Archive of the Hamburgisches Museum für Völkerkunde, File: SSE 1.

Thomas, D. H. 2000. *Skull Wars: Kennewick Man, Archaeology, and the Battle for Native American Identity*. New York: Basic Books.

Thomson, G. 1941. *Aeschylus and Athens: A Study in the Social Origins of Drama*. London: Lawrence and Wishart.

Tigorov, V. 1879. "Proekt programmy issledovania russkoi zemel'noi obschiny" (A project for studying the Russian rural community). *Otechestvennye Zapiski* 8: 235–54.

Tishkov, V. 1992. "The Crisis in Soviet Ethnography." *Current Anthropology* 4: 371–82.

Titmuss, R. 1972. *The Gift Relationship: From Human Blood to Social Policy*. New York: Vintage.

Tjon Sie Fat, L. A. and G. J. C. M. van Vliet. 1990. *Philipp von Siebold: Zijn Japanse Flora en Fauna* (*Philipp von Siebold: His Japanese Flora and Fauna*). Haarlem: H. J. W. Becht.

Tokarev, S. A. 1966. *Istoriia Russkoi etnographii. Dooktiabr'skii period* (*The history of Russian ethnography. The pre-revolutionary period*). Moscow: Nauka.

Tort, P. 1996. *Dictionnaire du darwinisme et de l'évolution*, 3 vols. Paris: Presses Universitaires de France.

Trigger, B. 1968. "Major Concepts of Archaeology in Historical Perspective." *Man* n.s. 3: 527–41.

—— 1984. "Alternative Archaeologies: Nationalist, Colonialist, Imperialist." *Man* n.s. 19: 355–70.

—— 1989. *A History of Archaeological Thought*. Cambridge, UK: Cambridge University Press.

Trotter, R., R. H. Needle, E. Goosby, C. Bates, and M. Singer. 2001. "A Methodological Model for Rapid Assessment, Response, and Evaluation: The RARE Program in Public Health." *Field Methods* 13: 137–59.

Trouillot, M.-R. 1991. "Anthropology and the Savage Slot." Pp. 17–44 in R. Fox, ed., *Recapturing Anthropology: Working in the Present*. Santa Fe, NM: School of American Research Press.

Truettner, W. H. 1979. *The Natural Man Observed: A Study of Catlin's Indian Gallery*. Washington, DC: Smithsonian Institution Press.

Tucker, W. H. 1994. *The Science and Politics of Racial Research*. Urbana: University of Illinois Press.

—— 2002. *The Funding of Scientific Racism: Wickliffe Draper and the Pioneer Fund*. Urbana, IL: University of Illinois Press.

Tully, J. 1993. *An Approach to Political Philosophy: Locke in Contexts*. Cambridge: Cambridge University Press.

Turner, R. S. 1993. "Vision Studies in Germany: Helmholtz versus Hering." *Osiris* 8: 80–103.

Turner, T. 2002. "Representation, Politics and Cultural Imagination in Indigenous Video: General Points and Kayapo Examples." Pp. 75–89 in F. Ginsburg et al., eds., *Media Worlds*. Berkeley: University of California Press.

Turner, V. 1967. *The Forest of Symbols*. Ithaca: Cornell University Press.

Turton, D. 1992. "Anthropology on Television: What Next?" Pp. 283–99 in P. Crawford and D. Turton, eds., *Film as Ethnography*. Manchester: Manchester University Press.

Tylor, E. B. 1866. "The Religion of Savages." *Fortnightly Review* 6: 71–86.

—— 1873. *Religion in Primitive Culture*. New York: Harper.

—— 1880. "President's Address." *Journal of the Anthropological Institute* 9: 443–58.

—— 1881. *Anthropology*. London: Macmillan.

—— 1888. "On a Method of Investigating the Development of Institutions, Applied to Laws of Marriage and Descent." *Journal of the Anthropological Institute* 18: 245–272.

—— 1905. "Professor Adolf Bastian." *Man* 5: 138–43.

—— 1910. "Anthropology." Pp. 108–19 in *The Encyclopaedia Britannica*, 11th Edition, vol. I. New York: The Encyclopaedia Britannica Company.

Underhill, P., et al. 2000. "Y Chromosome Variation and the History of Human Populations." *Nature Genetics* 26: 358–61.

Valentine, L. and R. Darnell, eds. 1999. *Theorizing the Americanist Tradition*. Toronto: University of Toronto Press.

van der Velde, P. 2000. *Een Indische Liefde: P. J. Veth (1814–1895) en de Inburgering van Nederlandse-Indië*. (A Love for the East Indies: P. J. Veth (1814–1895) and the Integration of the Dutch Indies.) Amsterdam: Balans.

van Dijk, C. 1992. "Tussen Koloniale Handel en Wetenschap: De Volkenkundige Musea in Nederland in de Negentiende Eeuw." (Between Colonial Trade and Science: The Anthropology Museums in The Netherlands in the Nineteenth Century) *Tijdschrift voor Geschiedenis* 105: 346–66.

van Gennep, A. 1905. "Ethnographie, folklore." *Mercure de France* 53(184): 608–12.

—— 1914a. "La signification du premier congrès d'ethnographie (Neuchatel)." *Mercure de France* 10(410): 322–32.

—— 1914b. *En Algerie*. Paris: Mercure de France.

van Wengen, C. 2002a. "Indonesian Collections at the National Museum of Ethnology in Leiden." Pp. 81–108 in R. Schefold and H. Vermeulen, eds., *Treasure Hunting? Collectors and Collections of Indonesian Artifacts*. Leiden: Research School of Asian, African, and Amerindian Studies (CNWS), University of Leiden/National Museum of Ethnology.

—— 2002b. "The Interaction Between Studies of Material Culture and Academic Anthropology in Leiden." In H. Vermeulen and J. Kommers, eds., *Tales from Academia: History of Anthropology in the Netherlands*. Saarbrücken: Verlag für Entwicklungspolitik.

—— 2002c. *Wat is er te doen in Volkenkunde? De Bewogen Geschiedenis van het Rjksmuseum voor Volkenkunde Leiden*. Leiden: Rjksmuseum voor Volkenkunde.

van Willigen, J. 2002. *Applied Anthropology: An Introduction*, 3rd edn. South Hadley, MA: Bergin & Garvey.

Vasilchiakov, A. I. 1881. *Sel'skii byt i sel'skoe khoziaistvo v Rossii* (Rural material culture and economy in Russia). St Petersburg: Tipografia M. M. Stasiulevicha.

Vermeulen, H. 2002. "Contingency and Continuity: Anthropology and Other Non-Western Studies in Leiden." Pp. 95–182 in H. Vermeulen and J. Kommers, eds., *Tales from Academia: History of Anthropology in the Netherlands*. Saarbrücken: Verlag für Entwicklungspolitik.

—— and J. Kommers. 2002. "Introduction: Histories of Anthropology in The Netherlands." Pp. 1–68 in H. Vermeulen and J. Kommers, eds., *Tales from Academia: History of Anthropology in the Netherlands*. Saarbrücken: Verlag für Entwicklungspolitik.

Vildé, B. 1938–39. "L'ethnologie française et le Musée de l'Homme" (French Ethnology at the Musée de l'Homme). *Aikakauskirja: Journal de la Société Finno-ougrienne*, vol. L.

Vincent, J. 1990. *Anthropology and Politics: Visions, Traditions, and Trends*. Tucson: University of Arizona Press.

Virchow, R. 1879. "Nubier." *Zeitschrift für Ethnologie* 11: 449–56.

Visweswaran, K. 1997. "Histories of Feminist Ethnography." *Annual Review of Anthropology* 26: 591–621.

Vitalis, R. 2002. "International Studies in America." *Items and Issues* 3(3–4): 1–2, 12–16.

Vitashevskii, N. A. 1929a. "Sposoby razlozheniia i sbora podatei v Yakutskoi obshchine" (The ways of imposing and collecting taxes in the Yakut community). Pp. 63–77 in D. M. Pavlinov, N. A. Vitashevskii and L. G. Levental', *Materialy po obuchnomu pravu i po obschestvennomu bytu iakutov*. Trudy Komissii po Izucheniu Yakutskoi ASSR Leningrad: Izdatel'stvo AN SSSR.

—— 1929b. "Yakutskie materialy dlia razrabotki voprosov embriologii prava" (The Yakut data for developing the issues of the embryology of law). Pp. 89–220 in D. M. Pavlinov, N. A.

Vitashevskii and L. G. Levental', *Materialy po obuchnomu pravu i po obschestvennomu bytu iakutov.* Trudy Komissii po Izucheniu Yakutskoi ASSR Leningrad: Izdatel'stvo AN SSSR.

Vogt, C. 1864. *Lectures on Man.* Philadelphia: Lippincott, Grambo.

Wagner, R. 1967. *The Curse of Souw.* Chicago: University of Chicago Press.

—— 1974. Are there groups in the New Guinea Highlands? Pp. 95–122 in M. Leaf, ed., *Frontiers of Anthropology.* New York: Van Nostrand.

—— 1975. *The Invention of Culture.* Chicago: University of Chicago Press.

Waiko, J. 1992. "Tugata: Culture, Identity, and Commitment." Pp. 233–66 in L. Foerstel and A. Gilliam, eds., *Confronting the Margaret Mead Legacy: Scholarship, Empire, and the South Pacific.* Philadelphia: Temple University Press.

Wallace, A. F. C. 1961. *Culture and Personality.* New York: Random House.

—— 1999. *Thomas Jefferson and the Indians: The Tragic Fate of the First Americans.* Cambridge, MA: Harvard University Press.

Wallerstein, I. 1974. *The Modern World-System.* New York: Academic Press.

—— et al. 1996. *Open the Social Sciences: Report of the Gulbenkian Commission on the Restructuring of the Social Sciences.* Stanford: Stanford University Press.

Warren, K. B. 1998. *Indigenous Movements and their Critics: Pan-Maya Activism in Guatemala.* Princeton: Princeton University Press.

Wartelle, J.-C. 2004. "La Société anthropologique de Paris de 1859 à 1920." *Revue d'histoire des sciences humaines* 10: 125–72.

Washburn, S. L. 1951. "The New Physical Anthropology." *Transactions of the New York Academy of Sciences.* Series II, 13: 298–304.

—— 1963. "The Study of Race." *American Anthropologist* n.s. 65: 521–31.

—— 1983. "Evolution of a Teacher." *Annual Review of Anthropology* 12: 1–24.

Wassén, S. H. 1932. "Le Musée Ethnographique de Göteborg et l'oeuvre d'Erland Nordenskiöld" (The Gothenburg Ethnographical Museum and the Legacy of Erland Nordenskiöld). Tucuman: Universidad Nacional, Instituto de etnología, Revista.

Watson, C. W. 1998 "In Anthropology, the Image Can Never Have the Last Say." Pamphlet in the Manchester University series "Groups for Debate in Anthropological Theory," P. Wade, ed. Manchester: Department of Social Anthropology.

Watson, J. 1970. "Society as Organized Flow: The Tairora Case." *Southwestern Journal of Anthropology* 26: 107–24.

Watters, D. R. and Zamora, O. F. 2002. "Expeditions, Expositions, Associations, and Museums in the Anthropological Career of C. V. Hartman." *Annals of Carnegie Museum*, 71(4): 261–99.

Wax, M. 1972. "Tenting with Malinowski." *American Sociological Review* 37(1): 1–13.

Wcislo, F. W. 1990. *Reforming Rural Russia: State, Local Society, and National Politics, 1855–1914.* Princeton: Princeton University Press.

Weaver, T. 1973. *To See Ourselves: Anthropology and Modern Issues.* New York: Scott, Foresman.

Weeks, M. D., Himmelgreen, M. Singer, S. Woolley, N. Romero-Daza, and M. Grier. 1996. "Community-based AIDS prevention: Preliminary outcomes of a program for African American and Latino injection drug users." *Journal of Drug Issues* 26: 561–90.

Weidenreich, F. 1946. "On Eugen Fischer." *Science* 104: 399.

Weikhart, R. 1995. "A Recently Discovered Darwin Letter on Social Darwinsim." *Isis* 86: 609–11.

Weinberger, E. 1994. "The Camera People." Pp. 3–26 in L. Taylor, ed., *Visualizing Anthropology: Selected Essays from V. A. R. 1990–1994.* New York/London: Routledge.

Weindling, P. 1989. *Health, Race and German Politics between National Unification and Nazism, 1870–1945*. New York: Cambridge University Press.

Weiner, A. 1980. "Reproduction: a Replacement for Reciprocity." *American Ethnologist* 7: 71–85.

Weiner, J. F. 1997. "Televisualist Anthropology: Representation, Aesthetics, Politics." *Current Anthropology* 38: 197–235.

Weiner, S., et al. 1998. "Evidence for the Use of Fire at Zhoukoudian." *Science* 281: 251–3.

Wendler, D. 1996. "Locke's Acceptance of Innate Concepts." *Australasian Journal of Philosophy*. 74: 467–83.

Werbner, R. 1984. "The Manchester School in South-Central Africa." *Annual Review of Anthropology* 13: 157–85.

Westermarck, E. 1891. *The History of Human Marriage*. London: Macmillan.

—— 1908a. *The Origin and Development of Moral Ideas*. London: Macmillan.

—— 1908b. "Sociology as a University Study." *Inauguration of the Martin White Professorships of Sociology*. London: University of London.

—— 1926. *Ritual and Belief in Morocco*. London: Macmillan.

—— 1930. *Wit and Wisdom in Morocco*. London: George Routledge and Sons.

—— 1932. *Ethical Relativity*. London: Kegan Paul, Trench, Trubner & Co.

—— 1936. "Methods in Social Anthropology." Huxley Memorial Lecture. *Journal of the Royal Anthropological Institute of Great Britain and Ireland* 66: 223–48.

Whitehead, T. L., and Price, L. 1986. "Summary: Sex and the Fieldwork Experience." Pp. 289–304 in T. L. Whitehead and M. E. Conaway, eds., *Self, Sex, and Gender in Cross-Cultural Fieldwork*. Urbana: University of Illinois Press.

Whiten, A., and C. Boesch. 2001. "The Cultures of Chimpanzees." *Scientific American* 284(1): 48–55.

Whorf, B. L. 1956. *Language, Culture and Reality: Selected Writings of Benjamin Lee Whorf*, ed. by John Carroll. Cambridge: MIT Press.

Whyte, L. L. 1960. *The Unconscious Before Freud*. Garden City, NY: Doubleday.

Wieviorka, M. 1995. *The Arena of Racism*. London: Sage.

Willey, G. R. and J. A. Sabloff. 1993. *A History of American Archaeology*, 3rd edn. New York: W. H. Freeman and Company.

Williams, E. 1985. "Anthropological Institutions in Nineteenth-Century France." *Isis* 76: 231–48.

Willis, W. 1974. "Skeletons in the Anthropological Closet." Pp. 284–312 in D. Hymes, ed., *Reinventing Anthropology*. New York: Vintage Books.

Winkelmann, I. 1966. "Die Bürgerliche Ethnographie im Dienste der Kolonialpolitik des Deutschen Reiches (1870–1918)." PhD Dissertation, Humboldt-Universität zu Berlin.

Winston, A. S. 1998. "Science in the Service of the Far Right: Henry E. Garrett, the IAAEE, and the Liberty Lobby." *Journal of Social Issues* 54: 179–210.

Winston, B. 1995. *Claiming the Real: The Documentary Film Revisited*. London: British Film Institute.

Wissler, C. 1938. *The American Indian: An Introduction to the Anthropology of the New World*, 3rd edn. New York: Oxford University Press.

Withey, L. 1989. *Voyages of Discovery: Captain Cook and the Exploration of the Pacific*. Berkeley: University of California Press.

Wolf, E. 1982. *Europe and the People without History*. Berkeley: University of California Press.

Wolf, J. de. 1999. "Colonial Ideologies and Ethnological Discourse: A Comparison of the United Faculties at Leiden and Utrecht." Pp. 307–25 in J. van Bremen and A. Shimizu, eds., *Anthropology and Colonialism in Asia and Oceania*. Surrey: Curzon.

Wolpoff, M. H. 1968. "Telanthropus and the Single Species Hypothesis." *American Anthropologist* 70: 477–93.

—— and R. Caspari. 1997. *Race and Human Evolution: A Fatal Attraction.* Boulder, CO: Westview Press.

Worboys, M. 1988. "The Discovery of Colonial Malnutrition between the Wars." Pp. 208–25 in D. Arnold, ed., *Imperial Medicine and Indigenous Societies.* Manchester: Manchester University Press.

Worobec, C. D. 1991. *Peasant Russia: Family and Community in the Post-Emancipation Period.* Princeton: Princeton University Press.

Worsley, P. 1957. *The Trumpet Shall Sound.* London: MacGibbon and Kee.

Wright, S. 1995. "Anthropology: Still the Uncomfortable Discipline?" Pp. 65–93 in A. Ahmed and C. Shore, eds., *The Future of Antyhropology.* London: Athlone.

Wulff, R. and S. Fiske. 1987. *Anthropological Praxis: Translating Knowledge into Action.* Boulder, CO: Westview Press.

Wynn, T. 1985. "Piaget, Stone Tools, and the Evolution of Human Intelligence." *World Archaeology* 17: 32–43.

—— 1995. "Handaxe Enigmas." *World Archaeology* 27: 10–24.

Xia, N. 1983. "A General Survey of China's Archaeological Work." *Beijing Review* 26(44): 21–5.

—— ed. 1986. *Zhongguo da baike quanshu: kaogu xue.* Beijing and Shanghai: Zhongguo da baike quanshu chubanshe.

Yefimenko, A. 1877. *Narodnye iuridicheskie obychai loparei, korelov i samoedov Arkhangel'skoi gubernii* (Popular legal customs of the Lopars, Korelians and Samoyed of the Archangelsk province). St Petersburg: Tipografiia V. Kirshbauma.

—— 1884. *Issledovania narodnoi zhizni* (*The studies on the people's life*). Vypusk pervyi: "Obychnoe pravo" Moscow: Izdanie V. I. Kasparova – Russkaia Tipo-litographia.

Young, C. 1975. "Observational Cinema." in P. Hockings, ed., *Principles of Visual Anthropology.* The Hague: Mouton.

Young, M. W. 2004. *Malinowski: Odyssey of an Anthropologist, 1884–1920.* New Haven: Yale University Press.

Zerilli, F. 1998 *Il lato oscuro dell'etnologia. Il contributo dell'antropologia naturalista al processo di istituzionalizzazione degli studi etnologici in Francia.* Rome: CISU.

Zilberman, Y. 1991. "Ethnographic Notebook: 'Hilma Granquist and Artas: A Finnish Anthropologist in Israel'." *Cambridge Anthropology*, 15(1): 56–69.

Zimmerman, A. 2001. *Anthropology and Anti-Humanism in Imperial Germany.* Chicago: University of Chicago Press.

Zuckerkandl, E. 1963. "Perspectives in Molecular Anthropology." Pp. 243–72 in S. L. Washburn, ed., *Classification and Human Evolution.* New York: Wenner-Gren Foundation.

Zwernemann, J. 1983. *Culture History and African Anthropology: A Century of Research in Germany and Austria.* Stockholm: Uppsala.

Index